The Myth and Reality
of German Warfare

FOREIGN MILITARY STUDIES

History is replete with examples of notable military campaigns and exceptional military leaders and theorists. Military professionals and students of the art and science of war cannot afford to ignore these sources of knowledge or limit their studies to the history of the U.S. armed forces. This series features original works, translations, and reprints of classics outside the American canon that promote a deeper understanding of international military theory and practice.

SERIES EDITOR: Roger Cirillo

An AUSA Book

THE MYTH
AND REALITY OF
GERMAN WARFARE

Operational Thinking from
Moltke the Elder to Heusinger

COLONEL GERHARD P. GROSS, BUNDESWEHR

EDITED BY MAJOR GENERAL DAVID T. ZABECKI, USA (RET.)

FOREWORD BY ROBERT M. CITINO

 UNIVERSITY PRESS OF KENTUCKY

Scholarly publisher for the Commonwealth,
serving Bellarmine University, Berea College, Centre College of Kentucky,
Eastern Kentucky University, The Filson Historical Society, Georgetown College,
Kentucky Historical Society, Kentucky State University, Morehead State University,
Murray State University, Northern Kentucky University, Transylvania University,
University of Kentucky, University of Louisville, and Western Kentucky University.
All rights reserved.

Editorial and Sales Offices: The University Press of Kentucky
663 South Limestone Street, Lexington, Kentucky 40508-4008
www.kentuckypress.com

Library of Congress Cataloging-in-Publication Data

Names: Gross, Gerhard Paul, 1958- author. | Zabecki, David T., editor.
Title: The myth and reality of German warfare : operational thinking from
    Moltke the Elder to Heusinger / Colonel Gerhard P. Gross, Bundeswehr ;
    edited by Major General David T. Zabecki, USA (Ret.) ; foreword by Robert
    M. Citino.
Description: Lexington, Kentucky : The University Press of Kentucky, 2016. |
    Series: Foreign military studies | Includes bibliographical references and
    index.
Identifiers: LCCN 2016025075| ISBN 9780813168371 (hardcover : alk. paper) |
    ISBN 9780813168388 (pdf) | ISBN 9780813168395 (epub)
Subjects: LCSH: Military planning—Germany—History—20th century. | Military
    planning—Germany—History—19th century. | Germany—History,
    Military—20th century. | Germany—History, Military—19th century.
Classification: LCC DD101.5 .G76 2016 | DDC 355.401—dc23
LC record available at https://lccn.loc.gov/2016025075

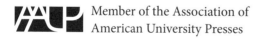

Contents

Color maps follow page 208

Foreword

The Prussian-German tradition in land warfare has generated more than its share of books over the centuries. Good books? That's another story.

Gerhard Gross's *The Myth and Reality of German Warfare* is one of the good ones—one of the best, in fact. Name any criteria by which to judge superior military historical scholarship, and this book has it: broad and deep primary source research; an author who combines scholarly academic training with the technical insight of an operator within the German military establishment (Gross is a colonel in the *Bundeswehr*); and a sustained and powerful argument for continuity in German military operations and operational thought from the mid-nineteenth century through the early NATO years. The original German book was an important and pathbreaking work when it first appeared in 2012, and scholars in the field immediately recognized it as such. I am pleased to see it appear in an English translation, which will make it available to entirely new audiences on this side of the Atlantic: historians, students, and of course a U.S. military establishment as interested as ever in the elusive German concept of "mission command."

The strengths of Gross's book are many, but perhaps most important is its periodization. As in all academic fields, military historians (and German military historians in particular) tend to produce temporally atomized works dealing with one man, one war, one battle or campaign. Writing a book with broad spectrum coverage in time, as Gross has done here, requires scholarly chops, deep expertise in more than one period, and the intellectual courage to go out on a limb and actually try to *say* something. Gross possesses all of these attributes in abundance. As you will see when you read this book, he is as authoritative when discussing the Battle of Königgrätz in 1866 as he is on the great Soviet offensive in Belorussia in 1944, Operation BAGRATION. He knows the thoughts of Carl von Clausewitz, Karl von Reyher, and Albrecht von Roon as well as he knows Heinz Guderian and Erich von Manstein. As a result, he can actually sustain an argument for *patterns of continuity over historical time*—which, it has always seemed to me, is the very point of historical studies.

His argument is essentially this: the German operational tradition—Germany's battlefield behavior—arose over time out of a well-defined historical and geographical matrix. First Prussia and then the German Reich were stuck in a tough spot in Central Europe, ringed by enemies and potential enemies. Germany faced not only the specter of two- or multi-front wars, but also the nightmare of the war of attrition, having to face coalitions of states that could outproduce it, outnumber it, and eventually grind it down in a contest of numbers and materiel. Out of this unforgiving confluence of factors, this "strategic dilemma," as Gross calls it, came a certain operational predilection, a "German way of war." Gross writes: "The military leadership repeatedly attempted to address Germany's strategic dilemma with operational solutions, which would compensate for the vulnerability of the country's central geographic position and its relative inferiority in manpower and resources."

Gross identifies the German solution clearly: waging war in a way that used speed, aggression, and surprise as force multipliers, allowing German armies to punch above their weight and to land heavy blows from unexpected directions. The Germans called this approach *Bewegungskrieg*—the war of movement. The term did not imply simple tactical maneuverability or a faster march rate, but rather maneuver on the operational level—the movement of large units like divisions, corps, and armies. Prussian commanders, and their later German descendants, sought to maneuver these formations in such a way that they could strike the mass of the enemy army a sharp—even annihilating—blow as rapidly as possible. It might involve a surprise assault against an unprotected flank, or both of them. On several notable occasions—as at Königgrätz (1866), Sedan (1870), or Tannenberg (1914)—it even resulted in entire Prussian or German armies getting into the rear of an enemy army, the dream scenario of any general schooled in the art. The desired end-state was something called the *Kesselschlacht*: literally, a "cauldron battle," but more specifically a battle of encirclement, one that hemmed in the enemy on all sides prior to destroying him through a series of "concentric operations."

This vibrant and aggressive operational posture imposed certain requirements on German armies: an extremely high level of battlefield aggression and an officer corps that tended to launch attacks no matter what the odds, to give just two examples. Consider the operational careers of Gerhard Leberecht von Blücher, for example, or Prince Friedrich Karl, the famed "Red Prince" of Königgrätz, or even someone we usually regard as a blunderer, General Hermann von François in the Tannenberg Campaign: these were the recurring patterns of the Prussian-German command personality: defending only as long as necessary, constantly looking for an opening in the defender's array, and, having found it, launching a vigorous attack.

Aggression alone was not enough, however. The Prussians and Germans also found over the centuries that conducting an operational-level war of movement required a flexible system of command that left a great deal of initiative in the hands of lower-ranking commanders. It is customary today to label this command system *Auftragstaktik* (mission tactics): the higher commander devised a general mission (*Auftrag*) and then left the means of achieving it to the officer on the spot. It is more accurate, however, to speak, as the Germans themselves did, of the "independence of the lower commander" (*Selbständigkeit der Unterführer*). A commander's ability to size up a situation and act on his own was an equalizer for a numerically weaker army, allowing it to grasp opportunities that might be lost if it had to wait for reports and orders to climb up and down the chain of command. Again, consider General Constantin von Alvensleben launching his III Corps into the attack at Mars-la-Tour in 1870 without orders from higher command echelons, or the commander of the 7th Panzer Division in the 1940 campaign, General Erwin Rommel, switching off the radio in his forward command post rather than receive the halt order from higher headquarters that he knew was coming. Once again, these men were the exemplars of an operational tradition that stressed action now over waiting to see how things might develop later, a doctrine that reminded the officer, in the words of the manual *Truppenführung,* that "the first criterion in war remains decisive action. Everyone, from the highest commander on down to the youngest soldier, must constantly be aware that inaction and neglect incriminate him more severely than any error in the choice of means."

Hard-hitting aggression, free-wheeling command and control, mobility above all: it was a formidable operational package. It had to be, since the Germans had decided early on that it was not enough merely to win. Rather, they must destroy the enemy force:

> To compensate for the disadvantages of space and inferiority in resources, as the General Staff saw it, they decided to exploit the advantage of interior lines resulting from Germany's central geographic position, combined with a high-quality army and a superior command-and-control system. This then became the guiding principle of their thinking. The underlying concepts of mobility, attack, initiative, establishment of the main effort, envelopment, surprise, and destruction had already been developed by Moltke the Elder for the conduct of a rapid war. The objective became one of destroying the enemy's forces at the border or in the adjacent territories through one or more rapid battles of envelopment. Destruction in the military sense was understood not as physical extermination, but rather the elimination of effective military power—through, for example, the taking of prisoners. Considering Germany's central geographic position, the German military leaders always focused on the elements of time and space in the development of their operational-strategic plans and the manning, arming, and equipping of the military force.

These characteristics, then, formed what Gross calls "the cornerstones of German operational thinking."

As Gross demonstrates in the course of this painstaking historical analysis, these preferences—for operational mobility, independent command, and winning a rapid victory to avoid the nightmare of a war of attrition against vastly superior enemies—remained more or less constant: from the age of Moltke (described here as a great synthesizer and field commander, rather than the master theoretician of war usually lionized by military historians); through Field Marshal Alfred von Schlieffen in the pre-1914 era; Generals Paul von Hindenburg and Erich Luden-dorff in World War I; General Hans von Seeckt in the Weimar period; and the great Panzer theoreticians and commanders of World War II. Indeed, this "Ger-man way of war" even survived 1945, carried over into the nascent Bundeswehr and NATO by General Adolf Heusinger, who had served as the chief of the Opera-tions Directorate (*Operationsabteilung*) in the Wehrmacht's General Staff during World War II.

Make no mistake, however. Gross does not exhibit any particular enthusiasm for this way of war. Rather, he is highly critical of it. Win or lose, the Germans stuck with this pattern of operational thought (and actual operations). And if it did not work—as in Helmuth von Moltke the Younger's 1914 Marne Campaign or Erich von Falkenhayn's attempt to "bleed the French" at Verdun in 1916, or Hit-ler's deranged attempt to conquer the globe in World War II—to give just a few examples, well, then, it could not be the fault of the pattern. It was the fault of indi-vidual commanders, who were lacking in the requisite genius or too enervated in spirit or who had never received that "drop of Samuel's oil" that anointed them and elevated them to a higher spiritual plane as commanders of armies and lead-ers of men. The Germans, Gross argues, "personalized" failure, actually going so far as to psychologize Moltke the Younger (too weak of character) and Falkenhayn (too hesitant and paralyzed by self-doubt). Hitler, of course, did them all a favor by being so apparently psychotic that it was hardly necessary to assassinate his character. The commanders of the Wehrmacht could have at Hitler as they liked in their memoirs, and by and large the world believed every defensive and self-exculpatory word they wrote.

But the German tradition contained other weaknesses. As Gross notes here, so focused were German officers on the particular problems of designing and exe-cuting a plan for rapid and total victory early on in any future conflict that they rarely thought about the higher realm of war: politics, coalition warfare, strat-egy, economics, logistics (or at least any long-term, sustained logistics, which they believed were unimportant since they intended to terminate the war victoriously within weeks). They preferred to leave all these thorny problems to someone else.

And once again, in World War II, they made the mistake—an existential mis-take, it turned out—of "leaving all these thorny problems" to Adolf Hitler. The army was, at the very least, complicit in the starvation and deaths of millions of Soviet citizens and POWs on the Eastern Front. Army officers—planners and commanders alike—supported this unique brand of "logistics," in which they would intentionally starve millions in the occupied territories in order to feed, clothe, and support German troops on campaign, freeing German armies to do what they did best: fight operational-level maneuver warfare and smash the Soviet army and state as rapidly as possible. The crimes in the east were not accidental, nor did they belong to Hitler alone.

Finally, this book deserves praise for the clarity of Gross's methodological approach. Books on doctrine—operational, tactical, or otherwise—abound in the military history profession. Writing about doctrine is one way to appear serious to a broader profession that distrusts campaign history and mocks it as "drum and trumpet" scholarship, the "old military history," which has supposedly been replaced and superseded by something newer and more worthy. Unfortunately, doctrinal history can be as interesting as watching paint dry, just as you would expect of a book that spends most of its pages explicating and dissecting an army's tactical and operational manuals (and I offer this criticism as one who has written books on doctrine).

While Gross certainly knows his way around the German army's technical literature and can analyze it in an interesting and convincing way, he also delves unabashedly here into actual campaigns and battles. Indeed, I am convinced that his approach is the only useful way to write about operational doctrine, which, after all, is nothing but a mountain of meaningless words until some commander and his army try to put it into practice. Battle is "lived doctrine"—and in turn, the outcome of battle can (or at least should) shape the evolution of doctrine. Put in different terms, Gross has elevated *praxis* to its rightful place in the study of war, standing alongside but certainly not subservient to the role of *theory*. In that sense, I might, with the author's indulgence, recommend *The Myth and Reality of German Warfare* as a complement to my own 2005 book, *The German Way of War,* which likewise emphasized the role of battle and campaign in formulating a military culture over time.

Gerhard Gross's book *The Myth and Reality of German Warfare* is one of the most important books ever written on German military history. The University Press of Kentucky should be proud to publish it in English translation.

Robert M. Citino
Military History Center
University of North Texas

Preface

Military operations have always been the hallmark of the German art of leadership. Generations of German General Staff officers were trained and educated in operational thinking. Following their orders, millions of German soldiers fought and died in the deserts of North Africa, at the gates of Paris, and in the vastness of Russia.

Individuals such as Helmuth von Moltke the Elder, Alfred Graf von Schlieffen, Hans von Seeckt, Erich von Manstein, and Adolf Heusinger, the first chief of staff of the *Bundeswehr,* personified operational command and control in the German Army. The battles of Königgrätz in 1866 and Tannenberg in 1914, the *Sichelschnitt* (Sickle Cut) in the France Campaign in 1940, the battles of encirclement in Russia in 1941, and Manstein's *Schlagen aus der Nachhand* (strike from the rear) during his Kharkov Counterstrike in 1943 are among the best-known examples of the German art of operational command and control. It is, therefore, not surprising that these battles are used as models for operational command and control training of officers both in Germany today and internationally. In 1999 the Joint and Combined Operations Working Group of the *Führungsakademie der Bundeswehr* (Bundeswehr Command and Staff College), in coordination with the French Army's *Service Historique de l'Armee de Terre* (Army Historical Service) compiled and published the *Grundsätze der Truppenführung im Lichte der Operationsgeschichte von vier Jahrhunderten* (Principles of Command and Control in the Light of Four Centuries of Operational History). These principles are used to instruct officers in the timeless concepts of command and control on the basis of selected historical examples. The emphasis is clearly on practical application.

Surprisingly, there has so far been no scholarly analysis of the history of German operational thinking. This study by Colonel Gerhard P. Gross, Ph.D., of the *Zentrum für Militärgeschichte und Sozialwissenschaften der Bundeswehr* (Bundeswehr Center for Military History and Social Science), fills that gap. Colonel Gross examines from a scholarly perspective the development of German operational thinking, from its origins to the establishment of the Bundeswehr. Published in Germany in 2012 as *Mythos und Wirklichkeit: Geschichte des operativen Denkens im deutschen Heer von Moltke d.Ä. bis Heusinger* (Myth and Reality: The History of Operational Thinking in the German Army from Moltke the Elder to Heusinger), the title indicates the extensive range covered by the book.

In his multi-perspective and diachronic examination of the operational thinking of five different German armies, Gross analyzes both the strengths and the conceptual failures, including the interdependencies between the operational idea and organization for war by society as a whole. His overview of the development and failure of operational thinking of German generals and the General Staff over a period of more than a century is based on a wide range of sources and literature. In the process, Gross dismantles cherished myths and replaces them with lines of continuity that run from the mid-nineteenth century to the mid-twentieth century. The study uncovers the political, social, strategic, and general economic reasons for the eventual failure of the "Operations Myth," and also the human and personal reasons for these developments. Simultaneously, the author offers an insightful explanation for Germany's failed attempt in the twentieth century to grow into a major and global power through the use of military means.

I commend Colonel Gross for his impressive research and the resulting reappraisal of the history of operational thinking in the German Army. Thanks also to the chief of our Era of the World Wars research branch, Professor Rolf-Dieter Müller, Ph.D., and the ZMSBw editorial staff, headed by Arnim Lang, Ph.D. Particular thanks go to Wilfried Rädisch (coordination), Carola Klinke (setting), Bernd Nogli and Frank Schemmerling (maps and organizational charts), and Knud Neuhoff and Marina Sandig (image procurement/image copyrights). Maurice Woynoski (image editing) supervised the work in cooperation with the editor of the German edition, Colonel (Ret.) Roland G. Foerster, Ph.D.

Colonel Hans-Hubertus Mack, Ph.D.
Director
Bundeswehr Center for Military History
and Social Science

Abbreviations and Special Terms

BArch	*Bundesarchiv*—The German Federal Archives
CINCENT	NATO Commander in Chief, Central Europe
D.V.E.	*Druckvorschriften-Etat*—Training Manual
F.u.G.	H.Dv. 487 *Führung und Gefecht der verbundenen Waffen* (1921)—Command and Combat of the Combined Arms
FOFA	Follow-on Forces Attack
Freiherr	Baron
FRG	Federal Republic of Germany
GDP	NATO General Defense Plan
GDR	German Democratic Republic—East Germany
geh.	*geheim*—secret
Gestapo	*Geheime Staatspolizei*—Secret State Police (Third Reich)
Graf	Count
H.Dv.	*Heeresdienstvorschrift*—Army Service Manual
Kaiser	Emperor
KTB	*Kriegstagebuch*—War Diary
KVP	*Kasernierte Volkspolizei*—People's Garrison Police
Luftwaffe	Air Force
NATO	North Atlantic Treaty Organization
N	*Nachlass*—Posthumous Papers
NS	*Nationalsozialismus*—National Socialism
NVA	*Nationale Volksarmee*—National People's Army, the armed forces of East Germany
OberOst	*Oberbefehlshaber Ost*—Supreme Command East (World War I)
OHL	*Oberste Heeresleitung*—Supreme Command of the Army (World War I)
OKH	*Oberkommando des Heeres*—Supreme Command of the Army (World War II)
OKW	*Oberkommando der Wehrmacht*—Supreme Command of the Wehrmacht (World War II)
Op.Abt.	*Operationsabteilung*—Operations Division
Panzer	Tank, Armored
Reich	Empire
Ritter	Knight

SA
: *Sturmabteilung*—Assault Detachments, the paramilitary force of the Nazi Party

SACEUR
: NATO Supreme Allied Commander, Europe

SED
: *Sozialistische Einheitspartei Deutschlands*—German Socialist Unity Party, the Communist Party of East Germany

SHAPE
: NATO Supreme Headquarters, Allied Powers Europe

SS
: *Schutzstaffel*—Protective Echelons, the umbrella organization for the Nazi Party's police and security forces, and its military forces, the *Waffen-SS*

T.A.
: *Truppenamt*—Troop Office, the clandestine General Staff of the Reichswehr

T.F.
: *Vorschrift Truppenführung*—Unit Command, the German Army's capstone doctrinal manual

T.F./A.
: H.Dv. 100/2 *Führungsgrundsätze des Heeres im Atomkrieg* (1956)—Army Command Principles for Nuclear War

T.F./G.
: H.Dv. 100/1 *Grundsätze der Truppenführung des Heeres* (1956)—Principles of Army Unit Command

T.F./B.
: H.Dv. 100/900 *Führungsbegriffe* (1977)—Command Concepts

Introduction

Is there a German way of war? While German historians either avoid this question or have in recent years unjustly reduced it to the idea of genocidal war of annihilation, Anglo-American and Israeli historians decades after the end of the Second World War continue to have lively and controversial discussions about German military warfare during the era of world wars. In addition to the scholarly interest, some authors have demonstrated an unmistakable intent to learn from German operational warfare, with the focus clearly being on German land warfare. For various reasons, German aerial and naval warfare play only a minor role, if any, in the considerations of military historians. Both the operational and tactical capabilities of the German land forces in coordination with the *Luftwaffe* during the Second World War are often put forth as primary examples from the history of war. While Geoffrey P. Megargee[1] and Shimon Naveh[2] give critical accounts of the *Wehrmacht*'s operational capabilities resulting from specific German command and control problems, and Naveh argues for the lack of a coherent theory of operational thinking,[3] others emphasize the extraordinary operational capabilities of the German Army. Trevor N. Depuy expressly focuses on the performance of the German Army in the nineteenth and twentieth centuries, speaking of the "institutionalization of military excellence" in the German General Staff.[4] And as Edward N. Luttwak describes the Soviet invasion of Afghanistan: "In fact, it was an operation very much in the German style: elegant, full of risks, and most profitable."[5]

Robert M. Citino goes even one step farther. He draws a direct line from the Schlieffen Plan to Desert Storm, the most successful American military operation of the post–World War II period. The key to that success was a well-planned and thought-out mobile war and a clear definition of the main effort—concepts familiar to any German officer.[6] Both Luttwak and Citino suggest that there is a time-transcendent German operational art, the main factors of which—defining the center of gravity, risk assessment, speed, and maneuver—have been largely adopted by American and Soviet officers.

At the same time, both authors revive the myth of the Schlieffen Plan as a well-organized recipe for victory that eliminated all risks. In Schlieffen's tradition, frictions, which according to Clausewitz have a significant impact on war, are eliminated through the planning process. The primacy of rapid operational success, then, results in a neglect of the strategic dimensions of war, such as economic warfare and propaganda. This theoretical concept, however, gives little consideration to post-conflict operations, such as people's war and partisan warfare. The Soviet Afghanistan Campaign analyzed by Luttwak, however, demonstrates that if the ensuing partisan warfare is not addressed in the general strategy of a rapid and mobile operation, the result will not necessarily guarantee victory, but rather can lead directly to defeat.

Most German military historians consider the analysis of red and blue arrows on operational plans inappropriate. The study of operational history is still linked with the notion of strident militarism. Such detailed analyses of operations is considered to be directly in the tradition of the apolitical approach to the study of war representative of the Military History Division of the Great General Staff and the Reich Archive during the periods of the two world wars. Such an action-oriented approach to deriving lessons learned, they argue, focused on the evaluation of war history examples for future application by the armed forces, and neglected the economic, social, cultural, and political dimensions of war. This results-oriented approach by the armed forces, therefore, was limited to exploiting historical lessons for current military plans and the education of soldiers, and served to form patterns of thought for the officer corps. But because they are rarely interested in military procedures, the modern critics of the operational approach often fail to consider the fact that the German Army's "operators" more often than not tended to neglect the logistics element, or completely disregard it, as did Schlieffen in his 1905 memorandum.

Stig Förster once cautioned that it was the task of the *Bundeswehr* to ensure that officers do not again focus unilaterally on the conduct of operations only within the framework of the grammar of war, without also taking into account the political foundations of their profession. This warning, however, should be understood in the context of the 1990s, when there was a strong demand within the German Army for a classic approach to the history of operations.[7] This, however, does not mean—as Förster explained—dispensing with a modern history of operations. In the course of the late 1990s discussion about the justification for a scholarly approach to the history of operations, Bernd Wegner correctly established that eliminating the history of operations from the military history canon was a serious error because it dangerously narrowed the historical analysis of war. A modern expansive approach to military history, therefore, should include an integrated but critical study of the history of operations.[8]

The history of operations does not justify itself on its own terms; rather, it should contribute to an increase in overall understanding. As Förster in effect argued: "It would be a mistake for historians and scholars to continue to ignore the research of specialists in this particular field, just as the history of battles and campaigns can no longer be written without consideration of the wider historical context."[9]

Sönke Neitzel also favors reintroducing the study of war proper into military history, without neglecting the questions of psychology, everyday life, and culture that have come to characterize the "New Military History."[10] He makes the case for a pluralism of research methods and approaches in the fields of political, operational, and cultural history. Referring to arguments advanced by Michael Geyer[11] and Stefan Felleckner,[12] Neitzel insists that paying attention to the "core of the war"—that is, to the dying and killing, the fighting, and the battle or the campaign—will result in "a stronger picture."[13]

During the 1980s the German Army experienced a revival of operational thinking that largely escaped the notice of historians. At the time, the chief of staff of the army, Lieutenant General Hans-Henning von Sandrart, thought that military leadership principles had been in the shadow of the concept of forward defense for far too long. He insisted that officers should think beyond the first battle of the Cold War General Defense Plan (GDP) and apply the principle of free operational command and control within the framework of an extensive overall defense and the follow-on battle. In the era of Flexible Response and Follow-on Forces Attack (FOFA), an independent theory of operations could no longer be ignored. Operational thinking had to be revived.[14] Consequently, Sandrart reintroduced the classical German General Staff ride, and in 1987 he issued the *Leitlinie für die operative Führung von Landstreitkräften in Mitteleuropa* (Guidelines for Operational Command and Control of Land Forces in Central Europe).[15] Subsequently, the guidelines were incorporated into the 1987 edition of Army Regulation H.Dv. 100/100 *Truppenführung*.

The critics reacted to this development. Martin Kutz, then an associate professor at the *Führungsakademie der Bundeswehr*, argued that the process of the modernization of operational command and control was not only an ideologically motivated campaign to revitalize traditionalist values, he also considered the exclusively military argument a revival of Schlieffen's patterns of thought as eternal concepts for action. Referring to German military history of the previous century, Kutz also severely criticized the focus on large-scale offensive operations without consideration of the economic, social, or political realities.[16] For him, a return to the operational thinking of the German General Staffs in the era of the two world wars was a dangerous and unwelcome development.

This study focuses on operational thinking in the German Army during the era of the two world wars. The concentration is on the army because in the prevailing German military thinking of the period ground forces were the decisive element in warfare. In the closed subculture of the military, the army, its general officers, and its General Staff officers developed their own subsystems. While during the era of world wars the continental thinking of German Army commanders did concede to the navy an independent albeit secondary role in bringing about a decision in war, they recognized only a supporting function for the Luftwaffe, primarily the tactical air support of the ground forces. Furthermore, neither the German Navy nor the Luftwaffe had developed a similar service-specific framework of operational thinking. They did, however, develop their own operational terminologies that were functions of their specific reliance on technology and operational space. In some areas these concepts overlapped with the ideas of the army. And although those concepts are not directly the subject of this study, we will consider them from the point of view of the army.

The time period we will evaluate is not limited to the era of world wars. We will consider developments from the mid-nineteenth century through to the beginnings of the Bundeswehr, attempting to achieve a smooth transition between the epochs. It is impossible to understand the operational thinking of Field Marshal Alfred Graf von Schlieffen, Colonel General Ludwig Beck, Colonel General Heinz Guderian, or Field Marshal Erich von Manstein without starting with the development of operational theory under Field Marshal Helmuth Graf von Moltke the Elder in the late nineteenth century. Nor is it possible to understand the early period of the Bundeswehr, from its establishment until the retirement of its first chief of staff, General Adolf Heusinger, without examining Heusinger's World War II experiences as the chief of the Operations Directorate of the General Staff of the *Oberkommando des Heeres* (Army High Command). Continuities in personnel reinforce conceptual continuities, despite structural changes. This is particularly true in the field of operational thinking, where the senior leaders of the "new Bundeswehr" were recruited from the operations departments of the three Wehrmacht services. This study, then, will follow both a structural-based and a personality-based approach. To the present day, the development of operational thinking has always been linked to individuals such as Moltke, Schlieffen, or Manstein, in addition to organizational actors like the General Staff.

Why are the military leadership of the German Army and many Anglo-American military historians so interested in the operational thinking in the German ground forces during the last two centuries? This is an especially interesting question considering the fact that the British and Americans were successful without a developed theory of the operational art, whereas the Germans were not successful in waging war based on such a theory. Did this German leadership philosophy in combination with new innovative tactical procedures—as frequently stated— enable the German forces during the two world wars to fight successfully for years despite their quantitative inferiority in personnel and materiel? Although there have been recent studies on the development of German tactics[17] that explain the significance of tactics for German operational art, there still has been no adequate answer to the questions of effectiveness, the development of German operational command and control, and the German thought behind it in the era of the world wars. What are the advantages and risks of what is known as the typical German practice of land warfare? What is the specific nature of German operational command and control, and in particular, of the operational thinking upon which it is based? Is there even such a thing as typical German operational thinking—and if so, why and how did this thinking develop in Germany during the past two centuries? Is German operational thinking a consequence of the political system and Germany's belated democratization, or is it rather proof of the fiercely debated German *Sonderweg* (special path)? Did Germany's central geostrategic position influence the development of operational thinking? And last but not least, was it a straight-line development?

How can a process like operational thinking be operationalized—in other words, applied on the battlefield? Although thinking is an abstract process that cannot be directly measured, its results are reflected in reality and thus can be analyzed. Contemporary doctrinal regulations, files, documents, and military literature are the windows to the understanding of both the theory and practice of operational thinking, just as are the military operational plans and their actual execution in war.

While during the early 1970s Manfried Rauchensteiner[18] and Josef Marholz[19] in a series of articles addressed operational thinking in Austria, and Anglo-American military historians continually discussed individual aspects of the questions of operational art, the most recent German works were for the most part decades old and addressed operational thinking from a purely military technocratic perspective. The heyday of the German military theorists ended in the 1930s. The few recent German studies, such as the article by General Dieter Brand,[20] do not reach beyond the military specialist level. Kutz, with his clear-cut article, has been the only writer to break out of this box. Contemporary young General Staff officers, who often emphasize that they never learned as much about German operational thinking in the era of world wars as they did when they attended the U.S. Army Command and General Staff College at Fort Leavenworth, or the British Army Staff College at Camberley, prefer to focus their own research papers on the lack of the strategic rather than the operational dimension of German warfare.[21]

The sources differ for the various periods. Record availability for the Reichswehr, the Wehrmacht, and the initial stages of the Bundeswehr is good. In contrast, with a few exceptions the files of *der Grosse Generalstab* (the Great General Staff) at the *Reichsarchiv/Heeresarchiv* (Reichs Archive/Army Archive) in Potsdam were destroyed in a British bombing raid in April 1945. The files of the *Kriegsgeschichtliche Forschungsanstalt* (War History Research Institute), however, did survive the war. In conjunction with the files on Schlieffen's operational thinking that have been found in the posthumous personal papers of General of Artillery Friedrich von Boetticher, they make it possible to reconstruct to a great extent Schlieffen's thinking and planning. The files from the era of Moltke the Elder, unfortunately, were destroyed. But thanks to the compilation of Moltke's writings made by the *Kriegsgeschichtliche Abteilung* (War History Division) of the Great General Staff just before the outbreak of the war in 1914, it is possible to reconstruct Moltke's operational ideas as well. Neither of these two important figures in the development of operational thinking before the First World War, Moltke the Elder and

Schlieffen, offered a coherent and working military theory. Unlike Moltke the Elder, Schlieffen advanced his views of warfare, such as Cannae or contemporary warfare, in the form of journal articles published after his retirement.

So far, then, there has been no diachronic, multi-perspective study of operational thinking in the five German armies from the mid-nineteenth century to the mid-twentieth century, which includes the interdependencies between operational thinking and the organization for war of society as a whole. It is, therefore, the objective of this study to close that gap by addressing the development of German operational thinking within the framework of the economic, political, and social environment. Such an approach is the only way to understand the continuities and discontinuities of the military history of ideas that is centered on the operational thinking in the German ground forces during the era of the world wars.

The military history analysis of operational thinking in the German Army should not aim at describing every one of the supposedly important or decisive operations. Rather, this study is about the development of operational thinking against the background of German military history during the world wars period as a whole. Readers expecting the Anglo-American "lessons learned" approach, or the traditional lines of the method of application approach, which has been applied to the German Reich and the Wehrmacht, and for which there has been frequent call to apply to the Bundeswehr, will lay the book aside disappointed.

1

Definitions

Tactics—Operations—Strategy

The first task of every theory is to clear up the muddled, and one can even say very confused, terms and concepts. Only if one has achieved agreement on the names and terms can one hope to advance to the consideration of things with clarity and ease. One can then be certain of always being at the same point of view as the reader.

—Carl von Clausewitz

What does operational thinking mean? To approach this topic it is necessary to define the terms "operation" and "operational," and to categorize them within the three levels of warfare that are recognized internationally at the beginning of the third millennium—those being the strategic, the tactical, and the operational. Simultaneously, we must also examine the effectiveness of the definitions of those terms. This is important for two reasons. Firstly, the meanings of terms change over the years, parallel to the variety of human spheres of life. Secondly, the military concepts of operation and operational have up to the present day seldom been examined in depth, and the understanding of those concepts remains very contradictory.

On the international level the definitions of these terms can vary widely because of differences in military cultures and linguistic conventions. Furthermore, German officers who may have had differing understandings of the various types of operations have used the terms over the decades without defining them or without differentiating them clearly. The reasons for this are partly because the military environment assumes a general understanding of the terms, and partly because a specific definition of the terms as applied to the various command echelons poses a very difficult problem. It is not surprising, therefore, that even the Prussian-German military doctrinal regulations, known for their linguistic accuracy, lacked a definition of "operation" for decades. For example, the 1910 edition of D.V.E. No. 53 *Grundzüge der höheren Truppenführung* (Fundamentals of Higher-Level Military Command), which in turn was based on the *Verordnungen für die höheren Truppenführer* (Regulations for Higher Troop Commanders) issued in 1869 by Field Marshall Helmuth von Moltke, notes the term "operation" only in passing in connection with the concentration of the force for battle. Regulation H.Dv. 487

Führung und Gefecht der verbundenen Waffen (Command and Combat of Combined Arms) issued in 1921 and 1923 by Colonel General Hans von Seeckt, and H.Dv. 300 *Truppenführung* (Command and Control of Forces), written in 1933 primarily by Colonel General Ludwig Beck and General Carl-Heinrich von Stülpnagel, did not include a reference to "operation" in the index. The only reference was to the operations order. Interestingly, only in April 1939 did the Luftwaffe's manual of army tactics define for the first time the term "operation."[1]

The 1962 edition of H.Dv. 100/1 *Truppenführung der Bundeswehr* (Command and Control of Bundeswehr Forces) did not elaborate on the term "operation," but mentioned it only in the chapter on command terms[2] in the context of higher-level command, and also in the manual's Annex 1. The term "operation" is defined for the first time in Bundeswehr regulations in the 1977 edition H.Dv. 100/900 *Führungsbegriffe* (Command Terms) as an action of a force connected in time and space that is always directed at a particular objective and may include maneuver, combat, and other actions of any type and any extent.

A primary reason for the decades-long lack of definition is that prior to the Bundeswehr there was no specific German doctrinal regulation for either the operational or the strategic levels of warfare. German Army regulations usually dealt with command at the tactical level. Only the *Grundzüge der höheren Truppenführung* (Fundamentals of Higher-Level Military Command) addressed the operational and strategic dimensions of war. But the preliminary efforts to extend this central regulation after the issuance of H.Dv. 487 were discontinued in the mid-1930s.[3] We will return to this issue later.[4]

Although the term "operation" was for the first time defined in a German Army regulation at the end of the 1970s, it has been used in military writings since the mid-nineteenth century. The great German military writers—Moltke the Elder, Sigismund von Schlichting, Colmar von der Goltz, Friedrich von Bernhardi, and Schlieffen—all used the term. Over the years a wide range of associated terms also appeared in the lexicon. Terms like operations plan, operational objective, operational base, operational target, line of operations, and operational level of command have been in use for more than a century. Others, like operational concept, deep operations, and free operations also have come into use during the past few decades.

The versatility of this lexical grouping is also reflected in the German lexicons and military handbooks. While officers often avoided fixing a definition in their regulations and writings or were not able to offer one, the lexicons and handbooks early on defined the term "operation" and its associated grouping. From the definitions offered in these various publications we can trace the evolution of the term over the past two centuries. With the exception of *Johann Hübners Zeitungs- und Conversationslexikon* of 1826, which only included the military meaning of the term, all standard lexicons over the years have listed the primary definition of "operation" in its medical context. The military meaning always was given at the end of the entry. Some lexicons, like *Brockhaus' Kleines Konversationslexikon* of 1905,[5] only offered the medical meaning.

Although an entry for "operation" is missing completely in the first edition of the *Brockhaus* of 1809,[6] the supplements to the first four editions of 1820 include the following definition: "In the language of war, operation is a synonym for an undertaking. The operations plan is the provisional draft, according to which the undertakings of a campaign will be established."[7] The *Brockhaus* edition of 1820 defines two central points for the understanding of an "operation" and "operational thinking" in this short entry: "On the one hand an operation is an active, targeted military act; on the other hand there is an underlying plan."

By contrast, *Hübners Zeitungs- und Conversationslexikon* defines an operation only as an attack against fortified enemy positions with the objective of forcing the opponent to attack.[8] Hübner's is a unique definition not shared by the other lexicons. The *Brockhaus* of 1839 defines operation concisely: "Among other things, the undertakings of an army during war are called operations, and the draft according to which they take place is called the operations plan."[9] *Herders Conversations-Lexikon* of 1857 goes a fundamental step beyond this and distinguishes between tactical operations directed at the battle, and strategic operations directed at the structure of the campaign.[10]

Pierer's Universal-Lexikon published four years later elaborated even further on the term. It defined the operation as an undertaking in war directed at the main body of the enemy and leading to the decision of the war. It also referred to the base of operations, the line of operations, and the operational objective.[11] Interestingly, Pierer three years before the 1866 Battle of Königgrätz attributed a war-deciding role to the operation.

Meyers Neues Konversations-Lexikon of 1866 defined for the first time offensive and defensive operations and assigned them—albeit not very convincingly—to the realms of tactics and strategy.[12] At the same time, the 1866 *Meyers* defined the term "operational" under its own headword to mean practical action, without giving it a military reference.

The 1908 edition of *Meyers Grosses Konversations-Lexikon* became more specific in a longer entry that described military operations as the maneuvers and actions of larger army elements, including marches, engagements, and battles. Operations could be conducted either along interior or exterior lines. The combination of operations up to the final decision, the destruction of the enemy, was a campaign.[13] With this definition *Meyers* introduced an additional dimension to the concept of an operation that corresponded to the spirit of the times—the operational objective was the military destruction of the enemy main body. When combined with the idea that operations are executed by larger army units, the operation came to be understood as being a higher level of warfare than tactics.

Interestingly, the concise military dictionaries of the Reich were not more specific in their definitions of operations than were the contemporary general lexicons. The 1901 edition of the *Militär-Lexikon*,[14] for example, defined the operation itself only briefly as the maneuver of army units, while the *Handwörterbuch der gesamten Militärwissenschaften*[15] of 1879 understood operation as army maneuvers directed at a decision in a narrower strategic sense. The *Handbuch für Heer und Flotte* stood out because it devoted so much space to the discussion of the term "operation" in the military language of the German Reich, and for the first time it explained the term "operational" in respect to the navy. Nonetheless, the author of the army section of the entry, General August Philipp Freiherr von Falkenhausen, declined to define "operations" specifically. He instead argued for replacing what he considered the outdated term of operations with *Herresbewegungen* (large-scale army maneuvers), because he believed that the term must always be understood in conjunction with strategy.[16] Falkenhausen's arguments presented in a standard military handbook of the time indicated that the term "operations" was still subject to much dispute in the military language at the beginning of the twentieth century, because it was not yet clearly differentiated from tactics and strategy.

The so-called *Weimarer Brockhaus* edition of 1932 marked a definite shift. It rejected the limitation of the term to land warfare, which had held sway until World War I. The entry for operation now read: "In war, a group of military actions which are closely related through the pursuit of a specific objective."[17] In 1939 the *Handbuch der neuzeitlichen Wehrwissenschaften* defined operation similarly but more precisely in terms of space and time: "An army maneuver in its entirety complete in itself in terms of objective, time, and space, mostly associated with larger combat actions."[18] In 1955 the first edition of *Brockhaus* after World War II almost—but not quite—copied this wording. Undoubtedly as a direct result of the experiences of World War II, the new definition replaced *Herresbewegung in ihrer Gesamtheit* (army movement in its entirety) with *grössere militärische Verbände* (larger military formations).[19]

During the succeeding thirty-six years the *Brockhaus* editors made very little change to the definition of operations. The editions of 1991 and 1998 generally adopted the 1955 definition.[20] These later editions did, however, define for the first time the adjective "operational" as strategic, as does the 1997 edition of the *Fremdwörter-Duden*.[21] The 1955 *Brockhaus* had not included an entry for operational, and the 1932 edition defined it only in the medical sense. Thus, this summary of the terms "operation" and "operational" in the German lexicons and military handbooks of the last two centuries illustrates how imprecise the formation of the two concepts has been up to the present.

Why has it been so difficult to define "operation" and "operational" in the military context? In large part it is because both words have undergone a continuing semantic change over the course of the last two centuries, and the definition of the term "operation" within the framework of warfare still seems to cause significant problems. Thus, it becomes necessary at this point to posit a short definition of tactics and strategy as applied to warfare.

The terms "tactics," the Greek *taktiké* (the art of formation and disposition), and "strategy," the Greek *strategós* (army leader), have been used almost exclusively in the military sense from the end of the eighteenth century to the middle of the twentieth century, and have since achieved even more general usage. While tactics is generally understood as a planned, calculated, and targeted short-term or medium-term action, strategy represents a long-term, designed, planned striving for an objective or a favorable end-state. Although both terms are of military origin, they have come to be used in various ways in the everyday spheres of sports, economics, and politics.

In the beginning there was tactics. Since classical antiquity, tactics has been a clearly defined military concept. It included the capability to conduct marches, establish camps, concentrate armies, and mobilize soldiers for battle. As a consequence of the complex development of European military organizations in the early modern era, the impetus emerged to distinguish between elementary tactics concerning the maneuvers of a battalion or a regiment, and higher-level tactics—sometimes called grand tactics.[22] Against the background of the mass armies that emerged during the course of the French Revolution and the Napoleonic Wars, military thinking in Europe reached a turning point in the late eighteenth century. Addressing the increasing complexity of warfare, military theorists like Georg Heinrich von Berenhorst, Heinrich von Lloyd, Heinrich von Bülow, Antoine de Jomini, and Carl von Clausewitz attempted to develop a theory of war that would cover all aspects of the military. In the course of this process it became a common approach at the beginning of the nineteenth century in Europe to subdivide warfare into tactics and strategy. The distinguishing criteria, however, were still unclear.

In the course of this complex process, strategy—the science of the army leader—became separated from tactics. Heinrich Berenhorst finally defined strategy as "the art of marching," and tactics as "the art of fighting."[23] Georg Wilhelm von Valentini, on the other hand, felt that such a separation was superficial, because there were transitions between both during their applications, and the differences, therefore, were only marginal.[24] For a long time the question of how to classify the two levels of warfare was subject to much debate. Bülow, who understood tactics as "everything in a war which has the enemy as the direct objective," and strategy as "all aspects where the enemy is the purpose or the indirect objective,"[25] subordinated strategy to tactics. Clausewitz, on the other hand, gave strategy precedence over tactics. In his book *Vom Kriege* he defined tactics as the "principles of how to use forces in battle," and strategy as "the principles of how to use battles for the purpose of war."[26] Simultaneously, Clausewitz saw an end-means relationship and a clear interdependence between tactics and strategy. His concept of strategy was directed at the overall picture, because next to the specifically military issues he assigned the decisive role to politics, the latter being the dominant factor occurring throughout all phases of war. But politics had to include in its strategic consideration the nature of the armed forces that it established.[27]

Jomini also influenced the thinking of German soldiers, but to a lesser extent than Clausewitz. In contrast to Clausewitz, he did not ask "What is war?" but rather "How do you conduct war?"[28] Considering the deep sense of uncertainty about the correct military leadership approach to varying war scenarios, this less philosophical but more practical approach appealed very much to the General Staff officers. It offered learnable rules rather than general elements of education designed to develop leadership capabilities. For Jomini, strategy was the art of warfare on the map, which encompassed the whole theater of war.[29] Jomini, however, excluded the social and political factors of warfare from his canon of immutable principles and limited the influence of political options on the start of a war.

Clausewitz's and Jomini's thoughts materially influenced the German military thinking through the end of World War II, but in combination they ultimately led to a dangerous dead end. Thus, a purely military understanding of strategy became dominant in Germany, rather than Clausewitz's concept based on the primacy of politics. Moltke the Elder laid the foundation for this development. He limited the influence of politics to the beginning and the end of a war. For Moltke and his successors the conduct of warfare itself was ultimately a purely military and apolitical act. As Moltke made unmistakably clear in the introduction to his work *Über Strategie*: "Politics uses war for the achievement of its goals. It has a decisive influence on the beginning and end of the war in the way that it reserves the right to increase its demands or be content with lesser success. Under such uncertainty strategy can be directed only at the highest objective that the available means provide. [Strategy] best works as a support to politics, only for the purpose of politics, but completely independent in its actions."[30]

While German military theoreticians and officers at the end of the nineteenth and the beginning of the twentieth century always quoted Clausewitz, his concepts were reduced to a random number of useful quotations.[31] Meanwhile, the influence of Jomini's works spread throughout the officer corps subcutaneously. It took two lost world wars to reawaken German thinking to the "real Clausewitz."[32] Even though Clausewitz's influence on German military strategy over the last two centuries has certainly been long overestimated,[33] he at least laid the foundations for, and also the limitations of, the German and Anglo-American concepts of strategy of the twenty-first century.

Even today, these concepts are not really fixed, neither for strategy per se, nor for military strategy. In accordance with the primacy of politics, strategy is characterized by the close connection between politics and warfare, while simultaneously integrating the economic, cultural, social, and religious factors. Strategy, therefore, is a political notion. But as it has for centuries, strategy still does not conform to an exact definition.[34] Currently, for example, the terms "strategy" [editor's note: sometimes called national strategy or grand strategy] and "military strategy" are frequently used synonymously today.[35] But military strategy implies a purely military approach and is a subset of the overall strategy. Because strategy must be understood more holistically, it must incorporate all the social and human elements and all possible fields of human interaction as they apply to warfare. Strategy is not limited to just the higher level of warfare; rather, it seeks to achieve military objectives without limitation to purely military matters.

This Janus-headed dichotomy is resolved through the primacy of politics as postulated by Clausewitz, an approach generally accepted today throughout the western world. The conflicts between military and political interests must be reconciled again and again in every new and complex situation that arises. Thus, strategy (national strategy) will mean, according to Edward Luttwak, "the regulation and consequences of human relations in the context of real or potential armed conflicts."[36] Likewise, military strategy will mean the uniform command and control of armed forces of a state or alliance in one or more theaters of war, with the objective of deciding the outcome of the war. As presently understood, national strategy does not necessarily focus on military victory; rather, it also relies on civil institutions for the resolution of conflicts.

While the development of the concept of strategy in Germany had long been shaped by the rejection of political primacy, the introduction of ever more modern weapons systems and means of communications has influenced the continuing development of tactics. The modern concept of tactics is still based on Clausewitz's definition that tactics deals with individual battles and the achievement of combat victory with armed forces, and on Jomini's definition that tactics means the maneuver of an army on the battlefield and the various formations in which soldiers are led in battle.[37] More recently tactics have come to be understood as the theory of the command and control of troops in combat, and in this sense it is usually understood more or less as procedure.[38] Tactics include the various forms of combat, such as attack and defense.

Under the influence of advances in armament technologies, new tactical concepts of combat have evolved, such as *Stosstrupptaktik* (Stormtroop Tactics, also called today fire and maneuver tactics) and *Raumverteidigung* (area defense, also known as defense-in-depth) during World War I, and the modern concepts of combined arms warfare. Simultaneously, the ongoing development over the centuries of modern weapons systems and the means of transportation and communications has made the deployment of troops far more complex. Compared to the maneuvering of an ancient Greek phalanx, modern deployments make ever higher demands on tactical command and control systems. But over and above the coordination of multiple systems in combined arms warfare, even individual weapons tactics have grown more complex. In all situations, the tactics applied must accommodate the most varied weather and terrain conditions. The tasks facing the Bundeswehr in the conduct of its new missions abroad, combined with the fact that political considerations assert ever greater influence on the execution of those missions in these theaters of deployment, may in the future lead to an extended concept of tactics beyond combat, resulting in a new spectrum of tasks. For the period under examination in this study, however, tactics shall be understood as the command and control of troops and military assets in space and time, and their combined actions in combat.

The "operational," the most recent level in the military leadership triad, emerged in military thinking only at the beginning of the nineteenth century. While tactics and strategy have migrated from military to civilian usage, the term "operation" derives from the Latin word *operatio,* meaning duty or work. Originally a purely civilian concept, it evolved only gradually into a specialized military term. It describes primarily an active action, and only secondarily an undertaking. In mathematics an operation stands for a calculation; in data processing for a working step; and in medicine for a surgical procedure. In the Anglo-Saxon group of languages the word "operation" is attributed to a direct action. Thus, we have the basis for the recurring misunderstanding of the term "operation" in the military sense. The military meaning of operation derives from the French *opéra-tion,* which according to the *Dictionnaire de l'académie française* means "the act of a power to achieve an effect, particularly concerning war, but also in politics, administration, finance, and trade, and as intentions, projects, and plans that will or have been executed."[39]

In German-speaking areas the term "operation" has meant the movement of troops since the end of the eighteenth century, a development that accompanied the advent of mass armies. Friedrich Meinert wrote in 1789 that a military operation was "any undertaking in a war with the objective of damaging the enemy, with or without the use of force" and that "its soul is the art of maneuvering."[40] Georg Venturini wrote that the operation belongs to the art of maneuver and teaches how to move armies.[41] Bülow, whose definition decisively influenced the development of the modern concept of the operation, and who defined it as close to strategy,[42] went even a step beyond, writing in 1799: "Any movement of an army which has the enemy as an immediate objective is called an operation. I say immediate, because otherwise any march could be called an operation."[43] Bülow integrated the operation into a geometric and therefore a calculable working hypothesis of operations in the wider sense, to include the line of operations, the base of operations, and the operational objective.

In contrast, Clausewitz was generally skeptical of Bühler's mathematical approach, and in particular of the significance of the base of operations.[44] Clausewitz understood an operation as an army maneuver in accordance with an operations plan, as developed in the context of a strategy. The task of strategy, then, was the selection of the line of operations, with all other operational forms assigned to the realm of tactics. Clausewitz distinguished between operations against lesser enemy concentrations and the main operation against the enemy's main body. The objective of an operation was of particular relevance for him. He favored the clear establishment of a center of gravity, with the direction for the main effort determined by the political objective: "I can only call an operation truly effective when it aims at the heart of the enemy monarchy. That means instead of gnawing at the borders, it must advance as far as possible as long as that direction remains open, and continue to focus all forces toward that objective."[45]

With these definitions Clausewitz, together with Bülow, established the foundation for the development of modern operational thinking in Germany over the course of the next two centuries. Nonetheless, the German military doctrinal regulations over that period show quite clearly that the terms "operation" and "operational" were never adequately defined until after the end of World War II—not for the army, or for the Luftwaffe, or for the navy.[46] In 1977 the Bundeswehr for the first time defined the term "operation" in H.Dv. 100/900 *Führungsbegriffe* (Command and Control Terms).[47] During the period of the two world wars especially, both terms were loaded down with an unmanageable variety of baggage. Both terms more often than not were determined by the thought of the individual user. As an adjective, operational has been used as a close equivalent to strategic—but sometimes closer to the tactical. It is, therefore, unsurprising that there are far more German definitions for operational[48] and operation than there are for strategy and tactics.[49]

At the starting point of this study, then, we can derive from the contemporary regulations and lexicon entries some key points about the terms "operation" and "operational." In the period under examination the terms have been used in a wide range of military contexts. The definitions vary and are somewhat imprecise, to the point of being almost completely avoided at times. Nonetheless, the operation and the operational level do remain consistently positioned between tactics and strategy. An operation is always a subordinate element of a much larger action. But the limits of such action are often undefined and fluid. It is, therefore, often difficult to determine the precise point at which the strategic level of warfare ends and the operational level begins. A strict boundary between tactics and operations also involves complex issues, because the latter has an effect on the outcome of the battle. Thus, phrases like operational-tactical level and operational-strategic level are often used.

An operation is closely connected with movement, be it a deployment, an advance, or a battle. Over the course of the twentieth century, mobile warfare has come to be closely associated with the operation and operational. Likewise, during the period of the world wars, operations have almost always been supported by air forces. There is also the distinction between smaller operations conducted by a few corps, and larger operations, which involve the main body of the army or even the entire land force. Operations comprise one theater of war, while strategy encompasses all theaters of war.

As a working hypothesis for this study, an operation will be understood as an independent military action to accomplish a strategic objective. The operation is orientated on the geographic situation and the maneuvering of the enemy. During the period of the world wars the operation was mostly a multiservice action, strategic in its approach and tactical in its execution. This definition indicates, therefore, that regardless of any ambiguities the conduct of a war is a strategic matter; the command and control of the forces in combat is a tactical matter; and the leadership of large formations in a theater of war is an operational matter.

The extent to which operations and tactics are interwoven into military practice can be seen in the German war plan of 1914. The Moltke Plan, based on Schlieffen's 1905 memorandum—generally known as the Schlieffen Plan—centered on a strategic-level defense in the east with only one field army. Simultaneously, France was supposed to be defeated decisively with the mass of the German armed forces within a few weeks' time in order to then defeat the Russians after a redeployment to the east. Within the context of this military strategy, the offensive through Belgium against France, as well as the Battle of Tannenberg in the east, were operations in separate theaters of war. They had different force strengths and operated in unequally sized spaces, but they were conducted under similar time pressures. By contrast, the surprise attack on Liège, which had become necessary because of the strategic factors resulting from the neutrality of Belgium, was a tactical action, the success of which had a decisive impact on the conduct of future German operations. That surprise attack on Liège, which had to be executed before the overall deployment could be completed, also had significant consequences for the overall strategy of the German Reich. It put the German operations under even greater time pressures and cost the leaders of the Reich precious time for the negotiation of potential political solutions.

The Moltke Plan illustrates the placement of the "operation" in the level of the leadership triad and the interdependencies between strategy, operations, and tactics. It also demonstrates that certain factors and constants, like space and time, influence or even determine operational considerations.

But what constitutes operational thinking today? A final, all-inclusive definition is still not possible because of the fluid meanings and usages of the terms "operation" and "operational." The concept of operational thinking oscillates between tactics and strategy. In the most general sense, operational thinking may be understood as the consideration of certain factors or constants, such as time, space, and forces, in conjunction with the deployment and command of larger formations in a theater of war. The overall purpose is to achieve strategic objectives.

2

Factors and Constants

Space, Time, and Forces

> The great constant in German history is the country's central position in Europe.
> Germany's fate is its geography.
>
> —Hagen Schulze

As suggested by the contemporary literature, German General Staff officers carried into the two world wars not only their marshal's batons in their rucksacks, but also Clausewitz's book *Vom Kriege*. Without any doubt the operational thinking of officers like Moltke the Elder, Schlieffen, Beck, Guderian, and Manstein was influenced by the study of classical and contemporary military theorists. Thorough analysis, however, indicates that the influence of military theory literature on the majority of the General Staff officers has been overemphasized. Instead, the factors of space, time, and forces played the decisive role in the development of operational thinking and tactics in the German Army. Those elements form the basis for any operation, and they therefore stand at the center of operational thinking. That thinking, in turn, was influenced by an increasingly expanding understanding of the economic and social parameters. Although the factors of space, time, and forces are interrelated and influence each other, time and space are especially interlinked because they establish the framework for warfighting. The commitment of forces, to include military equipment, combat vehicles, weapons, soldiers, and more recently intelligence and communications systems, must be oriented in terms of time and space. Thus, both military operations and tactical actions are always functions of time and space. In the process of operational thinking, both parameters can be calculated more easily based on the enemy's freedom of action than on one's own intent.[1]

Space and Time

As a first principle there is the shape (*Gestalt*) of the space, upon which time (*Zeit*) is dependent. Every geographical area is defined by both its shape and the time in which it can be traversed. The conditions of military geography, therefore, form a decisive factor in the planning and conduct of operations. In contrast to today's humanistic concepts of geography, which regard space as the projection of the area that forms the human habitat as defined by religious and ideological factors,[2] most General Staff officers up until a few decades ago regarded geographic space primarily in its natural and scientific terms. The assessment of space at the operational level and of terrain at the tactical level is always the first step in a military estimate of the situation. Terrain features such as mountains, plains, and seas, as well as infrastructure and weather factors, have a significant influence on warfighting, and are thus the essential foundations of the military decision-making process. In the course of the assessment of the situation, the enemy's armament posture is a variable that can be countered temporarily by the economic and personnel resources of the state. The physical shape of the space available for waging war, on the other hand, is a constant that can only be modified by reinforcing the terrain—for example, with fortifications. The importance that the German Army's leadership attached to the physical-material conditions of space for decision making and the conduct of warfare is illustrated in the fact that in the German General Staff a survey division (*Vermessungsabteilung*) reported directly to the chief of the General Staff. With their *Generalstabskarten* (General Staff maps) the personnel of that division[3] established the practical prerequisites for the operational-strategic plans of the German General Staff, and those plans were based on the geostrategic reality that Germany is situated in the center of Europe.

The geostrategic situation of a state, however, is not determined wholly by the natural physical characteristics of its area. Economic, social, and political factors also have a decisive influence.[4] The characteristics of an area are not static and unchangeable, because people alter an area through structural activity, and also through their perceptions. The latter changes depended on the political situation. The favorable trafficability or cultural interchange opportunities of a centrally positioned space can be regarded positively, but also negatively as a military threat to such central position. For many years the military area construct of the General Staff was based on an exclusively geographical conception, coupled with the perception of threat in the form of a two-front or multi-front war.

The General Staff never saw the opportunities, but always the potential risks and threats arising from the central position. Thus, we must consider here the question of whether or not this exclusively military area construct was the product of worst-case thinking. In the final analysis, the question of the outbreak of a two-front war was not a geographical but a political one. It is the function of politics to establish the general conditions that will prevent such a situation. The two-front war, therefore, was not a given by nature; rather, it was something that resulted from human actions, and could be influenced by such. Nonetheless, many of the General Staff officers—the operationally thinking group within the officer corps— saw the entire question fatalistically. That was exactly what the General Staff officers did when they made the central position advantage of interior lines the basis of their concept of strategic warfare and an important element in their concept of operational warfare.

Since the establishment of the German Reich in 1871, Germany's central position was seen as a threat in the paradigm of the military area construct. The Reich was the only one of the five great European powers that directly bordered three of its potential enemies: Russia in the east, Austria-Hungary in the southeast, and France in the west. There was no direct border with Great Britain, but the latter had the ability to cut off Germany from international trade by a naval blockade. Thus, many German political and military leaders compared Germany's geostrategic situation with that of Prussia before and during the Seven Years' War or even the Thirty Years' War. Chancellor of the Reich Otto von Bismarck got to the heart of the matter in 1888 when he said to the German Africa explorer Eugen Wolf: "Your map of Africa is very pretty, but my map of Africa lies in Europe. Here is Russia and here is France, and we are in the middle. This is my map of Africa."[5]

Based on such an analysis of the situation, Bismarck and his successors strove to prevent a two-front or even multi-front war through the establishment of alliances. Although the 1879 Dual Alliance with Austria-Hungary eliminated the risk of a multi-front war, the German political and military elites still saw the consequence of the central position as a two-front war, with the Russian and French Sword of Damocles hanging over Germany. The central position, therefore, reinforced the sense of threat that was widespread among the political and military elites of the Reich. They believed they were surrounded by a world of enemies.[6]

The loss of territory after the defeat in World War I did not greatly change Germany's geostrategic situation. As a consequence of the European order after 1918, Germany still had a common border with France, but now it also had one with Poland and Czechoslovakia, two powers with a combined long border and great military potential. Thus, as Germany's senior military leaders continued to see it, the country's central position still carried the threat of a two-front war. In 1937 the chief of the *Truppenamt* (Troop Office), General Ludwig Beck, assessed Germany's central position in the classical sense of the General Staff's military area construct as being one of the constants of German history. The territorial losses resulting from the Treaty of Versailles actually intensified the threat: "Without any doubt, the issue of space exists for Germany because of its central position in Europe, and perhaps will for all time; but especially since the territory changes of Versailles."[7] Beck's thinking exemplifies the military area construct.

Germany's 1945 defeat fundamentally changed the geostrategic situation in Europe. At the Potsdam Conference the Allies agreed in principle to the Curzon Line[8] as the western border of Russia, in conjunction with a westward compensation of territory for Poland up to the Oder River. The Oder–Neisse line thus became the de facto eastern border of Germany, and all German areas east of that line now came under Polish administration, or in northeastern Prussia under

Soviet administration. Germany, occupied by the Allies and separated into four occupation zones, no longer existed as a Great Power in the center of the continent.

The global political competition between the Soviet Union and Western Powers, which intensified during the years following World War II, had direct consequences for Germany. The country was cut into two states astride the north-south borderline of the two power blocs. The space that had been Germany thus moved from the center to the periphery. Operational-strategic factors made the Soviet Zone, which later became the German Democratic Republic, the staging area for the Warsaw Pact. The Western Zones, which later became the Federal Republic of Germany, became the glacis of NATO. Until the end of the 1950s, therefore, the territory of Germany was not seen as a subject by Germans, but as an object by the former victorious powers. To gain at least partial control over the area of the Federal Republic of Germany the government under Konrad Adenauer endeavored to establish army divisions and advanced the concept of the forward defense of Germany as an international interest of NATO.

Against this background, then, the key question within the General Staff from the foundation of the German Reich in 1871 until the end of World War II was whether a two-front war could be won—and if yes, how must it be conducted? Paradoxically, the German military found the solution to this dilemma, caused by geographical realities and faulty foreign policy, in the much-despised central position itself. As Schlieffen determined, the central position also offered strategic advantages: "Germany has the advantage in that it is situated in the middle between France and Russia, and it separates these allies from each other."[9]

The geostrategic situation of the Reich, then, opened up the opportunity to the General Staff for the conduct of a potential two-front war through the exploitation of interior lines. That, in turn, meant challenging enemies separated in space and time individually, and defeating them one after the other before they were able to exploit the advantages of concentric attack along exterior lines. An important requirement for the successful execution of such an operational and strategic formula was the possession of sufficient depth in Germany's own territory. The indisputable advantages of warfare on interior lines became lost if there was not enough space to defeat first one and then the other enemy.

Another important prerequisite for success was the rapid deployment of Germany's forces. Apart from a mobile army organization, the ability to do so primarily required very good traffic networks. According to the assessment of the General Staff, Germany met all prerequisites to conduct warfare on interior lines because the country's spatial west-to-east depth allowed for the timely movement of larger army formations from one front to the next and Germany's interior railroad grid was very robust. Despite Germany's defeat in 1918, the clandestine General Staff in the form of the Truppenamt still considered the pre–World War I general assumptions to be valid. As Beck put it in 1938: "So it came about that the space issue for the German armed forces waging war along interior lines in Central Europe did not have a retarding effect on our operational freedom. In contrast, it can be seen that a spacious and coherent central main theater of war was a great advantage for the [World War I] Central Powers, and allowed them to continue land warfare operations in three directions for more than four years."[10]

But warfare along interior lines also carried a great risk—the factor of time. In the event, it proved not possible during World War I for Germany to defeat one of the two opponents before the other could intervene effectively in the war. The result was an imminent catastrophe.

World War I exemplifies the compression of space and time, and it shows that a mental separation of space and time is somewhat artificial. Time as well as space influences all military actions, whether tactical, operational, or strategic. Consequently, there is a military-specific time construct that is expressed in the course of time acceleration. In the first part of the twentieth century this phenomenon affected the mobilization period, and in the second half it affected warning times. During the Cold War especially, this phenomenon reduced political reaction times. Furthermore, the time factor places limitations on the physical and psychological strength of soldiers and animals and the serviceability of weapons, vehicles, and other equipment. Traversing larger areas requires more time. Consequently, decisions and their execution in a tactical limited-area context are faster than operational and strategic decisions directed on larger areas.

Operational actions are focused more on the future than are tactical actions, and require more time for reconnaissance, planning, and execution. Larger troop bodies deployed in the execution of an operation cannot be halted or redirected without some difficulties; mistakes cannot be rectified, or only can be with great effort. Military leaders, therefore, must plan far ahead in time and space, but in so doing they lose their direct contact with the troops and the battle. Senior leaders are forced to ensure that their subordinate leaders at the point of the action act in the sense of the senior's intent. This can be achieved on the one hand by improvement of the means of communications, and on the other hand by directives that control largely independently acting subordinate commanders. The latter method, however, requires uniform training and education that results in a homogeneous collective thought process synchronized with that of the senior commanders. This individualization of command is, therefore, a factor in the acceleration of the time element.[11] Its importance in the development of operational thinking in Germany cannot be underestimated.

Although advanced signals technologies have facilitated faster communications over the years, advances in modern ground combat vehicles and air, naval, and submarine technologies also have accelerated the command process into the third spatial dimension, which of course expands the overall operational space. This acceleration puts ever greater pressures on the military decision makers, especially considering the increasing logistics requirements for modern weapons systems. Time pressures increase the potential for mistakes in the command process. As a result, the side that succeeds in establishing and keeping its enemy under time pressure will increase its own chances for success while simultaneously minimizing the enemy's. Gaining time for military actions, therefore, is a key to operational success.

If one of the opponents lacks time, he can acquire it by either capturing or giving up area. Both options, however, include risks that are not always calculable and can overcome purely military factors. The side operating on interior lines and surrounded by enemies, for example, cannot afford to give up major population centers, economically important territories, or sources of raw materials. Such considerations conflict with former thinking that divided one's own national territory simply into forward and rearward areas. The relinquishing of politically or culturally significant regions may endanger the inner political stability of the state. The lack of time and resulting requirements for gaining time, therefore, are nearly always issues confronting the side fighting on interior lines.

The side operating on exterior lines, on the other hand, frequently has the depth or the protection of the sea on one flank—which means an advantage in time. That side also can put its enemy under strong time pressure through a concentric, synchronized attack, or it can gain time by giving up area or by controlling the seaways. The opponent in such a position has easier access to worldwide resources, which can thus serve to compensate for any loss of an operationally-strategically important area. That side also can use blockades to cut off its opponent from crucial warfighting and life-sustaining resources. If the power in the central position is not totally self-sufficient, but like Germany only semi-self-sufficient and therefore dependent on the import of strategic raw materials like coal and oil as well as food, the geostrategic situation will allow that side to sustain the war for a limited time only. While the side operating on exterior lines can draw greater advantage as the duration of the war increases, the side operating on interior lines must endeavor to keep the war as short as possible. Thus, the war must be brought to a rapid decision before the enemy can bring his full power base to bear.

Time is a decisive factor, both for the side operating on interior lines and for the side operating on exterior lines. Nonetheless, the operational and strategic time pressures are much stronger on the side operating from the central position. The military has a key role to play in the modern social acceleration process, as social change speeds up significantly. This happens not only through the rapid provision of moral-political support, the acquisition of information, and the provision of personnel and equipment,[12] but also through the interdependency between modern weapons systems, operational plans, and warfare. The pressure for acceleration exerted on science, society, and politics by a situation of permanent military threat and the ever faster-running military decision-making process—for example, the mobilization of 1914—finally culminates in the commitment of all forces to achieve victory.

Forces

In combination, space and time impact military planning, materiel, and personnel, and also the foreign and security policy of a state. Owing to the time factor driving the requirement for a fast opening of a war, continental powers like France and Germany needed land forces that were already trained and available in great numbers right at the start of hostilities. Sea powers like Great Britain could act initially with small, rapidly deployable professional armies. In contrast to land powers, the maritime superiority of the sea powers gave them the time to raise and train an army. Compulsory military service, therefore, was not so much a policy inherent to the democracies, but rather one necessary for a major land power to commit a large force with trained reserves either at the front or in the hinterland. This was especially important for a continental power like Germany, which was at an overall manpower disadvantage relative to its potential enemies. Military leaders concluded, then, that the manpower numerical inferiority could only be compensated for by a temporary superiority achieved through the rapid establishment of a center of main effort at the front. While Moltke the Elder had been able to conduct the German wars of unification with a relative manpower superiority, he and his successors based their later plans after the foundation of the Reich in 1871 not only on a two-front war, but a two-front war fought with an inferior force ratio.

Apart from the parameters of space and time, the element of forces, therefore, was a major factor in operational thinking. Without taking time and space into consideration, the commitment of military forces is doomed to failure. Military leaders must therefore leverage their advantages in space and time to achieve success. Time, space, and force strength must all be synchronized. The numbers of deployed soldiers and their armament and support systems play a decisive role. The larger the deployed force, the more difficult will be its control and its orientation in space.

Smaller and more mobile armies with modern equipment and well-trained soldiers and subordinate leaders are less complicated to command and control and they therefore offer opportunities to conduct decisive, daring, and decision-seeking operations. Consequently, the side that is inferior in numbers can to a certain degree balance quantity with quality. Large mass forces also cause complex logistical problems, especially if they have to be supplied over long distances, across wide spaces, and under less than optimal traffic conditions.

The troop strengths of the Battles of Leuthen in 1757, Waterloo in 1815, and Königgrätz in 1866 show the extent to which the size of field armies in Europe grew within a little more than one hundred years. While at Leuthen 29,000 Prussians faced 66,000 Austrians, by Waterloo 72,000 French soldiers were opposed by 115,000 British and Prussians. The number of combatants nearly doubled in sixty years. On the battlefield at Königgrätz 206,000 Austrians and Saxons fought against 221,000 Prussians. That means Moltke the Elder alone led into the field nearly ten times as many soldiers in 1866 as Friedrich II (Frederick the Great) did at Leuthen almost one hundred years earlier. At the end of the nineteenth century the sizes of armed forces again increased dramatically. During the era of armies numbering in the millions, the Central Powers in 1914 entered World War I with 3.7 million soldiers and the Entente with 5.8 million. Over the course of the war France and the German Reich alone committed 8.5 million and 11 million soldiers, respectively, on the ground, on the seas, and in the air. The difficulties of commanding such huge masses of troops in an area ranging from Verdun in the west to Baku in the east, and from the North Sea to Palestine, were enormous. Simply moving and supplying such huge forces during the more than four years of the war was an enormous challenge to the military high commands of all sides.

Overshadowing these issues of command and supply of large mass armies remains the hard fact that in combat, battle, and war superiority of numbers is the cornerstone of all success. Every military commander, therefore, will endeavor to achieve the local/regional superiority of his forces. The side inferior in numbers has two options to balance the superior strength of his opponent: he can either use the advantages of the defense from fortified positions, or he can defeat elements of the enemy force by achieving and exploiting local numerical superiority. Both variations can result in a balance in forces. The defensive, as the passive form of combat, requires more time to accomplish this objective than the more initiative-based attack. Furthermore, there is the option of achieving a qualitative advantage over the enemy through superior training and command and control, in order to conduct fast and complex operations on the offensive. But even the most effective increases in quality cannot offset the power of the law of numbers—in other words, "the minority [force] with which one wishes to succeed [. . . must] at least be strong enough to defeat decisively at least such a significant part of the enemy force that the defeat of the latter and its consequences will achieve a balance of forces."[13]

Considering Germany's central situation, the factors of time and space during the period of the world wars were always the focus of operational-strategic plans and the armament and manpower policies of the German military leaders. Thus, the combined factors of time, space, and forces established both the context and also the decisive cornerstones of German operational thinking up to the end of the 1950s. These inseparably linked parameters have been regarded as constants by German General Staff officers up through the end of World War II in Europe. In certain extreme situations, they have even been regarded as determinants.[14] As the General Staff officers saw it, they could not change the factors established by nature and politics, except to a limited extent through conquest. Accordingly, the only remaining option was to develop a military policy within the framework of the given parameters that would allow a highly qualified force in terms of personnel and materiel to achieve a rapid victory during any two-front war fought with inferior numbers.

3

The Beginnings

Planning, Mobility, and a System of Expedients

Moltke: An Evolutionary Mind, Not a Revolutionary One

It all started with Moltke. That sentence summarizes his multiple contributions to the beginnings of operational thinking in Germany.[1] But Moltke really did not start it all. In contrast to the official line of the Military History Division of the Great General Staff, operational thinking actually arose from the advent of mass military forces armed with increased firepower in the form of individual hand-held firearms and artillery. This had been a development of the French Revolution and the resulting changes in society as a whole. Civic participation and warfare were combined. Although operational thinking is based on a military phenomenon, its roots actually come from a social phenomenon.

Helmuth von Moltke the Elder, the long-serving chief of the Great General Staff, was undoubtedly one of the authors of the development of operational thinking, initially in Prussia and then in Germany. Nevertheless, he cannot be counted among the great European military theoreticians, such as Clausewitz or Jomini, and he certainly is not the missing link between Clausewitz and Schlieffen. Moltke the Elder left no systematic body of military theory behind.[2] He was a pragmatist, a practitioner.

Before we search for a body of operational thinking specific to Moltke, some criticism of the sources of his military writings is in order. The majority of his writings were official directives or military study texts, which were meant to provide General Staff officers with additional training. Those writings often were jointly drafted in the General Staff and eventually received Moltke's approval. Today, it is no longer possible to distinguish his original contributions. Moltke's writings were collected by the General Staff's Military History Division and published posthumously during the years from 1892 to 1912. The General Staff officers who carried out this process wanted to emphasize the term "operation" in Moltke's works in order to establish a base of reference for the longer-term development in operational thinking. They also wanted to emphasize the significance of operations for future warfare. Owing to the World War II destruction of the *Reichsarchiv* and the resulting loss of documents, it is no longer possible today to verify whether or not certain passages from Moltke were reinterpreted to conform to the thoughts of the contemporary General Staff during the publication of those volumes, which were published in many parts. Such a possibility, however, cannot be ruled out. There are precedents for such revisionism. As Werner Hahlweg proved only in the 1950s, Friedrich Wilhelm Graf von Brühl distorted key passages from Clausewitz's *Vom Kriege* to change the relationship between the civilian government and military commanders in favor of supremacy of the military.[3] Schlieffen as well obscured the historical truth in his works where it did not conform to his ideas.[4]

Moltke used the term operation often, and most of the time in connection with the maneuvering of formations on the battlefield. In his writings, the term "operation" can often and simply be replaced by army-level maneuvering. He also frequently used the composite terms "operations plan," "lines of operations," and "operational objective." Moltke's term "operational objective," which was sometimes synonymous with battle objective, meant the enemy army, which had to be taken under fire.[5] What is essential to our questions is the fact that Moltke did not understand the operation as a level of warfare of its own between tactics and strategy, but rather he subsumed the operation into the field of strategy. Therefore, Moltke's operational thinking, which has been postulated in the literature for decades, can be understood only through an analysis of his concept of strategy. His paper "Über Strategie,"[6] in which he discussed Clausewitz and simultaneously established links between the categories of tactics—operations—strategy, is the only one of his writings that addresses in detail strategy and operations. According to Moltke's thinking, the primary functions of strategy as a means of achieving the political goal were those of providing the necessary armed forces and ensuring the success of the initial deployment. Conversely, Moltke considered the "use of the resources provided in wartime—i.e., the operations," as continuous functions.[7] While strategy was a part of politics for Clausewitz, Moltke considered it to be "entirely independent with respect to actions" during the phase from after the start of the war until the conclusion.[8] He later modified his point of view, making the following remark on Wilhelm von Blume's 1882 book, *Strategie: Eine Studie*: "The course of war is primarily characterized by its military aspects."[9] Despite this gradual modification, Moltke described different phases of war as being political ones at the beginning and at the end, and a purely military phase in between. As part of the latter, he considered the operation as an aggregate of military actions, such as a campaign, planned by the chief of the General Staff and issued as a directive order to the commander in chief of an army in the field.[10] Tactics determined the success of an operation by means of the battle. The enemy's independent will, which had to be broken, was a factor in both tactics and the operation. The initial deployment of the army, for which the operations plan was of central importance, was inextricably linked to the operations. In contrast to his later successor Schlieffen, however, Moltke held the opinion that the further course of the war could be planned only less thoroughly and required a situation-oriented execution of operations. "It is fairly safe to say that no operations plan goes beyond the first encounter with the main enemy force. Only laymen think they can recognize in the course of a campaign the consistent realization of the original idea that was conceived in every detail in advance, and realized fully until the end."[11]

Within this framework, Moltke understood strategy as a system of expedients and demands upon the military leadership to react to situational changes under the most adverse conditions. Logically, therefore, doctrines of a general kind as well as rules derived from such doctrines cannot be of any practical use for operational thinking. Instead, the commander, who has acquired knowledge through earlier military training and experience—be it from the study of war history or his own life experiences—must on the one hand have the theoretical knowledge, and on the other the ability to develop "the traits of both his spirit and his character freely and for practical application, like an artist."[12] To Moltke, operational command was logically an art that could only be learned incrementally. Moreover, mental flexibility, a quick grasp, and strength of character were for Moltke the basic prerequisites for operational commanders. Even though Moltke was certainly thinking in operational terms, he did not establish a theoretical model of operational thinking. Moltke the practitioner considered strategy-operations as an "application of knowledge to practical life" under constantly changing conditions.

On 29 October 1857, three days after his fifty-seventh birthday, Moltke, who in 1822 had transferred to the Prussian Army from Danish service, and who had been a German General Staff officer since 1833, was assigned as chief of the Great General Staff of the Prussian Army. It was the first time that a trained General Staff officer, who in contrast to his predecessors had served in Germany's Napoleonic-era Wars of Liberation, acceded to this post. Nobody in Berlin at that time guessed what effect this assignment would have on German history and the development of Prussian-German military affairs. At that time, the Prussian General Staff was not yet the efficient planning and command and control organization of later years, but rather a scientific-military think tank, without its own specific area of leadership competence within the Prussian War Ministry.[13]

Moltke the Elder, who had never commanded a battalion or even a regiment, and who therefore had no command experience, nevertheless seemed especially qualified for the post. He had experienced war in the Ottoman Empire as a young captain, and he had held several successful assignments in the General Staff with Troops. He also served as an adjutant to two different royal princes, and thus had excellent relations with the royal family. The new chief of the Great General Staff was regarded as an erudite officer with a universal education. As an author, however, he had made his name not primarily through works of military theory or military history, but through accounts of his travels in Turkey.

The *Allgemeine Kriegsschule* (General War School, the original name of the

General Carl von Clausewitz. Reproduction of a painting by Wach, printed by Meisenbach Riffarth and Company, Berlin, ca. 1820. *Library of Congress LC-USZ62-58866.*

Lieutenant General Gerhard von Scharnhorst. Portrait by Friedrich Bury, ca. 1812. *Bild 183-H28195.*

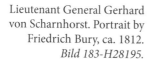

Field Marshal Helmuth Graf von Moltke at Versailles. *BArch/183-B0403-0049-001.*

The Great General Staff of the Prussian Army, 1870–1871. Field Marshal Helmuth Graf von Moltke, standing in the center, his arms folded. *hpk/Rud. Rogorsch.*

Kriegsakademie) had aroused Moltke's interest in geography. There, like all the other General Staff officers, he had received intense training in topography, a core competency of the General Staff. His geography instructor, Carl Ritter, had also instructed Clausewitz, August von Gneisenau, and Gerhard von Scharnhorst.[14] Ritter instilled in his officer students the understanding that geography was more than just a physical space, but rather a unity of the elements of physical and cultural geography.[15] Clausewitz was the director of the General War School during Moltke's period of training, but he was responsible primarily for administrative and disciplinary matters. Clausewitz never taught Moltke directly. As Moltke himself later wrote, he was formed as a young General Staff officer by his military history instructor Major Karl Ernst Freiherr von Canitz und Dallwitz, who himself had been a student of Clausewitz. This is significant because Canitz's teachings were connected with Clausewitz's works with respect to the *Vernichtungsgedankens*—the concept of destruction. In contrast to Clausewitz, however, and in accordance with the thinking of that era, Canitz advocated the thesis that the offensive was superior to the defensive.[16]

Today it is not possible to determine the exact extent to which Ritter's and Canitz's ideas influenced Moltke the Elder's operational thinking. Nevertheless, the fact that he identified these two as the instructors who influenced him in the most lasting manner points to the conclusion that at least some of their thoughts made their way into his own thinking. The General War School provided the young Moltke with the general concepts of war that were common to the Prussian Army, as derived from experiences from the Napoleonic Wars. In contrast to the period prior to World War I, the decision in the battle took the central but not the absolute position in this canon. Much in line with Jomini's thinking, the General War School instructors taught the advantages of interior lines and the principle of keeping one's forces together, while at the same time emphasizing the importance of freedom of maneuver and the advantages of flanking positions.[17]

Moltke's appointment as chief of the Great General Staff on the eve of the Prussian constitutional crisis of 1857 came at a time of military and political upheaval, which was to thrust Prussian and German history in a new direction. The new chief of staff faced a challenging situation shortly before Prince Regent Wilhelm took power. Many of the reforms of 1813–1814 had come to nothing, which suited the army's officers, who for the most part were members of the nobility. The forty-year-long reform logjam, which until relatively recently has been cited repeatedly in the literature, has been shown convincingly by Dierk Walter to be a mere legend which served as a founding myth that legitimized the establishment of the Reich.[18] There had, in fact, been an evolution, although not always a steady one, in the Prussian military since the Wars of Liberation. The army, however, had not developed into a parliamentary force, but remained very much a royal force army. The *Landwehr* (territorial reserve), which without any basis in reality was idealized into a national militia by bourgeois politicians, had, however, been integrated into the standing army. But simultaneously the Landwehr had been weakened by reorganization measures over the years, and the members of the officer corps voiced increasing criticism of the Landwehr as bourgeois, unsoldierly, and politically inefficient. The question was how a potentially revolutionary Landwehr could perform its secondary mission of protecting the Hohenzollern dynasty—which many officers actually considered its more important mission—in addition to serving its foreign and domestic policy functions?

Besides such political motives, the reasons favoring reform were primarily of a military nature. This dual military force structure system of line and Landwehr territorial reserve had for many years allowed impoverished Prussia to act as a European Great Power. But in contrast to the other European Great Powers, Prussia had not adjusted to its population increase from 11 to 18 million with a corresponding increase in army personnel. Rather, Prussia had kept its military personnel strength constant at approximately 150,000 since 1815. That in turn led to serious inequities in conscription, because not even one-third of the potential conscripts could be called up. The size of the regular army also was a handicap for a European Great Power at the end of the nineteenth century, one that limited its ability to act in the area of foreign policy. The French Army, for example, was twice as large, and the Russian Army was almost seven times as large as the Prussian Army. Prince Regent Wilhelm was determined to change that. Together with Bismarck and War Minister Field Marshal Albrecht Graf von Roon, Wilhelm pushed through the so-called Roon Reforms to modernize the army and increase the actual strength.[19]

This is not the place to examine all aspects of the Prussian constitutional crisis or to discuss its effects on German history. For the purpose of our study, however, it is important to take several key points into account. The actual strength of the army was increased from approximately 150,000 to 200,000 troops. The first line was strengthened, while the Landwehr was limited to the communications zone and garrison duty. A militia was no longer in question. The forces were reorganized in certain areas and further modernized, albeit rather slowly. At the same time, the steady if sometimes only partial process of professionalization, which had been going on for years, continued. Despite the reforms, however, the existing force structure of Prussia—and from 1871 onward of Germany—remained essentially unchanged and was fairly constant until World War I. Sudden, abrupt bursts of innovation did not take place, as they had in previous years. The result was the continuation of the Prussian system of the king as the commander in chief.

"March Separately, Strike Combined"

Roon's reforms were not able to solve the most important problem for German operational thinking: the personnel numerical inferiority in terms of a two-front or multi-front war. Although Prussia increased its annual recruitment quota considerably, there were political and economic reasons why the country avoided making full use of its defense potential. The same reasons carried over to the German Reich. But even the full application of Prussian-German defense potential would not have compensated for the resulting personnel numerical inferiority in the case where Prussia-Germany had to face an alliance of several Great Powers. This is because the other European Great Powers—singly at certain times, but more probably combined—had larger armed forces available in both war and peacetime than did Prussia-Germany. Therefore, the statement made so often in the literature that Moltke conducted his wars with numerical superiority is incorrect. During the Franco-Prussian War the Prussian Army was numerically superior to its adversary only at the beginning of the war in 1870, and Prussia by no means had been numerically superior in 1866.[20]

Thus, Moltke, like his predecessors, faced the numbers problem from the beginning. For one thing, the Prussian Army even following the reforms was a match for or superior to no more than one adversary in terms of personnel numbers. And on the other hand, the progressively increasing growth in personnel numbers brought with it the corresponding challenge of moving and controlling masses of soldiers. In the first case, Moltke could place his hope on politics in the personal skills of Bismarck. The question of how to move supplies and deploy, maneuver, and command a mass military force to produce victory could only be answered by himself, the chief of the Great General Staff. Moltke the Elder was not the only senior military leader in Europe who faced this problem, which arose from increasing population growth and the progressive industrialization of warfare. In contrast to other European military leaders, however, he was the one who first thought through and implemented in the most compelling way the tactical, strategic, and—especially important—operational consequences of these developments.

The new Prussian chief of staff was convinced that one's forces could never be too strong to bring about the decision.[21] It was, therefore, every commander's task to ensure the greatest numerical superiority possible in a battle. Securely deploying a large army with more than one hundred thousand soldiers onto the battlefield over long distances created not only transport problems, but also logistical problems in the broader sense. Moltke summarized it well in the *Verordningen für die höheren Truppenführer* (Regulations for Senior Troop Commanders): "Strictly speaking, very large force concentrations are a calamity. It is difficult to feed an army that is concentrated in one location, and impossible to billet it. It cannot march, nor operate, nor exist in the long run; it can only fight."[22]

Moltke, therefore, searched for the ways and means to ensure numerical superiority on the battlefield and to be able to maneuver and to control a mass military force while simultaneously ensuring its supplies. He believed firmly that final victory could only be achieved if these factors acted together. Moltke's solution to that problem, which has been embedded in the vocabulary of German officers ever since, was "March Separately, Strike Combined." It was not a new concept, but Moltke adapted it pragmatically to the current situation and applied it at the battles of Königgrätz and Sedan. He divided his force into several large field armies, which he led to the battlefield as far as possible along different approach routes, and then brought them together to bring about a decision. The dividing of the forces also offered a decisive operational time advantage, as Moltke explained in his essay "Über Marschtiefen" (On March Depths). He worked out the importance of the General Staff's calculating resources, the space, and the time lines, because separately moving elements of the force were capable of achieving higher march rates.[23]

Even though Moltke rejected the permanent concentration of forces during the approach march for ease of logistics and transportation, he insisted unconditionally upon such concentration for the battle. The new chief of staff, however, certainly did not underestimate the risks of a concentric attack on exterior lines. As Napoleon had demonstrated most effectively, an able adversary, through rapid changes of his army's positions, was capable of defeating individually the enemy's separately moving force elements before they could converge. Napoleon, therefore, always considered the force operating on interior lines to hold the advantage at the strategic level. We will examine this issue further in connection with the plans Moltke developed after the establishment of the German Reich for a potential two-front war against France and Russia.

Moltke the Elder's ideas contradicted those of Jomini, whose thinking predominated among military theoreticians until far into the nineteenth century, and who on principle rejected the concept of separate actions on exterior lines. Referring to Napoleon, Jomini stated that the French emperor's active and mobile warfare on interior lines had been extremely successful in defeating successive concentric attacks conducted on exterior lines. As already noted, Moltke's ideas were not new. Even if Friedrich II in exceptional circumstances had used the concentric control of separated units, Gerhard von Scharnhorst was the first to postulate concentric warfare.[24]

> The opinion that one must hold his forces together in war and that it is a principle of warfare that they should not be split is, thus, wrong. Rather, it is a general rule, albeit only for the abler [commanders], to spread out carefully while forcing the enemy to do the very same thing, and then to attack individual elements in a concentrated manner. The principle of strategy . . . therefore, demands never standing concentrated—but to fight in a concentrated way.[25]

Scharnhorst's ideas, which were shared by August Graf Neidhardt von Gneisenau, can be seen clearly in the concentric coalition campaign against Napo-

leon in 1813 and at the Battle of Leipzig.[26] While Clausewitz makes a comparison evaluating the advantages and the drawbacks of concentric warfare, Prince
Wilhelm, who later became the Prussian king and German Kaiser, explained in
1830 that the main principle of war is to "march separated, but strike together."[27]
This statement, which in all probability was formulated on behalf of the prince by
Moltke's predecessor as chief of the General Staff, General Karl von Reyher, shows
that Moltke's ideas were no break with his predecessors' military thinking.[28] As in
other areas, Moltke built upon the ideas that had been circulating for years among
the members of the General Staff. The emerging entirely new means of transportation now made it possible to apply and implement these ideas in a new way.

Railway and Telegraph: The Acceleration of Space and Time

The military use of the railway was the most important of these developments.[29]
Although many Prussian officers were initially skeptical about this innovative and
almost revolutionary means of transport, the General Staff recognized the significance of the railways early on, and from 1856 onward started drawing up railway
schedules for the transportation of forces.

Moltke himself pointed out the importance of the railways in a short publication as early as 1842.[30] But while his predecessors tended to focus on the practical
advantages of rail for logistics and the transport of soldiers, Moltke recognized
the operational-strategic potential of the railways—the speed that led to the saving of time and the gaining of space. The new means of transportation made space
smaller through its capability of crossing distances in less time. The limits on the
factors of time and space, which had existed for centuries in both the civilian and
the military worlds, were lifted.

As with the introduction of horses to warfare, the steam engine right from the
beginning obviously held an increased potential for expansion. This leap in quantity provided warfare with a certain increase in acceleration whose advantages
had to be applied. Although the control and supply of large force elements became
more flexible through the use of the railways, the integration of those forces into
the deployment plans presented new difficulties. Thus, the orderly transport of
large formations to the right location and the unloading of those forces at the right
moment required a significant amount of planning. While Moltke's predecessors
had recognized the importance of the railways and the telegraph for warfare, they
had not integrated these innovations into concrete war plans. Moltke the Elder
changed that. In 1859 for the first time he included the exact dates of the railway
transports into his deployment plan.[31] Consequently, the new chief of staff, who
was one of the first to make a realistic assessment of the use of railways in war,
established a special Railway Section in the General Staff in 1869. That section
drafted the time lines for the rail transports, thus working out the data upon which

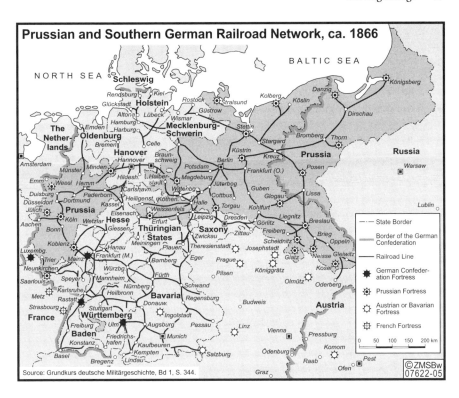

the mobilization plans were developed in the future. Furthermore, Moltke introduced transport exercises as part of the General Staff and force exercises.

The advanced capacity of the railways as a means of mass transportation can be seen in the Prussian-German deployment of 1870, when approximately 510,000 soldiers, some 160,000 horses, and more than 1,400 guns were transported into the lodgment areas by rail within only thirteen days. The new means of transport made the deployment faster and more precise, which in turn created the possibility of a quick opening of the war with superior numbers concentrated at the designated point. At the same time, the enormous planning workload considerably increased the managerial requirements in the headquarters, while reaction time decreased drastically. Mistakes that happened during deployment, therefore, could only be corrected with enormous difficulty, or not at all.

The time gained through the quick deployments could be used for political leverage, as in the Austro-Prussian War of 1866, or for operational leverage as in the Franco-Prussian War of 1870–1871. The possibility that rapid railway deployments would limit the political room for maneuver, as in fact happened in 1914 at the start of World War I, could not yet be foreseen in the middle of the nineteenth century. The expanding advantages of the railways also influenced another change in thinking over the years. Originally rail transport was seen as an advantage to the side conducting defensive operations on interior lines, but it increasingly became obvious that rail transport offered even greater advantages for conducting offensive operations on exterior lines.[32] General Staff officers, therefore, recognized quickly that the decisive advantage of the railways was not in supply transport, but rather in the immediate opening of the war. During the following decades the insight that the gain in time benefited the attacker reinforced an already existing preference for offensive warfare.

The electrical telegraph was another technical innovation that Prussia integrated into its concept of warfare. But because of their lack of qualified personnel and usable equipment, the potential provided by the telegraph could not be brought to bear where it would have been most advantageous for the command and control of military forces, on the enemy's territory.[33]

Both technical innovations compressed the factors of space and time. In the first case, they reduced only one's own space, because in the final analysis they accelerated only one's own force movements and communications. As soon as the forces entered the enemy's territory, the advantages ended either because the enemy destroyed his rail and communications facilities, or because the enemy's facilities were not compatible with one's own equipment. German forces managed in neither 1866 nor 1870–1871 to rebuild quickly the destroyed railway infrastructures in the enemies' countries. Therefore, as in the Napoleonic era, quickly advancing forces depended on supplies coming from their own country on horse carts. Meanwhile, the arriving supplies piled up at the unloading points.[34] Thus, until World War I the acceleration of the linked factors of space and time ended at the forward-most unloading points.

The Individualization of Command: Command by Directive

Dividing the army into several field armies operating remotely in space and time from the direct control of the commander in chief made necessary a new approach to command and control. Since it was not possible with nineteenth-century communications technology for one general to exercise direct control of the field armies operating at great distances from each other, Moltke the Elder decided to grant the commanders of major units far-reaching autonomy in the accomplishment of their tasks. Here, too, he used the mission-type command and control system that had become common practice in the General Staff since Scharnhorst and Gneisenau. Moltke adapted this system to the new realities.[35] He initiated the individualization of command and control by the means of mission-type command flowing from the senior-most level of command.[36] This system, which became known as *Auftragstaktik*, was integrated into all levels of command in the German Army over the next few decades.

Moltke flattened the hierarchical chain of command and the command levels by increasing individual responsibilities. This contributed essentially to the development of operational thinking, because henceforth command and control were exercised not only through orders, but also by the understanding of the common idea of the battle. The chief of the General Staff gave objective-oriented tasks to the force commanders and other commanders, without interfering with their detail planning, which they had to accomplish within the framework of the overall planning. Moltke's order for the invasion of Bohemia in 1866 and the freedom of action of the army's senior commanders are prime examples of this system of command and control: "From the point in time they face the enemy, the army commanders must use the army divisions entrusted to them according to their own discretion and the necessities of the situation, always taking into account the situations of the other divisions. Mutual support will become necessary through continued understanding."[37]

This procedure allowed commanders at the point of the action to react rapidly and flexibly to unforeseen events—"frictions," as Clausewitz called them. This required, however, that the superiors gave only orders that could be executed and that they refrained from micromanaging any details. While there were clear advantages to such a system, there also was a risk that the subordinate leaders would not act within the framework of the intent of their superior leaders, or that the subordinates would make mistakes. Moltke was willing to accept these risks for the obviously greater benefit to be derived. The basis for this type of leadership method included trust in the subordinates, the standardization of the education and training of the officer corps—especially the General Staff officers—and the ability of the members of the officer corps to assess situations individually and independently and make and execute the corresponding decisions.

The Prussian General Staff system ensured the success of this leadership principle. The four pillars of the system were the uniform training of the General Staff officers at the Kriegsakademie, the Great General Staff itself in Berlin, the *Generalstabsreisen* (General Staff rides), and the *Kriegsspielen* (war games).

The General Staff officers, being on the same organizational level, understood each other as a result of their training and education. The German armed forces' system of issuing orders has, since that time, contained a paragraph stating explicitly the *Absicht* (intent) of the superior commander. This remains a key element of Bundeswehr orders procedure to this day. This command and control procedure, which Moltke developed further, was based on the principle of historical-critical realism, which allowed every individual to act within certain limits.[38] The slowly developing individualization of the civil society made its way also into the military, where the classic mass infantry drills of the era of Friedrich II lost all meaning.

Moltke demanded initiative from his force commanders. Faced with the complexities of war, he considered actions characterized by initiative to be more important, despite the inherent potential for error, than the slavish execution of orders or waiting in ambiguous situations. He therefore explicitly demanded autonomous actions within the overall framework of the high command. "Numerous are the situations in which an officer must act according to his own judgment. It would be a serious mistake for him to wait for orders in moments when orders often cannot be given."[39] The advantages of directive command and control improved considerably the coordination of separate units, thereby minimizing the danger of being defeated by an adversary defending on interior lines because support did not materialize.

A mass military force divided into two independently acting forces, their rapid mobility and logistics support based on the railways, and the ability to exert command and control over the detached major units by means of directives show us two pillars of Moltke's thinking that were closely linked to the development of nineteenth-century society, and which made offensive operations possible. Together with the concentric attack on the exterior lines, they form the framework of Moltke's operational thinking.

Fire and Maneuver

In this section we will address another central point of Moltke's operational thinking that is closely linked to his overall focus on the enemy's army. For Moltke, the enemy's territory, including his capital, was the strategic objective of war. The enemy's army was the operational objective, meaning it was the target of any attack because it secured the objective of the war.[40] Moltke taught, then, that the battle was the most efficient means of destroying the enemy force. The battle was the focus of his concept of warfare, as well as the starting point of his concrete operational thinking. As he stated unequivocally in his regulations for senior commanders: "Victory in the decision brought about by force of arms is the most important factor in war. Victory alone breaks the enemy's will, forcing him to succumb to ours. Neither the occupation of an area of land nor the conquest of a certain location, but rather the destruction of the enemy force alone will usually be decisive."[41]

The accomplishment of such, however, was extremely difficult owing to the increased firepower of the mass military forces, and therefore required a new approach. For Moltke the solution lay in maneuvering. The conclusion derived from tactics that the strength of the enemy armies and increased firepower would very likely thwart a pure head-on attack led him to the solution of a mobile tactical defensive combined with a subsequent counterattack, which in turn would be based on a frontal attack to fix the base of envelopment of the enemy army's flank. Moltke also was convinced that it was necessary to divide his own forces because a tactical flanking maneuver immediately before the battle would be impossible owing to the range of the artillery and the infantry weapons of the committed troops. Moreover, he was convinced, like Napoleon, that an army should never be united immediately before the battle in sight of the enemy. For Moltke, the operation was perfect if his own, separately marching formations converged concentrically on the enemy's front and flank.

The *vollkommene Schlacht* (perfect battle) planned in such a manner, however, was also a function of masterly operational command on the one side and poor operational command on the other. It was, therefore, something fairly exceptional and not, as is constantly repeated today, the norm. When all factors were combined in the best possible way, such as at Königgrätz, strategy and operations achieved the optimal results. Moltke, who was a realist, consequently took the battles of Königgrätz and Sedan for what they were—exceptions to the norm. Thus, as he said to his officers during a tactical discussion in 1873: "If we succeed in attacking the enemy from two sides and in combining two columns on the battlefield, we can expect the greatest successes. That is what we did at Königgrätz in 1866. But can it be expected here? No! The enemy will evade such an attack or go on the offensive himself in order to use his superiority to overwhelm one of our separate army units."[42]

Moltke knew that there was no guarantee of victory. On the question of whether a battle should be conducted offensively or defensively, there were phases where he tended toward a mobile defense because of the increasing weapons effect. Thus, he wrote in 1874, commenting on the relatively high losses suffered during the Franco-Prussian War: "It is my conviction that the increase in firepower has given the tactical defensive a substantial advantage over the tactical offensive. It is true that we were always on the offensive during the 1870 campaign, and that we took the enemy's strongest positions, but at what cost!? Shifting onto the offensive only after having repelled several attacks by the enemy seems more promising to me."[43]

Of course Moltke still believed that a victorious defensive battle generally ended in offensive actions that brought about the decision. While on the tactical level Moltke preferred the defensive because of the increased weapons effects, he favored rapid, mobile, and offensive warfare with a clear concentration of effort at the operational level because it was now possible to combine the force elements concentrically on the battlefield, thanks to the new transportation technologies and the improved coordination systems. "While the tactical defensive is the stronger form, the strategic [operational] offensive is the more efficient form, which, alone, leads to the objective. . . . In short, one may say that the strategic [operational] offensive is the direct way to the objective, while the strategic [operational] defensive is the detour."[44]

Behind all these deliberations was Moltke's conviction that operations should bring about a rapid and fundamental decision—in other words, the overcoming of the enemy in battle. As Moltke wrote: "The objectives of war [can] never be reached in a more complete fashion than by battle. The primary objective must be to overcome the principal enemy force in the open air, i.e. by means of battle."[45] As a consequence and by intentionally neglecting secondary theaters, he emphasized the maximum possible concentration of forces and combat efficiency in the operational main effort in order to bring about a rapid decision. All other activities took second place to this goal. But in contrast to the Napoleonic era, the annihilation of the beaten enemy during the pursuit was hardly possible any longer because of increased weapons effects. Moltke, therefore, stressed the necessity of achieving, if possible, a total victory on the battlefield, thereby annihilating the enemy army.

The Objective of the Operation: The Rapid Battle of Annihilation

Entirely consistent with Clausewitz's ideas, victory for Moltke did not equal complete annihilation of his foe, which according to a popular contemporary interpretation meant the physical extinction of the enemy force. Rather, Moltke defined it as putting the enemy force in such a condition that "it can no longer continue the war."[46] Moltke, then, did not call for a *Vernichtungskrieg* (war of annihilation) in the sense of the later racial ideology of the National Socialists. Nor did his operational ideas lay the foundation for such a special kind of warfare of the twentieth century. Contrary to Clausewitz's understanding, the war aim for Moltke was solely based on achieving the elimination of the enemy force. One reason for this conviction certainly was the knowledge that in the middle of the "long nineteenth century" wars should be fought as rapidly as possible because of the size of the armed forces involved, the interruptions to trade and commerce, the speed of mobilization, and not least importantly Prussia's central position.[47] Even his comments on a long war, resulting from the experiences with the *Volkskrieg* (people's war) in France, did not change this fundamental conviction. That experience actually confirmed for Moltke his conviction that only a quick war was capable of preventing a prolonged shedding of blood and the resulting radicalization leading to a people's war. Nor were these operational considerations the only reasons why it was necessary to limit the war by ending it as quickly as possible. There also was the threat of an uncontrollable dissolution of constraints. Moltke, on the other hand, did not think it was possible to prevent a people's war absolutely. But at the same time he did not make the annihilation of the enemy's army in a decisive battle an absolute. As he explained it: "It greatly depends on the political situation whether it is right at the risk of heavy losses during a war to plan the battles in such a way that they aim for annihilation, or to choose the safe path and achieve the goal through a series of less decisive successes."[48]

The Primacy of Politics

The argument has been made repeatedly that Moltke, as a faithful student of Clausewitz, was a proponent of absolute war and was therefore primarily responsible for starting the process of the totalization of German warfare that began in the middle of the nineteenth century.[49] That argument, however, is surely a superficial one.[50] As previously noted, Moltke undoubtedly did not understand the primacy of politics in the same way Clausewitz did.[51] Rather, Moltke separated war from politics. When weapons spoke, politics had to remain silent. On the other hand, this conviction of Moltke's did not, as some historians continue to argue, remain unchallenged by the orthodoxy of German military thinking. By the turn of the century, for example, leading German officers such as the former Minister of War General Julius von Verdy du Vernois and Lieutenant General Rudolf von Caemmerer questioned in their writings Moltke's views about the influence of politics on operations.

Moltke did not want the "integrity of the conduct of operations" in the war threatened by politics, or even by the war minister, who, in Moltke's opinion, was only responsible for the provision of personnel and materiel. This latter point is forgotten frequently. Nonetheless, in war as well as in peace, Moltke always accepted the primacy of politics in the person of the king of Prussia and later the German Kaiser, Wilhelm I.[52] That distinguished Moltke from his successor, Alfred Graf von Waldersee, who was dismissed from office when he did not support the sovereign's political decisions. For Moltke, the Kaiser was the sovereign, and not the Reich chancellor, who embodied the highest political decision-making authority. Moltke's key memorandum, "Über die militärpolitische Lage" (On the Military-Political Situation) of 10 October 1879, offers impressive evidence for this. Moltke concluded his deliberations with the following sentences, often forgotten in the standard literature: "Your Imperial and Royal Highness may most graciously forgive me if it was the case that my assessment digressed. In the final analysis, the military sphere can no longer be separated from the political one. Would Your Majesty, being above both of these, proceed to a gracious evaluation of the idea I have developed."[53]

Such statements show that Moltke recognized an interdependence of military and political actions to the extent that the Kaiser was the sovereign and the commander in chief, and that he made the decisions after being advised by his closest military and political experts. According to Moltke's conviction, however, the command and control of the operations was solely the task of the chief of the General Staff. Nonetheless, the Kaiser as the commander in chief of the army was able to exert influence on the chief of staff at any time.[54]

The General Staff: The Center of Planning and Operational Leadership

By the middle of the nineteenth century, the era in which a commander was able to control a battle in the unity of space and time in Aristotle's sense was long over. The command and control of geographically widely spread mass military forces required not only qualified subordinate leaders, but also a general head-quarters and staff. This development, which was accelerated even more rapidly by advancing technology and increasing force levels during the nineteenth century, had started as early as the Napoleonic Wars. Moltke expanded the General Staff to become the main, permanent, and homogeneous planning and warfighting authority, for the purpose of enhancing the chief of the General Staff's command and control capability and planning competency. Since 2 June 1866, the chief of the General Staff had been commissioned by the king with the direct command and control of operations.[55] It is important to remember here that at the time Moltke assumed office he took over an existing planning and command and control organization that by European standards was already working together extremely well. It was a foundation upon which he could build.

The rise of the General Staff came at the time of growing specialization and professionalization in both civil society and the military. In the process, autonomous areas of competency emerged that faced each other with increasing incomprehension. The steadily growing division of labor and the increasing complexity of military procedures caused the military social structure to develop a life of its own. The resulting military subculture emerged within society. During the nineteenth century this process was accelerated by the gradual disintegration of the predominant position in society held by the nobility, the class which formerly had provided the soldiers and the rulers.[56] Many noblemen, especially Prussians, withdrew into the military, which was bound to the Kaiser by a specific code of honor and personal loyalty. Thanks to the victories in the German wars of unification, these soldiers occupied the most prestigious position in the German Reich.[57] A simultaneous development—one that is still continuing—was the emergence of the military rather than the ruling political leaders as the group with the specialist knowledge of warfare, and its prevention. Over the years, the German General Staff developed into a hotbed of this specialized knowledge. To this day in the Anglo-American literature the German General Staff is either overly celebrated[58] or portrayed as the beginning of the German Sonderweg (special path).[59] Many German historians likewise represent the operational command and control achievements of the General Staff in a favorable light through the use of such phrases as *Generalstabsmässig*—done in General Staff style.[60] It therefore is not surprising that the typical ideal construct of a General Staff is often based on the Prussian-German example.

At the time Moltke took over the General Staff, it was a department of the War Ministry, and the chief of the General Staff was the advisor to the war minister, not to the king. Although the chief of the General Staff was granted *Immediat-recht* (direct access to the sovereign) only in 1883, and the General Staff was not formally put on a par with the War Ministry until the end of the war in 1918, the General Staff under Moltke became one of the three primary corridors of power within the German military system. And there was a permanent competition with the other two, the Military Cabinet and the War Ministry. At the same time the General Staff acquired the sole, long-term planning competency for mobilization and deployment, as well as for the conduct of operations and warfighting. As will be shown later, mobilization during the course of this development lost its independent character and became a decisive act of operational planning within the framework of deployment.

It is particularly important at this point to consider the training and education system of General Staff officers in relation to the long-term development of the doctrine of operational leadership as applied to the tactical and operational levels in peacetime. As principal staff assistants, General Staff officers were to transmit the competencies they acquired in peacetime. Under Moltke the Generalstabsreisen (General Staff rides) became the main training tool. Not only did the staff rides simulate specific war scenarios, but they first and foremost provided the General Staff officers with tactical operational training, and thus conveyed an understanding of the operational dimensions of space and time. The intention was to guarantee a homogeneous level of training among this small military elite, which in turn would ensure consistency in command and control. The study of war history served the same purpose.

The evaluation of previous military campaigns had already begun in Scharnhorst's time, but Moltke intensified the practice with the focus on practical application. The intent of this approach to the study of war history was to extract during times of peace examples of successful warfighting for the training of those officers who did not have personal war experience, and also to derive lessons from war history for future warfare. Contrary to what has been written repeatedly, however, it was not Moltke who initiated this process.[61] The origins of this process can be traced back to the time of the Wars of Liberation, when Scharnhorst subjected individual campaigns of the Revolutionary Wars to examination in order to draw lessons from them.[62] Like many of his predecessors, Moltke personally studied war history extensively, and he promoted its intensified study as an element in the training of General Staff officers.

Initially a study subject of its own at the Prussian Kriegsakademie for training in operational-strategic thinking, the study of war history later came to serve the purpose of supplying material for tactics and strategy lessons within the framework of the application method. The objective of the application method, introduced by Julius von Verdy du Vernois, was for the student to develop his own nonschematic solution based on a specific military situation and the relevant circumstances. The result would be lessons learned for the future. The longevity of this ahistorical methodology resulted from the fact that tactics instructors at the *Reichswehr* officer training school were simultaneously the war history instructors. The Bundeswehr to this day needs to incorporate more war history examples in its training.[63]

Moltke's Operational Thinking in the Planning Stage and in War: The Battle of Königgrätz

In the following section the Battle of Königgrätz in 1866 will serve as the model as we briefly examine Moltke's operational thinking, from the practical application of the operations plan, through operational leadership during the war, to the successful conclusion of the battle. (See Plate 1.)

Königgrätz was the largest battle of the nineteenth century, and at the same time it was the last classically decisive battle in European military history. A study of this battle allows us to summarize, without getting lost in tactical details, Moltke's most important operational considerations against the backdrop of the reality of the war.[64] In order to do this we must draw back the veil of mythology cloaking the battle to reveal the key points of this study. The myth surrounding Königgrätz is the result of Prussia's rapid victory over a quantitatively and qualitatively superior Austria. Such an outcome was completely unexpected by the military experts of the day. According to Moltke, Prussia's geographical position—with its shallow depth of defense and its 450-kilometer semicircular border with the enemy territories of Saxony and Bohemia—did not allow for defensive warfare. At the same time, the concave deployment formation gave Prussia the opportunity to execute a concentric attack on exterior lines, whereas Austria and Saxony had the advantage of the defense on interior lines.

According to the contemporary theories of warfare, the advantage was clearly on the side of Saxony and Austria. Because Italy also declared war on Austria, only part of the Danube Monarchy's armed forces were deployed against Prussia. Moltke, on the other hand, ignored Austria's allies and sent most of the Prussian army against the main enemy, Austria.

This clear concentration of effort, combined with the concentric deployment, increased the time pressure and carried high risks. Therefore, it was not only for political but also for purely military reasons that a rapid victory had to be sought.

Moltke decided to invade Bohemia with three separate field armies: the Army of the Elbe and the First and the Second Armies. Although his operations plan was criticized by many high-ranking officers in the Prussian military, Moltke stuck to it. In the face of Austria's earlier mobilization, he decided to carry out in one single action mobilization, deployment, and the start of operations simultaneously. In doing so he would gain time, seize the initiative, and proceed immediately to the offensive after the deployment was completed. However, the concentric advance on Gitschin, close to Königgrätz, had to be precisely coordinated time-wise in order to achieve the planned linkup of the Prussian army on the battlefield so that the Austrian front and flank could be attacked simultaneously.

The weaknesses of the telegraph communications network and the logistical support system quickly became evident when the troops marched into Bohemia. But since Austria and Saxony did not succeed in attacking and defeating individually the separately acting Prussian field armies, and since Moltke through his con-trol of the operation prevented the linkup of the Prussian armies from happening too early, the battle ensued north of Königgrätz on 3 July 1866.

The battle began in the morning with the attack of the First Army and ended in the afternoon with the retreat of the Austrians and Saxons to Königgrätz. Despite some frictions, Moltke succeeded in uniting his armies concentrically on the bat-tlefield. While the First Army, with the support of the Army of the Elbe, fixed the enemy with a frontal attack, the Second Army successfully attacked the Austrians' deep and open right flank. The Army of the Elbe, however, failed in its attempt to envelop the allies' left wing. While that meant the plan to destroy the combined Austrians and Saxons by a double envelopment did not succeed, the Austrian Army nonetheless was defeated in the evening of 3 July. It was the last European battle of decision that effectively concluded a war. Without going deeply into the tactical details, the Prussian *Zündnagelgewehr* (needle gun) certainly had a signifi-cant impact on the tactical course of the battle. The independent shifting of the Austrian right flank also aided the attack of the Second Army.

In the final analysis, Moltke's heavily criticized operations plan proved success-ful. In the conduct of real-world operations, Moltke had most definitely not failed his "lieutenant's exam," as Friedrich Engels had predicted he would.[65] Moltke had accom-plished the unexpected, which itself was an important feature of the system of opera-tional thinking he initiated. And in so doing, he had surprised the enemy. Moltke succeeded in quickly uniting three field armies concentrically in time and space. And despite the deployment frictions with logistical support, communications, and the issuing of orders, he managed to do it in a chronologically effective sequence.

Much of the approach in the course of this operation was by no means mod-ern, particularly the logistical support. Rather, it was carried out in a manner more typical of the Napoleonic era. Nevertheless, the Battle of Königgrätz gave proof to the practicality of three key concepts: (1) the ability to move mass military forces faster by separating them; (2) the avoidance of the defender's increased firepower by flanking attacks, while simultaneously fixing the enemy frontally; and (3) the conduct of an operation by adapting to the situation.

The flexibility with which Moltke developed his operational plans is demon-strated by the fact that in 1870 he did not have his troops dogmatically deploy concentrically. Since he expected the battle to take place right at the beginning of the war and close to the border, he advanced his troops separately and finally con-centrated them for the Battle of Sedan.

The Limits of Operational Thinking: People's War

The Battle of Sedan is at the center of the mythology surrounding German opera-tional thinking in the nineteenth century. The victory at Sedan, which was memorialized in the German Reich with the annual observances of *Sedantag* (Sedan Day) on 2 September, was a testament to the triumph of Moltke's operational leadership.[66] But in the final analysis, the German Reich celebrated a lost victory. All too often the fact is forgotten that the triumphant victory at Sedan was not the sought-after battle of decision. Nor did it result in the conclusion of the war, as Königgrätz did. Instead, the victory at Sedan merged into a months-long people's war, which was, according to Dierk Walter, a "combination of national consciousness, civic participation, and universal conscription."[67] The French did not accept their defeat at Sedan as a battle of decision in the classical sense. (See Plate 2.)

It is important to bear in mind that the people's war in the context of the Franco-Prussian War cannot be compared to a *Franc-tireur* (guerrilla fighter) war. Rather, the Germans mainly fought against the regular, even though improvised, forces of the French Republic. Therefore, it would be too simplistic to consider the second phase of the Franco-Prussian War in the context of operational thinking only from the perspective of a people's war. There is no doubt that the German troops struggled greatly with the peripheral guerrilla war that developed a momentum of its own, which combined with fortress warfare, the fight for the lines of communication, the setting-in of a war of attrition, and the limited possibilities of chasing an enemy who dispersed and reorganized on every occasion. All of these were elements reminiscent of pre-Napoleonic warfare that were thought to have been overcome by operational warfare. Nonetheless, the German leadership ultimately maintained the initiative and, despite inferiority in numbers, defeated the individually attacking enemy forces one after the other by operating on interior lines. This and the victory at Sedan, along with the protracted struggle with the Franc-tireurs, who were considered dishonorable, shaped the collective German memory of the war of 1870–1871.

Nonetheless, the body of myth that grew around the Battle of Sedan and the other victories ultimately won from a position of inferiority obscured understanding in the German military that while the greatest operational victories may be able to bring about the decision in battles, such was not necessarily the case for wars in the face of mass mobilizations and people's war.[68] As long as the warring parties still had the resources to field new armies, battles that in the past would have produced decisions were reduced to ordinary battle victories without necessarily having any strategic impact. Thus, the limits of operational thinking became obvious. This does not mean, however, that individual battle victories, such as the German victory at Tannenberg in 1914 or the Russian victory outside of Moscow in 1941, would not have any strategic impact. Such victories strengthened the winner's perseverance and confidence, and influenced neutral states.

The idea that politics in the form of an excessive nationalism denied the success of operational thinking by simply reducing the alleged decisive battle to an isolated event was widely rejected and never accepted by many in the German military. People's war, combined with war of attrition and partisan warfare, seemed to be a problem that could be solved through operational leadership, albeit with great difficulty. The confusion initially expressed over the duration and the intensity of the French people's war eventually passed into obscurity in the light of victory and German unification. Moltke himself made sure that the prestige of the army was not damaged by the official accounts of the war. The chief of the General Staff, who had voiced concerns even before the beginning of the war that the French would not accept a great German victory because of their patriotism, was surprised when his concerns came true.[69] Later, he summed up the changed character of warfare when he prefaced the third volume of the official history of the Franco-Prussian War with the following statement:

> The times are over when, for dynastic purposes, small armies of regular soldiers marched off to fight in order to conquer a town, a stretch of land, and then moved into winter quarters or made peace. Today's wars call whole nations to arms, and hardly a family is not affected. Demands are made on all of the financial strength of the state, and no turn of the year puts an end to the ceaseless actions.[70]

While the wars of the 1850s and 1860s were still controllable cabinet wars that were decided by battles limited in time and space, the Franco-Prussian War, which had started as a conventional cabinet war, developed in its second phase into a people's war between an invading army and the improvised troops of the French Republic. That war had the support of large segments of the population. It appeared that the cabinet war preferred by Moltke, with its potential limitation of violence, was in the process of being replaced by potentially unlimited people's war.

Preemptive War

Based on the conviction that Germany was facing an ever-growing grand coalition of enemies, Moltke the Elder and his successors during the decades preceding the outbreak of the Great War in 1914 repeatedly recommended preemptive warfare to the leadership of the Reich. As justification, the chiefs of the General Staff frequently cited the example of Frederick the Great, who had started the Seven Years' War with an attack on Saxony in 1756 in order to preempt his enemies France, Austria, and Russia. Bismarck, who viewed a preemptive war as a potential political option and who temporarily threatened France with such a war, also referred to the example of Frederick during an address he made to the Reichstag on 4 November 1871. As Bismarck explained the "theory of a war of aggression for the purpose of defense": "such a defense through advance is very frequently and in most cases the most effective form of defense, and it is very useful for a country with such a central location in Europe, with three to four borders that potentially can be attacked, to follow the example of Frederick the Great."[71]

Bismarck's further statements made it clear that the decision for a preemptive war was a strategic and thus a political decision. As Bismarck argued, "if there is really no way to prevent a war, the government must choose the point in time at which a war can be fought with the fewest casualties and with the least danger for the country, for the nation."[72] But since he did not see the existence of the German Reich threatened, Bismarck flatly refused Moltke's and Waldersee's military rationale for avoiding a two-front war and their repeated calls for a preemptive war in 1875 and between 1887 and 1890.[73]

From today's perspective, it is difficult to say with certainty whether or not Schlieffen sought a preemptive war against France. Schlieffen, who consistently abstained from making political demands, was surely ready to fight a preemptive war, if so required by the political leaders. He did not, however, actively call for such a war.[74] On the contrary, Moltke the Younger strongly recommended several times to Wilhelm II and also to the Foreign Office a preemptive war against the Entente.[75] During all those years, the recommendations of the General Staff for preemptive warfare as a solution to the Reich's strategic dilemma were rejected by Germany's political leadership.

Leaving aside an assessment of a preemptive war from the perspective of international law, the question whether offense is the best defense has been asked time and again in military history.[76] Even Thucydides described discussions in ancient Sparta on whether to preempt Athens's increasing power by a preventive war. Frederick the Great's motto "better to preempt than to be preempted" is not a uniquely Prussian-German perspective. France, too, launched preemptive wars on its western borders in the seventeenth and eighteenth centuries, as did Great Britain when the Royal Navy attacked the Danish fleet close to Copenhagen in 1807. The decisive factor is always the political will to thwart imminent enemy aggression.

Preemptive war has an offensive operational dimension as well as a defensive strategic dimension. Consequently, it is always a war of aggression, even if it serves the purpose of defense. This is what distinguishes a preemptive war from a war of conquest, which time and again has been propagandized as preventive in order to justify the aggressor. Such was the case of the German attack on the Soviet Union in 1941. However, no special form of operational thinking is necessary for the conduct of a preemptive war, apart from the fact that it can never be fought from the defensive, but must be fought from the offensive. Consequently, operational thinking based on an offensive mobile conduct of operations, as was the case with German operational thinking, does not necessarily lead to a preemptive war or a war of aggression. Nonetheless, it undoubtedly establishes the prerequisites for the political leaders to consider such operations. This, however, applied to all European armies in the nineteenth century and at the beginning of the twentieth.

Deployment Planning, 1871–1888

With the unification of Germany a new major power emerged in the heart of Europe. That country bordered Austria, Russia, and France as well as Switzerland, the Netherlands, Belgium, Luxembourg, and Denmark. From the perspective of the military and political leadership, Germany's central geographic position inherently carried the danger of a multi- or two-front war. Such a threat was nothing new to the General Staff, since throughout its history Prussia too had lived with the potential threat of a multi-front war. Friedrich II had fought against Austria, Russia, and France. Yet despite all his successes in battle, in the end he only ensured the survival of Prussia thanks to the "Miracle of the House of Brandenburg." This ubiquitous memory remained alive in varying degrees of intensity over the years. The General Staff, therefore, expected from the political leadership that it would at least avoid the threat of a multi-front war by forming alliances.

As the armies of millions grew and nationalism became rampant, Moltke's ideas became more impractical against the backdrop of a possible people's war. He clearly expressed this to the Kaiser at the conclusion of the negotiations on the Dual Alliance on 10 October 1879. Despite France's increases in armament and personnel, Moltke did not consider France alone as a major threat. However, if France formed an alliance with another major power bordering Germany and then attacked, the survival of the Reich would be seriously at risk.[77] As Moltke wrote to the Kaiser shortly after the end of the Franco-Prussian War, "The most dangerous challenge to the continued existence of the new German Reich would be a simultaneous war against Russia and France."[78]

Ever since he took office, Moltke had worked on plans for a two-front war against either France and Austria[79] or France and Russia.[80] In 1859, Moltke for the first time developed a deployment scenario for a two-front war against Russia and France based on the idea of "turning against the first front with as few forces as possible, fighting on the other front with as many forces and as swiftly as possible, and then reconquering what would have been lost on the first front in the meantime."[81] The operational intention of warfare on interior lines, with a defense on the one side and an offensive on the other, reappears in a modified form in all the plans of the General Staff for a war against Russia and France until 1914, and even for a long time after that. The idea that Russia's expected slow mobilization would facilitate a concentric offensive against the Russian Army outside Warsaw also appears repeatedly in future plans.

Eleven years later, Moltke submitted a new draft plan for a two-front war against France and Russia that included an offensive in the west as well as in the east. For this purpose, he divided the German Army into two almost equally large contingents.[82] Still recognizing the potential of a people's war, however, he pointed out that even a rapid success in the battle against France would probably not end the war.[83] In 1877 for the first time the General Staff considered defensive warfare against France in the case of a war against Austria and France. Yet, during that same year the General Staff planned to begin with a quick offensive against France in a two-front war against France and Russia, since France would be ready for war earlier than slowly mobilizing Russia. Under that scenario Moltke wanted to deploy 520,000 soldiers in the west and only 80,000 in the east. Even though he expected a quick battle to take place in the third week of the war and he called for an early declaration of war on France (on the fifth mobilization day) to support the initiative, he did not believe that France, even after losing a "decisive battle," could be forced by military means to make peace. As he noted: "Even with the greatest successes, we can never expect a rapid end to the fighting on this front, as the last campaign [the Franco-Prussian War] has sufficiently shown."[84]

Thus, Moltke gave up on the idea—which he had first developed in 1859 and had modified significantly by 1871—of first destroying one enemy and then the other. Based on this thinking as reflected in later campaign plans, a future two-front war against France and Russia would have resulted in an offensively conducted defensive battle, even with Austrian and Hungarian support. Based on the geographically and sufficiently widespread interior lines, the German armies would have been deployed time and again for varying concentrations of effort from the west to the east and vice versa by way of the well-developed German rail network within the war zone, which itself had expanded to Central Europe. Once the enemy was exhausted, it would then be the task of diplomacy to bring about the peace.

In 1879 Moltke finally gave up on his original operational concept. Based on the noticeable increases in Russian mobilization speed, the forward concentration of Russian troops in Poland, and the strengthened French fortifications, Moltke decided to fight on the defensive in the west and on the offensive in the east. This operational paradigm shift was based, among other factors, on the insight that the long eastern border could be better protected through offensive rather than defensive action, and that the strengthening of the French fortifications would prevent a quick decision in the battle in the west. Consequently, three-fourths of the army was to deploy to the east and only one-fourth against France. The latter force would have the mission of repelling French attacks through the conduct of a mobile defense anchored on the German fortifications at Metz-Diedenhofen and Strasbourg, with the final defensive line on the Rhine. After the successful conduct of a battle of annihilation against the Russian Army in Poland, the offensive would not be continued toward Russia. Instead, the then-available forces would be redeployed for an offensive in the west. Moltke flatly ruled out a decisive defeat of

Russia because of the depth of the Russian territory and Russia's resulting operational possibilities.

Even after Germany concluded the alliance with Austria-Hungary, Moltke generally adhered to his operational concepts. The Dual Alliance, however, provided him with the opportunity to reinforce the German forces in the west. In 1880, 360,000 soldiers were allocated to deploy to the east and 330,000 to the west. The offensive planned as a concentric attack on the Russian Army in Poland was now to be launched simultaneously from Prussia and Galicia. Although the German forces were still inferior in numbers, the new grouping of forces in the west now provided the possibility of achieving a decisive battle. Simultaneously, Moltke with the support of Alfred Graf von Waldersee, his assistant chief of staff and eventual successor as chief of staff, now saw an opportunity to implement his basic idea of combining the tactical defense with the strategic offense in the west.[85] Moltke, however, was not able to win over the majority of the General Staff, because most of the General Staff officers favored a rapidly conducted offensive operation. Moltke's last deployment plan (*Aufmarschplan*), developed with Waldersee in 1888, followed the basic principle of the offensive in the east and the defensive in the west. With the further reinforcement of the forces in the west to two-thirds of the army, the opportunity for a major decisive battle was again within the realm of the possible. But until Moltke left office as chief of the General Staff in 1888, there was no change in his fundamental insight that even the most successfully decisive battle would not result in the immediate end of the war on one of the two fronts.

Conclusion

Moltke did not invent operational thinking in Germany, but he structuralized it by combining already existing individual ideas with the new technological innovations of his time—railroads and the telegraph. He thus responded to the tactical changes required to address mass military forces and the increase of firepower resulting from the technological improvements in artillery and infantry weapons.

Operational thinking was not only influenced by the tactical changes, but it also evolved from tactics. Tactical maneuvers such as the envelopment or the flank attack were transferred to the level of mass military forces and retained their designations, usually with the additional term "operational." As far as terms are concerned, therefore, it was hardly possible during Moltke's era to make a distinction between operations and tactics, and it was probably not even yet necessary for his contemporaries. This explains the existing confusion of terms, and at the same time makes it clear why it was so difficult to define the new phenomenon precisely. Things were in a state of flux; clarification and structuring were not yet possible.

Moltke made a distinction between the decision of a battle and of an operation. He saw the latter as maneuver executed with great speed thanks to the division of one's own forces into separately operating field armies under the direction of the General Staff. The separately operating armies were combined in the battle in order to achieve the mission objective, the annihilation of the enemy's army—in Clausewitz's terms, to destroy or to crush it. For Moltke, maneuver provided the opportunity to avoid the increased firepower of the mass military forces that gave the defender an advantage in battle. However, the maneuvers had to be executed and controlled quickly, and with the element of surprise. According to Moltke, operational command and control and operational thinking were not schematic patterns, but rather a situation-oriented system of operational actions and reactions (*Aushilfen*) based on maneuver, which would bring about a quick victory. In the final analysis, substantial elements of Moltke's operational concept were Napoleonic. Moltke adapted them to the new technologies.

The individualization of command and control initiated by Moltke was a reflection of the contemporary acceleration of social life, which should not be underestimated as a factor in the development of operational thinking in Germany. For example, the ever faster operational-strategic planning cycle forced the political players into ever faster decision-making processes, to which they finally yielded in a strange form of fatalism.

Moltke did not consider the operational as a separate level of warfare between tactics and strategy, but rather as a subordinate function of strategy. But while he skipped back and forth between the two terms, the term "operation" found its way into the language of the General Staff. In fact, it really only entered the discourse and the planning processes of the German General Staff under Moltke's later successor, Alfred Graf von Schlieffen.

The people's war of 1871 illustrated the limits of operational warfare focused on the quick decision of the war, since it ignored the decision of the battle brought about by operational measures while mobilizing the people in a nationalistic manner. This led to the intensification of what for centuries had been known as asymmetric or low-intensity warfare, which both then and even now caused major problems for regular armies and prolonged wars for unlimited periods. Thus, people's war illustrated that even excellently conducted operational warfare did not guarantee a quick decision of the war.

The General Staff largely ignored this reality, its selective evaluation and learning processes only focusing on the operation that ultimately would lead to victory with inferior numbers. For the most part, the General Staff only considered military problems on the operational-strategic level and rarely on the strategic-political level. In the final analysis, the General Staff, which Moltke had expanded during his tenure to become Germany's primary operational planning and command authority, lacked the necessary competencies to function at the political level.

Although the General Staff had acquired a central position within the power structure of the German military system, it did not have the vital competencies in the spheres of armament, personnel, or economic and financial preparations necessary to conduct grand strategic—in other words, political—warfare. These functions remained under the control of either the German Military Cabinet or the War Ministry.

Therefore, the all-encompassing access of the General Staff to the materiel and personnel military resources cited all too often in the literature is a myth. In peacetime, the General Staff was merely the highest planning authority, and in time of war it was the operational command and control center. Logically, it focused in peacetime on operational planning. But this planning almost inevitably led to the tendency to eliminate frictions by expanding the preliminary military considerations to the whole war. Despite the experiences of the Franco-Prussian War and the increased armament efforts of France, the General Staff held to the opinion that owing to Germany's central geographic position, a two-front war could only be won through mobile operational warfare. This becomes obvious from Moltke's deployment plans (*Aufmarschpläne*). In its considerations the General Staff ignored the people's war potentially looming in the future. It was, rather, the responsibility of the politicians to head off any probable war of attrition.

4

The Sword of Damocles

A Two-Front War

> Operation is movement.
>
> —Field Marshal Alfred Graf von Schlieffen

The Central Position

"Only make the right wing strong." Schlieffen on his deathbed probably did not utter that phrase addressed to his successor, as his followers long maintained. Nonetheless, those words express the tragedy of a man whose life's work was posthumously glorified either as a recipe for victory or condemned as the climax of Prussian-German militarism. Based on the studies of Gerhard Ritter in the 1950s,[1] schoolbooks and nonfiction texts to this day inform their readers that the German Reich entered the First World War in 1914 with the Schlieffen Plan as its operational and strategic plan. That plan failed at the Marne after Great Britain was forced to enter the war because of the German violation of Belgian and Luxembourg neutrality. This generally accepted interpretation has been challenged recently by American historian Terence Zuber. His theories on Schlieffen's operational plans, culminating in the thesis that there was no Schlieffen Plan, sparked an international debate.[2] Thanks to newly discovered source documents, however, previous concepts of Schlieffen's operational plans, and thus of operational thinking of the General Staff, have been reconsidered in the course of this debate.[3] Earlier, Annika Mombauer verified that the German General Staff in 1914 entered the war not with the Schlieffen Plan, but with an operational plan by Colonel General Helmuth von Moltke the Younger, which was a modification of Schlieffen's concepts in crucial areas.[4]

Before we turn to operational thinking before the First World War and the resulting operational and strategic plans, we must explain the geostrategic position of the German Reich in the late nineteenth century in terms of space, time, and forces. Situated in the center of Europe, Germany bordered its ally Austria-Hungary and Switzerland to the southeast and south. The mountain barrier of the Alps constituted a natural terrain obstacle against attacks from the south. Germany's northern borders were formed by the North and Baltic Seas, as well as by

Denmark on the Cimbrian Peninsula, which together with Sweden controlled the Baltic exits. In the east, the Reich shared a concave border measuring more than nine hundred kilometers with Russia, one of Germany's two main potential opponents. That eastern border offered no natural protection by major rivers or mountains. Furthermore, the areas of the country east of the Vistula, which extended to great depth, were vulnerable to being cut off. Therefore, defending East Prussia was difficult. In addition, Berlin itself was only three hundred kilometers from the eastern border, and only one hundred kilometers from the first natural obstacle, the Oder River. Although the geographic situation in the east seemed unfavorable at first glance, it also had its advantages for the Central Powers. At least there was the possibility of conducting a flank attack simultaneously from East Prussia and the Carpathian Mountains to defeat the Russian forces stationed in Congress Poland, which projected far into the territory of the Central Powers. However, the roughness of the terrain, dissected as it was by many rivers and marshes, as well as the vastness of the area, made such an operation very difficult. Simultaneously, the German railway network was not nearly as well developed in the east as it was in the west, which made a rapid eastern deployment considerably more difficult, if not impossible.

In the west, the Reich bordered Belgium, the Netherlands, Luxembourg, and France. The section of that border shared with the potentially most dangerous opponent, France, ran along the ridge of the Vosges Mountains to the foothills of the Ardennes in Lorraine. Both France and Germany had reinforced this border region with fortifications at Belfort, Epinal, Toul, and Verdun on the French side, and Strasbourg and Metz-Diedenhofen (Thionville) on the German side. If the French broke through the German lines, the next natural defense would be the Rhine. That, however, would mean accepting the loss of important industrial areas of the Rhineland. Given the geostrategic central position of the German Reich, one cannot dismiss the observation made by the Reich Archives: "No other Great Power, with the possible exception of Austria-Hungary, which had long stretches of its borders protected by high mountain ramparts, was in a similarly unfavorable situation from threat of attack as the German Reich."[5]

Based on this evaluation, which is understandable in terms of the geography, the military leadership of the German Reich developed a perception of space that fatalistically did not allow for any alternatives to a two-front war. That, in turn, influenced Germany's political decision makers. At the same time, the military professionalism of the General Staff, despite this fixation, prevented it from making plans for a case of war against either Russia or France alone, in parallel with plans for a two-front war. It was not until the mobilization year of 1913–1914 that the General Staff in response to the development of the political situation ceased to plan for a great eastern deployment.[6]

Furthermore, all operational and strategic plans of the General Staff for a two-front war were subject to the dictates of time, because of Germany's central position. Most German military theorists and the members of the General Staff believed that in the event of a two-front war the only alternatives were either a lengthy defensive war of attrition or a rapid offensive war of maneuver. According to the majority thinking, it was impossible to win a protracted war of attrition because of domestic and economic factors. Thanks to Germany's geographical dimensions and good railway infrastructure, the only chance for victory was to operate either defensively or offensively at selected strategic points through proactive and rapid actions based on interior lines. Germany's difficult military situation owing to unfavorable space and time factors became even more difficult because of the relative numerical inferiority of the personnel and materiel of Germany's land forces.

Proceeding from the reality of Germany's geostrategic situation, the first two chiefs of the German General Staff, Moltke the Elder and Waldersee, planned between 1871 and 1891 to respond to a two-front war by dividing the German armed forces between the Eastern and Western Fronts, using the German fortifications to conduct a mobile defense against France, and taking regional offensive actions against Russia in coordination with Germany's ally, Austria-Hungary. This defensive strategy was based on conducting limited offensive thrusts. The intent was not to achieve a total victory through a battle of annihilation.[7]

Dealing with the threat of a two-front war was a rather theoretical issue during the tenures of Moltke and Waldersee. The one exception was the crisis of 1887–1888, when both specifically demanded war against Russia. For their successors, however, a two-front war was a real issue, because of the political and ensuing military developments. In contrast to Moltke the Elder, who had always been able to wage his wars in the knowledge that he had excellent diplomatic support from Bismarck, his successors had to plan for a two-front war from a position of inferiority and under completely different political and military conditions.

Discourse and Definition

The established literature tends to reduce the development of operational thinking in the late nineteenth century to Schlieffen, while simultaneously suggesting that such thinking was straightforward and without any discussions within the officer corps since the time of Moltke the Elder. This picture fits the classic cliché that the General Staff, a monolithic institution intent on performance and focused solely on the will of the chief of the General Staff, was the only place for reflection on operational thinking.

But Schlieffen and the General Staff were not the only ones discussing the waging of a two-front war. Many active and retired officers, including General Friedrich von Bernhardi, General Alfred von Boguslawski, General Wilhelm von

Blume, Field Marshal Colmar von der Goltz, General Sigismund von Schlichting, and Austria-Hungary's General Alfred Krauss participated in the debate. During a public discourse that was unique in German military history, they discussed tactical, operational, and strategic processes for waging a future war with mass armies.

The discourse surrounding terms like operations and operational level of command was something akin to a Tower of Babel situation. Hardly any published book or journal article could do without one or the other of the terms, but only a few authors explained those terms at all. Since there was no official definition of operations in the Schlieffen era, the few explanations available provide the only insight into the development of the terms in the late nineteenth century. Boguslawski, for example, wrote: "Operations refer to an entirety of actions in a theater of war aiming at a particular objective. As a rule, they consist of marches, moving into positions, and battles. By no means does operation always include the method of attack; however, it is difficult to separate the idea of maneuver from this term."[8]

In contrast, von der Goltz referred to belligerent acts that were in a close, purposeful context: "Any such group of acts is composed of marches, buildups, and battles and are referred to as an 'operation.'"[9] The common feature of both definitions is that operations consist of multiple connected and purposeful acts and that the aspect of maneuver, which Moltke the Elder had emphasized, is at the center of an operation. None of the authors, however, classified an operation as the distinct level of war between the levels of tactics and strategy.

Lessons from Military History

Integrated into the discourse on how to best wage a two-front war, officers also discussed how to learn properly from military history. Evolving from the extended debate over the reform of infantry combat between the advocates of normal tactics (*Normaltaktik*) and those of mission-type command and control (*Auftragstaktik*),[10] historian Hans Delbrück and his military critics argued over whether Frederick II (the Great) had been a master of the strategy of annihilation, or a practitioner of the strategy of attrition.

This conflict, which lasted for decades and became known to history as the *Strategiestreit* (strategy debate),[11] rocked the military establishment for two reasons. On the one hand, a university professor as a knowledgeable layman was challenging the military's sacrosanct claim to authority on issues of military historiography. On the other hand, Delbrück questioned the tradition of Frederick's ideas of annihilation as postulated by the General Staff, and in so doing challenged the operational thinking of that body. Although Delbrück's arguments on the bipolar nature of the strategy of attrition and the strategy of annihilation were rejected fiercely at first, the General Staff eventually was forced to accept the theses of this "civilian strategist." Not the least part of Delbrück's argument was his methodical proof of the deficiencies in the military history works of the General Staff.[12] This concession, however, did not change the basic operational and strategic certainty regarding the relative superiority of the strategies of annihilation and attrition.

During the course of the strategy debate, officers in various forums discussed the question of how to apply to a future war the operational lessons learned from the Wars of German Unification. This exchange of opinions gave rise to a fierce discussion over the issue of whether there was a fundamental difference between warfare as conducted by Moltke and Napoleon, given that Moltke assembled his forces on the battlefield, whereas Napoleon assembled them before the battle.[13] This debate, which took place on several levels, had implications that are important for our understanding of the development of operational thinking. While the focus of the specific discussion was on the possibilities of the success of frontal attacks, the underlying context was—similar to the strategy debate—the question of the value of lessons learned from military history and the validity of timeless operational teachings.

Schlichting, for example, criticized anyone believing in a timeless theory of war that had been valid since at least the time of Frederick the Great. In Schlichting's opinion, strategy and operations were subject to permanent change, since each period was influenced by its own principles of leadership. Although he granted that Moltke the Elder developed an operational and strategic law that was quasi-universal, he considered its historical validity to be limited. Schlichting also thought that such a law had not existed before the Wars of German Unification, and generally would not be applicable in the future. He substantiated his thesis by citing the rapid development of arms, military equipment, means of transportation, and communications compared to the previous centuries. Simultaneously, Schlichting postulated an operational law governing a particular period, which if taught in an ideal way would result in standard operational thinking and standard command and control of armed forces.[14] Although Schlichting thus deliberately reduced the freedom of operational thinking in favor of a modern but not always "correct" form, and he advocated a narrower operational thinking based in the present, he nonetheless insisted on the extensive independence of the tactical leaders in selecting their courses of action.

Lieutenant General Wilhelm von Scherff opposed Schlichting's opinions. He argued against mission-type command and control and in favor of the schematic form of battle in tactics. Scherff also advocated relatively wide discretion for the senior leadership to exercise command and control through directives, thus postulating a more open form of operational thinking than Schlichting.[15] In the late nineteenth century the debate in the military literature about operational thinking between those two opposing positions was placed against the backdrop of the question of how the next war should be fought.

Other critics of Schlichting, including Colmar von der Goltz, Alfred von Boguslawski, and Alfred Krauss, accused him of making Moltke's operational teachings absolute, while neglecting older experiences. They expressly argued against focusing exclusively on recent war experiences, emphasizing instead the value of older experiences. Von der Goltz, in particular, argued that on principle victors were inclined to generalize for the future those procedures they had just applied. He also cautioned against the assumption that future wars would be decided rapidly through mobile operations. Although in his opinion rapid mobile warfare was the ideal to strive for, Goltz nonetheless expected the conduct of operations to be slow and rather awkward because of the reinforced French border fortifications, the rough terrain in the east, and the increase of armies of millions that were difficult to command and control.[16]

Although the General Staff and military writers tended to focus their analyses on the war experiences of the three victorious wars of unification, they by tradition also closely examined the experiences of more recent wars, to include the Boer War, the Russo-Japanese War, and the Balkan Wars. First and foremost, however, that analysis was limited to tactical evaluation and did not have a decisive influence on the development of operational thinking in the German Reich. Furthermore, the premise for any assessment was always its application to future German warfare.

Typically, the General Staff almost neglected the American Civil War in its deliberations, even though it had been history's first industrialized war. The General Staff was convinced that that war was completely different from the European theater of war, both in terms of its geographical and military conditions. And, of course, there was a certain cultural arrogance toward the "emigrants and upstarts" of the New World that probably contributed to this attitude. Although there is no conclusive evidence that Moltke the Elder really referred to the American Civil War as "two armed mobs chasing each other around the country, from which nothing could be learned,"[17] this quote does represent a common view within the German officer corps.[18] Why, according to the unspoken conviction of German General Staff officers, should an army that had convincingly demonstrated its tactical and operational competence in three wars and had become a model for many other armed forces learn something from the American Civil War—especially considering the incompetence of most American generals in operational matters? This was especially so considering that after the Civil War the American Army was only used to fight Native American tribes in the west.

Interior Lines, Center of Gravity, and Surprise

Despite all gradual differences, the core of the debate was the question that had puzzled Moltke the Elder: whether in the event of war a German army, inferior in numbers and pressed for time because of its central position, would be able to win a two-front war—and if so, how?

The extensive coverage in the military journals describes a model that on the one hand comes close to the plans of the General Staff, but on the other hand is distinctly different.[19] Basically, all authors because of the geographical situation of the German Reich rejected the concept of a defensive-oriented defense based on huge fortifications.[20] At the strategic level they all advocated warfare conducted on interior lines. That type of warfare made it possible to defeat various opponents individually and sequentially, despite the unfavorable force ratios. Lieutenant General Rudolf von Caemmerer got to the heart of the matter when he wrote:

> But during the ensuing actions the army which has advanced united must as a rule maneuver from one side to the other. That is to say, the side operating on the interior side will alternately advance in two opposite directions; and simultaneously, a small element based on circumstances will have to be committed to guard one side, while the main body delivers the blow on the other.[21]

It was necessary to defeat at an early stage the enemy who were separated in time and space, before they were able to support each other with coordinated attacks along the exterior. Goltz and Bernhardi, therefore, pointed out the risks of an interior line strategy. Considering the mass armies and the difficulties involved in achieving rapid and decisive victories, Goltz predicted major problems for a successful conduct of operations on interior lines. Although Bernhardi supported operations on interior lines, he also pointed out the utmost importance of making "the first victory as complete and as crushing a defeat as possible, so as to cripple for some considerable time the enemy first attacked. Every miscalculation in this respect may have injurious consequences."[22]

It was important, therefore, to assess exactly and to distribute the forces accordingly, since the German forces operating on interior lines between France and Russia would have to leave large elements behind to contain the defeated enemy for months, even after major and decisive wars. Fighting on interior lines, therefore, would necessarily require a systematic concentration of effort. "Superiority at the decisive point is the crucial test. Such superiority is attained by means of an unexpected concentration of forces."[23] Transferring the strategy onto the operational level without a systematic concentration of effort in combination with surprise was, therefore, very difficult.

Attack

Most of the German military theoreticians of the period rejected the idea of a defensively oriented conduct of operations, as Clausewitz and to some extent Moltke the Elder had in mind. Because of Germany's central position, the offensive would be the only way to achieve victory. That idea corresponded with the conviction that "the attack on its own" was what mattered. Consequently, operational thinking focused on the attack. Statements by Goltz, like "to wage war means to attack,"[24] or Bernhardi, such as "the issue of the next European war hangs in the balance of strategic offensive,"[25] represent the traditional understanding of the officer corps of the German Reich; but such thinking was also the prevailing opinion among the officers of allied and potentially enemy armies.[26]

The conduct of mobile offensive operations required offensive tactical warfare. The will to conduct offensive and maneuver operations played a considerable role in the development of the German Army's tactics. It was inevitable that the tactical attack as a prerequisite for offensive conduct of operations was considered of paramount importance.[27] Nevertheless, the proponents of offensive warfare did not forget the fact that the enhanced weapons effects had strengthened the defensive. But they argued that the moral and operational impacts of the attack were to overcome the tactical superiority of the defense. Bernhardi even went as far as to declare that under modern conditions the superiority of offensive warfare was greater than formerly.[28] As the history of war confirms, numerically inferior forces quite often have been able to defeat vastly superior enemies. To do so, however, it was necessary for the troops to have a high level of combat readiness, a strong psychological constitution regarding self-sacrifice, an irrepressible will to win, and the ability to concentrate efforts.

Many experts were of the opinion that the Russo-Japanese War of 1904–1905 confirmed the value of initiative and willpower as the central tactical and operational factors. As Lieutenant Colonel William Balck wrote, reflecting the opinion of many of his comrades:

> The war experiences clearly show the operational and tactical superiority of the offensive over the defense. The freedom to choose the location and time makes up for the advantages of a prepared battlefield. To wage war means to attack; to attack means to carry the fire forward to get as close to the enemy as possible. . . . The will to win can offset an imbalance in numbers. Not the one who is stronger, but the one who is more energetic has the best chances of succeeding.[29]

The attacker has the advantage of the initiative. It gives him a head start in space and time over the defender, and thus tactical and operational advantages, including concentration of effort in the main direction of attack of his choosing and ensuring the force and materiel superiority over the enemy at the decisive location, at the right time. Therefore, a surprise concentration of effort was the effective means for a numerically or even strategically inferior side to achieve at least a temporary tactical and operational superiority, while deliberately accepting certain risks. According to Goltz, German conduct of operations required a ruthless offensive, with a decisive battle conducted blow for blow.[30]

Combat Superiority

At first glance, the concept of defeating the enemy individually through successive attacks and by a concentration of efforts based on initiative and surprise, as well as the exploitation of interior lines, was an enticing proposition. On further reflection, however, it was a very risky approach, since it had to be executed under time pressure and with numerically inferior forces, both in manpower and equipment. But in addition to the concentration of efforts, the military writers of the period postulated a consistent enhancement in the quality of the force and command and control procedures as the solution for the central problem of Germany's capability to fight against superior forces. Again and again, examples from war history, like Frederick the Great at Leuthen, were used to emphasize the importance of superior command and control and to stress its ability, owing to the genius of the military commander, to offset the numerical superiority of the enemy. At the same time, myths grew around great battle commanders like Moltke and Friedrich II, celebrating their iron and indomitable wills and also their almost supernatural ability to grasp the situation by intuition and act accordingly. It was mostly taken for granted that Prusso-German officers had better mastery of the operational art than their potential enemies—or such was "proven" with the help of the selected historical examples.

Based on the German national character, there was no doubt that well-trained and well-commanded German soldiers were superior to their enemies. A smaller, high-quality army excellently trained in tactical matters was considered capable of executing the planned rapid operations and proficiently defeating the numerically superior enemy. Many writers marginalized numerical superiority by comparison with quality. Bernhardi qualified this idea by pointing out that it was impossible to quantify command and control, and that command and control no matter how superior would never be able to offset the effect of high numerical superiority. Bernhardi called it the "Law of Numbers."[31] Even an ideal elite army should not be numerically inferior by much to the enemy army. Since the early twentieth century, the public interested in military matters became increasingly aware of this insight. In order to win in such a situation it was necessary to attempt to increase all of the force's psychological, moral, and intellectual powers. Morale and will would be the last means against numerical superiority and fire.[32] While the debate in the contemporary military journals between the proponents and opponents of increasing military personnel strength remained open or undecided, the differences in opinion on that issue between the General Staff and the War Ministry were almost insurmountable. Emphasizing the high quality of the force and of command and control procedures, the War Ministry categorically rejected any further increase in personnel strength.[33]

Maneuver and Envelopment

All the elements of operational thinking, including attack, interior lines, main effort, initiative, and surprise, are directly connected with maneuver. While fire offers clear tactical and operational advantages to the side that is superior in materiel and personnel, the vast majority of German military theoreticians held the opinion that the maneuver element allowed the numerically inferior side with a mobile command and control system and well-trained forces to take the initiative, to concentrate its effort, and to respond quickly to changes in the situation. As postulated by Moltke, the conduct of mobile operations made it possible to combine separate field armies on the battlefield concentrically, and thus use the resulting envelopment to fight a battle of annihilation. Over the course of the years the question of whether success in a battle would more likely result from a breakthrough or from an envelopment remained a matter of fierce discussion. General Ludwig Freiherr von Falkenhausen, who for years discussed that issue in his writings, explained that the best way to cope with the dreaded positional warfare was through a flanking maneuver with simultaneous advances against the flanks and the rear of the enemy. Simultaneously, he cautioned that such a maneuver required great skill in command and control and a high-quality force. He concluded: "Bypassing and flanking are not universal remedies to achieve victory; they exist neither in warfare nor in medicine. What matters are correct and skilled application, forceful implementation of the means, and adaptation."[34]

Consequently, Falkenhausen demanded excellent training of the forces, combined with the simultaneous application of schematic rules and superior command and control systems. Even if with armies of millions the decisive aspects of warfare were not subject to change, operational command would have to adapt to the changing conditions.[35]

The debate, which over the course of the years increasingly centered on Bernhardi, culminated just prior to the First World War. Bernhardi, an open opponent of Schlieffen, criticized the unilateral focus on the envelopment concept and the ensuing battle of annihilation. Bernhardi insisted on including as an element of operational thinking the breakthrough, as both a tactical and operational method of attack. Essentially, however, he protested against a mechanical concept of war, which in his opinion Schlieffen advocated by unilaterally committing himself to one operational procedure.[36] Bernhardi argued for granting the commander freedom of action in the conduct of operations. He regarded warfare as an art and not as a science—which he accused Schlieffen of doing. Consequently, Bernhardi categorically rejected an operational system or a recipe for victory, because "Anyone going to war with the idea of wishing to conquer by a definite system will scarcely cover himself with glory."[37]

Schlieffen's Operational Thinking

Before going into Schlieffen's operational thinking and the resulting operational and strategic plans, we should briefly examine the man himself. Schlieffen was born on 28 February 1833. After completing his *Abitur* (secondary school completion and university entrance qualification certificate), he started his career as an officer. He was assigned to the General Staff after he graduated from the Allgemeine Kriegsschule. His career followed the usual General Staff pattern, routinely alternating between troop assignments, service in the General Staff with troops, and on the Great General Staff. After his tenure as a regimental commander he was promoted to a position as a division chief in the General Staff. In 1888 he was promoted to *Oberquartiermeister* (deputy chief of staff) and understudy to Waldersee. On 7 February 1891, Schlieffen was appointed chief of the General Staff of the German Army. The high level of esteem in which he was held can be seen by the fact that after his retirement in 1906 he was promoted in 1911 to the rank of field marshal even though he had never conducted a victorious battle as a commander.

During his tenure as chief of the General Staff, Schlieffen did not participate in the military theory debates of the Reich, although he followed them closely. It was only after his retirement, probably in order to secure and preserve his life's work,[38] that he went public with his operational ideas, most of which were published in the form of war history studies.

For decades these classical studies by the military retiree shaped our image of Schlieffen. This was especially the case after the significant files on the operational thinking of the General Staff during the Schlieffen era—including the General Staff rides, the war games, the deployment plans, and further operational deliberations—were believed to have been lost as a consequence of the World War II destruction of the papers and documents of the Army Archive. Only secondary documents survived. Thus, for years the very limited number of surviving files on the operational plans of the Great General Staff under Schlieffen, combined with his literary legacy and the accompanying myths and demonizations, distorted the views of Schlieffen's operational thinking. The new sources discovered during the course of the discussion about Schlieffen's operational plans that was triggered by Terence Zuber[39] facilitated a reevaluation of Schlieffen's operational thinking in some aspects—but not necessarily in the fundamental way advocated by Zuber.[40]

Schlieffen did not posit a definition of the concept of operation, neither in the regulations issued during his tenure, nor in his later writings. He did, however, use the terms operation (*Operation*), operational (*operativ*), and operate (*operieren*) regularly. What can be deduced from his writing is that Schlieffen understood an operation as a targeted maneuver of major army units within a given area. Transferred to his war plans, warfare on interior lines with a changing concentration of effort was the strategic level, and warfare against France was the operational level. He did not clearly distinguish operations from tactics and strategy. This, however, does not mean, as Wallach mistakenly concluded, that Schlieffen obscured the differences between tactical action and operational maneuver by merging them in the battle, and "that elements which had previously been clearly distinguished from one another lost their meaning."[41] As we have already discussed, there was no clear distinction among the three levels of command during the Schlieffen era, and he did not introduce such a distinction, although it was often argued that he had done so.[42]

Like Moltke, Schlieffen did not leave a written body of operational doctrine. Schlieffen's followers later derived such from his writings, and presented the results as a recipe for victory. Schlieffen brought operational thinking in Germany to a temporary first level, and left an imprint on it that lasted for decades.

Shortly after the start of his term in office in 1891, Schlieffen came out from under the shadow of his powerful predecessor and developed his own operational-strategic concept for a two-front war. His basic strategic assumption for such a war was the premise that Germany would not be able to win a long war of attrition.[43] Like Bernhardi and Goltz, he considered a war resulting in lengthy and exhausting trench warfare possible and even probable. Schlieffen saw not only the economic difficulties arising from a blockade against Germany, but also the domestic dangers of a potential revolutionary transformation of the civilian workforce.[44] Owing to the dangers that a war of attrition posed for Germany, Schlieffen intended to prevent such a lengthy war and also to end any future war as quickly as possible in order to avoid the anticipated impact of a blockade, which would require some time to take effect.[45] Consequently, his operational thinking focused on those efforts necessary to achieve a rapid decision of the war.[46]

Unlike his predecessors, Schlieffen did not want to cut the Gordian knot of a two-front war by using defensive means. For him, the offensive was the only option for preventing a lengthy war of attrition, which he was convinced would be impossible to win. The increasingly prevailing fixation on the unilateral conduct of offensive operations was in accordance with the prevailing zeitgeist in Wilhelmine Germany for solving political problems through offensive means. Many key players in politics, the military, and the economy were glad that the blight of stagnation had been blown away with ascension to the throne of the dynamic young Kaiser Wilhelm II. The drive to tackle "the law of constriction" (*Gesetz der Enge*) was no longer cautious and protective, but rather offensive, with the objective being Germany's rise to world power status. To achieve that objective, the political and military elites of the Reich were ready, if necessary, to wage an offensive two-front war, which was considered inevitable. In accordance with the "law of the initiative" (*Gesetz der Initiative*), the offensive as a self-determined action was better suited to enforce Germany's will by violence than was the passive acceptance of the defensive and its accompanying wait-and-see attitude.

Warfare in the event of a two-front war had to be guided by factors like political environment, space, time, and Germany's own military capacities, as well as those of the enemy. In the final discussion of the *Generalstabsreise Ost* in 1901, Schlieffen summarized his own strategic and operational credo based on those determinants as follows:

> Germany has the advantage of being located in the middle between France and Russia, separating those allies from each other. Yet it would give up that advantage as soon as it split up its army and left itself outnumbered by each of its enemies. Germany, therefore, must aim to defeat the first while the other is only pinned down. Afterward, when the first opponent is defeated, Germany must achieve superiority in numbers in the other theater, using the railway which will be pernicious to the other enemy as well. The first strike must be carried out with full force, and a truly decisive battle must be fought.[47]

With those words Schlieffen announced to his General Staff officers what in his opinion were the sacrosanct base assumptions regarding the German Army's possibility of waging a rapid two-front war. Schlieffen's solution for the Reich's strategic dilemma was short and crisp: Using interior lines and the good German railway network to divide a two-front war into two successive one-front wars, with his forces enjoying superiority on each front.

To execute such a strategy, one of the two opponents had to be defeated decisively and, above all, very quickly. That could be achieved only through offensive and not defensive actions. In addition to the conduct of offensive operations, it also required offensive tactical training for the units of the German armed forces.[48]

Owing to the rapid French mobilization and the lack of operational depth of the French defensive area, Schlieffen decided to attack France first. From the very beginning, the planned operation would be under extreme time pressure. If the French were not decisively defeated before the Russian Army began to attack, it would spell disaster. Over the course of the years the rapid decisive battle against France became the focus of Schlieffen's operational thinking. A settlement with one of the main opponents, if possible Russia, was the focus of his strategic thinking. The result was the paradox that although the strategic interest of the German Reich was in the east, for operational considerations the decision of the war would be sought in the west.[49]

The Battle

The idea of the battle of annihilation was closely connected to the conviction that the outnumbered opponent had a chance to win only if he thoroughly defeated elements of his opponents' forces, against whom he was able to muster local superiority, if possible through surprise.[50] Otherwise, the surviving enemy forces would threaten him again and again and he would never have the opportunity to attack the enemy on the second front with any chance of winning. Schlieffen, in accordance with Moltke the Elder and the contemporary military thinking, considered the rapid battle of annihilation to be the only chance of achieving victory in a two-front war, given the realities of space, time, and the forces of the Reich.

The purpose of the decisive battle was to neutralize the enemy army as a power factor. The assumption that Schlieffen considered only one gigantic decisive battle as the objective of his operational thinking, which has been quite common since the publication of Wallach's book, *The Dogma of the Battle of Annihilation,* is an oversimplification, however. Such a monocausal view of Schlieffen's operational thinking suggests a battle in the classical tactical sense. But because of the mass armies now committed and the spatial constraints of the battle space, such a battle was no longer possible. The concept of Schlieffen's intended operationally decisive battle was a sequence of several individual battles lasting several days, with some of them merging into each other. The dimensions of the battlefield, or rather the battle space, went beyond all previously known battlefields. Newly discovered files of his *Generalstabsreisen* (General Staff rides) and his *Schlussaufgaben* (key taskings) confirm that Schlieffen did not assume that there would be only one single major battle of annihilation.[51] There is, however, no doubt that his operational thinking centered on the decision of the battle in the sense of destroying the enemy's army, if possible in an area close to the border. He was convinced that a war could only be ended by neutralizing the enemy's army. Schlieffen considered surprise an important prerequisite for any success.

Schlieffen's unilateral fixation on the decision of the battle goes far beyond the ideas of Moltke the Elder. The former effectively rejected the principle that victory in a battle was just one of many options of a strategy to end a war.[52] Schlieffen's *Planspiele* (map exercises) indicate that he did not necessarily assume that a successfully decisive battle in the west would result in an instant peace settlement, since even after such a victory over the French Army he planned to leave considerable force elements in the west. Altogether, these map exercises show a much more flexible and less dogmatic Schlieffen than the one portrayed by Ritter and Wallach. Political considerations were very much a part of his estimates of the situation. At times, when the center of gravity shifted from east to west, and during periods of considerations and decisions among the leadership of the Reich regarding a rapprochement with Russia or Great Britain, such factors were reflected directly in Schlieffen's operations planning.

Annihilation

A rapid battle of annihilation was the key objective of the conduct of operations. For the theoretical basis for this concept Schlieffen turned to Moltke and especially Clausewitz, whose work he reduced to the idea of annihilation:[53] "apart from the high ethical and psychological significance of [Clausewitz's] works, it is the emphasis on the idea of destruction permeating all his writings which gives them their permanent value. It is actually thanks to Clausewitz that the idea of an honest war was kept alive in the Prussian officer corps throughout the long period of peace. In his spiritual development Moltke closely followed Clausewitz, from whom he began to transcend."[54]

Schlieffen's understanding of destruction was in agreement with the general opinion in the German Reich. It was not the extinction of the political or economic existence of a state, rather it was the defeat of the enemy army, which in turn was entangled in the idea that the enemy army represented the entire personnel, materiel, and moral force of that state. As with many other things in the discourse about two-front warfare, the question of whether or not a planned and rapid destruction was indeed possible remained a point of contention. Even Bernhardi pointedly argued that a total destruction of the enemy army was but a very exceptional occurrence.[55] The intended destruction of the enemy army, however, was not an original German concept; it was also an objective in the thinking of France, Russia, and Great Britain.[56]

As previously noted, however, destruction was not to be understood as physical extinction, but rather as the neutralization of the enemy's army as a means of conducting war. Goltz, for example, wrote: "'Defeat' and 'destruction' must not be taken to mean actually killing off or putting all of the enemy's fighting men entirely hors de combat." And, "By 'destruction' we imply that we reduce the enemy to such a physical and moral state that he feels himself incapable of continuing the struggle."[57] This understanding of the concept of destruction as the incapacitation of hostile armed forces on an operational level had been widely understood in the late nineteenth century among the German public with an interest in military affairs. There could be no question of the extinction of an entire population strata in a European war. Military history literature after the Second World War made the German concept of destruction into an absolute.[58] Wallach's *The Dogma of the Battle of Annihilation* was at the vanguard of this development.[59] Much current thinking, then, traces the annihilation doctrine, or the cult of annihilation,[60] as a linear development from the German annihilation strategy in the 1904–1908 genocidal war of annihilation in Namibia,[61] via the Schlieffen Plan, to the Wehrmacht's racist war of annihilation in the Soviet Union during the Second World War—all within the framework of the Sonderweg (special path) thesis.

It is indisputable that the Wehrmacht's racist war of annihilation against the Soviet Union was in no way compatible with the ideals of the *kaiserlichen Armee* (Imperial Army).[62] The question, then, is when did destruction in the sense of incapacitation turn into annihilation without boundaries? Certainly, the General Staff did not develop the Schlieffen Plan as a racially driven war of annihilation. But did not initial developmental tendencies toward a physical destruction of the enemy loom as early as at the end of the Kaiser's Reich? Given the experiences of the Franco-Prussian War, there were already some in Germany who, fearing a people's war, went beyond the concept of an operational war of annihilation.[63] The majority opinion of the military was reflected in the remarks of Wilhelm von Blume, commenting on the outbreak of a people's war following the decision of the conventional battle:

> Such a scenario could only be successful as long as the enemy believed in it and submitted to it without appealing to the sword. Warfare while avoiding bloodshed is a contradiction in itself. At present, only the most reckless use of all means acceptable in international law to defeat the enemy conforms to the seriousness of the situation in which the war positions the state, and the extent to which the national interests are at stake. To wage a war in this context is the means to reduce its sufferings.[64]

Cannae or Leuthen?

Given the fire superiority of the defender, both Schlieffen and Moltke the Elder considered uncompromising envelopment operations to be the only chance for a successful battle of annihilation, especially taking into account the numerical inferiority of the German armed forces. Thus, the iron will to envelop became the second pillar of Schlieffen's operational thinking on the battle of annihilation.

The conduct of mobile operations was the prerequisite for a successful envelopment followed by a battle of annihilation under time pressure. Consequently, maneuver, combined with the related elements of a concentration of effort and surprise, was the backbone of a battle of annihilation and envelopment. Schlieffen's operational thinking cannot be understood without the factor of maneuver. Like Moltke the Elder, he was convinced that the successful command and control of mass armies was only possible through maneuver.[65] In one of his last Schlussaufgaben, Schlieffen categorically pointed out to his General Staff officers: "It is a law that by occupying positions one does not win battles; this is achieved only by maneuver."[66]

Operational envelopment is closely linked to maneuver. In Schlieffen's opinion, the only chance for victory was through a simultaneous attack on the flank and front of the enemy. Consequently, Schlieffen lectured his General Staff officers accordingly on the operational-strategic position of the German Reich: "Therefore, we will have to operate with our smaller army in such a way as to attack not only an enemy wing with the strongest possible forces, but also to threaten seriously the enemy's fallback lines, the sensitivity of which increases disproportionately with the size of his army. This is the only way to achieve genuinely decisive results and rapidly end the campaign. And doing so is essential for us, especially in the event of a war on two fronts."[67]

After his retirement, Schlieffen even went as far as to say to General Hugo von Freytag-Loringhoven: "The attack against the flank is the substance of the whole history of war."[68]

The envelopment concept was not the result of Schlieffen's historical studies, but of his evaluation of Germany's operational-strategic situation. His writings about Cannae and the Wars of Liberation, which he wrote after his time in office, served primarily as historical confirmation of his already existing operational ideas. At the same time, Schlieffen used his writings in an attempt to put pressure on his successor, Colonel General Helmuth von Moltke the Younger, and thus prevent him from abandoning the envelopment concept.[69] Even as chief of the General Staff, Schlieffen used the public as a means to convey his ideas when he had the War History Division (*Kriegsgeschichtliche Abteilung*) of the General Staff prove the extraordinary importance of envelopment in the 1903 monograph *Der Schlachterfolg*.

Schlieffen's *Cannae* monograph holds a special position in this context. On the one hand, he used the Battle of Cannae to prove that even an army inferior in numbers could destroy a superior enemy by means of a double envelopment. On the other hand, no other of his writings had such a profound influence on the operational thinking of his time. While the Cannae principle became the symbol of an ideal operation, especially for junior officers far into the twentieth century,[70] it still symbolizes for his critics Schlieffen's unrestricted operational megalomania.[71] As is often the case when his operational thinking is discussed, both his admirers and his critics fail to maintain the required distance from his statements. There is no doubt that Schlieffen stretched the historical truth to substantiate his theories. He qualified elements of his writings when he stated that it would always be desirable to have superiority in numbers for the double envelopment,[72] or when he definitively declared: "A perfect Battle of Cannae is only rarely to be found in history, because it requires a Hannibal on the one side and a Terentius Varro on the other, who cooperate in their way to achieve a great purpose."[73]

Such words are no ideal rationale for a recipe for victory, or a dogmatic battle of annihilation. Furthermore, the focus on Cannae obscures the fact that the point of reference for Schlieffen's war history analysis was not the ancient world, but the age of Frederick the Great. Shortly after the unification of the German Reich, the Prussian-dominated General Staff started to analyze Frederick's wars, drawing in the process parallels between the situation of Prussia in the mid-eighteenth century and that of Germany in the late nineteenth. Even though the analogy was artificial and history never repeats itself, it must be acknowledged that the geostrategic position of Prussia and Germany were quite similar, since Prussia as the core nation of the Reich was situated in the center of Europe. During Frederick's time, Prussia was inferior in both personnel and materiel to its potential enemies in a multi-front war. According to the thinking of that time, the General Staff looked for the factors that had made the Prussian victory in the Seven Years' War possible.

As is often the case when attempting to apply history to the present, the assessment confirmed their analysis of the situation: war was only possible through a battle of annihilation based on an operational envelopment, and the genius of the commander was of utmost importance for such a victory. The manifest conclusion was the fundamental importance of the battle for the success of the war. As a logical consequence, therefore, Schlieffen substantiated his operational thinking with the example of the 1757 Battle of Leuthen. After his victory at Rossbach, Frederick II rapidly redeployed his troops on interior lines from west to east and won the battle with a flank attack, although inferior in numbers.

In the thinking of many German officers, the historical analogy was not an artificial one, considering Germany's geostrategic position. Within this selective process, however, the key point was completely ignored that it was not the success of Frederick II in the battles that led to peace, but rather the general fatigue of the parties to the war—a deeply political process. In contrast, Schlieffen himself spoke of the "Leuthen Program."[74] As Schlieffen wrote, it was only under ideal conditions that a modern Cannae was conceivable. According to the General Staff, a limitation to a unilateral envelopment was practical. In the end, Leuthen symbolized the operational envelopment plan that was the basis of Schlieffen's memorandum of 1905.[75]

Quality and Quantity

In addition to a functioning command and control system, the operational envelopments planned by Schlieffen required a high-quality force whose numbers were relatively adequate against the potential enemy. The General Staff did not doubt the importance of the quality of the army. As early as during Schlieffen's time, an increasing number of voices cautioned that Germany's relative inferiority in numbers had reached the critical threshold that was necessary to execute the operations as planned. It appears that for Schlieffen himself this development was not so dramatic, since ultimately he did not urge the War Ministry to expand the size of the army, even though such growth would have been of fundamental importance to his operational plans. Caught in the departmental egoism conflicts of the German Reich, Schlieffen accepted without complaint the statement of War Minister Karl von Einem that the development of the army was complete. This shows clearly that the General Staff, despite being the planning and warfighting authority of the German Reich, had hardly any influence on the management of the personnel and materiel resources required for the execution of those plans. But how was Schlieffen to convince a war minister who refused an expansion of the army for financial and domestic political reasons if the General Staff did not inform him of its operational plans? Also, Schlieffen did not want to dilute the monarchist character of the army by admitting too many bourgeois officers into an expanded armed forces.[76] Moltke the Younger was the first chief of staff to inform the war minister of the General Staff's plans, doing so in an effort to justify his requirements for personnel increases. But Moltke too failed to get authorization for the substantial troop reinforcements necessary for the planned operations. Like his predecessor, Schlieffen, he was convinced that the better quality of the German troops and their leadership would more or less make up for the numerical deficiency.[77]

Planning and Command and Control

Schlieffen systematically continued the expansion of the General Staff begun under Moltke the Elder. Schlieffen increased the number of departments from eleven to sixteen.[78] The tasks of the General Staff included the description and mapping of the country, as well as gathering information about foreign armies (Section IIIb), and the wartime preparation of the troops. Above all, the General Staff concentrated on mobilization and the conduct of war. In addition to the tactical and strategic training of the General Staff officers, the chief of the General Staff was responsible for the operational and strategic war planning of the German Army. The implementation of the General Staff's operational thought into specific military plans was accomplished through the preparation of updated *Aufmarschanweisungen* (deployment directives) for the individual field armies. These directives were issued by the *Aufmarschabteilung* (Deployment Department)[79] on 1 April, the beginning of each new mobilization year.[80] Preliminary to that process, the Railway Department planned the German Army's rail deployment based on the top-secret *Direktiven für den Aufmarsch* (directives for deployment), which were issued by the chief of the General Staff in November/December of the previous calendar year.[81] This process was repeated every year. The *Aufmarschpläne* (deployment plans) were usually destroyed at the end of the mobilization year, along with the General Staff's other obsolete top-secret documents.[82]

The planning efforts of the few General Staff officers dedicated to the mobilization plans were enormous.[83] These requirements increased even further as Schlief-

Great General Staff, 1913

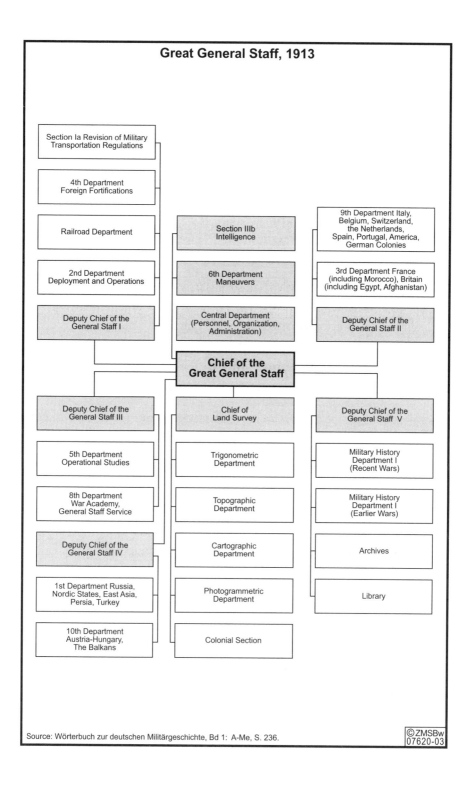

Section Ia Revision of Military Transportation Regulations

4th Department Foreign Fortifications

Railroad Department

2nd Department Deployment and Operations

Deputy Chief of the General Staff I

Section IIIb Intelligence

6th Department Maneuvers

Central Department (Personnel, Organization, Administration)

9th Department Italy, Belgium, Switzerland, the Netherlands, Spain, Portugal, America, German Colonies

3rd Department France (including Morocco), Britain (including Egypt, Afghanistan)

Deputy Chief of the General Staff II

Chief of the Great General Staff

Deputy Chief of the General Staff III

5th Department Operational Studies

8th Department War Academy, General Staff Service

Deputy Chief of the General Staff IV

1st Department Russia, Nordic States, East Asia, Persia, Turkey

10th Department Austria-Hungary, The Balkans

Chief of Land Survey

Trigonometric Department

Topographic Department

Cartographic Department

Photogrammetric Department

Colonial Section

Deputy Chief of the General Staff V

Military History Department I (Recent Wars)

Military History Department I (Earlier Wars)

Archives

Library

Source: Wörterbuch zur deutschen Militärgeschichte, Bd 1: A-Me, S. 236.

fen and his officers made every effort to accommodate in their plans the current technological advances and trends as a hedge against potential incalculables. In this way Schlieffen attempted to eliminate chance, or Clausewitzian friction, which he could not afford, given the critically small time window for his plans. In the end, mobilization, deployment, operation, and battle were compressed into a single grand planned action.[84] These plans were designed not only to prevent frictions, but also to influence the decisions of the enemy by using the initiative to force him to react.

This, however, is not a specifically German concept. According to Barry Posen, it is inherent to forms of military organization. From the perspective of organizational theory, organizations, including the military, tend to structure their processes in accordance with standing operating procedures to prevent friction. The key factor is the intent to execute decisions free of outside interference. This includes both external interference from the enemy and domestic influence from political officials. Such thinking prefers the offensive over the defensive. The latter only allows for reaction, and in the process the "imperative of action" (*Gesetz des Handelns*) is transferred to the enemy for long periods of time. The defender becomes the object and not the subject of events, and the number of incalculable frictions increases accordingly. In contrast, the offensive offers the possibility of wresting the initiative from the enemy through planning and executing one's own tactical and operational actions as autonomously as possible—and in so doing limiting misunderstandings and mistakes to a minimum. Consequently, military leadership prefers an offensive over a defensive doctrine.[85] Within this framework, mission-type command and control (*Führen nach Auftrag*), which has characterized the German army up to the present, appears to be what it is—a system of expedients.

The operations planned under Schlieffen necessarily required tight leadership. According to his concepts, the modern commander sat in a central room and exercised his command and control function via a large network of telephones. This necessarily restricted freedom of action at the operational level of command, but did not deviate from the execution of the plan. Since the commander had hardly any influence over the operations after he gave orders to execute the plan, all his subordinate officers had to be trained and educated in his operational understanding to enable them to act flexibly in the spirit of the higher commander when frictions did occur. According to Schlieffen, there was a need for action in this respect, since: "if [the synchronization among the commanders] does not happen, the campaign will easily end unfavorably, as experience has shown. Each army commander or commanding general assumes the obligation of internalizing the line of thought of the supreme commander. This obligation is a rather great one, especially considering that the fate of the battles largely depends on it."[86]

Although Schlieffen emphasized the independence of the subordinate commanders as the classical German principle of command and control, he stressed this principle with unusual sharpness: "This is all quite nice, but the subordinate leaders must understand the responsibility heaped upon them."[87] This burden that Auftragstaktik (mission-type command and control) placed on subordinates, and which has often been ignored by its many advocates, has rarely been explained so pointedly and by someone with such command competence. Thus, modern General Staff officers were no longer heroic fighters and commanders who led and inspired their soldiers on horseback and through personal example; rather, they were "professionals with extensive state-of-the-art training who practiced the trade of war as scientific art."[88]

But the General Staff was only one, albeit important, institution of several in the overall military structure of the German Reich. Apart from the navy, with whom neither Schlieffen nor his successor coordinated in any detail on the Reich's war plans,[89] there also was the Military Cabinet, responsible for the personnel management of the officers and also the staff for the imperial command authority, and the War Ministry, responsible for the personnel size of the army and the procurement of armaments. The war minister represented the imperial chancellor at the Reichstag in affairs concerning the armed forces. This constellation prevented the General Staff, which as the youngest of the three branches was involved in a running turf battle with the War Ministry, from developing strategic plans, since it lacked the required scope of authority and responsibility. Furthermore, it was the responsibility of the Kaiser, who as commander in chief of the armed forces stood above the three branches, to coordinate the strategic war plans. Kaiser Wilhelm II did not live up to this responsibility, and the three branches, therefore, worked and planned in parallel but often at cross-purposes. This system, which was linked to the German government through the Kaiser and the war minister only, restricted the General Staff to the operational planning level in peacetime and was not suited to developing an overall strategic planning component for the Reich.

This reality does not conform at all to the image of the all-embracing power position enjoyed by the General Staff as the "founder of the German Reich," an image that the General Staff itself had cultivated since 1871. The image of an organization of monolithic thought and planning, where nameless General Staff officers like components of a well-oiled machine devoted themselves to the will of their chief without discussion, is in no way based on reality. Yet, this is the image that was cultivated by the writings of the members of the "Schlieffen School" during the 1920s and 1930s. Although our knowledge of the inner circle of the General Staff—about fifteen officers—is limited because of their strict secrecy and the loss of files, these people did have differing operational ideas, which reflected generational conflicts. There are many indicators that for quite some time Schlieffen had considered the organization of the German Army as it had been developed by his predecessors to be wrong, and that he only waited for an opportunity to implement his new ideas.[90]

Schlieffen can be seen as the advocate of a generation of officers who agreed only to a limited extent with the ideas and the defensive orientation of "The Immortal Moltke." Rather, they believed in more offensive solutions to the problem of a two-front war. Against this backdrop, Moltke's often-cited horrified and negative response to the new plans developed by Schlieffen appear in a different light, and can be compared to Schlieffen's response to the new ideas of his successor after the end of his own tenure in office.[91] Those reservations culminated in Schlieffen's famous memorandum of 1905. As the final discussions of the *Grosse Generalstabsreise West* of 1904 show,[92] Schlieffen's operational plans had been well criticized during the final years of his tenure. It is probably an irony of fate that Schlieffen, who himself had been a member of a younger faction eager for change, was confronted with the same phenomenon as he was leaving office. These generational conflicts, however, are evidence that the General Staff was not ruled by uniformly dogmatic opinion; rather, there was quite a range of differing operational and strategic concepts.

Aufmarschpläne—Deployment Plans

When Schlieffen succeeded Waldersee as chief of the General Staff in 1891, he had several years of experience in a key position responsible for the preparation of deployment plans based on an offensive-defense posture in the east and the west, with the center of gravity being in the east. Schlieffen's assumption of office coincided with a crucial change in European politics. The rapprochement between Russia and France, which had been in the making for years, resulted in an alliance similar to the Dual Alliance between Germany and Austria. For Schlieffen, the hypothetical military threat of a two-front war became a realistic scenario.

Just a few months after he assumed office, Schlieffen wrote a memorandum questioning the plans of his predecessors. Only a year later he expressed doubts whether the Russian Army could be defeated and destroyed in the deployment as planned. The Russians' improved railway infrastructure would enable them to deploy more rapidly, and supported by the completed fortifications of the Narew Line, the only possibility to defeat them would be a frontal attack. And that course of action virtually excluded the possibility of inflicting an annihilating defeat on the Russians. For the foreseeable future, therefore, no military decision could be expected in the east, especially since the Russian forces would be able to withdraw into the depths of the vast Russian countryside. Given the fact that, thanks to improvements in railway technology, France would be able to complete its mobilization before the Germans and then launch an attack at a very early stage, Schlieffen considered France the more dangerous enemy that had to be defeated through a rapid and decisive battle. As a consequence, Schlieffen in 1892 fundamentally changed the deployment plans of his predecessors by shifting most of the German forces, and thus the operational center of gravity, to the west.[93]

Schlieffen based his memorandum of 1894 on a rapid French offensive. Since he did not believe in the efficacy of a lengthy defensive, and he feared the French could break through the German front, he wanted to defeat the French Army through a large-scale meeting engagement by accelerating the German deployment and launching into an immediate offensive. As he noted, this plan was based on his conviction that "in order to win we must try to be superior at the point of contact. We will only have a chance to do so, however, if we determine the operations, and not if we wait passively to learn what the enemy has determined for us."[94]

If contrary to expectations the French did not attack, Schlieffen intended to use massive heavy artillery to break through the French fortification system near Nancy. But Schlieffen quickly realized that a breakthrough near Nancy would not be possible. Thus, in his memorandum of 2 August 1897 he gave up the idea of breaking through the French fortification system, stating clearly that a German offensive against France would have to be conducted over a route where it would have to overcome as few fortifications as possible. Having weighed all the possibilities, the only solution for Schlieffen was a northern outflanking of Verdun. Since the gap between the Vosges Mountains and the Belgian-Luxembourg border prevented a broad deployment of the German Army, he concluded that "an offensive swinging around Verdun should not hesitate to violate the neutrality not only of Luxembourg, but also of Belgium."[95] The objective of the German offensive was to attack the rearward lines of the French Army, cut it off from Paris, and then destroy it. That was the first time Schlieffen put into writing the idea of an envelopment of the French fortification system. In his 1897 memorandum there was not yet any mention of a wide-area offensive enveloping Paris itself.

Although Schlieffen since 1892 had decided in favor of offensive operations against France, the General Staff continued to work on a *Grosser Ostaufmarsch* (Great Eastern Deployment) scenario. In addition to the General Staff Ride West, Schlieffen also conducted a General Staff Ride East each year. At the same time, war games and final operational problems (Schlussaufgaben) were used to work through all imaginable warfare scenarios in the east, especially the problems of rail transport and the railway network, which was less developed in the east than in the west. Consultations with Germany's ally Austria-Hungary remained vaguely limited to a German attack from East Prussia on the Narew River sector. A coordinated operations plan did not exist. Each ally planned his own war independently, and only with vague information from the other ally.[96]

The deployment plans, General Staff rides, and the war games of the years before 1904–1905 indicate that Schlieffen generally adhered to the envelopment idea, although he realized its risks. His operational intentions, however, varied depending on the expected intentions of the French leadership, and he did not focus solely on large-scale envelopment. Schlieffen cautioned against too wide of an envelopment "since the deployment has a dual task—counterattack if the enemy advances immediately after having completed his deployment, and attack if he remains standing behind his fortifications."[97]

Those words go to the heart of the problem of Schlieffen's operational planning. What was to be done if the French remained in their fortifications and played for time? What was to be done if the Russians mobilized sooner than expected? If that happened, Schlieffen's entire strategic concept, which had been based on a rapid redeployment of German forces from the west to the east, would collapse. In that case disaster would be inevitable, since the German forces would hardly be able to hold off a concentric Franco-Russian attack. Schlieffen thus became convinced that an immediate German offensive forcing the French Army into a decisive battle was the only solution to the problem.

In 1902, when Schlieffen thought that the French had learned about the German envelopment plan and would prepare appropriate countermeasures, he decided to change his operational planning. During the mobilization year of 1902–1903, the German Army was to deploy much of its force—the Second to Sixth Armies, with eighteen army corps—directly to the French-Luxembourg border. The First Army was to be used for remote flanking security. Schlieffen intended to attack simultaneously both Nancy and the front between Toul and Verdun. He wanted to destroy the expected French attack against the German northern flank with a flank attack by the German field armies on the right wing. After securing victory there, the right wing was to cross the Meuse downriver of Verdun and proceed against the rearward lines of the French Army.[98] Thus, Schlieffen planned to combine the envelopment operation with a counterattack and a frontal attack.[99] Schlieffen maintained this basic idea for the deployment of the mobilization year 1904–1905 as well. The plans of that year indicated a reinforced left and a weakened right wing, which did not deploy too far to the north. That approach would have enabled Schlieffen to conduct both a powerful counterattack in Lorraine and an offensive supported by a frontal attack aiming at a decisive battle in the Verdun sector.[100]

Both options were feasible and indicate the high degree of flexibility inherent in Schlieffen's operational planning. At that point, however, the chief of the German General Staff was not yet planning a far-reaching offensive through Belgium. That changed with the 1905–1906 mobilization year. In contrast to the deployment of the previous year, it was no longer only eight army corps and six reserve divisions, but seventeen army and two-and-a-half reserve corps that would deploy north of Diedenhofen to the Dutch border. Never before in his deployment plans had Schlieffen so directly focused on the right attack wing. This reflects the distribution of forces specified in the memorandum of 1905. The chief of the General Staff had now decided against a mere northern outflanking of Verdun and in favor of a large-scale envelopment by the German right wing to Lille, through Belgium, in the direction of Brussels. And for the first time he was determined to violate Dutch neutrality in the event of war.

Why did Schlieffen change his previous operational planning concepts and in 1904 order a deployment plan with such far-reaching political and serious operational risks? According to Gerhard Ritter, Schlieffen made this difficult decision neither in response to changed French plans, nor with consideration of the development of the political situation as influenced by the Russo-Japanese War, but rather proactively for purely military reasons. Ritter painted the picture of a "simple soldier" who ignored political developments and decisions, or did not take them into account in his planning. He acted quasi-autonomously as a pure military technocrat. Recently discovered sources, however, indicate that it was both political considerations and the then recent information about the enemy's situation that led Schlieffen in late 1904 to make substantial changes to the German deployment plan. Since the midsummer of 1904, the General Staff's Section IIIb had been convinced that the deployment of the French left wing had been shifted to the north, and that a French offensive had become improbable because of the Russo-Japanese War.

> A French offensive, which had been probable until 1904, no longer seemed likely considering the Russo-Japanese War. Rather, it had to be expected that the French would not attack immediately after the outbreak of a war. Instead, they would marshal probably behind their fortifications and expect the attack by the Germans. They might presume that the German right wing would bypass their fortification front on the north. For marshaling, it seemed more convenient to move the deployment rapidly to the north, instead of massing the main body opposite Alsace-Lorraine, as had been expected to that point.[101]

Based on this estimate of the enemy's situation, Schlieffen had to assume that without Russian support the French would no longer act cautiously offensive, as had previously been expected, but rather defensively, and that they also would reinforce their left wing. Considering this change in the overall situation, it is understandable why Schlieffen, during the postmortem session of the first General Staff ride of 1904, questioned his previously favored northern envelopment of Verdun to Mézières. He realized the danger that the German Army might not be able to force the French to withdraw from their fortified positions. Despite the disadvantages involved—the violation of Dutch neutrality and the loss of surprise because of the long approach routes through northern Belgium—Schlieffen for the first time considered an attack with the majority of the German Army on the less fortified front of Verdun–Lille. Such a large-scale envelopment would enable the German units to envelop the French fortification system completely, which, given that the French had introduced an extensive modernization program for their fortification belt as a reaction to the changed strategic situation, was the *sine qua non* condition in Schlieffen's operational planning.[102]

As we have seen, Schlieffen during the Great General Staff Ride West of 1905 simulated his new operational concept against his best General Staff officers. The positive results—as Schlieffen saw them—were reflected in the deployment planning for the 1906–1907 mobilization year, the last one under his responsibility as chief of the General Staff. Thus, Schlieffen again reinforced the right wheeling flank for *Aufmarsch West I*, the state of war with France. The initial operational objectives—the First Army was to cover the right flank against Antwerp and the Second Army was to advance toward Brussels—indicate the wide range of the German right wing envelopment intended by Schlieffen. According to the orders: "The entire army, except the Seventh Army, makes a right wheel through Belgium. The left wing (Eighth Army) follows Metz and covers the left flank of the army if necessary in a fortified position against Verdun."[103] The wording does not allow for a different interpretation. Schlieffen clearly planned a large-scale envelopment operation, including all of Belgium and some parts of the Netherlands.

Altogether, Schlieffen made fundamental changes to the operational plans four times during his tenure as chief of the General Staff. In 1892 he shifted the operational focus from east to west. In 1894 he finally abandoned the defensive orientation of his predecessors and planned for a rapid offensive in the form of a frontal attack against the French Army. After 1897 Schlieffen at first wanted to bypass the French fortifications north of Verdun, but from 1899 and especially from 1904 he intended to bypass the entire French fortification line.

The German officer corps, however, did not let Schlieffen's plans go unchallenged, as the Schlieffen School suggested after 1918 and as was since accepted and reinterpreted without reservation by Schlieffen's critics after 1945. Leading military theorists of the time, including Goltz and Bernhardi, doubted the practicability of Schlieffen's plans. Field Marshal Gottlieb von Haesler argued that France would not let itself be captured "like a cat in a sack."[104] As early as in 1895, the former senior quartermaster, Major General Martin Köpke, cautioned with almost prophetic foresight: "In any event, there are enough signs that the war of the future will look different than that of 1870–1871. Rapid victories of decisive importance are not to be expected. The army and the people will have to get used to this unpleasant reality early on."[105]

The Schlieffen Plan

In February 1906, Schlieffen gave his successor, Helmuth von Moltke the Younger, a memorandum entitled "War Against France."[106] This memorandum became famous under the name of the Schlieffen Plan. It was not, as often claimed, however, Schlieffen's plan for a two-front war. Rather, it was a campaign plan for a war against France. According to Jehuda Wallach, the memorandum was based on a two-front war. But Wallach mistakenly assumed that Cannae and not Leuthen was the working model for Schlieffen's plan, and he also offered other misinterpretations of Schlieffen's operational thinking.[107] Wallach's interpretations of Schlieffen, which for decades have shaped Schlieffen's image in history, are in many places based on unsupportable foundations.

The memorandum was not the deployment plan of 1906, but rather a study of ideas for an optimum operations plan in the event of a single-front war against France. Schlieffen also intended the memorandum as his legacy to his successor, Moltke the Younger, who Schlieffen felt had been imposed on him. Although in principle Moltke shared Schlieffen's basic ideas, including the establishment of a center of gravity in the west and the rapid destruction of the French after the envelopment of their fortification system, he rejected a dogmatic fixation on envelopment. He also insisted that it was necessary to fix the enemy frontally more solidly before the envelopment could succeed. In Schlieffen's opinion, however, Moltke's ideas threatened the credibility of his life's work. Schlieffen therefore decided to record for history his position in no uncertain terms. In so doing he expressly reminded his successor of his basic operational ideas and advanced further proposals and execution guidelines for a potential war against France.[108] Schlieffen's memorandum was not a topical operations plan, but a feasible scenario for operations against France based on the deployment and mobilization plans of 1906–1907. It was also a précis of his operational thinking, combined with a subtle suggestion to Moltke the Younger to push for an increase in overall troop strength.

Schlieffen did not plan a "Super Cannae," as has so often been mistakenly claimed in the historical literature. Rather, he planned a "Super Leuthen." Based on the assessment that France would restrict itself to the defensive, the entire German Army was to deploy in the west with a strong right and a weak left wing.[109] The ratio between right and left wings was seven-to-one. Having completed the deployment, the right wing was to march on the Metz–Wesel line through Belgium, Luxembourg, and the Netherlands. The objective was to bypass the French fortification system and the main French positions, which had been extended to the northwest to Mezieres and La Fere. Upon executing the wide envelopment, the right wing would then turn to the south to attack west of Namur. The Metz-Diedenhofen fortress was the pivot between the two wings. The left wing was

Military Solution to the Problem of the German Reich's Central Position: The Schlieffen Plan

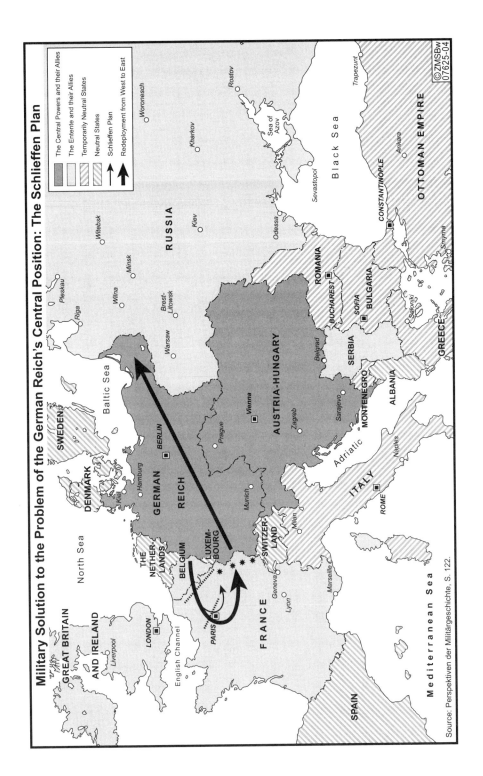

Legend:
- The Central Powers and their Allies
- The Entente and their Allies
- Temporarily Neutral States
- Neutral States
- Schlieffen Plan
- Redeployment from West to East

© ZMSBw
076Z5-04

Source: Perspektiven der Militärgeschichte, S. 122.

tasked with advancing to Nancy and containing the French forces in order to cover the left flank of the subsequent advance.

The German advance was based on an ambitious schedule. The schedule required reaching the French-Belgian border as early as the twenty-second day. After successfully breaking through the French border defenses, several major battles of encirclement would be fought in the border area to defeat the French Army. If the German forces failed to achieve Schlieffen's hoped-for annihilating defeat of the French west of the Oise, or if the French retreated to the south, the plan then called for an envelopment of Paris from the west. By turning back toward the east after the thirty-first day, the Germans would push the French forces up against the western side of their own fortifications, ultimately defeating the French through a major battle of annihilation.

The offensive was planned as a continuous chain of attacks. The entire operations plan was not only under extreme time pressure, there also was the possibility of French counterattacks in sectors such as the Upper Rhine. Schlieffen deflected those concerns by stating that the decisive battle would take place on the right wing. The French, therefore, would rapidly break off any counterattacks against the German left wing. In his final memorandum, written in 1912 during his retirement, Schlieffen was even prepared to give up East Prussia in favor of being able to execute a gigantic envelopment movement that reached the Channel coast. He justified this change of strategy with the often quoted remark: "The fate of Austria is to be decided ultimately not on the Bug, but on the Seine!"[110] Up to the present day that memorandum of 1912, which Schlieffen completed on 28 December, only a few days before he died, has been cited frequently as proof of his exaggerated operational planning. But the critics forget that this was a study prepared by an ill man nearly eighty years old, one who had been deliberately cut off from any information since his retirement, and whose anger about his successor had only increased as the effects of age took their toll.

Contrary to the widespread opinion in the historical literature, Schlieffen did not want to fight the decisive battle deep inside France, but as a sequence of major battles of envelopment near the border.[111] Hence, his memorandum was basically a deployment plan that extended to the French-Belgian border for the frontier battles he expected to fight in the French border area. It was not an operations plan for the follow-on phase. This can be understood easily from the outline of the memorandum published by Gerhard Ritter in 1956. Of the fifteen total pages of his memorandum, Schlieffen devotes only two to the operations plans after the frontier battles, while he uses almost ten pages for his estimates of the situation and the advance to the frontier battles—not including his deliberations on force strength. In contrast to his detailed explanations on the advance through Belgium, he also wrote: "If the Germans allow [the French] to proceed farther in this direction [to the south] the result would be an endless war. We must by all means press the French eastward against the Mosel forts, against the Jura, and against Swiss terrain, by attacking their left flank. The French Army must be annihilated."[112]

These thoughts were in agreement with Moltke. Any further operations planning remained open. Schlieffen's frequently noted increased emphasis on orderliness ends with the first decisive battles. The memorandum was not a detailed recipe for victory, planned through to the end.

The memorandum of 1905 clearly stated the most important elements of operational thought—movement, attack, speed, initiative, main effort, encirclement, surprise, and annihilation—that had been prevalent in Germany since Moltke the Elder. It also pointed out the inherent risks and deficiencies. Was it really possible to eliminate all friction? Would the French really allow their actions to be dictated by their enemy? Was the German infantry capable of executing the marches required for a rapid advance under combat conditions? Were the technical resources available to support the conduct of rapid mobile operations? How were the attacking forces to be provided with logistical support? What was the German Army's level of motorization, and thus its capability to act independently of the railway network? Was the German Army's force strength sufficient for the offensive? How was the war to be ended, given the possibility of a people's war following the successful battles? Who would execute the highly rapid operations, given that the high rates of fire of modern automatic weapons made it no longer possible to use cavalry in that role? And last but not least, did alternative courses of action exist in the event of defeat, and was there a danger of getting bogged down in a lengthy war of attrition?

Neither Schlieffen nor Moltke nor the contemporary military theorists provided adequate answers to those questions. Schlieffen ignored those problems by including force units that only existed on paper, as he had done in some of his war games. The western encirclement of Paris is a typical example. Or, Schlieffen took it for granted that the infantry would achieve the high degree of marching efficiency required to execute the ambitious schedule under battle conditions. According to Schlieffen, the roads in the area of the advance were well-maintained, and the forces would just have to make great efforts.

One solution to that problem would have been the widespread motorization of the German units, which would have greatly increased operational mobility and speed. That did not happen, but it would be somewhat shortsighted to cite this as an example of a general technophobia among the German military leadership. There is no doubt that in the decades preceding the First World War the German Army was not at all comfortable with the quick succession of technological innovations and the resulting effects on warfare. But there most probably was an explicit sense of technophobia among Bernhardi and others.[113] A prime example for that is the sense of crisis over the efficacy of the attack, caused by the increased introduction of automatic weapons. The German Army's response to that challenge was to solve the problem by resorting to moral factors, rather than turning to technical innovations.[114] A strong spirit in the attack and iron will would prove the limits of technology and overcome the problem of defending against the enemy's fire from automatic weapons.

Schlieffen's vision of a modern operational level of command was criticized as well. According to Hermann Giehrl, there was a danger that the modern means of communications would reduce the commander to a technocrat or a bureaucrat. Not only the commander's command and control capability, but even more gravely that of the entire officer corps would be called into question.[115]

There is no doubt that over the years the Reich had missed or misjudged important developments in artillery and automatic weapons and even made grave mistakes.[116] There can be no question, however, of a general technophobia. According to Eric Brose, it is shortsighted to attribute Germany's defeat in the First World War primarily to inadequate technical innovation and incorrect economic decisions in conjunction with tactical mistakes. The actual picture is rather more ambivalent. While the War Ministry initially evaluated the warfighting efficacy of new technical innovations and often took the conservative approach of waiting for such innovations to mature in civilian use, the General Staff forced the introduction of new technologies. Contrary to the widespread technophobia of the German military leadership frequently cited in the historical literature, Schlieffen had a more open mind about modern technical innovations than his various comments taken out of context by his critics have led us to conclude. Those comments referred primarily to future developments in infantry small arms and automatic weapons, and cannot be extrapolated as a general assessment of the use of technology in warfare. Schlieffen actually considered modern means of communications, motor vehicles, motorcycles, and airships to be indispensable command and control technologies for the modern commander who would control operations from an innovative communications center far removed from the front lines.

Nor were Schlieffen's technological interests limited to the communications tools necessary for mobile operations. Over the course of decades he supported the introduction of heavy, high-angle-firing artillery pieces. This development continued under his successor, culminating in 1914 shortly before the outbreak of the war in the introduction of the 42cm *Mörser* (heavy howitzer) popularly called *Die Dicke Bertha* (Big Bertha). The General Staff also paid particular attention to railway technology as a necessary prerequisite for the execution of operational-strategic warfare on interior lines. There is no doubt that the General Staff and the German Army were functioning at the state-of-the-art level with railway technology. The management procedures developed in the General Staff's Railway Department for controlling the movements of large masses of forces constituted an operational, strategic, and technological core competency.

In contrast, however, the German Army lacked the technical equipment necessary for conducting tactical and operational warfare on and off the roads. The introduction of trucks went very slowly and was not a key priority for the military leadership. The reason for this was that the trucks of the period lacked off-road capability and were generally underpowered. Furthermore, the General Staff planned to requisition civilian trucks in time of war, thereby saving money during peacetime. At the beginning of the war in 1914, therefore, the German Army did not have the motorized transport capacity required to conduct rapid operational envelopments.

Reconnaissance was another important command and control asset at the operational level. The invention of aircraft and airships offered the General Staff considerably expanded capabilities for tightly focused command and control systems. Until the outbreak of the war in 1914, Germany increasingly relied on Zeppelins. The use of aircraft for aerial reconnaissance was expedited during the tenure of Moltke the Younger, and was generally up to the technical standards of that time. Thus, on the eve of the First World War the picture of the German Army's use and development of technical tools for operational warfare was an ambivalent one. In the area of mobility, the key capability for rapid operational warfare, the German Army was up to date with railway technology on the one hand, but sadly deficient in motorization and off-road capabilities on the other hand. That was a shortcoming that was impossible to rectify during the course of the war.[117] Schlieffen himself shrugged off the army's logistical problems, stating: "On the other hand, there should be no lack of food. Rich Belgium and rich Northern France can supply a lot, and if the right pressure is applied, they will provide the supplies they lack from outside sources."[118]

Aside from the fact that Schlieffen did not mention the supply of munitions and material, and he intended to ensure the supply of food by pressuring the civilian populations, he showed an alarming disinterest in logistical issues. His approach is reminiscent of warfare in the era of Frederick the Great, rather than of warfare in the era of armies of millions.[119]

Schlieffen was not the only one with an obvious blind spot for logistics. While civilians with an interest in military issues and the General Staff engaged in fierce discussions about a great variety of tactical and operational issues, they hardly talked about the logistical difficulties of offensive operational warfare. Operational and tactical factors clearly overshadowed the logistical factors of operational thinking. This phenomenon derives from the fact that until the beginning of the First World War, German armed forces fought their battles either on German territory or in immediately adjacent regions. And this, of course, was a function of the central position in Europe of Germany and its predecessor states. During the Franco-Prussian War of 1870–1871 it was possible to supply the troops from the depots throughout the war. Concentric offensive operations beyond the Central European regions, whose success greatly depended on perfect logistical support, were not a common operational and strategic concern of the German Army. The British Army, on the other hand, could not conduct offensive operations outside the British Isles without a solid logistical system in place from the start. Wilhelm von Blime was the only German commentator to point out the logistic uncertainties of mobile warfare:

> Apart from the restricting activities of the enemy, [friendly] troops will only be able to move freely in the area [of operations] with secured living conditions as long as they have the means to overcome natural obstacles, to satisfy their requirements, and to supply the necessary materials themselves, or are provided with them, or find them in the [enemy's territory]. The support the theater might provide is extremely valuable, but not sufficient for requirements of all kinds (for example, replacement of munitions), any army strength, and any war situation. Therefore, operational capability is ensured only to the degree it is possible to exist without any support.[120]

The General Staff, however, ignored Blume's clear conclusions on the necessary logistical support for operations. In the final few years before the First World War, the General Staff studied logistical requirements for operational warfare by using several standard examples from the nineteenth century. It came to the conclusion that with the increase of the armies to a strength of millions it had become more difficult to supply the forces. As a result, operations in states with few support resources would restrict the conduct of operations. At the same time, the General Staff argued that during the execution of rapid and mobile warfare the troops would have to make do with a minimum of supplies. As in the Napoleonic era, the troops had to rely primarily on living off the countryside, and they would have to do so without any consideration for the local civilian populations.[121]

As British historian Hew Strachan correctly emphasizes, those conclusions show that the General Staff did not develop a logistical concept to support operational mobile warfare. Instead, they simply ignored the inevitable consequences.[122] As a result, logistical problems were marginalized in operational planning.

Neither Schlieffen in his memorandums and war games nor other military officers thought through to the end the question of how to conclude the war after the victorious battle. They virtually blocked out the idea that the decision of the battle would not necessarily produce the decision of the war, given that a subsequent people's war and war of attrition were unwinnable in the opinion of all the German experts. For many German officers, as well as many officers in other European armies, the solution to the problem was to focus on moral and psychological factors.[123] The aggressive iron will to win, coupled with a fresh spirit of the attack, the *"Furor Teutonicus,"* but with more rifles, would make up for the disadvantages of Germany's geostrategic position and numerical inferiority. Or, as Schlieffen said to his colleagues in the postmortem session of the last war game under his tenure: "This [flank attack] requires a confident commander, an iron character, a tenacious will to win, and a force that is clearly aware of the either-or [consequences]."[124]

War Games

Schlieffen's operational thinking was not as narrow-mindedly dogmatic as Ritter and especially Wallach have suggested. In the late 1950s Professor Eberhard Kessel of Mainz criticized Ritter's interpretation, pointing out that Schlieffen's war games, final operational problems, and General Staff rides included a large number of alternate courses of action. Kessel had been able to read the relevant documents before the Army Archive was destroyed in 1944.[125] The records of two recently discovered war games from 1905 that were prepared at the same time as Schlieffen's famous memorandum confirm Kessel's analysis. The first war game was based on the scenario that, despite the Russo-Japanese War, Russia in cooperation with France waged war against Germany and Austria-Hungary. In the postmortem session of that war game Schlieffen addressed the fundamental issue of a two-front war: the shifting of German forces on interior lines. His deliberations are of fundamental importance for the assessment of his operational thinking, as the following lengthy quote indicates:

> This theory of the decisive battle plays an important role, since war with France and Russia has become a threat to Germany. In theory it goes something like this: We throw all our strength against France, fight a decisive battle there, which of course ends in our favor, and in the evening of the day of battle, or in the early morning of the next day at the latest, the railroad trains are ready and waiting. The victors head east to fight a new decisive battle at the Vistula, Neman, or Narew Rivers. To my satisfaction, one of you gentlemen took the trouble to prove that currently wars do not proceed in this way. After the battle comes . . . the pursuit, and it may sometimes continue for quite a long time. At the least one probably can consider Sedan as the decisive battle. . . . If on 2 September 1870 the German armies had been transported from Sedan to the Vistula, what would have become of the 1870 campaign in France?

Proceeding from this point, Schlieffen explained to his colleagues with the help of recent examples from the Russo-Japanese War that an immediate troop withdrawal after a victorious decisive battle was not easy. He continued: "If we intend to wage war in France for months we cannot stand back and watch [the

Russians] march across the Vistula, Oder, and Elbe Rivers [while we] continue to wage war in France. This is absolutely impossible. If we are unable to withdraw forces after the decision, we will have to attempt to drive the Russians back right from the start of the war."[126]

These passages confirm that Schlieffen was well aware of the problems associated with a lengthy war in France. It is especially interesting to note here that Schlieffen, who never talked about battles of annihilation in this context but only decisive battles, did not believe that he would have to annihilate the enemy after the battle. Furthermore, he refused to give up major areas of German territory in the east, which he considered to be completely unacceptable, and he also thought of conducting an offensive defense in the east from the very beginning of the war.

The last war game conducted by Schlieffen personally in December 1905 indicates just how flexible elements of his operational and strategic plans were, in contrast to the repeated arguments to the contrary. Schlieffen based this 1905 war game on what he personally thought was the improbable scenario of a war between Germany and its ally Austria-Hungary on one side, and France, Russia, and Great Britain on the other. This scenario is extremely interesting for us, considering the German deployment plans of 1914. As he considered simultaneous offensives on both the Western and Eastern Fronts impossible to conduct alone, Schlieffen planned a strategic defense on both fronts in order to defeat within the shortest time possible first the one and then the other aggressor through counter-attacks.[127] That 1905 war game shows that Schlieffen did not reject the strategic defensive in certain war situations.

A comparison between the 1905 memorandum and the two war games of that year shows the astonishing spectrum of Schlieffen's operational thinking. It is, therefore, necessary to rethink the common wisdom of Schlieffen as a narrow-minded military dogmatist, as he has been portrayed in the literature for so many years.

The Moltke Plan

Owing to considerable differences in operational issues, and also probably because of personal differences,[128] Moltke the Younger shortly after he entered office in 1906 avoided any contact with Schlieffen, nor did he ask his predecessor for advice.[129] Nevertheless, Moltke did adhere to the basic operational and strategic principles developed by Schlieffen, since he did not see any better alternatives for the challenge of a two-front war. Moltke the Younger also divided the two-front war into two single-front wars. First, France was to be defeated through a major envelopment operation, and then the attack on Russia would follow. Moltke, however, deviated from the plans of his predecessor in important details and changed key elements of the deployment plans.[130]

Moltke took into account the changes in the geostrategic situation and at the operational level during the time since he assumed office. While Schlieffen was able to discount as improbable a war against Russia, France, and Great Britain all together, Moltke had to take into account antagonism of these powers toward Germany. From the very beginning Moltke questioned two key premises of Schlieffen's planned large-scale envelopment. Moltke did not exclude the possibility of a lengthy war. Even as early as 1905 he told the Kaiser: "It will be a people's war that cannot be won in one decisive battle, but will turn into a long and tedious struggle with a nation that will not give up before the strength of its entire people has been broken. Our own people too will be utterly exhausted, even if we should be victorious."[131]

Furthermore, Moltke unlike Schlieffen anticipated an early French offensive.[132] Moltke's reservations about Schlieffen's plans were so strong that as early as the mobilization year of 1908–1909 he abandoned the passage through Holland, because he considered the Netherlands to be the economic windpipe of Germany in any war. Further developing what in his mind was the correct western offensive, he decided in the following years that a surprise attack on Liège would be necessary.[133] That, however, would put German operations under even greater time pressure and also would prevent almost any opportunity for a political solution in the event of war.[134]

The astonishingly speedy reconstitution of the Russian Army after 1905 increased the danger of a two-front war in Moltke's opinion, and caused him to reinforce the units intended for deployment in East Prussia.[135] Despite this change in the situation, he continued to focus on the west. With the mobilization year of 1913–1914, however, he discontinued planning for a great eastern deployment, because based on the then current political situation he discounted any possibility of an isolated German-Russian war without French involvement. In addition to the political reasons, railway-related factors probably contributed to this decision. Given the preparations for the new transport plan, with which the General Staff intended to speed up the deployment by three days, the Railway Department was unable to devote the necessary planning efforts to a great eastern deployment as well.[136]

As the General Staff received increasing intelligence indicating that in the event of war the French Army would immediately launch a major offensive in Lorraine, Moltke reinforced the German troops in Alsace-Lorraine beginning in the mobilization year of 1909–1910. For political reasons he did not want to give up either that region or East Prussia. During the mobilization year of 1913–1914 the two field armies on the German left wing with six army corps and two reserve corps would face seventeen army corps and nine reserve corps on the French right attack wing. According to Moltke's plans, the German right wing had to bring about the decision, despite the corps that would deploy southeast of the Metz fortress. The corps allocated to the left wing were to repel the French offensive and prevent the deployment of stronger French units to the French left wing by pinning down the forces on the French right. In the event of a massive French attack toward Lorraine, Moltke was even prepared to give up the German envelopment through Belgium. As he reasoned, the opportunity to destroy the bulk of the French Army in Lorraine rapidly would make the right wing envelopment unnecessary.[137]

In early August 1914, therefore, seven-eighths of the German Army deployed in the west, and one-eighth in the east. At first glance this deployment appears to have been in accordance with Schlieffen's plans of 1905. To the present day a great deal of the historical research still supports the conclusion that Germany started the war with the Schlieffen Plan. Wallach supported this conclusion,[138] but recent research seriously challenges this long-held assumption.[139] Moltke's operations plan against France differed in essential elements from that of his predecessor. The essential differences were the reinforcement of the German left wing, the abandoning of the passage through Holland, and the rapid conquest of Liège. Thus, in 1914 the German soldiers did not enter the field with a Schlieffen Plan, but with a Moltke Plan.

Moltke's shifts in the center of gravity were based on a fundamental operational disagreement with Schlieffen. Moltke did not want to commit himself before the war broke out to a single operations plan—the great envelopment of Belgium. He wanted to keep other operational options open. In his opinion the war would present other options in addition to the envelopment.[140] Even as early as during Schlieffen's tenure, Moltke argued with Schlieffen about the possibilities of achieving a direct breakthrough, which he thought would be a viable option in any future war. While Schlieffen wanted to impose his will on the enemy by all means available and maintain the absolute initiative, Moltke planned to force the French Army into battle and defeat them at the first opportunity. He wanted victory anywhere he could get it. This was a more reactive approach to the conduct of operations, and contrasted with Schlieffen's more active approach of imposing the imperative of action on the enemy. In the style of his uncle, Moltke the Elder, the younger Moltke wanted to combine the advantages of the defensive with a subsequent offensive, while simultaneously opening a window for political negotiations for the Reich government. Inherent in Moltke's approach, however, was the danger of becoming dependent on the enemy's actions, which in turn called into question the entire strategic concept of a divided two-front war.[141]

Nonetheless, Moltke the Younger's concept of a more mobile conduct of operations was closer to the operational thinking of his uncle than to that of Schlieffen.[142] This can be seen clearly in the railway plans that were in effect shortly before the outbreak of the war. In addition to pushing the rail deployment to ensure that fully mobilized units remained in their garrisons until the political situation was clarified, Moltke intended to expand the switch lines for a rapid deployment on interior lines from east to west and vice versa. This indicates that the General Staff intended to keep all operational and strategic options open in any future war.

Moltke the Younger also differed from Schlieffen in his estimation of the duration of a future war. Like his uncle, he believed a lengthy war was a distinct possibility. At times he even had doubts about a German victory.[143] Although Moltke the Younger and the entire German Army leadership based their hopes for victory in the unequal fight on the morale and fighting quality of the German soldier, their latent doubts do not fit the exaggerated image of the excessive voluntarism of the Great General Staff before the First World War as it has been presented in the historical literature.

During the first weeks of the war in 1914, Moltke the Younger's self-doubts probably affected the conduct of his leadership. They did not, however, affect his operational capabilities. One, then, must concur completely with Hermann Gackenholz's assessment: "The autonomy, completeness, and consistency of Moltke's plans for the western campaign are proof of a high degree of strategic [operational] capabilities."[144]

Conclusions

The development of German operational thinking had largely matured by the time the First World War broke out. The key elements evolved over decades during a discourse both inside and outside the General Staff. As an exponent of a younger generation of officers with a more aggressive stance, Schlieffen continued to adhere to the decisive elements of maneuver, attack, speed, initiative, main effort, encirclement, surprise, and annihilation, which all were based on ideas of Moltke the Elder. Schlieffen even combined them into a single package encompassing tactics, operations, and military strategy. But Schlieffen did not introduce the concept of three specific command echelons—tactics, operations, and strategy—commonly recognized today. Unlike Goltz or Boguslawski, Schlieffen did not offer a specific definition of operations. The otherwise always correct chief of the General Staff did not think such was necessary, neither in the published regulations nor in his studies.

Schlieffen's operational thinking, therefore, is revealed in his war games, final operational problems (*Schlussaufgaben*), memorandums (*Denkschriften*), and the General Staff rides during his tenure, rather than in the body of writings he produced after his retirement. Newly discovered primary records indicate a chief of the General Staff who was much more flexible and thought more politically than the historical literature to date would lead us to believe. These new sources also clarify that not only the interested military public but also the General Staff, which generally has been considered a monolithic block, engaged in fierce debates about future warfare in a two-front war scenario and the development of operational thinking in general. The military leadership of the German Reich considered Schlieffen's ideas quite controversial. The main elements of his operational and strategic doctrine were:

1. To pursue war not defensively and reactively, but to take the offensive and wage the kind of warfare based on seizing the initiative.
2. To use interior lines to divide the two-front war into two single-front wars, which would then be waged one after the other.
3. To establish a center of gravity through an offensive in the west and a delay in the east.
4. To conduct rapid battles of annihilation with the strong right wing after the envelopment of the French fortification system and the successful passage through Luxembourg, the Netherlands, and Belgian territory.
5. Following the victory in the west, to transport the victorious units to the Eastern Front using the railways, and then defeat the enemy that had been delayed initially.

This doctrine, which was based on the assumption that Germany would not be able to win a lengthy war of attrition, was basically accepted by Schlieffen's critics both inside and outside of the General Staff.[145] A violation of Belgium's neutrality had never been debated in the General Staff. It was accepted without reservation as an absolute necessity. Points of dissension that could not be ignored, however, existed over details, such as the overemphasis on the envelopment. This is particularly true for Schlieffen's successor. Moltke the Younger did not completely embrace Schlieffen's unilateral fixation on the envelopment. He did not want to change the conditions according to his terms and impose his will on his enemies by all means; rather, he wanted to respond flexibly to the situation. In this respect, Moltke was closer to his uncle's operational thinking than to Schlieffen's. Naturally, these differing ideas were reflected in Moltke the Younger's deployment plans.

The thoughts of Schlieffen and most German military theorists, including Moltke, focused on the decision of the battle. In the broadest sense, Schlieffen understood it as the decision of the war. Although Schlieffen's operational plans now seem far less dogmatic than had been previously assumed, they still betray the weaknesses of German operational thinking. In addition to the conviction that the enemy's numerical superiority could be compensated for with a higher quality force and superior command and control systems based on moral and psychological factors, the unilateral overemphasis on the tactical and operational parameters at the cost of the logistical parameters was another major weakness.

The fact that the operational plans ended after the initial victorious battles and that no further dispositions existed for any potentially necessary further warfare or for any subsequent deliberations to end the war is another fundamental deficiency of German operational thinking, developed from transferring tactical conditions to the operational level. This line of thinking provided a close linkage to tactics, but it did not ensure adequate consideration of the strategic dimension. In addition to the rejection of anything political and the negation of the primacy of politics in warfare, the reason for this deficiency was the extreme departmental egoism that characterized the German Reich. This departmental egoism regularly prevented interdepartmental coordination. It was not only the navy and army leadership that did not communicate with each other; the General Staff and the War Ministry limited their cooperation to an absolutely minimum necessary level, and often worked more against instead of with each other. Although Schlieffen certainly included political factors in his planning to a greater degree than what had been assumed previously, he did not cross the existing lines of his department. Since the General Staff had only very limited access beyond the operational and strategic levels to all the functional areas that were important for the conduct of warfare, it focused on the deployment and operations plans. This deliberate isolation, which was in part intentional and in part inherent in the system, prevented the true linkage between operational and strategic levels and caused the General Staff to suffer from tunnel vision.

To what extent did the General Staff officers surrounding their chief shut their eyes to and deliberately disconnect themselves from reality? And to what degree were exchanges of opinion nipped in the bud because of departmental egoism, thus preventing overall strategic planning for the Reich? These are still open questions that historians must try to resolve. One thing is certain, however. It would be a grave error to deny that Schlieffen, Moltke the Younger, and their General Staff officers had the intellectual capabilities to develop a comprehensive operational-strategic concept.[146] The General Staff was well aware of the high level of risk inherent in their operational plans for a two-front war. Such plans, therefore, were not regarded as a recipe for victory, but rather as an emergency solution for a perceived impasse in a potentially deteriorating situation.

Any failure of the operational doctrine in an actual war, however, carried grave domestic and foreign policy risks. In the event of a serious defeat, there was the strong possibility that the consequences would be a destabilization of Germany's ruling system, and, in the worst case, an end of the Hohenzollern monarchy and with it the loss of the army's position of power. The only alternative would have been to attempt to make the leadership of the Reich understand the hopelessness of a two-front war, and therefore cause them to change Germany's foreign policy. That approach, however, conflicted with the self-image of the German General

Staff officers and also would have called into question the position of the General Staff and the army itself within the German Reich.

Therefore, Schlieffen and his successor developed an operational doctrine based on maneuver, with the objective of undermining the enemy's strategic potential and preventing its full application. The question was, however, did Germany have the rapid mobile forces necessary to execute those operational plans?

5

Bitter Awakening

World War I

> The main characteristic of an offensive battle is the envelopment or bypassing, which is to say the actual conduct of the battle.
>
> —Carl von Clausewitz

The West

"In the evening, we were moved forward to the first line to check any renewed thrust. The British, however, seemed to have had enough. Our success that day was that we had managed to hold our position. Still, the battlefield looked dreadful, with corpses, mostly British, lying there in droves. The fighting had been so very fierce that neither side took prisoners."[1]

This was not the type of maneuver warfare the General Staff had planned and prepared for, but rather it was the long, drawn-out war of attrition that Schlieffen had attempted to prevent through his operational doctrine. From the autumn of 1914 onward, the war on the Western Front—and a year later in some sectors of the Eastern Front—had frozen into a system of positions echeloned in depth over a length of hundreds of kilometers. Soldiers were struggling for every foot of ground using poison gas, heavy artillery, flamethrowers, and machine guns. For the first time in military history, they fought in all dimensions of space, being simultaneously undermined by engineers and bombarded by aircraft. At the same time, the British naval blockade cut off the Reich from overseas trade.

Moltke the Younger had turned out to be right when he predicted a lengthy people's war. The worst-case scenario of the General Staff had become a reality, and neither the military nor the political decision makers were in any way prepared for it. They could find scant consolation in the fact that their enemies also had been taken by surprise by this development. What were the reasons for this fundamental change? Was it caused by the departure from reality cited by Martin Kutz; or was the General Staff incapable of developing a concept of the war that matched reality?

In order to answer these questions it is necessary to give a brief recapitulation of the military events during the initial weeks of the war. During the sixteen days following the start of the mobilization on 2 August 1914, some 1.6 million German soldiers were deployed along the western German border in seven field armies. Five of those armies were on the right wing, and two were deployed on the left wing southeast of the Metz-Diedenhofen fortifications. In accordance with the German operational plans, the center of gravity of the initial deployment was along the Belgian border. The Belgian fortress of Liège was captured on 16 August. On 18 August, two weeks after the German declaration of war on France, the German main attack wing, consisting of the First, Second, and Third Armies, began to advance. (See Plate 6.)

Three days later, the German troops arrived at the French-Belgian border. As had been expected by Schlieffen and Moltke the Younger, border battles took place with French and British units. The German troops, who advanced along the entire front, including in Lorraine and the Ardennes, were able to defeat their enemies during what became known as the Battle of the Frontiers, but they did not manage to encircle and crush them as planned. The German forces merely achieved the "ordinary victories" that Schlieffen had feared. The Belgian Army, which fell back toward Antwerp, was not destroyed. The Allied forces withdrew south in the direction of Paris, pursued by the units of the German main attack wing.[2] In the course of this pursuit, the advancing First Army passed Paris to the east, instead of to the west as originally planned.[3] The French high command seized the opportunity and attacked the right flank of the German attack wing on 6 September.[4] That was the beginning of the Allied counteroffensive along the entire front from Verdun to Paris. In the opinion of the senior department chiefs of the *Oberste Heeresleitung* (Army Supreme Command, or OHL), the hoped-for decisive battle was imminent.[5]

The key event took place outside Paris. On 6 September, the newly formed French Sixth Army attacked from Paris against the right flank of the First Army. Colonel General Alexander von Kluck found himself forced to withdraw his units in order to repulse the attack. As a consequence of this withdrawal, a gap of almost fifty kilometers opened between the German First and Second Armies, into which French and British forces advanced. There was a real risk of the German right wing being encircled and annihilated. Consequently, OHL ordered a general withdrawal to reestablish a unified front. The Battle of the Marne ended on 9 September.[6] Germany had been defeated in the sought-for decisive battle. (See Plate 7.)

During the following weeks the warring sides attempted in vain to outflank each other to the north in what became known as the "Race to the Sea." That ended in October 1914 as both sides arrived at the Channel coast near Ostend. The Western Front then froze into a system of trench positions hundreds of kilometers long, running from the border of Switzerland to the North Sea.

While the offensive in the west reached its culmination outside Paris, the Russian offensive started more quickly than expected. The French, meanwhile, had done everything to exploit the advantages of operating on exterior lines in conjunction with an early Russian attack in order to render the expected German attack in the west more difficult through concentric operations. As a result, OHL was forced to deal with crises on the Western and Eastern Fronts at the same time. Owing to the early Russian offensive, Germany was caught in the very strategic vise against which the General Staff had been preparing for years.

The East

In the strategic calculations of the Reich's military command, the east was merely a secondary theater of war. For that reason, only one-eighth of the German land forces, the Eighth Army of approximately 120,000 soldiers under the command of Colonel General Maximilian Graf von Prittwitz und Gaffron, deployed to the areas east of the Vistula River.[7] There was no coordinated operations plan with the Austro-Hungarian Army. The two alliance partners each planned their own war separately, only vaguely aware of what their confederates intended.[8] The German side had anticipated an attack on East Prussia by two Russian field armies of approximately 360,000 soldiers each, separated by the Masurian Lakes and thus operating independently. Consequently, the German units were outnumbered by the Russians about three-to-one.

The General Staff treated the Russian Army with a mixture of respect and disdain. While it acknowledged that the soldiers were capable of putting up a tough defense, it considered the operational capabilities of the officer corps to be mediocre.[9] In an assessment memorandum dated October 1913, the General Staff evaluated the Russian command as methodically slow, with their troop movements always progressing very haltingly. The assessment concluded: "For that reason, in a clash with the Russians the German command may venture on maneuvers that it would not get away with if facing a more evenly matched opponent."[10] On the basis of that assessment, the German command intended to attack and defeat the Russian armies successively through a distinct concentration of effort in offensive and mobile combat management. The Germans would make use of their extensive and well-maintained railway network and skillfully exploit interior lines. Schlieffen had run through such a scenario during several General Staff rides, but he had not developed a detailed defensive plan.[11] On the contrary, the *Aufmarschanweisung* (deployment directives) for the Eighth Army expressly stated that its commanding general would direct operations as he saw fit.[12] In all circumstances, Prittwitz was to maintain the initiative. As Moltke expressly said to Prittwitz: "When the Russians come, do not on any account go on the defensive, but take the offensive, offensive, offensive."[13] The German units were only allowed to withdraw to the line of the Vistula River if there was an imminent threat of the Eighth Army being annihilated.[14]

More quickly than had been expected by OHL, the Russian First (Njemen) Army, responding to intense French diplomatic pressure,[15] advanced to the north of the Masurian Lakes as early as 15 August.[16] Separated from the First Army by this natural obstacle and lagging behind it by a few days, the Second (Narew) Army marched from the south toward the East Prussian border.[17] Prittwitz decided to attack the First Army first with the bulk of the Eighth Army near Gumbinnen on 20 August 1914.[18] In the course of that battle Prittwitz received a message reporting that the Second Army had completed its initial deployment and was about to attack farther to the west than expected. The danger of being encircled caused Prittwitz to break off the ongoing battle and to withdraw his army to the Vistula River line.

Although the withdrawal was covered under the *Aufmarschanweisung,* Moltke—who had been less than pleased for some time with the hesitant leadership of the Eighth Army—relieved Prittwitz of command on 22 August. This is not the place for a discussion of the pros and cons of this decision that were later debated in the German military literature.[19] Nonetheless, it should be noted that owing to differences of opinion with OHL, the command of the Eighth Army was assigned to Paul von Hindenburg and Erich Ludendorff, who Moltke expected to provide more decisive leadership and, above all else, victories. That was the beginning of the rise of the two men, who were then little known outside the military establishment. That was about to change, however. On 31 August, the new commanding general of the Eighth Army reported to the Kaiser the annihilation of the Russian Second Army. (See Plate 5.)

How could such a victory have been achieved? Outnumbered, 153,000 German soldiers had faced 191,000 Russians, with a second Russian army behind the German forces. And what then were the resulting military and political consequences? Proceeding from the deployment already initiated under Prittwitz, and being very well informed about everything their enemies were doing through aerial and radio reconnaissance, Ludendorff and Hindenburg stripped the front facing the Russian First Army, which was slowly advancing on Königsberg. They left only a thin cavalry screen. Then, concentrating all of their forces, the Eighth Army attacked the Russian Second Army in its flanks, encircling it near Tannenberg and crushing it completely between 26 and 30 August.[20] That was the birth of the "Heroes of Tannenberg" legend. The battle was scarcely over when it was already being compared to Cannae, and Hindenburg and Ludendorff were being feted as the true heirs of Schlieffen.[21] Most importantly at that point, Germany despite the failure of the offensive in the west still had victorious leaders to hold up to their own people, as well as to Germany's allies and enemies.

From the military perspective, a major defeat had been inflicted on the Russians and the "Russian steamroller" had been stopped. In the meantime, the Austro-Hungarian Army in Galicia was threatened with imminent disaster.[22] In the following weeks the German Eighth Army, which meanwhile had been reinforced with units from the west, was able to support the Austro-Hungarian forces in stopping the Russian advance.[23] Yet, the victory at the Battle of Tannenberg also had profound, long-term psychological, historical, and strategic repercussions. Thus, the latent feelings of superiority over the Russian troops and their leaders that had prevailed among German soldiers and their leaders prior to the outbreak of the war were confirmed. And that mind-set continued into World War II.

Assessment

The German attack on France and the strategic concept of forcing the issue to achieve an early decision had failed. Did this mean that the operational concept of the General Staff developed over several years was obsolete? Had it failed in the reality of war?

When we examine against the framework of operational thinking the German operations in the west and in the east during the initial months of the war, the resulting picture is ambiguous. Based on his operational notions, Moltke the Younger had reinforced the left wing of the German front and therefore had abandoned an even stronger concentration of effort on the right wing. His critics later accused him of having lacked the will necessary to achieve an unconditional concentration of effort. Down to the present day it has been impossible to determine conclusively whether or not any more troops could even have been concentrated on the right wing, considering the difficult traffic conditions and logistical problems.[24]

Surprise definitely had been achieved at the beginning of the offensive. Yet operational surprise, like tactical surprise, loses its advantages when the enemy has enough time to react, and that very development played out during the summer of 1914. During the frontier battles the effect of surprise on the Allies caused by the German right attack wing, which was swinging unexpectedly far to the west and was numerically very strong, passed its zenith.[25] Consequently, once the French high command recognized the center of gravity of the German attack, they shifted troops along their interior lines from the disputed eastern border areas to Paris. This dramatically altered the force ratio between the German and the Franco-British units in favor of the Allies. As a result, at the beginning of the Battle of the Marne on 5 September, the 24.5 German divisions on the right wing faced 41 Allied divisions.[26] The element of surprise was lost. Within the few days during which their window of opportunity existed, the German forces did not succeed in encircling and annihilating the enemy armies as planned. As Schlieffen had feared, the Allied units retreated, evading a decisive battle only to launch a counterattack outside Paris when the German advance had reached its culminating point.

There were two reasons for the German inability to exploit the element of surprise. In addition to the fact that machine guns and modern artillery had now
made the tactical defensive clearly superior to the offensive, the German attack
divisions were simply too slow to encircle the enemy units. Even so, the soldiers of
the First Army had marched under combat conditions at an average of more than
twenty-three kilometers per day for more than three weeks. That meant that on the
thirty-first day of mobilization they arrived not just at the Amiens–La Fere–Rethel
line, as planned by Schlieffen, but already outside Paris. This was an enormous
achievement considering the prevailing mid-summer temperatures. Despite this
high rate of march and problems with repairing the destroyed railway network in
Belgium and northern France, the logistics system still functioned fairly well. As
in the past, however, the troops were forced to live off the country. Among other
things, that caused problems with the Belgian civilian population and was one of
several reasons for the German atrocities in Belgium during the advance in 1914.[27]

During the course of the operation, OHL progressively lost the initiative.
Owing to major communications problems, Moltke and his staff never had a current picture of the situation. In some cases, the situational information received at
OHL was more than twenty-four hours old. There were also considerable communications problems between the field armies.[28] Germany, therefore, paid dearly for
the General Staff's failure to increase the rate of introduction and adoption of the
most current command and control technical assets. The kind of close command
and control of units Schlieffen had in mind was difficult to achieve without such
state-of-the-art technologies. It was precisely to deal with this type of situation
that Moltke the Elder had introduced the technique of leadership by directives in
the German Army. In August 1914, however, that leadership model failed almost
completely in the crucial situations on the Western Front.

Moltke the Younger himself was out of his depth. The complexity of the situation and the problems of commanding and controlling an army numbering
millions were heretofore completely unknown and something no one had ever
trained for. Based on his own personality, he exercised command in a rather hesitant manner and employed what could be called a cooperative style of leadership. However, he received no thanks from his immediate subordinates, especially
those on the right attack wing. As a result, the individual commanders, including the First Army's Kluck and the Second Army's Field Marshal Karl von Bülow,
gave too much rein to their personal animosities toward each other. It sometimes
seemed they were fighting each other rather than together.[29] When the First Army
was put under the operational control of the Second Army, that only exacerbated
the problems rather than solving them. In Lorraine, meanwhile, the frictions
between Prussian and Bavarian officers turned into open conflict.[30] This was perhaps inevitable, considering that the German Army was still a force composed of
contingents of previously independent states, and that even after more than forty

years the unification of the Reich was as yet far from a completed fact in the minds of many people. Thus, the lack of mobility combined with the coordination problems resulting from both inadequate communications systems and personal animosities prevented the German forces from encircling and annihilating the enemy forces during the frontier battles.

This reveals a crucial weakness in German operational thinking. The war was merciless in demonstrating that military operations are executed smoothly only on paper, and that the General Staff had not developed a comprehensive and conclusive concept for the command and control of an army numbering in the millions.

Schlieffen's conviction that a general would be able to command operations on the basis of preconceived planning and far from the front with telephones and the belief in the excellent command capability of German General Staff officers were both exposed as chimeras by the reality of the war. This resulted not only from a dogmatic faith in the planning of the General Staff, but also from the structural problems of the Reich, which became glaringly obvious during the very first weeks of the war. German Crown Prince Wilhelm and Bavarian Crown Prince Rupprecht had assumed command of field armies for dynastic reasons. Crown Prince Wilhelm in particular lacked the necessary military qualifications for this task. Although traditionally in Germany a strong chief of staff was assigned to a dynastic commanding general to function as the true commander of the field army, the increasingly fast and complex sequences of war operations made misunderstandings and communications problems inherent in this system. This was compounded by the requirement for balancing federal political considerations in filling the top military positions. The problem of a loss of control by field army commanders, who sometimes acted willfully and not in accordance with the intent of the supreme command, became obvious during the Battle of the Marne. The solution to that problem was the establishment of army groups as an operational command and control echelon over multiple armies.

Nonetheless, the Reich's structural leadership problems in the event of war were most clearly apparent in the person of the supreme commander in chief, the Kaiser himself. Under the constitution Wilhelm II held the supreme command authority over both the navy and army. Yet owing to a lack of military qualifications, he was inherently incapable of performing those functions, including the development of a joint strategy. Even Wilhelm's efforts to enforce coordination between the General Staff and the Admiralty Staff for a hypothetical occupation of Denmark, which might have become necessary in consequence of a British attack, failed because of the professional jealousies between the army and navy.[31] The Kaiser doggedly held on to the power of command over "his navy" until the summer of 1918. At the beginning of mobilization in 1914, however, he appointed the chief of the Prussian General Staff, Moltke the Younger, as the chief of the General Staff of the German Field Army (Feldheer), and thus responsible for the command of

Field Marshal Alfred Graf von Schlieffen. Portrait photo, ca. 1910. *BArch/183-R18084*.

Kaiser Maneuver 1906 in Mecklenburg. Chief of Staff Helmuth von Moltke and Kaiser Wilhelm II. 1906. Photographer: Oscar Tellgmann. *BArch/136-C0087*.

Field Marshal Paul von Hindenburg with his staff. Erich Ludendorff (*left*) and Lieutenant Max Hoffmann (*right*), ca. 1914/1915. Photographer: o.Ang. *BArch 146-1993-132-12A*.

General Erich von Falkenhayn.
Undated portrait photo.
BArch/146-2004-0023.

the army at the imperial level during the war. In so doing, Wilhelm essentially ceded to Moltke the command authority vested in the Kaiser by the constitution.

The *Oberste Heeresleitung* (OHL) was established as the agency for the conduct of the ground war.[32] It was a component of the *Grossen Hauptquartier* (Grand Headquarters).[33] During the war, the Kaiser remained at the Grand Headquarters with few interruptions, primarily to create the impression that Wilhelm II commanded operations following the old Prussian tradition. In truth, the Kaiser went hunting and played skat.

The Grand Headquarters was a symbol of the unsolved structural defects of the Reich's outmoded constitutional system. In the end, it was actually a combination of military command center and imperial court, from which the political leaders of the Reich—the chancellor and the state secretary for foreign affairs— withdrew after a few months to continue their official business in Berlin. Thus, the Kaiser lived in the society of his own court, which was dominated by a military environment, but far from the suffering of the soldiers in the trenches, the hunger of the families at home, and political realities in Berlin.[34]

The Grand Headquarters, which changed its location fairly frequently during the course of the war, was also a focus of intrigues on which every chief of OHL had to keep an eye at all times. Moltke the Younger in particular, who could never feel certain of the support of Wilhelm II, was forced right from the outbreak of the war to keep a watchful eye on the moods prevailing in the Grand Headquarters. The Prussian minister of war, General Erich von Falkenhayn, who became Moltke's successor, was consistently calling his leadership into question. How could an overall strategy, which had not been drawn up in peacetime, and was now urgently needed after the failure of the Moltke Plan, be developed in such an atmosphere? Moltke the Younger literally had to fight simultaneously on several different fronts, for the early Russian attack had imposed a two-front war on Germany from the very beginning.

In contrast to the Western Front, the German forces in the east achieved major successes early on. Tannenberg conformed to the classic German ideal of a battle of encirclement, conducted with outnumbered forces and resulting in the annihilation of the enemy. Only a few days after the termination of the battle Tannenberg was being regarded as evidence for the validity of the German operational doctrine. The tremendous success of Hindenburg and Ludendorff confirmed to everyone who wanted to believe such that it was not the German operational doctrine, but the leadership errors of a few individuals that had caused the failure in the west. In justifying this conclusion, however, several significant differences between the initial situation on the Western Front and that on the Eastern Front were willfully ignored.

Unlike in the west, the German divisions in the east with their heavy artillery had definitely superior firepower and tactical superiority. Moreover, the senior

Russian command after winning the initial border battles underestimated its enemy and failed to conduct the proper reconnaissance. The German senior command, in contrast, had a clear picture of the situation provided by its own aerial reconnaissance assets. And because German signals intelligence gave Hindenburg and Ludendorff a solid assessment of their enemy's operational intent, they therefore were able to ensure that their own operations retained the element of surprise. This is a factor that can scarcely be overestimated. Prior to the war the General Staff had war-gamed all conceivable situational developments in East Prussia and worked out an operational scheme for the defense of that area that the German senior command could use as a base. And finally, there was the key fact that Schlieffen himself had pointed out—that for a Cannae you need not only a Hannibal but also a Terentius Varro. In the case of the Battle of Tannenberg, he was Alexander Samsonov, and he can be considered as the personification of the Russian senior command acting slowly and prone to operational mistakes. Interestingly enough, another key aspect of the Battle of Tannenberg is rarely examined. Tannenberg was a defensive battle, which the Eighth Army won primarily because of its better intelligence and railway networks on interior lines. Tannenberg, therefore, cannot be cited as an example of a successful offensively conducted operation.

Without discounting the command achievements of Hindenburg and Ludendorff, we must remember that the conditions for the execution of operational thinking were easier in the east than in the west. Nonetheless, "The Duo," as Hindenburg and Ludendorff came to be called, did not succeed in encircling and destroying the Russian armies through the offensively conducted follow-on battles at the Masurian Lakes or outside Łódź. The German senior command also learned on the Eastern Front that without a well-established railway network its troops could not move fast enough in enemy territory to encircle and annihilate the Russian forces, which managed to withdraw adroitly despite inadequate road systems. Even during the first months of the war the crucial condition on which the operational German doctrine was based, the ability of the German forces to move more quickly than their enemies, turned out to be incorrect. Thus, in the west the French, with a good railway system at their disposal, were able to shift their troops more quickly than the marching Germans could move. In the east, owing to the inferior road system, it was impossible to encircle the Russian units as they fell back into the depths of their own territory.

Although the Battle of Tannenberg in East Prussia was a successful example of the exploitation of space and time in a "Schlieffen Plan in miniature," the Entente still managed to achieve its strategic objective despite the Russian defeat. Wilhelm II extolled the highly acclaimed operational triumph when he said to Hindenburg, "You have accomplished a feat of arms which, almost unparalleled in history, has won you and your troops everlasting renown for all time."[35] Those words, however, concealed the Reich's strategic defeat that was bound inseparably to that opera-

tional victory. After all, when disaster threatened in the east, Moltke had redeployed two army corps from the Western Front to the Eastern Front.[36] At the time
of the Battle of Tannenberg those units were still traveling by train and were badly
missed during the fighting at the Marne. The French calculation, then, had worked
out. The early Russian attack had forced OHL to relinquish some reserves to the
east, thus preventing the absolute strategic concentration of effort demanded by
Schlieffen, and at least aimed for by Moltke. Despite their operational victory in
the east, the Germans were strategically defeated by offensives conducted almost
simultaneously on exterior lines. To this day, these circumstances tend to be
glossed over in the relevant military literature in favor of a German operational
hagiography.[37]

Maneuver

An intense debate over the reasons for the defeat commenced only a few hours
after the end of the Battle of the Marne. Moltke the Younger was very quickly designated the guilty party responsible for the debacle, and a replacement for him
was found in Falkenhayn. The obvious personalization of the guilt demonstrated
that the mistakes of individuals and not the operational thinking underlying the
planning were supposed to be the cause of the defeat. As a consequence, a critical
examination of the operational planning and the operational thinking underlying
it did not take place. Although the mainstays of German military thinking were
not called into question, the military and political command of the Reich had
to admit to itself that after the failure of the Moltke Plan Germany was forced to
conduct precisely that drawn-out war of attrition it had tried so hard to prevent
through its operational and strategic planning. Neither the army and the navy nor
the political leadership had any plans prepared for this situation, although Moltke
the Younger had been anticipating a more lengthy war for quite some time. Yet,
the opportunity of developing an overall economic, political, and social strategy
in response to the failure of the war plans the army and navy had developed independently of each other was allowed to pass.[38] The Kaiser, whose task it should
have been to bring together purposefully the diverging individual concerns into a
comprehensive strategic approach, was incapable of doing so. As a result, the army
and the navy with few exceptions both continued to wage their own war during
the subsequent years.[39]

The new chief of OHL, General Erich von Falkenhayn, was faced with a
dilemma at the end of the first year of the war. Strategically, he saw the center
of gravity quite definitely on the Western Front against France, and particularly
against Britain. Yet, any maneuvering and therefore any realistic offensive operations were impossible there because of the high rates of fire from machine guns
and rapid-firing artillery pieces with modern recoil systems. Falkenhayn learned

Eastern Front, 1915

SWEDEN

STOCKHOLM

Source: Birken/Gerlach,
Atlas und Lexikon zum
Ersten Weltkrieg,
T. 1: Karten.

BALTIC SEA

**Commander-in-Chief East:
Hindenburg**

0   50   100   150   200 km

Army Groups:
Hindenburg,
Prinz Leopold

Helsingfors

SAINT PETERSBURG ■

6th Army

Reval

ESTONIA

Nowgorod

Dorpat

LIVLAND

Pskow

**RUSSIAN
EMPIRE**

Windau

Courland

Riga

Libau

Mitau

Neman Army

Dünaburg

**NORTHWESTERN
FRONT (Alekseev)**

Dvina   *Witebsk*

Memel

Group Lauenstein

Tauroggen

Aug. 8
Kowno

10th Army

Wilna

LITHUANIA

10th Army

Königsberg

8th Army

Olita   Sept. 19

Minsk   *Mogilev*

Danzig

Lötzen

Grodno

12th Army

WESTERN FRONT

**Army Group
Gallwitz**

Baranowitschi

Bobruisk

Graudenz

Lomscha

**GERMAN
REICH**

Thorn

**Nowo
Georgiewsk**

Ostrolenka

Posen

1st/2nd Army

Brest Litowsk
Aug. 26

Pinsk

9th Army

Lodz

Warsaw

5th Army

POLAND
Army
Detachment
Woyrsch

Iwangorod

4th Army   *Kowel*

Volhynia

Breslau

Lublin   *Cholm*

**1st Austro-Hungarian
Royal and Imperial Army**

Luck

Rowno

Shitomir

Kattowitz

*Rawa
Ruska*

Dubno

**Army Group
Mackensen**

Pless

Teschen

Cracow

*Tarnów
Gorlice*

Army of
the Bug*

3rd Army

**SOUTHWESTERN
FRONT (Ivanow)**

Winniza

**4th Austro-Hungarian
Royal and Imperial Army**

11th Army

Lemberg

8th Army

Tarnopol

UKRAINE

Brünn

**3rd Austro-Hungarian
Royal and Imperial Army**

Przemysl

Stryj

Halicz

11th Army

**Kamenez-
Poldolsk**

**2nd Austro-Hungarian
Royal and Imperial Army**

Munkács   *Kolomea*

Chotin

Theiss

Southern Army

Czernowitz

9th Army
Dnjestr

VIENNA
■

**Army Group
Linsingen**

Danube

AUSTRIA-HUNGARY

Detachment
Pflanzer-Baltin

Pruth

Budapest ■

Graz

**Army Group
Böhm-Ermolli**

Klausenburg

©ZMSBw
07616-03

—— Front in late April   ▪▪▪▪▪ Front in late May   ▬▬▬ Front on 11 July   ▬▬▬ Front on 9 September   ══ Front in November

☼ German Fortresses   ★ Austrian Fortresses   ✦ Russian Fortresses

* from July 1915:
Army of the Bug (Linsingen)

this lesson the hard way during the German offensives in Flanders, which resulted in heavy losses. On the Eastern Front, where the trench system was less densely developed and the Central Powers had the advantage in artillery, there was an opportunity for decisive operational warfare. But that was inconsistent with the notions of the prewar era. After all, the General Staff had decided against decisive operations in the east owing to poor road conditions and to the geographical position of Russia, which allowed the Russian Army to withdraw into the depths of their national territory. Falkenhayn, who followed the tradition of his predecessors closely, did not believe in a major decisive battle in the east either. In contrast to Hindenburg and Ludendorff, who argued that battles of encirclement resulting in annihilation were possible because of the favorable space-forces ratio in the east, Falkenhayn considered a decisive victory against Russia to be doubtful. He merely expected that the Central Powers could achieve only "major local successes."[40] He found his opinion justified by the Battle of Łódź[41] and the Winter Battle of the Masurian Lakes,[42] in which the Russian command demonstrated its operational maneuver capability, skillfully withdrawing its units from the planned encirclements.

In contrast to the German Supreme Command in the East (*Oberost*), Falkenhayn considered the Eastern Front a secondary theater of war. He was firmly convinced that the war would be decided in the west. Accordingly, the strategic center of gravity in the war should be there. For that reason, Falkenhayn—in the tradition of Schlieffen—was only prepared to operate offensively to a limited extent in the east. In contrast to Hindenburg and Ludendorff, he did not plan for a "Super Cannae" in the east, but merely intended to crush the Russian offensive capability temporarily through operations adapted to that front's geographical conditions and the logistical capabilities, thus establishing a glacis in the east that would enable him to shift the center of gravity back to the west in the following year.

Following along wholly in the tradition of Moltke the Elder, the new chief of OHL intended to secure terrain and thereby buy time. He planned to use this approach—together with a chess-like castling move along interior lines—as the basis for an offensive in the west. Consequently, Falkenhayn rejected the Oberost recommendation to shift the strategic center of gravity to the east, saying: "All victories in the east that can be won at the expense of our position in the west are worthless."[43]

Over the course of the succeeding years, a fierce controversy raged between pro-western and pro-eastern advocates about whether the strategic center of gravity should be on the Western or the Eastern Front, and over the proper operational conduct of the war in the east. That debate only ended in 1916 with the resignation of Falkenhayn and the establishment of the "Third OHL" under The Duo of Hindenburg and Ludendorff.[44] The fact that once they were in overall command even Hindenburg and Ludendorff did not shift the strategic center of gravity from the

Western to the Eastern Front shows that this conflict was largely a function of the personal ambitions of the protagonists.

In the following section, we will examine German operational warfare in the east on the basis of two examples: the Central Powers offensive in the summer of 1915, and the Romania Campaign of 1916–1917.

Considering the critical situation of the Austro-Hungarian Empire after the debacle of its army in Galicia,[45] OHL found itself constrained by having to provide military support to Austria-Hungary. Any further defeats of the Austro-Hungarian forces might induce Italy and Romania to enter the war on the side of the Entente. Thus, the strategic situation forced Falkenhayn to turn toward what he still considered the secondary theater of war on the Eastern Front. Wholly in accordance with German operational doctrine, he planned to resolve the dire situation in the east through offensive operational warfare. He regarded any merely defensive support of Austro-Hungary as being out of the question. Consequently, Falkenhayn in 1915 decided to shift the German center of gravity temporarily to the Eastern Front. Thus, the operational army reserve formed recently through internal restructuring was used not for offensives against Serbia or in the west, but instead marshaled largely near Gorlice–Tarnów. The newly established Eleventh Army, consisting of eight infantry divisions under Colonel General August von Mackensen, and the Austro-Hungarian Fourth Army were ordered to force the collapse of the Russian Carpathian Front by launching an offensive in its rear. Simultaneously, Oberost was to contain the Russian armies in the north and feint an offensive against Riga by an attack in Courland.

On 2 May 1915, after several hours of heavy artillery fire, German and Austro-Hungarian units penetrated the Russian positions after only three days.[46] In the course of the following days and weeks this breakthrough developed into a major offensive, which the Central Powers resolutely reinforced by bringing up additional reserves—despite the entry of Italy into the war and the Entente counterattacks in the west in Artois. After taking back Przemyśl and Lemburg (Lwów), Falkenhayn at the end of June decided to force the collapse of the Russian Narev–Vistula Front through a pincer attack, with Oberost attacking from the north and the Eleventh Army attacking from the south. The two arms of the pincer were to meet north of Warsaw, encircling and annihilating the Russian armies.

These plans caused another flare-up in the operational differences between Oberost and OHL. Hindenburg and Ludendorff rejected Falkenhayn's operations plan as inadequate. Instead, they proposed a more far-reaching envelopment operation via Kovno. From there the Russian Army was to be rolled up from the rear, hopefully resulting in a victory decisive for the outcome of the war.[47] Falkenhayn, who considered the Russians to have more stamina than did his critics, managed to get the Kaiser to support his line of thought.[48] During the following weeks Falkenhayn's doubts were borne out. The encirclement failed, as the Russian units destroyed all traffic routes and fell back skillfully. Owing to the exhaustion of their troops and their overlong lines of supply, the German attack divisions were unable to encircle and annihilate the Russian forces. Thus, the planned operational encirclement became merely a head-on encounter, in which the enemy was pushed back to the east.

At the end of 1915 the exhausted forces of the Central Powers shifted to the defensive along the line between Czernowitz and Riga. Although the Russian forces lost more than 2.5 million men during the offensive, their army essentially survived. The Central Powers had achieved the greatest operational success of World War I, but no decisively annihilating victory. Such an outcome had never been the intention of OHL, but Falkenhayn at the least had partially achieved his strategic objectives.

Although the victories did not wring peace from Russia, they did at least prevent the entry of Romania into the war, if not that of Italy. Moreover, the military successes in the east caused Bulgaria to enter the war on the side of the Central Powers. That secured the victory over Serbia and, as a result, established a link with the Ottoman Empire. Falkenhayn regarded the establishment of a glacis extending far into Russia, which in turn facilitated a concentration of effort in the west in 1916, as a most important victory.

As expected, Falkenhayn on the one side and Hindenburg and Ludendorff on the other differed profoundly in their evaluation of the results of this operation. Whereas the latter accused Falkenhayn of having failed strategically, because he had not made use of a unique chance to achieve the utter defeat and annihilation of Russia, the chief of OHL thought that his conclusion was justified by the fact that the Russians could evade battle at any time by withdrawing into the interior of their country. Falkenhayn therefore remained convinced that the overall victory in the war could only be won in the west. This concept forced hundreds of thousands of French and German soldiers into the bloodbath of Verdun a few months later.

The offensive in the east had revealed the limits of operational action, which we tend to discount to this day. As Schlieffen had predicted, the majority of the Russian field armies were able to elude all attempts at encirclement, and thus their annihilation, by withdrawing into the interior of their country. The final results also owed considerably to the Russians' adroitness at using their rear depth successfully for delaying actions in combination with an orderly withdrawal into the interior. The Russians were very good at that. Although contemporary observers such as Gallwitz gave detailed descriptions of these same skills, which German soldiers in World War II faced time and again,[49] many General Staff officers refused to take note of the clear evidence. On the contrary, they developed an excessive sense of superiority based on the successes achieved by the outnumbered German forces. Even more significant than the Russians' skills at delaying action was the fact that the vastness of the Tsarist Empire, in conjunction with poor and sometimes dreadful lines of communications, placed severe limitations on the conduct of maneuver operations in the east. Whereas the German railway network made quick transportation movements and a concentration of effort possible within Germany, the extremely poorly developed Russian traffic network substantially impeded maneuver operations. Thus, at a distance of approximately 120 kilometers away from the nearest railway unloading point, the logistical support system was at times brought to a standstill.

Particularly startling was the fact that in the east the speed of the advancing troops was not enough to enable them to encircle the retreating enemy units. The cavalry, which by then had become doomed to insignificance on the Western Front, was unable to execute this task on the Eastern Front either. While it managed to achieve a certain importance in the fighting in Courland, the effects of automatic weapons made it impossible for the cavalry to make its mark on the conduct of maneuver operations even in Russia. Maneuver warfare in that theater was characterized by the marching pace of infantrymen and the horse-drawn artillery guns and carts plodding along on poor tracks far from the farthest forward railway unloading point.[50] Thus, the walking pace and the vast expanse of Russia imposed tight limits on maneuver warfare. The rapid, deep encirclement operations of a decisive nature, which were postulated by operational doctrine and absolutely essential for the annihilation of the Russian Army, only took place on paper and in the heads of some General Staff officers in the circles of Hindenburg and Ludendorff. In reality, an annihilation of the Russian Army in the east was impossible because of the space-time-forces ratio, just as Schlieffen and Falkenhayn had foreseen.

For that reason, the General Staff in its prewar planning had never contemplated pursuing the defeated armies into the interior of Russia. Since the time of Moltke the Elder, all operational plans for a war against the Russian Empire ended with a victory over the Russian forces in Congress Poland at the most; or as Moltke the Elder put it: "Following up a victory in the Kingdom of Poland into the interior of Russia would not be in our interest."[51] Thus, the prevailing operational conditions frustrated the maneuver warfare calculations made by Hindenburg, Ludendorff, and other General Staff officers. The Central Powers offensive had mercilessly exposed the crucial weakness of German operational doctrine. The attacking units did not have sufficient maneuverability to be able to execute the crucial task of operational thinking—the encirclement and subsequent annihilation of the surrounded enemy forces.

Although the 1916 campaign against Romania was described by the combatants as a "fine war," and after World War I was featured in military specialist journals and the memorial literature as a "model of generalship,"[52] that campaign also exposed the limited nature of German operational warfare.[53]

In the summer of 1916 the Central Powers found themselves in one of the worst strategic crises of the Great War. The German offensive at Verdun and the Austro-Hungarian offensive in Italy had both failed. At the Somme, the German troops were only able to counter the British offensive by drawing on their last reserves of strength. Russia's Brusilov offensive brought the Central Powers to the verge of a disastrous defeat in the east. Germany and Austria-Hungary had badly underestimated the resources and the reorganizational and operational capabilities of the Russians.[54] The Central Powers were able to prevent the Brusilov offensive from succeeding only by committing all available reserve forces. At the very moment when OHL assumed that the crisis was over, Romania entered the war on the side of the Entente on 27 August 1916. Falkenhayn, who had at that point no longer expected a Romanian entry into the war, was taken completely by surprise.[55] The Kaiser, who learned of the bad news while playing skat in the evening, was severely shocked and wanted to sue for peace at once.[56] Completely out of his depth in such a situation, the Kaiser dismissed Falkenhayn and appointed Hindenburg as chief of the General Staff, with Ludendorff as first quartermaster general.[57] Faced with this precarious situation, and the new leadership at the Third OHL, the Central Powers on 6 September finally agreed to entrust Wilhelm II—and thus OHL—with the operational direction of the operations of all the Central Powers forces.[58]

Based on the plans of the previous Second OHL, Hindenburg and Ludendorff decided on an unambiguous concentration of effort and an immediate offensive against Romania. Wholly in accordance with German operational doctrine, the newly established Ninth Army, together with Austro-Hungarian units under the command of Falkenhayn,[59] was to annihilate the Romanian forces, which were more numerous but clearly inferior in weapons and equipment. The Romanians had penetrated into Transylvania with a double envelopment. Subsequently, the German units were to cross the Carpathian Mountains and—together with the German, Bulgarian, and Turkish units that were advancing from the south under the command of Mackensen—annihilate the Romanians.

As happened all too often, however, reality failed to conform with the plans. While Falkenhayn did succeed in defeating the Romanian troops in Transylvania despite being outnumbered, the double envelopment resulting in the annihilation of the Romanian troops failed. Once again, an attempt at achieving a Cannae had fallen flat. Even though Mackensen was successfully marching into the Dobrudzha region, Falkenhayn's units did not manage to fight their way as quickly as planned through the Carpathian passes. He only achieved his breakthrough after several attempts. Falkenhayn in coordination with Mackensen's army, which by then had crossed the Danube River, did manage to catch the Romanian forces in their rear and flanks and crush them in front of Bucharest. Nonetheless, the majority of the Romanian troops managed to escape from the encirclement and later in coordination with Russian forces established a new front on the Vltava River. The Central Powers were now able to draw on the oil fields near Ploiesti and the Romanian food resources. By the end of 1916, despite heavy losses, they finally managed to stabilize the situation on the Eastern Front.[60]

The Central Powers offensive against Romania, which was predominantly executed by German units, was a model of operational maneuver warfare against a numerically or materially superior enemy, the type of operation which the German General Staff habitually planned and trained for. Yet was the war against Romania truly such a perfect example of the German operational doctrine? Did this highly successful offensive at least bear out German operational principles? Certainly the Romania Campaign was a major military victory, which, considering the difficult initial strategic situation, can hardly be overrated. The large, yet not too large, theater of war was almost ideally suited to operational warfare according to the theories of Friedrich Ratzel,[61] the founder of German geopolitics, and enabled the German Army to leverage its superior tactical and operational leadership in offensive maneuver warfare. The German forces, however, still did not succeed in annihilating the materially inferior and badly led Romanian units. The several attempts at a double envelopment failed, owing to the exhaustion of the soldiers, to the dramatically deteriorating logistical situation caused by an overextension of the supply lines, and to the geographical and weather conditions. Again and again, the enemy managed to escape being encircled and annihilated because the German divisions were unable to advance quickly enough.

In Romania, too, the measure of all things was the marching pace of the infantryman. In the end, the Romanian Army was merely driven back in a head-on collision, as had been the Russian Army in 1915. Thus, the Romania Campaign is a perfect example of the dual-natured German conduct of World War I. The German Army's vaunted tactical-operational superiority ran up against the operational-strategic limitations inherent in the German conduct of the war.

As in Poland in 1915, the German Army, which had been designed for operations close to the border, ran up against the limits of its geographical reach, both logistically and operationally, in Romania. Operational warfare in the east was not restricted only by these problems, however. In contrast to the Western Front, Germany conducted a coalition war in the east. In addition to national sensitivities—the Austrians considered the Germans to be arrogant, and the Germans regarded the Austrians as incompetent in military matters—and personal problems between Hötzendorf and Falkenhayn, the training and equipment status among the Central Powers forces differed considerably. In the opinion of the Germans, many of the Austro-Hungarian divisions, let alone the Ottoman and Bulgarian divisions, were unsuited to fast-paced operations. Another factor that had a particularly adverse effect, one that was of crucial significance for German maneuver warfare, was the inadequate operational training of the officers of Germany's allies. That resulted in repeated disconnects in the command and control procedures. The Germans tried to eliminate that problem by assigning liaison officers and putting German officers in command positions in the other armies.[62]

On the one hand, the Romania Campaign showed how Mackensen managed to keep an army consisting of German, Austro-Hungarian, Bulgarian, and Ottoman elements successfully under operational control. On the other hand, it illustrated that OHL largely committed German units and that German divisions served as the bracing struts in the mixed-force armies. Yet all those efforts only solved the existing surface problems. The Austrians, who felt that the German Reich had let them down since the beginning of the war, repeatedly felt humiliated by the arrogant and overbearing manner of their alliance partners. They complained of this quite often.[63] For the entire duration of the war, OHL was unsuccessful in developing adequate command structures for coalition warfare.[64]

The conduct of the war in the east also exposed another weakness of operational thinking, aside from the fact that the operational capabilities did not match the strategic objectives. Space was reduced to its purely geographical dimension. As in the cabinet wars of the eighteenth century, the operational planning was done in a virtual vacuum, devoid of people. The resident population in the theater of war was ignored, as it was of no significance for operational warfare. Such was the opinion of the majority of the General Staff officers. Considering the experience of the people's war during the Franco-Prussian War of 1870–1871, this is really quite amazing. This phenomenon can be explained, however, by the notion that through a rapid operational conduct of the war it would presumably be ended quickly, and the outbreak of a people's war would thus be prevented.

The vast geographical dimensions of the war—in 1915, German troops fought in France, Russia, the Balkans, and in the Ottoman Empire—as well as the fact that Germany and her allies were forced to conduct a long-drawn war of attrition should have been cause enough for a revision of the operational doctrine. Such was not the case, however. The Romania Campaign was seen as the proof of the correctness of German operational thinking. Nonetheless, the wartime experiences influenced the further development of operational thinking after World War I. Both the enlisted soldiers and the officers experienced a veritable culture shock by what they considered the hygienic and cultural backwardness of the areas the German Army occupied.[65] In the soldiers this manifested itself in a lasting feeling of military superiority, after having gained their major victories from a position of numerical inferiority. Whereas the Germans had feared the "Russian steamroller" prior to the start of the war,[66] they subsequently began to underestimate the Russian Army. The fierce fighting and the dogged Russian resistance, as well as the experience of the Brusilov offensive, should have disabused them of that notion.[67] Over the years, the fighting and the military capabilities of the tsar's army, as well as the problems of operational warfare on the "forgotten front," increasingly took a back seat when compared to the battles of attrition that had been fought in the west. German propaganda also did its best to ensure that this image of the Russians became firmly fixed in the minds of the soldiers.

Breakthrough

At the end of 1914, an unbroken trench system echeloned in depth extended over hundreds of kilometers between the Swiss border and the Belgian North Sea coast. Maneuver warfare in the west had come to an end that autumn with the failure of the German attempts at a breakthrough in Flanders. The fire of automatic weapons not only imposed tight limitations on the psychological elements—will and aggressive spirit—but also squashed any chance of operational maneuver on the Western Front. Maneuvering was brought to a standstill in the sort of trench warfare that Schlieffen had wanted to avoid at all costs. Consequently, it was not the operational and strategic aspects of space, but rather the tactical advantages and disadvantages of the terrain in the battle area that now dominated the thinking of OHL. Despite the General Staff's fixation on operational maneuver warfare, the fact that this scenario too had been discussed long before the beginning of World War I is shown by the words of Major General Ernst Köpke, senior quartermaster in the Great General Staff, who in 1895 wrote: "[In] positional warfare [trench warfare]—a battle for long fronts of fortified field positions—it will be necessary to conduct a successful siege of major fortifications, otherwise we will not be able to achieve any successes against the French. Hopefully, we will not then lack the intellectual and material preparation necessary for this, and will find ourselves well-trained and equipped for this type of fighting at the crucial moment."[68]

Despite the experiences of positional warfare in the Russo-Japanese War of 1904–1905, and contrary to the choir of maneuver warfare advocates, Köpke remained a single voice crying in the wilderness with those prophetic words. Consequently, the German Army, like its enemies, entered the war insufficiently prepared for lengthy trench warfare. For that reason, OHL from 1915 onward found itself confronted with the fact that it needed to develop a defensive concept suitable for modern weapons systems, including machine guns, artillery, gas, and aircraft. Conversely, it also had to adapt the method of attack used up to that point to the realities of a defensive system echeloned in depth. And not the least, the limited resources of the Reich had to be taken into account. Positional warfare forced OHL to reappraise the ratio of attack to defense. Inevitably, the focus of tactical considerations now shifted toward the latter. In the subsequent years the Germans continuously developed an area defensive system that enabled them to beat back the major Allied attacks at the Somme, in Champagne, and in Flanders, albeit with heavy losses.[69]

OHL not only had to solve unfamiliar tactical problems, it also needed to win a drawn-out war of attrition for which it was not at all prepared. The operational and strategic conditions under which OHL had to conduct such a war were obvious. For one thing, the Germans and their allies were inferior to their enemies in both personnel numbers and equipment. Moreover, this disparity would continue to deteriorate to their disadvantage if the war lasted longer, and it would only be possible to compensate for a limited period of time through innovative defensive procedures and superior command and control concepts. Considering the inequality in resources, time was on the side of the Entente. Thus, as in prewar planning, the time factor was the driving element for rapid maneuver warfare. An operational attack approach aimed at the annihilation of an enemy force required at least temporary local superiority. But in order to prosecute the sought-after operational maneuver warfare, the enemy's trench system first had to be penetrated. As a starting point, then, it was necessary to solve the tactical problem of a breakthrough.

Under Schlieffen and the dogmatic fixation on encirclement, the problem of the breakthrough had not been examined in depth either by the General Staff or by the members of the informed public. The entire concept of a breakthrough met with so much disapproval that in the *Instruktionen für die höheren Truppenführer* (Instructions for Senior Commanders), which had been revised during the Schlieffen era, as well as in other training manuals, the word "breakthrough" did not occur at all.[70] Nor was the breakthrough a topic in the contemporary military literature of that time. The purpose and objective of a tactical or operational breakthrough was discussed only rarely. The critics of the breakthrough—Schlieffen prominently among them—argued that because of the increasing fire effect a breakthrough against an enemy in good shape and at an only slightly inferior strength level would be next to impossible.[71] Moreover, even in the event of an initial success, the defenders would seal off the breach and annihilate with flanking fire any attackers who had broken through.

Only Bernhardi supported including the breakthrough as an element of operational thinking, thereby intentionally assuming a position opposed to that of Schlieffen. While the latter clearly favored the encirclement concept, he did not completely exclude the utility of a breakthrough into a gap detected in a long front of positions under certain rare exceptional conditions. Nonetheless, Schlieffen had in mind an operational breakthrough as a consequence of enemy mistakes, rather than a tactical breakthrough.

In 1905 Schlieffen, presumably owing to differences of opinion with his successor, supported his hypotheses with a war history study based on the chances of a tactical or operational breakthrough. With only two exceptions, he drew as supporting evidence examples from the era of Friedrich II and the Wars of Liberation. He came to the conclusion that owing to the increasing fire effect during the period under investigation, no tactical breakthrough with any significant success had been achieved. Schlieffen did point out, however, that war history was a very limited tool for drawing definite conclusions concerning future wars. Therefore, despite the increased fire effect, a tactical or operational breakthrough might be possible under certain conditions; but any lasting success, such as achieved through an encirclement, would be improbable. Schlieffen therefore considered it "a mistake to . . . base one's whole approach on the success of a breakthrough, regardless of whether it is supposed to be tactical or operational, although it can truly only consist of taking advantage of a favorable moment."[72]

His successor merely took note of Schlieffen's views. Although Moltke the Younger continued to adhere basically to the encirclement concept, he was no longer prepared to accept a one sided fixation. When Moltke planned the Kaiser Maneuver of 1905, he made the troops train for a breakthrough. He also annoyed Schlieffen by taking advantage of Schlieffen's riding accident to draw up an order to the commanding generals in which he expressly pointed out the importance of a frontal attack in conjunction with an encirclement.

Consequently, frontal attacks, and thus tactical breakthroughs aimed at deciding a battle, were increasingly exercised under Moltke the Younger during the last years of peace, including during the Kaiser Maneuvers of 1912 and 1913.[73] Thus, the breakthrough gained more importance in the canon of operational thinking than under Schlieffen. Although the encirclement still remained the *conditio sine qua non* of German operational thinking, Moltke the Younger no longer ruled out a tactical breakthrough extended to an operational level. This change of focus in operational thinking is illustrated by his final remarks on the Kaiser Maneuver of 1913, in which he stated:

> An operational intent which is based on the success of a battle break-through from the outset is only justified where no attack against one or both enemy wings can be carried out. If this option is not available, then we certainly have to aim at a frontal victory or at least we need to push the enemy back frontally. Under favorable conditions, this may result in a tactical breakthrough by individual elements. This will only become crucial if we succeed in widening [the breakthrough], if we can turn the local breakthrough into a battle breakthrough along a wide front.[74]

Not even Schlieffen could continue to rule out the necessity of a breakthrough, considering the development of armies numbering in the millions and the resulting widths of potential positions. In his "Schlieffen Plan" of 1912, he mentioned the possibility of a breakthrough on the French front opposite the German main attack wing. In continuation of his theses of 1905, he planned for breakthroughs in great width and in several places. The next step, then, was to consist not of turning the enemy front from the flank, but of seeking a decision through encirclement operations conducted far to the enemy's rear.

Among other reasons, the breakthrough concept had long been suppressed in Germany because—all experts were of one mind on this—any success not only required effective surprise, but also a clear superiority in manpower and materiel. Those were conditions that Germany could not then meet. Moreover, according to Krafft von Dellmensingen, a breakthrough as a form of attack by superior numbers did not offer a chance of achieving a decisive operational success. It would always be merely a precondition for a subsequent encirclement operation. For that reason, the German General Staff always regarded the breakthrough only as *ultima ratio.*[75]

Yet within only the first few weeks of World War I, OHL was forced to accept that a breakthrough would be an indispensable condition for a return to maneuver warfare. The German Army found itself confronted with the question of how to break through a trench system with an increasing in-depth structure, and subsequently destroy the defender's reserves positioned beyond the range of German artillery in a follow-on battle of maneuver. The success of an attack, then, depended on whether or not a breakthrough succeeded before the defender was able to concentrate his reserves at the point of the breakthrough. This time pressure turned the tactical mobility of the troops into the crucial factor of combat management.

For Falkenhayn, time became the measure of all things, not only on the tactical but also on the strategic level. He was convinced that Germany and her alliance partners had to win the war no later than the end of 1916 or the beginning of 1917, because otherwise the Entente powers would emerge as the winner of the war owing to their superior resources. It therefore was necessary to develop a strategic concept that would make a military victory in combination with political gains possible in the end.

The Second OHL and the Third OHL represent two different strategic concepts that employed different operational procedures. What they had in common was that Falkenhayn in 1916 and his successors in 1918 only took the initiative in the west when the threat by Russia had been eliminated, at least temporarily in the case of the Second OHL and completely in the case of the Third OHL. A concentration of effort on the Western Front had thus become possible.

Based on the relative strengths of the forces involved, Falkenhayn considered a peace resulting from a German military victory to be impossible. Consequently, as Moltke the Elder had planned for a two-front war, Falkenhayn aimed for a negotiated solution at the end of 1916 or beginning of 1917, subsequent to one or more successful battles. Taking into account the public opinion in Germany, such a solution had to go beyond the *status quo ante* of August 1914, and could only be successfully executed from a position of strength.[76] As we have already noted, Falkenhayn did not believe in a military solution in the east, despite the opportunities for operational warfare there. In his opinion, only a major success on the Western Front would achieve the strategic effect he wanted.

From the beginning of 1915 OHL planned for a decisive breakthrough in the west, and the various army groups submitted several proposals. Lieutenant General Konrad Krafft von Dellmensingen, for example, wanted to break through near Arras, separate the French and British forces from each other, and push the British units into the sea. Lieutenant General Hermann von Kuhl proposed an attack on the Aisne River, with operations being extended to Paris after a successful breakthrough.[77] Falkenhayn also tasked Colonel Hans von Seeckt, who as chief of staff of the III Army Corps had directed a successful German attack near Soissons in January 1915, with working out a breakthrough plan for the Western Front. Like Krafft von Dellmensingen, Seeckt suggested a breakthrough along the Allied forces' boundary between Arras and Albert, in order to separate the British from the French. For the breakthrough, which was planned for a width of twenty-five kilometers, Seeckt estimated that a field army with a strength of five army corps would be necessary, followed by another nine army corps in a second wave that would continue the attack in depth and simultaneously secure the flanks. As with the other proposals, Seeckt anticipated considerable difficulties in the execution of his course of action, and he did not expect it to succeed quickly.[78] At the same time he also emphasized that a breakthrough on the Somme would provide a chance for initiating a decisive operation.

It is clear that, faced with trench warfare, the General Staff finally grasped that a tactical breakthrough was now a prerequisite for a transition to operational maneuver warfare. Three conditions had to be met for a successful breakthrough. One: a diversionary attack far from the actual breakthrough sector was required to pin down the enemy's operational reserves. Two: the attack would have to be launched with surprise and maximum force, supported by heavy artillery. And Three: after a successful initial breakthrough, the attack would have to be sustained with a continuous supply of reserves.

Convinced by Seeckt's reasoning, Falkenhayn tasked him with the planning of the Central Powers' first major operational breakthrough on the Eastern Front, near Gorlice–Tarnów. Although the breakthrough in the east was successful against an enemy armed with inferior artillery, the chief of OHL did not consider that something similar could be tactically executed in the west. Experience had shown as much during the German defensive battle in Champagne during the autumn of 1915, when the French had failed to break through the German defense-in-depth system despite their far superior numerical strength. Falkenhayn's reservations call to mind the similar arguments advanced by breakthrough opponents before the war. According to Falkenhayn, an enemy with unimpaired morale and almost equal in strength would quickly seal off any breakthrough and annihilate any penetrating attackers with flanking fire.[79] Moreover, he noted that OHL did not have available the thirty divisions considered necessary for a major operational breakthrough.[80] The chief of OHL, therefore, planned instead to execute a local break-in at Verdun—a place of national importance for France—to lure the French Army into a counterattack. Falkenhayn judged that the French forces were suffering from low morale resulting from their defeats that autumn. Once German forces established favorable defensive positions after reaching the heights surrounding Verdun, the French counterattack would then be pounded to pieces by artillery fire. The intention was to turn Verdun into a *Blutmühle* (Blood Mill) for the French army, without exposing the German forces to excessive losses. OHL also intended to commit its operational reserves to repulse the anticipated British counterattack to relieve the French, thus decisively weakening the British Army as well. Britain's anticipated defeat on the Western Front, in combination with the *uneingeschränkten U-Boot-Krieg* (unrestricted submarine warfare), was supposed to force Britain to sue for peace.[81]

The German attack was deliberately not planned as a breakthrough battle. That would have resulted in huge German losses, which Germany could not afford. In the final analysis, Falkenhayn wanted to wear down the Entente before the Reich was worn down. Falkenhayn's plans were based on the analysis of the last Entente attacks, during which the attacking French forces suffered three times higher losses than the German defenders.

The Verdun attack began on 21 February 1916. But the pressure of events forced Falkenhayn to drop his initial strategic scheme of ensuring that the enemy was bled dry in their counterattack. What Falkenhayn had not anticipated was that the breakthrough concept took on a life of its own during the course of the Verdun battle, and a failure to achieve that breakthrough would have been a propaganda defeat. But the German forces did not yet have the tactical assets which would have enabled them to force a breakthrough. All the attacks, which by then had become a matter of gaining merely some few meters, were foiled by the fire of automatic weapons. In the end, the assault on Verdun in the spring of 1916 turned into a debacle and cost the lives of hundreds of thousands of German and French soldiers. The defeat at Verdun also meant the failure of Falkenhayn's operational-strategic concept. His dismissal was now only a matter of time.

Falkenhayn's successors, Hindenburg and Ludendorff, were ready and waiting in the wings. Their strategic ideas were completely opposed to those of their predecessor. They intended to achieve a peace from a victorious position after a great annihilating German victory. They were convinced that Falkenhayn had thrown away that kind of victory in the east. Yet, before the beginning of a major offensive, the Western Front, which was on the verge of collapse under Allied attacks, had to be stabilized and Russia had to be forced into a peace settlement.

The tactical problem was solved by the Third OHL through the perfection of the defense-in-depth system, which enabled the German Army in the west to repulse the Allied offensives in several terrible battles of attrition.[82] The strategic problem was solved through the acceleration of the internal collapse of the Tsarist

Empire. After all, the Bolshevists, who had come to power with German support, seemed ready for a separate peace. In addition, the Italians had been defeated at the Isonzo River and forced to fall back to the Tagliamento River. At first glance, an outside observer by the end of 1917 might have concluded that the Central Powers had won on points the military struggle during the fourth year of the war. However, a realistic evaluation of the situation made matters appear in a completely different light. The Ottoman Army was in retreat in Iraq and Palestine, the Bulgarian forces were clearly war-weary, and the Austro-Hungarian Army was only a shadow of its former self. The economic situation of the Central Powers was badly strained owing to the Allied maritime blockade.

The blockade also had a direct effect on the political mood in the Reich. Famine during the winter of 1917–1918 resulted in a major wave of strikes in January 1918. In 1917, the first mutinies occurred in the High Seas Fleet. The January strikes in particular were seen as a warning sign by the German command. They were a dramatic way of making OHL realize that Bolshevism, and thus the revolution, could become a real danger to the Reich. Problems within the military itself also multiplied. The personnel replacement situation was extremely tense. Although the frontline troops had withstood the pressure of Allied attacks, the majority of the soldiers were war-weary and feared a continuation of trench warfare. "Malingering," as Ludendorff himself put it, was rampant within the army. The essential question of whether the troops would be able to endure another year of relentless defensive battles or whether they would collapse remained unanswered. Yet the crucial factor in the Third OHL's decision in favor of a major offensive was that the unrestricted submarine warfare, which had been begun with such high hopes, had not only failed but had resulted in the United States finally entering the war on the side of the Entente. With its enormous material and manpower resources, this new ally of France and Britain more than compensated the Entente for the withdrawal of Russia from the war.

Considering the growing war-weariness of their own troops and the continuously increasing superiority of the Entente in all areas, Hindenburg and Ludendorff regarded a successful permanent defense as tantamount to a defeat. The peace with Russia led OHL to hope that a large-scale offensive operation in the west could still wrest from the enemy a peace settlement based on a military victory. As opposed to their predecessor, Hindenburg and Ludendorff considered a negotiated peace to be out of the question. Yet a decision had to be reached before American troops in significant numbers were able to intervene in the fighting in France. Consequently, as in 1914, the operational planning took place under enormous time pressure. By January 1918 the operational planning started the previous autumn was complete. The operational objective was the annihilation of the British Army, as Ludendorff was convinced that the British operated more awkwardly than the French.

Even during the planning phase it became obvious that Ludendorff as an organizer was out of his depth in the operational-strategic level of the offensive. He did not know how to resolve the dilemma between the necessary tactics for a breakthrough, the operational freedom of maneuver for the planned encirclement and annihilation of the British Army, and a strategic option for a peace based on a military victory. It was only logical that Ludendorff, who had no political concept for the ending of the war beyond "all or nothing," reverted step by step to what he really knew inside out: tactics and organization. After the war, he was to defend this decision by stating: "Tactics had to be given priority over pure strategy. Without tactical success, there would be no such thing. A strategy which does not take this into consideration is condemned to failure right from the outset."[83]

As opposed to Schlieffen, Ludendorff planned not one decisive attack, but rather a sequence of several offensives. Ludendorff did not expect a singular thrust in which everything would be staked on one throw to result in a successful outcome. Presumably, he also shrank from the risk involved. He described the nature of the upcoming offensive to the Kaiser and the imperial chancellor as follows: "Nobody should think that we will have an offensive as in Galicia or Italy; rather, it will be a tremendous struggle which will begin in one place, be continued in another, and take a long time."[84]

The focus of Ludendorff's deliberations was on the success of a tactical breakthrough, which in this war no side had as yet managed to achieve. For that reason, he decided at the end of January 1918 on an offensive on either side of St. Quentin. He selected that point of attack because it offered the best chance for a tactical breakthrough owing to the weakness of the enemy defenses there, and not because a successful breakthrough there would expand the viable operational alternatives. Irritated by the underlying criticism of his decision being focused on tactical instead of operational reasons, the pro-eastern Ludendorff told the pro-westerners: "I cannot abide the term operation. We'll just bash a hole in the middle and then see what happens. That's what we did in Russia."[85] Words like those were enough to make Schlieffen turn in his grave. After all, in his fixation on tactical success while ignoring operational considerations, Ludendorff shook the foundations of German operational thinking and jeopardized the military and political purpose of the whole offensive by directing a breakthrough at an operationally unfavorable point.[86]

Yet considering the lack of success of all the attempts at a breakthrough on the Western Front, Ludendorff really had no other option, for without a tactical breakthrough there would be no subsequent operation. A decisive factor, however, was the location of the intended breakthrough. Owing to some extent to the immobility of the German Army, the selection of that point had a significant influence on the development of the follow-on operation. Despite all criticism, if the breakthrough succeeded, then the attack against the juncture between the British and

French armies at least offered the opportunities to separate the Entente forces, roll up the British southern wing, and in a further phase annihilate the British Army.

As a prerequisite for a successful breakthrough, the German Army during the previous few years had developed a new mobile attack doctrine. In contrast to the Entente, which put armor on cannons and machine guns and installed them in tracked vehicles, the Germans developed artillery and infantry tactics with the conventional means at their disposal. The command and control principle was based on the recently developed Stormtroop Tactics.[87] Its cornerstones were mobility, flexibility, speed, and surprise. The infantry tactics were integrated with the newly developed artillery procedures, which eliminated the necessity for registration fire.[88] That in turn made it possible to reduce the length of the preliminary artillery preparation—which was now much more accurate and effective—to only a few hours, thus ensuring that the element of surprise was maintained.[89]

German tank development only began in reaction to the initial use of that weapon by the British in September 1916. The heavy Type A7V Panzer, which was the first German model developed, experienced a number of developmental problems and only entered service in small numbers (nine vehicles) on 21 March 1918. Because of the tank's low priority in the Hindenburg Program, which focused on a defensive posture in the west in 1917, there was no acceleration of Panzer development that year. In retrospect, that would have been very useful. By 1918, shortages in the defense industry further restricted tank development. Moreover, inefficient coordination of the work done in research and development resulted in ineffective parallel designs, which in turn limited the buildup of a tank force during the last year of the war. In the end, the German Panzer force was largely equipped with captured Allied tanks. Altogether, twenty German Type A7V tanks and approximately twenty captured tanks faced more than three thousand Allied tanks in 1918.[90]

Following an excellent organizational preparation, which nonetheless was unable to remedy the essential structural shortcomings in the mobility of the assault units,[91] the German offensive began with Operation MICHAEL on 21 March 1918.[92] Although the attack resulted in major tactical successes, heretofore unprecedented on the Western Front, the attempt to turn the tactical breakthrough into an operational one failed. In the end, the Allies managed to hold the front and—as expected—were able to bring up reserves more quickly than the Germans could reinforce their attack.

Thus, despite all tactical successes, the German attack did not solve the problem of a breakthrough of a fortified trench system. As in maneuver warfare, mobility was lacking at a tactical level. Consequently, the Germans only sporadically managed to move the artillery units forward in time to successfully continue the attack. The problem was moving the guns over the shattered terrain that they themselves had earlier laid waste. Whereas the measure of all things in operational maneuver warfare was the marching pace of the infantry, in a breakthrough it was the plodding forward of the horse-drawn artillery.

Ludendorff also committed fundamental operational leadership errors. Because the attack made better progress south of the Somme, he shifted the main effort from its original sector north of the Somme to the south, which originally was supposed to be only a supporting attack. That meant that he initiated a second battle against the French before the British Army was defeated, a blatant violation of the operational principle of the concentration of effort. Even while the battle raged, Ludendorff was being criticized for his one-sided concentration on the tactical level while neglecting the operational level. After the war and down to the present, the eccentric planning of the offensive has been regarded as a major cause of its failure.[93] The follow-on attacks—GEORGETTE, BLÜCHER, GOERZ, and YORCK, as well as GNEISENAU, HAMMERSCHLAG, and HAGEN—sometimes resulted in impressive tactical break-ins, but never in operational breakthroughs, much less in strategic victories.[94] Operation BLÜCHER, for example, had been planned as a diversionary attack and was only expanded when it achieved unanticipated great tactical success. There was no clear operational line connecting the offensives at all. Depending on their success, OHL allowed successful attacks to continue instead of focusing on clear operational objectives. Consequently, Operation MICHAEL and all the follow-on offensives got lost in an eccentric operational void. In the end, the German forces won engagements, but no battles that were decisive for the outcome of the war. One cannot help thinking that the General Staff in the person of Ludendorff focused exclusively on the tactical challenges of trench warfare while completely forgetting the operational skills, or that German thinking at that point included no options at all for solving the problem of trench warfare. (See Plate 8.)

Both conclusions are supported by the fact that in five years of war OHL did not manage to develop any strategic concept for ending the war beyond Ludendorff's all-or-nothing approach. There is no evidence whatsoever for an overall German strategy. It is true that the navy finally established a Central Navy Operations Staff within the Grand Headquarters in the summer of 1918. And only a few months earlier the Admiralty Staff had committed the most modern units of the fleet to the high-risk capture of the Baltic Islands. Operation ALBION was the only truly joint army-navy operation of the war, yet it was conducted in a quite obviously secondary theater, and even then merely to score a point in an ongoing internal power struggle with the command of the High Seas Fleet.[95]

The German political leadership, in the person of a chancellor at Ludendorff's mercy, refrained from taking a stand and, like the virtually indifferent Kaiser, relied completely on OHL, and thus on a purely military solution. Yet what was such a solution to look like even after a conclusively annihilating victory over the British Army? Did OHL truly believe that Britain or France would be prepared to accept a peace based on a German military victory while American reinforcements continued to arrive in Europe? Would such an enforced peace not require that the whole of France be occupied at the very least—something which German military forces simply were not in a position to do? One cannot help thinking that within OHL faith and will dominated not only tactics and operations, but also strategy and politics. The Third OHL had no realistic political conception of how to end the war. It becomes increasingly obvious that the officers there had lost any sense of reality.

In the end, OHL secured tactical territorial gains at the price of higher numbers of casualties than even in the defensive battles of 1917.[96] When the Entente forces started their counteroffensive in mid-July, the German units were no longer capable of putting up a resistance. After the "Black Day of the German Army" on 8 August 1918, the German forces began a retreat that ended in the Armistice of 11 November 1918. In the last year of the war, Germany had staked everything on a victory-enforced peace, and thus on a "great battle for France"—and lost.

Conclusion

The First World War was an acid test for the operational thinking developed in the Reich. If a strict standard is applied to the requirements posited by the General Staff for operational thinking, then it must be said to have failed. Operational thinking had not stood the test. This fact cannot be obscured, even by the individual operational triumphs, such as the Battle of Tannenberg. That battle—which had been elevated to near-sacred status as the "Cannae of the East"—was actually not an offensive battle of encirclement, planned as such within the framework of operational thinking; rather, it was a defensive battle. Not the least, Tannenberg was a strategic defeat, because OHL, fearing a disaster in East Prussia, moved reinforcements from the Western to the Eastern Front, and those forces were then badly missed in France in the further course of the war.

In the German operational center of gravity, the Western Front, neither a single nor a double encirclement succeeded, much less a decisive battle of annihilation. On the contrary, at the culminating point of the 1914 offensive, the German attack wing suffered a major defeat at the Battle of the Marne. The Reich certainly did not lose the war in front of Paris. Still, the fiasco on the Marne revealed the conspicuous tactical, operational, and strategic weaknesses of the German Army. The German troops, still all too frequently attacking in "drill formation," sustained terrible losses from machine gun and artillery fire. From the very beginning of the war, this fire imposed narrow, insurmountable limits on the moral values—the determination and aggressive spirit that were supposed to compensate for the superior strength of the enemy. Thus, the reality of the war exposed the absurdity of a great deal of the peacetime training.

Like the Admiralty Staff, the General Staff initially found it difficult to shift from planning to leadership.[97] The application of operational thinking to operational leadership did not go smoothly. The General Staff, a purely planning organization in peacetime, failed to develop an adequate set of instruments for the command and control of an army numbering in the millions and lacking sufficient means of communications. Yet, the firm, centralized command of an operation of the kind that Schlieffen had envisioned was to some extent inconsistent with the system of leadership by directives used in the German Army at the operational level. The deliberate independence of the higher command level, in combination with human shortcomings, such as a craving for recognition and personal animosities, resulted in frictions that repeatedly impeded the progress of operations under extreme time pressures.

The defeat at the Marne in early September 1914 forced the military and political leaders of the Reich to accept that Schlieffen's solution for the Reich's strategic dilemma had failed. The attempt to circumvent the superior potential of the enemy nations by exploiting interior lines and separating the two-front war into two rapid offensive operations to be executed sequentially while maintaining the upper hand locally had not succeeded. Simultaneously, trench warfare on the Western Front forced the previously ignored concept of the breakthrough to the forefront of German tactical and operational thinking. Yet, not even the German attack procedures developed during the war solved the breakthrough problem. German units only achieved breakthroughs in the east.

The further course of events in the war also showed that major large-area operations in Russia did not result in decisive victories either. In the end, the eastern offensives culminated in the depths of the vast Russian territories. A military decision in the east, therefore, was not possible because of the prevailing operational conditions that frustrated the German military scheme based on maneuver warfare. The limitations of the German conduct of the war led the German High Command toward trying to achieve a strategic decision in the east through political calculations. Thus, the Great War exposed the tactical limits of operational thinking in the west, and its strategic limits in the east.

Germany's critical weaknesses were very clear after only the first few weeks of World War I. The German Army lacked the mobility required to turn its theoretical planning into reality. The General Staff had underestimated the interdependence between the time pressures at the operational-strategic level and the mobility of the troops required for the execution of operations. They thus failed to recognize that mobility was not only the most important, but the decisive factor in the conduct of operations. In rapid mobile warfare conducted under time pressure over large areas, the army that is supposed to inflict a crushing defeat on an enemy must have not only well-trained and -equipped units, but especially highly mobile ones. Yet the German Army did not have such units. The cavalry could not assume the mobility function. Consequently, the marching pace of the infantry and the maneuverability of the artillery determined the speed of any attack. That meant that an encirclement of forces conducting an orderly retreat was impossible, unless the enemy made glaring mistakes. During World War I, therefore, the German Army never succeeded in conducting an offensive battle of encirclement ending in the annihilation of the attacked enemy, neither on the Western Front nor on the Eastern.

Putting it succinctly, the German Army lacked the mobility as well as the means of communications for the mobile command and control of armies numbering in the millions that were required to enable it to make its theoretical plans become reality. Still, despite all the early technical deficiencies of tanks, the 1918 Allied offensives in the west demonstrated that the mobile conduct of attacks was once again coming within the bounds of possibility. The interpretation of Eric Brose, who reduces the German defeat to a widespread technophobia among the military leadership and the resulting errors of judgment in economic and armaments matters, does not advance the argument far enough.[98]

Nonetheless, the war relentlessly exposed the tremendous disparity between what the German Army was able to achieve based on careful and realistic calculations, and what was demanded of it. Aspirations and reality in the German military and political command echelons were at variance with each other, both before and then near the end of the war. As suggested by Martin Kutz, the General Staff's denial of reality prior to the war was only one step removed from the Third OHL's complete escape from reality at the end. Thus, it was only logical and consistent for Ludendorff, who in crucial phases put tactics ahead of operations, to postulate—as in tactics—an iron will as the solution for the strategic dilemma of numerical and materiel inferiority. But in so doing, he tried to ignore the fact that in World War I the daily conditions of an industrialized war of the masses imposed extremely narrow limits on personal will. An even more spectacular effect on the development of operational thinking in the war resulted from Ludendorff's tendency "to solve all issues of political life by military means."[99] And in so doing, he negated any influence whatsoever of political circumstances on the operational-strategic level of warfare.

The Great War also exposed another weakness of the German Army's operational thinking. In the tradition of Friedrich II, the logistics and transportation elements of German operational planning were designed for warfare close to the borders, a function of the central position of the German Reich. Neither in the west nor in the east had the prewar operational plans extended beyond a depth of approximately four hundred kilometers from the German borders. The expansion of the war in the east, in the Balkans, and in the Ottoman Empire went far beyond the areas upon which the plans were originally based. Consequently, logistical problems in the virtually impassable terrain of the east imposed tight limitations on the conduct of mobile operations. During the war, the logistical support options were adapted to operational planning only very slowly, and often inadequately.

Despite these shortcomings, it should be noted that the German Army achieved great feats in the transitional area between tactics and operations. All criticism aside, the Battle of Tannenberg first had to be won. Taking into account the German capabilities, the 1915 offensive in Russia and the 1916 Romania Campaign are both examples of successful operational leadership. Within the limits of the available options, OHL demonstrated an enormous capacity for innovation in some areas, as for example in the development of new tactical procedures for defense and attack.

Nonetheless, at the operational-strategic level the Great War revealed the one-sided tactical and operational fixation that was at the core of German operational thinking, and that had its origins in the political-military system of the Reich. Prior to and during World War I, Germany failed to develop an overall strategy. Such would have required a clear evaluation of areas and resources. Both evaluations, however, were conducted only selectively by various agencies, such as the General Staff and Admiralty Staff. Locked into a permanent struggle for power, the agencies of army and navy acting under the Kaiser paralyzed each other in their fight over resources. Mutual distrust and departmental conceits were often more important than national interests. Schlieffen, for example, during his period in office never informed the minister of war of his operational plans, although the latter was responsible for the army's personnel and armament. Moltke the Younger in 1912 was the first chief of the General Staff to notify the minister of war of his war plans. Talks with the senior political level on operational-strategic issues were also an exception.

Under the constitution of the Reich, the operational-strategic plans should have been brought together in the person of the Kaiser. This, however, was implemented only inadequately. No attempt was made to scrutinize the plans of the chief of his General Staff as to their inherent political risks. Wilhelm II as the supreme commander was incapable of coordinating military and political leadership, either in peacetime or in war, in such a way that an overall strategy for the Reich was developed that might address a potential war of attrition. At the end of the Great War, Lieutenant General Wilhelm Groener, former head of the General Staff's Railway Department, then chief of the *Kriegsamt* (War Office), and later Reichswehr Minister, drove home the point when he wrote: "Owing to the great material increases of the last decades, our entire nation had been massively deluded into thinking that our strength was invincible. Before we had adequately secured our continental position in Europe, we already had plunged headlong into world politics, for which our military preparations were by no means sufficient."[100]

But with such an interpretation of the situation, Groener would not have been able to convince a majority in German military circles, not even shortly before the end of the war.

6

Old Wine in New Wineskins

Operational Thinking in the Reichswehr and the Wehrmacht between Reality and Utopia

The Search for Causes

World War I mercilessly exposed the weaknesses of German operational think-ing and caused the operations experts of the army to fall into a military identity crisis. The question of whether in the face of positional warfare rapid and mobile warfare was still even possible touched the core of the German Army's military thinking. The overwhelming majority of the military was convinced that numeri-cally superior enemy forces could only be overcome by rapidly conducted opera-tions. That was the only feasible foundation for Germany's military power politics, and closely related to that, the place of the army within the Reich's structure. In 1938 Waldemar Erfurth summed up these considerations in an article published in the journal *Militärwissenschaftliche Rundschau* (Military Science Review): "The mobile use of armed forces is tantamount to increasing their numbers."[1] Thus, the mobility of the troops and command and control personnel, in combination with moral factors, such as will and faith, were to continue to compensate for the supe-rior strategic resources of potential wartime enemies. This, however, was to be effected through offensive action. After all, the offensives of 1918 had shown that mobile attacks were still possible.

It was logically inevitable that the search for the cause of the failure in World War I that started immediately at the end of the war would become overshadowed by the self-interest-driven process of coming to terms with the past. And that in turn provided the evidence for the irrefutability of German operational thinking, and thus ensured its future efficacy. This process was reflected in the literature by rationalizations,[2] such as: "in the field we were unconquered; we won the battles, but for various non-military reasons the enemies won the war,"[3] or the Kaiser's Army was "not conquered, although it had been numerically inferior."[4]

Correspondingly, the reasons identified for the defeat of the "unconquered army in the field" were the inadequate mobilization of society, the "Stab in the Back" by the socialists of the fighting forces, and the "watering down" of the Schlieffen Plan, which was supposed to have been a recipe for victory. And as the Schlieffen Plan was diluted, the same thing happened to operational thinking.

But the key questions of whether the German Army was even able to achieve the operationally required mobility and speed necessary to destroy the enemy, and whether even to pursue world power politics from Germany's inferior resource base, were ignored despite the obvious answers indicated by the war. The debates conducted by historians like Hans Delbrück were personalized by the military from the very start.[5] There were two reasons for that. Firstly, in German operational thinking it was the commander and not an operations staff who was credited with the capability of making quick and correct operational decisions. Secondly—and this was the decisive point—a personalized search for the guilty parties prevented a general discussion of the basic correctness of operational thinking from even taking place.

At the center of the debate was the question of the consequences of OHL's actions during the first weeks of the war on the subsequent course of the war. Most of the contemporary participants in the debate quickly found an answer to that question. The culprit was Schlieffen's successor, Moltke the Younger, who had died in 1916 and therefore could not defend himself against his critics. Moltke was accused of having watered down the recipe for victory that Schlieffen had entrusted to him, thus giving away sure victory.[6] Moltke's critics also claimed that he was a weak decision maker. Leading proponents of the Schlieffen School, like Groener and Kuhl, eulogized in their writings a virtual idealization of Schlieffen's operational planning, which they claimed had held the "secret of victory."[7] Their position was given particular support by the fact that the Reichsarchiv, into which the War Historical Departments of the General Staff had been incorporated, compiled an account of the first weeks of the war on the Western Front that focused on Moltke's mistakes. In personalizing the guilt, the Reichsarchiv in effect officially prevented any questioning of operational thinking itself.[8] This approach, however, did not go unchallenged. A smaller group, whose most prominent exponent was Georg Wetzell, the former chief of OHL's Operations Department III, took the position that Moltke the Younger had quite correctly made the right decisions during the final years before the start of the war. Considering the military and political developments at the time, Moltke adapted the Schlieffen Plan to the then current situation. Wetzell's group also argued that Moltke had adhered to Schlieffen's basic principles.[9]

Moltke's successors were not spared either in the process of the personalization and psychological analysis of the German defeat. Even up to the mid-1930s the Kriegsgeschichtliche Forschungsanstalt (War History Research Institute), which continued the Reichsarchiv's historical works on the Great War, accused Falkenhayn of abandoning the strategy of annihilation during the Battle of Verdun for the sake of a strategy of attrition. The Forschungsanstalt even betrayed an exaggerated antipathy toward Hindenburg and Ludendorff. The criticisms of Moltke the Younger and Falkenhayn were ultimately even supported by psychopathological personality assessments of the two.[10]

Colonel General Hans von Seeckt. *BArch 146-1970-085-36.*

General Joachim von Stülpnagel (facing camera).

Lieutenant General Wilhelm Adam.
BArch 183-H04143.

Defense Minister Lieutenant General (Ret.) Wilhelm Groener.
BArch 102-05353.

Major General Kurt Freiherr
von Hammerstein-Equord.
Photographer: G. Pahl.
BArch 102-02019.

General Wilhelm Heye (chief of the Army Command), Defense Minister Otto Gessler, and
Admiral Hans Zenker (chief of the Naval Command) at the maneuvers of the 6th Infantry
Division and 3rd Cavalry Division in Westphalia in 1927. Photographer: Oscar Tellgmann.
BArch 136-1353.

Wilhelm Marx's criticism offers an example of the power of this kind of politics of memory, as it was pursued by the various parties: "For some 13 years, the oratory 'Cannae' has been performed continuously in German military literature. Ever new soloists keep singing new tunes, again and again the choirs join in with their dirges. Even every *Fähnrich* (officer candidate) is taught at the military schools that there would have been a super Cannae on the Western Front in 1914 except for the incompetence of the German commanders."[11]

Such was taught not only at the military schools but also in 1935 at the recently established Wehrmacht Academy. The failure of the initial offensive in 1914 was, apart from a lack of the means of communications, the failure of the higher command authorities and their inadequate leadership skills. The incitements leveled at Falkenhayn culminated in the charge that he himself had doubted his aptitude as a military commander, and that he therefore ultimately became an advocate of the strategy of attrition at Verdun.[12]

By personalizing the guilt, a general debate on the fundamental correctness of German operational thinking was largely and successfully avoided.[13] Consequently, the lessons of the Great War—that Germany was not able to compensate for its inferior manpower and materiel resources by superior operational command and tactical innovations, and was therefore not capable of winning a war of attrition—could be ignored.

Evidence suggests that an unbiased analysis of the overall strategic situation of the Reich was not conducted because a realistic estimate of the situation of the military and economic potential against the strategic balance of forces inevitably would have led to the abandonment of Germany's claim to Great Power status. The recognition of this truth, therefore, would have resulted in Germany's abandonment of Great Power politics based on military power. Such, however, was *inconceivable* to the apolitically socialized German military elite, who clung to the concept of operational warfare being free of political considerations. Even after Germany's defeat in the Great War, they could not bring themselves to consider developing strategy shaped by the primacy of politics. The military elite, rather, preferred to maintain the illusion that it was possible to overcome the superior resources of the enemy coalition by offensive operational warfare. According to the convictions of the military elite, therefore, it was only necessary to adjust just a few of the tactical and operational parameters in order for Germany to regain its Great Power status.[14] The main problem was the restrictions imposed on the German military by the Treaty of Versailles, which limited Germany to a force of one hundred thousand soldiers and prohibited compulsory military service, the General Staff, aircraft, submarines, and tanks.[15]

There were, however, differing ideas on how to reach this goal. There was general agreement that the Reichswehr, contrary to the concept of the victorious powers, should not be established as a border guard force, but rather as a military power instrument for external conflicts. Since this task could not be accomplished with an army of one hundred thousand soldiers, at no time was German military thinking between 1919 and 1935 guided by the military framework of the Versailles Treaty.

Concepts of War

Starting from the experiences of the Great War and the political-military situation resulting from the Versailles Treaty, different concepts of war evolved through the mid-1920s that were closely associated with the operational-strategic perceptions of individuals such as Walther Reinhardt, Hans von Seeckt, and Joachim von Stülpnagel. This process was mirrored in a wide range of military publications. Against the backdrop of the industrialization of the war and the difficulties with discipline during the last months of 1918,[16] the contemporary literature discussed a potential economic war. But the discussion particularly focused on tactical-operational issues apart from the psychological factors of future warfare.[17] The discussions about the war of the future took place throughout Europe as well as in Germany, and the core of the debate centered on whether operational warfare was still possible in an environment of positional warfare, and how future war was to be waged.[18]

The personalization of the guilt for the loss of the war effectively limited any fundamental challenge to operational thinking, which according to the convictions of its proponents would be an undesirable development in German military ideas. Nonetheless, some of the participants in the debate were convinced that any future war would be fought with mass forces and huge amounts of materiel, and would lead inevitably to positional warfare. Such a war of attrition could then only be won by mobilizing all national resources and through an unwavering fighting spirit and the will to persevere on the part of the people.[19] Others considered that in contrast to the Great War, the extensive application of all technical means, such as tanks, aircraft, etc., was the only viable approach to revive operational warfare.[20] A third group still was convinced that positional warfare could be overcome by making selective modifications to operational thinking, such as a stronger concentration of effort, movements in larger areas, a more systematic use of surprise, and the conduct of successful breakthroughs.[21] However, the precondition for successful warfare in the future—and this was what all participants in the debate implicitly agreed upon—was to recover the control over the course of the war that the military had lost.

The overwhelming majority of contributions to the debate drew on the experiences of the Great War and tacitly assumed that a stable, military-friendly system of government was an indispensable prerequisite for successful operational warfare. Reversing the equation, there was no question that an autocratic system inevitably depended on the military successes of operational doctrine. Any thought was dismissed, however, that it might become necessary again to have the national ruler sent to Holland by train because his security could not be guaranteed by the army, either inside or outside of Germany.

All the key points in the debate were reflected in the operational deliberations of the leaders of the *Reichsheer* during the interwar period. Even the *Chef der Heeresleitung* (chief of the Army Command), Major General Walther Reinhardt, continued to believe that the attack offered the only chance for a decisive victory. He viewed any future war as a continuation of the mass war of 1914–1918. In his opinion, automatic weapons fire rather than maneuver would dominate the battlefield. Hence, he believed firepower to be the key to success.

Reinhardt considered that mobile operational warfare was outdated and that large-scale mobile envelopment operations could not be conducted in the future. He believed that mass and materiel warfare was bound to lead to positional warfare. The front lines and the homeland had to be prepared for such warfare, he said. In order to transition from positional warfare to decisive battle, which Reinhardt also advocated, he argued for a strong concentration of effort to achieve a large-scale breakthrough.[22] The attack, however, would not be a rapid and mobile one, but would be carried out slowly while methodically moving forward artillery fire support from tanks. Reinhardt's notions very much resembled the ideas that were then being discussed in France. Reinhardt's operational thinking had a stronger focus on the transition to tactics than had been the case in prewar thinking. Considering the Great War experiences with positional warfare and limited tactical and operational mobility, Reinhardt advocated a revision of German tactical and operational ideas.[23]

As a consequence of the *Kapp Putsch,* Reinhardt resigned as the chief of the Army Command in March 1920. His successor, Colonel General Hans von Seeckt, was chief of the Army Command from 1920 to 1926. In contrast to Reinhardt's static thinking based on the idea of positional warfare, Seeckt advocated mobile, operational warfare. Seeckt's concept of war had a major influence on the Reichswehr. During World War I, Seeckt had been one of the German Army's greatest field army chiefs of staff. He served primarily on the Eastern Front and later in the Ottoman Empire. After the war he transformed the disbanded General Staff into the newly established *Allgemeines Truppenamt* (General Troop Office) and served as its chief until March 1920. From June 1920 until his retirement in October 1926, Seeckt served as chief of the Army Command. During those years, he played a decisive role in the buildup and orientation of the new Reichsheer. Under his aegis, the German Army developed into a "state within the state," shielded from all political influences. Simultaneously, he shaped the Reichsheer as a "school battalion of a modern army," making it a cadre army and an elite military force. By structuring the force with a high percentage of staff officers and by training soldiers to be ready to assume next higher levels of command, Seeckt intended to facilitate the rapid buildup of a larger army to defend against any attack, or in preparation for the repudiation of the restrictions of the Treaty of Versailles. Seeckt, however, did not plan the then evolving Reichsheer as the foundation for a mass military force, but rather as a two-hundred-thousand-strong professional army, because his operational doctrine could only be executed by a force of such a manageable size. In addition to the operational army, Seeckt wanted to establish national defense forces on the basis of general military service. Those forces, which would be mobilized in the case of a war, would serve as a personnel pool and would only be used to repel an invasion if the professional army was unable to bring about a decision.[24] Seeckt also considered it a major advantage that a smaller professional army, as opposed to a mass military force, could always be equipped with the most modern weapons and equipment.[25]

The clandestine buildup of a German air force, as well as the secret pilot, tank, and chemical warfare training conducted in the Soviet Union, were started during Seeckt's tenure in office. Those measures advanced the goal of making the German Army—which the victorious World War I powers had intended as border control and police forces for domestic deployment—capable again of waging war, and in the process developing into the armed forces of a modern Great Power.[26]

Seeckt's concept of war was based primarily on an analysis of the experiences of the Great War. However, he identified neither deficiencies in the operational doctrine nor a specific incorrect assessment of enemy forces as the reasons for Germany's defeat. He was convinced that it had not been possible to achieve the intended rapid decision—the only way to ensure victory—because of the difficulties in the command and control system and the inferior quality and the immobility of the mass army. No army in the field during the war had been able to execute rapid decisive operations.[27] When Seeckt looked for the reason for Germany's defeat, he found it in the mass army.

The Treaty of Versailles restrictions on personnel strength most certainly contributed to Seeckt's rejection of mass military forces and his preference for a small, mobile, elite force manned by highly qualified troops. Most of all, however, Seeckt addressed the problems of the command and control capabilities of the mass force that had been apparent even before the Great War.[28] Even at that time doubts were expressed that a mobile operational command and control system was possible for armies exceeding a certain size. As armies grew to forces of millions, Seeckt concluded that the operational thinking that originally had been developed for the command and control of larger masses of armies in the middle of the nineteenth century had finally reached its limits. Because of their sheer size, the armies lost their mobility. Thus, two key elements of German operational thinking were finally brought into question.

According to Seeckt's thinking, the lower quality of the mass military force combined with the increased weapons' effects and the simultaneous increase of troop numbers led inevitably to positional warfare. In the competition between the increased numbers of troops and materiel, the latter gained the upper hand.[29] Victory or defeat, therefore, was not determined by battlefield successes, but rather by superior economic and manpower resources.

Seeckt, however, did not draw the conclusion that Germany had to abandon its Great Power political aspirations because of its inferior resources and the resulting military circumstances—a situation exacerbated by the Treaty of Versailles. Without submitting plausible evidence for this conclusion in his writings, Seeckt was convinced that a people's army was not able to meet the requirements of a modern war, and that therefore the era of mass military forces was over. He argued, then, that it was again possible to bring about a decision with a fast-moving, mobile, highly qualified, and immediately deployable army. That ideally would happen on the enemy's territory, before mobilized masses could be set in motion.[30] Consequently, Seeckt believed that the future belonged to high-quality, more mobile, and thus smaller armies.[31]

Even before the provisions of the Treaty of Versailles became known in February 1919, Seeckt had developed his initial thoughts on the concept of a professional, operational army, which formed the basis of his later ideas.[32] As chief of the Army Command he proceeded strictly in accordance with his operational thinking and on the basis of a professional and focused analysis of the tactical experiences of the war. He guided the development of the offensive tactics that were necessary to support his concept of operational warfare. As in the case of his operational thinking, Seeckt's tactical thinking followed a line of continuity that compensated for numerical inferiority with mobility. Mobile warfare was at the core of Seeckt's thinking, although he did not rule out positional warfare completely. In contrast to the prewar doctrinal regulations, he placed greater emphasis on *Verteidiging* (defense) and on *Hinhaltenden Gefecht* (delaying combat). Positional warfare, however, was to be avoided in the future if at all possible. Seeckt's guiding principle was: "Less than ever does the salvation of the weaker side lie in rigid defense, but rather in mobile attack."[33] The operations manual *Führung und Gefecht der verbundenen Waffen* (Command and Control of the Combined Arms—*F.u.G.*),[34] adopted by Seeckt in 1921–1923, was steeped in this spirit. It assigned the decisive function in battle to combined arms combat.[35]

Convinced of the superiority of German pre–World War I doctrine,[36] Seeckt incorporated elements from the prewar regulations into the new *F.u.G.*[37] He did not do so in an uncritical manner, but rather he took the wartime experiences into account. Thus, Seeckt's tactical and operational thinking embodied change and continuity simultaneously.[38] *Das F.u.G.* focused on the tactical, not the operational, level, while briefly touching on certain aspects of operational warfare.

Seeckt advocated mobile defense as well as rapid, wide-ranging, and decisive offensive operations.[39] He did not want soldiers in a mass military force, but an elite force consisting of well-trained and highly motivated combatants. The lack of the modern tools of combat would be compensated for by Auftragstaktik (mission-type command and control) and mobile warfare. Defensive operations were only "justified against a vastly superior enemy, and in order to facilitate an attack at some other place or at a later time."[40] Battle group and Stormtroop-type tactics that had been developed during the war were further developed for offensive operations. Essentially, Seeckt planned for a strategic defensive, with a mobile professional army tactically and operationally capable of executing offensive operations at the highest level.[41]

According to Seeckt, any future war would start with the air forces fighting for air supremacy. While the air battle was still raging, the immediately deployable elite army would advance into the enemy's territory through rapid operational attacks and close air support, with the mission of destroying the enemy's army before its leadership could bring its numerical manpower and materiel superiority to bear in the long run. If, however, that initial strike did not produce a military decision, then the national *levée en masse* mobilized in the meantime would be committed.[42] The objective of this form of warfare was to prevent the enemy's superior strategic forces from becoming effectively engaged.

Despite Germany's defeat in the Great War, Seeckt unwaveringly held on to Schlieffen's concept of defeating the enemy's forces through rapid, mobile operations before the enemy states were able to engage their superior resources. Seeckt was convinced of the absolute superiority of the German approach to conducting mobile warfare at the beginning of the war in 1914, and he therefore intended to increase the operational tempo even further.[43] He believed that a professional army that was immediately deployable without any mobilization delays was the key means to achieve this. Seeckt wanted to correct the German Army's obvious lack of mobility during the Great War with motor vehicles, motorized infantry, aircraft, and combat-effective cavalry. Seeckt particularly assigned a special role to the cavalry. As he saw it, the horse soldier had not yet been replaced by the motorized soldier.[44] Despite the experiences of the Great War, he even planned to commit cavalry to a main combat mission on the enemy's flanks and rear.[45] With such thinking, of course, Seeckt betrayed himself as a supporter of the cavalry in the heated debate on the significance and future of the cavalry. In 1927 that debate escalated into a dispute over the retention of the lance.[46] Seeckt's position was probably a function of the Versailles Treaty provisions that allowed the Reichsheer to field three cavalry divisions. Another reason was the fact that at the time the cavalry was the only truly mobile means of operational warfare as Seeckt envisioned it.

It is important to remember here that the conduct of offensive operations requires the capability and the means for tactical attack. The Reichswehr did not have all the necessary means available. As in the case of World War I, the Reichs-wehr's mobility was limited to horses, the feet of soldiers, and the railways. The only exception was that the Reichswehr now had a few more trucks. In the final analysis, Seeckt had neither the means nor a conclusive concept for the tactical execution of his operational ideas. Yet, the required means for that sort of combat existed already in the form of the tank. The problem, however, was that tanks were still too immobile, they did not have communications systems, and of course the Reichswehr was forbidden to have tanks. Nonetheless, there were no practical restrictions on the theoretical development of the tactical and operational use of tanks. Apart from the discussions on the future of the cavalry, therefore, the question of how to use a fighting vehicle was at the center of the military theory debate in Germany during the years that followed.[47] Some officers, such as Major (later Colonel General) Heinz Guderian, were convinced that the potential of fighting vehicles and aircraft was still a long way from being exploited fully for modern mobile warfare. They believed that tanks had to be included in future operational considerations and training procedures.[48]

The importance Seeckt devoted to operational training in the Reichsheer can be seen not only in the *Führerreisen* (leaders' rides) he initiated for the training of general officers, but also in the development of the doctrinal manual *Leitlinien für die obere Führung im Kriege* (Guidelines for Higher Commands in Time of War). Since the manual on command and control of the combined arms (*F.u.G.*) only dealt with the tactical level, this new manual was intended to address the higher command levels as a continuation of the *Grundzüge der höheren Truppenführung* (Fundamentals of Higher-Level Military Command). The work developed by Colonel Konstantin Hierl on behalf of the Truppenamt is a unique testimony to the operational thinking of the Reichswehr at the beginning of the 1920s. Even down to its specific wording it remains completely faithful to classical operational thinking.[49] The author, however, did not finish the important chapters on the subjects of *Volkskrieg* (people's war) and *kleiner Krieg* (smaller wars). But the wording and composition of the *Grundzüge* does suggest that Hierl did not attach any particular importance to those topics in 1923, because as in Schlieffen's time the objective of all operations was the destruction of the enemy's forces. Politics was still regarded as having no influence on the command and control of operations. As for the problem of manpower inferiority, the guiding principle still was to compensate for the enemy's superiority to a certain extent with a higher quality of command and control and troops, combined with the rapid conduct of operations. The particular importance of psychological factors and the unconditional will to victory was emphasized repeatedly in the context of the numerical inferiority of manpower and materiel.

What was new in the *Grundzüge* was the explicit requirement that the army's operational plan—the execution of which was not to be developed in detail—had to be included in the Reich's strategic war plan. That most likely resulted from the experience of World War I. The Reichsheer's overwhelming inferiority in manpower numbers also undoubtedly contributed to the particular emphasis on the center of gravity: "The guiding thought of the operations plan must correspond with the utmost consistency to the distribution of forces, particularly the choice of the center of gravity during the strategic buildup. The more unfavorable the entire balance of forces, the more uncompromisingly all other considerations must support the main effort."[50]

The emphasis on the significance of communication links for the higher commands also traces back to the wartime experiences. Defense was only dealt with briefly, and withdrawal was treated as a rather irksome duty. The *Grundzüge* did not treat positional warfare as an inevitable consequence of modern weapons systems, but rather as the result of an indecisive frontal clash between two mass military forces. Positional warfare was to be avoided if at all possible, because the advantages of high-quality troops would be wasted in static fighting. "Great generals leading good troops have always avoided positional warfare as far as possible, and have sought to develop their genius freely in mobile warfare."[51]

In the chapter titled "Army Maneuvering" Hierl discussed the significance of motorization for operational command and control. He described the potentials for rapid transport by motor vehicles, while pointing out that these depended on a hard-surfaced road network. Another drawback was that owing to their high speed, motor vehicles could not be used along with horse-drawn vehicles, which were not well suited for rapid mobile warfare without additional support. He also stressed that fighting vehicles did not have the capability of making longer marches. In conclusion, the *Grundzüge* did not assign any major significance for mobile warfare to either tanks or motor vehicles.

The *Grundzüge* identified the ability to marshal separately marching units at the right place, at the right time, and functionally structured as an outstanding capability of the operational commander. Envelopment and breakthrough operations were addressed in great detail, with the envelopment always the preferred maneuver whenever possible. In summary, the *Grundzüge* stressed: "In operations, just as little as in tactics, the success of the attack depends very little on attempting a specific approach. Exterior and interior lines, envelopment and breakthrough counterbalance each other. Any attack operation is based on the given situation. The choice of the correct attack operation and its energetic execution will result in success. Strong confidence in one's own superior powers and the unquenchable will to win form the moral basis for the success of any attack."[52]

Much space was devoted to defense, while the manual demonstrably noted that any defensive operation aimed at bringing about a decision inevitably had to lead to an offensive operation. The continuity with prewar doctrine became particularly evident in the section on the battle. The battle itself was still at the center of operational thinking, since the will of the enemy could only be broken by the force of arms. According to the *Grundzüge,* the object of the battle is the destruction of the enemy. The element of surprise had a major influence on the outcome of the battle. And in order to achieve this, the *Grundzüge* favored an operational flank attack, while not excluding the frontal attack. The battle came at the end of the operation, and the tactical success in the battle determined its outcome. This was an explicit interlocking of the tactical and the operational levels. Entirely in accordance with Schlieffen's ideas, emphasis was placed on victory in the decisive battle as the final objective of an operation, while stressing, "the battle of armies exists for its own sake, for the sake of victory which is pursued in [the battle]."[53]

With both its restorative and innovative elements, Hierl's *Grundzüge* mirrored the conflict among the leaders of the Reichswehr during the 1920s. Vastly inferior to all potential enemies in terms of manpower and materiel numbers, the Reichswehr developed modern, innovative tactics focused on maneuver and combined arms combat. But with regard to operational thinking, the Reichswehr was caught between restorative and innovative concepts, and it clung to utopian plans for being able to conduct large-scale operational warfare. Those plans, however, were still deeply rooted in Schlieffen's ideas and were only selectively modernized based on the World War I experiences. A typical example is the acceptance of the breakthrough. Accordingly, defense only played a minor role in Hierl's manuscript. Just as in Schlieffen's time, the focus of the *Grundzüge* was the operational attack with the objective of achieving an envelopment. At that point the restorative element of Hierl's thinking is particularly obvious. After all, World War I had led to the abandonment of the envelopment as the only valid option.[54]

Without generally questioning the importance of mobility in warfare, alternative tactical and operational concepts, such as delaying combat, breakthrough, and defense, were openly discussed in German military journals as early as in the middle 1920s.[55] As the discussion progressed, the interlinking of the operational breakthrough with the subsequent operational envelopment came increasingly to the fore.

A doctrinal regulation that, contrary to the general view, held onto the dogma of envelopment was no longer acceptable to the majority of the Reichswehr leaders by the mid-1920s. Hierl's *Grundzüge* was heavily criticized by Lieutenant Colonel Joachim von Stülpnagel, and the chief of the Truppenamt recommended against issuing the draft as an official regulation. Seeckt concurred, in part because the leaders' and General Staff rides would continue to provide the primary vehicle for operational training. For security reasons, Hierl was even prohibited from publishing his effort privately.[56] That fact, therefore, indicates that what Hierl had drafted was the German operational doctrine for a possible war of the future, at least in a rudimentary form.

Much of the literature describes Seeckt's operational doctrine as a "renaissance of classical warfare,"[57] but one that turned out to be a chimera.[58] Both parts of that statement are accurate. Seeckt largely planned and thought along the lines of Schlieffen's operational categories. And as in Schlieffen's time, mobility and speed combined with excellent leadership skills were the cornerstones of Seeckt's operational thinking.

The focus on mobile warfare can at least in part be explained by Seeckt's operational experiences on the Eastern Front. As someone who served extensively on that front, the limitations on operational warfare resulting from the lack of mobility of the German divisions would have made an indelible impression on Seeckt. This, however, was not quite the case.

Seeckt intended to conduct a mobile war that essentially was still determined by the marching pace of the infantry, and only supported by the air force. He overestimated the operational mobility of larger infantry units. His references to the significance of combat-effective cavalry as a means of mobile warfare also appear out of touch, considering the fact that the cavalry had not been able to accomplish that task during the Great War. In the final analysis, Seeckt's tactical-operational doctrine did not solve the problem of operational warfare that World War I had exposed—the lack of mobility and speed. His concept of operational warfare, which was based on a higher tempo and greater mobility than in World War I, simply lacked the technical means to make it possible. And any attempt to explain the role of the cavalry in Seeckt's operational doctrine as an anticipation of the operational employment of tanks in World War II falls short.[59] There was no room for operational armored units in Seeckt's plans.

It would be wrong, however, to accuse Seeckt, given his proven intellectual skills, of conceiving ideas of war that were completely divorced from reality. The "Gospel of Mobility" that Seeckt imposed on the Reichsheer is only understandable if one takes into account that in considering Germany's central geographic position, he perceived the areas close to the borders as the Reichsheer's exclusive area of deployment—as had been the thinking prior to World War I. Thanks to the existing rail network, rapid movement would have been possible then, even in the border regions in the west or the east.

Seeckt was not alone in his thinking. In his book *Der Mensch und die Schlacht der Zukunft* (Man and the Battle of the Future), George Soldan also argued for a high-tech and mobile professional army, similar to the British example. In Soldan's opinion, only such an army would be able to meet the requirements of modern mobile warfare. He predicted the future war as a "miracle of mobility." For Soldan, the army of the future had only one task: to end the war through battles of annihilation. A reviewer summarized Soldan's core thesis in the journal *Militärwochenblatt* (Military Weekly) with the following words: "In war history, therefore, we do not have an age of positional warfare ahead of us, but an age of the strategy of annihilation. Whoever does not annihilate the enemy's army in the first weeks of

the campaign, and does not hit the adversary's army of millions at the very beginning, has lost the war."[60]

Seeckt's "military utopianism," which was diametrically opposed to the real
defense capabilities of the Reichswehr, did not pass unchallenged. Reacting to
Germany's apparent military impotence in the face of the French occupation of
the Ruhr in 1923, the younger Truppenamt officers by the middle of the 1920s
increasingly came to the realization that the army would not be able to defend
Germany effectively in the case of a French or Polish attack. The primary exponent
of this group, later known as "the Fronde," was Stülpnagel. As chief of the Heeres-
abteilung (Army Department) of the Operationsabteilung (Operations Division)
of the clandestine General Staff in the form of the Truppenamt, he was not a military lightweight. He held a key position in the further development of operational
thinking. Dissatisfied with Seeckt's operational-strategic war planning, Stülpnagel
presented his ideas about future war to the officers of the Reichswehramt in February 1924. The presentation under the title "Gedanken über den Krieg der Zukunft"
(Thoughts on the War of the Future) was a direct challenge to Seeckt and the operational traditionalists in the army's leadership.[61] Stülpnagel's integration of people's
war as a conflict that affects society as a whole into operational warfare and his
rejection of rapid, offensive operations aimed at destroying the enemy constituted
a fundamental break with the traditional operational thinking as passed down by
the chief of the Army Command from the Kaiser's time.

It is worthwhile to take a closer look at Stülpnagel's theories, which he distrib-
uted a few weeks later in the Truppenamt, and the resulting deliberations on his
theories. For one thing, his ideas had radical consequences for society and under
no circumstances could be implemented in a democracy. It was, however, a new
operational approach, and we can identify the differences and commonalities with
classical operational thinking.

Stülpnagel's concept was based on a "systematically planned and deliberately
conducted war of liberation."[62] He believed that without considerable rearmament
effort Germany was not capable of fighting such a war, neither at present nor in the
foreseeable future. He also said that any future war would be one against the German people as a whole, the country's nerve centers and sources of power, and not
just against the army. Consequently, Stülpnagel argued that the Reichswehr and
the people had to wage the war together with military means, and that the civilian
population in this fight would have to submit to the will of the military. Considering the German military's significant inferiority in manpower and materiel—
a disadvantage that could not be compensated for by the quality of the troops
and the leadership—Stülpnagel doubted that it was possible for the Reichswehr to
wage a war in the foreseeable future with any prospect of success based strictly on
Schlieffen's ideas. A new strategic concept, therefore, had to be developed based on
the strategic realities and not on wishful thinking.

Stülpnagel anticipated the war of the future in two phases. Firstly, it was essential to buy time in order to ensure the mobilization of manpower and materiel for the formation of a field army and to create the political conditions for other powers—for example, Russia—to intervene on Germany's behalf. That buying of time would be achieved through the strategic defensive by means of a strategy of attrition. Contrary to Schlieffen, therefore, Stülpnagel's first objective was not the annihilation of the enemy, but rather "the uprising of the whole people for liberation in the most primitive defensive battle."[63] By abandoning a rapid, decisive initial offensive, Stülpnagel abandoned what had been a pillar of German operational thinking since Schlieffen. Doing so, however, required that the war had to be fought entirely on German territory, where the enemy would be worn down gradually in the fight for time.

In order to accomplish this, Stülpnagel planned to expand the successful tactical defense that had been developed during the final two years of World War I into operational area warfare in depth. Initially, the enemy that marched into Germany would be fought in the border regions by small, rapid, mobile battle groups that would not attempt to set the conditions for a decisive battle. The enemy would be worn down slowly through delaying combat, which in turn would weaken him systematically in terms of materiel and morale. That kind of border warfare and guerrilla warfare, prepared for systematically in time of peace, would be waged ruthlessly with boldness and rigor by the population under the leadership of retired officers.[64] Stülpnagel also called for the destruction of important transportation infrastructure, as well as the chemical contamination of tactically and operationally decisive areas. Simultaneously, the enemy would be demoralized further through the conduct of an organized people's war, which would include clandestine acts of sabotage.

In the final extremities of such a people's war, Stülpnagel argued that the sense of national hatred should be leveraged to the extreme, without shying away from any forms of murder or sabotage.[65] He did think, however, that by openly wearing identification badges the members of the civilian population could identify themselves as combatants according to the Hague Convention of Land Warfare.[66]

Stülpnagel did not succumb to the illusion that the civilian population would fight such a people's war with great enthusiasm, especially since warfare of that sort would necessarily result in severe retaliation measures. Nonetheless, he thought that the German people would have to bear the burden for the sake of the national war of liberation. There was no other option—defeat the enemy or perish. Thus, Stülpnagel called for the transformation of the Weimar Republic into an authoritarian state unreservedly committed to the war of liberation—a state that eliminated anything pacifistic or atypically German; a state that raised the youth to hate the external enemy; and a state that systematically committed the civilian population to war. Stülpnagel believed that was the only way to marshal the total power of the people, upon which his operational planning was based. For the logical development of the new ideas of warfare, the integration of the civilian population into the battle was the *sine qua non* of successful operational warfare. This radicalization of warfare as advocated by Stülpnagel, which in so many areas became reality during World War II, was contrary to Seeckt's operational ideas and the conviction that it was the army and not the people that waged war. From Seeckt's perspective, the use of force was reserved for the military.

In his study of the Reichswehr, Wilhelm Deist reduced Stülpnagel's operational concept solely to his concept of the people's war, explaining that Stülpnagel substituted warfare conducted by an operational army as advocated by Seeckt with a national war of liberation carefully prepared in detail. Deist, therefore, argued that one could not speak of a renaissance of operational warfare in the works of Stülpnagel.[67] But Deist's analysis falls short. It is certainly true that Stülpnagel accused the traditionalists around Seeckt of having stopped the evolution of their operational thinking with Schlieffen's doctrine of annihilation fought between modern and approximately equivalent mass military forces. And Stülpnagel also denied that there was a recipe for victory that could be derived from history. He was convinced that the war of the future would differ significantly from all the previous wars.

Despite all of his criticism of the old patterns of thought, even Stülpnagel could not escape from his military socialization as a member of the General Staff and divorce himself completely from German classical operational thinking. That explains why he drew on Moltke the Younger's operational ideas when he postulated that, based on the military situation, a defensive operation with a subsequent offensive was the Reichswehr's only effective operational option for a future war. Therefore, despite all the probabilities of success that Stülpnagel predicted for guerrilla and people's war, he too was strongly convinced that it was not possible to achieve a decision in war solely by the means of a defensive people's war. He considered that the fight to win time merely served to achieve a balance of forces, to win allies for the continuation of the war, and, most of all, to build up Germany's field army. As soon as those goals were reached, Stülpnagel planned to shift from the defensive fight for time to the offensive fight to bring about a decision. At that point, according to Stülpnagel, "the decisive battle had to be fought the way Schlieffen taught it."[68]

The objective of the second phase of Stülpnagel's operational doctrine was the annihilation of the demoralized enemy armed forces. He planned the offensive as a combined attack by mobile units, heavy artillery, and air support. Although Germany did not have an air force at the time, Stülpnagel included tactical as well as operational air war as decisive factors in warfare. He advocated clear coordination with the navy in the common war effort. A supreme commander would direct the deployment of the navy, which was not an end in itself, but rather in support of the army.

The contrast between Stülpnagel's concepts of the people's war and the actual decisive battle could not be greater. His phrasing and choice of words were reminiscent of Schlieffen—whom he referred to as the great master—and reflected the long-lasting operational influence of the General Staff:

> So now let us address the real operations, which will allow the intellectually superior commander to defeat even a stronger enemy. Concepts such as the exploitation of interior lines, eccentric withdrawal [withdrawal along multiple diverging axes], and others are gaining increased importance again. The old basic doctrine of the concentration of forces at the decisive point while weakening other sectors must be at the forefront of our thinking at all times. The result will be gaps in the front, which can only be filled by cavalry or the militias. We must accept those gaps deliberately, because the fear of gaps prevented Cannae-like operations during the World War. . . . It is obvious that such a fight places the highest demands on the willpower of the commander and the quality of the troops.[69]

Thus, Stülpnagel too held the opinion that the army in the field had to achieve the decision through operational warfare according to classical German operational thinking. As Michael Geyer has argued, however, it is impossible to speak really of a "defensive Cannae" or a "defensive Blitzkrieg."[70] Considering the Reichswehr's significant manpower and materiel inferiority, the people's war was comparable to modern initial skirmishes and was merely intended to allow time to build up a combat-capable operational army. That meant that Stülpnagel deliberately accepted heavy losses among the civilian population. Thus, the strategy of attrition only laid the groundwork for a subsequent strategy of annihilation. As Gil-li Vardi has quite correctly argued, Stülpnagel did not break with tradition, nor even introduce a new revolutionary concept.[71] For Stülpnagel the people's war was merely a means to an end, the only realistic chance to win time. His objective was and continued to be the decisive battle. The older literature generally discounts this point because of the long-standing fixation on the concept of people's war. Stülpnagel's only real innovation was in attempting to integrate two military concepts into the battle of annihilation. Up to that point those two concepts—people's war and mobile warfare—had been considered diametrically opposed and mutually exclusive. Stülpnagel's concept was initially to exploit people's war for the strategy of attrition, but only to achieve a delay. Ultimately the decision would be achieved in the battle fought by the army and led by General Staff officers.

Stülpnagel's doctrine was unique in its radicalism, as it attempted to combine Moltke the Elder's operational thinking and the concept of people's war. In order to effect the latter, Stülpnagel called for no less than the complete reorganization of the state into an authoritarian nationalist system dominated by the military and an extensive rearmament program. These were thoughts that Ludendorff too repeatedly expounded in his writings from the middle of the 1930s. It is, however, doubtful that it would have been possible to put Stülpnagel's operational planning into practice, not only for political and social reasons, but for military reasons as well. Stülpnagel's close associates in the Army Department doubted the military success of the type of operational zone defense he advocated.[72] Even Stülpnagel himself considered the form of warfare he postulated as merely a heroic gesture to be made in the immediate future. In the final analysis, therefore, neither Seeckt's nor Stülpnagel's operational ideas could be implemented in the milieu of the Weimar Republic, although for different reasons.

The concepts of war that existed simultaneously in the Reichsheer, and the operational concepts deriving from those ideas, show an Army Command searching for the correct approach to warfare in the future. The fact that that approach was a matter of controversy even inside the Truppenamt can be seen in the commentary to Hierl's *Grundzüge der höheren Truppenführung*. While the chief of the Truppenamt's Section T-4 considered Hierl's writing to be excellent, Stülpnagel, when asked to give his comments as chief of Section T-1, responded with scathing criticism:

> Colonel Hierl's work is excellent; parts of it are brilliantly written and suited to train the leaders for a new war with the instruments of power of the army of 1914. . . . These instruments of power are not at our disposal, neither now nor in the next decade. . . . Hierl's work follows Schlieffen's train of thought. Schlieffen prepares for the war with mass military forces. Is it conceivable that in the future war we will face our enemies with "masses"? Having been raised in the military tradition of Schlieffen myself, it is difficult for me to have to speak out against its practical application today.[73]

Although Stülpnagel continued to call for the adherence to the principle of the great battle of annihilation, his ideas on how to get there differed from the classical Schlieffen approach. Stülpnagel argued that only by accepting that Germany had to wage the war from the position of the weaker party would it be possible to win any future war.[74]

The debate on future warfare, and therefore on the focus of operational thinking in the Reichsheer, continued without interruption during the following years. Because of his critical attitude, Stülpnagel bore personal consequences. Kicked upstairs in the classical manner, he was promoted to colonel in February 1926 and transferred to Brunswick as a regimental commander.

Seeckt's and Stülpnagel's concepts differed on key issues. While Stülpnagel

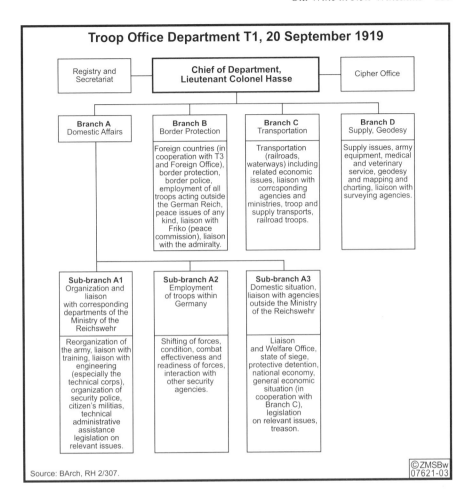

wanted to abandon the army's monopoly on the use of force and replace it with "the military leaders' claim to leadership in society," Seeckt insisted on the professional army's exclusive right to use force, involving the population at most on the sidelines of the battle. For Stülpnagel, however, the army in the final analysis was only one instrument. It was, however, the decisive one. Stülpnagel's concept did include the use of force by civilians. Both concepts aimed to guarantee the military's claim to power in society, albeit in different ways. In operational terms, the significant difference was the fact that Seeckt immediately sought a rapid decision with the operational army, while Stülpnagel wanted first to remain on the defensive in order to attrit the enemy, and then defeat him operationally through a counterattack. Thus, Seeckt adhered to Schlieffen's theories, while Stülpnagel followed more closely those of Moltke the Elder. Both doctrines, however, held in common the principle that the decision ultimately would be achieved during the attack in a battle of annihilation. This point has been widely overlooked in the literature, with the exception of Vardi's recent study.[75] The differences between the two doctrines are not in their objective, but rather in the way to achieve that objective.

The primacy of politics in operational warfare was not a factor in any of the operational concepts of those years. On the contrary, the military, especially according to Stülpnagel's ideas, was to extend its influence over politics to conform it to the conduct of operations as intended by the military. In the final analysis, the "people" were to sacrifice themselves with probable heavy losses during the people's war initial phase of the battle, while the army regrouped and held its fire until it was time to deliver the final blow.

Planning and Training

Faced with the Reichsheer's hopeless military inferiority, two operational doctrines had evolved by the middle of the 1920s that during the subsequent years were advocated by different factions of the officer corps. Stülpnagel's ideas first influenced the war games called *Westkrieg* in 1924 and *Ostkrieg* in 1925, and in the process demonstrated how Janis-faced his concepts were under operational conditions. In conjunction with waging a people's war in the west, offensively conducted operations against Poland in the east attempted to compensate for Germany's numerical inferiority with high-quality troops and superior command and control. Germany's systematic military buildup starting in 1924–1925 also served the same purpose.[76]

The idea that the entire Truppenamt unanimously supported Stülpnagel's ideas is not correct. The members of the Truppenamt vigorously debated about operational mobile warfare. This was corroborated by a study made in 1926 with Stülpnagel's express approval by Major Friedrich von Rabenau entitled *Die operative Beweglichkeit eines Heeres und ihre Erfolgsaussichten gegenüber moderner Waffenwirkung* (The Operational Mobility of Ground Forces and Their Prospects for Success in the Face of Modern Weapons Effects). While Rabenau made a sincere effort to produce a synthesis between operational mobile warfare and people's war, in the end he reduced his operational-strategic approach to Schlieffen's concept of a two-front war: defensive on one front, offensive on the other.

According to Rabenau, the forces deployed in a chessboard pattern on the main front remain defensive, while the weaker enemy is defeated by offensive operations using the elements of surprise, envelopment, and a thrust into the enemy's rear. Rabenau assumed that the French, owing to their slow and immobile form of warfare, would give the German formations the space and time necessary to conduct mobile operations. Such operations absolutely depended on modern means of transport—the railway and motor vehicles—and mobile command and control procedures supported by the latest communications systems. The enemy who was superior in equipment and manpower would be defeated by applying these principles, which were the pillars of classical German operational thinking. Rabenau's analysis continued Schlieffen's traditions. There was, however, one essential point where Rabenau went beyond the latter's concepts. He replaced Schlieffen's joint front with continuously moving formations capable of executing sudden and surprising concentrations of effort. Thus, Rabenau dramatically extended German operational doctrine, laying the conceptual groundwork for the Wehrmacht's motorized mobile warfare.

Although Stülpnagel's successor, Colonel Werner von Blomberg (later field marshal and Reich war minister), tested elements of his predecessor's ideas in war games, Michael Geyer's assumption that Stülpnagel's operational doctrine became the basis of the Reichsheer's operational planning after Seeckt retired is not correct. In general, much of the literature to this point has attached too much influence to Stülpnagel's ideas on the development of German operational thinking. One reason is the fact that the bulk of the relevant records on this question were destroyed during World War II, and those sources that fortunately did survive have too often been incorrectly interpreted or accepted as absolute truth. For another reason, many historians, including Michael Geyer in his still widely regarded study *Aufrüstung oder Sicherheit,* unfortunately used the military technical terms in rather imprecise manners, and Geyer sometimes did not accurately interpret the context of the inner workings of the General Staff and its internal networks and animosities. Thus, Geyer characterized the Truppenamt's *Winterstudien* (winter studies) of the years of 1927–1928 and 1928–1929 as "*Operationskriegsspiele*" (operational war games), "*Erprobungskriegsspiele*" (trial war games), or "*Organisationskriegsspiele*" (organizational war games). Those terms did not exist in the military vocabulary of the time.

It seems necessary, therefore, to conduct a quick overview of the training material the German Army used in the years following World War I. According to Lieutenant General Kurt von Hammerstein-Equord, who succeeded Blomberg as director of the Truppenamt and held that position until the end of October 1930, there was a striking difference between *Studien* (studies), such as the above noted winter studies, and *Kriegsspiele* (war games). As Hammerstein wrote: "I think it is necessary to make a clear distinction at all times as to whether you want to simulate operationally—which necessarily means that you must not take into account the real conditions—or whether you want to make a study—which means that you absolutely must include the real world conditions. In that case, the consequence is that in taking into account our weakness, no decisive operations are possible. Mixing both only leads to incorrect conclusions."[77]

These Kriegsspiele, which gained increasing importance in the Reichsheer and were developed continuously over the years, were never formalized in a regulation, specifically to avoid even the slightest element of standardization. The

Kriegsspiele were created during the Kaiser's time as a tool to train military leaders. They were especially important to the Reichsheer, because of the impossibility of conducting major exercises with large formations owing to the lack of money and low force strengths. Thus, the Kriegsspiele developed into integral elements of the interwar period training programs because they made it possible to exercise with prohibited weapons and equipment. Over the course of the years, different training activities were incorporated under the term Kriegsspiel.[78] The characteristic feature of the Kriegsspiele was the fact that with a few exceptions they were conducted without troops. The type of Kriegsspiel that is particularly relevant to our discussion is the one that exercised situational assessments and decision making based on free play between two sides, with "Red" usually playing the enemy and "Blue" the friendly forces. The senior officer conducting the exercise played through the participating officers' decisions to the end, evaluated them, and then presented his own *Leitungslösung* (director's solution). Kriegsspiele, however, were also used as instruments to troubleshoot warfighting problems. The Wehrmacht used them increasingly to resolve practical operational questions or to prepare campaigns, such as the Operation BARBAROSSA invasion of the Soviet Union.[79]

The *Winterstudie* (winter study) of 1927–1928 was based on a hypothetical Polish attack on Germany, which the Reichsheer was to fend off with its 1927 armament levels. The study came to the conclusion that the Reichsheer would be able to resist for only a short time, despite giving up considerable amounts of territory. The winter study of 1928–1929 was based on the situation of a two-front war with France and Poland, in which France only used its *armée de couverture* (covering army), and the Polish Army was tied down largely by a Soviet attack. The result, as recorded by the Truppenamt, was that while the Reichsheer would be able to delay the attack successfully with the armament levels expected to be reached in April 1933, decisive battles would be possible neither in the west nor in the east. It was impossible, therefore, to win a war.[80]

These winter studies also served to verify the status of the territorial reserve and border security organizations. Although the Truppenamt supported the continued existence of those organizations,[81] it nonetheless was critical of the low combat power of the border security service.[82] Geyer's assertion that the primary purpose of the winter studies had been to exercise Stülpnagel's doctrine of people's war is somewhat overstated. On the contrary, the winter studies focused on the deployable army in the field. The capacity of the entire population was not considered a necessary factor in the establishment of armament levels, and only the capacity of the population of East Prussia was thought necessary for military purposes. Operational considerations were generally less important in both the 1927–1928 and 1928–1929 studies, although they did demonstrate the futility of a defense against France or Poland, or both countries in a two-front war. At the end of the 1920s the Reichswehr still faced an operational-strategic dilemma that, according to the convictions of its leaders, could be solved only through a buildup of manpower and materiel. In late June 1927, the Reichsheer's military leaders drew up a mobilization plan for a field army of twenty-one divisions under the cover name of A-Plan (*Aufstellungsplan*—buildup plan).[83] Nonetheless, there was an open debate in the fashion of the old German military tradition over the Reichsheer's basic ability to wage war and also to conduct a simultaneous buildup. Thus, based on the assumption that the Reichsheer must be able to defend itself against Poland and France, the studies concluded that it would not be possible to commit the Reichsheer without increases in manpower and equipment: "A buildup is indispensable if wc havc to fight."[84]

The Truppenamt conducted these deliberations at the end of the 1920s in an environment of changing foreign and domestic policies. The political-military thinking, which in Seeckt's time had been focused on Versailles and Germany's political isolation, had changed largely because of the 1925 Locarno Treaty. The Reich's foreign political isolation was broken, and the improved economic conditions made it possible to almost double the military budget between 1924 and 1928.[85]

During this transitional phase, Wilhelm Groener took over as minister of the Reichswehr in January 1928. He had clear ideas about the Reich's future defense policy. His thinking was based on the insight that Germany "had been ready neither politically nor economically and socially for the World War, which went beyond everything that could have been imagined, and the fighting therefore was doomed from the beginning."[86]

Groener worked simultaneously to make the military subordinate to the Weimar Republic's overall policies and to adapt the Reichswehr's capacities to the Reich's foreign policy. He also showed a deeper understanding for the complexity of modern warfare, but he declared at the same time that the central goal of German policy had to be based on establishing voluntary military service. In contrast to many of his old comrades in arms, Groener understood that modern military affairs depended on the framework of civilian conditions. From an operational perspective, Groener was in the direct line with Schlieffen and Seeckt. Groener could foresee only a short war because of the worldwide economic interconnections. Given France's superiority, Groener was convinced of the futility of a war with that state, and he was determined to guide the operational planning for the future exclusively toward a defense against Poland. But although the leading Reichsheer officers began to accept the Reich's factual military situation—largely because Seeckt's and Stülpnagel's operational doctrines were not realistic—they did not agree with Groener either. When Blomberg wanted to issue guidelines for further operational planning of a delaying defense against France based on the results of the winter studies, Groener prevented him from doing so, even though the Reichswehr Ministry had agreed previously.[87]

Thus, the Reichswehr Ministry imposed its statutory authority when Groener on April 1930 issued his directive "Die Aufgaben der Wehrmacht" (The Functions of the Armed Forces), which detailed the guiding principles of defense policy to the senior navy and army commanders.[88] Groener emphasized that the military did not have the status of being a function in itself, but rather it was an instrument of the political leadership, from which its functions derived. Based on the military's strength, it would operate only in a limited number of crisis situations. Besides fighting against civil unrest and fending off illegal border incursions, the military would be used for defensive purposes only, and then only when doing so made sense from both a military and a political perspective. Implied in all this was that no futile battles would be fought. The doctrine included, however, the option of making active use of the military when a favorable opportunity presented itself. To execute the specified missions, it would be necessary to establish close operational coordination between the navy and the army at the ministerial command level, combined with close coordination with the Foreign Office.[89] The previous operational plans that had been based on heroic and utopian ideas were modified into a realistic defensive strategy as ordered by the political leadership:

> What we first of all must eliminate from all deliberations is the idea that we might be able to fight against France. From the military perspective, we will be so inferior to France for the foreseeable future that any effort to fight would be tantamount to accelerated suicide. Things are different in the east. There, I perceive the possibility that we might in the foreseeable future reach an armament capability level that makes it possible to defend our borders with some prospect of success.[90]

In Groener's view, the future work of the Truppenamt should be dominated by practical work instead of unrealistic paper exercises and war games. Groener cited as examples *Fall KORFANTY* (Case KORFANTY) against Franc-tireurs and *Fall PILSUDSKI* (Case PILSUDSKI) against regular Polish troops. The ideas of Groener and his chief of the Office of Ministerial Affairs, General Kurt von Schleicher, met with resistance within the Reichsheer's leadership. Groener tried to weaken that leadership by a skillful manipulation of personnel management policy.[91]

During those years the coordination between the army leadership and the Foreign Office was satisfactory from the diplomats' perspective. They even credited the soldiers with a sober assessment of the situation and with turning away from the romanticism of the past.[92] But the judgment of the Foreign Office was at least partly wrong. Groener's and Schleicher's ideas about the Reichswehr being an instrument of overall security policy that should be used only in limited situations resonated hardly at all with the Reichswehr's leaders. Just like Stülpnagel's people's war doctrine, the newer ideas merely amounted to episodes in the development of German operational thinking. The military was not ready to accept any political influence derived from realism on their conduct of operations, and with it the partial reduction of their power. Nor in the foreseeable future would they abandon the idea of abrogating the Versailles restrictions, and with that a future Germany with restored strength and Great Power status.

Despite the fact that Groener ruled out large-scale warfare, the Truppenamt continued to cultivate the idea that war meant large-scale offensive or counterattack operations, and it trained to those scenarios in its war games. Those exercises, however, more often served as operational training for leaders rather than resolving real operational problems. Political-military realism, which had only started to have some influence, started to wane again by the beginning of the 1930s. Training and exercises continued based on traditional operational command, and the Truppenamt and the leaders' staff rides were structured in such a way that it was the only feasible approach. None of the war games that were played reflected the current political situation or the Reichsheer's manpower and equipment situation, but rather demonstrated the way the army's senior leadership and selected command personnel were thinking in operational terms. This is significant because the list of the participants in these Kriegsspiele reads like a *Who's Who* of the World War II generals. Significantly, Hammerstein-Equord's first words during the final discussion of the 1930 Truppenamt staff ride set the tone of the program: "The purpose of this year's Truppenamt staff ride was to play through *decisive operations*. When the initial situation was conceived, therefore, it was not based on the factual force ratios or on today's political situation. Only the existing borders were real, in order to have a well defined [exercise] area."[93]

Without going into detail on the individual Kriegsspiele, it is important to note that they all were conducted within the framework of traditional operational thinking.[94] The director's solutions always posited attacks or counterattacks into an open flank after a successful delaying defensive battle. What was emphasized was the importance of establishing through one's own conduct of the operations opportunities for envelopment, and then exploiting those opportunities. This implied deliberately assuming high risk to turn inferiority into a local superiority by concentrating all forces. The standard solutions repeatedly were based on rapid movement, striking power, envelopment operations, and clear concentrations of effort. A delaying resistance was conducted only at the beginning of the operation, after which a deliberately executed counterattack was driven into the flank. The war games continually exercised the connection between area and time, the courage to execute quick decisions under uncertainty, rapid maneuver, and command and control.

The Kriegsspiele served, as Hammerstein explained, to develop operational thinking and therefore did not need to be based on real political situations. They were training for the future, thus demonstrating that the Reichsheer's leadership remained committed to classical operational thinking. And that remained based on Schlieffen's doctrine that the weaker side could undermine the enemy's capabilities only through a quick offensive, followed by a battle of annihilation, thereby winning the war. According to the final discussion of the 1933 leaders' staff ride: "It is the weaker party that must not give up the thought of destroying the enemy. For them, it is the only way out. What must be strived for is not a heroic defense, but a decisive victory, as paradoxical as that may sound."[95]

The development of the doctrinal regulations ran parallel to the development of the Kriegsspiele. Manual H.Dv. 300 *Truppenführung* (Troop Leading–*T.F.*) was essentially drafted by Ludwig Beck, who as a colonel general later served as army chief of staff.[96] Issued in 1933, it was a replacement for the earlier H.Dv. 487 *Führung und Gefecht der verbundenen Waffen* (Command and Control of the Combined Arms in Combat—*F.u.G.*). Like the *F.u.G.* it replaced, *T.F.* dealt essentially with the practical level, based on the assumption of the armament, equipment, and personnel strength of an unrestricted armed forces. No distinction was made between either a people's army or a professional army. Since operational and tactical thinking were often interwoven, the influence of *T.F.* as well as of the earlier *F.u.G.* on the further development of German operational thinking must not be underestimated. The most important elements of this pioneering doctrinal regulation were as follows:

T.F. addressed those commanders it considered to comprise the senior leadership level, and who commanded independent formations. According to *T.F.*, the infantry and cavalry divisions were the smallest elements capable of operational independence.

As noted, *T.F.* was not an entirely new creation, but was based on *F.u.G.* in many points. Thus, *T.F.* expressly stressed the significance of combined arms combat for mobile warfare. *T.F.*, however, did not address positional warfare at all. Together with the operational form of *hinhaltender Widerstand* (delaying resistance), *Verteidigung* (defense) was subsumed under the term of *Abwehr* (the defensive). Overall, *T.F.* attributed a more important role to the Abwehr than did previous doctrinal publications. German warfare, then, was adapted to the Reich's military realities and more oriented toward defense.[97] To speak of a one-sided emphasis on the defensive, however, or even a change of priorities in the relation between attack and defense, would be an exaggeration.

F.u.G. had been somewhat ambiguous about the efficacy of fighting vehicles and the debate about the cavalry's future. *T.F.*, on the other hand, was more precise about the implications of motor vehicles. Even though the manual was far from assigning an operational significance to tanks, it did state, "Combat by the other arms must follow the fighting vehicles in their attack sectors."[98] That sentence freed the fighting vehicles for the first time from their dependence on the infantry, which went back to World War I thinking. Notwithstanding, the infantry remained the principal arm. The objective tied to combined arms combat was to deliver sufficient striking power and firepower against the enemy during an attack to bring about a decision. Tanks and the air force continued to have the task of supporting the infantry in the conduct of mobile combat operations.

T.F. did not answer the question of whether tanks should be used as slow and heavy weapons accompanying infantry, or as quick and mobile main weapons systems in independent formations.[99] In the later 1930s that problem would become the catalyst in the debate about the motorization of the German Army.

In accordance with classical German operational thinking, Beck's first sentence in *T.F.* postulated that military leadership was based on knowledge, practice, and intuition: "Warfare is an art, a free and creative activity founded on scientific principles."[100] Without overworking Schlieffen's remark about "Samuel's droplet of anointing oil," Beck too stressed that a senior commander must have an innate ability beyond rational consideration—a genius able to grasp situations by intuition and dominate the war as a personality through his "emotionally determined willpower."[101] As logic shows, however, it was not possible to lay down such capabilities in a written regulation.

Logically, this second effort to codify a doctrinal regulation for the basics of higher command was doomed from the start as well. The manual *Die höhere Truppenführung* (Higher Troop Leading) was supposed to be issued in 1931 as a complement to *T.F.* Major General (Ret.) Paul Schürmann submitted a first draft in September 1930 under the title *Gedanken über Krieg- und Truppenführung* (Thoughts About Warfare and Troop Leading). As he indicated, it was based on the "basic principles of higher-level military leadership" and on Hierl's earlier draft. Schürmann's draft, which copied entire passages verbatim from Hierl, was entirely in Schlieffen's spirit. Attack, surprise, envelopment, concentration of effort, and especially maneuver were the key points of focus. The passages on defense were rather meager. Schürmann granted that armored formations were an effective striking power. But despite their potential for independent commitment, he considered their function to be the support of infantry to achieve a breakthrough.

On the other hand, Schürmann attributed an important function to the cavalry in mobile warfare. In combination with other arms, it was even a decisive element in the outcome of battles—and the outcome of battles, according to Schürmann, was the objective of all operations. While he granted that the air force had some influence, his discussion of this "influence" took up no more than half a page. The Truppenamt criticized Schürmann for holding on to the "good old formulations of old regulations, as well as to Clausewitz, Moltke, and Schlieffen." Meanwhile, Major General (later Field Marshal) Walther von Brauchitsch, an expert commissioned by the director of the Army Training Department, said that the directive needed "more Schlieffen."[102] The Truppenamt, however, considered Schürmann's draft merely as a source of inspiration at best for a future doctrinal regulation.

That future document was never written, because in 1935 Beck as chief of the Truppenamt issued provisional orders to stop work on a doctrinal regulation for higher-level military leadership. Aside from the criticism of Schürmann's initial draft, another key factor contributing to that decision was the Truppenamt's conviction that operational leadership training should be continued through the Kriegsspiele and the leaders' staff rides. The following insight was decisive: "The famous anointing oil cannot be filled into bottles, nor can the qualities of being a commander in chief be cast into regulations."[103]

Mass Army and Offensive Army

When the National Socialists took power in 1933, the buildup of a mass military force that had been planned under Groener was already under way. At the same time, thinking started shifting slowly back to the attack, which, combined with a renaissance of the factors of will and morale, often went in step with National Socialist ideology.[104] The theory of total operational war was advocated repeatedly in literature, had been postulated as early as the Reichswehr era, and was then adopted by the Wehrmacht prior to World War II.[105] That theory, however, was not conclusive, nor was it corroborated by the key sources on operational thinking of the 1920s and 1930s. The discussion in Germany about the increasingly total nature of warfare started with the publication of Ludendorff's book *Der totale Krieg*, which indeed influenced Hitler's concepts of warfare. It did not, however, greatly influence operational thinking, because the idea was in no way militarily innovative.[106] Thus, Karl Linnebach in his study on war of annihilation postulated the political objective of war as "the destruction of an enemy state, or if need be, even the annihilation of the enemy's people."[107] These, however, were not operational but rather political requirements of warfare. By the start of World War II, German officers essentially associated total war with a combination of a national-totalitarian ideology and the strategic preparations of the war economy,[108] rather than ideological warfare as advocated by National Socialist dogma.[109] There was no connection at all to operational thinking. The army's leaders were thinking along the classical lines of the Kaiser's era. While the military critics accepted the increasingly total and unlimited nature of warfare as a given fact, they also discussed it as a problem related to a people's war. That type of war was introduced into the Truppenamt's operational thinking in only a limited way by Stülpnagel in the middle 1920s. But even in Stülpnagel's concept, the war in the final analysis was not won by means of a people's war, but as a consequence of operations by the regular army that waged a war of annihilation. The arms buildup that started after Hitler's seizure of power coincided with the interests of the Reichswehr's leaders. It also partially corresponded with their and the *Führer*'s objectives and served the purpose of being able to win a war of annihilation, whether initially on the defensive or subsequently on the offensive. The army's leaders did not anticipate or wish for, any influence exerted by the Führer on operations, let alone the element of political primacy vested in him personally. Corresponding to the two-pillar model, operational warfare was and remained the domain of the General Staff officers. The idea of the army and the military leadership was to remain in charge of the war on the battlefield, while the Führer and the party were to assure the home front's support for the war.

The arms buildup was essentially directed by the Truppenamt's chief, Beck, who was appointed to that office in October 1933. It was based on a threat perception that went back to the nineteenth century and which had been aggravated by the trauma of Germany's defeat in World War I. This "complex of fear," as Klaus-Jürgen Müller termed it, is reflected in Beck's assessment: "Our military situation demands the rapid elimination of our state of complete defenselessness. An attack by us must become our neighbors' risk."[110] The new political leaders and the generals also agreed to pursue a revisionist policy that restored Germany's Great Power status. The generals defined that status as essentially tantamount to military strength.

Beck, an "advocate of a conscript army controlled by the traditional military elite,"[111] considered the Reichsheer as the core of the future Wehrmacht. He rejected both the concept of a people's army, with a political-ideological orientation, as well as a militia force. Based on the Reichswehr's plans,[112] Beck's "December Program"[113] conceived a peacetime army of twenty-one divisions, totaling 300,000 soldiers.[114] This *Risiko-Heer* (risk army) would be capable of prosecuting a potentially successful defensive war on multiple fronts, which would deter potential enemies, and in so doing secure the continuing arms buildup.[115] In wartime the army would expand to sixty-seven divisions, to include a motorized light division, an armored formation, and corps-level support troops. With Hitler's approval, the buildup of the army started based on Beck's "December Program."

The buildup program had foreign and domestic policy implications, as well as an operational element. In the foreign policy area, the German arms buildup program was intended to alarm the other European Great Powers, even if the defensive character of that buildup only served to defend German territory during the years from 1933 to 1934.[116] In the domestic policy realm, the establishment of the new Wehrmacht was the task of the officer corps, not that of the Nazi Party's paramilitary *Sturmabteilungen*—the SA.[117] The command of the conscript army, therefore, lay with the old military elite, which protected its now outdated role as the nation's only organization under arms. From an operational perspective, replacing the militia and border troops with a two-tier Wehrmacht model as Stülpnagel had advocated was a decision in favor of classical operational doctrine. The decision against a mass military force was at the same time a decision against an elite military force such as Seeckt had advocated. The Truppenamt did not share Seeckt's conviction that operational leadership was possible only with a small elite force. Despite its defensive character, Beck's December Program, with its motorized light division and its armored formation, was the core of the offensive military force that would result from the first stage of the military buildup. Furthermore, Beck laid the foundations for the conduct of mobile operations as early as the end of 1934 with the establishment of the Inspectorate of Motorized Forces, the Panzer Experimental Formations, and the order to establish the Armored Forces.

The reintroduction of general conscription on 16 March 1935 supplied the manpower for an accelerated transformation from a defensive to an offensive military force capable of conducting a decisive offensive war.[118] The next stage in the buildup started in the autumn of 1935, following a proposal by the General Staff. (The Truppenamt had been redesignated the General Staff on 1 July 1935.) The objective was a peacetime army of thirty-six divisions, which in wartime would expand to seventy-three divisions. With a projected end-strength of 1.4 million to be reached in 1940–1942, the force would have almost as many personnel as the Kaiser's army. This accelerated buildup was in full synchronization with Hitler's war plans, but it disrupted the balance between a forced, quantity-focused buildup and a slow, continuous, quality-focused buildup. Owing to the shortage of strategic resources, Germany was only capable of conducting either a rapid, quantity-focused buildup without reserves and stable supplies or a slow, quality-focused buildup.

This question led to strong disagreement between the General Staff under Beck, who advocated a forced, quantity-focused arms buildup, and the *Allgemeinen Heeresamt* (General Army Office) under Colonel General Friedrich Fromm, who advocated a continuous arms buildup. The General Staff under Beck eventually won the conflict. This decision in favor of quantity over quality was fully consistent with the General Staff's thinking, which, as in Schlieffen's time, wanted to avoid a long war because of the Reich's shortage of resources and because the country's internal stability was not a sure thing. The General Staff wanted to win a short war through operational mobility.[119] They did not anticipate another long-drawn "world war of attrition," but rather a continental European war characterized by a rapid succession of attacks in Germany's border areas. Thus, the reinforcement of Germany's offensive power became the army's main preoccupation.

Beck consequently geared the army for a potential two-front offensive war that could be fought after the weakness imposed by the Versailles sanctions had been overcome. Fromm, based on the World War I experience, did not believe in the efficacy of offensive mobile warfare. He worried about the vulnerability of a high-tech spearhead without effective infantry support. For financial and economic reasons he criticized the accelerated arms buildup that he believed would overstress the Reich's resources. Fromm could not, however, overcome Beck's position. Thus, by the middle of the 1930s it was the chief of the General Staff and not the chief of the General Army Office who was in charge of rearmament. This was a change from the Schlieffen era. Despite all demands for mobility and the establishment of an armored force, the Wehrmacht essentially remained an infantry army. At the end of the planned arms buildup the German Army during the mobilization years 1940–1941 was supposed to have three armored divisions and three light motorized divisions. But it also would have seventy-two infantry divisions whose mobility, as in World War I, was defined by the infantryman's pace and the trot of the horse-drawn artillery.

What was the General Staff's idea about any future war after the phase of weakness of the first years of arms buildup had been overcome? As in the Kaiser's era, the waging of war was primarily the task of the army, and not the navy. The newly established Luftwaffe would support the army. Even if some army officers were convinced that the Luftwaffe should play an operationally significant role, the majority of officers held to the opinion that the Luftwaffe's primary mission should be support of the army on the battlefield once air superiority was achieved.[120] The Luftwaffe generally developed along those lines. Despite initial considerations for the establishment of a long-range aerial arm, by the mid-1930s the Luftwaffe had emerged as an efficient, offensive, medium-range aerial force to support the army. Although the Luftwaffe was also supposed to be capable of flying operational missions of its own, its main purpose was to support the army in ground combat. According to Horst Boog, the term "operation" had a different connotation for the Luftwaffe.[121] Despite the conception of the air force as a central support arm, the Luftwaffe's leadership also considered that the war against the enemy's centers of gravity was operational in nature.

By the middle of the 1930s the key elements of mobile warfare were defined as concentration of effort and envelopment, combined with breakthrough and surprise.[122] The coordination between separate army elements to achieve an envelopment was discussed not only at the General Staff level, but also in the military journals of the period. While Waldemar Erfurth openly favored envelopment,[123] M. Ludwig[124] and F. Lindemann[125] were rather skeptical about decisive envelopment operations. What remained unclear in the debate was the question of whether or not the breakthrough was a precondition for the envelopment, and how a tactical breakthrough could be forced and exploited into an operational breakthrough. Many critics considered the breakthrough separate from the envelopment, rather than distinct stages of one joint operation. At the same time, the Luftwaffe claimed that in mobile warfare the attack was henceforth only possible with aerial support, because the Luftwaffe alone was able to attack the enemy through a vertical envelopment.[126]

Several different sources allow us to reconstruct the General Staff's concept of warfare in the middle 1930s, despite the fact that many of the records were lost during World War II. There was unanimity about the idea that Germany needed a mass military force based on conscription to advance its Great Power claims. Seeckt's operational doctrine, based on a small, technically sophisticated professional army executing a "lightning-like" war was rejected as unreasonable and impractical for any war to come. As Lieutenant Colonel Gerhard Matzky noted during a lecture at the Wehrmacht Academy in 1935, it had not been the mass military force itself that was responsible for Germany's defeat during the Great War, but rather the poor leaders who had been unable to shape and command that mass military force.[127] In accordance with the practice that had been in vogue for years of laying personal blame on specific individuals, Matzky argued that all that was necessary for success in war was improved operational command combined with the application of mobility assets. Logically, the introduction of armored vehicles and aircraft was necessary for warfare. Matzky emphasized air superiority in particular as a decisive factor and a key objective for future warfare.[128]

There also was unanimity of thought that a future war would have to be quick and decisive. Therefore, a rapid offensive on the enemy's territory with the objective of a speedy battle of annihilation was an essential goal, although defense would play a more important role than it had during the era prior to World War I. The study *Der künftige Krieg nach den Ansichten des Auslandes* (The Future War in the View of Foreign Countries)[129] was conducted for the chief of the Army Command by Colonel Carl-Heinrich von Stülpnagel, the director of the Foreign Armies Division at the Truppenamt. Stülpnagel was a close colleague of Beck. From that study we can derive insights into the Truppenamt's concept of the conduct of operations, and also how it tried to win support for its arms buildup initiatives. At the very beginning Stülpnagel echoed Beck's arguments for a high-priority arms buildup that would result in the ability to conduct initial operations before the enemy's armaments industry could gear up. "For states with little raw material supplies and a wartime industry that cannot evolve very fast, the compulsion to conduct this kind of war is especially strong. A determined initial [offensive] operation will easily break through the enemy's presumably weak border security. . . . This solution, therefore, is unanimously considered the type of modern warfare to be sought."[130]

The attack was to be conducted by a thrust into the enemy's rear and flank. It would be preceded, if necessary, by a breakthrough that would be successively exploited into an operational envelopment. Concentration of effort and surprise were emphasized as the core elements of operational warfare, augmented by motorization on the battlefield and in the air. The combat posture during the deployment was supposed to facilitate rapid and situation-specific regrouping. Mobile warfare with a mass military force was possible, it was argued, only with high-quality *Sonderverbänden* (Special Forces), under which Stülpnagel included all motorized formations.[131] Thus, not small, high-quality armies, but modern mass military forces were the backbone of the future war, but it was essential that those armies be mobile. Stülpnagel did go one decisive step beyond classical German operational thinking. For him, the primary objective of operational action was no longer the annihilation of the enemy force, but rather the annihilation of the enemy's centers of gravity and "the destruction of the enemy people."[132] The term "annihilation," however, was not meant in the physical sense of the word, but rather the annihilation of the people's ability to wage war.

Operational command of rapid formations also was the theme of a lecture given by Lieutenant Colonel Willi Schneckenburger at the Wehrmacht Academy in February 1936.[133] He identified highly mobile formations as the indispensable means for the conduct of the German style of warfare on interior lines. Combined with the Luftwaffe, he argued, such forces were able to make quick concentrations of effort resulting in decisive combat action. According to Schneckenburger, the most important elements of operational warfare were "surprise, speed, the ruthless breakthrough or envelopment of newly forming defensive lines, the massive use of fighting vehicles against the deep flank and the rear of the enemy, the rapid transfer of supplies, and coordination with superior aerial forces."[134]

All three officers unanimously advocated the return to a mass military force. At the same time, they emphasized the importance of the Luftwaffe, and especially of motorized units for the conduct of mobile operational warfare. There was, however, disagreement on the precise use of motorized formations, especially the armored units of the future.

The army's officer corps had for years been engaged in a highly controversial debate over whether tanks were auxiliary weapons of the infantry or should be used operationally in armored formations. That debate spilled over into the contemporary media. The specialized literature to this day links that debate in a very imperfect way to the names of Guderian as the promoter and Beck as the opponent of the operational use of tanks. Before we take a closer look at that dispute, which is the source of legends, it is necessary to take a very brief look at the discussion on the use of tanks within the informed public sector.

Bernhardi had discussed the significance of tanks in mobile warfare of the future only a few years after the end of World War I.[135] Since the Reichsheer was not allowed to have tanks, the German military journals of the period enthusiastically reported both the French thinking that regarded tanks as infantry support weapons, and therefore preferred heavy but immobile tanks, and also the British ideas that favored lightweight and medium-sized tanks committed in independent formations.[136] The significance of tanks for mobile warfare was first discussed by Guderian in a 1927 article titled "Bewegliche Truppenkörper" (Mobile Troop Elements). Referring to the British position, Guderian argued that World War I had demonstrated that the infantry and cavalry did not have enough striking power relative to the firepower of modern defensive weapons, and therefore were incapable of achieving a rapid decision through force of arms. Such a decision, however, could be achieved by fighting vehicles in combination with aircraft. Guderian thus argued in favor of an independently deployed fighting vehicle formation supported by air forces. As Guderian wrote:

> Never before, and as far back as anyone can remember, has mobility been so promising as now in the time of the [internal combustion] engine and the radio. The technological advances virtually force themselves upon the soldier. Therefore, we can by no means believe that positional warfare will be the style of the fighting of the future. Rather, we are going to do our utmost to compensate for the lack of numbers and military equipment with mobility. We must try to penetrate the secrets of mobile warfare, and not just in the ordinary, but the extraordinarily mobile warfare—the war of surprising means, of the full use of the plentiful technical tools of our time.[137]

Years before the Wehrmacht had tanks of its own, Guderian with those words explained the potential tanks offered for an operational doctrine that was geared toward rapid decisions. Were tanks the means of mobile warfare that World War I lacked, and which in the future would make it possible to realize operational doctrine—a doctrine that was still regarded as correct? That question was answered in the affirmative by almost all officers who dealt with the subject over the course of the following years. But the debate still continued fiercely over the essential question of whether tanks should be used as infantry support or in operationally independent armored formations.

Fromm, the chief of the General Army Office, argued in favor of strengthening the classical infantry component. He was convinced that tanks served the infantry best by making it possible for the latter to break into the enemy's system of positions. For Fromm, the armored formations, like the artillery, were essentially infantry support arms used for limited counterthrusts.[138] Fromm was not alone in that opinion. The *Organisationsabteilung* (Organizational Division) of the Army General Staff also was convinced that the infantry would be the main arm of a future war, and that armored formations were only an expedient that, when committed en masse, could in certain cases force the decision of the battle.[139] George Soldan also favored the tactical adaptation of tanks to the infantry. He thought that the operational use of tanks was a logical exception, although he favored coordination with the infantry. Soldan, therefore, thought it wrong to orient the actions of the other arms on the operational use of tanks.[140]

Other officers, such as Guderian, Walther Nehring (who was later a general of Panzer troops), and Walter Spannenkrebs (who later became a major general), advocated the operational use of tanks. Based on observations of foreign armies, the experience from the war, and their own ideas, they developed a tactical-operational concept for the operational use of tanks.[141] That concept was based on the Stormtroop and battle group tactics that the Germans had developed and used successfully in World War I.[142] The basic elements of such tactics were speed and surprise, in conformance with traditional German operational thinking.[143] Tanks were not to be dispersed; rather, when concentrated for a tactical assault in large numbers they could lead to an operational decision. The Panzer arm was to force the breakthrough principally with support from the Luftwaffe, engineers, motorized infantry, and artillery. Owing to its own striking power in a combined arms battle, the Panzer arm could operate detached from the infantry's slower assault tempo. The requirements for success were concentration of effort, suitable terrain, surprise, and the commitment of large numbers in sufficient depth and breadth. The primary targets of the tank assault were the enemy's antitank defenses, artillery, reserves, and command and control centers throughout the depth of the defensive zone. After the successful breakthrough, Panzer divisions that were combined in an armored corps were to move against the enemy's flank and rear and conduct envelopment operations to achieve the decision of the battle.[144] As Nehring postulated the expectations for the operational use of tanks: "Rapid armored formations combined with strong air forces will be efficient weapons of war. It follows that such formations can be entrusted with the execution of independent operational tasks."[145]

General Carl-Heinrich
von Stülpnagel.
BArch/183-R63893.

Reich Chancellor Adolf Hitler in conversation with Reichswehr Minister Werner von Blomberg and Propaganda Minister Dr. Goebbels in 1934. *Bild 102-00765.*

Colonel General Werner Freiherr von Fritsch, commander in chief of the German Army, and General Ludwig Beck, chief of the Army General Staff, during maneuvers in Mecklenburg in 1937. Photographer: Oscar Tellgmann. *BArch/136-B3516.*

The development of the operational use of tanks, however, was not the work of Guderian alone, based on the influence of Basil Liddell Hart.[146] Rather, it was the product of a group of many officers,[147] in contrast to what for decades has been reported in the historical literature about the German Panzer forces.[148] Austria's General Ludwig Ritter von Eimannsberger deserves special mention here. He was one of the first to postulate the operational use of armored formations in his unpublished book, summarizing the future use of tanks with the following words:

> My theory is based on the operational use of tanks as main weapons systems. The Panzer division is a new operational unit composed of all arms, albeit with the armored vehicle as the main weapon. For the operational breakthrough, the motorized division will coordinate with the Panzer division and dislocate [the enemy's] antitank forces. [My] book advocates the close cooperation between armored vehicles and aircraft.[149]

Eimannsberger's manuscript largely influenced Guderian's ideas about the operational use of tanks.[150] While James Corum admits that Guderian exerted an evident influence on the development of tank operational doctrine, he also notes that the latter, like Ludendorff, was a complete egoist and self-promoter. "If Guderian had been a modest man and never written a word about himself, he would have gone down in history as an excellent general, a first-rate tactician, and a man who played a central role in establishing and developing the first Panzer divisions. But Guderian was far from modest."[151]

Guderian's often repeated claim that he had to force the acceptance of the operational use of tanks against the opposition of the traditionalist group around Beck in the General Staff has not held up under more current studies.[152] In his most recent study on Beck, Klaus-Jürgen Müller disproves once and for all the legend that Beck had not recognized the significance of operational armored forces, and that he had opposed on principle the establishment of the Panzer Force.[153] Müller explains the friction between Beck and Guderian in terms of the disagreements within the military leadership itself, and the deep personal antipathy between both officers. According to Müller, Beck in his memoranda had called for even more tanks than did Guderian, and had been open to the operational use of tanks as a weapons system. Beck, after all, had worked for the accelerated establishment of an offensive-capable military force, one whose core was supposed to be a strong, operationally oriented tank element. Beck did not support the early establishment of single-arm Panzer divisions as advocated by Guderian. Rather, Beck supported the option of establishing combined armored and motorized formations, as advocated by his deputy chief of staff, Major General (later Field Marshal) Erich von Manstein.[154] Looking back at the 1935 Truppenamt staff ride, Beck clearly criticized the incorrect use of the armored corps. He spoke in favor of making the Panzer divisions that would be used for the first phase of the attack subordinate to the infantry. At the same time, Beck in his final summary emphasized that the high value of the Panzer divisions lay "in the envelopment toward the flank and the rear or against front lines, where they have the mission of exploiting success already achieved—that is, turning a break-in into a breakthrough."[155]

Nevertheless, Beck over the course of time became more and more inclined toward the establishment of modern Panzer divisions. Thus, in January 1936 Beck, as a proponent of a "multi-functional, flexible branch structure," logically and flatly rejected the General Army Office's idea to use tanks as infantry auxiliary weapons, advocating instead the establishment of battalions consisting of forty-eight fighting vehicles.[156] The requirement for mobility also influenced the tanks' overall design parameters. In contrast to France, therefore, Germany developed fast and lightweight tanks.[157] Despite all the technical progress, one constant factor of German military thinking remained unchanged: the conviction that it was not technology, but rather psychological and moral factors that decided the final outcome of war, and that they would make German victories possible in situations where Germany was inferior in terms of manpower and materiel.[158]

Fromm's was just one of several critical voices who argued against adopting an exaggerated and one-sided offensive posture, while neglecting the defensive as Germany had before 1914. The officer corps was not at all unanimous about operational issues. General of Artillery (later Field Marshal) Wilhelm Ritter von Leeb warned against adopting an overly doctrinaire concept of attack. The controversy was argued openly in the pages of *Militärwissenschaftliche Rundschau,* culminating in 1936 with Beck forbidding the journal from printing further contributions by Guderian.[159] That gave Leeb the opportunity to lay out his ideas in a series of individual articles that were later published in book form as *Die Abwehr* (The Defensive).[160] Leeb considered the defense to be an important and very valuable method of warfare because of the Reich's geographic position and its inferiority compared to its potential enemies. He continued to argue that the importance of defense had increased dramatically since the Great War, and that the increased weapons effects opened up new operational and tactical opportunities for the successful conduct of combat. While defense alone did not produce success in an absolute war,[161] it made possible the concentration of effort through delaying resistance and, in combination with the advantages of interior lines, the effort to achieve a decision. To secure one's own mobility, Leeb advocated a defensive area with a pronounced disposition in depth. Delaying tactics would be used in the initial fighting. Leeb also placed great importance on antitank defenses in depth. Counterattacks would be conducted by motorized reserves and tanks.

Leeb expanded the mobile defense concept of World War I by integrating tanks. The combination of delay and defense in a defensive zone of great depth was his answer to attack by rapid armored formations. Although Leeb thought that the attack was more consistent with a soldier's basic nature than defense, his line of argument culminated with the warning: "[The defense] must not be pushed into the background, as before the [world] war, rather it must be given due importance in the training and education of leaders and the forces as a reflection of our political and military situation."[162]

Leeb's appeal fell on deaf ears at the time. The traditional idea of winning a war through rapid offensives prevailed. Any doubts about this concept were suppressed at the highest command levels. Thus, the commander in chief of the army, Colonel General Werner Freiherr von Fritsch, wrote in the introduction to the third edition of Schlieffen's *Cannae*: "Today, it is generally recognized that the concept of annihilation itself was not wrong, but that it was the insufficient means through which it was attempted that was the cause of failure."[163]

Thus, the operational concept remained the same. The only thing that changed was the execution at the tactical-operational level. Motorization made that possible. The elements of the attack—fire and maneuver—which had been separate during World War I, were now combined in tanks, thus providing the means to overcome positional warfare through rapid and decisive operations. Tanks were the element of mobile warfare that had been missing in World War I.

Planning, War Games, and Studies

Operational plans changed when the Reichswehr was transformed into the Wehrmacht. The purpose of the military was no longer defense against an enemy attack or the use of the armed force at a favorable moment; rather, the purpose of the Wehrmacht was the offensive conduct of a continental, multi-front war. The years from 1935 to 1937 were a period of overall economic crisis and change in the foreign policy state of affairs, both of which were caused by the deliberate military buildup. It also was during that period that the army's operational plans finally reached their decisive level of development. Logically, the plans were oriented on the real political conditions. As a consequence of the German-Polish Non-Aggression Pact of 26 January 1934, the *Wehrmachtskriegsspiel* (Wehrmacht war game) of January 1934 was the last one that was based on the threat of a two-front war with Poland and France.[164]

As the army built up, the General Staff's level of expectation expanded from the planning of a sanction-based Central European war, to a pan-European, multi-front war. Now it was no longer the states of eastern Central Europe, but the Great Powers of France and the Soviet Union that became the focus of operational planning for a classical two-front war. This was also a reaction to the Soviet-French-Czech alliance treaties of May 1935. Concrete plans against a Russian attack or a German offensive against the Soviet Union were, however, not worked out while a potential two-front war was played through in the Kriegsspiele and studies.

Thus, in May 1935, in answer to a request from the *Wehrmachtamt* (Armed Forces Office), the General Staff's *Abteilung Fremde Heer* (Foreign Armies Division) analyzed the scenario of a two-front war against France and the Soviet Union, with Poland remaining politically neutral. The Russian attack was anticipated to come through Czechoslovakia or via Lithuania and Romania. In that same year and under the assumption of a similar scenario, *Wehrkreis* I (Defense District I) in East Prussia played through a preemptive attack on Lithuania designed to thwart a Soviet attack. Deeply rooted in classical operational thinking, the war gamers emphasized speed and surprise, and especially the initiation of the war without warning,[165] as the criteria for success.[166]

As the Wehrmacht grew, the General Staff's operational options increased accordingly. Offensive operational possibilities and long-term operational planning expanded during those years. The use of the delaying resistance and a subsequent counteroffensive, as played in the Wehrmachtskriegsspiel of 1934, were no longer emphasized. The focus of the defensive area shifted to the west, along what was known as the Roer–Rhine–Black Forest line, with the objective of securing the strategically important armaments-producing areas and containing the enemy. The General Staff also used Kriegsspiele and studies to plan the buildup systematically from 1935 onward. The objective was always the culmination of the military buildup in 1940–1941.[167]

War Minister Blomberg fixed the plans for the next few years in the *Weisung für die einheitliche Kriegsvorbereitung der Wehrmacht* (Directive for Standard War Preparations of the Wehrmacht), issued on 24 June 1937. The focus of the major European powers at that point had shifted from the center to the periphery because of the Spanish Civil War, Italy's continued expansionism in East Africa, and continued Japanese aggression in China. That shift left Germany greater freedom of action. Blomberg noted that even if there was no imminent danger of war, and even if Germany was not planning a war, it was nonetheless important to be prepared for every contingency, and if necessary, to be able to exploit a politically favorable situation.

In addition to a few specific instances, such as *Fall OTTO* (Case OTTO—the invasion of Austria), the directive described a pair of two-front war scenarios for which preparations had to be made. *Fall ROT* (Case RED) was a two-front war against France on the one hand, and against Czechoslovakia and the Soviet Union on the other. In the west, the French offensive was to be blocked by mobile forces on the Roer–Rhine–Black Forest line. *Fall GRÜN* was based on the same scenario as *Fall ROT,* with the sole difference that the imminent attack by the enemy coalition would be preempted by a surprise attack on Czechoslovakia. The operational objective was the quick destruction of the Czech armed forces and the occupation of Bohemia and Moravia. The strategic purpose was to eliminate early on the threat in the rear to the campaign in the west by taking out the airbases the

Soviet Union could use for attacking Germany. It was explicitly emphasized, however, that the political and international legal requirements had to be met prior to launching any attack.

Blomberg's directive alone was clearly offensive in nature. The discussion was no longer about self-defense, but about a potential multi-front war that the Wehrmacht would prosecute offensively. It was, however, no master plan comparable to Schlieffen's. The directive left open all the imaginably possible options for war in the east and in the west. What was lacking was a strategic-operational framework for the conduct of the attacks in the west and east. Thus, Blomberg's directive was no new version of the Schlieffen Plan; rather, it was based on the operational mobility available to Germany's military leadership. The establishment of the West Wall defensive line that could be held with a small number of forces, however, gives rise to the conclusion that Hitler was primarily interested in an offensive in the east.

Although France was considered to be the main enemy of a future war, Czechoslovakia repeatedly was at the center of the operational planning for a potential two-front war. Over the years the General Staff drafted several studies and operational plans for an invasion of Czechoslovakia as part of a Central European conflict. In the spring of 1935 Beck played through a concentric counteroffensive against Czechoslovakia as a component of a two-front war. The proposed solutions revealed differing views about the chances of success of a war against Czechoslovakia. Manstein, in agreement with Beck, was rather skeptical about the prospect of a rapid German offensive operation against mobilized Czech forces. Other participants in the exercise, much to Beck's chagrin, concluded that the prospects were good for a quick and decisive operation.[168]

This particular Truppenamt staff ride showed that while there was a basic consensus on operational thinking among the leading officers, they assessed the prospects of success and the specifics of the execution quite differently. Those responsible for operations were by no means a monolithic block.

The extension of the French and German fortification networks along the German western border, along with the *Anschluss* (annexation) of Austria in 1938, changed the strategic situations of the Reich and of Czechoslovakia. The General Staff now no longer anticipated a French surprise attack, but rather a deliberate offensive following French mobilization. The General Staff assessed the greatest risk to be a French attack into southwestern Germany, across the Rhine and then thrusting toward the Czech border. The plan to counter such a move was to mount a delaying resistance, and then destroy the advancing French forces through a major operational counterattack into the French flank, somewhere in the area between Heilbronn and Würzburg.

Beck intensified operational planning for a war against Czechoslovakia based on Blomberg's 1937 directive and its amendment issued that December, which postulated war only after the Wehrmacht reached full operational readiness, and only if a premature two-front war—which Germany could not have won at the time—could be avoided. The 1938 Truppenamt staff ride was planned to simulate a period of several months and was conducted largely as a written exercise. Beck gave it the classified name *Führung eines Angriffskrieges gegen die Tschechoslowakie einschliesslich Aufmarsch* (Offensive War Against Czechoslovakia Including Deployment.)[169] The scenario was based on a multi-front war. In coordination with Hungary as an ally, the attack against the Czech Army was launched concentrically, with the deployment logically coming from the west. The objective of the operation was the destruction of the Czech armed forces. All mobile formations were committed to the operation.[170] The Luftwaffe had the mission of disrupting the Czech deployment and supporting Germany's forces.

Beck, like Hitler, advocated a "solution to the Czech problem," albeit not at the price of a continental war. Even during the war game Beck began to adapt the operational plans against Czechoslovakia to the new situation that existed after the Austrian Anschluss. When Hitler stated that it was his "unconditional will" to break Czechoslovakia apart and ordered preparations for a military action in a 30 May 1938 amendment to the *Fall GRÜN* directive, Beck warned against a long war that Germany could not win. Contrary to Beck's convictions, however, the result of the war game indicated that the Western Front could repel a French attack for more than fourteen days without support, and that Germany could win a war against Czechoslovakia during that time.[171] That result also confirmed the conviction held by the commander in chief of the army and many other General Staff officers that Germany was able to fight a successful two-front war.[172] Beck did not share that assessment and he resigned on 18 August 1938, after first having voiced his contrary opinion in several memoranda.

Later in 1938 the Munich Agreement resulted in the peaceful annexation of the Sudetenland into Greater Germany. As a result, the question of the Wehrmacht's ability to achieve rapid operational success against the Czech Army in a two-front war during the summer of 1938 remained unanswered.

While the General Staff's operational planning was proceeding, the army's commanders intensified operational training and advanced the training of the General Staff officers in every respect.[173] All the studies, war games, and operational plans made during the years before the start of World War II emphasized classical operational thinking in the form of the attack against a superior enemy, with a clear concentration of effort and particular emphasis on coordination with the Luftwaffe in support of the army.[174] The role played by the commanders and the significance of the art of operational leadership was emphasized repeatedly. During the final discussion of the VI Army Corps' 1938 General Staff ride, the commanding general, Major General Georg von Sodenstern, commented on operational leadership:

I am speaking of an art, for indeed, soldiers become artists in long-range operations! Only few attain the level of artistic skill. Often they suffer the hard fate of Count Schlieffen, which then becomes their people's fate too. They do not get the chance to prove their skills, and they have to entrust weak hands with their tremendous intellectual legacy. Few are those who acquire more than the ordinary technical knowledge of the General Staff. Few are those who, with visionary eyes, anticipate the enemy's actions, as Hannibal once did at Carthage, and have that enemy march into the iron grip of their enveloping wings. They are the ones about whom the late General von Seeckt once said that they knew about "last things."[175]

A few years before the start of World War II, every German General Staff officer knew that although modern weapons technology was important, in the end it would be the leader who would decide victory or defeat.

The Conflict Over Senior-Level Organization

Shortly after the end of World War I, criticism of the inadequate command structure before and during the war was raised in conjunction with the personalization of the guilt for losing the war. Even though in the Weimar Republic changes to the senior-level organization that had been prescribed by the Treaty of Versailles were only possible to a limited degree, the Reichswehr as early as in the 1920s started considering the development of a comprehensive command and control organization for the entire armed forces in any future war—a *Wehrmachtführungsstab* (Wehrmacht Operations Staff).[176]

Groener and General Kurt Schleicher initiated the process of establishing an integrated Wehrmacht leadership. After Hitler seized power, that process was continued by Blomberg as the Wehrmacht's commander in chief, with the objective of centralizing functions and power. The Wehrmacht war games initiated by Blomberg also served the same purpose. Thus, thought was given in the 1934 Wehrmacht war game to the powers of the senior political and military leadership in time of war. The side of the blue forces was played by the chief of the Wehrmacht supported by a Wehrmacht staff. That staff included an operations division that executed the decisions made by the German War Cabinet and issued the relevant strategic directives to the chiefs of the Naval and Army Commands and to the Luftwaffe.[177] The Army Command, however, did not concur with those ideas. The army's leadership believed that any future war would be a continental European land war, and logically the army leadership should be responsible for operational planning and the command and control of overall operations. The struggle to establish the senior-level organization, therefore, was not only a struggle to maintain the historical identity of the General Staff within the German armed forces,

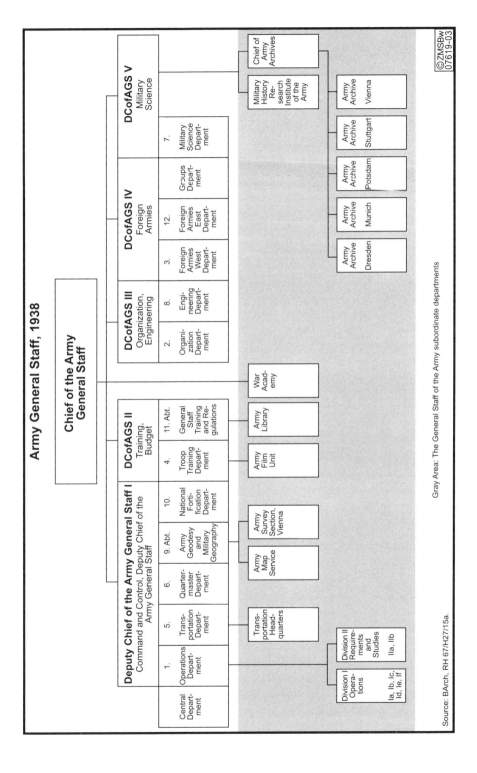

Army General Staff, 1938

Chief of the Army General Staff

Deputy Chief of the Army General Staff I
Command and Control, Deputy Chief of the Army General Staff

1. Operations Department	5. Transportation Department	6. Quartermaster Department	9. Abt. Army Geodesy and Military Geography	10. National Fortification Department

- Central Department
- Division I Operations — Ia, Ib, Ic, Id, Ie, If
- Division II Requirements and Studies — IIa, IIb
- Transportation Headquarters
- Army Map Service
- Army Survey Section, Vienna

DCofAGS II
Training, Budget

4. Troop Training Department	11. Abt. General Staff Training and Regulations

- Army Film Unit
- Army Library
- War Academy

DCofAGS III
Organization, Engineering

2. Organization Department	8. Engineering Department

DCofAGS IV
Foreign Armies

3. Foreign Armies West Department	12. Foreign Armies East Department	Groups Department

DCofAGS V
Military Science

7. Military Science Department

- Military History Research Institute of the Army
- Chief of Army Archives
  - Army Archive Dresden
  - Army Archive Munich
  - Army Archive Potsdam
  - Army Archive Stuttgart
  - Army Archive Vienna

Gray Area: The General Staff of the Army subordinate departments

Source: BArch, RH 67/H27/15a.

©ZMSBw
07619-03

but also Beck's attempt to prevent the intervention of politics into operations, which based on his convictions was the exclusive domain of the General Staff.

The General Staff found itself on the defensive from the very beginning in this "multi-front conflict." The decision to establish the Luftwaffe as the third independent branch of the Wehrmacht and to transfer the responsibility for operational air war to the newly established Luftwaffe General Staff caused the Army General Staff to lose immediate access to the aerial assets, but it also diluted its exclusivity as a "German General Staff." The leading position of the Army General Staff, hitherto undisputed within the Reich's military structure, was challenged from the very beginning by the Luftwaffe's commander in chief, Hermann Göring. Contrary to the officers of the Army General Staff, Göring also held many of the highest offices of the state and the National Socialist German Workers' Party. The threat to the position of the Army General Staff as the decision maker in operational matters resulted from the combination of Göring's political and military authority, coupled with his thirst for power. That threat, however, was underestimated at first. The officers in the Army General Staff had been brought up in the traditional ways of thinking, and they considered themselves as the only ones truly qualified to make and execute operational decisions. They initially underestimated the new Luftwaffe General Staff and they looked down on the new organization with a certain degree of arrogance, although its members were recruited from the Army General Staff itself. Clinging entirely to their continental thinking, the Army General Staff officers were convinced that the Luftwaffe was merely an auxiliary arm of the army. The Luftwaffe General Staff, however, started thinking along Wehrmacht lines early on, not the least as a result of their doctrine of operational air war. In contrast, the Army General Staff as a functional elite continued to focus on the operational-strategic aspects of warfare. The Army General Staff officers received only cursory training, if any at all, in strategy. Nonetheless, there was common agreement within the General Staff that under no circumstances would any more powers be ceded to any newly established Wehrmacht leadership.

Beck was generally off the mark when he equated the General Staff of the 1930s with the Great General Staff of the Kaiser's era. The position of chief of the Army General Staff that emerged after the renunciation of the Versailles Treaty did not have the powers that Schlieffen had had. He had no command authority, either in peace or in war. In contrast to his predecessors, he was merely the principal advisor and assistant to the commander in chief of the army, and did not have direct access to the head of state. However, as the deputy of the commander in chief of the army, the chief of the General Staff held a dominant position in the military hierarchy owing to the broad range of his functions. In addition to the education and training of General Staff officers, he was entrusted with all planning and preparations for operational land warfare and national defense. Within the General Staff, the Operations Division was the prominent element.[178]

Blomberg's 2 May 1935 directive to the General Staff to prepare an operational study for a surprise attack on Czechoslovakia triggered an escalation in the dispute over the Wehrmacht's senior-level organization.[179] Even though Blomberg and the Wehrmachtamt (Armed Forces Office)—the new designation of the former *Ministeramt* (Ministerial Office)—confirmed the significance of the army in relation to the Luftwaffe and the navy, there was still a considerable mistrust of the Wehrmachtamt's ideas, particularly in the Army General Staff under Beck. Beck, who kept comparing the Army General Staff to the old Great General Staff, was not ready to relinquish the reins of the General Staff's original function of operational planning. This was particularly so because, as opposed to the old Great General Staff, the current General Staff now had to function under a commander in chief of the army.

In several memoranda written over the following years, Beck and the army commander in chief, Colonel General Werner Freiherr von Fritsch, argued against Blomberg's efforts to establish a central Wehrmacht leadership. In the course of this dispute Fritsch in 1937 called for the "establishment of a comprehensive agreement on operational *Gesamtkriegführung* (conduct of overall warfare) by delegating to the Army High Command the authority to process all relevant proposals."[180] Beck and Fritsch did succeed in blocking Blomberg's plans to establish a Wehrmacht General Staff and to take over the command and control of Wehrmacht maneuvers. They also managed to undermine the Wehrmacht Academy that Blomberg had established by boycotting it to such a degree that it closed in 1938. They were not, however, able to push through their principal initiative that would establish the commander in chief of the army as the primary advisor to the commander in chief of the Wehrmacht on all key issues of overall warfare. Thus, General Wilhelm Keitel, chief of the Wehrmachtamt in the Ministry of the Reichswehr, in his 19 April 1938 memorandum "Die Kriegsführung als Problem der Organisation" (Warfare as an Organizational Problem), emphasized the specific warfighting importance of the army for Germany's continental power. By no means, however, did Keitel indicate a primacy in favor of the army. He argued that none of the branches of the Wehrmacht could be entrusted with the command and control of overall warfare from the beginning of hostilities.[181] Only an *Oberkommando der Wehrmacht* (Wehrmacht High Command) would be capable of doing so, he argued.

At first glance, the issue of the senior-level organization, and thus the question of operational command and control, was resolved according to Blomberg's desired solution when Hitler assumed direct command of the Wehrmacht and the dictator himself took over the positions of the "Reich War Minister and Commander in Chief of the *Wehrmacht*." He did that in 1938 immediately after Blomberg's dismissal resulting from the Blomberg-Fritsch Affair. At that point the Wehrmacht lost its effective independence. The functions of the Ministry of the

Reichswehr were taken over by the High Commands of the Luftwaffe, Navy and Army, as well as by the Oberkommando der Wehrmacht, which all were directly subordinate to Hitler.[182]

Political and military power was now concentrated in one hand, even more strongly than it had been during the Kaiser's Reich. Such a concentration of power had been called for often during the interwar period, harkening back to the era of Frederick the Great. The new result, however, was still inadequate for the tremendously increased tasks of modern warfare. War as an event that affected society as a whole had grown in complexity to the degree that it could no longer be controlled by only one person. One solution to that problem might have been an institutional separation of the military and political leadership under the principle of the primacy of politics, combined with the establishment of a central warfighting command authority over all the Wehrmacht's services. What happened instead was just as in the period of the Kaiser's Reich: a large number of agencies immediately subordinate to Hitler evolved and competed with each other, and at times even worked against each other.[183]

With the emergence of the Oberkommando der Wehrmacht (OKW) from the Wehrmachtamt, Hitler created for himself a personal military staff led by General Wilhelm Keitel, who assumed the ministerial functions of the former Reich war minister. Keitel, however, only exercised command authority on behalf of Hitler. OKW was not a unified command and control warfighting organization as its name suggested. Within OKW, operational and strategic planning was conducted by the *Wehrmachtführungsamt* (Wehrmacht Operations Office).[184] Its chief, Colonel (later Colonel General) Alfred Jodl, had direct access to Hitler and increasingly rose to become his real primary military advisor during the war. However, the *Abteilung Landesverteidigung* (National Defense Branch) of the Wehrmacht Operations Office never was a Wehrmacht General Staff. The three services of the Wehrmacht, each of which had an assistant branch chief in the Abteilung Landesverteidigung, knew how to prevent this from happening.

Despite the rejection of the army commanders' claims to leadership, the chiefs of the three Wehrmacht services and their General Staffs retained far-ranging powers, particularly in operational areas. At the beginning of the war in 1939, the Wehrmacht was far from conducting unified operational warfare. The dispute over the senior-level organization had broad consequences for the officer corps. Beck, for example, prohibited his officers from having official contact with OKW, while within OKW the Army General Staff was regarded as a bastion of the classical Prussian traditions, whose only objective was to preserve its antiquated social status privileges. The Oberkommando des Heeres (Army High Command—OKH) perceived the Wehrmacht High Command as a threat to the army's constitutional position within the Reich. There is where the gap opened between the conservative OKH and the Nazi revolutionary officers in OKW. That gap only continued to widen throughout World War II. The personal fallout from this conflict caused divisions in the officer corps and allowed Hitler to play the respective parties off against each other.[185]

Hitler's accumulation of military offices, however, did not result in the clearly structured senior-level organization of the Wehrmacht that many had advocated during the interwar period, as based on the experiences of World War I. This resulted on the one hand from the diverging power interests of the Wehrmacht services, and on the other hand from Hitler, who quite in the spirit of the poly-cratic "Führer State," exploited the conflicting interests and power struggles by stoking the competition over roles and missions to strengthen his own position of power. Not the least owing to internal military power struggles, therefore, Germany entered World War II just as it had World War I, without a functioning political-military organization at the senior-most level.

Conclusion

Despite the territorial cessions and the military and economic sanctions of the Treaty of Versailles, Germany was still a potential Great Power, even after its defeat in World War I. The reclaiming of Great Power status was, therefore, an indispensable objective of the Reich's military elite.[186] That would be achieved by means of classic power politics, as "in the days of the Kaiser," and if necessary, even with the use of military force. Compared to Germany's pre–World War I situation, however, the level of the Reich's manpower and materiel inferiority had been dramatically exacerbated. The Reichsheer only had one hundred thousand soldiers. Conscription, tanks, and aircraft were prohibited. But the war had proved that Schlieffen was right on at least one point: Germany was not able to win a lengthy war of attrition. The attempt to compensate for inferiority of resources with tactical-operational innovations had also failed. The recognition of this truth should have resulted in the abandonment of Great Power politics based on military might. Such, however, was inconceivable for Germany's military elite.

Furthermore, even after the lost war the issue of including political considerations in the conduct of operations was anathema for those officers who had been raised and socialized apolitically. The development of a modern strategic framework consistent with the primacy of politics as the controlling factor of warfare was unimaginable to that officer corps. Unwaveringly, German officers clung to the principle of conducting military operations free of political influence. The operational level of warfare was and would remain the exclusive domain of the military. Despite the defeat in World War I, there was no question that the military had a grasp on the correct leadership concept in the form of German operational thinking.

In an effort to prepare for future wars, the operations experts continued to try "to pour new wine into old wineskins" by finding means and approaches for a war against a superior coalition of enemies. Thus, the selective evaluation of the wartime experiences that started immediately after the end of World War I almost inevitably led to the confirmation of the principles of mobile operational warfare and the primacy of the attack, concepts basically unchanged from before the war. The inconsistent application of those principles, combined with leadership failures and the watering down of the Schlieffen Plan, the neglect of technique, and finally the *Dolchstoss* (dagger thrust) right at the end of the war were identified as reasons for Germany's defeat. Because operational warfare was seen in Germany as an art, and the commander was considered an artist, the personalization of the guilt for the loss of the war guaranteed that the operational doctrine itself would not be blamed, but rather the failure of individual "artists." Owing to the officer corps' socialization, this rationalization was unanimously accepted, since it shifted the blame onto a few individuals while securing the hope of a resurgence of the Reich and the position of the officer corps in society. But it also deflected any examination of the true causes of Germany's defeat.

While on the one hand the Reichswehr largely rejected a realistic causal study on the operational-strategic level, on the other hand it analyzed the tactical lessons of the war in a professional and focused manner. But this incomplete assessment affected not only the tactical but also the conceptual operational foundations of the Reichsheer's leadership. The resulting line of continuity that counterbalanced numerical superiority with tactical and operational mobility is very clear here.

During Seeckt's time the Reichswehr, in reality hopelessly inferior to its potential enemies, operated simultaneously at a realistic tactical and a utopian operational-strategic level. While the tactical innovations that resulted from the continuing developments of combined arms warfare shaped German Army tactics for years, the return to operational thinking also led to frustrations and a crisis in operational theory during the Seeckt era. Considering the Reich's overwhelming military inferiority, officers like Joachim von Stülpnagel called for a realistic estimate of the situation. Those officers doubted the chances of success for Seeckt's small, elite army, which in a future war was supposed to destroy the enemy through a mobile and offensive battle conducted according to the classical German concept of operations. Their idea of warfare was not classical operational war as Schlieffen had taught it, but rather the integration of people's warfare, irregular units, and societal war with operational warfare.

Nonetheless, Stülpnagel's concept also was closely related to the classical German operational doctrine, because he too thought that it was the regular army that would achieve the decision of the war in a major battle of annihilation. This radicalization of warfare advocated by Stülpnagel, which in many ways came to fruition during World War II, ran contrary to Seeckt's traditional operational ideas and the latter's convictions that the army and not the people should fight the war and that the use of force was therefore reserved for the military. Yet, Seeckt's operational doctrine of prosecuting a lightning-like and victorious war with a small, technologically sophisticated, and mobile professional army before the enemies' military and social resources could develop to their full potential was in the final analysis a radicalization of Schlieffen's classical operational concept based on initial operational speed that proceeded at maximum tempo from the outset. It was not, as Wallach argued, a doctrine of its own. It was, in fact, the exact opposite of the idea of total war that Stülpnagel or even Ludendorff had in mind. A total, socially unrestrained war that ultimately could not be controlled by the military was not in the interests of the wide majority of the German officer corps. Such a war, after all, would also challenge the military's social position as the nation's sole body to bear arms. In the end, and in consequence of Germany's real strategic situation, neither Stülpnagel's nor Seeckt's operational ideas were feasible, albeit for different reasons.

The process initiated by Groener for coordinating operational plans with German foreign policy and the Reich's real strategic situation was supported only in part by the army's leadership. Deeply rooted in classical operational thinking and in contrast to Groener, the army's leadership developed only a limited understanding of the concept of overall warfare that went beyond the operational military level. They therefore continued to reject the notion of the subordination of the military and its plans to the primacy of Germany's overall policy.

As shown by the war games conducted at the end of the 1920s and the beginning of the 1930s, the Reichsheer's operational thinking once more demonstrated classical operational mobile warfare based on offensive action, even though more consideration was given to the defense and to delaying combat than during the years prior to 1914. Surprise, concentration of effort, envelopment, annihilation, the central position, operations on interior lines, and generalship combined with the belief in a quick and decisive battle to neutralize the enemy's resources were the foundations of this kind of operational thinking. And although the breakthrough as the prerequisite for a successful envelopment remained a source of great controversy within the Reich, it too became increasingly important. Slowly, the breakthrough in combination with a subsequent operational envelopment came to be seen as a comprehensive and integrated operation.

During the years following Hitler's seizure of power in 1933, the German Army under Beck and Fritsch was grounded on the basis of this operational doctrine, despite the residual opposition from within the ranks. Logically, an offensive operational doctrine, which during the 1920s and early 1930s had been overshadowed temporarily by more defensive attitudes, once again gained primacy during the Wehrmacht's increasing military buildup. The objective was to establish a mass and offensive military force that during a continental European two-front or multi-front war would be able to force a quick decision from a position of inferiority. Opinions differed, however, on whether such would be possible in reality. Economic, financial, and materiel factors became secondary to the primacy of the operational thinking traditionally prevalent in the German General Staff. Logically, a policy of broad-based rearmament for a short war was pursued instead of a deep-based rearmament program for a long war.

In general, it is quite apparent that the new structure of the German Army was a resurgence of the Kaiser's Army, augmented by military technology and organizational innovation. That approach also applied to operational thinking. The patterns of thought were not as monolithic within the officer corps as the scholarly literature keeps suggesting; there were, in fact, differing points of view. One example was the relation between defense and attack, which was even discussed in the media. But the German Army's operational thinking was still rooted in the classical operational concepts of the Kaiser's Reich.

The key difference was that the military equipment necessary for rapid mobile warfare so sorely lacking in World War I was now available in the form of the tank, aircraft, and motorization in general. Nonetheless, the debate still raged on how to use the tank, whether in support of the infantry or as an operationally independent arm in the form of Panzer divisions. By 1937–1938 the latter had clearly emerged as the favored option. Nonetheless, operational innovation evolved slowly, as it had during the nineteenth century. The evolution progressed in the face of opposition from those who advocated the tactical innovations, such as Stormtroop and battle group tactics, which the Germans had developed during World War I. Even as late as the start of World War II in 1939, there was no comprehensive concept of *Blitzkrieg*.[187] Despite all the problems, the tactical-operational innovation process that started during World War I and was reflected in the postwar doctrinal manuals *Führung und Gefecht der verbundenen Waffen* and *Truppenführung,* as well as in the development of tank doctrine, was not as cumbersome as military learning processes are often said to be. Compared to other European countries, the process in Germany proceeded fairly rapidly and with determination.

In contrast to the period of the Kaiser's Reich, the Army General Staff of the 1930s managed to control the rearmament process on the basis of operational objectives. But as the only real operational-strategic planning body, it gradually lost importance in the face of technical weapons developments and the growing significance of the coordination between the three Wehrmacht services of the navy, Luftwaffe, and army. All attempts failed to retain the Army General Staff's unique leadership position on operational issues, and thus to secure its traditional position of power within the military structure. During the buildup of a mass and offensive military force and the struggle of the army and the General Staff to retain their position of power within the overall military structure, they still clung to the Wilhelmine thinking of a single-dimensional concept of power, that being military power. Thus, there was a fundamental debate between the Army General Staff and OKW on whether operational considerations should be subordinate to political imperatives, or wartime operations should be based on operational-strategic imperatives. Beck's resignation in reaction to the Blomberg-Fritsch Affair and the German war plans against Czechoslovakia, as well as Hitler's assumption of the direct supreme military command, decided that issue to the detriment of the Army Command and the General Staff. In subsequent years, the political leadership in the person of Hitler increasingly intervened in the General Staff's realm of operational planning. After Beck's resignation, "the forcible coordination of the Wehrmacht in the field of operational planning" occurred rapidly and without any friction, according to Wilhelm Deist.[188] Yet, a central military planning and command authority, which had been so sorely lacking during World War I, had not been established either. And that was a gap that Hitler exploited skillfully.

7

Lost Victories, or the Limits of Operational Thinking

A war launched by Germany would immediately cause other countries to intervene in support of the attacked country. In a war against a world coalition, Germany would be defeated and then be at the mercy of vengeful victors.
— Colonel General Ludwig Beck

The Concept of Blitzkrieg

A quarter-century after the start of World War I the German Reich started World War II with the 1 September 1939 attack on Poland. While most officers of the Wehrmacht welcomed the war as a step in the revisionist objective of reclaiming Germany's Great Power status, the war from the very beginning was, for Hitler and the National Socialist regime, an ideological racial war of extermination for the purpose of gaining *Lebensraum* (living space) in the east. The Wehrmacht prosecuted this war until the bitter end in May 1945.

When bells rang out all over Germany in the summer of 1940, no one could have foreseen the Wehrmacht's unconditional surrender only a few years in the future. The large majority of Germans reacted with astonishment and satisfaction to the defeat of France after a campaign of only forty days, followed by the signing of the armistice on 22 June 1940 in the Compiègne Forest—in the same railway car in which Germany had surrendered on 11 November 1918. For the German majority, the symbolic act of French subjugation in that historic salon car wiped out the humiliation of World War I. At that point the concordance between population and the National Socialist regime was at its peak. The unexpectedly rapid success over the strongest military power in Europe was preceded by the victory over Poland in the autumn of 1939 and the conquest of Denmark and Norway earlier in 1940. German and international media immediately called the German conduct of the war "Blitzkrieg."

Up to that point the word Blitzkrieg—which has now entered many languages as a synonym for a rapid mobile war—characterized the military successes of the Wehrmacht in the opening years of World War II. This was largely the result of National Socialist propaganda, which, until the 1941 defeats suffered in Russia, used the term as an expression of German superiority and the invincibility of the Wehrmacht. The term Blitzkrieg, tightly linked with the *Panzer*, was not coined in the Anglo-Saxon world, as often claimed, but actually appeared in German military publications as early as the mid-1930s.[1] It was, however, never introduced into the official terminology of the Wehrmacht. The "anarchy of interpretation"[2] of the term that arose after World War II can be limited to the tactical-operational and strategic framework of our discussion here.

On the strategic level the theory has been debated for years that Hitler promoted a "German Blitzkrieg strategy" to achieve world domination, and that he intended to keep conflicts localized to avoid a lengthy multiple-front war, while isolating potential opponents through foreign policy maneuvers and then defeating them one by one. The individual conquests were to be separated by pauses to exploit the conquered territories economically and to avoid overtaxing German economic capacities. Parallel to the foreign and economic policy measures, the Nazi Party planned to mobilize the German population internally for the support of the war. The objective was to use a focused, broad-based armament (*Breitenrüstung*) approach to develop a strategic first strike capability. The Blitzkrieg concept allegedly was developed by the Wehrmacht as a practical method of execution. Following a surprise start of the war, rapid envelopment operations with Luftwaffe support were intended to force a quick decision. At first glance this fascinating and striking thesis that Hitler developed a program for winning world supremacy, or that he had tried to execute such a step-by-step plan, ties together various pieces of the existing puzzle into one neat picture—but those pieces fit only superficially.[3] There is no doubt that Germany pursued not a "deep" but rather a "broad" armament policy. Nor is there any doubt that Hitler intended to conquer Lebensraum in the east. There also is proof that Hitler harbored ideas of world rule going beyond that. And last but not least, the German General Staff since Schlieffen's time tried to counter both operationally and strategically the superior potentials of a coalition of opponents in a two- or multiple-front war through the conduct of rapid operations to achieve a final decision. But all these factors stand separately and were not systematically linked in an integrated Blitzkrieg strategy. Michael Salewski correctly identified the step-by-step model as monocausal.[4] Timothy Mason assessed the theory of the Blitzkrieg strategy as an after-the-fact fictional construct to explain the initial successes of the National Socialist regime. As Professor Sir Hew Strachan stated most clearly: "Blitzkrieg, therefore, may have had some meaning at a purely operational level, but as an overall strategic and economic concept it was nonexistent."[5]

Nonetheless, there were indeed some underlying principles of German warfare in the first phase of World War II, and they were not new. They all derived from the tradition of German operational thinking.[6] Blitzkrieg is the synonym for a qualitatively new step in traditional German operational command and control. Thanks to motorization in the air and on land, the maneuver that was the foundation of German operational thinking regained dominance over firepower. The mobility that was so painfully lacking in World War I now facilitated the execution of German operational thinking in a new dimension. Such was noted as early as the summer of 1940 in the article "Revolution der Kriegführung,"[7] written by Friedrich von Rabenau, a former subordinate of Stülpnagel in the Truppenamt, and now a general officer and chief of the Army Archives (*Heeresarchive*). Rabenau pointed out that the use of tanks and aircraft had undoubtedly influenced the campaigns against Poland and France, just as any war introduces something new. But in the end, the ultimate truths of the art of war that at times over the years had been lost sight of were reconfirmed. The foundation of the great successes, then, had been operational doctrine as practiced in Germany since Schlieffen, based on achieving a rapid decision of the war by destroying the enemy forces in battle through the establishment of a main effort and an envelopment. The instrument for the execution of that doctrine was maneuver warfare, which resulted in high-tempo actions, and was now even more greatly accelerated through modern warfighting technologies. The trench warfare of World War I had been an aberration resulting from the inability of the opposing sides to force through operational maneuver warfare. According to Rabenau, it was thanks to Seeckt that the concept of maneuver warfare remained firmly anchored in the German Army's operational thinking over the years, despite all resistance: "Seeckt knew what he was doing. He preserved the decisive heritage of the General Staff until such time as that knowledge could once again become viable action. The trend of maneuver warfare continued to follow Schlieffen's old ultimate truth—the battle of Cannae's idea of envelopment and destruction by encirclement."[8]

The war, therefore, undoubtedly brought about many new concepts, but they did not replace the classic conduct of operations. In contrast, the early campaigns in the west and the east reharmonized command options and military capabilities—which had not been the situation during World War I. That harmonization facilitated the acceleration of maneuver warfare with modern military capabilities. The fundamental truths that had fallen into question during World War I were revalidated "through the work of a genius."[9] This reference to the "Führer's genius" was a factor in the decision of OKW (Wehrmacht High Command) to block the publication of a study that sang the praises of Schlieffen and Seeckt too highly. As Jodl put it, "Our victories are certainly not due only to having rediscovered Schlieffen and Seeckt."[10]

The efforts of OKW to credit the early victories to the Führer's abilities as a superior military commander cannot obscure the fact that since Schlieffen the General Staff had believed that the only chance to counter the enemy's superior manpower and materiel resources and to destroy his army was through the conduct of rapid, decisive offensive operations. The experience of the lengthy war of attrition of World War I confirmed to the operations experts in the Truppenamt and later the revived General Staff especially that Germany could not win such a long war and that it must be avoided by any means. The contrary warning voices in the military journals and inside the General Staff itself were in the minority. Among them were the chief of the Economic Staff, General Georg Thomas, who dismissed the belief in a short war as wishful thinking. Those critics stood in the tradition of men like Walther Reinhardt and George Soldan, who saw future wars as trench fighting and protracted wars of attrition.[11] As shown by the results of the Truppenamt staff ride of 1938,[12] even Ludwig Beck's argument did not receive wide support when in July of that year he criticized the feasibility of a Blitzkrieg-like operation in an invasion of Czechoslovakia. Almost one year before the start of World War II, most participants in that 1938 staff ride thought like Walther von Brauchitsch that a two-front war was winnable.[13]

There were, however, no operational plans for a well-considered, sustainable, and consecutive Blitzkrieg strategy. In contrast to 1914, the German Reich entered World War II in 1939 without a developed war plan for the conduct of a two-front war. There was no Schlieffen Plan or Moltke Plan in the General Staff files. Any consideration of an overall strategy for a two-front war with Poland and the Western Powers had been blocked categorically by Hitler.[14] The attack on Poland was not an integral component of an overall strategic concept. An analysis of the planning and conduct of both campaigns shows that the victories over Poland and France were indeed based on traditional German operational thinking, but they were not the result of a well-considered, long-term Blitzkrieg strategy. Instead they were based on short-term to mid-term operational plans and on the exploitation of the enemy's mistakes.

Offensive—Unplanned: Blitzkrieg Wars

After Hitler ordered the preparation for an attack of Poland at the end of April/ beginning of May 1939, the General Staff had only a few months' time to draft the Case WHITE (*Fall WEISS*) operational plan. As Colonel Günther Blumen-tritt noted, the initial operational situation was very favorable for the Wehrmacht: "The conformation of the frontier embraced Poland on three sides. The country was crushed, as between two mighty arms. In the north, East Prussia extended far toward the east, and from its southern border encircling forces could press south-ward toward Warsaw and Brest-Litovsk. On the other hand, the Polish-Slovakian frontier in the south invited a thrust from south to north, toward Kraków and Lemburg."[15]

The concept of destroying larger enemy force concentrations in Poland by a simultaneous pincer attack from the north and south was nothing new for the German military. The General Staff had discussed just such an operation prior to and early during World War I. Both Schlieffen and Falkenhayn rejected such a pincer attack as infeasible, owing to the difficult geographic conditions and the low mobility of the forces. Now, however, tanks and aircraft gave the Wehrmacht capabilities that seemed to make a pincer attack possible. The General Staff, there-fore, planned to destroy the majority of the Polish Army through a concentrated attack with Army Group South (*Heeresgruppe Süd*) from Silesia and Army Group North (*Heeresgruppe Nord*) from East Prussia. The linkup of the two pincer wings would occur near Warsaw. During a General Staff ride in May 1939, General of Artillery Franz Halder conducted a map maneuver exercise for the pincer attack on Poland, supported by the Western Powers, Lithuania, and the Soviet Union.[16] The objective of the exercise was:

> An examination of how far the . . . ambitious set of operations plans can be achieved through a surprising penetration of *massed rapid forces*; how the issues arising from the *movement* and *supply* of strong mechanized and motorized assets can be resolved; how the *Panzer and motorized divi-sions* operating in the *depth* of the enemy's territory following the pen-etration will be able to exploit and expand their success until the mass of the divisions deploying on schedule from Silesia will have off-loaded, reached the front, and be able to intervene there; how the [Polish] forces deployed in the Vistula bend can be destroyed quickly; and how favor-able initial positions for the operations *east* of the Vistula can be won.[17]

The purpose of the map exercise as described by Halder indicates that early in the summer of 1939 the General Staff had indeed developed an operational concept for an attack, but the execution lacked solutions for many of the basic issues concerning the core of the conduct of the tank-supported mobile opera-tions. The results of the General Staff ride were disillusioning for OKH. The opera-tional objective of destroying the forces west of the Vistula rapidly had not been achieved. The reasons that surfaced during the exercise's postmortem session were a lack of confidence in the operational abilities of the mobile units combined with the concern about threats to the flanks. An unnecessary reorganization of forces resulting from the establishment of a faulty main effort also caused increased loss of time and wear and tear on equipment. In order to prevent such problems in the future, Halder ordered that the security of the flanks would be left to the follow-on infantry units. In addition, the motorized units were to attack even more rap-idly and relentlessly in the operationally most favorable direction to destroy the enemy.[18] Halder's solution, in the tradition of German operational thinking, was to destroy the enemy through a rapid and mobile envelopment. But at the same time it also was a break with the ideas of Schlieffen, who had given great impor-tance to the security of the flanks. While the army required the direct support of the Luftwaffe in the tactical battles, the Luftwaffe itself planned at first to focus its maximum concentration of airpower against the enemy's deploying forces. Based on the Luftwaffe's own doctrine, that mission took priority over the direct support of army forces.

The 1939 staff ride showed that the General Staff understood the issues of the practical execution of German operational doctrine, considering the army's varying levels of motorization. But the solution arrived at was a further acceleration of maneuver with acceptance of the recognized greater risk. True to tradition, the solution also ignored totally the logistical issues connected with such offensive operations. The initial situation posited for the staff ride also shows that the General Staff, despite Hitler's assurances to the contrary, did not exclude the possibility of a two- or multiple-front war as a result of a German attack on Poland. Consequently, the rapid destruction of the Polish Army at the bend of the Vistula was the *conditio sine qua non* for the continuation of the war. After completion of that operation any Soviet units intervening in the battle would be fought east of the Vistula,[19] while at the same time the Germans would redeploy reinforcements to the Western Front.

Hitler on 22 August 1939 largely dismissed the worries of the generals about a lengthy and ultimately unwinnable two-front war when he once again informed the Wehrmacht's senior leadership of his "relentless determination" to wage a war of conquest in the east, and simultaneously he announced the signing of the Hitler-Stalin Pact. He again insisted that the Western Powers would not intervene in the conflict.[20] Although many of those present at the meeting heard Hitler's assurances with considerable concern, the military leadership without dissent yielded the strategic leadership to the Führer. They even encouraged him in his plans when, despite the sobering results of the Army General Staff ride, they assured him that they would be able to conclude a war against Poland within a few weeks' time.[21]

Meanwhile, the army's commanders reacted to the recognized deficiencies with increased troop training and scheduled an extended marching and field training exercise for September 1939.[22] But it would not come to that. On 1 September 1939, after a short mobilization phase, the Wehrmacht, in accordance with the Case WHITE deployment directive of 15 June 1939,[23] attacked Poland without prior declaration of war. In field strength the German force of 1.5 million soldiers was only slightly superior to the Polish Army's 1.3 million. But the German Army had 3,600 tanks while the Polish Army had only 750. Of the fifty-four German divisions, fifteen were fully motorized and capable of conducting rapid operations. The German air superiority was overwhelming as well. Nine hundred mostly obsolescent Polish aircraft faced nineteen hundred German. Thus, the Wehrmacht had a significantly higher level of motorization, which facilitated the rapid and mobile conduct of operations as planned by the General Staff.

Deployed to encircle the Polish units west of the Vistula, the main attacking units of Army Groups North and South broke through the Polish defense. The decisive thrust was the frontal breakthrough by the Tenth Army in the southern sector, which established the required conditions for the extensive envelopment. The linear Polish defense was vulnerable to the German operations that were based on rapid thrusts by the Panzer units, supported by tactical air power. On 14 September the pincer arms closed on Warsaw. (See Plate 11.)

West of the Polish capital the surrounded Polish units at the Bzura River tried but failed to break through the encirclement. Fearing that the Polish Army could not be completely destroyed west of the Vistula, OKH on 11 September initiated a second pincer operation that was to close east of the Bug River. The Soviet invasion of Poland on 17 September put an end to that operation. After the fall of Warsaw the last Polish units capitulated on 6 October 1939.[24]

Within a few weeks the German Army had achieved its operational objective of attacking from both sides and completely destroying the majority of the Polish forces west of the Vistula. The Wehrmacht attributed its success to the perfect execution of the operational doctrine developed by Schlieffen and Moltke the Elder. The chief of the General Staff of the First Air Fleet, Major General Wilhelm Speidel, clearly expressed that idea in a lecture he gave for party and military elites in Prague on 16 November 1939. The pincer operation in the Poland Campaign, as Speidel put it, was a perfect example of a skillfully exploited, large-scale envelopment operation on exterior lines. In the spirit of Moltke the Elder, the soldiers had marched separately and succeeded unified. Schlieffen's dictum that "the operation must not result in an ordinary victory, but rather in total destruction"[25] was always in the forefront. According to Speidel, what that in fact meant was not merely the destruction of the opponents' ground forces, but of his total armed forces. The Luftwaffe had contributed to that objective through the operational destruction of the enemy's air force. Furthermore, the Luftwaffe supported the operational objective of destroying the enemy's infrastructure, reserves, and logistics. Only then was the Luftwaffe able to provide tactical support to the army.

Speidel expressly noted that a rapid victory had been necessary for political reasons, a reference to the Western Allies' declaration of war on 3 September 1939. Despite Hitler's assurances, the Wehrmacht had to conduct the Poland Campaign under the threat of a two-front war. In the very sense of Schlieffen's operational thinking, the objective then was to defeat quickly the one and then the other enemy. But in contrast to 1914, the 1939 attack on Poland was not part of a general strategic plan. As opposed to the Schlieffen Plan or the Moltke Plan, which were developed for two-front wars, the current campaign was designed as an isolated area attack on a single enemy. It was only because of the unanticipated entry of the Western Powers into the war that the geographically limited one-front war became a two-front war in a matter of weeks. Although the German General Staff had not planned for such, it nonetheless succeeded on the strategic level in completing the first phase of a Schlieffen Plan in reverse. One of the two opponents had been dealt an annihilating defeat, and the German Army was now capable of launching a massive attack against the second opponent in a single-front war without being concerned about the threat to its rear. Consequently, the bulk of the German Army was redeployed to the west.

After the swift victory over Poland and the alliance with the Soviet Union, Germany now only faced a single-front war against France on the continent. As in 1914, the German Reich was not prepared to fight a world war when Great Britain eventually entered the war. The German political and military leadership had not learned any lessons from the experience of World War I. There was no overall strategic German war plan in 1939. Neither the German Navy nor the Luftwaffe, therefore, had the military capabilities for fighting a war against Great Britain.[26]

In his personal war diary Manstein summarized in a nutshell the lack of willingness of the military and political leadership to learn the lessons of military conflict management. On 24 October 1939 he wrote:

> The victory over England, if she remains determined to proceed, can only be achieved by sea or air. Any prior victory on the ground to eliminate her continental assets (which might lead her to abandon the race) will be the prerequisite for this if we are not to be able to block England effectively with our fleet and air force. . . . But this question should have been addressed *before* we entered into a war, facing the question as early as 1939 of whether we would be up to the task in terms of armaments and especially the inner resoluteness and strength of the army. In the end, of course, the politician must decide whether he must start the war under any risk, because the war might otherwise be forced on him at a later time under even more unfavorable conditions.[27]

The Army General Staff, as predicted by its former chief, Ludwig Beck, was overcome by the development. Mentally unprepared for a campaign against France, they had not prepared an operations plan for an offensive in the west. An aggravating factor was the significant tactical and training deficiencies exposed by the Poland Campaign—deficiencies that the earlier Army General Staff ride had predicted. The army's materiel and equipment were inadequate as well.

The issues were mainly the result of the Wehrmacht's abbreviated buildup. In 1939 the army entered the war with varying levels of mobility, unequal equipment, and a highly divergent level of training. Only a few "elite units" were equipped with high-quality assets, were well-trained, and were capable of conducting mobile warfare without restrictions. Of the 157 German Army divisions, just sixteen were fully motorized.[28] The remaining 90 percent of the German Army units advanced on foot or on horse, as in World War I, and for the most part did not have arms any better than in World War I.[29] The image of a "fully motorized Ger-

Military Solution to the Problem of Germany's Central Position in the Second World War: The Revision of the Schlieffen Plan

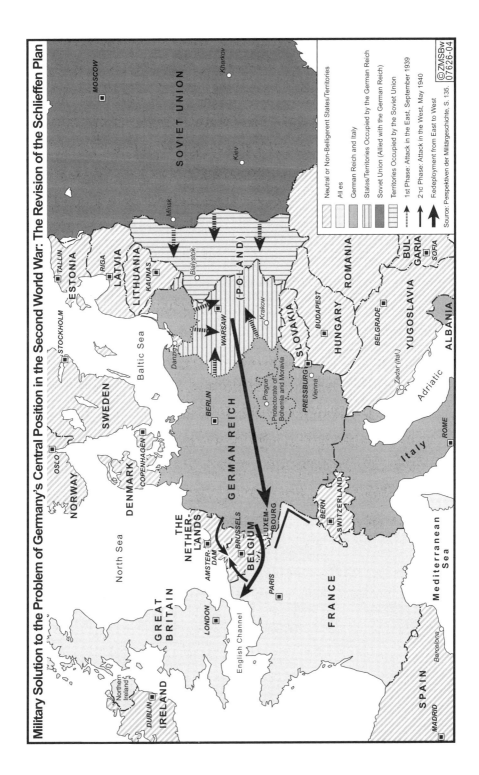

Neutral or Non-Belligerent States/Territories

All es

German Reich and Italy

States/Territories Occupied by the German Reich

Soviet Union (Allied with the German Reich)

Territories Occupied by the Soviet Union

1st Phase: Attack in the East, September 1939

2nd Phase: Attack in the West, May 1940

Redeployment from East to West

Source: Perspektiven der Militärgeschichte, S. 135.

© ZMSBw
07626-04

man Blitzkrieg Army," which still lingers in many minds to this day, is the product of a National Socialist propaganda lie. In reality the German Army was an army of horses, using more than double the number of horses they had used in World War I. The great majority of the soldiers received only a few weeks of training and were far from the image of the young, dynamic frontline fighters of National Socialist propaganda. In total, only 77 divisions were fully operational, among them the ten Panzer and six motorized divisions—that is, only five divisions more than the Germans had available for the Operation MICHAEL offensive in 1918.[30] The German Army entered the war as a two-class army in terms of motorization and equipment.[31] Tactical-operational thinking also hung on this divide, because in the minds of generals of 1939 the new ideas of deploying rapid troops conflicted with their war experiences as young officers during World War I. What made matters even more difficult was that the expansion of the officer corps had been so fast and so great that no *unité de doctrine* existed any longer.

The Poland Campaign exposed the inadequate training level of the troops, and the typical frictions were far greater than those usually expected at the beginning of a war. The negative consequences of the Wehrmacht's rapid buildup thus became very clear. In contrast to the soldiers of World War I, glaring deficiencies appeared in the ability of the 1939 soldiers to master mission procedures and the methods of attack. Even elements of the Panzer forces were unable to master combined arms operations in front of Warsaw and at the Bzura.[32] As in the last war, the deficiencies in the defensive battles were especially striking. Because such deficiencies were attributed among other factors to inadequate determination on the part of the troops, OKH on 15 December 1939 eliminated delaying resistance (*Hinhaltenden Widerstand*) as an approved form of combat.[33] The chief of the General Staff noted that the infantry had not even come close to the training levels of 1914.[34]

OKH responded with a large-scale training program.[35] In addition to leadership training, combined arms operations and combat power were the focus of the troop exercises. Simultaneously OKH issued several revised regulations and tactical instructions, which in part drew upon the experiences of World War I.[36] The infantry was restructured and better armed to increase its combat power.[37] One especially considerable deficiency exposed by the Poland Campaign was the inability of many officers, even some at the operational command level, to cope with their duties. Consequently, commanders were trained in dedicated courses for the conduct of combined arms operations.[38] The objective of the training was to improve the capability of the mid-level officers in the chain of command to execute the operational concepts developed by the General Staff.

While the training initiative produced initial successes, the materiel situation deteriorated dramatically in certain war-critical sectors. As in World War I, the trucks required for the swift conduct of operations were not available in sufficient numbers. The German Army had only 120,000 trucks to provide the logistical supply so urgently needed for rapid and mobile operations. Because of the severe shortages of rubber, an improvement in automotive assets could not be counted on for the foreseeable future. Since Germany's fuel situation also was tense, Halder in February 1940 even considered a rigorous "demotorization program."[39]

While the German Army did everything to increase the striking capability of the units, the General Staff started the operational planning for an offensive against France. But an immediate attack as had been intended in the Schlieffen Plan and was now being demanded by Hitler was not possible because of the man-power and equipment limitations. The General Staff worked out several opera-tional plans right up until the start of the German western offensive in May 1940. Those plans did not consider a direct breakthrough of the French Maginot Line fortifications. That decision was based largely on the memory of the failure of the 1914 German offensive in Lorraine.[40]

When the German General Staff started to plan an offensive in the west after the completion of operations in Poland, they were faced with the same situation as prior to World War I—the territory of the Benelux countries was the only transit area for an attack on France. The World War I experiences of the officers on both sides, who were then lieutenants and captains and were now general officers, influ-enced and even crucially determined both sets of operational plans.

The Allied planners were almost certain that the Wehrmacht would once again attempt the Schlieffen Plan. With the French right flank secured by the Maginot Line, and the center being the geographic barrier of the Meuse and the Ardennes, which had been a first-rate terrain obstacle in World War I, a repetition of the German offensive through Flanders—an area suitable for tanks—seemed strongly logical. For the purpose of providing timely assistance to the attacked Belgians and preventing combat action on French soil as in the First World War, the Allied generals decided to respond to a German attack by advancing with their left wing into Belgium and the Netherlands, and with their right anchored on the Magi-not Line, and then halting the German units along the Dyle River line and near Breda.[41]

On the German side, too, Schlieffen was present at the map table. At first glance, therefore, it is not surprising to see that the early deployment directives in many respects were similar to a slightly updated Schlieffen Plan, which had been adjusted to the speed of the tank. The similarity, however, is only superficial. While Schlieffen intended to fight a rapid battle of destruction, and he considered space only as a short-term means for achieving success in battle, the objective of the initial 1940 deployment directives was to "gain as much space in the Neth-erlands, Belgium, and northern France as possible, as the basis for fighting an advantageous aerial and naval war against England, and [for establishing] a wide frontal zone of the vital Ruhr area."[42]

When the battle of annihilation failed and the lost race to the sea made it impossible to occupy the central strategic positions on the Channel, the General Staff officers who were captives of their own World War I experiences merely planned to drive back the Allied units head-on, with the objective of achieving a medium- or long-term gain of operational-strategic space facing the British coast.[43] This was in no small part the result of directions from Hitler, who repeatedly interfered with the planning—which he had not done in the Poland Campaign. The result produced by the General Staff, however, was just what the Allies expected.

Hitler was dissatisfied with the operational drafts produced by the General Staff. Those plans appeared to him to be too limited and lacked the element of surprise. He rejected them as the "thoughts of a war school cadet."[44] Even if this criticism was a bit excessive, it could not be dismissed from a technical military perspective. Apart from a clear formation of a center of gravity, the operational plans lacked the courage to accept risk that was characteristic of German operational thinking, and therefore lacked the "famous operational spark." Had the initial plans been executed, they most likely would have produced only tactical, but not operational success. The German operational planners, shaped by their World War I experience as young officers on the Western Front, all held the enemy in great respect. A comprehensive study will show whether the unimaginative drafts of the General Staff were indeed, as Frieser suspects, an act of opposition, or rather were owing to the respect for the former enemy.

The chief of staff of Army Group A, Eric von Manstein, did not concur with the predictable plans. The decisive factor for him was "that the striking power of the army should be a *unique* one against an equal opponent."[45] As Schlieffen would have seen it, therefore, the decisive striking power must not be used to gain control of a coastal strip or to fight a larger enemy force, but to achieve the critical success necessary to drive through to the point of full decision on the ground. OKH lacked the will to force such a battle of annihilation and decision. Even worse, as Manstein saw it, was the lack of belief in the victory. This criticism, however, should be regarded with reservation, considering the personal differences between Manstein and Halder.[46] What cannot be denied is the validity of Manstein's fundamental criticism of OKH's abandonment of the will to achieve a decision, and in particular of the General Staff's surrendering one of the supporting pillars of German operational thinking.

As late as October 1939 Manstein described the operational situation in the west as extremely unfavorable because of the confined space in the area of operations and the enemy's options for preventing rapid successes through terrain obstacles and fortifications and through counterattacks. In the spring of 1940 Manstein developed an operations plan that was based on the key elements of traditional German operational thinking: envelopment, establishment of main effort, initiative, rapid action, attack, surprise, willingness to assume risk, and mobility. The element of surprise was of special significance, based on placing the attack at the center of the main effort through the clever use of space and time at a key point completely unexpected by the enemy, but a point of operational-strategic importance.

Manstein's plan—later known as the *Sichelschnitt* (Sickle Cut)—was the one actually executed in May 1940. It focused on engaging in a rapid, surprising, and decisive battle of annihilation, in complete accordance with Schlieffen's thinking. Based on the assumptions of the Allies, German units were to feign a repetition of the Moltke Plan of 1914, including a move into the Netherlands. That feint would confirm the Allies' assessment of the anticipated German attack and induce them to advance their forces into Belgium. Meanwhile, strong German motorized units would advance to Sedan through the allegedly impassable forests of the Ardennes, a space that World War I had shown to be difficult to pass through, and if at all, only very slowly and under great threat from the air. But that area was above the northern terminus of the Maginot Line. There were only isolated defensive positions farther along the border between Belgium and France. After a successful breakthrough at the Ardennes, the German attack would continue westward to the estuary of the Somme, while the Allied units already in Belgium would be encircled and defeated in a gigantic battle of annihilation.[47]

The General Staff did not concur with Manstein's daring plans and refused to forward them to Hitler via OKW. Halder, who had a deep personal aversion for Manstein, resolved the issue in a classical manner. Manstein was "kicked upstairs" to a higher position on the Eastern Front. Halder, meanwhile, slowly grew to accept Manstein's operational concepts as the result of his own map exercises. Somewhat conspiratorially, Halder found an opportunity to introduce Hitler to the operational concept. Coincidentally, Hitler himself had been considering the idea of a breakthrough near Sedan.[48] Hitler finally agreed with these ideas. But as Frieser has argued convincingly, and as demonstrated through Hitler's actions during the campaign, the Führer only understood the tactical and not the operational dimension of the Sichelschnitt plan.

Building on Manstein's concepts, the General Staff in mid-February 1940 started the operational planning for the western offensive, Case YELLOW (*Fall GELB*). The plan included without scruple the violation of the neutrality of the Benelux states. In contrast to the previous operational plans, the absolutely critical factors of space and time made the new plan a highly risky matter. The time factor played the key role. The thrust of the motorized units had to be executed as quickly as possible, along a few easily blockable routes, and under a high level of threat from the air. If the Meuse River was not taken on the fifth attack day at the latest, the Allies would see through the German operations plan and be able to initiate the necessary countermeasures. In addition, the motorized units had to advance without delay and in a single bound against the Somme to complete the encirclement. The entire maneuver would have to be executed without flank security—exactly as Halder had concluded in his postmortem session of the 1939 Army General Staff ride.

As the operational plans of the General Staff clearly show, the breakthrough as the precondition for the subsequent envelopment and annihilation of the enemy forces had become the absolute foundation of operational thinking. Without a successful tactical-operational breakthrough, nothing else counted. But the necessary elements for a successful breakthrough included surprise, the subsequent establishment of a main effort, and a swift tactical attack procedure. Only when the imperative of action (*Gesetz des Handelns*) could be maintained by uninterrupted maintenance of the initiative would success be achievable under the conditions of high risk.

Compared to the Poland Campaign, the Wehrmacht started the offensive on 10 May 1940 relatively weaker in both manpower and materiel—and in the decisive sectors even inferior in quality.[49] While in the north Army Group B feinted a rerun of the Schlieffen Plan, Army Group C in the south kept on the defensive. The main attack in the center was executed by Army Group A. The mass of the motorized units and of the Luftwaffe was deployed there. After the Luftwaffe destroyed the enemy's air forces on the ground and established air superiority, it then could provide the tactical support for the breakthrough at Sedan. The Luftwaffe managed to accomplish that by the third day of attack. Only six days later, on 19 May, the German Panzer spearheads reached the coast near Abbeville. The Allied units in Belgium were encircled.

But the complete annihilation of the enemy forces failed, especially in the case of the British Expeditionary Force. The halt of the Panzer units[50] allowed the British leadership to evacuate the majority of their soldiers to Great Britain via Dunkirk, which reduced Manstein's attempted strategic victory to an ordinary operational one.[51] There was no Cannae. In Halder's opinion, that was achieved later during Case RED (*Fall ROT*), the second phase of the France Campaign.[52] After successfully regrouping, the German forces on 5 June broke through the French positions on the Somme and advanced in a Schlieffen-like manner to the south and across the rear of the Maginot Line, which in the meantime had been attacked and breached by Army Group C.[53] The French Army subsequently was defeated in a huge battle of annihilation, and France lost the war. (See Plate 12.)

The success of the Battle of France was the product of not only German operational skill and Allied mistakes, but also the training program initiated after the Poland Campaign. Thanks to that initiative, the France Campaign resulted in a triumph of tactical-operational tank deployment in combined arms mobile warfare.[54] It took the Wehrmacht only six weeks to defeat the western Allied forces, which still had been operating largely based on the concepts of World War I.

Conducting mobile operations, the Panzers broke through the French positions after establishing a surprise main effort at the Meuse. German forces combined infantry Stormtroop Tactics with the shock power of the Panzers, supported by the dive-bombers as "flying artillery."[55] The primary reason for the success of the France Campaign, however, was not because of the cumbersome infantry divisions, but rather because of the motorized "elite divisions" committed to the center of main effort. Regardless of open flanks, they thrust to operational depth to crush the enemy's reserves and encircle and destroy his units. The infantry for the most part marched behind the Panzer units. The gaps that opened up between the rapidly advancing motorized units and the ponderous infantry divisions—which as in World War I were still dependent on the marching pace of the soldiers—were greater during the France Campaign than during the Poland Campaign.

Strong disagreements arose between the senior leadership of Army Group A, which wanted to adapt the advance to the speed of the infantry divisions, and the commanders of Panzer units, including Guderian and Major General Erwin Rommel. Continually referring to the concept of Auftragstaktik (mission-oriented tactics), the Panzer leaders pressed the attack in the absence of orders and without flank security. Just as Kluck had done in front of Paris or François had at Tannenberg during World War I, Guderian and Rommel acted high-handedly and interpreted the conduct of operations in their own favor. Rommel especially commanded his division like a company commander. In the end, success proved them right.

The disagreement over another use of Panzer units finally culminated in the famous halt order at Dunkirk, when the commander in chief of Army Group A, Colonel General Gerd von Rundstedt, stopped the offensive for fear of a flank attack and to allow the infantry divisions to close up. That order triggered an open break between the traditionalists and the progressives along the fault line of the best way to deploy the mobile units. It was a conflict that had grown over the years and had been suppressed only on the surface. Even though in the early spring of 1940 there was no question in the General Staff about the much-vaunted uniform operational thinking, the fault line nonetheless ran through all echelons of command and reflected the struggles for relative status within the military hierarchy. OKH, the General Staff, and the commanders of the Panzer divisions all insisted on continuing the advance, while Hitler and OKW favored slowing down the tank units. OKH could not assert itself against the subordinate army group because Hitler supported Rundstedt's opinion.

The France Campaign thus exposed the operational leadership deficiencies of the General Staff that were already evident during World War I. The staff did not always succeed in executing its operational concepts, but whether they were right or wrong is not the point here. As in World War I, the leaders in the field forced a *fait accompli* on the operational leadership. This partial dilution of authority resulted from the mission-type command and control principle, and to a certain degree was inherent in the German command style, which in complex situations expressly allowed for independent and self-reliant battle command in order to execute the higher command's intent. But such was not always the case during the France Campaign. In the decisive phases the General Staff appears to have been driven by the front-line commanders, much as had Moltke the Younger in 1914. Halder's rather cautious attitude in such critical situations—for example, the successful breakthrough at Sedan—surely contributed to this situation, as did Hitler's increasing "interference" into the conduct of operations. Nothing of the sort was anticipated in the concept of directive-based command and control. In effect, it challenged the General Staff's authority over operational leadership, its primary domain, more fundamentally than any out-of-control division commander or stubborn army group commander in chief ever could have done. Compounding this situation was the fact that the Wehrmacht's rapid buildup resulted in inadequate operational training of the higher command echelons. Ultimately, that training inevitably took place as learning by doing during the Poland and France Campaigns, and thus became more and more common over the course of time. But it would be superficial to draw the conclusion that Rommel and Guderian had not received sufficient operational training.[56]

The decisive structural operational problem of how to reconcile the various attack speeds was suppressed against the background of the internal struggles for power and the ecstasy of the victory. But the consequences of this omission would come back to haunt the German Army's leadership in a most dramatic way during Operation BARBAROSSA.

Offensive: The "Planned Blitzkrieg Wars"

Hitler was at the peak of his power following the successful France Campaign. His hope that Great Britain would make peace with Germany and let him act on the continent at his own discretion did not come to pass, however. Hitler planned a landing in Great Britain, but Operation SEA LION (SEELÖWE) became unfeasible when the Germans were defeated in the air during the Battle of Britain. The strategic stalemate between the two adversaries exposed a dilemma that Napoleon had faced, one that consequently neither the political nor the military leadership of the Reich since Schlieffen had considered in their operational-strategic plans. In this situation the commanders of the army and navy saw one option for attacking Great Britain in the Mediterranean, thus shifting the strategic center of gravity to the periphery. That potential Mediterranean alternative strategy, however, quickly faded into the background in favor of a continental solution. Shortly after the end of the France Campaign, Halder was not excluding consideration of a war against the Soviet Union to force it to recognize Germany's hegemony on the continent—

even under the risk of a two-front war. What then was the situation in the east in the summer of 1940?

After the campaign against Poland ended, OKH left only a few units based in the east, because a Russian attack was not thought imminent. During the subsequent German campaign in the west the Russians shored up the security of their "western glacis" by annexing the Baltic States into the Soviet Union, demanding the cession of Bessarabia, and deploying additional Red Army units to the occupied areas. In response, the General Staff drew up routine operational plans for a war with the Soviet Union. Halder assigned the preparation of those plans to the headquarters of the Eighteenth Army, which had been repositioned in East Prussia after the completion of the France Campaign. The General Staff's objective was to establish a striking power in the east to ward off any Russian attack. The defense was to be mobile and offensively conducted. The territorial security guarantees that had been given to the countries in the east also played a role in Halder's thinking. Nor did he believe in a rapid victory over Great Britain. Thus, Halder's routine planning focused on the potential enemy in the east, and since the beginning of July 1940 he had had the Operations Division of the General Staff examine the option of a war against the Soviet Union to force its recognition of Germany's hegemony over Europe.[57] In a classic German manner, such a campaign was to be conducted with rapid, decisive operations. Functioning within the framework of its own institutional norms, the General Staff independently and without any influence by Hitler started the contingency planning against the potentially most dangerous opponent on the continent—therefore accepting the possibility of a two-front war. Based on traditional German operational-strategic thinking, the planners believed that a short two-front war was both acceptable and feasible. Their considerations were based on the slowly growing doubts about defeating Great Britain through an indirect strategy. Based on the experience of World War I, a lengthier war of attrition against Great Britain allied with the United States would only be possible if Germany could first secure the raw materials and the industrial centers of the Soviet Union.

After Hitler's unsuccessful "peace approach" (*Friedensavancen*) to Great Britain, he issued on 22 July the initial order for the solution of the "Russian Problem." At that point the routine plans for a war against the Soviet Union beyond a mere defense were already in existence.[58] Over the course of the subsequent days and weeks those plans merged with Hitler's decisive intent to conduct a "war for living space" (*Lebensraumkrieg*).[59] In strategic terms, Hitler tied the war for Lebensraum to the fight against Great Britain, whose dominance on the continent was to be ended through a victory over the Soviet Union. Simultaneously, the objectives were to deter the United States from entering the war, to relieve Japan from a potential conflict with America, and to secure economically exploitable colonial areas to support a lengthy world war. This war aimed not at preemptively neutralizing the Russian military machine, but at asserting Germany's hegemony on the continent through the victory over the Soviet Union and at providing the starting position for the continued conduct of warfare. In contrast to former and current revisionist arguments that the attack of the Soviet Union was a preventive war, it was in fact a war of aggression, conducted for the expansion of power, which turned into an ideological war of racial annihilation for Lebensraum in the east.[60]

On 31 July 1940, Hitler finally announced his intention of crushing the Soviet Union. Halder noted in his war diary: "In the course of this conflict Russia must be knocked out. Spring of 1941. The faster we destroy Russia the better."[61]

The decision to initiate plans for an attack on the Soviet Union gave Hitler a strategic alternative to direct warfare against Great Britain. Over the following months he held both options open without making a final decision. The General Staff also continued to develop both options. In addition to the initial studies for an eastern campaign, work continued on the Mediterranean plans, to include an attack on Gibraltar. Nonetheless, a number of incalculable factors of a two-front war continued to concern the General Staff, despite all the outward confidence. Not the least of these concerns was the fact that Halder and Brauchitsch were not sure that Great Britain could indeed be neutralized by a German victory over Russia. The level of risk in the west was not to be underestimated, especially in the Mediterranean region.[62]

The plans for a war against the Soviet Union were not only advanced by the Army General Staff, which had the overall lead, but also by the navy, the Luftwaffe, and OKW. Navy commander in chief Grand Admiral Erich Raeder voiced opposition against a change of strategy, and the navy consequently was assigned only the minor mission of securing the shipping in the Baltic Sea. The navy's center of gravity would continue to be a naval war against Great Britain.[63] The Luftwaffe was directed to cooperate with the army. The initial task would be the elimination of the Soviet Air Force. The direct support of army operations was only the second priority. There were no plans for aerial attacks on Russian economic and armament centers.[64]

Immediately after Hitler informed OKH of his intent, the General Staff under Major General Erich Marcks intensified the operational planning. The initial considerations for a campaign against the Soviet Union had already indicated that the vast territorial expanse of the country and strategic and economic factors would have a decisive influence on operational planning. Based on Germany's blockade experience during World War I, it would be necessary for Germany to gain control of the industrial centers of Moscow and Leningrad, the raw material and industrial regions of the Caucasus and the Urals, and most absolutely Russia's grain center of the Ukraine in order to sustain a multi-year war of attrition. The traumatic German experience of the hunger winters of World War I and the conviction that the German population would not be able to support itself made the "nutritional

Grand Admiral Erich Raeder (commander in chief of the German Navy), Field Marshal Wilhelm Keitel (chief of the Wehrmacht High Command), Field Marshal Erhard Milch (general inspector of the Luftwaffe), and Colonel General Friedrich Fromm (chief of Army Armament and commander in chief of the Wehrmacht Replacement Army) at a state ceremony with Adolf Hitler in October 1940. Photographer: Heinrich Hoffmann. *BArch/183-1983-0210-507.*

On the Soviet front: the commander in chief of Army Group North, Field Marshal Wilhelm Ritter von Leeb, and the commander in chief of the Eighteenth Army, Colonel General Georg von Küchler, at an artillery forward observation post near Krasnoye Selo in September 1941. Photographer: Schröter. *BArch/183-B12786.*

Hitler and his staff at the Führer Headquarters in May–June 1940. *BArch/183-R99057*.

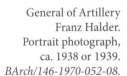

General of Artillery
Franz Halder.
Portrait photograph,
ca. 1938 or 1939.
BArch/146-1970-052-08.

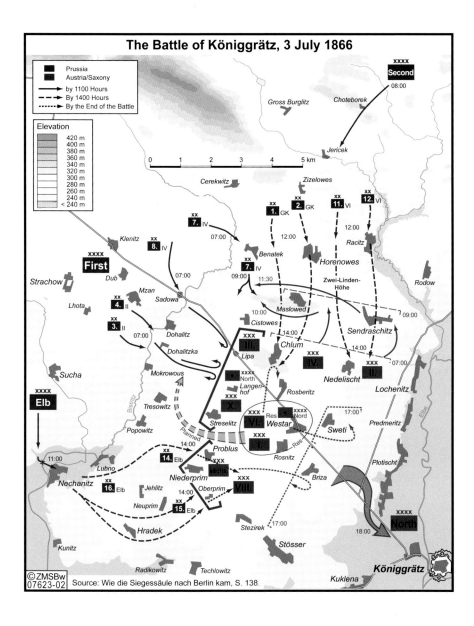

The Battle of Königgrätz, 3 July 1866

Prussia
Austria/Saxony

→ by 1100 Hours
- - → By 1400 Hours
····→ By the End of the Battle

Elevation
420 m
400 m
380 m
360 m
340 m
320 m
300 m
280 m
260 m
240 m
< 240 m

0 1 2 3 4 5 km

©ZMSBw
07623-02 Source: Wie die Siegessäule nach Berlin kam, S. 138.

Plate 1.

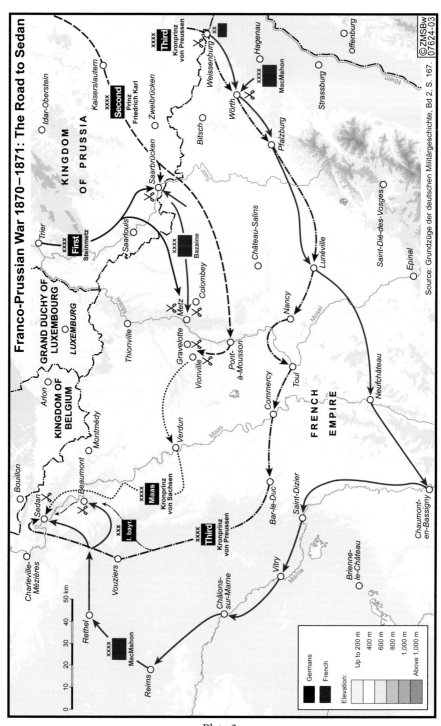

Franco-Prussian War 1870–1871: The Road to Sedan

©ZMSBw
07624-03

Source: Grundzüge der deutschen Militärgeschichte, Bd 2, S. 167.

Plate 2.

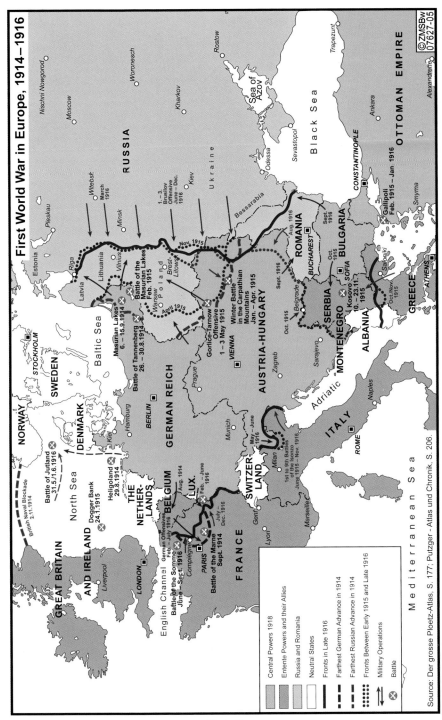

First World War in Europe, 1914–1916

OTTOMAN EMPIRE

RUSSIA

Trapezunt
Rostow
Nischni Nowgorod
Moscow
Woronesch
Kharkov
Sea of AZOV

Black Sea

Ukraine

Kiev
1.–3.
Brusilow
Offensive
June–Dec.
1916
Bessarabia
Odessa
Sevastopol
Ankara
Smyrna
Alexandrette

Pleskau
Estonia
Witebsk
March
1916
Minsk
Aug. 1916

Nov. 1915

Riga
Latvia
Lithuania
Vilnius
Brest-Litowsk
Poland
Warsaw
April 1915

Battle of the
Masurian Lakes
Feb. 1915

ROMANIA
BUCHAREST
Oct. 1915
Belgrade
Sept. 1916
Oct. 1915

CONSTANTINOPLE
Gallipoli
Feb. 1915 – Jan. 1916

Gorlice-Tarnow
Offensive
1–3 May 1915

Winter Battle
in the Carpathian
Mountains
Jan. – Apr. 1915

BULGARIA
SOFIA
Kosovo
10. – 23.11.
1915

Saloniki
Oct./Nov.
1915

Baltic Sea

Masurian Lakes
6. – 15.9.1914
Battle of Tannenberg
26. – 30.8.1914

VIENNA
AUSTRIA-HUNGARY
Zagreb
Sarajevo
SERBIA
MONTENEGRO
ALBANIA
GREECE
ATHENS

SWEDEN
STOCKHOLM

DENMARK
Kiel
Hamburg
BERLIN
GERMAN REICH
Prague
Munich

NORWAY

North Sea

Battle of Jutland
31.5./1.6.1916
Heligoland
29.8.1914
Dogger Bank
24.1.1915
British Naval Blockade
2.11.1914

GREAT BRITAIN
AND IRELAND
Liverpool
LONDON

THE
NETHER-
LANDS
BELGIUM
LUX.

Aug. 1914

English Channel

German Offensive
Feb. – July 1916
Battle of the Somme
June – Sept. 1916
Compiègne
PARIS
Battle of the Marne
Sept. 1914

Feb. – June
1916
July –
Dec. 1916

FRANCE

SWITZER-
LAND

Genf
Lyon
Marseille

Milan
1st to 9th Battles
of the Isonzo
June 1915 – Nov. 1916.
May – June
1916

ITALY
ROME
Naples

Adriatic

Mediterranean Sea

©ZMSBw
07627–05

Central Powers 1918
Entente Powers and their Allies
Russia and Romania
Neutral States
Fronts in Late 1916
Farthest German Advance in 1914
Farthest Russian Advance in 1914
Fronts Between Early 1915 and Late 1916
Military Operations
Battle

Source: Der grosse Ploetz-Atlas, S. 177; Putzger - Atlas und Chronik, S. 206.

Plate 3.

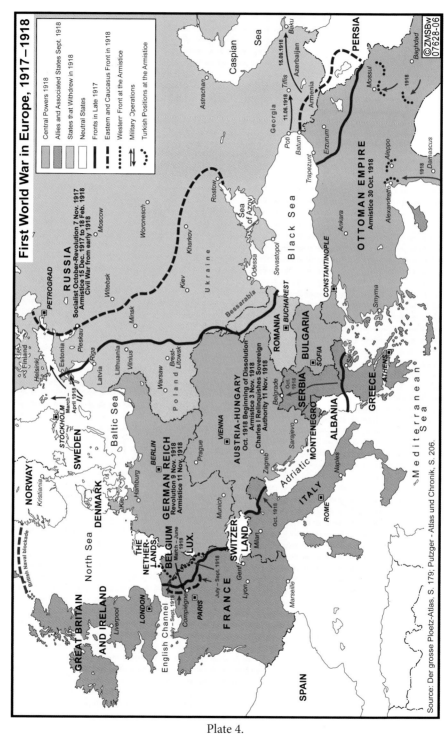

First World War in Europe, 1917–1918

Legend:
- Central Powers 1918
- Allies and Associated States Sept. 1918
- States that Withdrew in 1918
- Neutral States
- Fronts in Late 1917
- Eastern and Caucasus Front in 1918
- Western Front at the Armistice
- Military Operations
- Turkish Positions at the Armistice

©ZMSBw
07628-06

RUSSIA
Socialist October-Revolution 7 Nov. 1917
Armistice 15 Dec. 1917 to 18 Feb. 1918
Civil War from early 1918

PETROGRAD

Caspian Sea

PERSIA
Baghdad

Astrachan

Moscow

Woronesch

Kharkov

Kiev

Ukraine

Witebsk

Minsk

Rostow

Sea of Azov

Sevastopol

Odessa

Bessarabia

Black Sea

Georgia
Poti
11.06.1918 Tiflis
Batum
Trapezunt
Erzurum
Armenia
Azerbaijan
15.09.1918 Baku
Mossul
1918
Damascus

OTTOMAN EMPIRE
Armistice 30 Oct. 1918

Ankara
Smyrna
Aleppo
Alexandrette
1918

Finland
Helsinki

Estonia
Pleskau
Riga
Latvia
Lithuania
Vilnius

STOCKHOLM
March–
April 1918

SWEDEN

Baltic Sea

Warsaw
Poland
Brest-Litowsk

ROMANIA
BUCHAREST
BULGARIA
SOFIA

Belgrade
Oct. 1918
SERBIA
MONTENEGRO
Sarajevo
Zagreb

Adriatic Sea

ALBANIA

GREECE
Saloniki
ATHENS

CONSTANTINOPLE

Mediterranean Sea

NORWAY
Kristiania

DENMARK

North Sea

GERMAN REICH
Revolution 9 Nov. 1918
Armistice 11 Nov. 1918

BERLIN
Hamburg
Kiel

Prague
Munich

AUSTRIA-HUNGARY
Oct. 1918 Beginning of Dissolution
Armistice 3 Nov. 1918
Charles I Relinquishes Sovereign
Authority 11 Nov. 1918

VIENNA

ITALY
Naples
ROME
Milan
Oct. 1918

British Naval blockade

GREAT BRITAIN AND IRELAND
Liverpool
LONDON

English Channel

THE NETHER-LANDS
BELGIUM
LUX.
Gent
Compiègne
PARIS
July–Sept. 1918
July–Sept. 1918

March–June 1918

SWITZER-LAND

FRANCE
Lyon
Marseille

SPAIN

Source: Der grosse Ploetz-Atlas, S. 179; Putzger - Atlas und Chronik, S. 206.

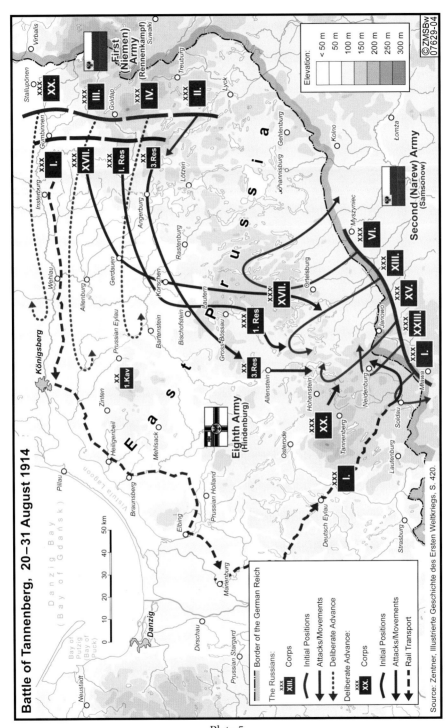

Battle of Tannenberg, 20–31 August 1914

Elevation:
< 50 m
50 m
100 m
150 m
200 m
250 m
300 m

First (Niemen) Army (Rennenkampf)

Second (Narew) Army (Samsonow)

Eighth Army (Hindenburg)

The Russians:
XIII. ⟶ Corps
Initial Positions
Attacks/Movements
Deliberate Advance:

Deliberate Advance:
XX. ⟶ Corps
Initial Positions
Attacks/Movements
Rail Transport

Border of the German Reich

©ZMSBw
07629-04

Source: Zentner, Illustrierte Geschichte des Ersten Weltkriegs, S. 420.

Plate 5.

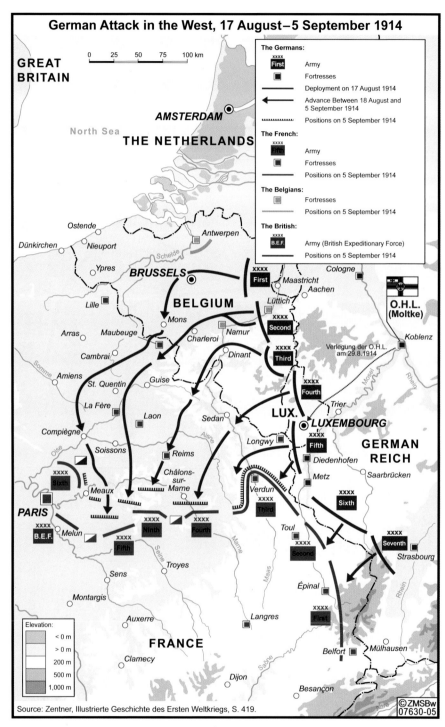

German Attack in the West, 17 August–5 September 1914

Legend	
The Germans:	
First	Army
■	Fortresses
	Deployment on 17 August 1914
◄──	Advance Between 18 August and 5 September 1914
....	Positions on 5 September 1914
The French:	
Fifth	Army
■	Fortresses
──	Positions on 5 September 1914
The Belgians:	
■	Fortresses
──	Positions on 5 September 1914
The British:	
B.E.F.	Army (British Expeditionary Force)
──	Positions on 5 September 1914

Source: Zentner, Illustrierte Geschichte des Ersten Weltkriegs, S. 419.

© ZMSBw
07630-05

Plate 6.

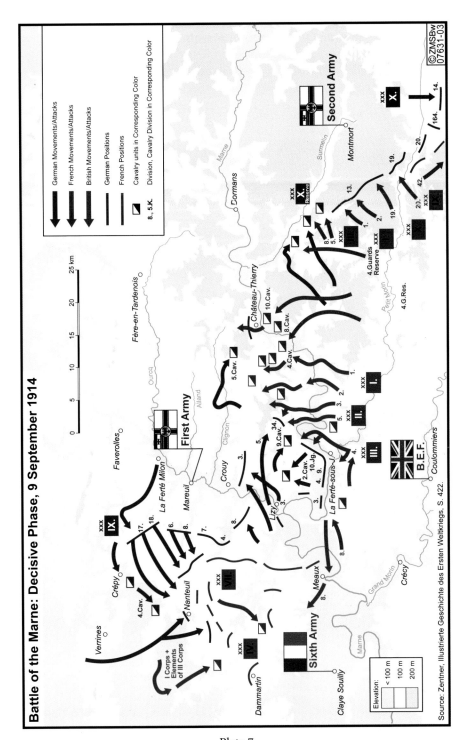

Battle of the Marne: Decisive Phase, 9 September 1914

German Movements/Attacks

French Movements/Attacks

British Movements/Attacks

German Positions

French Positions

Cavalry units in Corresponding Color

Division, Cavalry Division in Corresponding Color

8., 5.K.

0   5   10   15   20   25 km

Elevation:
< 100 m
100 m
200 m

Source: Zentner, Illustrierte Geschichte des Ersten Weltkriegs, S. 422.

©ZMSBw
07631-03

Second Army

First Army

Sixth Army

B.E.F.

Plate 7.

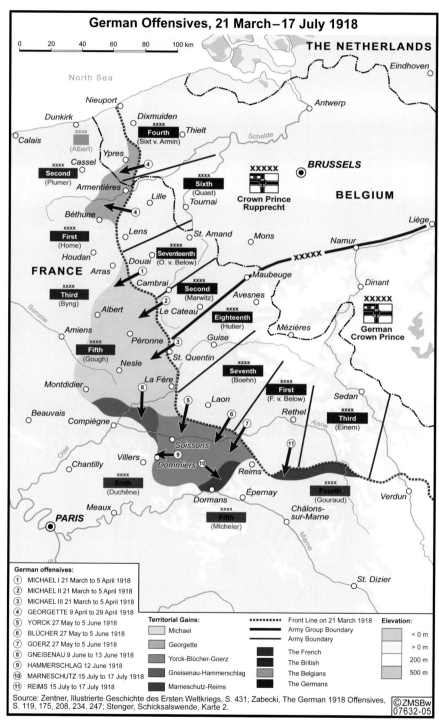

German Offensives, 21 March–17 July 1918

0   20   40   60   80   100 km

THE NETHERLANDS

North Sea

Eindhoven

Nieuport

Dunkirk

Calais

Dixmuiden

Fourth
(Sixt v. Armin)

Thielt

Schelde

Antwerp

(Albert)

Ypres

Cassel

Second
(Plumer)

Armentières

Béthune

First
(Home)

Houdan

FRANCE

Arras

Lille

Tournai

Sixth
(Quast)

BRUSSELS

XXXXX
Crown Prince
Rupprecht

BELGIUM

Liège

Lens

St. Amand

Mons

Namur

Seventeenth
(O. v. Below)

Douai

Maubeuge

Dinant

Cambrai

Second
(Marwitz)

Avesnes

Albert

Le Cateau

Eighteenth
(Hutier)

Amiens

Péronne

Guise

Mézières

Fifth
(Gough)

Nesle

St. Quentin

XXXXX
German
Crown Prince

Montdidier

La Fère

Seventh
(Boehn)

Laon

First
(F. v. Below)

Sedan

Beauvais

Compiègne

Chantilly

Villers

Soissons

Dommiers

Reims

Rethel

Third
(Einem)

Verdun

Sixth
(Duchêne)

Dormans

Épernay

Châlons-
sur-Marne

Meaux

PARIS

Fifth
(Micheler)

St. Dizier

German offensives:
- ① MICHAEL I 21 March to 5 April 1918
- ② MICHAEL II 21 March to 5 April 1918
- ③ MICHAEL III 21 March to 5 April 1918
- ④ GEORGETTE 9 April to 29 April 1918
- ⑤ YORCK 27 May to 5 June 1918
- ⑥ BLÜCHER 27 May to 5 June 1918
- ⑦ GOERZ 27 May to 5 June 1918
- ⑧ GNEISENAU 9 June to 13 June 1918
- ⑨ HAMMERSCHLAG 12 June 1918
- ⑩ MARNESCHUTZ 15 July to 17 July 1918
- ⑪ REIMS 15 July to 17 July 1918

Territorial Gains:
- Michael
- Georgette
- Yorck-Blücher-Goerz
- Gneisenau-Hammerschlag
- Marneschutz-Reims

•••••• Front Line on 21 March 1918
Army Group Boundary
Army Boundary

The French
The British
The Belgians
The Germans

Elevation:
< 0 m
> 0 m
200 m
500 m

Source: Zentner, Illustrierte Geschichte des Ersten Weltkriegs, S. 431; Zabecki, The German 1918 Offensives, S. 119, 175, 208, 234, 247; Stenger, Schicksalswende, Karte 2.

©ZMSBw
07632-05

Plate 8.

Second World War in Europe, 1939 to 1942

① The Netherlands
② Belgium
③ Switzerland
④ Albania
⑤ Protectorate of Bohemia and Moravia

ICELAND
Faroe-Islands
Shetland-Islands
Orkney-Islands
GREAT BRITAIN
IRELAND
Birmingham
Coventry
LONDON
Dover
Brest
BRUSSELS
Nantes
Orléans
FRANCE
Vichy
Bordeaux
Hendaye
»ETAT FRANÇAISE«
Marseille
SPAIN
Barcelona
Balearic Islands
ALGIERS
Bône
TUNIS
Algeria
Gabes
TRIPOLI
Libya

NORWAY
Narvik 6.40
Namsos 5.40
Andalsnes
Dombås
Lillehammer
Bergen
OSLO
Stavanger
Kristiansund 4.40
Aalborg 4.40
DENMARK
COPENHAGEN
North Sea
Baltic Sea
Gdingen
Königsberg
Danzig
Hamburg
Stettin
BERLIN
GERMAN REICH
Cologne
LUX.
Frankfurt
Strassburg
Munich
Vienna
Prague ⑤
Lidice
SLOVAKIA
BUDAPEST
HUNGARY
Agram
BELGRADE
YUGOSLAVIA
Sarajevo
Nisch
Venice
ITALY
ROME
Sardinia
Corsica 11.42
Toulon 27.11.42
11.42
Sicily
Pantelleria
Malta
Bizerte
9.11.42
Tunisia
Africa Corps from Feb 1941

Kirkenes
Petsamo
Murmansk
Kiruna
Gällivare
Salla
Luleå
Archangel
SWEDEN
FINLAND
Drontheim
HELSINKI
Viipuri
Hanko
Leningrad
Tichwin
STOCKHOLM
REVAL
Estonia
RIGA
Kalinin
Latvia
Lithuania
Smolensk
KAUNAS
Minsk
Brjansk
Posen
Bialystok
Brest-Litowsk
Kutno
Breslau
WARSAW
POLAND
Krakow
Lwow
Kiev
Uman
Lidice
Gomel
Kursk
Orel
Tula 11.41
Woronesch
MOSCOW 11.41
Gorki
Stalingrad 23.8.42
Kharkov
Krementschug
Rostov
8.42
Odessa
Perekop
Feodosia
Tuapse
Maikop
Sevastopol
Black Sea
ROMANIA
BUCHAREST
BULGARIA
SOFIA
TIRANA ④
Janina
Saloniki
Istanbul
ANKARA
TURKEY
GREECE
Cape Matapan 3.41
ATHENS
Dodekanes
Crete 5.41 6.41
Cyprus
Haleb 7.41
SYRIA
BEIRUT
DAMASCUS
LEBANON 7.41
Palestine
JERUSALEM
Port Said
Suez
Jordan
Trans-
5.41
Derna
Tobruk
Sollum
Benghasi 3.–4.41
Alexandria
El Alamein
Cairo
El Agheila
Marsa el-Brega
Egypt
1.41
3.41
1.–2.42
6.42
5.–6.41
4.–11.41
6.–11.42
Mediterranean Sea

8.11.42
12.11.42
11.42

SOVIET UNION

Kirov Railway

Legend:

- Axis Powers and Danzig at the Beginning of the War in 1939
- Allies of the Axis Powers in 1941

Advance of the Axis Powers and their Allies
- 1 Sept. to 6 Oct 1939
- Late June 1940
- Late December 1941
- Mid-November 1942
- → Attacks of the Axis Powers and their Allies
- ○ Encircled Polish and Russian Forces
- ⚓ Air Landings

POLAND Allies at the Beginning of the War
- Territory of the Western Allies, November 1940
- Territory Occupied by Western Allies, November 1942
- Soviet Union at the Beginning of the German Attack on 22 June 1941
- Neutral States
- Vichy France from 10 July 1940 (including Colonial Territories)
- → Allied Attacks
- --→ Allied Retreats
- → Soviet Advance 1939 and 1940
- 1.42 Allied Positions in Africa
- ⚓ Air Landings

- Greek-Italian Front, April 1941
- --- State Borders at the Beginning of the War on 1 Sept. 1939

0 200 400 600 km

© ZMSBw
07634-05

Source: Putzger - Atlas und Chronik, S. 234.

Plate 9.

Second World War in Europe, 1942 to 1945

① The Netherlands
② Belgium
③ Switzerland

Source: Putzger - Atlas und Chronik, S. 235.

Allies and Territories Occupied by Allies in Late 1942
Allied Advance:
Early October 1943
Mid-December 1944
End of the War May 1945
→ Allied Attacks
7.43 Dates of Seizure by Allied Forces
O Encircled German forces

States Neutral until Early 1945
States Neutral until the End of the War
26.2.45 Dates of Declaration of War on Germany

Areas held by German Troops Within and Outside of Reich Territory at the End of the War
Farthest Advance of the Axis Powers, November 1942
→ Axis Powers' Attacks
---→ Axis Powers' Retreats
—·— State Borders in November 1942

0   200   400   600 km

©ZMSBw
07635-05

Plate 10.

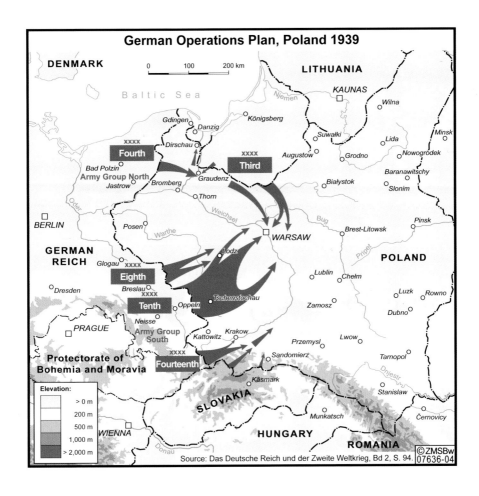

German Operations Plan, Poland 1939

DENMARK

Baltic Sea

LITHUANIA

KAUNAS

Wilna

Gdingen

Danzig

Königsberg

Suwałki

Lida

Minsk

XXXX
Fourth

Dirschau

Augustow

Grodno

Nowogrodek

Bad Polzin

Army Group North

Jastrow

Bromberg

Graudenz

XXXX
Third

Białystok

Baranawitschy

Slonim

Thorn

Weichsel

Bug

BERLIN

Posen

Warthe

WARSAW

Brest-Litowsk

Pripet

Pinsk

GERMAN
REICH

Glogau

XXXX
Eighth

Lodz

POLAND

Lublin

Chelm

Dresden

Breslau

XXXX
Tenth

Oppeln

Tschenstochau

Zamosz

Luzk

Rowno

Dubno

Neisse

PRAGUE

**Army Group
South**

Kattowitz

Krakow

Przemysl

Lwow

Tarnopol

XXXX
Fourteenth

Sandomierz

Dnjestr

**Protectorate of
Bohemia and Moravia**

Käsmark

Stanislaw

SLOVAKIA

Černovicy

WIENNA

Munkatsch

Elevation:
> 0 m
200 m
500 m
1,000 m
> 2,000 m

HUNGARY

ROMANIA

Donau

Source: Das Deutsche Reich und der Zweite Weltkrieg, Bd 2, S. 94.

©ZMSBw
07636-04

0   100   200 km

Plate 11.

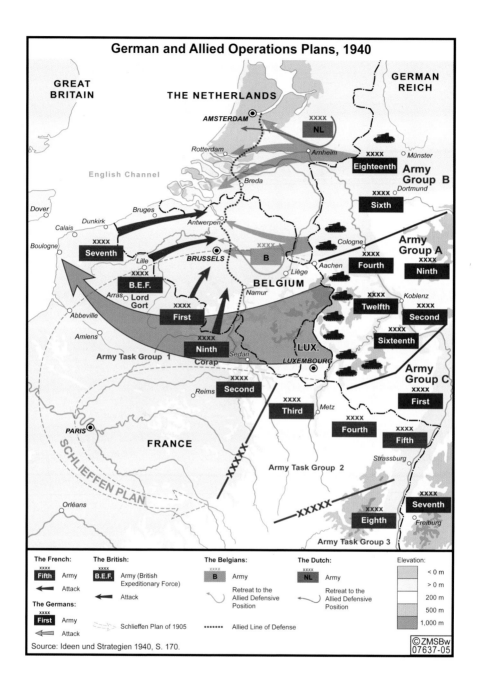

German and Allied Operations Plans, 1940

GREAT BRITAIN

THE NETHERLANDS

GERMAN REICH

AMSTERDAM

Rotterdam

Arnheim

Münster

XXXX NL

English Channel

Breda

XXXX Eighteenth

Army Group B

Dover

Bruges

Antwerpen

Dortmund

XXXX Sixth

Calais

Dunkirk

Boulogne

XXXX Seventh

Lille

BRUSSELS

XXXX B

Cologne

Army Group A

XXXX B.E.F. Lord Gort

Arras

BELGIUM

Liège

Aachen

XXXX Fourth

XXXX Ninth

Abbeville

XXXX First

Namur

XXXX Twelfth

Koblenz

XXXX Second

Amiens

XXXX Ninth

Corap

Sedan

LUX.

LUXEMBOURG

XXXX Sixteenth

Army Task Group 1

Army Group C

Reims

XXXX Second

XXXX Third

Metz

XXXX First

PARIS

FRANCE

XXXX Fourth

XXXX Fifth

Strassburg

SCHLIEFFEN PLAN

Army Task Group 2

Orléans

XXXXX

XXXX Eighth

XXXX Seventh

Freiburg

Army Task Group 3

The French:	The British:	The Belgians:	The Dutch:	Elevation:
Fifth — Army	B.E.F. — Army (British Expeditionary Force)	B — Army	NL — Army	< 0 m
← Attack	← Attack	Retreat to the Allied Defensive Position	Retreat to the Allied Defensive Position	> 0 m
The Germans:				200 m
First — Army		Schlieffen Plan of 1905	Allied Line of Defense	500 m
⇐ Attack				1,000 m

Source: Ideen und Strategien 1940, S. 170.

©ZMSBw
07637-05

Plate 12.

Operations Draft East (Major General Marcks), 5 August 1940

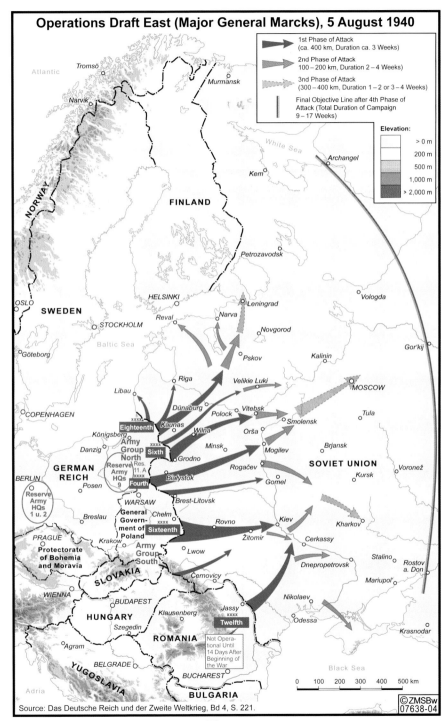

1st Phase of Attack
(ca. 400 km, Duration ca. 3 Weeks)

2nd Phase of Attack
100 – 200 km, Duration 2 – 4 Weeks)

3nd Phase of Attack
(300 – 400 km, Duration 1 – 2 or 3 – 4 Weeks)

**Final Objective Line after 4th Phase of
Attack (Total Duration of Campaign
9 – 17 Weeks)**

Elevation:

> 0 m
200 m
500 m
1,000 m
> 2,000 m

Source: Das Deutsche Reich und der Zweite Weltkrieg, Bd 4, S. 221.

©ZMSBw
07638-04

Plate 13.

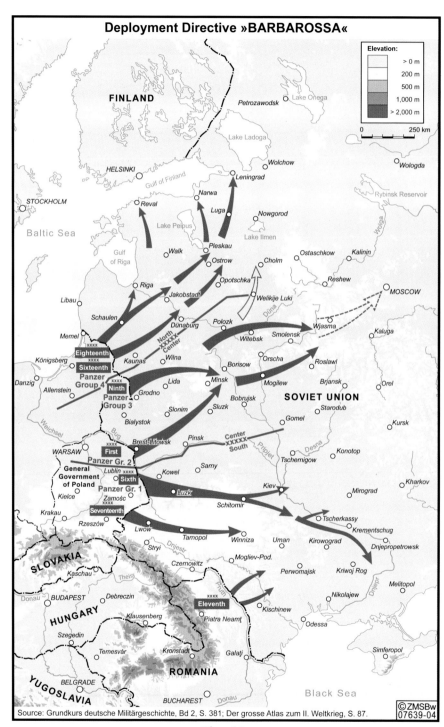

Deployment Directive »BARBAROSSA«

Elevation:
> 0 m
200 m
500 m
1,000 m
> 2,000 m

0   250 km

Source: Grundkurs deutsche Militärgeschichte, Bd 2, S. 381; Der grosse Atlas zum II. Weltkrieg, S. 87.

©ZMSBw
07639-04

Plate 14.

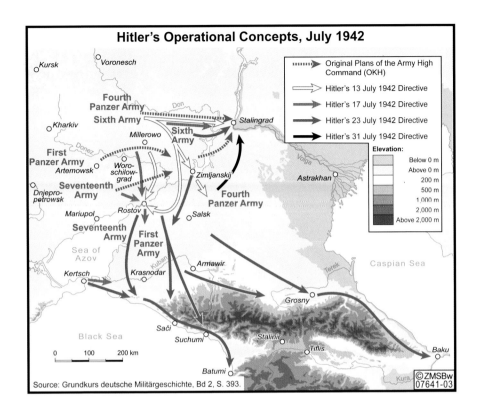

Hitler's Operational Concepts, July 1942

Original Plans of the Army High Command (OKH)

Hitler's 13 July 1942 Directive

Hitler's 17 July 1942 Directive

Hitler's 23 July 1942 Directive

Hitler's 31 July 1942 Directive

Elevation:

Below 0 m
Above 0 m
200 m
500 m
1,000 m
2,000 m
Above 2,000 m

Kursk
Voronesch
Kharkiv
Fourth Panzer Army
Sixth Army
Millerowo
Sixth Army
Don
Stalingrad
First Panzer Army
Artemowsk
Woro-schilow-grad
Donez
Zimljanskij
Volga
Astrakhan
Seventeenth Army
Dnjepro-petrowsk
Mariupol
Rostov
Salsk
Fourth Panzer Army
Seventeenth Army
First Panzer Army
Sea of Azov
Kertsch
Krasnodar
Kuban
Armawir
Terek
Caspian Sea
Grosny
Black Sea
Sači
Suchumi
Stalinir
Tiflis
Baku
0   100   200 km
Batumi
Kura
©ZMSBw
07641-03

Source: Grundkurs deutsche Militärgeschichte, Bd 2, S. 393.

Plate 15.

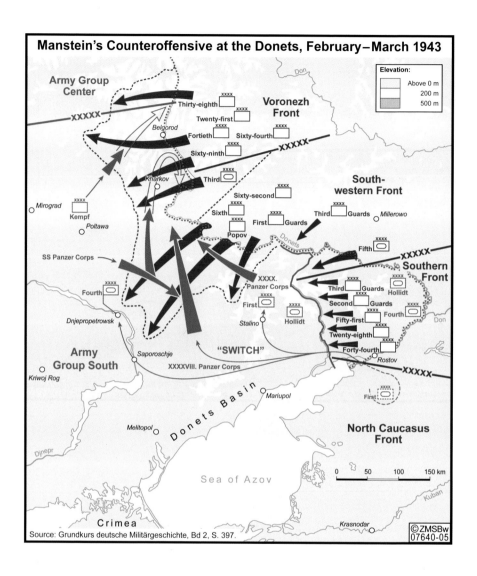

Manstein's Counteroffensive at the Donets, February–March 1943

Elevation:
- Above 0 m
- 200 m
- 500 m

Army Group Center

Don

XXXXX

Thirty-eighth XXXX

Twenty-first XXXX

Voronezh Front

Belgorod

Fortieth XXXX   Sixty-fourth XXXX

Sixty-ninth XXXX

XXXXX

Kharkov

Third XXXX

Sixty-second XXXX

South-western Front

Mirograd

Kempf XXXX

Poltawa

Sixth XXXX

First XXXX Guards

Popov XXXX

Third XXXX Guards   Millerowo

SS Panzer Corps

Fifth XXXX

XXXXX

Southern Front

Fourth XXXX

XXXX. Panzer Corps

First XXXX

Third XXXX Guards   Hollidt XXXX

Second XXXX Guards

Fourth XXXX

Dnjepropetrowsk

Stalino   Hollidt XXXX

Fifty-first XXXX

Twenty-eighth XXXX

Don

Army Group South

Saporoschje   "SWITCH"

Forty-fourth XXXX

Rostov

XXXXVIII. Panzer Corps

XXXXX

Kriwoj Rog

First XXXX

Donets Basin

Mariupol

Melitopol

North Caucasus Front

Djnepr

0   50   100   150 km

Sea of Azov

Crimea

Krasnodar

Kuban

Source: Grundkurs deutsche Militärgeschichte, Bd 2, S. 397.

©ZMSBw
07640-05

Plate 16.

war" (*Ernährungskrieg*) and the seizure of the granary of Russia a major priority. Such was a focus of consideration not only for Hitler and the various economic authorities, but also for General Georg Thomas at OKW and for the director of the Policy Branch of the OKW Economic Staff, Colonel Wilhelm Becker. The capture of the Ukraine, then, was not a question of if, but of when.[65]

In contrast to OKH, OKW made intense efforts to deal with the economic warfare issue in conjunction with operational warfare. Although the navy had the lead in any military trade war, the World War I experience and the actions of the Third OHL in the war's final years made it clear that the capture of areas critical to the war effort, especially the food production areas, was a prerequisite for the victorious prosecution of a lengthy war of attrition. While OKH stuck primarily to its operational thinking based on rapidly undermining the enemy's resources, OKW took a more "modern" approach and planned for a multi-year war of attrition—knowing such a form of warfare might lead to "the total shattering, even the extermination of sectors of the enemy as an ultimate goal," and be devoid of any "chivalrous concept of war." Thus, the war would necessarily evolve into a war of annihilation, regardless of any moral or international legal considerations.[66] (See Plate 13.)

Although these thoughts arose from a military utilitarianism, there is a striking similarity to National Socialist ideology. It was then only a small step to the insertion of National Socialist ideology into the operational-strategic planning process. If and to what extent OKH was informed of OKW's operational-economic war plans—considering the tensions between them—has not been studied sufficiently. What is certain is that Halder flatly refused to accommodate any "economic demands on the conduct of operations," since such ran contrary to the army's operational thinking.[67] But the broad-based economic factors that would secure the Greater German Reich's autonomy in a longer war of attrition against Great Britain and the United States were designed to establish tight limits on the conduct of operations—a fact that the chief of the General Staff ignored for a long time.

From the very beginning operational planning at the General Staff suffered from the fact that Hitler and OKH did not agree on the operational objective. While Hitler predominantly focused on the capture of the military-economic areas and the political centers, the General Staff—following traditional operational thinking—focused on the annihilation of the enemy's army. Hitler did, however, support the two parallel pincer operations toward Kiev and Moscow (and later Leningrad). Those operations would be followed by an offensive against the oil-producing area near Baku. Thus, Hitler established the centers of gravity on the wings, with the capture of the Baltic States in the north and the Ukraine and later Baku in the south. Halder did not concur with those ideas, and planned the center of gravity in the center, with a thrust toward Moscow. His objective was to destroy the central Russian railway network by capturing Moscow, and then to annihilate the Soviet reserve forces that he was convinced were massed in front of Moscow. For Halder the attacks on Kiev and Leningrad served only as flank security for the main operation.

General Erich Marcks submitted the "Operations Draft East" at the beginning of August.[68] Although the plan included the capture of the economic regions in the south and north of the Soviet Union, the focus was on the capture of Moscow. The fall of the capital as the political and economic center of the Soviet Union would accelerate the country's demise. After taking the city and having annihilated the Soviet units in the north, the plan was to combine forces with Army Group South and attack the Ukraine in a gigantic pincer movement, finally reaching the Rostov–Archangel line, from which the Soviet industrial areas in the Urals were to be destroyed by the Luftwaffe.

To advance the planning process in accordance with his own ideas, Halder at the beginning of August assigned as the overall planning coordinator Lieutenant General Friedrich Paulus, a recognized operations expert and Panzer specialist. Paulus shepherded the operational planning and successfully played it through in several map exercises.[69] During this phase of the planning Hitler did not comment on the plans for the war against the Soviet Union. Only after the talks with Soviet foreign minister Vyacheslav Molotov failed in November did Hitler use the occasion of a briefing at OKH on 5 December to make it clear that hegemony in Europe had to be established in the fight against Russia. The Führer accepted Halder's operational plans in principle, emphasizing that the Soviet forces had to be broken up and then defeated in detail.[70] But Hitler left open the question of the establishment of the center of gravity, especially regarding the attack on Moscow. He also declared that the coming spring was the most favorable period for the campaign.

That, however, was not a definitive decision on the conduct of operations, because Hitler continued to consider the option of establishing the war's strategic center of gravity in the Mediterranean.[71] Over the course of the following weeks he decided against the "Mediterranean Alternative Strategy" and in favor of the attack in the east. The deployment to Libya of the German Africa Corps under Rommel in February 1941 and the Operation MARITA Balkans Campaign in April 1941 were essentially only efforts to help stabilize Germany's ally Italy. For Hitler, the Mediterranean as a secondary theater of war had only a peripheral status in the fight to gain time.[72]

On 18 December 1940, Führer Directive No. 21 prepared by OKW fixed the operational intent for a campaign against the Soviet Union. Hitler dictated his operational concepts in person. Thus, the center of gravity remained in the center, but not as an advance toward Moscow. Rather, the intent was to turn to the north and in coordination with Army Group North annihilate the Soviet forces in the north and capture the Baltic States and Leningrad. The first phase of the offensive was intended to destroy the Soviet units west of the Dnepr–Dvina line. The offensive against Moscow was to follow only after completion of that operation and after a logistical pause and reorganization. "Only a surprisingly rapid breakdown of the Russian resistance could justify aiming at both targets simultaneously."[73] Halder remained convinced that his operational concept was correct, but he also accepted its subordination. He was optimistic that developments would prove him right. Halder also repeatedly tried to add changes in his favor on the working level, which over the months produced planning frictions. But Halder could not get around Hitler's insistence on focusing on economic and ideological factors and his repeated declaration that Moscow was absolutely immaterial to him. Furthermore, Hitler detached the Twelfth Army from Army Group South and committed it to the Balkans Campaign. That made Halder's planned envelopment operation by Army Group South impossible to execute.[74] (See Plate 14.)

The Führer on 8 June 1941 largely confirmed his operational-strategic concept in the final deployment directive for Operation BARBAROSSA. There was no mention of a main thrust at Moscow. The offensive's centers of gravity were on the wings.[75] But in the end the operational plan was really a compromise between the differing operational ideas, lacking a clearly established center of gravity. This was owing to the fact that during no phase of planning had Hitler and OKH reached an agreement on the operational objective of the campaign. While Halder considered the annihilation of the enemy's forces as the operational objective, Hitler, although talking of the destruction of the Red Army, saw the ultimate goal as the capture of the economically important areas for the war effort. Guderian got to the heart of this dilemma in his memoirs: "Three army groups, each of approximately the same strength, were to attack with diverging objectives; no single clear operational objective seemed to be there. Seen from a professional perspective, this did not at all appear promising."[76]

The question of how the Soviet Union would be forced to make peace after the annihilation of the Red Army remained unresolved. The conflict between Halder and Hitler over the operations shook the very foundations of the General Staff's operational thinking. Hitler discounted the dogma of annihilating the enemy's forces through a decisive battle as the operational objective in favor of economic and ideological gains. The question then follows as to why both Halder and Brauchitsch allowed Hitler to interfere unopposed into what had been the exclusive domain of the General Staff since the time of Moltke the Elder. Undoubtedly, Halder recognized the validity of Hitler's strategic decisions up to that point. Despite many warnings to the contrary, the Führer had advanced the Great Power ambitions of the German officer corps far more rapidly than they had thought possible. Considering the position of power Hitler had achieved through these successes, Halder doubted his ability to defend his own convictions against not only the Führer, but also against OKW and the Luftwaffe. The overall situation led Halder to believe that he could only prevent Hitler's interference in the conduct of operations by delaying a final decision until the campaign was well under way. Convinced of the outstanding operational expertise of the General Staff, Halder waited for a crisis, at which point he would assert his superior competence and experience. Then, Halder was convinced, he would be able to present the only correct operational solution.[77] As historian Manfred Messerschmidt put it, the successes then would make Hitler go along in the direction intended by the General Staff.[78] It was a hope that would prove deceptive.

Right from the start, Operation BARBAROSSA was designed as a Blitzkrieg. Fast, decision-seeking operations would destroy the Red Army en masse as early as during the initial frontier battles. Apart from the space factor, the time factor played a decisive role. General Marcks estimated a required time of nine to seventeen weeks for the entire campaign.[79] With the attack starting in early summer, Halder expected it to end by autumn 1941—after approximately eight to ten weeks. Hitler assumed up to twenty-one weeks. Many foreign observers agreed with the German assessments.[80] The belief in a rapid victory suppressed the army leadership's concerns for the consequences of a two-front war that the attack might set off. As they saw it, the opportunity was good for dealing with the Soviet Union quickly, thus avoiding a two-front war and then dealing with a follow-on one-front war at the right time.

How did the operations experts come to believe this, considering the vast depth of Russian space that opened up like a funnel toward the east, interspersed with many rivers perpendicular to the direction of advance, and with poor transportation infrastructure compared to the west? From the start the German General Staff planned the campaign based on relative inferiority. They underestimated not only the real strength,[81] but also the military strength[82] of the Red Army. The General Staff was not overly concerned by the prospect of having to launch the attack from a position of inferiority. That corresponded with the German concept of war since the time of Schlieffen. Naturally, the qualitative superiority of materiel, troops, and especially of the commanders were basic assumptions. Furthermore, Hitler and his generals assessed the military strength of the Soviet units as low,[83] because the Soviet conduct of the wars against Poland in 1920 and against Finland in 1939–1940 had exposed the Red Army's weak leadership at the mid-level and higher command echelons. Those more recent observations reinforced the German experiences from World War I, when numerically inferior German forces had defeated the tsarist troops on the Eastern Front secondary theater of war, and had captured large areas of Russia. Such experiences nourished the certainty of Germany's superior military leadership, and the illusion of the internal fragility of the multiethnic Russian state.[84] Thus, the concept of duplicating the "railway deployment of 1918" became a central element of OKH plans, as Marcks planned to execute the Russia Campaign with a similar railway deployment.

The contempt for the Red Army's leadership capabilities was less an individual heritage from World War I—the minority of the senior Wehrmacht officers had eastern war experience—and more of a social construct, not based on the operational experience of the last world war, but on a stereotypical view of the enemy.[85] The simple Russian soldier was considered to be inferior to his German counterpart. Racial ideology certainly played a part here. The great bravery of the Russian soldiers and their ability to fight under the most adverse conditions was largely ignored,[86] as was the inexhaustible Russian reservoir of manpower and the vastness of the Russian space, of which Moltke the Elder, Schlieffen, and Falkenhayn had all expressly warned.[87] The image of the feared Russian steamroller of 1914 was replaced by the 1940 figure of the colossus on shaky foundations. Considering this largely artificial assessment of the enemy, it is little surprise that the General Staff ignored any facts that did not fit their preconceived image—facts, for example, like the Soviet victory over the Japanese Sixth Army at the Khalkh River battle in August 1939.[88]

This was a great mistake, since the Khalkh River battle demonstrated the Red Army's ability to conduct combined arms warfare with mechanized units and air support. Even when the alleged war experience did exert significant influence, the real reasons for Germany's feeling of superiority came from the military successes against Poland and especially against France. After the victory in the west, the Wehrmacht was convinced that the rapid, air-supported Panzer operations by the "elite units" were the solution—in other words, compensating for numerical inferiority with mobility. That concept seemed only to need some incremental improvements. The crisis of the attack appeared to be surmountable. Consequently, during the run-up to Operation BARBAROSSA the number of Panzer divisions increased, while the number of tanks per division decreased accordingly.[89] The resulting decrease in thrusting power was accepted because it was compensated for by strengthening the Panzer division's infantry elements with additional infantry and motorcycle units. Another compensation was the improvement of mobility by increasing the number of motorized units. The enemy zone of defense would be broken into by combined arms, which would then facilitate the subsequent exploitation by the Panzer units to operational depth.[90] As in the campaign against France, surprise and initiative were the weapons of choice.

At the tactical-operational level the Red Army would be defeated through a double envelopment by rapidly mobile units. This classic operational procedure was called a *Kesselschlacht* (cauldron battle). The requirement for a successful double envelopment was the seizure of the initiative and the will to force the imperative of action upon the enemy. The Kesselschlacht could be fought offensively as well as defensively, the 1914 Battle of Tannenberg being an example of the latter.[91]

The key was the freedom of action necessary to achieve the intended operational objective within the available time and space. A successful Kesselschlacht—and this was an absolute condition of German operational thinking—could be won despite being outnumbered. The essential condition for the success of a double envelopment was the concentration of the attack units in the smallest possible space to ensure a local, if temporary, superiority at the center of gravity. After effecting an initial breakthrough, the attack had to be advanced in depth rapidly, regardless of open flanks. Such, of course, required complex coordination measures. But the whole thing depended on a smooth and fast start, and then the forward advance of the offensive wedges while maintaining the advantages of freedom of action and initiative, leading to the defeat of the enemy in depth. The close coordination between the tactical and the operational levels of leadership and the uniform command procedures of the committed Wehrmacht elements were absolute conditions for success.[92]

The majority of the German military elite was convinced that the mobile and swift conduct of operations facilitated by the combination of tanks and aircraft guaranteed operational-strategic success. This form of operational warfare termed Blitzkrieg, which corresponded to the army's classical operational thinking since the time of Moltke the Elder, put the emphasis on speed and mobility to compensate for inferiority in manpower and materiel. The motorization of warfighting equipment both on the ground and in the air made possible the conduct of rapid, mobile, and extended-area operations upon which such operational thinking was based, but which could not have been executed fully during World War I because of mobility limitations.

Consequently, the most important parameters of traditional German thinking, which included mobility, attack, initiative, center of gravity establishment, envelopment, surprise, and destruction, now all came together in the Wehrmacht's operational command and control system called Blitzkrieg. All of these parameters are key elements in the Operation BARBAROSSA plans. Marcks stressed that surprise, rapid action, and mobility were the principles of success for the attacks in the Eastern Campaign. The objective of operations in depth was, apart from destroying the enemy's supply and communications lines, the double envelopment and destruction of the enemy's military forces. Owing to the size of the operations area and the strength of the Red Army, the BARBAROSSA plan did not anticipate one but several *Kesselschlachten*—a "sequence of Cannaes." This form of operations was based on the General Staff's intent to force the imperative of action upon the enemy and to seize the initiative. But because of insufficient coordination between OKH and Hitler, the establishment of the center of gravity was diluted correspondingly.

The German political and military leadership both assumed that the Soviet economy would break down after the loss of the regions to be occupied. That conviction was reinforced on the one hand by the experiences of World War I, and on the other hand by relying on outdated information that "proved" through ideological determination the inferiority of Bolshevism. Other indicators were ignored because they did not fit into the desired situational picture. The August 1940 military-geographic study of the Soviet Union, for example, provided a realistic picture of the Soviet industrial capacities and warned that the Soviet Union would not break down after the loss of its western industrial regions, because of the buildup of the modern industrial centers in Siberia. The warning of the military geographers about the depth of the operational area and the difficult climatic conditions for motorized warfare were for the most part shoved aside and only rudimentarily integrated into the situational assessment against the background of the World War I experiences and the German innate feeling of superiority. An unbiased situational assessment was hardly possible because of a combination of assumed warfighting experience, racial-ideological blindness, and self-overestimation. Thus, the verification of assumptions inherent to a well-ordered military situational assessment did not take place.

A further issue, one closely connected to operational thinking, was not resolved for the attack against the Soviet Union. The conduct of rapid and mobile operations absolutely required an agile, expansive, and mobile logistical system to cope with the vast area of the operations. In the period between the world wars this core problem of German operational thinking had been suppressed by the primacy of purely operational factors, although the acceleration of the rates of advance through motorization had increased logistical requirements even more.[93] The transition from transportation by rail to motor vehicles that accompanied the troops in the field was still incomplete in the German Army, despite the experiences of World War I.[94] Simultaneously, the long-standing weaknesses in the German railroad system had not been corrected.[95]

With only a few exceptions, Halder being among the most noteworthy, the General Staff had no great interest in logistical issues.[96] Although all forms of logistics had gained enormous importance in modern mobile warfare, the transfer or promotion of an officer to the branches of transport or supply—which were considered second-rate—was almost always considered a "punitive transfer" by the "victim."[97]

Traditionally, the operational thinking and logistics system of the German Army were adapted to the areas in Central Europe adjacent to the country's borders. World War I exposed the limitations of this system. Nonetheless, the belief was widespread that during the pending operations in the east any logistical problems could always be mastered through Germany's vaunted improvisational capabilities. The operations experts took refuge in the idea that the suppliers (*die Versorger*) would somehow always manage to "conjure up" a logistical solution.[98]

The preparations for Operation BARBAROSSA pushed the primacy of operations to its limits. The task was to ensure the logistical supply of more than 3 million soldiers, approximately five hundred thousand vehicles, and nearly three hundred thousand horses over a vast area of operations, and for a rapid offensive in an area far beyond the dimensions of any previous German military operation. In addition, the vast geographical expanse, poor traffic conditions, meager infrastructure, and climatic extremes of Russia were far different than the conditions in Central or Western Europe, upon which the German concept of the conduct of operations was developed. Furthermore, the time constraints compressed the logistical planning process. The operation required the rapid and mobile supply of the fast assault units over an initial attack breadth of two thousand kilometers, widening like a funnel to more than three thousand kilometers as the operation progressed toward the east. The operational objectives diverged from the center and were more than fifteen hundred kilometers away from the initial bases. The key challenge was the efficient supply of the motorized units, because the Soviet railway network would be usable only on a limited basis during the initial weeks of the campaign.

The General Staff anticipated supply problems during the campaign, but they assessed such issues as negligible because of the planned short duration of the Blitzkrieg. According to the operational experts, logistics was not a factor that would delay significantly or even endanger the success of the operations.[99] The logistical system, therefore, was geared for a short campaign. For the initial, war-deciding phase of the campaign, the General Staff assumed that the supply system would operate with trucks on the roads. The quartermaster general, General Eduard Wagner, developed a special supply system based on a five-hundred-kilometer operational depth, twice any depth achieved in World War I.[100] This required that the troops, as in the eighteenth century, forage for their food in the countryside for the four to five months the operation was estimated to last, because the available transport capacity and the width of the operational area allowed only fuel, ammunition, and spare parts to be forwarded via bulk transport.[101] That was the only way to ensure the functioning of the required rapid supply system. Each army group was allocated enough trucks for about twenty thousand tons of bulk transport for their equipment. The subsequent second phase of the campaign would have to be supplied via the repaired railroad system, and after a longer operational pause for logistical reorganization. Thus, the greatest risks were assumed in the area of logistics. The fully motorized supply system that would be required for the rapid and mobile operations as planned simply did not exist in the Wehrmacht.[102] Despite all the recognized difficulties, neither the General Staff nor Hitler expected that transport or supply problems would seriously endanger the operations. According to old tradition, logistical problems were considered negligible.[103] If problems arose at all, they would only appear after a longer duration. Based on the German leaders' assumption of the certainty of superiority and victory, nobody really believed in the possibility of a long campaign. As at the start of World War I, they expected to be home for Christmas.[104]

Despite the obvious risks, only a few feared a *finis Germaniae* on the eve of the assault on the Soviet Union, as was widely reported after the war. The mood was rather typical of that of Propaganda Minister Joseph Goebbels, who wrote in his diary on 16 June 1941:

> They [the Soviets] have available about 180 to 200 divisions, maybe a little less, approximately as many as we have. They are absolutely not comparable to us in terms of personnel and materiel quality. The thrust will take place at several places initially. They will simply be rolled up. The Führer estimates about four months for the action; I estimate much less. Bolshevism will collapse like a house of cards. We face an unprecedented triumph. We must act. Moscow wants to stay out of the war until Europe is tired and bled dry.[105]

Supported by Romanian units, the Wehrmacht started its attack with Army Groups South, Center, and North in the early morning hours of 22 June 1941. The surprise, which according to operational thinking was a decisive condition for operational success, worked because the Wehrmacht, contrary to international law, attacked the Soviet Union without a declaration of war and Stalin had ignored all the indicators and warnings of a German attack.

The early days of the attack produced significant successes. The Luftwaffe destroyed nearly a quarter of the eight thousand Soviet aircraft and within a few days achieved air superiority. That in turn created the opportunity for tactical air support of the ground forces. By the beginning of July the German spearheads had penetrated as much as four hundred kilometers into Russian territory. The confidence of victory spread among the German leadership. Halder believed the operational objective of the first phase of attack, the destruction of the Soviet forces in the sector up to the Dvina and Dnepr Rivers, had been achieved. On 3 July he wrote in his personal war diary: "It is not saying too much if I claim that the Russian campaign will have been won within fourteen days. Of course, it will not be completed by then. The vastness of the area and the persistence of the fiercely conducted resistance will continue to make demands on us."[106]

Very rarely had a chief of the German General Staff assessed the situation as glaringly wrong as did Halder in those days. Surely the Red Army had sustained great losses of manpower and materiel. Army Group Center, under Field Marshal Fedor von Bock, attacked in the center of the main effort with thrusts by Panzer Group Two under Guderian and Panzer Group Three under Colonel General Hermann Hoth. They fought huge Cannae-like battles with their Panzers at Bialystok and Minsk.[107] Army Group South, however, advanced only slowly because of the unexpectedly persistent Soviet resistance. The Russian forces suffered great losses, but could neither be encircled nor destroyed. And although Army Group North broke through the Soviet defensive positions faster than in the south, the Soviet units managed to evade the planned encirclement in the Baltic States by withdrawing to the east.

Both army groups on the flanks had not yet achieved operational freedom; they only managed to push the Soviet units back frontally. Thus, the initial operational objective of destroying the Soviet units in the border regions was not achieved. The striking power of the Red Army remained unbroken. The subsequent success in the encirclement battle of Smolensk did not change the situation.[108]

This first phase of the Russian Campaign already showed that, as in the France Campaign, the largely horse-drawn German infantry divisions did not have the speed and mobility to keep up with the advances of the motorized units. The forward movement of the infantry divisions responsible for destroying the Red Army forces in the encirclements became an operational problem, because the Panzer units could not continue their advance before the infantry closed up. A controversy between the exponents of the Panzer and infantry factions flared up very quickly over the conduct of operations, and in particular on the formation of encirclements. The question of whether large-scale or smaller-scale encirclements should be formed developed into an operational doctrine dispute. While Panzer generals Hoth and Guderian, supported by Bock, favored large encirclements reaching far into the east, OKH and Hitler together with the commanding generals of the infantry field armies favored smaller encirclements, which could be cleared out faster.[109] This controversy paralyzed the conduct of operations from the beginning of the campaign. The decision by OKH to form smaller encirclements was based on the requirements of the infantry units, but it also served to rein in the Panzer generals. As the France Campaign had demonstrated, the Panzer commanders, in "good Prussian tradition," had a tendency to develop their own uncontrollable momentum. But OKH, remembering all too well the unauthorized actions of the commanders on the German right wing in August–September 1914, intended in this campaign to control the army groups and field armies in a strict operational sense by keeping them on a short leash. Contrary to the spirit of command through directives, Halder recommended to the commanding generals of the army groups that they should impose tight controls and force their wills upon the tactical conduct of their subordinate armies.[110]

The frontline commanders objected to OKH's principle of centralized command, which they identified with Brauchitsch and Halder. The field commanders also blamed OKH rather than Hitler for any operationally incorrect decisions, all the more so as the advance started to stall in the face of the increasingly persistent Russian resistance. Simultaneously, the fighting became more ferocious. Gradually, the General Staff's ostentatious confidence of victory was replaced by a more sober assessment of the situation. Although the spearhead of Army Group North was only one hundred kilometers from Leningrad, and the attack in the south was making progress as well, the destruction of the Red Army was still out of reach. As in World War I, and as predicted by Schlieffen and Moltke the Elder, the majority of the Soviet armies evaded envelopment by withdrawing to the east. Simultaneously, the German problems accumulated. The losses in personnel and materiel were far above the anticipated levels. Supply difficulties arose first, and then partisan attacks became frequent in the sectors behind the front. Finally, the General Staff and Hitler could no longer close their eyes to reality. They had absolutely underestimated the Red Army's military strength and the manpower and materiel figures. As Halder wrote in his war diary on 11 August 1941: "At the start of war we estimated about 200 enemy divisions. Currently we count 360. These divisions are certainly not armed and equipped in our sense, and they are often under inadequate tactical command. But they are there. And if a dozen are destroyed, the Russians will raise up another dozen. And they gain the time to do this by sitting close to their sources of power, while we move farther and farther away from ours."[111]

This rather commonplace operational insight about war against Russia had been made repeatedly by Moltke the Elder and Schlieffen. About the time that the land bridge to Smolensk was established, Halder made the comment in his war diary that the disagreement between him and Hitler over the second phase of the campaign had broken out openly. Hitler wanted to exploit the situation as he planned by destroying the Soviet units hanging back in the north and particularly in the south, and therefore capturing the economically critical areas for the war effort. Halder, on the other hand, continued to advocate for Moscow as the objective of the attack. As Adolf Heusinger, the chief of OKH's Operations Department, put it, Halder wanted to execute his pet concept in front of the Soviet capital by destroying the Red Army on a reversed front through a battle of annihilation.[112] Such would be in accordance with classical German operational thinking, achieving a Cannae-like victory the Germans had not yet been able to accomplish. Halder believed that such a strike would regain the initiative. The Soviet units remaining far to the west would eventually "rot away."[113]

The power struggle that ensued between Hitler and OKH was decided in Hitler's favor.[114] All Halder's efforts to change Hitler's plan through indirect interference remained unsuccessful. Army Group Center received orders to continue the offensive with their infantry divisions only. Simultaneously, the Panzer groups were ordered to turn south and destroy the Soviet units in the Ukraine. For Halder, that order meant the end of operations and the transition to tactics—and ultimately to positional warfare.[115]

Initially the attacks appeared successful. The German units in the north reached Leningrad.[116] On Hitler's order, however, the city was not captured. It was to be encircled and then starved out. In the south the initial successes exceeded all previous victories. During the encirclement battle of Kiev alone more than 650,000 Russian soldiers became prisoners of war.[117] As soon as the end of the Battle of Kiev the Panzer units on Hitler's orders were concentrated immediately for an attack on Moscow. Hitler at that point had made a typically intuitive decision that agreed with Halder's thinking. Even before the beginning of winter the Soviet units remaining east of Smolensk were to be destroyed through a large-scale double envelopment. Addressing the problems that the slower-moving infantry divisions experienced during the battles of the previous weeks, Bock planned to attach individual infantry divisions to the Panzer groups. Operation TYPHOON was supposed to start as soon as possible, but the deployment of the Panzer units was delayed because of the start of the muddy season in Russia.

Not only the climatic conditions, but also the manpower and materiel situation weakened Army Group Center. While the Soviet Union continued to raise new units without interruption, the Germans were exhausted. The situation for trucks and tanks had deteriorated dramatically. Supply shortages, especially fuel, occurred because of the inadequacy of the rail network.[118] Despite all efforts, mobility and military strength were not at full levels by the start of the attack on 30 September 1941. Nevertheless, the Panzer groups once more achieved a double envelopment of large Soviet units in the double battle of Vyazma and Bryansk.[119] And again, more than 670,000 Russian soldiers became prisoners of war. The path to Moscow laid open for the German forces, but the units had only 50 percent of their military strength left. The attack on the Russian capital finally ground to a halt within sight of Moscow itself because of the ferocious resistance put up by the Soviet units, and also because of the shortage of German forces, exhaustion, and cold temperatures reaching more than 20 degrees below zero Celsius [−4 degrees Fahrenheit].

On multiple occasions beforehand, Army Group Center had pointed out the condition of the troops and demanded the cancellation of the attack. But the General Staff was still haunted by the ghost of the lost Battle of the Marne. This time around they were determined not to interrupt a successful battle. The orders were to hold out to the last man. But the German offensive had already passed its culminating point. When the Red Army on 5 December caught the German leadership by surprise, launching a counteroffensive with freshly deployed and winter battle–proven units, the Blitzkrieg against the Soviet Union failed.[120] Over the subsequent weeks the German soldiers, without winter clothing and badly supplied, fought for their very lives.

According to Halder, the Soviet offensive led to the largest crisis of the war. Although the Red Army drove the Wehrmacht back as much as 150 kilometers toward the west, the Soviets did not achieve a decisive operational success. In consequence of this crisis, a radical personnel reshuffle took place within the German Army leadership. Bock and Rundstedt were replaced and Brauchitsch dismissed as commander in chief of the army. Consequently, Hitler assumed the direct command of the German Army himself.

By the end of the 1941 Soviet Winter Offensive, the German Army in the East (*Ostheer*) lost some one-third of its manpower and nearly 90 percent of its tanks. Although those losses could not be replaced completely until the spring of 1942 and the army was significantly weakened, Hitler planned a large-scale offensive in the south of Russia in addition to the capture of Leningrad. The plan consisted of four phases: (1) the capture of Voronezh; (2) the destruction of the Soviet units between Don and Donets; (3) the capture of Stalingrad through a pincer operation; and after the completion of the third phase, the final phase (4) would be a thrust via the Caucasus to the oilfields along the Caspian Sea.[121] The plan was published in Führer Directive No. 41 in the spring of 1942. It once again demonstrated Hitler's operational intent directed at the seizure of territory—an intent now supported by Halder.[122] The aim of the strategy was to capture the economic bases for raw materials in order to equip Germany for a lengthier war against the maritime powers of Great Britain and the United States. (See Plate 15.)

These ambitious objectives had to be reconciled with the army's poor state of readiness. By the end of 1941 the army had been pushed back to its 1940 armament levels, and in some areas even to the levels of the start of the war in 1939.[123] Because of the drastic reductions in overall motorized assets, the army was able to maintain motorization levels only in selected elements of the mobile units. That, in turn, widened the gap between the mobile units and the slower infantry divisions. The German Army, therefore, increasingly evolved into a two-speed army, with all the resulting consequences for the tactical-operational conduct of the war. According to OKH reports, only eight to eleven of the 162 divisions were fully mission-capable, including only two Panzer and three infantry divisions. Seventy-three divisions were only capable of defensive actions.[124] (At the start of the campaign in June 1941 twenty-one Panzer divisions had been fully mission-capable.) Because of the manpower and materiel shortages, it was not possible then to assemble attack forces at the level of the summer of 1941. The German Army in the East was only a shadow of its former self. This was "a poor man's state of affairs that bears no relationship to the size of our military programs."[125] The mobility of the German Army in the East, which was the essential requirement for the conduct of offensive mobile operations, was far more limited than it had been in 1941.

Despite the bad logistical situation, the warnings raised by the Sixth Army were simply ignored in the face of the strategic situation. The Sixth Army anticipated great difficulties in making the thrust to the Don because of the lack of foodstuffs along the route of advance and the long and overextended supply lines that would impede rapid operations.[126] OKH raised a number of concerns about Hitler's overly ambitious plans and the current strategic situation, especially since Germany now had declared war on the United States, thereby expanding the European war to a world war. The only chance OKH now saw for avoiding a lengthy two-front war and the war of attrition that it could not win was a victory over the Soviet Union and the capture of the Russian strategic resources. The decision in Russia had to be forced in 1942. As in World War I, time pressure now hung over the planning process like the Sword of Damocles.

Case BLUE (*Fall BLAU*) started after the successful encirclement battle of Khar-kov. The Soviet armies, however, withdrew skillfully and could not be destroyed. The German offensive increasingly degenerated into a deep thrust into empty space, even more so as Hitler repeatedly passed up the opportunity to establish a main effort in favor of secondary objectives. Not the least, Hitler's deployments with weakened flanks made it impossible to achieve the original intention of a double envelopment.[127] The most significant of Hitler's decisions was to move up the offensive against the Caucasus, which originally had been planned for after the capture of Stalingrad. Hitler ordered the execution of both operations simultane-ously, decisively weakening German overall offensive power, which should have been concentrated at the center of gravity according to classical operational think-ing. The attempt to conduct both operations at the same time diluted the signifi-cant level of local superiority necessary to fight a battle of encirclement. As Bernd Wegner noted, "The splitting of the operation into two suboffensives diverging from each other in a rectangle made inevitable a dramatically increasing deterio-ration of the relation between the space gained and forces committed."[128] Halder too saw that—as in 1918—the overextended German front, now forty-five hun-dred kilometers in length and with long supply routes and wide-open and thinly secured flanks, could not withstand a Soviet counterattack.

When the German attack on Stalingrad stalled, urban fighting ensued. The Sixth Army, which had inadequate infantry forces, could not win in such a situa-tion. A serious leadership crisis resulted. At the end of September Hitler dismissed Halder. Only a few weeks later the Red Army started their counteroffensive, over-running the Romanian defensive positions on the flanks of the Sixth Army and encircling Stalingrad.[129] Hitler forbade Paulus from attempting a breakout. When a relief offensive failed as well, the Sixth Army surrendered at the end of January and beginning of February 1943.

The following phase of operations was a great achievement of operational com-mand, as the German Army conducted a controlled withdrawal from the Caucasus region to Rostov, and from the Kuban bridgehead to the Goth's Head (*Gotenkopf*) fallback position.[130] But that did not resolve the situation at the southern front com-pletely. A further Soviet offensive thrusting at the Crimea aimed to destroy Army Group South completely. Manstein crushed that operation in a manner reminis-cent of his earlier Sickle Cut plan. He attacked the advanced Russian spearheads concentrically, which consequently destabilized the front in the south.

But it was not only in the east that the Wehrmacht had lost the initiative and suffered serious defeats. Britain's Lieutenant General Bernard L. Montgomery defeated Rommel's Africa Corps at the beginning of November 1942 in the battle near El Alamein, forcing Rommel and his units to retreat across the top of North Africa.[131]

At the culminating point of the war the Allies had inflicted serious losses upon the Wehrmacht, from which the German forces would not be able to recover. The Wehrmacht had lost its capability to conduct operational-strategic offensives. Now, the ambitious offensive plans against the British in the Mediterranean and India became obsolete. Those plans had been worked out by OKH and OKW on Hitler's orders prior to the start of Operation BARBAROSSA. Nothing demonstrates the operational-strategic hubris of the Wehrmacht leadership in those days better than Führer Directive No. 32, "Preparations for the Period Following BARBAROSSA." In addition to the capture of Gibraltar, an intermediate pincer operation from Bulgaria via Turkey and from Libya against the British position in Egypt was planned without any realistic considerations of logistics and geography.[132] A deployment in Afghanistan against India also was in preparation, to which OKH intended to commit seventeen divisions.[133] These grandiose operational plans were just Halder's style. At the beginning of July 1941 he spoke in support of a pincer operation against the land bridge between the Euphrates and the Nile, with a secondary thrust against the Caucasus.[134] The fact that Paulus presented detailed operational studies after only a few weeks' time shows how seriously OKH took these plans.[135] It also illustrates the extent to which the loss of the grip on reality had affected the operational thinking of the General Staff, and their resulting overestimation of the Wehrmacht's capabilities. Operation BARBAROSSA exposed not only the striking tactical-operational weaknesses, but also the operational-strategic flaws inherent in the German concept of the conduct of operations. In their assessment of space and time, the General Staff let themselves be guided not by real facts, but by illusions. According to Hans Meier-Welcker, they had not been "able to imagine the power and the possibilities of the Russian space."[136]

What Hitler and the General Staff shared was the conviction that the Soviet Union would be defeated in a short campaign. This approach—based on classical German operational thinking—assumed that it would be possible to evade the Soviets' potential strengths before they could bring them to bear. The disregard of the factors of space and time for the eastern theater of war—similar to what Ludendorff and Hindenburg did during World War I—gained the upper hand in German thinking, in combination with the old stereotypes of the enemy and notions of German superiority. The consequence was a complete underestimation of the Red Army's manpower and materiel strengths,[137] as well as the lack of a realistic assessment of the Soviet Union as a spatial entity and its climatic conditions.[138] Furthermore, the leadership rivalries between OKH and Hitler prevented a focused conduct of operations.

The operations plan, which intended a rapid breakthrough of the Soviet defensive lines along the border and then the destruction of the Red Army through thrusts into Russia's depth followed by a double envelopment, had failed. Right from the start the General Staff had not planned for a gigantic Cannae-like operation in Russia. The aim instead was to weaken the Red Army through many "small Cannaes," and then confront it in a decisive battle in front of Moscow. On the one hand, these ideas of Halder's that were based on classical German operational thinking were unsuccessful because Hitler's operational-strategic plans were focused on gaining space, and not on the destruction of the enemy forces. They also failed because of an absolute overestimation of German resources and capabilities and an underestimation of the Soviet potentials and the vast spatial expanse of Russian territory. During the decisive phase of the campaign, when German losses exceeded all the previous forecasts, the hubris of the German leadership even went to such an extreme that Hitler held newly produced tanks back from the east for an attack in North Africa. He even redeployed the Second Air Fleet to the Mediterranean prior to the start of the offensive against Moscow.[139]

The campaign also exposed the German tactical-operational deficiencies that had surfaced during the earlier France Campaign, and which had not been corrected but only ignored. Since these were structural deficiencies resulting from Germany's limited resource base, they were impossible to correct. Germany was not able to motorize its army completely.

The limited financial resources and the shortages of raw materials only permitted a partial mechanization. Consequently, there were only a few motorized units and many nonmotorized ones.

The nonmotorized infantry divisions were too slow for the conduct of mobile operations. They were hardly able to keep up with the pace of the Panzer units thrusting deeply forward. Their march tempo was determined, as in World War I, by the infantrymen's marching pace and the trudging along of the horse-drawn carriages. The infantry's slow mobility also weakened tactical coordination, because the mobility of combined arms combat must always adapt to the slowest element.[140] The result was a reduced capability to execute encirclement battles rapidly and maintain operational momentum, because the Panzer units could only disengage from the encirclements when the infantry units arrived. It was, therefore, frequently impossible to turn tactical successes into operational ones. The lengthy retention of the Panzer groups during the second clearing-out phase of an encirclement battle significantly restricted the follow-on sequences of the planned operations. All too often tactics dominated operations. And, considering the small number of Panzer groups, the infantry divisions even had to play a direct role in the execution of the envelopments. Consequently, this limited the speed of an enveloping movement to the marching pace of the infantryman. The operations plans had not sufficiently considered the different marching speeds of the Panzer and infantry divisions.

Whether and where encirclements were achieved was ultimately a function of the command and control mistakes made by the Soviet troop commanders. The planned large encirclements were rather an exception, because of the infantry's lacking mobility. Many small encirclements were executed. Quite often those encirclements started to deteriorate because their eastern closure could only be achieved by the Panzer units, which in turn could not close the encirclement because of the lack of infantry. Despite the great tactical successes, classic battles of annihilation failed to materialize.[141] Day by day the distances increased between the rapid Panzer units and the slowly marching infantry. This meant that the rearward lines of communications of the mobile units could not be secured adequately. As a consequence, the transportation units had to move through the mobile units' rear battle areas, which had not yet been cleared of the enemy. The transport units suffered heavy losses, which made the already problematic supply situation even worse. Attempts to resolve this dilemma did not yield results.[142]

Finally, the Russia Campaign destroyed the image of the "German Blitzkrieg Army" that had been trumpeted by National Socialist propaganda. The German Army of World War II was, in fact, an army of horses with an advance tempo largely adapted to the marching capability of man and horse. The mobility of tanks and dive-bombers, the latter at least partly providing the mobile artillery element that had been missing in World War I, formed only the narrow steel spearhead of a wooden spear. In truth, a two-class army fought in Russia, with dreadful losses of manpower and materiel that could not be replaced during the course of the ongoing war.

The Defensive between Movement and the Halt

The catastrophic defeats in the Caucasus and at Stalingrad forced the German leadership to reassess the strategic situation. They recognized the change in the situation that resulted from the defeats in the east and the landings of the Western Allies in North Africa. Individual voices even spoke of a turning point in the war. But the transformation of this insight into an overall strategic concept for the further conduct of the war did not happen.[143] A new operational approach, or "even the will for a strategic reshaping of the overall situation was not discernible."[144] Instead, the leadership again and again expressed the hope of being able to shift to an offensive. Reality, however, showed that such hopes were pure fantasy.

A third summer offensive in the eastern theater of war was out of the question. The manpower and materiel losses had been too huge. In 1943 Hitler himself only talked about "changing tactics on a small scale." The German leadership had to concede to the inevitability of defensive action, Germany's greatly unloved type of combat, reminiscent of World War I. How could it be conducted?

In principle, two defense variations were possible—a static defense or a tactical-operational mobile defense. While the static defense adapted from the trench warfare of World War I is associated with Hitler, Manstein represents mobile operational defense. The Führer had already imposed his ideas of static-linear defense on OKH during the defensive battles of December 1941, when he forbade larger evasive maneuvers. As in World War I, will and belief were supposed to compensate for the lack of manpower and materiel. Not the least of all, the soldiers had to render fanatic resistance and fight for every foot of ground, "to the last man standing."[145] Hitler clearly defined his concept in a Führer Order he issued for the preparation of the defense battles in the winter of 1942. He forbade a defensive system echeloned in depth and ordered a linear main front line analogous to the World War I battles up to 1916. That line had to be held at all costs. This stood Hitler in the very tradition of Falkenhayn and his defensive doctrine up through 1916. Evasive action was forbidden without Hitler's express consent. That restricted significantly or even made impossible any conduct of an operationally mobile defensive battle. Hitler explicitly justified his order on the experience of World War I: "I am purposefully returning . . . to this type of defense, as it was successfully practiced in the hard defensive battles of World War I, especially up to the end of 1916. Intentional echelonments in depth were only made when the enemy's material superiority became overwhelming. This superiority of the enemy was incomparably higher than is now the fact at any point of the Eastern Front."[146]

Hitler strictly forbade a mobile operational defense because the local commanders repeatedly used what limited leeway they had for a mobile tactical defense, despite the Führer's order to defend on a static line, constantly harkening back to the trench warfare of World War I.[147] In his Führer Order on "General Tasks for the Defense," issued 8 September 1942, he again argued for his credo of rigid defense, citing his own warfighting experiences:

> So-called operationally evasive movements, unless they lead to a well-prepared and better rearward position, cannot improve the overall situation, but only make it worse, because the enemy's forces will not be attrited by such actions. As a consequence, the sector of the front to be held increases from any resulting salient. But even when the resulting rearward position is shorter, the enemy still profits because the force ratio always remains the same. . . . There always has been and will be only one means for the defender who is numerically inferior to improve his situation—he must inflict such losses on the attacker from a well-fortified position as possible, so that the enemy eventually is bled dry.[148]

This statement and others similar were based completely on the experience of trench warfare in World War I and in total opposition to classical German operational thinking. One of the pillars of that thinking was the belief that inferiority in

Field Marshal Erich von Manstein and General Dietrich von Choltitz studying maps in June–July 1942. Photographer: Horster. *BArch/101I-231-0731-19.*

manpower and materiel could only be compensated for through mobile warfare. The conflicts, then, between Hitler and the army's generals and the General Staff were intractable.

Hitler continued to justify his position based on the enemy's air superiority, which impeded movement, especially in the west. He continued to believe in the superior approach of his pursuit of strategic war economy objectives.[149] Although Hitler himself was not completely wrong in accusing his generals of thinking only operationally and not in overall strategic terms, he nonetheless was a product of his personal experiences of war. He permitted mobile operational defensive actions only in the most dire of emergencies.

That happened in the course of the Soviet offensive against Army Group South in January–February 1943. While the Sixth Army was fighting their desperate battle of encirclement at Stalingrad, the Red Army started an offensive in the southern sector of the Eastern Front. The operational objective was the encirclement and destruction of Army Group South by thrusting toward the Black Sea, after first reaching the Dnepr crossing points. Following a successful breakthrough of the defense lines of Germany's Italian and Hungarian allies, the Soviet tank units made a thrust toward the west into a 150-kilometer-wide gap. Manstein, who had just been assigned as the commander in chief of Army Group South, did not see any possibility for his numerically inferior forces to close the gap. In the classic

General Heinz Guderian in his armored command carrier during the Battle of France in May 1940; front left an Enigma cryptographic machine. Photographer: E. Borchert. *BArch/101I-769-0229-12A*.

Field Marshal Erwin Rommel and his chief of staff, General Fritz Bayerlein, during the Battle of Tobruk in June 1942. Photographer: Moosmüller. *BArch/146-1977-158-07.*

German operational tradition, he decided to resolve the situation by attacking. He planned to clear out the Don–Donets bend near Rostov and then retreat to the Mius position. Once the overall front line was shortened, Manstein intended to redeploy the Fourth Panzer Army to the left wing of Army Group South. As a result, the Soviet units would be advancing into a funnel. Once the Soviet offensive culminated, the Soviet forces would be attacked and destroyed by a concentric thrust into their open flank by several Panzer divisions. The situation was nearly hopeless, and after a series of fierce arguments Hitler finally granted Manstein the freedom to execute his operational plan.

The Soviet lines of communications were vastly overextended, and the German attack on 21 February 1943 came as a complete surprise. Within weeks the Russian tank armies were destroyed, Kharkov was recaptured, and the front was pushed forward to the Donets again.[150] With this counterstrike from a position of inferiority Manstein achieved one of the most brilliant operational successes of World War II. He prevented not only the destruction of Army Group South, but also the breakdown of the entire Eastern Front.

Manstein's operation still greatly fascinates military historians throughout the world, but especially in Germany.[151] It is the prime example of shifting positions on interior lines and then launching a second strike from the rear (*Schlagen aus der Nachhand*).[152] Manstein applied all the principles upon which German operational thinking was based. He skillfully used space and time to marshal his units for a concentric attack on interior lines, forcing the attacking enemy to overextend his front and lay his flanks open. (See Plate 16.)

When the Soviet attack reached culmination, Manstein attacked while focusing the main effort. Simultaneously, he had an intelligence advantage over his enemy, which he consequently used to achieve surprise. As a result, Manstein regained the initiative and forced the imperative of action upon the enemy.

These classical pillars of German operational thinking also include a high level of willingness to assume risk and the conviction of the superiority of German tactical and operational leadership and mission-type command and control procedures. Nonetheless, two key elements for the early German successes in World War II that often have been overlooked in the historical literature were local German air superiority and the serious command and control mistakes made by the Soviet side.

Despite Manstein's great successes over the subsequent months, Hitler categorically rejected all of his suggestions for the conduct of a mobile operational defense on the Eastern Front because he was not prepared to risk the loss of the Donets area, which was important for Germany's war economy. In the debate over a second strike from the rear (*Schlagen aus der Nachhand*) versus an initial strike (*Schlagen aus der Vorhand*), Hitler opted for the latter.[153] The resulting Operation CITADEL was intended to destroy the Red Army units deployed on the leading edge of the salient near Kursk through a pincer attack. But that attack failed because of the Soviet defense.[154] The Battle of Kursk was the last great German offensive on the Eastern Front. But from the start Hitler only had intended to inflict great damage on the Red Army. He did not intend a Schlieffenesque decisive battle. Thus, the battle really was not what Manstein later called a "wasted victory" (*verschenkter Sieg*).[155] The Battle of Kursk represents the end of the German operational initiative in the east, not only because of the operational-tactical situation on the Eastern Front, but also because of the change in strategy that Hitler initiated prior to the battle. By November the military failures of 1943 had led the German war leadership to shift the strategic center of gravity from the Eastern to the Western or Southwestern Front. The Second Front was already *ante portas* (Before the Gates), and already affected overall strategy, and thus the operations and Germany's conduct of the war.

The operational-strategic initiative had been lost. The Wehrmacht was in the midst of a continental defensive battle for Fortress Europe and playing for time. Hitler now made his final decision to conduct a rigid holding operation in the east. As at the start of World War I, the east was to be held and the west to be defeated. While on the operational level Hitler was not willing to trade space for reserves or for gains in time, he was very much willing to do so on the strategic level.

Hitler's objective was to ward off an Allied landing in Western Europe and then use the forces that then would be freed up to shift back to the offensives in the east. Strategically, his concepts of space and time corresponded with those of Schlieffen. Even as late as the winter of 1944, after the failure of the Ardennes Offensive, he still planned to launch a large counteroffensive to the south with the German forces encircled in Kurland. Frieser argues that Hitler had allowed the formation of that encirclement for the purpose of having a strategic bridgehead from which to launch the "final victory."[156]

Hitler's new strategy was reflected in his senior leadership assignments. He relieved Manstein and the commander in chief of Army Group A, Field Marshal Ewald von Kleist. He justified the changes of leadership and strategy to Manstein during the latter's change of command ceremony with the words: "In the east, the time for large-scale operations . . . has come to an end. What is only important now is holding rigidly."[157] As their successors Hitler appointed two stalwarts of many defensive battles, Field Marshal Walter Model and Colonel General Ferdinand Schörner. Hitler also stated: "The idea of freely operating in an unoccupied area is nonsense."[158]

In the period that followed, Hitler repeatedly interfered with the operational command of the army groups and field armies. During the fighting near the Neve River at the end of December 1943, he prohibited the Sixteenth Army from conducting a timely withdrawal to more favorable blocking positions, which facilitated in turn the Red Army's broad thrust.[159] As the war drew on, Hitler's stand-and-fight orders increased. In March 1944 the concept of stubborn holding reached its climax with the order to establish fortified points (*festen Plätzen*) that would pin the enemy down.[160] With very few exceptions, Hitler rejected all efforts to establish an operational reserve for the conduct of mobile operational defense by the shortening of the front lines. In mid-1944, for example, Army Group Center had made such a recommendation to withdraw its front line behind the Berezina and into the Biber position.[161] Hitler instead ordered Army Group Center to establish a rigid and linear defense based on fortified points.

Nonetheless, the commanders in the field continued to interpret Hitler's orders in the sense of mobile tactical defense if there was any possible way to do so. It helped that according to German doctrinal regulations several types of tactical combat operations were possible in such situations. Apart from an actively conducted delaying operation, there were the options of a mobile or a static defensive operation based on a system of positions. While the Wehrmacht units in front of Moscow were still insufficiently trained in mobile defensive procedures and in delaying resistance, the crises they faced made them rely increasingly on such tactics, pragmatically applying Leeb's prewar concepts. The capability to improvise had to substitute for the lack of manpower, materiel, and adequate training. In the process, the Panzer units lost their significance as an operational attack force.[162] The Panzers were always deployed for counterattacks limited in time and space. The decisive antitank elements in the defense became the antiaircraft guns, such as the 88mm Flak gun, and the assault guns originally developed as assault artillery and tank destroyers.[163] As in World War I, infantry and artillery carried the main weight of the defense. Where Allied air superiority allowed, the few mechanized combat groups consisting of tanks, mechanized infantry, and armored artillery were able to conduct counterattacks against fragmented enemy elements as long as those forces were still on the move and had not yet established defensive positions.[164] The imbalance increased between the few motorized units and motorized infantry divisions, on the one hand, and the mass of the relatively immobile infantry and *Volksgrenadier* divisions on the other. The *Large Battle Procedures* (*Grosskampfverfahren*) issued at the end of 1944 were a return to the defensive concepts of 1917–1918.[165] As at the end of World War I, the troops were conducting tactically mobile fights within their sectors. Whenever possible, they evacuated their forward-most positions before they could be observed by the enemy and before the Soviet artillery started to fire.[166] The overall defensive battles were conducted from the base of the main line of resistance (*Hauptkampflinie*),[167] which had to be held with all available forces.[168]

Similar to the military leadership in World War I, Hitler interspersed his operational-strategic decisions with appeals to morale and offensive spirit.[169] Such demands were always couched in National Socialist rhetoric.[170] Will was reinforced by belief in the Führer: "The prerequisite for aggressive success is the

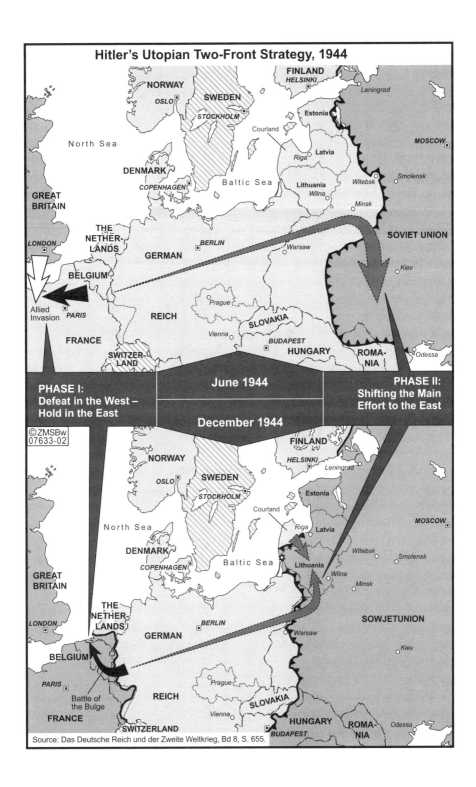

Hitler's Utopian Two-Front Strategy, 1944

PHASE I:
Defeat in the West –
Hold in the East

June 1944

December 1944

PHASE II:
Shifting the Main
Effort to the East

©ZMSBw
07633-02

Source: Das Deutsche Reich und der Zweite Weltkrieg, Bd 8, S. 655.

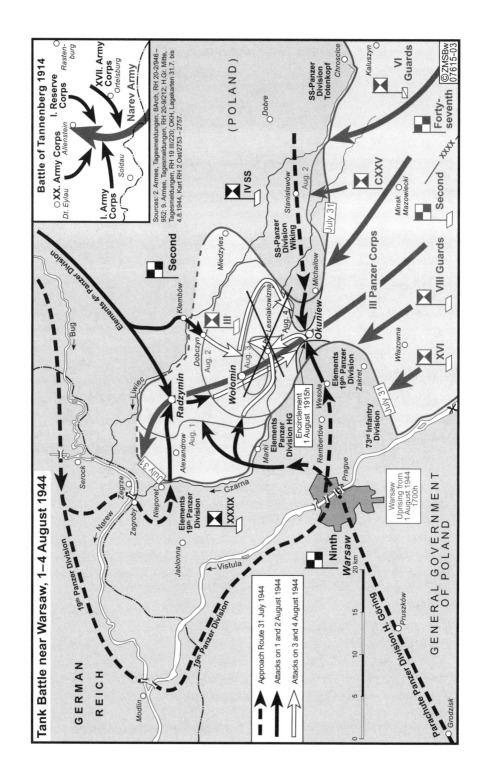

Tank Battle near Warsaw, 1–4 August 1944

Battle of Tannenberg 1914

○ XX. Army Corps *Allenstein*
I. Reserve Corps

XVII. Army Corps *Ortelsburg*

Rastenburg

Narev Army

I. Army Corps *Soldau*

Dt. Eylau

Sources: 2. Armee, Tagesmeldungen, BArch, RH 20-2/946 – 952; 9. Armee, Tagesmeldungen, RH 20-9/212; H.Gr. Mitte, Tagesmeldungen, RH 19 III/220; OKH, Lagekarten 31.7. bis 4.8.1944, Kart RH 2 Ost/2753 – 2757.

©ZMSBw
07615-03

(P O L A N D)

Chroscice

Kaluszyn

VI Guards

SS-Panzer Division Totenkopf

Dobre

Forty-seventh

IV SS

Stanisławów
Aug. 2

CXXV

July 31

Second

Minsk Mazowiecki

Miedzyles

SS-Panzer Division Wiking

III Panzer Corps

Michałow

VIII Guards

Klembów

III

Second

Elements 4th panzer Division

Dobczyn Aug. 2
Aug. 3
Lesniakowizna
Aug. 4

Okuniew

XVI

Wlazowna

← Bug

Wolomin

Aug. 3

Radzymin
Aug. 1

Elements 19th Panzer Division

Zakret

July 31

← Liwiec

Alexandrow
Aug. 1

← Czarna

Marki

Elements Panzer Division HG

Rembertów *Wesola*

Encirclement
1 August 1915h

73rd Infantry Division

Prague

Serock

Zegrze

Narew

Nieporet

July 31

Elements 19th Panzer Division

Zagroby

XXXIX

G E R M A N

Warsaw
Uprising from
1 August 1944
1700h

Jablonna

← Vistula

Ninth

Warsaw

20 km

R E I C H

19th Panzer Division

19th Panzer Division

Modlin

G E N E R A L   G O V E R N M E N T
O F   P O L A N D

Pruszków

parachute Panzer Division H. Göring

Grodzisk

0   5   10   15

Approach Route 31 July 1944

Attacks on 1 and 2 August 1944

Attacks on 3 and 4 August 1944

belief in our National Socialist Reich. . . . Belief in the idea given to us by the Führer."[171]

When the defeats accumulated and the military leadership feared losing control over the soldiers, they introduced military police units to enforce strict discipline without compromise.[172] Simultaneously, they increased their appeals to the soldiers' perseverance, trumpeting the invincibility of the German soldier.[173] As in World War I, when the manpower and materiel need to achieve victory were lacking, the World War II leadership fell back on the allegedly unlimited and renewable spiritual and psychological resources of the soldiers. During the final years of World War I, "patriotic instruction" (*Vaterländische Unterricht*) had been used to support the tactical innovations. During the final years of World War II the National Socialist leadership rose to the level of becoming an equal partner with the tactical-operational leadership. This development reached its apex in the manual H.Dv. 130/20 *The National Socialist Leadership,* which established "Nazi political officers as an *independent* functional area *equal* to military-tactical leadership for the training and command of the regiment."[174] The objective was to have fanatic fighters defeating the enemy's materiel superiority through their will and belief.

Apart from the smaller mobile counterthrusts,[175] there is another Eastern Front example of the German Army's ability to conduct mobile operational defense, an example largely overlooked until recently. Following the Red Army's major victory over Army Group Center at the end of July 1944, the Soviets were on the point of conquering the area around Warsaw as a springboard for a follow-on offensive toward the Baltic Sea. Without consulting with Hitler, Model decided that the situation required the destruction of the most advanced Soviet tank units through a concentric counterattack conducted by four Panzer divisions. As Manstein had done earlier, Model stripped the other hard-fought-over sectors of the front line, conducted a difficult redeployment of his numerically inferior attacking units, and then launched a successful counterattack.[176] The Red Army's attempt to take Warsaw by a *coup de main* failed, and the threatened collapse of the German front was averted. Model's victory surprised not only the Soviets, but the Polish Home Army (*Armia Krajowa*) as well, sealing the fate of the Polish resistance in Warsaw. The Warsaw Rising had started when the Soviet armored spearheads reached the outskirts of the city, but during the next several weeks it was brutally suppressed by the Germans, as the Soviet forces remained stalled on the east bank of the Vistula.[177]

In the west the Wehrmacht generals remained convinced that, because of the German system of mobile command and control, they would remain superior against the clumsily and methodically operating Allies in any open battle. The condition for any such success, however, was the unified commitment of all available motorized units, holding them together under all circumstances, and avoiding splitting up and parceling out the Panzers among the infantry units. At times, such was the practice on the Eastern Front.[178]

The Allies' successful breakout from their extended landing bridgeheads in Normandy offered the OB-West (*Oberbefelshaber West*—Commander in Chief, West), Field Marshal Günther von Kluge, the opportunity to launch an attack against the western flank of the American forces that were advancing to the south and east. By thrusting toward Avranches, the objective of Operation LÜTTICH was to cut off the rearward lines of the advanced Allied units and then encircle and destroy them. Seeing the opportunity to eliminate the opposing forces, Hitler supported the attack, although it ran contrary to his previous concepts. In this case he probably was influenced by Model's successful operational defense in front of Warsaw. Kluge concentrated three Panzer divisions with 140 tanks and sixty assault guns.[179] But because of the Allies' overwhelming air superiority, the Panzers could only deploy at night, and thus the assembly of the forces for the operation was delayed. At the same time, however, Kluge pushed to start the attack as soon as possible, because the concentration of the large Panzer units could not be screened from Allied air reconnaissance for very long.

The Allies, meanwhile, had intercepted and decoded the German radio traffic.[180] Recognizing the German intentions, they prepared their defense. Starting on the night of 6–7 August 1944, the German attack was crushed by massive Allied air strikes within a few kilometers of their line of departure. Jodl reported to Hitler that more than one thousand Allied fighter-bombers had pushed the German troops into the ground and the attack had to be broken off.[181] Earlier, the Allied air forces had caught the German fighter-bomber units committed to support the counterattack at their bases and destroyed them on the ground. Operation LÜTTICH was finally cancelled after the Allies started their own Operation TOTALIZE counterattack toward Falaise. The encirclement of major German forces was imminent.[182]

The Avranches counterattack shows that by the end of World War II an operational mobile defense conducted by numerically inferior forces could only succeed if certain parameters were met—most importantly surprise. Any such counterattack did not have a chance without surprise. In this case, surprise had been impossible because of the Allies' radio reconnaissance system, but the German leadership did not know about that. And, of course, Operation LÜTTICH showed that mobile operations were bound to fail when the enemy had overwhelming air superiority. The high mobility of the Panzer units on the ground was trumped by the superior mobility of the fighter-bombers in the air. Without sufficient air support, mobile operations were not possible, either in the offense or the defense. The subsequent German Ardennes Offensive proved this once more. Consciously executed during bad weather conditions, that attack broke down when the weather cleared and the Allies brought their air superiority to bear.

In the final phase of the war the operational readiness of the German forces was severely limited, not only by the Allies' command of the air, but also by Germany's lack of fuel. Such shortages threatened the termination of the Luftwaffe's air operations and the halting of the Panzers. Although the few Hungarian oilfields in German hands had been destroyed by Allied air raids, Hitler ordered an offensive in Hungary. This final offensive operation of the Wehrmacht failed in the face of Soviet resistance. But even if the Hungary Offensive had succeeded, it would not have resolved the fuel problem. Allied strategic bomber units would have prevented the Germans from resuming production. And even then, German infrastructure had been almost completely destroyed by the air raids, and that would have impeded if not prevented the transport of the fuel to the fighting fronts.

The conduct of mobile operational defensive operations was also limited by the varying and inadequate equipment of the units. Because the nonmotorized and largely horse-drawn infantry divisions had to be given the option of using a system of positions or other field fortifications for defense purposes, that drastically limited the mobility of any operational defense, which since the end of World War II has come to be seen as a panacea.[183] The progressive demotorization of the infantry divisions happened not because of a lack of combat vehicles, but because of a lack of fuel. Only main effort units were equipped with sufficient motorized combat vehicles. While the enemy continually increased the motorization of their units, the Wehrmacht deteriorated into an army of horses. The dramatically accelerating process of the Wehrmacht's immobility continued over the course of the war. At the end, for example, the Third Panzer Army had sixty thousand horses but no tanks. The conduct of rapid mobile operations became impossible.

Hitler: A Military Commander?

The confusion of the overlapping responsibilities within the top military echelons did not end with the beginning of the war, but rather was made worse by Hitler.[184] Initially, the Führer had only pushed the Wehrmacht's alignment with the National Socialist state (*Gleichschaltung*) very cautiously, and before the war he did not encroach upon the military commanders' areas of responsibility. During the course of the war, however, he interfered increasingly with the leadership of the armed forces. His claims to leadership in operational matters were strengthened by the rapid success against Poland, and especially by the triumph over France. Hitler attributed the latter to "his operational plan," which he had pushed through against the technical objections of OKH, and particularly the Army General Staff.

Consequently, Hitler left no doubt during the course of the preparations for the attack on the Soviet Union that he would not leave the conduct of the war in the east to OKH.[185] Already he had withdrawn four theaters of war—Norway,

France, Africa, and the Balkans—from the responsibility of OKH, placing them under the control of OKW. Thus, OKH was no longer the high command of the army, but only of the German Army in the East. Within the General Staff, the Operations Department under Major General Adolf Heusinger was responsible for the operational planning. The actual work was carried out by the department's 1st Branch.[186] The central position of the Operations Department in the structure of the General Staff indicates the importance of the conduct of operations for the General Staff's thinking. All the other departments did the groundwork for the Operations Department. The chief of the Operations Department was also the deputy of the chief of the General Staff. Within OKW the Department for National Defense controlled the OKW theaters of war in a manner similar to the Army General Staff's Operations Department. With the exception of intelligence, all other areas necessary for the conduct of the war, such as supply and reserve forces, were withdrawn from the control of the commander in chief of the army.

Right from the beginning of the war the center of power within the army leadership shifted away from the commander in chief of the army to the chief of the Army General Staff. This in part was the result of Brauchitsch's weak leadership, which became more obvious as the war went on; but it also resulted from the institutional conditions of the system. The chief of the Army General Staff, as the deputy of the commander in chief of the army, was armed with unquestioned competence in all issues of the planning and conduct of the war. He therefore logically filled the power vacuum left by Brauchitsch in OKH and against Hitler.

Halder, who accepted Hitler's claim to strategic competence from the beginning, and therefore never attempted to assert leadership at that level as Beck did, refrained from participating in the framing of the strategic objectives. Instead, he concentrated on the core task of the General Staff as he saw it, which was operational planning and command. Halder's assumption that he would be able to establish factual supremacy in operational matters through his technical expertise, and thus be able to assert influence on the strategic process, was stymied by Hitler's enormous will for power. Halder's hope that Hitler would not continue to interfere with operational planning proved to be all in vain. During the planning phase of Operation BARBAROSSA Halder learned that not only did Hitler's central operational objectives differ from his own, but that the Führer interfered increasingly and aggressively into the operational planning. In the previous months Halder himself had prepared the way for Hitler by ruthlessly interfering with the operational planning of the field army level commanders, increasingly limiting their functions to the tactical level. With the groundwork laid, it was easy for Hitler later to prevent any strong group of generals from coalescing against him who could have demanded participation at the political level in the Prussian sense. In the end, Halder and the Army General Staff gave in to Hitler's claim to power and became increasingly subordinated to the National Socialist machinery of power. Halder's efforts to keep an eye on the opposition did not change the situation.[187]

In contrast, Hitler very early on doubted the operational competence of OKH. In the autumn of 1938 an open argument broke out for the first time between the Führer and the chief of the General Staff. The conflict was over the operational plans being developed in preparation for an attack on Czechoslovakia. The clash ended in a terrible disaster for OKH.[188] Hitler was disappointed in the attack plan, which he found much too conventional, and he was very angry at Halder's stubborn insistence on sticking to the plan. In response, Hitler forced through his own ideas, which corresponded to the actual deployment of the enemy's forces. The resulting loss of face for the military leadership caused widespread apprehension throughout the army, which was only compounded by Brauchitsch's embarrassing declaration of loyalty to Hitler.[189]

Hitler constantly felt disappointed by the army. His already inherent lack of trust in the operational competence of the Army General Staff was increased by the planning chaos in the run-up to Operation YELLOW, and it colored his attitude toward Halder during the preparations for the attack on the Soviet Union. As Hitler saw it, the General Staff's recurring doubts on issues, such as the threats to the flanks by potential Soviet attacks from the Pripyat Marshes, confirmed his conviction—the more so since his situational assessment had proved right during the campaign.[190]

The creeping disempowerment of the General Staff advanced to the next level when, after reaching Smolensk, Hitler imposed his operational objectives against Halder's opposition. Hitler thus designated the operation's center of gravity as being to the south and north, rather than Moscow. As Hitler bluntly stated: "The army's 18 August proposal for the continuing operations in the east does not correspond to my intent. I order the following."[191] That illustrates how ruthlessly the Führer disregarded OKH's ideas. At the same time, it also was a blow against the authority of Brauchitsch, whose weakness Hitler exploited mercilessly. Halder was so angered by the affront that he suggested to Brauchitsch that they jointly ask Hitler to dismiss them. But Brauchitsch declined. Hitler won the decisive test of strength against the army leadership and he asserted his by then unchallengeable claim to the command of operational matters as well. Robert Kershaw aptly describes Hitler's strategy as a "destructive blow" against OKH and the General Staff.[192] After the German Army's defeat in front of Moscow on 19 December 1941, Hitler's dismissal of Brauchitsch and his personal assumption of direct command of the German Army was only the next and final logical step in a virtually completed process.

When Hitler took over the direct command of the army, his elimination of all the operational command opposition was complete. Hitler icily rejected all later efforts by Manstein and by the chief of the General Staff, Kurt Zeitzler, to restore

the General Staff's operational freedom of action or to designate an overall commander in chief of the army for at least the Eastern Front.[193] The Führer did not
yield one inch from his claim to absolute command and authority. During the subsequent years he even expanded that authority to the lower command echelons.
Hitler even went so far as to encourage competition between various elements of
the armed forces and OKW. In dealings with his generals, Hitler repeatedly and
skillfully asserted his will through his instinctive ability to judge character and to
recognize human weaknesses. Throughout the course of the war he surrounded
himself only with weak characters. From 1942, if not earlier, open opposition in
meetings was impossible.

What enabled Hitler to take over the army leadership, and what was the basis
for his military self-perception? He never underwent General Staff or even an
officer's training. He was a lance corporal (*Gefreiter*) at the end of World War
I. Serving mostly as a runner, he was awarded the Iron Cross First Class. This
"training" qualified him, like millions of other front fighters of World War I, as
merely an armchair strategist. But there was a bit more to Hitler than that. Apart
from his experiences of trench warfare on the Western Front, he had for a military layman an extraordinary strategic instinct and a nearly lexicon-like grasp of
detailed knowledge acquired through his intense studies of the military literature. Thanks to his good memory, he repeatedly trumped military officers with
his command of the facts.[194] As a consequence, not only certain members of his
military entourage, but he himself increasingly came to believe in his military
capabilities.

Hitler was also convinced that he had more personal experience of war than
the majority of his generals. Again and again, especially during his fits of rage, he
gave free rein to his offensive and insulting contempt for the former "swivel-chair
staff officers" who were now the general officers standing before him. After having
reproached Halder for his lack of relentlessness, he scornfully threw the words at
him: "What do you, Herr Halder, who during World War I sat in the same chair,
intend to tell me about the troops—you, who does not even wear the Black Wound
Badge?"[195]

Without discussing the question here of why Halder or other senior officers
in similar situations endured Hitler's tirades without complaint, we cannot ignore
that Hitler's reproaches were in fact accurate concerning a large number of these
senior officers. A not inconsiderable number of the senior-most army leaders had
indeed served in headquarters billets during World War I, or had fought as artil-
lerists not directly in the trenches.[196] But the fact that the majority of General Staff
officers had worked on staffs behind the front in World War I was not a function
of their individual cowardice, as Hitler implied in his accusations. Rather, it was
the German Army's long-standing policy of assigning those officers highly trained
in planning and command to functions where they could best contribute to the

prosecution of the war. It was a deliberate decision to avoid unnecessarily risking the highly qualified operators.[197]

The dilution of the army senior leadership's power only became possible after Hitler had achieved his early successes in the war and the "Führer Myth" grew to include Hitler's operational capabilities—allegedly the "greatest military leader of all time." Because of his early successes, many General Staff officers, who in the course of their training had been indoctrinated repeatedly with the concept of the intuitive rather than the rationally definable capabilities of the military commander, came to accept the notion that Hitler had been "anointed by Samuel," so to speak, and was therefore a genuine "natural talent." As Jodl explained to Heusinger, it was undeniable that the Führer had been mostly correct in his strategic instincts.[198] Even if Jodl's statements can be dismissed as those of a lackey in Hitler's immediate entourage, Eduard Wagner's comments in October 1941 were widely shared: "Again and again I wonder about the military assessment by the Führer. This time, he interferes in a decisive manner into the course of the operations. And up to now he always has been right. The great successes in the south are the result of his solution."[199] Wagner's words reflected both amazement and confidence in Hitler's operational capabilities. Nonetheless, Hitler's initial successes that were based partly on decisions he forced through against the reservations of the military professionals were not the result of "Samuel's anointment," but rather of the goddess of fortune.

The Führer himself believed that the early success in the war confirmed his capability as a military commander. In his hubris Hitler told Brauchitsch when he relieved him as commander in chief of the army: "Everyone can do this bit of operational conduct."[200] In a private conversation after he personally took over the command of the army Hitler also told Brauchitsch that he had expansive political aims, apart from the direct conduct of operations: "The task of the army commander in chief is to educate the army in a National Socialist perspective. I do not know any army general who could perform this task as I would wish it. That is why I have decided to assume the command of the army myself."[201]

That was the voice of Hitler's aversion to the army's conservative leadership that had grown within him over the years. And as his self-confidence as a military commander grew, his aversion to the generals grew accordingly. He eventually grew to mistrust them completely.[202] As a National Socialist revolutionary, Hitler despised the Prussian military aristocracy and their reactionary attitudes. He could, for example, barely mask his personal animosity toward Manstein, the classic representative of the Prussian military nobility and exponent of mobile operations.[203] In conversations with Reich Propaganda Minister Joseph Goebbels, Hitler increasingly dropped negative comments about the generals, who allegedly lied to him often and whom he regarded as disgusting.[204] The Führer was especially dismissive of the General Staff as a "special caste of particularly high-nosed, nobility airheads and national pests, full of sterile infertility, devoid of ideas, and cowards with concepts derived from such characteristics."[205] After captured German officers established the National Committee for a Free Germany (*Nationalkomitee Freies Deutschland*) and the Federation of German Officers (*Bund Deutscher Offiziere*), and then the failed assassination attempt of July 1944, the General Staff was in Hitler's mind a nest of malice and betrayal.[206]

Considering this background, it is no wonder that Hitler counted increasingly on a group of younger or middle-aged generals of rather lower-middle-class origins, like Eduard Dietl and Ferdinand Schörner.[207] They stood by their Führer loyally, partly out of ideological conviction or career opportunism, but also out of corruptibility.[208]

Hitler asserted without compromise his claim to absolute leadership over the chief of the Army General Staff. During the Eastern Campaign he reduced the army chief step by step to the role of a conveyor of orders and an operational supernumerary.[209] The dismissal of Halder in September 1942 and the subsequent appointment of Major General Kurt Zeitzler advanced this development farther. Zeitzler, a loyal follower of Hitler who the Führer expected to clean out the General Staff in short order,[210] was quickly given the nickname "*Hitlerjunge Quex*" within OKH.[211] Zeitzler was a simple infantry officer, and he had not been recruited from the inner circle of operators to fill the central position in the army's operational command. Thus, Zeitzler encountered distrust from the beginning, especially when he ostentatiously declared to the officers of the General Staff during his inauguration into office that everyone not unquestioningly believing in the Führer and demonstrating such in public would not have a future in the General Staff. Who, then, could wonder that the officers in the Operations Department referred to Halder as "the last chief of the General Staff"?

According to his Führer Principle (*Führerprinzip*), Hitler's approach to command was very centralized and hierarchical. His orders were to be executed without discussion. He had no truck with the classical German operational concepts of directive-based command and control. He demanded that the higher command echelons issue clear and unambiguous orders. The soldier's duty of obedience forbade any actions at the discretion of a subordinate unit. The senior command echelons were expected to intervene ruthlessly in the details. In so doing, of course, Hitler handicapped one of the most important elements of German operational thinking.[212]

Based on Schlieffen's concept of the modern military commander, Hitler did not lead from the front, but via telephone and telex from his headquarters far behind the lines. With this leadership from the rear (*Führen von hinten*), he was closer to Schlieffen than he was to Manstein and other generals who commanded from the front. But in contrast to Schlieffen, Hitler interfered with the smallest tactical-operational details in the conduct of operations. Rapid command decisions based upon on-site knowledge, which despite all the criticism of the method was the decisive strength of mission-type command, became increasingly impossible, even at the tactical level.

Contrary to what has been argued repeatedly since the war, Hitler's approach to command did not necessarily have only negative effects. During both World War I and World War II the very individual interpretations of the mission at hand did not always produce success. While on the operational level order-type command (*Befehlstaktik*) replaced mission-type command (*Auftragstaktik*), the troop-level commanders whenever possible conducted mission-type command on the tactical level.

Parallel to Hitler's growing distrust of the army generals, they also lost faith in the final victory and the Führer as the military defeats piled up. As Hitler noted, not without some justification, the euphoria from the early military success that supposedly resulted from the Führer's operational-strategic capabilities was first replaced by skepticism and then by open criticism of Hitler's leadership, his command decisions, and his operational abilities. But such complaints were uttered mostly internally, rarely openly. Hitler's critics reacted like a seismograph to the development of the military situation.

Within the General Staff any residual trust in the Führer slowly turned into consternation at his command decisions, his fits of rage, and his harsh reproaches about the incompetence of his officers. When Hitler ordered the thrust at the Caucasus against Halder's advice, and before the operations against Stalingrad had been completed, Halder noted in his diary with annoyance: "The habitual underestimation of the enemy's options starts to take on grotesque forms and becomes dangerous. It becomes more and more unbearable. There can be no question of serious work anymore. The characteristics of [Hitler's] leadership are pathological reactions, moments' impressions, and a complete lack of assessment by the [military] leadership structure."[213]

As the members of the General Staff came to see it according to Heusinger, Hitler not only made the wrong operational decisions more frequently, he increasingly controlled the organs of military leadership, losing himself in the smallest tactical details without caring about the larger operational picture. The "greatest military commander of all time" (*grösste Heldherr aller Zeiten*) determined the tactical details and thus lost sight of the overall situation—if he ever had it at all.[214] Thus, Heusinger thought that Hitler "absolutely lacked [an understanding of] the concepts of space and time."[215]

Here the question arises of why Heusinger and his Operational Department personnel continued to follow Hitler without opposition. Were they merely career-oriented technocrats of power? The charge that Hitler lacked the understanding of the decisive operational factors of space and time goes to the heart of the misunderstanding between the Führer and the army leadership. While Hitler initially thought strategically and oriented his objectives on the population and economic centers, the General Staff in strict accordance with the principles of traditional German operational thinking considered the annihilation of the opposing army as the foremost operational objective. This fundamental contrast can be seen in Operation BLUE. Hitler, based on the World War I experience of the German expansion toward the Caucasus in 1918 in order to gain the oil resources,[216] bluntly explained that he would have to terminate the war without access to the Caucasus oil.[217] In contrast, Halder undauntedly maintained the credo of German operational thinking, even after it was clear that World War II had been lost, when he wrote: "Owing to their training, the German operational leadership saw [their task] as defeating the live forces of the enemy, and not the possession of oil fields."[218]

During the early years of the war this fundamental conflict between Hitler and the army leadership could be papered over by both sides with the combat successes that had been achieved under high risk. But with the subsequent defeats in the east and the loss of the initiative, the conflict broke out into the open. From the professional military perspective, Hitler made more and more disastrous decisions—with his absurd offensive operations, his halt orders, and his prohibition against the conduct of an operational mobile defense. From Hitler's perspective in contrast, the generals had no understanding of strategy and were not capable of thinking in an overall strategic perspective. They always were ready for operational reasons to give up areas that were vitally important to the war effort.

There was a core element of truth to the allegations leveled by both sides. Hitler's operational leadership mistakes and wrong decisions outweighed by far the command successes he did achieve. Just a partial list of these failures on the Eastern Front include the operationally senseless order to capture Stalingrad, Hitler's hapless reaction to the Soviet counteroffensive, and the prohibition of the encircled Sixth Army from breaking out. Hitler's wrong decisions, resulting in the frontal offensive at Kursk and the rigid and linear defense in the east that culminated in the annihilation of Army Group Center in the summer of 1944 were, according to Karl-Heinz Frieser, the low point of the operational art of leadership.[219] Hitler's blunders in the west included the 1944 Ardennes Offensive and the deployment of larger units to the North African theater of war in 1943 when the situation there was already hopeless.

Those operations failed because Hitler ultimately lacked operational understanding. Planned envelopment operations failed again and again because of the weakness of the force committed on the flanks and unnecessary concentrations at the main effort. The Führer routinely failed to establish a clear main effort, or shifted it during the offensive. Operation BLUE is a prime example. Furthermore, he squandered many of the few mechanized units upon which the entire conduct of mobile operations was based by launching useless frontal attacks to capture cities like Voronezh or Stalingrad. He completely underestimated the enemy's capabilities and overestimated his own. He issued orders down to the battalion level that were hesitant, chaotic, unclear, and sometimes contradictory. Hitler's tendency for making decisions without sufficient predictability in the planning process also increased as he relied more and more on intuition and impulse. In the defensive, the rigid holding of lines repeatedly resulted in catastrophes and heavy losses. The fact that from 1943 on the German Army in the East suffered such grave materiel losses that it was capable of conducting only limited mobile defensive operations is in no way an excuse for Hitler's unprofessional leadership.

Hitler's lack of understanding of the operational-strategic linkages became particularly evident when he shifted the strategic center of gravity from the Eastern to the Western Front in 1943. That strategic decision was not followed up with the necessary operational decision. Hitler refused to make the decision to achieve the strategically necessary gain in time by the conduct of a mobile area defense in the east, even consciously accepting the loss of area. Instead, he wanted to do both, gain time and retain area, and in so doing he lost both. One explanation for this absurd behavior is certainly that the stubborn holding on in the east was the central precondition for Hitler's real overriding strategic goal—the extermination of the Jews in the camps of the east.[220]

But Hitler's operational weaknesses were paralleled unmistakably by those of the General Staff. For evidence one only needs to examine closely the planning chaos in the run-up to the France Campaign and the unfocused establishment of the main effort during Operation BARBAROSSA.

Along with such failures there were also great successes, such as the Sickle Cut (*Sichelschnitt*) maneuver in 1940, and the "Castling Movement" (*Rochade*) at Kharkov and the second strike from the rear in the winter of 1943. The latter two operations are closely associated with Manstein, certainly the Wehrmacht's most brilliant operational expert. Rommel is often mentioned in the same breath with Manstein. His operations, studied and admired to this day in Great Britain and the United States,[221] reflect many of the elements of German operational thinking, including surprise, mobile warfare, establishment of a main effort, seizing the initiative without compromise, and the attempt to force the imperative of action upon the enemy. But on the other hand, Rommel, who never received General Staff training and never served on a General Staff, rather acted and commanded like a company commander or battalion commander on the tactical level. His command principle reflected the close connection between tactics and operations.

The Prussian aristocrat Manstein, socialized in the General Staff and an excellent military expert, and line officer Rommel, of southern German lower-middle-class descent, not only personify two completely different types of officers, they also represent two fundamental structural weaknesses of German operational thinking that were mercilessly laid bare by modern warfare. Rommel represents the disregard for logistics structurally inherent in German operational thinking.[222] Manstein represents the operation-centered conduct of warfare focused on the decision of the battle, with occasional single-dimensional thinking for the overall strategic framework. Hitler, therefore, was correct when he complained that his generals seldom thought strategically but only in an operational perspective.

On the other hand, the postwar argument advanced by the generals that Germany lost World War II because Hitler was both a strategic and an operational dilettante is too self-serving. While Hitler recognized the strategic problems of the two-front war, and he had learned the lesson from World War I that only by securing a raw material and industrial base could Germany conduct a longer war of attrition—and he consequently aligned his operations according to that strategic criteria—the vast majority of the generals did not think beyond the annihilation of the enemy's forces. It was, therefore, difficult for the generals to understand why Hitler subordinated the conduct of operations to the overall strategic necessity of capturing the raw material resources of the Caucasus even though the forces available were insufficient for such operations. Thus, as the generals often failed to consider the strategic dimensions of warfare, Hitler in turn repeatedly ignored the simplest operational principles.

In what Bernd Wegner called their "paper victories" (*erschriebene Siegen*), the Wehrmacht elite after the war tended to suppress their own strategic failures and blamed the dead Führer for all the wrong operational and strategic decisions. They failed to recognize that Hitler had an astonishing strategic instinct as well as a particular view of strategic developments that set him well apart from the mass of his military entourage.[223] In general, Hitler's thinking about some matters was more modern than that of his General Staff officers, who could not break free from the reins of their traditional operational thinking.[224] They focused completely on operations, largely ignoring the new dimensions of modern warfare that encompassed the whole society. The fact remains, however, that in the initial phase of the war Hitler acted reasonably and with some luck within a limited military-strategic framework. Before and during the war, however, he never developed an overall and comprehensive strategic concept for the geographic situation and the economic capabilities of the Reich. His inability to design an overall strategy, to communicate it, and to develop operations from it was similar to the inability of those aristocratic army generals he despised so much.

Operational War of Annihilation?

In a double sense, Operation BARBAROSSA was designed from the beginning as a war of annihilation. From the operational perspective, the objective was—just as in the tradition of German operational thinking—the rapid annihilation of the enemy forces. Annihilation in the military sense here is understood not as physical extermination, but as the elimination of the enemy's army as an instrument for the prosecution of war. By 30 March 1941 at the latest, the German military leaders must have known that their classical operational approach to the conduct of war was in the coming campaign being linked to and would be used as an instrument of an ideological war.

In a memorable speech on that day Hitler disclosed to the generals the particular quality of the war being planned, one diametrically distinguished from the "normal wars" being fought in Northern and Western Europe and in Africa. The objective was not only—as Napoleon had once tried—the breaking of the Russian position as a major European power and the termination of Great Britain's dominance on the continent. The actual objective instead was the smashing of the Soviet Union and the decimation and enslavement of the Soviet population for the purpose of seizing Lebensraum in the east.[225] Doing so would achieve for Germany a strategic-economic position as a world power for the further fight against Great Britain and the United States. Inseparably tied to that objective was the ideological objective of the pending war—the physical annihilation of those ideologically "lethal enemies" (*Todfeinde*), Bolshevism and Jewry.[226] According to Johannes Hürter, "The military concept of annihilating the enemy forces was extended to the political concept of annihilating an ideology and an empire."[227]

Hitler, therefore, demanded from his generals nothing less than the abandonment of the traditional rules and standards of European warfare. The fact that they very well understood his intentions and the racial and ideological character of the imminent campaign is betrayed in one of Halder's diary entries: "The fight will be very different from the fight in the west. In the future, severity in the east will be a form of leniency."[228] Although Hitler did not cite details of the planned procedures, his listeners had to understand full well from the experiences of the SS methods in the occupation of Poland just what Hitler intended in his war for Lebensraum.

The military elite accepted Hitler's concepts for such a "racial-ideological war of annihilation" (*rassenideologisched Vernichtungskrieg*) and a "colonial war of exploitation" (*kolonialen Ausbeutungskrieg*) without criticism or comment, but also without enthusiasm.[229] Some of them undoubtedly focused their thoughts on their operational tasks in the coming campaign, rather than on the law of warfare issues. The question of whether a two-front war, the nightmare of the German military elite, really had been preempted as Hitler claimed was certainly on the minds of many general officers. The feelings of German superiority, reinforced from many directions, managed to overcome the existing skepticism, though.

OKW at least understood the character of the coming war. While OKH saw the classical operational objective in the annihilation of the enemy forces, OKW officers around Keitel drew from Germany's blockade experiences during World War I, and they therefore were thinking in terms of the totalization of warfare, far surpassing the annihilation of the enemy's military forces. In April 1938, OKW had issued a memorandum titled "Die Kriegführung als Problem der Organisation" (The Conduct of War as an Organizational Problem), which advocated the conscious totalization of warfare in any future military conflict. As stated in the memorandum's appendix, "Was ist der Krieg der Zukunft?" (What Is the War of the Future?): "The war will be conducted through all available means, not only with weapons but also with propaganda and the economy. It will be directed at the enemy's armed forces, at the materiel sources of the enemy's power, and at the psychological strength of his people. The guiding principle of its conduct must by necessity know no law."[230]

This justification, in combination with the National Socialist ideology of Lebensraum, led directly to the military's accepting as factual the German state's imaginary need for self-defense that went far beyond Frederick the Great's concept of "presumed self-defense" (*Putativnotwehr*). That, in turn, forced the adaptation and the outright violation of the existing standards of the international laws of war.

In the run-up to the attack on the Soviet Union, the German leadership prepared the ground for the ideological war of annihilation by supplementing, amending, or annulling various existing laws, regulations, and orders. These included the "Decree on the Exercise of War Jurisdiction" (Erlass über die Ausübung der Kriegsgerichtsbarkeit), the "Guidelines for the Conduct of the Forces in Russia" (Richtlinien für das Verhalten der Truppe in Russland), and the "Guidelines for the Treatment of Political Commissars" (Richtlinien für die Behandlung politischer Kommissare). As the campaign progressed, however, the forces in the field lodged so many protests about the regime of terror imposed by the SS Special Action Groups (*SS-Einsatzgruppen*) that OKH could no longer close its eyes to the consequences of those orders and decrees.[231] Although the Poland Campaign had not been conducted as an all-out war of annihilation,[232] it set the stage in many respects for the racial-ideological war of annihilation against the Soviet Union.[233]

Hitler's decision to replace the military administration of the occupied areas in Poland with a civil administration run by the SS and the police was very accommodating for the army leadership, which had reacted rather cautiously and with only a few protests to the incidents in Poland. The army leadership saw this division of powers (*Gewaltenteilung*) as an opportunity to avoid involvement in any anticipated atrocities, while at the same time leaving the military free to focus on operational matters. Prior to the start of Operation BARBAROSSA, OKW, OKH, and the SS had reached an agreement that the execution of the Führer's political tasks was the responsibility of the SS and not the army.[234]

Despite all the initial confidence of victory, there were military uncertainties based on classical German operational thinking inherent in Operation BARBAROSSA for which the army had no definitive solutions. Those uncertainties were part of the underlying and accepted "package of risks" (*Riskopakets*) that evolved with the development of German operational doctrine. Apart from the never resolved problem of logistics, the major risk was the relative weakness of the German force. Even though fighting outnumbered had been a core element of German operational thinking since Schlieffen, the law of numbers still influenced every military action. German doctrine was based on ensuring local superiority through the establishment of the correct main effort. Every military leader, therefore, had a vested interest in increasing the strength of the combat units.

After Reichsführer-SS Heinrich Himmler and Brauchitsch cleared the disputes over the SS murders in Poland, both sides started negotiations about how to secure the rearward areas during the upcoming BARBAROSSA campaign. Owing to manpower shortages, the army leadership was eager to reduce its responsibilities in the rear. Consequently, the SS took those duties over from the army.[235] That meant that OKH had no need to establish stronger security forces or even to task the frontline units with securing the rear areas. The acceptance of the SS regime of terror in the occupied areas was the price the army leadership had to pay for improving the strength of the forward forces. OKH was prepared to pay that price, but it was a short-term gain that carried a very heavy mortgage. In the end, however, the SS maintained their regime of terror with the participation of Wehrmacht elements, which led directly to the partisan warfare that was conducted with great brutality. On the Wehrmacht's side, the need to establish the military security of its own supply transports in the occupied hinterland, which was at least partially sanctioned by international law, was combined with an occupation policy that was based on racial-ideological annihilation. Even though relatively few Wehrmacht soldiers as members of the rear area force protection units participated directly in the annihilation actions, the commanders in chief of the army groups and the commanders of the field armies and their staffs knew about those measures and accepted the war crimes in order to maintain their own freedom of operations.[236]

The logistics problem shows even more clearly how OKH tried to remedy the never rectified flaw in its operational concepts by adopting the criminal notions of National Socialist ideology. Because of the lack of transport capacity and the vast extension of the operational space, the rapidly advancing forces could be supplied only alternatively with either ammunition, spare parts, fuel, or food. The decision, then, was that the troops would live off the country, since the war was expected to be of short duration. Without such a solution, it would have been impossible to supply the combat units, and therefore the rapid operations as planned would not have been possible. The General Staff had no other realistic alternative than to revert to that centuries-old practice of the European and German armies. The traditional technique of foraging in the occupied areas also supported Operation BARBAROSSA's National Socialist objective of waging economic warfare in the east. The commandeering of local resources had been one of the decisive planning objectives for the assault on the Soviet Union right from the start. To prevent the hunger winters Germany had experienced during World War I, which in the end had destabilized the Reich, the Ministry for Nutrition and the other agencies concerned with these issues decided to prosecute a hunger strategy against the Soviet population. Immediately after the beginning of the attack all available foodstuffs, with the exception of those required by the German troops, were to be transported from the captured areas back to the Reich. The consequent deaths of large numbers of the Soviet civilian population was not only deliberately accepted, but even endorsed.[237] This added a criminal dimension to the General Staff's solution for the supply of the advancing forces. The military decision makers in OKH were deterred by neither this nor the logistical consequences of a motorized army foraging in the field.

The General Staff assumed that the troops would be able to sustain themselves with the twenty daily rations they carried, plus whatever they could forage. But by basing their assumptions on the agricultural conditions in the border areas adjacent to Central Europe, they completely misjudged the completely different levels of support that the Soviet Union would be able to provide. While Army Groups South and North advanced through agricultural areas, Army Group Center in the main effort had to push through heavily wooded areas with little agriculture. Commandeering food from the country was thus very difficult for Army Group Center. They were forced to radically and ruthlessly "eat up" entire regions, with catastrophic consequences for the local population. Despite that, the General Staff, in a classical German combination of disinterest and underestimation of logistical problems, kept pressing the main effort in the center. The General Staff officers, focused on their operations, were not interested in feeding the local population. It was a solution quite in the tradition of German operational thinking.

Schlieffen had disregarded logistical issues, largely ignoring materiel and ammunition supply, and transferring the burden for food supply to the populations of the captured areas. He had no interest at all in just how those people were to meet the German demands. In the event that the local population would not comply with the German demands, Schlieffen explained that they would be "put under useful pressure . . . to bring in supplies, even from the outside, which [the troops] might lack."[238] This means that Schlieffen implicitly assumed that the troops would have to use pressure to ensure the flow of food supplies. The extent to which Schlieffen would have been willing to exert pressure on the enemy population cannot be deduced from the existing records. However, there can be no question that Schlieffen and his successors during World War I would have used hunger and therefore an annihilation strategy up to the level of the extermination of the Russian population, as the Germans later planned for and did in Operation BARBAROSSA.

Schlieffen's heirs, in contrast, adopted such a course of action for utilitarian reasons, within the framework of the National Socialist doctrine of Lebensraum.

In so doing, they acquiesced in the crimes inflicted upon the Soviet population. The experiences of World War II illustrate clearly that the army leadership in the course of the annihilation war in the east was willing to solve the structural problems of German operational thinking by ignoring both the traditional military code of honor and the basic standards of international law.

It is, however, only possible to prove the instrumentalization of National Socialist ideology in the conduct of military operations in the case of the siege of Leningrad. At the beginning of the attack Leningrad was one of the most important operational objectives for Hitler, but not for the General Staff, which saw Moscow as the operational objective of Operation BARBAROSSA. They considered the offensive in the north as only a flank security mission. In contrast, the Führer wanted to capture the city on the Neva not only because of its economic and maritime strategic importance, but also because of its ideological significance as the birthplace of the Bolshevik Revolution. According to Hitler, "Moscow and Leningrad must be razed to the ground to prevent people remaining who we will have to feed through the winter."[239] Again and again he demanded the capture of Leningrad, while the General Staff only planned to envelop the city because the available forces were running short after only a few weeks into the attack. Following a series of severe battles, Army Group North at the beginning of September finally succeeded in completing a large-scale encirclement of the metropolis.

The capture of the city seemed to be only a question of time when Hitler finally shifted the main effort of the German offensive to Moscow. Army Group North then had to detach the bulk of its mobile units and the VIII Air Corps to support the attack on the Soviet capital. The capture of Leningrad was now out of the question. The Eighteenth Army deployed in front of Leningrad was incapable of taking the city with just their infantry forces. After making a few small improvements to its front-line positions, the Eighteenth Army went over to the defensive. The operational objective was now to starve the city out through a siege and force it to surrender. That, however, was almost impossible, because although Leningrad was cut off from its land lines, it could be supplied via Lake Ladoga.

The intentions of the German military leadership varied. Early on in the attack OKW and OKH had combined their operational, economic, and ideological objectives. After the fall of Leningrad they planned to drive out and starve the surviving population, and then completely destroy the city. Wagner's sardonic remark about letting "the Petersburgers stew in their own juice"[240] obscured the intent to allocate the limited food reserves to friendly forces, but not to the Soviet population. Therefore, any breakout attempts by Russian civilians had to be prevented.

Neither the units in the field nor the commanders of the army groups were informed initially about OKH's intentions, which coincided with Hitler's ideological plans of annihilation, and the consequent change in the conduct of operations. The commander in chief of Army Group North, Wilhelm von Leeb,[241] assumed for example that the siege of Leningrad complied with international law at the time, and that it was a legitimate and classic military way to capture the city.[242] That would include the evacuation of the civilian population under certain conditions. Leeb repeatedly complained about the ruthless siege measures used against the civilian population, and he demanded that they be given the opportunity to leave the city.[243] But his requests to Brauchitsch and probably also to Hitler were answered in the negative.[244]

Thus, a purely military operation insidiously had turned into an ideologically driven operation of physical extermination against the population of Leningrad. The army senior leadership not only knew about it, but supported it. By the time the German siege ring was broken in 1944 some 1 million people had died. The reasons for the operation as it evolved are complex. On the one hand, it was driven by the National Socialist racial ideas that were widespread among the military leadership. Right from the start of the attack on the Soviet Union, for example, the commander of the Eighteenth Army and later commander in chief of Army Group North, Field Marshal Georg von Küchler, set the stage for the centuries-old struggle between Slavs and Teutons when he told his soldiers: "Since Genghis Khan Asian hordes have tried to advance against the racially superior Teutons and drive them out of their ancestral soil. But the current war is not only a fight between two racially different peoples; it is more than that. It is a fight between two ideologies, that is, Nationalism [sic] and Bolshevism."[245]

On the other hand, the decision apart from racial ideology was based primarily on practical reasons of military command and control operational procedure. Considering Germany's limited capabilities, neither Hitler nor the military senior leadership were prepared to commit the manpower and materiel necessary to capture the city, or even the food supply to feed the population. Thus, military utility combined with economic and ideological influences were the driving factors that resulted in the criminal conduct of operations.

As illustrated by other examples, the army leadership was willing to conduct its military operations through criminal means in order to compensate partially for the structural weaknesses of German operational doctrine, including drastic inferiority in manpower and inadequate logistics. Economic war, racial war, and conduct of operations were linked to each other, and reinforced and legitimized each other. The partial totalization and criminalization of operational thinking in the context of the racial-ideological war of annihilation became possible only by abandoning the traditional military values and standards. This deterioration in values resulted from the prejudices that developed in the German Reich and especially during World War I about the Russian and Jewish peoples, whom National Socialist ideology refused to recognize as humans. In contrast to the campaigns in Western, Southern, and Northern Europe, the conduct of war in the east showed no consideration for these "subhumans" (Untermenschen), even on the operational level. The army leadership, then, exploited that opportunity to minimize the weaknesses in German operational doctrine by resorting to criminal actions. Thus, the concept of the operational-strategic annihilation of the enemy forces, which in no way initially included the compulsory killing of all the enemy soldiers, evolved into the indiscriminate physical annihilation of Soviet civilians and soldiers as a necessary evil.

Conclusions

When on 1 September 1939 the German Reich started a new attempt to reshape the political map of Europe in its favor, it entered the war without a prepared overall plan. This was a sharp contrast to the start of World War I. In the autumn of 1939 neither the political nor the military leadership of the Reich had a strategic concept of Blitzkrieg. On the contrary, the operations plans for the attack on Poland were drafted only a few months before the start of the assault, and the plans against France only after the victory over Poland. The plans for the capture of Denmark and Norway, Operation WESERÜBUNG, were drafted after the assault on Poland. But even when the General Staff or OKW started to draft the attack plans on short notice, they did not act in a vacuum. The operational planning of the Army General Staff was based on traditional German operational thinking, which had been cultivated and developed over the years, and was dominated by the military thinking of the General Staff officers. But the lack of mobility and the combat realities on the tactical and operational levels during World War I had thwarted the execution of the General Staff's theoretical operational plans. During the interwar years that problem seemed to have been solved by the introduction of tanks, trucks, and aircraft. Under Hitler the maxim of the Army General Staff became one of undercutting the enemy's superior resources and potential by achieving a decision as fast as possible on the battlefield, thereby ending the war quickly.

But the rapid successes in the unintended "Blitz Wars" against Poland and France obscured the fact that the mobility problem had only been solved on the surface. At the start of the attack in 1940, only sixteen of the 157 divisions available in the west were fully motorized, and therefore fully capable of conducting mobile operations. Ninety percent of the German army's divisions had no greater mobility than their World War I predecessors. Their speed was determined by the infantrymen's marching pace, accompanied by the trudging along of the horse-drawn vehicles.

The German Army was a two-class force, not only for mobility but also for weapons. In 1940 some of the older soldiers fought with the same weapons they had used in World War I. The partial modernization and the semiobsolescent weapons were not primarily the result of the Wehrmacht's rapid buildup over a period of only five years, but also resulted from the structural limitations of Germany's strategic potential. Thus, the German Reich in May 1940 could only manage to bring about eighty divisions up to full operational capability, and only then by straining all its resources. The same thing happened during World War I, before the Spring Offensive of 1918. The image of a German "fully motorized Blitzkrieg army," which is still widely believed in both Germany and abroad to this day, was the result of a skillful National Socialist propaganda campaign—one whose effects remain. Those fully motorized units included the divisions of the *Waffen-SS*, which were under the operational control of OKH. Those divisions had all been fully motorized on Hitler's orders by the start of the France Campaign.

Although as in World War I the railway on the strategic level was the main means of long-distance transport for large troop redeployments on interior lines, the Wehrmacht at the tactical-operational level remained a horse-drawn army, just as the Kaiser's Army had been. During World War II the Germany Army deployed even more horses than it had during World War I. The varying levels of motorization forced the operational experts of the Army General Staff to reevaluate the time factor. The question was how to execute rapid and mobile operations with an army of varying qualities and that moved at two different speeds. The General Staff officers found the answer in their classical operational thinking rooted in Schlieffen. During the Poland and France Campaigns, they accepted the assumption of risk to establish a center of gravity with the elite motorized units, supported by tactical air power. By forcing the breakthrough at the decisive point, they won the decisive battle. Combined with surprise, that central element of the German concept of operations, the victories over Poland and France became a triumph of German operational thinking. Schlieffen's successors necessarily extended his envelopment doctrine to include the tactical-operational breakthrough, which he had rejected.

However, the successes of the early war years, unanticipated by the majority of the General Staff officers, cannot obscure the fact that the core flaws of German operational thinking were unresolved at the start of World War II. The war against the Soviet Union bluntly exposed the weaknesses of that school of thought. The Wehrmacht had failed to achieve the level of motorization necessary for the execution of their operational doctrine. The consequence was that the mobile units more often than not were forced to adapt their rates of advance to the slow infantry divisions that were motorized either partly or not at all. The decisive battles of annihilation sought by the General Staff remained unfought. Instead, Germany continued to rely on a combination of the establishment of a center of gravity, the will to retain the initiative, and its superior operational leadership. Traditionally applied to equalize the manpower disparity, that approach ultimately foundered on its own limitations. It was a repetition of what had happened during World War I, when the German Army tried to conduct a war beyond the Central European areas adjacent to Germany's borders. In the depths of Russia during World War II, air superiority could be maintained only locally at best.

The Russia Campaign also illustrates the operational hubris that resulted from the feelings of superiority after the victory over France, combined with the experiences against Russian forces during World War I. Many officers believed that Germany had defeated Russia "with its left hand" (*mit der linken Hand*). Those notions, however, were quickly dispelled, because the operational planners ignored the warnings of Moltke the Elder and Schlieffen about the depth of Russian space and the tenacity of Russian soldiers in the defense—warnings that should have been verified by the experience of the last world war. Such faulty assumptions were reinforced by the widespread National Socialist ideology about the superiority of the German over the Slavic race. Contributing to this disconnect from reality was the fact that the majority of the Wehrmacht colonels and generals had gained their warfighting experience in the trench warfare on the Western Front, and not in the mobile warfare on the Eastern Front between 1914 and 1918.

The unilateral focus on the operational element of warfare reinforced the traditional disregard of logistics in German operational thinking. While on the tactical level some of the lessons of World War I had been learned and applied, the operational experts continued to ignore the supply issues, largely because during the trench warfare of 1914 to 1918 the rail system had been adequate to support logistical requirements. The crucial role of logistics in modern mechanized warfare was seldom a discussion topic on any agenda. As with the overall operational planning, the General Staff was prepared to accept high logistical risks. As a consequence, a logistical system to support the conduct of rapid mobile operations was developed only for the initial stage of the Eastern Campaign. The traditional approaches to logistical support, tailored to operations in Central Europe adjacent to the German border, were modified somewhat, but were still completely inadequate for the attack on the Soviet Union. Starting with the second phase of Operation BARBAROSSA, and especially in the sector of Army Group Center, the low levels of motorization and the inadequate transport capacities forced the troops to forage for their food, as armies had done in the seventeenth and eighteenth centuries. And that, of course, negatively affected the local populations. Living off the countryside, as armies had done up through Napoleon's time, also complemented the National Socialist ideological goals for Operation BARBAROSSA by carrying economic warfare to the east, starving hundreds of thousands of Russian civilians in the process. Ultimately, OKH was willing to resort to criminal measures to compensate for a never rectified defect in their operational concepts.

Operation BARBAROSSA also exposed the structural strategic flaw inherent in German operational thinking. Ever since Schlieffen, overemphasis on the operational level had resulted in the neglect of the strategic level. This led to single-dimensional military thinking in the General Staff, which in turn gave Hitler the opportunity to neutralize that institution, first on the operational-strategic level, and then later on the operational-tactical level. In so doing, he personally assumed operational command and even partial tactical control over the army. Apart from the power struggle over the top-level structure and the competing claims to leadership between OKW and OKH, the paralysis of the General Staff in its own sphere of competence also resulted from the differences in operational ideas between those two headquarters. As in Schlieffen's time, for example, OKH centered the conduct of operations exclusively on the decision of the battle. OKH only modernized its operational thinking in some aspects concerning improved mobility at the tactical-operational level. They nonetheless unfailingly held to the objective of forcing a quick decision of the war through a succession of victorious battles of annihilation, fought in the areas adjacent to the German border. The army leadership continued to believe that rapidly destabilizing the enemy base of power was the only solution to Germany's strategic dilemma, thus preventing a long war of attrition and a people's war. OKW, on the other hand, did not on the basis of the experiences of World War I reject the concept of a lengthy war of attrition, an economic war, and a people's war. This strategic thinking of OKW that rather coincided with Hitler's strategic and economic "ideas of capturing and controlling space" was relatively foreign to the operational experts of the Army General Staff. They only adapted those factors of modern, mechanized warfare to their traditional concept of the conduct of operations.

By overemphasizing the purely operational factors, the General Staff ignored crucial aspects of modern mechanized warfare. In order to execute their operational concepts, the Army General Staff ultimately was prepared to resort to criminal means in the prosecution of the war in order to compensate for the structural weaknesses of German operational doctrine, including the neglect of logistics and the dramatic manpower disparity. They accepted and even endorsed the starvation of Russian prisoners of war and large parts of the population. As a consequence, the war against the Soviet Union—in contrast to the campaigns in the west—degenerated into a war of annihilation. In the course of that struggle, the opposing forces were rendered incapable of fighting, which of course was a return to the annihilation concept.

The General Staff and the operational experts, such as Manstein, largely suppressed any such apprehensions over Germany's conduct of the war, as well as the strategic realities. Boxed into the classical operational thinking focused on the decision of the battle, they saw themselves robbed of their victories by Hitler's rigid stand-and-fight orders in the defensive, and by his faulty operational-strategic configuration in the offensive. It was Hitler, and not the single-dimensional operational-strategic thinking, as Manstein suggested after World War II, that squandered the operational successes of the army and the General Staff, resulting in the "Lost Victories" (*verlornen Siegen*). And as happened following World War I, the personalization of the blame deflected attention from the structural deficiencies of German operational thinking in World War II.

The complete underestimation of the enemy, in combination with the overestimation of Germany's own capabilities, also illustrates that the loss of reality attributed to OHL in World War I was paralleled by an almost identical loss of reality by the Wehrmacht leadership during World War II.

8

Operational Thinking in the Age of the Atom

Each type of command and control of armed forces rests on the shoulders of its predecessors, forming a link of a chain.

—Colonel i.G. Ernst Golling

Studying the Causes and Coping with the Past

The Wehrmacht surrendered on 8 May 1945. For the second time within the space of just under thirty years the German armed forces had lost a world war. Germany, which subsequently was occupied by the Allies, was demilitarized and divided into four occupation zones. With that second defeat it lost its position as a major power in Europe. In contrast to 1918, there was no question in 1945 about the defeat. This time it was total and the surrender was unconditional. Moreover, Germany was overwhelmingly discredited morally because of the mass murder of 6 million Jews and the war of annihilation waged by the Wehrmacht in the east and in the Balkans based on racial ideology. Despite that moral burden, the majority of the German population still regarded the end of the war as a defeat. Forty years were to pass until Germany's liberation from National Socialism was addressed openly, although even then there were still critical objections. The turning point was a speech before the Bundestag delivered on 8 May 1985 by the Federal Republic of Germany's President Richard von Weizsäcker.

The reappraisal of the recent past was addressed in highly different ways in the two German states. For ideological reasons and based on the fascist model, no distinction was made in the German Democratic Republic (GDR—East Germany) between the Wehrmacht under fascism and the National Socialist system. Right from the very start of the postwar period, therefore, World War II was classified as a war of annihilation.[1] In the Federal Republic of Germany (BRD—West Germany), however, the Wehrmacht and the National Socialist state were for many years considered two separate spheres. The responsibility for the war and the associated crimes were not attached to the Wehrmacht, but rather exclusively to the SS or to Adolf Hitler. Personalization of the blame permitted issuing the military a blank check, as had been the case in the aftermath of World War I.[2] While the image of the "Clean Wehrmacht" was fostered in the Federal Republic, the Democratic Republic assigned the adjective fascist to the Wehrmacht from the very beginning.

The study of the war was not popular in postwar Germany. Because of the economic distress and the beginning of the Cold War along with the Iron Curtain that
divided Germany into two states, as well as the totality of the defeat, there was no
public analysis of the military reasons for the defeat of the sort that had been conducted during the Weimar Republic. This in no small measure was owing to the
fact that there no longer was a German armed forces, and therefore there was no
real public interest in—nor financial support for—such a study. Furthermore, the
former officers faced the problem of establishing themselves in civilian occupa-
tions, or they remained prisoners of war for many years.[3] The former Wehrmacht
leaders increasingly encountered criticism from the public media in response to
the war crimes trials during the immediate postwar period, and that in turn led
to the question of how close the relationship had been between the military and
National Socialism.[4]

It was only during the late 1940s that the first memoirs of famous generals,
such as Manstein's *Verlorene Siegen* (Lost Victories) or Guderian's *Erinnerungen
eines Soldaten* (Memories of a Soldier—published in English as *Panzer Leader*),
were published in the Federal Republic of Germany. Those books addressed in
public for the first time the reasons for Germany's defeat. In *Verlorene Siegen* Manstein established the programmatic line of argument. It was not the military and
therefore operational thinking that failed, but rather it was Hitler, the military dilettante. The shortages of materiel and manpower, adverse weather conditions, and
geography repeatedly were cited as the reasons for the military failures.[5] Other former officers who had held the senior-most command assignments, such as Colonel General Franz Halder, Beck's successor as chief of General Staff, or Lieutenant
General Adolf Heusinger, the former chief of the General Staff's Operations Division, tried to address the dilemma of the army's leadership in the National Socialist state. In their self-justifying writings they were torn between moral obligations
and obedience.[6]

Largely unnoticed by the West German public, former high-ranking German officers as early as January 1946 were addressing the thinking of the Wehrmacht in cooperation with the Operational History (German) Section of the U.S.
Army's Historical Division. Initially established to analyze American operations
in Europe, the Wehrmacht's tactical and operational experience in the east quickly
became the focus of American interest at the start of the Cold War.[7] Headed by
Halder, who enjoyed the confidence of the Americans, and including the circle
of other senior German officers from the prisoner of war camps of the Western
Allies, they created "paper victories" (*erschriebene Siegen*)—as Bernd Wegner
called them—that gave a clear shape to German World War II historiography. That
process took place in parallel with the discussion about German rearmament and
the publication of the first public German military periodicals.[8]

The prevailing line of thought in those years was that World War II had been waged by "the Führer," who failed completely, both morally and militarily. The personalization of the blame made it possible to keep the Wehrmacht's "shield of honor" clean, and also to evade the debate about the German military's approach to command and control and the associated operational doctrine after 1918. That juggling act accomplished the paradox of the military leaders claiming the credit for the operational successes, such as the Battle of France, while at the same time blaming the Führer for the defeats, by portraying Hitler as a dilettante who was unwilling to listen to professional advice.[9] Although some of the old, irreconcilable personal and professional conflicts among the army leadership resurfaced, such as the friction between Halder and Manstein, the former high-ranking military officers as a whole managed to convey to the public their own image of the Wehrmacht, which at the time was central to the debate over German rearmament. In addition to shaping the history of World War II along the same lines as the work of the former Reich Archive, the American-sponsored studies were designed primarily to "hand down to posterity without alteration the art of leadership as defined and developed by the German General Staff over the generations."[10] Thus, the intent was no more and no less than ensuring the continuity of the operational thinking of the German Army.

From the very beginning, that also was the objective of the principal postwar military periodical, *Europäische Sicherheit. Rundschau der Wehrwissenschaften* (European Security: Defense Studies Review), which had been established as a forum for discussion about rearmament.[11] The introductory editorial of the first issue in 1951 clearly described an unaltered agenda of German operational thinking that was separate from politics: "The active involvement of West Germany in European defense is a passionately debated issue of our day. It is not only a moral and a political problem, but rather it is primarily a military problem."[12]

According to the editorial, it was the objective of the journal to correct the lack of military understanding in Germany and to provide information about the military lessons learned from World War II. It is, therefore, hardly surprising to find in the journal's first issues an article by Halder's successor, Colonel General Kurt Zeitzler, and a contribution by the former president of the War History Research Institute of the Army (*Kriegsgeschichtliche Forschungsanstalt des Heeres*), Wolfgang Foerster, titled "Zur geschichtlichen Rolle des preussisch-deutschen Generalstabes" (On the Historical Role of the Prussian-German General Staff).[13] Also included was a preface by Halder entitled "Das Ringen um die militärische Entscheidungen im 2. Weltkriege" (The Struggle for Military Decisions in World War II).[14]

The article "Operationen" by former general Georg von Sodenstern published in early 1953 shows a clear intent to ensure the continuity of traditional operational thinking.[15] Following an introduction that addresses Moltke the Elder and Schlieffen, Sodenstern placed the operation within the triad of tactics, operations, and strategy. He also argued that the fact that the Western Allies won World War II without recognizing the operational as a distinct level of command did not in any way justify ignoring the operational level of warfare in the future. Examining the Western concept of strategy, Sodenstern confirmed that the soldier is not sovereign in strategic command and control issues, while at the same time he stressed the importance of the operational level: "It is the quintessential realm of the art of military leadership, in which the field commander must contend directly with the 'independent will of the enemy' [*unabhängigen Willen des Gegners*] and his means of power by making superior use of space, time, and the elements of armed force available to him."[16]

Eight years after the end of World War II, which had clearly demonstrated the limits of operational thinking, Sodenstern was once again advocating the classical German concept of operations and unreservedly rejecting any political influence on the conduct of operations. In his opinion, the field commander must have full command of the instruments of power available to him, which was consistent with the thinking during Schlieffen's time. The emphasis still remained on the inherent leadership skills of the field commander, although both world wars had demonstrated convincingly that even the most brilliant operations failed to compensate for an enemy's superior resources. There was, therefore, no advance in operational thinking toward an integrated overall strategy. Sodenstern did not advocate an innovative reorientation, but rather a revision to the old lines of operational thinking. In the Soviet-occupied German Democratic Republic, meanwhile, there had not yet emerged a similar public platform for such a debate.

Continuity

During the Allied Potsdam Conference in July 1945, even as the first subtle indicators of the coming Cold War appeared on the horizon, the Allies agreed to demilitarize Germany and to deprive it of any opportunity for a new passage at arms. By restricting and controlling the occupied country's resources, the Allies intended to prevent permanently any resurgence of Prussian-German militarism. But Allied unity quickly collapsed under the emerging East-West conflict.

The evolving global political antagonism between the Soviet Union and the Western Powers had direct implications for Germany, which was divided into two sub-states along the north to south border between the two blocs. From an operational-strategic perspective, the Soviet Occupation Zone, and later the German Democratic Republic, became the forward deployment area of the Warsaw Pact; while the former Western Zones of Occupation and later the Federal Republic of Germany turned into the glacis of NATO.

The Soviet Union covertly started forming paramilitary police forces in its occupation zone as early as 1948.[17] While the French viewed the idea of West

German armament in response to the Russian activities with the greatest distrust, the British and especially the Americans gave serious consideration to a reactivation of West German military potential in the face of the Soviet Union's apparent conventional military superiority. That development was accelerated by the 1950–1953 Korean War, which very clearly and drastically exposed the conventional inferiority of America and its allies. Given the Soviet threat, the first federal chancellor of the young Federal Republic of Germany, Konrad Adenauer, also supported the rearmament of West Germany. Simultaneously, he hoped that the Federal Republic would regain its full sovereignty and enhance its status within the international community by making a military contribution. And, of course, the defense of West Germany was a rather important issue for Adenauer. As early as 1953–1954, the chancellor understood that the nuclearization of warfare by the Western Allies would leave Germany a nuclear battlefield in any war. By reinforcing the West's conventional armed forces, Adenauer hoped to improve the defensive capabilities of the Western Alliance, and thereby raise the nuclear threshold in Germany's favor.[18] Adenauer took the initial steps even before the process of the integration of the West German armed forces into the Western Alliance structures—either via the European Defense Community or via NATO—was clarified. He did so despite a massive internal wave of protest against German rearmament. In 1950, Adenauer established the Schwerin Agency (*Dienststelle Schwerin*), which that October became the Blank Office (*Amt Blank*), charged with initiating the planning for the new Bundeswehr. In accordance with the American requirements to form "the Wehrmacht without Hitler and in a democracy" (*die Wehrmacht ohne Hitler in einer Demokratie*), the federal government planned ultimately to field twelve mechanized divisions, which, based on the Eastern Front experience of World War II, would be designed and organized for operational defense against the Soviet field armies.[19] The intent was to establish a new armed forces that was designed to have the lethality of the former Wehrmacht while at the same time being diametrically different in their internal structure, and especially in being subject to parliamentary control.[20] The structural changes in the form of military service in a democratic armed forces and the continuity in tactical-operational thinking for the defense of the sovereignty and territorial integrity of the young Federal Republic were two sides of the same coin.

Under such conditions it was no surprise that a renaissance of traditional operational thinking was advocated in the West German military journals of the early 1950s. Likewise, even though there was no support in the federal government for resurrecting the tradition of the German General Staff, it was also clear that many of the key senior positions in the newly established Bundeswehr, and especially the army, would have to be manned by former operations experts of the Wehrmacht.[21] Thus, the names of the trailblazers of the new German Army read like the *Who's Who* of the former General Staff Operations Division, and were headed by their former chief, Adolf Heusinger.

Heusinger, who volunteered to join the Kaiser's Army in 1915 and became a member of the Reichswehr in 1920, served in various assignments in the Operations Division upon completion of Principal Staff Assistant Training (*Führerge-hilfenausbildung*), the Reichswehr's clandestine General Staff officers' course. He became the chief of the Operations Division in August 1940. A sympathizer with the opposition to Hitler, Heusinger was arrested by the Gestapo following the failed attempt to assassinate Hitler in July 1944. Heusinger was then dismissed from office, although there was no direct evidence of his involvement in the opposition. Following the war Heusinger was first a staff member in the Operational History Program, and from 1948 to 1950 he was the chief of the Reconnaissance Division of the Gehlen Organization—West Germany's embryonic intelligence agency.[22]

After having worked in the background as an advisor to the federal government for several years, Heusinger became the head of the Military Directorate of the Blank Office. During the early phases of German rearmament Heusinger recruited several other members of the former General Staff Operations Division, including Colonel Bogislaw von Bonin, who later became NATO's Commander in Chief, Center (CINCENT); Colonel Johann Adolf Graf von Kielmansegg; and Lieutenant Colonel Ulrich de Maizière, who later became chief of staff of the Bundeswehr. Without going into the details of recruitment for the key divisions of the German General Staff over the years, it is sufficient to say that the organization functioned as an "old boy network." Markus Pöhlmann has defined such a structure as: "an informal, strategically structured relationship of loyalty comprising more than two persons. Beyond the optimization of the interpersonal and purely professional effectiveness of such a small group, it also serves both the promotion of the advancement of its individual members and the group's hegemonic position of power."[23]

Consequently, personal dependencies and animosities coexisted in this system, which simultaneously influenced the selection of its membership.[24] From a certain level of command upward, the issue was no longer only aptitude, qualification, and performance, but rather acceptance grounded in the institutional environment. On the one hand, the apparent dominance of the operations experts in the Blank Office[25] and the newly established Bundeswehr was a function of the requirements laid down by the Western Allies, who expected powerful German military units fit for operational defense to be raised within a minimum amount of time. To meet such requirements and to recruit qualified command personnel, the federal government had to rely on the operationally trained officers of the Wehrmacht. Owing to the personnel system, as well as the command and control structure of the German Army, they were mainly to be found among the former

General Staff officers. And of that group, the officers of the Operations Division were the elite, the nucleus of the General Staff. Closely linked together, they functioned as a classical and self-sustaining military old boy network. Consequently, the General Staff Operations Division officers moved up into the senior positions of the new German Army, although most of them did not have any Eastern Front warfighting experience as force commanders, and thus actually fell far short of meeting the second set of requirements of the senior leadership optimal profile.[26] The limited consideration given to former force commanders who had served on the Eastern Front was not only a function of the precedence given to the former Operations Division General Staff officers, but also of a general sense of mistrust of those officers who had returned from Soviet captivity. Thus, the revival of the Prussian-German officer corps ran in parallel with the resurrection of traditional operational thinking. Both processes were advanced primarily by officers who had served in the west or in senior leadership positions during World War II.[27]

Depending on their specific functions, those former General Staff officers who had served in senior leadership positions during World War II were, in fact, more or less closely connected with the Wehrmacht's criminal activities in the east. They had provided their military expertise to the National Socialist state as apolitical military technocrats. The prevalent attitude in the early 1950s, which distinguished between the Clean Wehrmacht and the criminal National Socialist system, facilitated the dominance of the early Bundeswehr by such officers. Paradoxically, all of the senior-most officers were scrutinized by a selection board, a process unique in German postwar history. But that board certainly did not examine any questions concerning the Wehrmacht's involvement in the Holocaust, or the Wehrmacht's criminal wartime activities in the east. Nor was the question addressed of how Heusinger could serve in four German armies (Kaiserheer, Reichswehr, Wehrmacht, and Bundeswehr) with highly different governmental and social systems while remaining true to himself.

The integration of the so-called office generals and officers—among them the former lieutenant general Hans Speidel—who never commanded any major formations, who had maintained apolitical attitudes under National Socialism, and who were anchored in the traditions of the General Staff, in turn guaranteed that the primacy of civilian political leadership would be accepted without reservation under the new and totally different political structures.[28] Thus, the selection board's qualified acceptance of Heusinger, ruling that he was acceptable for Bundeswehr service but not in the position of commander in chief of the army, was not a vote of distrust in Heusinger's activities under National Socialism, but rather the result of the fact that he had only been assigned to the General Staff during the war and had not held a command assignment at the front. He therefore did not have the necessary leadership qualifications for highest command.[29]

As early as the late 1940s Heusinger submitted several memoranda about the security situation of Germany and Europe, apparently in close association with various American agencies.[30] Among them was the 1949 paper "Die Bedeutung des Alpengebietes im Fall eines kriegerischen Ost-West-Konflikts" (The Importance of the Alpine Area in the Case of a Warlike East-West Conflict). Heusinger always based his memoranda on the overall strategic situation, from the Persian Gulf to the North Cape. He identified the area in the center of Europe, between the Alps and the Baltic Sea, as the key region in the struggle between East and West. Consequently, Germany was at the center of his operational hypothesis, which focused on countering a Soviet attack against Western Europe.

Heusinger and all the other former operations experts addressing this subject were faced with a strategic situation completely new to them. The division of Germany had shifted the two German states from the center to the periphery of the antagonistic power blocs. Moreover, until the late 1950s the territory of Germany was no longer a subject of the Germans, but rather an object of the Allies. It was no longer the central position of Germany and the threat of a two-front war that kept West German operations experts awake at night, but instead the country's marginal position as a glacis of the Anglo-Americans, whose strategic focal point was the North Atlantic and its peripheral regions. Thus, the decisive geostrategic prerequisite for the development of operational thinking since the days of Schlieffen had ceased to exist. For the West German operations experts the Federal Republic no longer faced the threat of a two-front war. The new geostrategic conditions no longer required a rapid offensive under time pressure to evade the superior resources of the enemy, but rather a defense that linked the protection of friendly territory with the time bought to deploy the superior capabilities of the Western Alliance.

Given the new geostrategic situation, the existing military force ratios, and the clear political guidelines, a surprise start to a war in order to move the fighting immediately to the enemy's territory and then to bring about a rapid decision was no longer a viable option, even though it had been the core element of German operational thinking since the days of Schlieffen. That old central component of German operational thinking that linked to the strategic level was now obsolete. Thus, the West German operations experts had to deal with the challenge of thinking and acting in the future at the operational-strategic level as a maritime rather than as a continental power. They had to adapt to the concepts of their former enemies in the west. In the future, the objective would no longer be a rapid offensive into the enemy's territory, but a defense to buy time for the deployment of the Allies' resources. If the strategy of deterrence failed, then it would no longer be a matter of a strategy of annihilation, but rather a strategy of attrition in its most comprehensive sense.

Owing to their military-technocratic and apolitical backgrounds, the loss of one of the core elements of traditional German operational thinking and the rethinking of the new operational-strategic situation were not difficult for Heus-inger and his associates. That was even more the case because they were firmly convinced that the second central component of operational thinking that linked to the tactical level was still effective under the changed geostrategic conditions. The conduct of mobile operations based on superior command and control proce-dures, initiative, flanking attack, and envelopment were still the keys to success on the battlefield. Since Germany's new allies had neither the operational systems nor any experience fighting against numerically superior Soviet forces, Heusinger and the other former German General Staff officers seized the opportunity to apply their operational skills and experience to the defense of the West, to the advantage of the Federal Republic. And in the process, they necessarily would enhance their own social status. That point was particularly important because the Germans ini-tially were merely tolerated junior partners in the Western Alliance, rather than being the hegemon of a coalition, as they had been during the two world wars.

Based on the foundation of German operational thinking, combined with the lessons learned from fighting against the Soviet Union, Heusinger rejected the concept of an exclusively static defense because of the Alliance's lack of military capacities, the clear manpower superiority of the Soviet armed forces, and the indefensible terrain along a front of more than eight hundred kilometers.[31] Fur-thermore, the territory of the Federal Republic of Germany was a narrow zone, with a maximum width of 425 kilometers in the south and 125 kilometers in the northern area around Hamburg. There were just a few favorable geographic defensive opportunities east of the Rhine River.[32] In all his memoranda, includ-ing "Die Verteidigung Westeuropas 1949/50" (The Defense of Western Europe in 1949–1950), Heusinger postulated a mobile and offensively oriented defense. The essential cornerstones of his operational thinking were summarized in the "Him-meroder Denkschrift" (Himmerod Memorandum), which was drafted for Ade-nauer by a body of military experts. Heusinger was a member of that group, and the memorandum's operational elements were primarily his contribution. He was convinced that a single, comprehensive operational plan was the prerequisite for the successful defense of Western Europe, and thus of the Federal Republic of Ger-many. At the time the memorandum was prepared, such a plan was not possible because of Russia's overwhelming numerical superiority.

Heusinger's concept was to conduct the overall defense of Western Europe as far to the east as possible, because of the very limited depth of the defensive zone. A high state of readiness and rapid defensive capabilities were necessary because of the potential of a surprise attack by the Soviets. According to Heusinger, the defense of Western Europe would focus on three areas of main operational effort: the Dardanelles, to deny the Soviets access to the Mediterranean Sea and the west-ern supply routes; the area of southern Scandinavia, Denmark, and Schleswig-Holstein; and the area of southern Germany, the Alps, and Tagliamento. The latter region included northern Italy. Along with the area in the north around Schleswig-Holstein, which controlled the Baltic Sea approaches and denied the Soviets access to the Atlantic, the two defensive areas in the north and south offered the opportunity to counter the threat to the Allied flanks posed by a Russian advance to the west from either of those approaches.

The conduct of the defense was to be mobile and offensively oriented, in order to pin down the enemy forces along their front and then destroy them by flanking attacks from the south and the north, supported by Allied air forces. This was based on the traditional principle of Schlagen aus der Nachhand (strike from the rear), developed during World War II. Nuclear weapons were not included in this concept for the Central European battlefield. Nuclear weapons were only considered for attacks against interior Soviet targets, such as the Baku oilfields. The attacker in Central Europe was to be defeated with conventional means, primarily armored and armored infantry divisions. Heusinger estimated that about twenty-five to thirty fully operational and ready divisions, including twelve German Panzer divisions, were required for a successful defense between the rivers Elbe and Rhine. This "armored fist" would force the Soviets to abandon any hope of a rapid thrust to the Atlantic. Based on Heusinger's plan, the West would conduct a counteroffensive as soon as the reinforcements arrived from the United States. In addition to destroying the approaching Soviet follow-on forces, the Allied air forces also would be required to provide direct support to the ground combat forces in the defense.[33]

Heusinger's deliberations were based on the premise that, just as during World War II, the Soviet field armies would be highly vulnerable to mobile operations, even despite their clear numerical advantage. The Western Allies, therefore, would be able to counter a Soviet advance with German support and German operational know-how. What is striking is Heusinger's ignoring nuclear weapons. Part of the reason is that for a long period of time he was for security reasons not privy to the Americans' nuclear operational planning. There was, however, a dilemma in Heusinger's thinking that was not to be underestimated. Should his operational plans ever be executed in any future war, the Federal Republic would not be just the main bulwark of the Western defense, it also would be the primary battlefield of the mobile defense. That was the price for the return of national sovereignty and membership in NATO, with its accompanying military security guarantees. Such, of course, was not in the interests of the federal government. Heusinger was well aware that Germany's contribution to the defense of the West would turn the Federal Republic into the actual battlefield. He believed, however, that this approach would increase conventional deterrence and correspondingly reduce the threat of a war.

If a war did break out, however, it would be necessary to defend as far to the east as possible, and to launch a counteroffensive in order to shift the fighting into

East Germany as quickly as possible.[34] Here, then, was the line of continuity to the classical German operational concepts of shifting the war to the enemy's territory as soon as possible by an offensive. In the 1950s, Heusinger's operational concepts were well in line with those of the Western Alliance, which were based on a "forward strategy" aimed at conducting a mobile defense as far to the east as possible.[35] This operational concept was supported by most of the former German officers, including retired General of Panzer Troops Gerhard Graf von Schwerin, Adenauer's advisor on security policy and head of the working staff on military issues, code-named the *Zentrale für Heimatdienst* (Center for Homeland Service). Schwerin likewise recommended to the federal government a mobile defense, rather than a static defense.[36]

As in the past, however, there were differing opinions on the matter. Retired General of Panzer Troops Fridolin von Senger und Etterlin, for example, declared that "the period of envelopment battles that can be won by operationally superior planning was over."[37] His criticism, however, was rejected simply and concisely with the counterargument that the issue was not one of envelopment battles, but rather of mobile defense. Other former high-ranking Wehrmacht generals, with whom Heusinger had discussed the buildup planning, interjected themselves into the debate, offering criticism and unsolicited advice. They did so despite the confidentiality restrictions Heusinger had placed on their earlier discussions. Heusinger, however, rejected even Manstein's repeated insistence on a different task organization for the future new German Army. Heusinger made it clear to his old comrades that he would not be dissuaded from his plans, even by critical comments in the media.[38]

The federal government not only accepted the Himmerod Memorandum's recommendations for the internal structure of the new West German armed forces; it also accepted the document's operational and strategic concepts and even made them public.[39] With Heusinger in the lead, the Blank Office continued to be the base of the operational planning for the defense of the Federal Republic of Germany in the years to follow. The objective was to establish for the Allies the operational importance of the West German divisions. Under no circumstances were inferior German units to serve merely as the cannon fodder of the Allies, as the French were still advocating.[40] Nonetheless, the criticism of those plans, which inevitably were to turn Germany into the zone of mobile warfare, did not fade. In the spring of 1955 the debate even cost the staunchest internal critic of those operational concepts his job. As early as 1952, Bonin repeatedly criticized the German defensive concept on the principle that it was not socially acceptable. Bonin argued that Heusinger's concept of conducting mobile warfare with armored units on the territory of the Federal Republic of Germany was not feasible because of the conflicting ideas of the Allies and American dilettantism in military matters. Bonin, therefore, recommended in a July 1954 memorandum the establishment of a defensive zone to a depth of forty to fifty kilometers along the Inner-German Border (IGB).[41] So-called antitank divisions (*Panzerabwehrdivisionen*), supported by machine guns, heavy engineer forces, and especially antitank guns, would fight the defensive battle in that zone.[42] He further recommended up to six Panzer divisions as a mobile counterattack reserve to destroy any enemy forces that managed to penetrate the zone. This defensive barrier was designed to slow down a Soviet advance until the Allied forces could deploy. Bonin's concept of national defense conducted as an immediate forward defense along the IGB was based on the lack of offensive capability of the West German armed forces and the principle of transparency for the Soviets.[43] Bonin hoped that such an approach would reduce the tensions between the two blocs, not preclude any future reunification of the two German states, and ensure inner-German acceptance of rearmament.[44] Moreover, he considered illusory the official position that the establishment of the Bundeswehr could be accomplished within two years. Bonin's ideas were rejected by the Blank Office, for both operational and foreign policy reasons. Heusinger did not believe that it was possible to repel with antitank blocking positions any attacker who had the freedom to select the point of his main effort. Mobile defense was the only way to block such an attack. Politically, Bonin's plans based on German neutrality were seen as jeopardizing the overriding objective of the integration of the Bonn Republic into the Western community.

The "Bonin Case" showed that West German military leaders objected to a national go-it-alone approach, because they believed that the defense of the Federal Republic of Germany was only possible within the NATO alliance. Bonin, however, was not dismissed because he held operational opinions contrary to the majority of officers in the Blank Office, but because he went to the public with them, made the internal debate public, and thus destroyed the image of the unity of the officer corps being projected to the outside world.

Between 1950 and the establishment of the Bundeswehr in 1955, the development of operational planning in the Federal Republic of Germany can only be understood in context with the developments in the fields of security and foreign policy that were related to the integration of West Germany and its future armed forces, as well as the future military involvement of the United States in Europe. There was consensus among the Western Allies that German forces would not be established on a national basis, but rather integrated within the alliance structure in a closely controlled way. A German ally that might become too independent and might lean toward neutrality had to be avoided by all means.

The failure of the 1950–1952 European Defense Community initiative made it possible for the Federal Republic of Germany to assert not only its own sovereignty, but also its equal status within the NATO alliance. During that period the German officers who engaged in the initial consultations with the Allies faced totally different problems. Because of the lack of defense funding, the Americans since 1948 had been developing operational ideas diametrically opposed to those of the Germans. Thus, the American military initially planned to conduct the delay at the Rhine River and eventually block any Soviet advance on the Pyrenees. Until the lost territory was recaptured through a major counteroffensive, the Russian attackers were to be decimated by nuclear strikes.[45] Such plans, of course, were not at all in the interest of the Germans, who vehemently resisted the American concepts that were being advocated primarily by the U.S. Air Force. The Germans, however, failed to grasp the full dimension of the American ideas on nuclear warfare, because they had almost no precise information about those nuclear weapons or their employment.

Digression: Moscow and East Berlin

While former Wehrmacht officers in western Germany developed their own traditionally oriented operational ideas even before the formal establishment of the Federal Republic of Germany, the new federal government seized upon those ideas because they supported the political plans for rearmament. In eastern Germany, however, former Wehrmacht General Staff officers had no such comparable influence on the tactical-operational thinking of the evolving armed forces of the German Democratic Republic. Among other reasons, this resulted from the politically and ideologically motivated change of elites in the Soviet Occupation Zone, which affected the military, particularly at the operational level of command. For ideological reasons, former Reichswehr officers who had served in World War II as staff officers of the Wehrmacht were unacceptable to the East German Socialist Unity Party (SED) as leadership cadre for the People's Garrison Police (*Kasernierte Volkspolizie*—KVP), the forerunner of the GDR's armed forces.

It was not possible, however, to achieve the proletarian-military recruiting ideal that was to be the foundation of the new East German armed forces because of the lack of qualified cadre among the acceptable socialist circles. During the initial stages of the buildup, therefore, the SED was forced to draw upon some combat-experienced former Wehrmacht officers. As World War II had progressed, the lower ranks of the German officer corps had opened increasingly to candidates from the middle class and the proletarian strata of society. This had been done deliberately by the National Socialist German Workers' Party, as a step in the evolution of a National Socialist People's Army.[46] There were, therefore, a sufficient number of these younger officers in eastern Germany who had been commissioned from the ranks, and who had not come from traditionally socially desired circles. These former officers were quite willing to serve with the KVP.[47] Among the former wartime officers there were just a few who had command experience at the operational level. Former members of the Wehrmacht General Staff with operational level command and control training, along with all other former Wehrmacht officers, were considered to be corrupted by fascism, or at least ideologically suspect. Their integration into the KVP was out of the question. Thus, during the transitional period, and until younger candidates graduated from the Soviet military academies, only those higher-ranking officers who had belonged to the Soviet-sponsored National Committee for a Free Germany (*Nationalkomitte Freies Deutschland*) were used to establish the new East German armed forces— and even those officers were dismissed after only a few years. Mainly there were five general officers, including Lieutenant General Vincenz Müller, who had been released from Soviet captivity in 1948 under the "Action 5 + 100" program.[48] But even those former senior officers, who were committed to socialism and were considered ideologically unobjectionable, had been socialized into the Wehrmacht and thus German operational thinking. Like their former comrades in the West, they were convinced of the superiority of the Wehrmacht's tactical and operational command and control system over that of the Soviet Army, even after Germany's defeat.[49]

Because of a lack of Soviet doctrinal regulations, the units of the KVP initially adapted their tactical ideas to those of the Wehrmacht, which the Soviets accepted and even partly supported. That changed over the years as East Germany was integrated into the Warsaw Pact and increasingly adopted Russian military technology.

From the outset the East German forces were unambiguously oriented on Soviet thinking at the operational level. In 1952, the second edition of the Red Army's *Field Service Regulations* became the official doctrine. The KVP's four planned corps of two infantry and one Panzer division each were established in accordance with Soviet military doctrine. That included equipment, ideology, and personnel policies. During the immediate postwar period Soviet military doctrine was based on communist ideology, and most especially on the trauma of the German invasion in the summer of 1941 and the subsequent war on Russian soil that resulted in enormous human losses and material damage. In the future, a surprise attack had to be prevented at all costs. The Soviet Army, therefore, had to be superior to any potential attacker right from the beginning of a war. It then had to seize the initiative and transition to the strategic offensive against the enemy's territory as early as possible in the war's initial phase. The Soviets attempted to compensate with superior conventional capabilities for America's nuclear monopoly, which existed until 1949. Consequently, the Soviet military leaders focused on conventional warfare, which for ideological reasons also offered the opportunity for a political reconstruction of Europe. Armored and mechanized formations, supported by air power, were supposed to penetrate the enemy's tactical defensive area and subsequently destroy the opposing armed forces by conducting rapid and deep operations.

To execute this doctrine the Soviet Army from 1946 on consistently increased the motorization levels of its units, transforming their mechanized corps of World War II into mechanized divisions.[50] Because organizational structures and equipment were already geared toward combined arms combat, the resulting newer units had improved mobility and increased firepower, resulting in greater overall striking power. The new Soviet divisions matched the West European divisions in many respects. The Soviet military leaders expected the newly increased mobility to result in a significant acceleration of future operations, and a correspondingly shorter duration. Given those propositions, traditional German operational thinking was adopted by the KVP and its successor, the National People's Army (*Nationale Volksarmee*—NVA). The future officers in the GDR accepted this process, not only because of ideological orientation, but also because they recognized certain analogies between Soviet and German operational thinking.

The similarities between the Soviet conduct of operations and classical German operational thinking are obvious. As in the German General Staff, the Soviet side also wanted to use mobility to set the rules, to seize the initiative, and to neutralize the enemy's firepower—which after 1945 was primarily American nuclear weapons. The partial alignment between the Russian and the German operational mind-sets resulted not only from the Russian analysis of German operations during World War II, but also from the clandestine German-Soviet military cooperation during the period of the Reichswehr. Russian officers at that time had the opportunity to learn about German operational thinking in the Reichswehr beyond what information they could derive from the specialist military journals. As in Germany, the Soviets after World War I deliberated intensively on the future of warfare, looking for a solution to regain the lost freedom of maneuver. In the process, the Soviets also profited from the experiences of the 1917–1922 Russian Civil War and the 1919–1921 Polish-Russian War.

As in the Reichswehr, the Russian internal discussion about future warfare oscillated between the strategy of attrition and the strategy of annihilation. General Michail Tuchačevsky, chief of the General Staff of the Red Army, supported the strategy of annihilation. For political and other reasons, he did not want the evolving capabilities of modern weapons systems, such as armored vehicles and aircraft, to limit his options for offensive operational warfare to a strategy of attrition. By the early 1930s the advocates of the annihilation strategy in the Red Army prevailed. In the process, the Soviets developed the theory of "deep operations." It was based on combined arms combat and the execution of a breakthrough in the attack that was calculated exactly to a specific width and depth of the attack zone. Integral to such a combined attack, armored units would operate independently and deeply in the rear of the enemy's defensive zone.[51]

Many similar ideas are found in German operational thinking. The extent to which German ideas were incorporated into the development of the Soviet doctrine has not yet been fully analyzed.[52] It is certain, however, that there was a robust exchange between the Reichswehr and the Red Army in the late 1920s and early 1930s, and that the Soviets adopted many ideas from Germany. The Reichswehr officers at the time admitted that most of their Russian counterparts on temporary duty in Germany had an excellent knowledge of German tactical and operational concepts. As Erich Pruck noted, "The Red commanders were familiar with the teachings of Clausewitz, Moltke, and Schlieffen. Their planning was dominated by attack, breakthrough, and envelopment."[53] Tuchačevsky even went so far as to refer to the Reichswehr as the master of the Red Army, because the Germans had provided substantial support to the buildup of the Soviet armed forces. The Soviets greatly appreciated their German partners, especially in the field of tactical and operational training. They therefore endeavored to adopt the Reichswehr's training methods in those fields. Consequently, German officers on temporary exchange duty in the Soviet Union repeatedly noted numerous common features of German and Soviet military thinking. "The war situations," as General Werner von Blomberg put it in his trip report following a visit to the Soviet Union in 1928, "showed almost entirely a perception of the operational and tactical principles equivalent to our own."[54] The Russian infantry manual of 1927 largely resembled the Reichswehr's *Das F.u.G.*, particularly in its emphasis of the significance of speed and surprise. The Russian *Field Service Regulations* of 1920 also explicitly stressed mobile warfare, with outflanking, envelopment, concentration of effort, and breakthrough.[55] The similarities, then, are hardly surprising. On the German side, progress in operational thinking was fostered by the analysis of Soviet regulations on fast-moving formations. The findings, however, failed to change in any significant way the German operational ideas on command and control. The Russian ideas did, however, influence German thinking on air warfare, air defense, gas warfare, and engineer forces. The Soviet Union's techniques of socializing the population to military matters by the use of mass propaganda and sophisticated technical assets did have an effect on the new "politically oriented" officers, such as Blomberg and Reichenau. It is, therefore, not at all accurate to talk of a one-sided exchange of military theory during this period, as many Germans did following World War II.[56]

Although most of the Russian officers who received advanced training in Germany or at the foreign bases of the Reichswehr in Russia later fell victim to Stalin's purges, the tactical-operational ideas they developed lived on in the Soviet Union. During World War II they were refined based on the experiences of Germany's initially successful execution of operational warfare. There was, however, one decisive difference in the respective operational concepts of the two armies. Rather than basing their operational procedures on mission-type command and control, the Soviets instead adopted the order-oriented approach. Therefore, flexible and situationally oriented command and control was neither common nor feasible in the Red Army because it conflicted with the direct supervision by the

Communist Party. Despite being grounded in a sound theoretical background, the Soviet conduct of operations was constrained significantly, which in turn contributed to the successes the Wehrmacht achieved from a position of numerical inferiority.

The Nuclearization of Operational Thinking[57]

At exactly the same time that Heusinger and his staff believed they had reached an understanding with their American counterparts about the feasibility of the Western Alliance adopting the German approach to operational planning for a mobile and offensively oriented defense, NATO in 1954 changed its military strategy.[58] Up to that point nuclear weapons had always been regarded exclusively as political instruments at the strategic level; but henceforth they would be tactical weapons. In the future any act of war by the Soviets in Europe would be answered by a lethal counterattack—"Massive Retaliation"—by the launching of both tactical and strategic nuclear weapons. This new military strategy did not emerge suddenly; rather, it evolved slowly, beginning in the early 1950s and driven by the conventional numerical inferiority of NATO's forces, the financial difficulties of the Western states, and the operability of the first Soviet nuclear weapons.[59] The plans to make tactical nuclear weapons available to the operational commanders, to which they officially had not had access prior to 1955, were largely unknown to the German military leaders. Therefore, this change that challenged the foundations of German operational planning astonished them. The mobile and offensively oriented conventional defensive battle was now a moot point.

The warfighting concept of the Alliance, based on its nuclear superiority, postulated a nuclear exchange between both blocs during the first thirty days of a conflict. That would be followed by operations using tactical nuclear weapons in a second phase. The parallel concepts of conventional defense and the strategic use of nuclear weapons had now merged. Within the evolving operational doctrine that assumed the use of tactical nuclear weapons, the conventional units now had the primary task of surviving the initial nuclear strikes as unscathed as possible, and then preventing the rapid overrun of Europe. Simultaneously, the Allied air forces had the mission of establishing air superiority and delivering nuclear counterattacks.[60] The ground forces had the mission of fighting dispersed from prepared positions in order to force the enemy to concentrate his forces, where they then could be destroyed by tactical nuclear strikes. Germany would be the battlefield on which such a war was fought. For the Federal Republic of Germany, then, the decisive question became one of where such a defensive operation would be conducted. Unless NATO had German support, the only option NATO saw was to stop the Soviet formations along the Rhine–IJssel line. With the units of a newly established German Army, however, a forward defense along the Trave Canal–

Elbe and Weser–Lech line would be possible. Then the targeting of the tactical nuclear weapons that were supposed to replace the armored units as the "backbone of the defense" would be possible to the east of the territory of the Federal Republic.

Metaphorically speaking, the conventional forces assumed the function of a "shield," which was to protect the nuclear strike forces and force the aggressor to concentrate his troops, which then would be destroyed by the "sword" of the Alliance—the nuclear weapons and their delivery systems.[61] The Allied air forces were the primary warfighting component under this concept because they had the nuclear delivery systems. Although this new military strategy was not accepted without serious reservations within the Alliance, and the land forces commanders challenged its underlying reliance on air power, NATO in the mid-1950s did not see any other option than the early commitment of nuclear weapons, given the Soviets' overwhelming conventional superiority. Eighteen NATO divisions faced eighty-two Soviet divisions. What everyone obscured, however, was the understanding that the risk of the nuclear devastation of Germany was being balanced against "the hope that nuclear deterrence would prevent that from happening."[62]

The German leaders only started to get a general idea about the new strategic concepts in early 1955, via indirect channels and through Speidel's contacts in NATO. Even though the Germans did not yet have full access to the Alliance's classified plans, Heusinger and the other operations experts in the Blank Office had to realize by then that any of their operational planning for the defense of the Federal Republic that failed to integrate nuclear weapons would fall short of the reality of the future. This realization not only gave many West Germans sleepless nights, it also mobilized the resistance against West German rearmament, with hundreds of thousands supporting the "Without Me Movement" (*Ohne-mich-Bewegung*). Given the dilemma of Germany as a battlefield, Heusinger likewise had a problem with the use of nuclear weapons as a means of defense. He did not believe that nuclear weapons would make conventional weapons obsolete. After all, their use challenged his operational concepts upon which the establishment of the Bundeswehr was based. Moreover, he rejected the idea of using nuclear weapons right from the start of the war in the event that deterrence failed. In addition to realizing the consequences of the use of nuclear weapons on the battlefield of Germany, Heusinger was concerned about the effect on the execution of German operational command and control. Nonetheless, the triad of tactics, operations, and strategy upon which the German General Staff officers believed that the well-balanced application of the superior German operational command and control was based started disintegrating with the nuclearization of conventional warfare. But as always in the past, the General Staff officers had different perspectives on the details of the operational concepts. While Heusinger held to his classical operational concepts, de Maizière and the younger officers, who already had been in the United States for training, supported the adaptation of operational thinking to the nuclearization of warfare, and they rejected the sharp separation between nuclear and conventional warfare that was the common point of view of the older officers.[63]

Nonetheless, Heusinger and his colleagues could not veto the Allied plans for relying on nuclear weapons, which had inevitable consequences for German operational thinking. This was all the more so because following Germany's admission to NATO the operational level of command was no longer in German national hands. The peacetime operational planning and wartime execution of operational command and control were now in the hands of NATO's Supreme Allied Commander Europe (SACEUR), and his subordinate regional combined commanders. The air force CARTE BLANCHE exercise held in June 1955 demonstrated how the Alliance visualized nuclear warfighting of the future.[64] It was at that point at the latest when the Germans fully realized the extent to which the Alliance planned to rely on nuclear weapons in the future, and the crucial role the air forces would play in the delivery of those weapons. The traditionally prominent position of the army within the German armed services seemed to be challenged by this development. The commanders of the new Luftwaffe, in turn, willingly seized upon the opportunity to advance the relative status of their service in the internal military ranking.

The year the Bundeswehr was established Heusinger's operational ideas faced increasingly heavy resistance. The primary reason was that the Federal Republic's contribution to NATO's defense in the form of twelve armored divisions was based on the traditional operational thinking, which now had to be reconciled with the nuclearization of conventional warfare. The increasing political and social resistance against German rearmament was also a factor. Moreover, German officers newly assigned to NATO headquarters realized that while the Alliance was willing to commit land forces to mobile operations in a nuclear war,[65] it simultaneously was starting to distance itself from those German operational ideas that were incompatible with the thinking of the rest of the Allies.[66] In Bonn there was a growing recognition that the forward defense along the Iron Curtain as Heusinger planned it was no longer compatible with the nuclear strategy advanced by the Alliance, because NATO did not have the necessary conventional forces.[67] Many in Germany also came to the gradual understanding that NATO, albeit reluctantly, could do without German forces, but it could not do without nuclear weapons to defend Europe. The federal government recognized that as a member of NATO it had to accept the principles of the Alliance's nuclear-strategic concepts.[68]

German operational thinking had reached a point of crisis. The changes in the geostrategic situation already had rendered the operational-strategic component of that thinking obsolete. Now the tactical-operational core of traditional German operational thinking, and with it the foundation of the professional identity of the General Staff officers, threatened to collapse under the nuclearization of warfare.

How could the traditional German concepts of operational command and control be exercised in an unlimited nuclear war that would initiate immediately at all levels at the very start of hostilities? How could Germany, as a junior partner, and one burdened with the odium of being a former enemy, advance its own operational doctrine within the Alliance? How should German soldiers be trained and educated for such warfare? And most critically, how could the reality of a nuclear war on German territory be explained to the German people?

The military leaders, for the most part, believed that answering that last question was primarily the responsibility of the politicians, although the military recognized its obligation to provide support in the form of rationale and information.[69] That also was the case when it came to determining the internal structure of the armed forces. Traditionally, the German approach had been to stress the superiority of man over machine, as a means for compensating for any enemy's superiority in manpower and materiel. The German Army, therefore, promoted the independence of the individual soldier through mission-type tactics and patriotic instruction. That approach was used as early as World War I, when warfare had evolved to the point where senior-level commanders no longed exerted any direct influence on the front lines. Pursuing that conceptual idea, the solution for waging a total nuclear war was found in the new organizational and leadership philosophy of "Inner Leadership" (*innere Führung*), which combined in a single person traditional soldier bravery with the freedom of the individual and the responsibility of the citizen. That made possible the command and control system and the commitment of that soldier in the chaotic environment of nuclear war.[70]

Although the majority of the German operational experts accepted the political deterrence function of nuclear weapons, it was difficult for them to imagine that there might be a total nuclearization of warfare itself. But it was not just the new strategy pursued by the Alliance that made them rethink the matter. The estimate of the enemy situation also played its part here. Based on the lessons learned from World War II, the Soviets had not only improved their own weapons systems and pushed ahead with the motorization of their formations, they above all had developed a far more flexible command and control system. In so doing, that altered to their own advantage the decisive parameters upon which German operational planning was based. That, in turn, challenged the efficacy of Heusinger's conventional operation plans. And as a result, the central component of German operational thinking, which sought to counter the enemy's greater manpower and materiel through superior operational planning and command and control, was reduced significantly.

In the autumn of 1956 the problems encountered during the establishment of the Bundeswehr forced the federal government to prolong the buildup phase. At the same time, the decision was made to reduce the tenure of compulsory military service from eighteen to twelve months, and to field as few as ten divisions

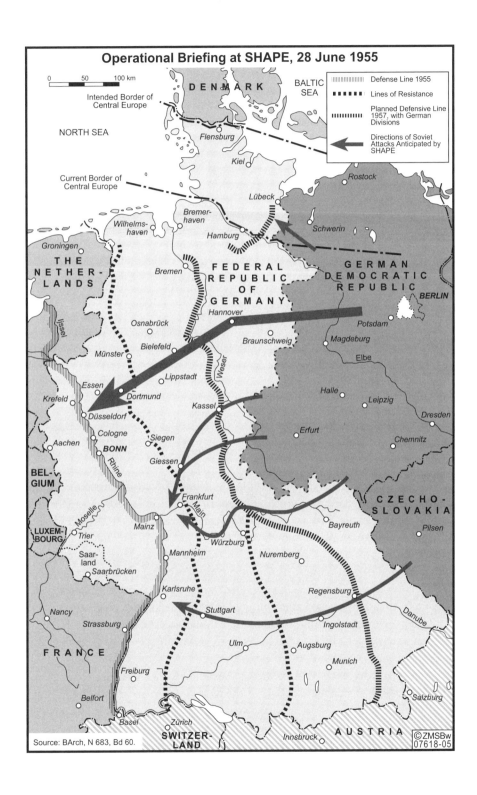

Operational Briefing at SHAPE, 28 June 1955

Legend:
- Defense Line 1955
- Lines of Resistance
- Planned Defensive Line 1957, with German Divisions
- Directions of Soviet Attacks Anticipated by SHAPE

Intended Border of Central Europe

Current Border of Central Europe

NORTH SEA

BALTIC SEA

DENMARK

Flensburg

Kiel

Rostock

Lübeck

Schwerin

Bremer-haven

Wilhelms-haven

Hamburg

Groningen

THE NETHER-LANDS

Bremen

FEDERAL REPUBLIC OF GERMANY

GERMAN DEMOCRATIC REPUBLIC

BERLIN

Münster

Osnabrück

Hannover

Braunschweig

Potsdam

Magdeburg

Bielefeld

Lippstadt

Weser

Elbe

Essen

Krefeld

Dortmund

Düsseldorf

Kassel

Halle

Leipzig

Dresden

Cologne

Siegen

Erfurt

Chemnitz

Aachen

BONN

Rhine

Giessen

BEL-GIUM

Frankfurt

Main

CZECHO-SLOVAKIA

LUXEM-BOURG

Trier

Moselle

Mainz

Würzburg

Bayreuth

Pilsen

Saar-land

Saarbrücken

Mannheim

Nuremberg

Karlsruhe

Nancy

Strassburg

Stuttgart

Regensburg

Danube

Ingolstadt

FRANCE

Ulm

Augsburg

Munich

Freiburg

Belfort

Salzburg

Basel

Zürich

SWITZER-LAND

Innsbruck

AUSTRIA

0   50   100 km

Source: BArch, N 683, Bd 60.

©ZMSBw
07618-05

for the time being, only four of which would be Panzer divisions. Those changes, combined with the assumption by SACEUR of the operational level of command and control when West Germany joined NATO, forced the operations experts to change their mind-set. Heusinger supported the concept of graduated response by the Alliance as an alternative to immediate nuclear war, and as the political-strategic environment evolved over the years he continually adjusted German operational planning.

The planners turned their attention to the second phase of a possible war. While the objective of the first phase was only to survive, the German planners, like many of their colleagues in the Alliance, still believed that they would be able to fight and win a war on the tactical-operational level following the first nuclear exchange. In response, they modified a decisive parameter of the traditional operational thinking. As after World War I, they concluded that mobility was the solution to the problem. Combined with a greater dispersion of the combat units and improvements in armor, increased mobility would provide the highest possible level of protection against nuclear strikes. It was a path out of the doctrinal crisis. The German planners also modified traditional operational thinking by sharing knowledge with their new allies and partially integrating tactical nuclear weapons into the conduct of operations, by treating them as artillery weapons with enhanced effect.[71] With integrated nuclear capabilities, better protection, and increased mobility, the new divisions would be the only units capable of conducting lightning-like operations. Thus, it all came back to the Panzer divisions as the backbone of the defense.

A key point for the planners was the requirement for well-trained and responsive commanders to execute such a nuclear mobile defense. That in turn guaranteed the continued requirement for Army General Staff officers, who would make an essentially German contribution to the Alliance, as well as support the army's claim to primacy in its competition with the Luftwaffe. It is interesting to see how Heusinger used the new face of war to justify the enhanced quality of leadership. He postulated that the use of tactical nuclear weapons made new and unprecedented demands on command and control, which in the tradition of classical German operational thinking remained an art rather than an exact science.[72] Heusinger thus emphasized the importance of those key operational planners and leaders within the military leadership. Simultaneously, Heusinger urged the Bundeswehr's senior officers who had served in World War II to recognize this new face of war.

Heusinger continually and untiringly explained this modified operational doctrine to both the civilian leaders of the federal government and the military leaders of the Alliance. While nuclear weapons would be of great importance in any future war, they would not be decisive alone. The enemy would still have to be defeated through a counterattack on land, and also from the sea. As he said, "The era of sophisticated armies and navies is not past" ("Die Zeit der hochmodernen Heere und Kriegsmarinen ist nicht vorüber").[73] A case in point is an operational alternative study conducted by the Army Command Staff in October 1959 that addressed Heusinger's and Speidel's ideas on counterattack operations. Based on the German operational tradition, and reminiscent of the encirclement battles of the Wehrmacht, Soviet attacking forces were to be destroyed by a pincer attack executed from the area of Hamburg in the north and from Nuremberg–Amberg in the south, and converging in the vicinity of Magdeburg. The study also identified other offensive options. But aside from the political sensitivity of such operational plans, they could not have been executed with the forces available at the time.[74] They did demonstrate, however, the intention of the army leadership not to concede passively to the Luftwaffe the exclusive role in the operational and strategic offensive.

Heusinger's arguments for the central importance of the army and navy in any future war also were directed at the efforts of the Luftwaffe to assume the primary position within the armed forces.[75] In the course of this internal power struggle, the Luftwaffe, under its chief of staff, Lieutenant General Josef Kammhuber, considered itself primarily to be the "nuclear sword of the Alliance," and therefore was oriented internationally. The army, on the other hand, focused on the national defense of the German territory.

The buildup of the new army reflected the transition from the old to the new operational doctrine. While the Panzer divisions were structured initially for conventional mobile warfare, the requirements of warfare in a nuclear environment led to the development of smaller, highly mobile combat units that combined increased firepower and mobility to ensure their survival during the first phase of the war, and their combat power for the second phase. During this process the Germans drew lessons from World War II and combined them with the American "Pentomic Structure" concepts for nuclear warfighting.[76]

As a result, the Wehrmacht's organization into battle groups was abandoned in favor of the brigade structure. Manstein had advocated such an approach as early as 1955.[77] Heusinger, who was now the chief of staff of the Bundeswehr (*Generalinspekteur der Bundeswehr*), and Lieutenant General Hans Röttiger, the chief of staff of the army (*Inspekteur des Heeres*) together implemented the brigade structure by 1959, despite internal resistance. The brigade was officially defined as the smallest operational unit capable of independently conducting combined arms combat and having its own logistical support. Under the new structure, the division now functioned as a small corps, supporting its brigades in combat. The resulting "Division 59" was organized into three brigades, which were capable of both conventional and nuclear warfighting. Starting that year the armies of the other Alliance partners also adopted that concept as the NATO standard division.[78]

New army doctrinal regulations were developed as the materiel and man-

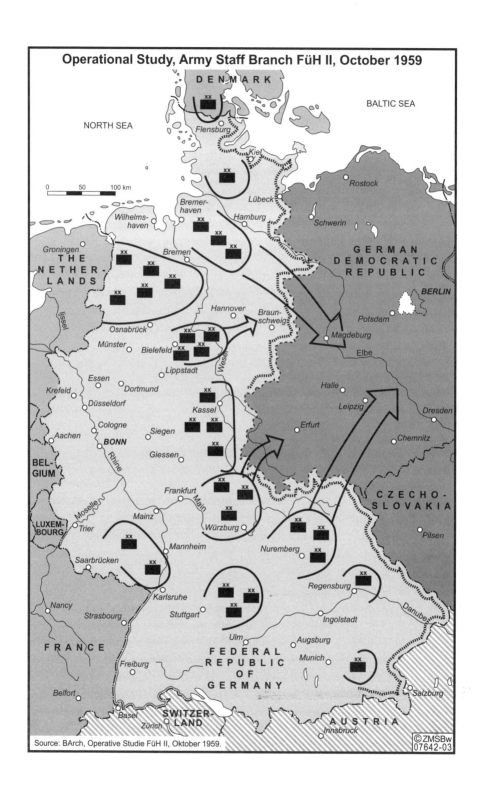

Operational Study, Army Staff Branch FüH II, October 1959

Source: BArch, Operative Studie FüH II, Oktober 1959.

©ZMSBw
07642-03

power of the land forces were built up, but no new manual for operational command and control appeared initially. One reason was that operational command and control was now in the hands of NATO's SACEUR. Another reason was that it had been German standard practice for decades to impart the operational principles of command and control through the training of General Staff officers.[79]

Even though no new operational command and control manual existed, the most important operational concepts were still in the old pre-war *Truppenführung* (*T.F.*) manual. Although that manual primarily addressed the middle level of command and control, the principles therein also applied to the lower tactical and the higher operational levels of command. Therefore, the most important components of German operational thinking were defined in the old *Truppenführung*, although they were based on the strategic concepts, the political situation, and the tactical doctrine of its day.

The initial efforts to write an updated replacement for the 1933 version of H.Dv. 300/1 *Truppenführung* began as early as the start of the 1950s. In 1952 retired General of Infantry Theodor Busse submitted a draft for combined arms combat, titled *Waffen im Bewegungskrieg* (Arms in Mobile War). It was based largely on the 1933 *T.F.* Busse's opening remarks in the preface indicate the draft's restorative character: "This regulation assumes a fully motorized Wehrmacht whose field army includes foot divisions consisting of motorized and partly motorized units."[80] But Busse's comments also betray an appalling lack of understanding of the face of modern war and the level of motorization of modern armies in the 1950s. It is no surprise, therefore, that Busse's draft failed to meet expectations. Based on his preliminary work, a new draft of *Truppenführung* was started in 1954. The new version followed in the tradition of its predecessors, *F.u.G.* and *T.F.* The principles of command and control, as well as combined arms combat, were codified in the new version. In March 1956, H.Dv. 100/1 *Grundsätze der Truppenführung des Heeres* (Principles of Army Unit Command—*T.F./G.*) was published. It was based in large part on the 1933 edition of *Truppenführung*, combined with the German warfighting experience of World War II and the Allies' concepts of nonnuclear warfare at the middle level of command. During the same period the army also developed H.Dv. 100/2 *Führungsgrundsätze des Heeres im Atomkrieg* (Army Command Principles for Nuclear War—*T.F./A.*). The separate manual was justified by the fact that the development of nuclear weapons was still in a state of flux. The other NATO states took a similar approach in the development of their doctrinal manuals during the mid-1950s.

Owing to the short editing time and the insufficient information provided by the Western Alliance, the 1956 edition of *T.F.* was incomplete in many respects and oriented toward a rear-looking analysis of the warfighting experience. What is noteworthy here is that for the first time military command and control was divided into the three distinct levels of strategy, operations, and tactics, based on

Heusinger's operational ideas and the military *Zeitgeist* of the mid-1950s. The manual assigned supreme command to the strategic level, which included the coordination of all senior-most military and political authorities of the state or the alliance. Command and control of the forces in combat and on the battlefield was the task of the lower level, the tactical. It included the command and control of regiments, battle groups, battalions, and companies. "The higher command level is the operational. It is of a purely military character and conforms to the policy and guidance of the supreme command level. It deals with committing armed forces to battle, their command and control on the battlefield, and with the establishment of military fundamentals. In general, it comprises all military command functions of the major units down to and including the division (brigade)."[81]

Based on the recent warfighting experiences, these comments aptly describe the range of military thinking in the German Army during the early years of the Bundeswehr. While the strategic level of command was adapted to the political realities, the operational and the tactical levels largely carried on the traditions of the Wehrmacht and the Kaiser's Army. There was, however, discontinuity on two decisive points. The operational level of command was defined expressly as being of a purely military character. The highly operational-strategic elements that had characterized German operational thinking since Schlieffen, but which never had been precisely defined or clearly identified, now vanished and were absorbed into strategy. Simultaneously, operational command and control was extended downward, to include the corps and even the division, to accommodate the new brigade structure. This expansion of the range of the tactical level assured by definition a German role in operational level command vis-à-vis the NATO SACEUR.

Although nuclear warfare was not addressed directly in the 1956 edition of *T.F.,* like its predecessors it was full of references to operational thought. In some cases entire passages were carried forward verbatim from previous doctrinal regulations. The continuity of traditional German operational thinking was clearly invoked in the new manual's opening sentences: "One can never be strong enough when it comes to bringing about a decision. . . . The weaker force may be the stronger one at the decisive point. Thanks to speed, mobility . . . surprise, deception, and maneuver. If one manages to hit the enemy in his most vulnerable spots, in the flanks and rear for example, the effect achieved can be great, even though friendly forces are fighting outnumbered."[82]

The operational ideas of Heusinger and his staff were reflected even more directly in H.Dv. 100/2 *Führungsgrundsätze des Heeres zum Atomkrieg.* The authors of that manual rejected categorically the greater influence of nuclear weapons on operations and command and control. Nuclear weapons alone were not the decisive elements of success in battle. They were just another means of combat, for those situations where conventional means did not suffice. The efforts in H.Dv. 100/2 to maintain the status quo of command and control are obvious: "Nuclear

The old and the new German armies. Retired field marshal Erich von Manstein with Franz-Josef Strauss (*right*), the defense minister of the Federal Republic of Germany. Bonn, 1957. *BArch/Bild 183-45526-0001.*

Theodor Blank hands the letters of appointment to the first general officers of the Bundeswehr, Hans Speidel (*second from left*) and Adolf Heusinger (*left*), on 12 November 1955. *Bild 183-34150-0001.*

weapons *do not annul* the traditional *command and control principles*; rather, they just alter the details of their execution, as well as the tactics and techniques of combat. This does not mean, however, abandoning the previous doctrine, but just *adjusting to the new elements that have emerged.*"[83]

In fact, the 1956 edition of *T.F.* was already obsolete when it was issued. As early as 1957 an army study group started working on a new command and control doctrinal regulation. The 1959 edition of *Truppenführung* was oriented on the Division 59 structure. It too was based on conventional rather than nuclear warfare, although an initial reference to nuclear warfare was included. Nuclear warfare was addressed in both the 1960 edition of *T.F.*, the so-called "Red *Truppenführung*," and the 1961 edition of H.Dv. 100/2 *Führungsgrundsätze des Heeres für die atomare Kriegführung* (Army Command Principles for Nuclear Warfare). As directed by the army chief of staff, both manuals were oriented toward mobile warfare with fully mechanized units. Even though the manuals addressed the intermediate command level and tactical warfare, they applied accordingly to the higher operational command levels.[84]

In this respect, the 1959 edition of *T.F.* differed clearly from the 1956 edition. Drawing from the experiences of the recent war, the latter edition precisely defined strategy, operations, and tactics, as well as supreme, higher, and lower command levels. Although the 1959 and 1960 editions of *T.F.* dispensed with definitions of levels of command based on the three levels of warfare, they did introduce the alternative concept of higher, intermediate, and lower levels of command. The lower (regiments, battalions, and companies) and the intermediate (brigades and divisions) levels of command dealt with tactics and conducted combined arms combat. The higher command level, which in the 1956 edition of *T.F.* was identified as the supreme command level, was the function of the Allied combined commands and their component armies and army groups. The overall control of operations and battles was the task of the higher command level. In contrast to the 1956 edition of *T.F.*, the operational command level finally was shifted from the national to the international range of tasks.

That was a significant break with classical military thinking in the German Army. And that break was a function of the political and military realities in the Federal Republic of Germany, the Bundeswehr, and the NATO alliance.[85] Integrated into the coalition as a junior partner, the operational level of command now came under the decision-making authority of the hegemon of the alliance. In both world wars Germany had performed that function, quite frequently to the disadvantage of its own allies. In NATO, that role was now held by the United States, which, in contrast to the Germans, gave its partners a greater say—up to the level of nuclear warfare—than the German General Staff ever gave to its allies.

The 1959 and 1960 editions of *T.F.* were merged in the 1962 edition of H.Dv. 100/1 *Truppenführung*. It was the first common doctrinal regulation on the conduct of both conventional and nuclear battle. Designed for the intermediate level of command, it defined the concepts of warfighting and commanding major units, and established principles for the sensible coordination of the individual services in a war fought in a nuclear environment.[86] Although the 1962 edition of *T.F.* marked the provisional end point of classical German operational thought, the key elements of such thinking were modified for the tactical level in a nuclear environment. As in Beck's day, the 1962 manual emphasized specifically that command and control of armed forces is an art. Concentration of effort, surprise, initiative, and freedom of action continued to be defined as the basis of success. As in the past, the dogma of mobility prevailed, although nuclear weapons had now increased the importance of firepower. According to German ideas, both the classical flanking envelopment and the modern vertical envelopment by airborne forces were still of great importance at the tactical level.[87] Although command and control of operations was now placed at NATO level, the 1962 *Truppenführung* would serve as the foundation of that command and control for the subsequent decades.[88]

Parallel to those doctrinal developments, the new minister of defense, Franz-Josef Strauss, pushed for equipping the Bundeswehr with nuclear delivery systems. Although the Luftwaffe initially profited, the army also fielded nuclear delivery systems. Simultaneously, Heusinger and Röttiger routinely cautioned against putting all of Europe's eggs in the nuclear basket. The politically desirable doctrine of forward defense could only be achieved if the conventional forces were strengthened.[89] Moreover, the two generals endorsed an even balance among the conventional armed forces, because they still clung to the idea that blocking forces were capable of stopping an attack without necessarily using nuclear weapons.[90] During the 1960s that dogma was repeated by the German Army's leaders like a mantra. And since the late 1950s it was not only the Germans who advocated this position. What was the sense of defending Europe with "massive retaliation" when afterward neither the country nor the population would exist?

That dilemma worried the German military. Their solution was a strong conventional forward defense designed to minimize the use of nuclear weapons, and if possible, avoid their use on German territory completely. During war games and General Staff rides, the operations experts of the army tried to develop solutions to the dilemma in the historical tradition of the General Staff, which of course no longer existed in the Bundeswehr. Thus, the army vice chief of staff, Major General Joachim Schwatlo Gesterding, declared after the 1960 Army General Staff ride that the war game had demonstrated that operational warfare was still possible, even despite the resulting losses and obstructions after the use of tactical nuclear weapons. The Luftwaffe considered that idea quixotic. The chaos that followed a nuclear war would make any organized conduct of operations impossible. As Luftwaffe chief of staff General Josef Kammhuber put it, conventional land operations would be an illusion. Following the first exchange of nuclear strikes the only thing left to operate on would be in the hospitals.[91] As cynical as that comment was, however, it was close to reality. It was a reality that had been ignored in the design of the 1960 war game. And by deliberately ignoring the implications of warfare for the national infrastructure and the population, it also represented a striking sense of continuity with the planning of the German General Staff for the past 150 years.[92]

The unease of Germany's American ally over the tendency toward automatic massive retaliation also increased.[93] War games conducted in the United States, particularly Exercise ST. LOUIS, indicated that the warfare contemplated by NATO in the second phase of a nuclear war was based on illusions. After nuclear strikes, the soldiers would have neither the physical nor the psychological capability to defend or attack at the necessary level.[94] Thus, the SACEUR from 1956 to 1963, U.S. Air Force general Lauris Norstad, advocated far greater flexibility. He did so in contrast to the U.S. Army's concept of "mobile defense," which was based on German mobile operational thinking despite the obsession with the nuclear-strategic option.[95] The American concept of mobile combat operations, however, differed from the German doctrine on one basic point. The Americans considered the Federal Republic of Germany as a large delaying zone that could be used fully for the conduct of mobile defense, while that was exactly what the German concept of forward defense intended to prevent.

Although Heusinger took the reality of the NATO alliance into consideration and oriented the reconstruction of the German Army toward a land combat force capable of fighting a nuclear war, he also remained loyal to previous principles and continued to advocate a graduated deterrence combined with the concurrent strengthening of the conventional forces. When the development toward "flexible response" became apparent with the beginning of the Kennedy administration, Heusinger, who in the meantime had become the chairman of NATO's Military Committee, saw his premise confirmed. Heusinger's response to a presentation by Lieutenant General Burkhard Müller-Hillebrand at the NATO Defense College in the spring of 1962 indicates just how strongly he supported this development. He agreed with Müller-Hillebrand that conventional war is always overshadowed by the threat of an escalation to nuclear weapons, and that the tactics must be oriented accordingly. Heusinger also praised Müller-Hillebrand's comments on the conduct of conventional combat and forward defense, and he expressed his hope that a balance of power between the blocs could be achieved by a stronger conventional force. Heusinger concluded by saying: "The current development with its greater emphasis on the necessity for conventional forces fills me with some satisfaction, because I repeatedly have fought for this idea since 1956, although it often has been decried as obsolete."[96]

Heusinger's satisfaction, however, cannot obscure the fact that his operational

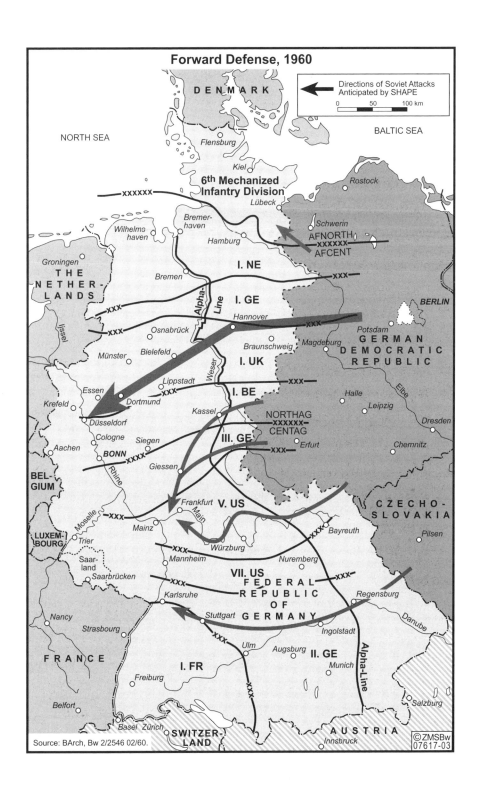

Forward Defense, 1960

Directions of Soviet Attacks
Anticipated by SHAPE

0   50   100 km

DENMARK

NORTH SEA

BALTIC SEA

Flensburg

Kiel

**6th Mechanized
Infantry Division**

Lübeck

Rostock

Schwerin

AFNORTH
xxxxxx
AFCENT

Bremer-
haven

Wilhelms-
haven

Hamburg

Groningen

I. NE

Bremen

THE
NETHER-
LANDS

Alpha-Line

I. GE

Hannover

Osnabrück

BERLIN

Potsdam

GERMAN
DEMOCRATIC
REPUBLIC

Münster

Bielefeld

Braunschweig

Magdeburg

Weser

I. UK

Ijssel

Lippstadt

I. BE

Essen

Halle

Leipzig

Elbe

Krefeld

Dortmund

Dresden

Kassel

NORTHAG
xxxxxx
CENTAG

Düsseldorf

Cologne

Siegen

III. GE

Erfurt

Chemnitz

Aachen

BONN

Rhine

Giessen

BEL-
GIUM

Frankfurt

V. US

CZECHO-
SLOVAKIA

Moselle

Main

Mainz

LUXEM-
BOURG

Trier

Würzburg

Bayreuth

Pilsen

Saar-
land

Mannheim

Nuremberg

Saarbrücken

VII. US
F E D E R A L
R E P U B L I C
O F
G E R M A N Y

Regensburg

Karlsruhe

Danube

Nancy

Stuttgart

Strasbourg

Ingolstadt

Ulm

Augsburg

II. GE

Alpha-Line

I. FR

Munich

Freiburg

Belfort

Salzburg

FRANCE

Basel Zürich SWITZER-
LAND

AUSTRIA

Innsbruck

©ZMSBw
07617-03

Source: BArch, Bw 2/2546 02/60.

concept was still unfeasible, both for economic factors and the fact that even the start of the shift from a strategy of massive retaliation to one of flexible response failed to solve the fundamental dilemma of nuclear warfare on German territory.[97] Even under the most favorable conditions, there always was the risk of "*sich zu Tode zu siegen*" (winning oneself to death).

Conclusions

The faith in the superiority of German operational thinking did not vanish with the surrender of the Wehrmacht on 8 May 1945. It lived on, both in the minds of the former General Staff officers of the Operations Division and, later, in the officers of the Bundeswehr and in the *Landser* pulp magazines of the postwar period. The title of the 1961 issue No. 28 of the *Landser* magazine echoed the multiple myths of German operational thinking: "Generalfeldmarschall Erich von Manstein. Der Schlieffen des Zweiten Weltkrieges" (Field Marshal Erich von Manstein: The Schlieffen of World War II).[98] In that issue Hans-Peter Sertl suggested that Manstein was the practitioner of the formula for victory that had been developed by Schlieffen. However, the execution of that formula failed because of the incompetence of Moltke the Younger during World War I and the military incompetence of Hitler during World War II. In Sertl's opinion, the reasons for Germany's defeat in World War II were not to be found in its operational doctrine, but rather in its faulty execution or in its rejection by Hitler, who handicapped the most ingenious operational expert since Schlieffen in the performance of his duties. This opinion, which was widespread during the postwar period, combines the "myth of the clean Wehrmacht" with the personalization of the blame assigned to the Führer. The parallels with the efforts in the 1920s to explain the defeat in World War I are clear. After the two lost world wars, the personalization of the guilt actually served to deflect from the actual reasons for the breakdowns. In contrast to the 1920s, the case of Hitler required no graphological and physiological post-mortem expert analyses, such as those that were conducted on Falkenhayn. The civilian Hitler was discredited sufficiently and exclusively enough by his atrocious policies and the Holocaust.

Unlike the downfall of 1918, that of 1945 changed fundamentally a central element of German operational thinking. Germany no longer existed as a single geographic state structure. Divided into two states, Germany moved from being the center of Europe to being the border between two hostile world power blocs. Thus, the central position and the threat to Germany of a two-front war, upon which the thinking of the General Staff had been based, ceased to exist. And as a result, the operational-strategic cornerstone of German operational thought disappeared—the concept of overcoming the enemy's superiority potential from a position of manpower and materiel inferiority by achieving a rapid decision of the war, thereby avoiding a war of attrition that Germany would have been unable to win. As a result, the need for a quick decision of the war that had dominated German military thinking since Schlieffen, and which had never been challenged politically, was now obsolete.

The soldiers of both German states faced a novel political and geostrategic situation. Those in the East had to integrate into a continental alliance, while those in the West had to integrate into a maritime alliance—a first in German history. Thus, the conditions for introducing each country's operational ideas into their respective alliances were very different on either side of the Iron Curtain. The Red Army dominated operational thinking in the East. It was only during the few years of the transitional period that some former higher-ranking Wehrmacht officers, all of whom had been members of the National Committee for a Free Germany and had acceptable ideological convictions, were employed in the field of operational command and control. It was not possible, however, for those officers to develop their own operational concepts, or even to pursue classical German operational thinking.

After a short period of silence, and even prior to formal West German rearmament, former Wehrmacht officers were participating in the discussions about the operational warfare concepts of the Western Alliance. The fundamental operational-strategic component of German operational thinking had ceased to exist as a result of the changed geostrategic situation, and the West German operational experts no longer had to work toward the objective of a rapid offensive conducted on enemy territory. And although the objective now was to ensure the slow buildup of the military potential of the Western Alliance through the conduct of the defensive within NATO's future structure, the German planners remained convinced of the superiority of German operational-tactical doctrine over that of both their allies in the near future and their former and potentially future enemies in the East. They held to that belief despite Germany's defeats in both world wars. Pursuing the operational tradition of the Wehrmacht, the trailblazers of the Bundeswehr, most of whom had served in the Operations Division of the Army General Staff, planned for a mobile defense based completely on motorized armored units against a numerically far superior enemy. The anticipated Soviet major attack would be slowed down in the center by a combination of mobile operations and close air support, and then destroyed by flank attacks from the north and the south.

The fact that in the north Schleswig-Holstein, Denmark, and South Scandinavia, and in the south Tagliamento, the Alps, southern Germany, and the Dardanelles were included as areas of main operational defensive efforts by Heusinger and his staff indicated the importance those planners attached to Western Europe and its peripheral regions for the defense of West Germany.

Faced with the danger that, based on the geostrategic situation, the NATO alliance would consider Germany merely as an operational delaying zone and bat-tlefield in a future war, the German military planners in coordination with the federal government thus insisted on defending West Germany as far to the east as possible, even before Germany formally joined NATO.

Despite this operational-strategic opening, the German operational plans were still characterized by the tradition of German operational thinking. As in the days of the Wehrmacht, the objectives were to compensate for numerical inferiority and to achieve victory by superior command and control, surprise, envelopment, flank attack, seizure of the initiative, and dictating the course of the action. The intent was to integrate this central tactical-operational component of the German system of thought into NATO as the German contribution to the art of command and control, thus securing Germany's status within the alliance.

Initially, Heusinger and his colleagues could not accept the idea that by drop-ping the atomic bomb on Hiroshima the United States had introduced an "ultimate weapon" into the conduct of warfare, one that inevitably required fundamental changes in operational thinking. The question then became how one should fight conventionally and exercise operational command and control in a nuclear war. The continued existence of classical operational thinking depended on the answer to that question. The initial German solution to the problem was simply to shift the use of nuclear weapons from the operational to the strategic level of war. Such weapons would be used far away in Russia, should deterrence fail. Thus, the effects of nuclear weapons on the conduct of warfare and their effects on the population of West Germany could be ignored. And as a result, classical tactical-operational warfare in the German theater was still possible in the future.

That self-deceptive illusion collapsed when Germany was admitted to the Western Alliance and was given access to NATO's defense planning. Despite the integration of the West German divisions, the alliance still believed that it was only possible to defend Western Europe with an early and massive use of tacti-cal nuclear weapons. In the future, the ground forces would serve as the shield to protect the nuclear sword of the air forces. As the significance of ground combat operations faded into the background, Germany itself would become not only a conventional theater of war, but also a nuclear one. In the subsequent years Heus-inger and his staff were forced to accept the fact that they were left with only a narrow operational range, especially considering that the operational level of command in the alliance was no longer at the national level, but at the interna-tional level.

Moreover, under the classical allocation of missions and roles the Luftwaffe had supported the ground forces in combined arms combat. Now those roles were reversed. In the future, as many German officers perceived it, the army was threat-ened with being reduced to the thankless task of a security guard for the Luftwaffe. The army was in danger of losing the longstanding struggle for manpower and materiel resources, as well as losing its primacy in operational-strategic design. This was all the more so since the Luftwaffe declared unequivocally that operations were no longer possible in future war.

In response, Heusinger and his closest colleagues adjusted the German operational doctrine for nuclear warfare by assigning the function of reinforced artillery to the tactical nuclear weapons. And similar to the period following World War I, they also saw increased mobility as the solution to the operational problem. Simultaneously, they continually advocated abandoning the strategy of massive retaliation in favor of graduated response. They were convinced that with those adjustments mobile warfare with armored formations under nuclear conditions would still be possible. They were not alone in the alliance. In the United States and Great Britain land forces also continued to plan for conventional war, despite the nuclear threat and although various war games showed that in any nuclear war there would be complete chaos without any opportunity to exercise command and control.

The Germans recognized that the failure of deterrence and any resulting nuclear war that was even limited only to Central Europe would have disastrous consequences for their country. "The execution of such plans, however, inevitably means the end of the German nation, perhaps also of Europe. The paradoxical case would become reality. A part of the army survives and achieves a debatable 'victory.' The nation being defended, however, is basically exterminated. . . . According to these studies, the victory of the free world over oppression means a Golgotha for the German people."[99]

Thus, it was not warfare but deterrence that would dominate the military thinking to serve the best interests of Germany. But it is necessary to square the circle here. While a credible conventional and nuclear deterrence capability with a low threshold for the use of nuclear weapons was required on the one hand, it was absolutely necessary to prevent the use of nuclear weapons by all means in order to secure the survival of the German population.

Initially the German Army's new doctrinal regulations continued the traditions of German operational thinking and were completely geared to the classical conduct of leadership in mobile warfare. Nuclear warfare was ignored. The army's operational concepts were reflected in the revised manuals and in the proposals for the organizational structure of the Bundeswehr. Panzer divisions were to form the core of the new army and, according to the 1956 edition of *Truppenführung,* would continue to operate in classical mobile warfare. Nuclear warfare still was ignored in the revised edition of 1959, which was based on the Division 59 structure optimized for mobile warfare. Nuclear warfare was treated separately in the 1960 edition. It was only in the 1962 *Truppenführung* that conventional and nuclear warfare were combined, making it Germany's first doctrinal regulation for the conduct of war in a nuclear environment.

Truppenführung 1959 and 1962 also marked a temporary ending point of German operational thinking. Both manuals assigned operational command and control functions to NATO's international level of command, and thus eventually to the American hegemon of the alliance. Nevertheless, German officers assigned to NATO exerted significant influence on the operational planning of the alliance by integrating traditional German concepts. But it would still be more than twenty years before the chief of staff of the German Army, Lieutenant General Hans-Henning von Sandrart, revived operational thinking in the German Army in the mid-1980s.

Conclusion

The history of operational thinking is the great narrative of the German Army during the era of the world wars and beyond. It consists of multiple interconnected themes, and it transcends the two lost world wars. The influence of that thinking, both in its components and its entirety, is still felt today—especially in the English-speaking world, and up through the 1980s in the Bundeswehr itself. Because of differing military cultural concepts, the boundaries between tactics, operations, and strategy are sometimes blurred. One of the issues that continually arise, however, is the condemnation of that special German approach to operational thinking as a significantly contributing factor to the strategy of the annihilation of civilian populations that culminated in Operation BARBAROSSA. But as in all history, the narrative is never completely black or white, but rather plays out in shades of gray. And this is much the case for the development of German operational thinking. Its advance has been a continuous process with roots reaching back to the mid-nineteenth century. With the establishment of the German Reich in 1870, the German military leadership was convinced that determining factors like geography, relative manpower and material inferiority, the existing world powers, and Germany's aspirations to become one of those powers were the foundations upon which German operational-strategic planning was based, and remained so until the end of World War II.

Operational thinking originally developed out of the need to exercise decentralized command and control of larger masses of troops over longer distances. By the end of the nineteenth century such methods were also seen as a military solution for the execution of a two- or a multi-front war conducted at the German border, or in the adjacent regions of Central Europe. To compensate for the disadvantages of space and inferiority in resources, as the General Staff saw it, they decided to exploit the advantage of interior lines resulting from Germany's central geographic position, combined with a high-quality army and a superior command and control system. This, then, became the guiding principle of their thinking. The underlying concepts of mobility, attack, initiative, establishment of the main effort, envelopment, surprise, and destruction had already been developed by Moltke the Elder for the conduct of a rapid war. The objective became one of destroying the enemy's forces at the border or in the adjacent territories through one or more rapid battles of envelopment. Destruction in the military sense was understood not as physical extermination but rather as the elimination of effective military power—through, for example, the taking of prisoners. Considering Germany's central geographic position, the German military leaders always focused on the elements of time and space in the development of their operational-strategic plans and the manning, arming, and equipping of the military force. These, then, formed the cornerstones of German operational thinking.

The military leadership repeatedly attempted to address Germany's strategic dilemma with operational solutions, which would compensate for the vulnerability of the country's central geographic position and its relative inferiority in manpower and resources. In the process, they analyzed carefully the lessons learned from previous wars, like World War I, and modified the technological and tactical-operational methods to address anticipated future warfare. The continuous efforts to improve efficiency resulted in the system of modern operational mobile warfare. The dynamics of this process can be seen clearly in the framework of the planning and the conduct of operations.

The German senior military leadership was convinced that as long as a defensive posture led inevitably to a lengthy war of attrition that could not be won, the offensive was the only viable solution in the event of war. Within the triad of strategy, operations, and tactics, operations were the key to the rapid execution of the war. Decisive battles of destruction resulting from fast and mobile operations were the keys to preventing the enemy's buildup and the neutralization of his superior potential in resources. Thus, time pressures determined all operational considerations and plans. The will to maintain or regain the offensive initiative was, therefore, the traditional foundation of the tactical-operational thinking of the German Army during both world wars. That offensive concept did not develop in a political or intellectual vacuum. Rather, it was based on the Reich's foreign policy that aspired to world power status, combined with the general belief that "the attack has always been the German way of fighting."[1]

Those lines of continuity were not disrupted by Germany's defeat in World War I. As early as in 1918 the German military elite began to seek answers to the questions of how the result of the Great War could be corrected, and how a future war could be won. Collectively refusing to face reality, they suppressed the actual strategic fact underlying the defeat, Germany's inferior force potential. That process of selective rationalization culminated in the conviction that Germany's tactical-operational approach had been right and that the failure was caused by individuals. Clinging to the certainty that the German Army had been "unbeaten in the field" (*im Felde unbesiegt*), there was a broad consensus that the Reich's lost Great Power status must be recovered. The only disagreements were on how to accomplish that.

What specific lessons, then, did the German military leadership draw from the experience of World War I? Starting from the premise that rapid operational attack was the answer to the risks inherent in Germany's central geographic position, the military's limited focus was confined to the tightly encompassed framework of its professional analysis procedures. There was little actual rethinking involved in that process.[2] The key question was the same as it had been during World War I: How could mobility be restored to the offensive? That was the basic approach to German operational thinking. Guderian, the advocate of rapid mobile forces, seemed to have cut through the Gordian knot that was entwined in the elements of time, central geographic position, and relative inferiority of manpower and materiel. The crisis of attack apparently had been resolved. The German Army, therefore, started World War II with large-scale offensive operations. They did so despite the experience of World War I and the fact that during the 1930s enormous expenditures had been invested in the expansion of fortifications, while simultaneously neglecting the development of defensive doctrine. In contrast to World War II, the military leadership of the Kaiser's Reich had started World War I with a detailed operational plan, and they thought the Schlieffen-Moltke Plan would be the recipe for success. When that failed, the resulting disillusionment was great indeed. In 1940 German forces again attacked in the West, but this time only with a plan drafted on short notice—the "Sickle Cut." And when France was defeated after only six weeks, the result was euphoria.

Both events—the defeat of 1918 and the victory of 1940—resulted in a diverging learning behavior among the military leadership. In World War I the German Army had developed mobile, combined arms defense and attack tactics only after running up against the stalemate of trench warfare. Following the victory over France in World War II, they came to believe that they now held the operational key to victory—Blitzkrieg. In the winter of 1941 that dream died in the vastness of Russian space. Once more, German troops inadequately trained in mobile defense procedures were thrown back on the defensive. In both world wars the tactical-operational concepts that prevailed at the start were quickly subjected to the merciless test of reality, a test that could be passed only in the crucible of war.

During both World War I and World War II the German Army was forced to develop defense concepts adapted to the contemporary means of combat and their own limited resources. While during World War I the Third OHL of Hindenburg and Ludendorff combined the experiences of the frontline troops with its own ideas on mobile defense in response to the high losses, Hitler, like Hindenburg's predecessor Falkenhayn, categorically refused to allow the forces in the field to conduct mobile defensive operations. Instead he ordered linear defense, explicitly referencing Falkenhayn's concepts. The field commanders interpreted Hitler's orders as liberally as possible in favor of the conduct of mobile combat operations, wherever possible yielding space to compensate for their weaknesses in manpower and materiel. But more and more often the innovative tactical-operational concepts developed on the front lines were rejected by the Führer, as he reached back to the experiences of World War I.

Hitler was successful in forcing through his concepts because many of the generals of World War II had served in World War I, and they too had been shaped by experiences similar to Hitler's. For their generation slogans like "1918 Never Again!" and "Retreat to the Marne" represented the command and control failures of the generals of that war, failures that had led to Germany's defeat. The 1914 Battle of the Marne, for example, was a fight that had been broken off far too early. It was such command mistakes that the lieutenants of that war, now as generals, wanted to avoid at all costs. They therefore complied with the stand-fast orders, even in the most desperate situations.

The command practices of many senior officers in World War II cannot be understood without also understanding their World War I experiences and the military socialization process that shaped them. At times during World War II they refought World War I in the exact same places, but this time with more modern weapons systems. The return to the tactical and operational ideas of World War I can be seen in the 15 January 1945 reissue of *Merkblatt* 18b/43, "Der Sturmangriff. Kriegserfahrungen eines Frontoffiziers von 1917" (Instruction Sheet 18b/32, The Assault: Combat Experiences of a Frontline Officer of 1917). In the preface to that reissued instruction sheet, Guderian wrote: "The principles of assaults are the same today as then."[3] Considering the military situation in January 1945, Guderian's comment betrays the inability of the German military leadership to face reality.

As a consequence of the deteriorating situation from 1944 on, the German Army conducted defensive operations based on the 1916–1917 *Grosskampfverfahren* (Large Battle Procedure), updated to include antitank defense tactics and techniques. But while in 1916 and 1917 the Third OHL worked to reduce heavy losses by replacing soldiers with machines in the defense, the army leadership of World War II in sharp contrast conducted an increasingly personnel-intensive warfare, justified by the slogan "People Against Tanks" (*Menschen gegen Panzer*). Tactical innovations that also influenced operational warfare, such as happened during World War I, only took place on a very limited basis during World War II.

During both world wars the German Army operated under the concept of mission-type command and control, even when Hitler specifically forbade the use of Auftragstaktik on the operational level, and then down to the tactical. It is doubtful if and to what extent the lower command echelons followed those orders. Likewise, it is questionable whether the young officers at the end of the war were even capable of conducting mission-type command, considering their very limited training.

When the operational approaches to solve the problem of Germany's relative inferiority in warfighting potential proved inadequate, the German leadership in both world wars shifted to an attempt to compensate for that shortcoming through higher levels of operational readiness. They also tried to reinforce the soldiers' wills to hold out through appeals to the alleged unlimited potencies of will and fighting spirit. As the commander in chief of Army Group B, Field Marshal Walter Model, wrote to his commanders on 29 March 1945: "The war will not be won by calculation, and not by the execution of duty alone. What is decisive is the *will* to win and *belief* in it! . . . To be a commander means: to believe."[4] And since the German Army in World War I had failed in its efforts to mobilize the national will to hold out, Hitler and the Nazi Party took over from the Wehrmacht all the functions of ideological indoctrination. The orientation of the Wehrmacht soldiers, in comparison to that of the frontline soldiers of World War I, was reconfigured by National Socialist ideology. As an article in a 1942 issue of *Militär-Wochenblatt* put it: "We do not have the same warfighting experience as in 1914. The new element in this war is political experience. It stems from our mentality and our soul. National Socialism is the key to understanding this."[5]

In World War I, OHL focused primarily on tactical innovation, although patriotic education (*Vaterländischer Unterricht*) was introduced near the end of the war. During World War II, however, ideological command progressively became the equal of tactical-operational command. An order issued by Field Marshal Ferdinand Schörner on 20 January 1945 is typical: "Every day proves more and more that the war cannot be won with tactical measures alone. The more we come closer to our native soil, the stronger the moral powers of belief, faith, and holy fanaticism must rise to the foreground."[6] By the end of the war, therefore, the appeals were no longer to professional military leadership, but rather just to hold out. A large element of that "persuasive power" was based on the threat of raw force.

The Germans believed that the foundation of mobile operational defense was not only the excellent training of the General Staff officers, but also quality training of the troops. While the Prussian-German Army of 1914 was largely well-trained and under professional command based on the ideas of the period, it was a force that was quite different from the Wehrmacht. The German Army of World War II was in many ways only a marginally improved version of the World War I army. Significant deficiencies in training and command were apparent as early as the Poland Campaign. That should not have come as a surprise. In the short time following 1935 the complexity of the tasks and the more modern weapons systems made it impossible to train the entire army to the level that had been achieved by the Prussian-German troops during the long period of peacetime before World War I. The post-1935 focus, therefore, was only on a few selected units. Those mobile units formed the spearhead of the German assaults. During the Eastern Campaign, when all the deployed divisions were in combat, that concept very quickly ran up against its own limits. The Panzer divisions were absorbed by Russian space, which expanded toward the east like a trapezoid. The disparity between the motorized elite units and the mass of nonmotorized infantry divisions became more and more obvious as the war progressed. Right until the end of the war the few well-equipped units formed the backbone of the German Army. But in the face of Allied air superiority, they were capable of conducting only limited mobile operations. And even then, the mobile units could not counterbalance the Allies' superiority in manpower and materiel.

Germany's defeat in World War II resulted in the division of the country. The armies of both German successor states were integrated into the military alliances of their respective coalitions. Thus, the basis of the German operational thinking was lost. It was no longer possible to think in terms of counteracting an enemy's superior resources in manpower and materiel by conducting rapid and decisive wars to prevent a lengthy war of attrition that Germany could not win. That necessity to conduct rapid and decisive warfare that had preoccupied German military thinking since Schlieffen, and which was never questioned politically because of the central geographic position of the German Reich, was now obsolete.

Nonetheless, the requirement for mobile operations still played a role in the West German defense concepts of the 1950s. The interest of the Western Powers in the warfighting experiences of the German Army on the Eastern Front provided the former Operations Department General Staff officers who were the future general officers of the Bundeswehr with the opportunity to make an original German contribution to the defense of NATO. And even though the German operational concepts did not exactly conform to NATO's defense plans for using nuclear weapons, they remained a firm element in the collective psyche of the German former General Staff officers. Even after two lost world wars the Bundeswehr's operational experts clung to the fundamentals of traditional German operational thinking, and the German operational command and control principles were still well respected within NATO circles. It is not surprising, therefore, that on 21 December 1962, the fiftieth anniversary of Schlieffen's death, the commandant of the Bundeswehr's *Führungsakademie* (Command and Staff College), Major General Ulrich de Maizière, commented on the interaction between the military and politics by noting that Schlieffen had found "an operational solution appropriate to his times that accommodated the changes in the political and military developments. Schlieffen's aim was the variability of the solutions within the framework of the basic paradigm."[7]

In the 1980s, German operational thinking experienced a renewed, albeit short, renaissance in the face of the reality of the changed international situation. The result was the 1987 *Leitlinie für die operative Führung von Landstreitkräften in Mitteleuropa* (Guidelines for Operational Command and Control of Ground Forces in Central Europe). That document was followed in 1994 by the first principles for the operational command and control of ground forces, and some years later by the *Grundsätze der freien Operation* (Principles of Free Operations).

That revival is associated closely with Lieutenant General Hans-Henning von Sandrart, the army chief of staff at the time. It was not, however, necessarily a direct consequence of the revival of military thinking in the United States from the late 1970s. Over the years the leading military thinkers in America had come to think of nuclear weapons as primarily a strategic instrument of political escalation. In the process, their significance declined as tactical-operational instruments at the battlefield level. Combined with the experiences from the recent Vietnam War and the Israeli experiences in the 1973 Yom Kippur War, the American armed forces had become increasingly dissatisfied over the years with the static frontal defense in Europe as delineated in the NATO General Defense Plan (GDP). Parallel to these developments, the German Army's leadership saw the opportunity to revive the concepts of mobile operations, which had faded into the background but were never completely abandoned. That revival was based on the successful examples of operational warfare of the past, especially from World War II; but the inherent systemic weaknesses that had been ignored or addressed only marginally in the past were again not addressed. This new reassessment focused primarily on the tactical-operational level of German operational thinking, and largely excluded the operational-strategic level.

What is surprising in that development is that the doctrine with which the Germans lost two world wars within thirty years was once again being advocated, but without confronting directly the weaknesses in that doctrine that contributed to those defeats. Undoubtedly the German Army fought successfully up to a point in the two world wars, despite its relative inferiority in manpower and materiel. The enemy coalitions the Germans faced were greatly superior, initially while the Germans were on the offensive during the France Campaign of 1940, and during the later years of the war when they were on the defensive. But whatever successes the German Army achieved were primarily the result of the tactical virtuosity of the soldiers and officers in the field, and only secondarily the product of the operational efforts of the General Staff officers.

The decisive weakness of German operational thinking was inherent in its very structure. Initially developed out of the necessity to project mass armies over large distances on the tactical-operational level, the concept was further developed under Schlieffen at the operational-strategic level as a solution to the problem of conducting a war from a position of relative inferiority. But the tactics as originally developed did not translate directly to the operational-strategic level, although the operation as binding link between tactics and strategy has both operational-strategic and tactical-operational dimensions. It was at the higher command level of "grand tactics" where the elements of mobility, attack, initiative, establishment of the main effort, envelopment, surprise, and destruction came into play the most. By focusing on the operational level of command the German General Staff consequently neglected the strategic level. In the minds of most German General Staff officers operational-strategic thought was a mere shadow.

The reasons for such a development must be sought in the German officers' relations to politics, because strategic thinking at its very core is political thinking. But for the General Staff officers political thinking was always secondary to military thinking. Civilian political thinking was largely foreign to them, even when during peacetime they accepted political decisions, albeit unwillingly. In time of war, however, they quickly claimed the mantle of leadership, in accordance with their interpretation of Clausewitz. Those officers socialized during the era of the empire largely agreed in their basic political attitudes with the domestic and foreign political positions of the Kaiser and his government. The aim was to establish Germany as a world power, with the help of the military if necessary. The defeat in World War I did not alter that any. It is important to note here that at the start of World War I the use of military force was considered a legitimate instrument of foreign policy in the rest of Europe, as well as in Germany.

In the minds of most General Staff officers during the period of the world wars—with the exception of a short interval during the Weimar Republic—there were no viable political solutions to compensate for the limitations of Germany's force potential. Thinking in the political realm was something not expected of the senior ranks of the military leadership, either during the period of the Kaiser's Reich or during the National Socialist regime. This sharp division was built into the senior-level structure of the Reich itself: the military hierarchy ran parallel to the political, merging only in the person of the Kaiser, and later the Führer. The strategic level, therefore, was concentrated solely at the top position. The leadership structure, which had been carried forward from the time of Frederick the Great, culminated in the principle of *roi connétable* (the king as the supreme commander). Kaiser Wilhelm II, however, was never capable of fulfilling that role, although Hitler did to a certain extent through the modern command, control, and communications systems. The basic principle itself, however, was inadequate for the conduct of modern industrial war, and especially "Total War," which required the integration of a nation's entire economic, political, and military resources. The German structure was even more dysfunctional because the leaderships of the Wehrmacht's individual components were locked into a paralyzing competition with each other. Those internal power struggles prevented the emergence of a senior military structure adapted to modern industrialized warfare.

The largely smooth interaction between the political and military leadership was in no way the function of the military's unconditional loyalty to the political system. Rather, it was the result of the corresponding political objectives in domestic and international affairs. Whenever the military leadership saw a threat to its power position within the Reich, it was always ready to intervene in domestic or foreign policy issues. While they often succeeded in doing so during specific periods of the Kaiser's Reich or the Weimar Republic, Hitler established the unequivocal policy primacy of the National Socialist regime at the expense of the Wehrmacht by the time of Beck's retirement at the latest. From that point on, most German General Staff officers, despite their personal reservations, came to see themselves as mere flywheels in a well-oiled military machine that executed the requirements of the political leadership. It is not surprising, therefore, that the Army General Staff blatantly ignored the strategic level of warfare and focused dogmatically on the operational level.

As Martin Kutz noted, it was during this "poor man's war" that the General Staff officers finally saw an opportunity to resolve the challenge of Germany's relative strategic inferiority. But as a consequence of the lack of strategic thinking, glaringly poor strategic decisions were made during the first half of World War II. Those errors culminated first in the faulty orders issued by a politician with no higher-level military training, and then by his operational neutralization of the General Staff. By that time Beck, who was one of the few General Staff officers to think strategically in the modern sense, was already in retirement and deeply involved in the Opposition that would lead to 20 July 1944. Because of their continental orientation during the era of the world wars, the army senior leadership never developed a strategic concept for an overall war that integrated the navy. The army leaders ignored the navy and naval warfare, although maritime power was absolutely essential for acquiring and maintaining Germany's status as a world power.

Further problems resulted from the lack of strategic thinking and the consequent focus on rapid and decisive battles at the tactical-operational level. The doctrine of rapid battles conducted along Germany's border, or in the immediately adjacent territories, reached and then exceeded its limitations as the fighting expanded beyond Central Europe. At that point the Germans ran up against "the tyranny of logistics." The original operational thinking was based on a logistics system adapted to one or more rapid battles of annihilation within no more than one hundred to two hundred kilometers of Germany's borders. Up until World War II, German forces were expected to live off the land in the country where they were operating. As soon as the war extended beyond that depth, the logistical system exceeded the limits of its technical resources, and finally retarded the execution of the wide-area envelopment operations upon which German operational doctrine was based. Surprisingly, this connection was ignored completely by the General Staff officers, who focused exclusively on the operational conduct of battles. Even up through the Bundeswehr an assignment to a logistical position was considered detrimental to an officer's career. One reason for that prevailing attitude lay in the training of German officers that emphasized their roles as active combatants. Another reason is most likely based on the indirect recognition of Germany's inadequate potential in resources. The General Staff officers found the solution to the logistics problem in the mobile battle and the rapidly conducted war of decision, which in turn minimized the persistent technical logistics questions. When logistics problems put Operation BARBAROSSA at risk, the General Staff tacitly accepted the conduct of criminal warfare against the Russian civilian population in order to ensure the success of the overall operation.

In addition to time and forces, the factor of space played a key role in the German operational thinking. The military experts working toward Germany's position as a world power failed to recognize that the essential prerequisite for Germany's domination of Europe was the elimination of Russia as a power. Moltke the Elder, Schlieffen, and even Falkenhayn, partially in recognition of Napoleon's experience, avoided conducting a war in the vast expanse of Russian space. Their successors, however, saw no problems or only minor problems in a war against the Soviet Union, largely based on a misreading of their own experience with Russian armed forces between 1914 and 1918. The post–World War I German operations experts extended a doctrine originally developed for achieving a rapid decision on Germany's borders or in the close adjacent territories. In doing so, they extrapolated from tactics to the operational and strategic levels without having the necessary assets and power resources.

The German Army had developed the concept of the rapid establishment of the main effort, supported by the will to maintain the initiative, as the means to compensate for having to fight from a position of relative inferiority. The operations experts believed their system to be superior, but sooner or later it had to fail when it ran up against the "law of numbers" and Germany's vulnerable geographic position. The General Staff officers largely avoided recognizing the reality that even with the most excellent of tactical-operational command and control systems they still might not be able to defeat an enemy coalition superior in manpower and materiel resources. Their thinking in large part was driven by the belief that any admission of Germany's military limitations would have been tantamount to admitting military incompetence, and therefore would have threatened their own position of power within the Reich.

The dogmatic focus on the rapid and successful battle of annihilation was intended to solve not only Germany's strategic problems, but also to limit any war to a cabinet war, preventing a people's war and therefore eliminating political influence from the conduct of the war. In the final analysis, German operational thinking during the era of the world wars, and even in the minds of some of its advocates up through the 1980s, was based on warfare in a vacuum, where neither the population nor politics, but only the military moved across the chessboard. Such concepts, based on eighteenth-century cabinet wars, however, had already been reduced to the level of absurdity by the realities of the Franco-Prussian War, and finally by World War II. But the General Staff continually suppressed such a realization.

It remains to be noted that the Bundeswehr, despite its devotion to classical German operational thinking during the 1980s, soon abandoned the one-sided orientation toward operational warfare. From the Bundeswehr's beginning, its officers and particularly its General Staff officers received joint training at the *Führungsakademie der Bundeswehr* (Command and Staff College) across all the individual services. Simultaneously, great emphasis was placed on leadership development, civic education (*innere Führung*), and political-military (Pol-Mil) training. The General Staff officers were assigned to the integrated NATO headquarters from the very beginning. From early on, the military operational experts engaged in give-and-take debate with other officers in all branches of the Bundeswehr, and with the civilian political leaders of the defense establishment. Over the years the old elite of operational experts was replaced by a new elite of political-military officers. Today it is the political-military officers, rather than the operations experts, who follow the Bundeswehr's premier career track. Thus, nearly all chiefs of staff of the Bundeswehr, including those from the army, have been primarily political-military officers. Germany's participation in NATO has most certainly been the primary cause of this development.

Thus, there are no unambiguous answers to the question of a uniquely German form of operational thinking. Certainly there are German roots, based in Prussia's and later the German Reich's political intent to become a Great Power without having the necessary resources to achieve that goal. Those shortcomings in turn led directly to the political leadership and the military command and control structure to discount the strategic dimension. But all states strive to enhance their positions of power, even if their resources are not equal to their aspirations. Mission-type command and control procedure is the core element of classical German operational thinking. What often is overlooked is that as early as World War I, Auftragstaktik, as the name implies, was a tactical rather than an operational procedure. At the operational level an excess of command freedom can lead quickly to disaster, as OHL experienced at the Marne in 1914 during the first few weeks of the war. During the initial weeks of World War II's Operation BARBAROSSA, the General Staff limited the operational freedoms of the divisional commanders and chiefs of staff, and correspondingly increased control from the top. They did so even before Hitler subsequently restricted operational freedom even more.

Other cornerstones of German operational thinking, including envelopment, mobility, speed, surprise, and annihilation, developed out of tactics and the conviction that the offensive was the superior form of combat. Those elements of warfighting are recognized by all armies; it is their individual application that makes the difference. The Germans, however, emphasized initiative and freedom of action far more than most other armies. In particular, the pressure to establish an absolute main effort in situations of relative inferiority, the willingness to assume a high level of risk, and the rapid annihilation of the enemy's force seem to be the primary characteristics of the German Army. But that approach has precedents in military history, especially from Napoleon. It is not the sole invention of the German General Staff. And many of the other elements attributed to German operational thinking can be found in the doctrines of other continental powers, like the Soviet Union. But owing to Germany's relative inferiority in manpower and materiel, the General Staff offices for centuries planned to conduct rapid and mobile operations as a means to undermine the superior force potential of an enemy coalition of maritime powers capable of conducting a longer war. This is especially important to understand in conjunction with the close exchange of thoughts between the Reichswehr and the Red Army during the 1920s. Additional scholarly analysis, however, will be required to determine the extent to which German operational thinking, in combination with the Soviet Union's strategic-geographic position, influenced the Russians. Even given the many apparent parallels with characteristic German operational thinking, such instances cannot establish conclusively the degree of direct influence.

Although German operational thinking undoubtedly had underlying structural flaws based on its inadequate integration with an overall strategy corresponding to Germany's limited force potential, and although the failure in logistics opened the gate for the criminal conduct of Operation BARBAROSSA, German operational doctrine per se was not based on criminal intent focused on the total annihilation of entire populations. German operational doctrine was a military attempt to solve the strategic dilemma of achieving continental hegemony without having a sufficient economic, military, and political power base. It was based on the inability of the German military and the political elites during the era of the world wars to recognize and accept Germany's real and limited power.

German operational thinking always assumed high risks, threatening at times the very existence of the Reich. And it certainly was no recipe for success. In the end it was only a makeshift. It was a doctrine for the "poor man's war," a poor man who strove for his place in the sun (*Platz an der Sonne*).

Notes

Introduction

1. Geoffrey P. Megargee, *Inside Hitler's High Command* (Lawrence, Kans., 2000), 230–236.

2. Cf. Shimon Naveh, *In Pursuit of Military Excellence: The Evolution of Operational Theory* (London, 1997).

3. Ibid., 128.

4. Trevor N. Dupuy, *A Genius for War: The German Army and General Staff, 1807–1945* (New York, 1977), 54–70.

5. Edward N. Luttwak, *The Pentagon and the Art of War: The Question of Military Reform* (New York, 1984), 112.

6. Robert M. Citino, *Blitzkrieg to Desert Storm: The Evolution of Operational Warfare* (Lawrence, Kans., 2004), 289.

7. Stig Förster, "'Vom Kriege.' Überlegungen zu einer modernen Militärgeschichte," in *Was ist Militärgeschichte?*, edited by Benjamin Ziemann and Thomas Kühne (Paderborn, 2000), 265–282.

8. Bernd Wegner, "Wozu Operationsgeschichte?," in *Was ist Militärgeschichte?*, edited by Benjamin Ziemann and Thomas Kühne (Paderborn, 2000), 105–113.

9. Stig Förster, *The Battlefield: Towards a Modern History of War* (London, 2008), 22.

10. Cf. Sönke Neitzel, "Militärgeschichte ohne Krieg? Eine Standortbestimmung der deutschen Militärgeschichtsschreibung über das Zeitalter der Weltkriege," in *Geschichte der Politik. Alte und neue Wege,* ed. Hans-Christof Kraus and Thomas Nicklas, Historische Zeitschrift, Beih. 44 (Munich, 2007), 287–308, and Sönke Neitzel, "Des Forschens noch wert? Anmerkungen zur Operationsgeschichte der Waffen-SS," *Militärgeschichtliche Zeitschrift* 61, no. 2 (2002): 403–429.

11. Cf. Michael Geyer, "Eine Kriegsgeschichte, die vom Tod spricht," in *Physische Gewalt. Studien zur Geschichte der Neuzeit,* ed. Thomas Lindenberger and Alf Lüdtke (Frankfurt a.M., 1995), 136–161.

12. Cf. Stefan Felleckner, *Kampf. Ein vernachlässigter Bereich der Militärgeschichte* (Berlin, 2004).

13. Neitzel, "Militärgeschichte ohne Krieg?" 308.

14. Hans-Henning von Sandrart, "Vorwort zu den Denkschriften," in *Denkschriften zu Fragen der operativen Führung* (N.p: n.p., 1987), 11–17.

15. BMVg, *Leitlinie für die operative Führung von Landstreitkräften in Mitteleuropa,* 1987.

16. Martin Kutz, ed., *Realitätsflucht und Aggression im deutschen Militär* (Baden-Baden, 1990), 49–86.

17. For a comprehensive view of the era of world wars, see Gerhard P. Gross, "Das Dogma der Beweglichkeit. Überlegungen zur Genese der deutschen Heerestaktik im Zeitalter der Weltkriege," *Erster Weltkrieg—Zweiter Weltkrieg. Ein Vergleich. Krieg, Kriegser-*

lebnis, Kriegserfahrung in Deutschland, ed. Bruno Thoss and Hans-Erich Volkmann, Im Auftrag des Militärgeschichtlichen Forschungsamtes (Paderborn, 2002), 143–166. On the development in the First World War, see Ralf Raths, V*om Massensturm zur Stosstrupptaktik. Die deutsche Landkriegtaktik im Spiegel von Dienstvorschriften und Publizistik 1906 bis 1918* (Berlin, 2009). And also see Christian Stachelbeck, *Militärische Effektivität im Ersten Weltkrieg. Die 11. Bayerische Infanteriedivision 1915 bis 1918* (Paderborn, 2010).

18. Manfried Rauchensteiner, "Zum 'operativen Denken' in Österreich 1814–1914," *Österreichische Militärische Zeitschrift* (1974): 121–127, 207–210, 285–291, 379–389, 473–478.

19. Josef Marholz, "Die Entwicklung der operativen Führung," *Österreichische Militärische Zeitschrift* (1973): 107–113, 195–204, 369–376, 458–461.

20. Dieter Brand, "Grundsätze operativer Führung," in *Denkschriften zu Fragen der operativen Führung* (N.p: n.p., 1987).

21. Christian Freuding, "Organizing for War: Strategic Culture and the Organization of High Command in Britain and Germany, 1850–1945: A Comparative Perspective," *Defence Studies* 10, no. 3 (2010): 431–460.

1. Definitions: Tactics—Operations—Strategy

The epigraph to this chapter is drawn from Carl von Clausewitz, *Vom Kriege. Hinterlassenes Werk des Generals Carl von Clausewitz,* 16th ed., ed. Werner Hahlweg, Vollst. Ausg. im Urtext mit erneut erw. historisch-kritischer Würdigung (Bonn, 1952), 175.

1. *Handbuch für Heerestaktik,* vol. 1, *Grundbegriffe* (Berlin, 1939), 12.

2. Ironically, this chapter is preceded by Johann Wolfgang von Goethe's quote, "Wer klare Begriffe hat, kann befehlen" (He who has clear concepts can command), from his *Maxims and Reflections,* Abt. "Allgemeines, Ethisches, Literarisches," XL, No. 733.

3. For the first time there is the attempt to distinguish the three command levels of tactics, operations, and strategy. "Strategy means the art of the military commander, the art to see, think, and command in a military way to defeat the enemy. Tactics is the theory of how to apply the armed forces in the preparation and conduct of the battle. Operations mean a military undertaking directed at a martial purpose that corresponds to the basic rules of strategy and tactics" (Major General Schürmann, "Gedanken über Krieg- und Truppenführung," 1930, BArch, RH 2/2901, 164).

4. See chapter 6, "Old Wine in New Wineskins: Operational Thinking in the Reichswehr and the Wehrmacht Between Reality and Utopia."

5. *Brockhaus' Kleines Konversations-Lexikon,* vol. 2, 5th ed. (Leipzig, 1911), 311.

6. Cf. *Conversations-Lexikon, oder kurzgefasstes Handwörterbuch für die in der gesellschaftlichen Unterhaltung aus den Wissenschaften und Künsten vorkommenden Gegenstände mit beständiger Rücksicht auf die Ereignisse der älteren und neueren Zeit,* 6 vols., 2 subsequent vols. (Leipzig, 1809–1811).

7. Supplements to the *Conversations-Lexikon,* 1:242.

8. Johann Hübner, *Johann Hübners Zeitungs- und Conversations-Lexikon: Ein vaterländisches Handwörterbuch,* Part 3, M–R, 31st ed. (Leipzig, 1826), 396.

9. "Operation," *Brockhaus Bilder-Conversations-Lexikon,* vol. 3 (Leipzig, 1839), 343.

10. *Herders Conversations-Lexikon,* vol. 4 (Freiburg i.Br., 1856), 403.

11. *Pierer's Universal-Lexikon,* vol. 12 (Altenburg, 1861), 307.

12. *Meyers Neues Konversations-Lexikon: Ein Wörterbuch des allgemeinen Wissens,* vol. 15 (Hildburghausen, 1867), 315.

13. *Meyers Grosses Konversations-Lexikon,* vol. 15 (Leipzig, 1908), 72f.

14. *Militär-Lexikon: Handwörterbuch der Militärwissenschaften* (Berlin, 1901), 655f.

15. Bernhard von Poten, *Handwörterbuch der gesamten Militärwissenschaften,* vol. 7 (Leipzig, 1878), 259f.

16. *Handbuch für Heer und Flotte: Enzyklopädie der Kriegswissenschaften und verwandter Gebiete,* vol. 1, ed. Georg von Alten (Leipzig, 1909), 873.

17. *Der Grosse Brockhaus: Handbuch des Wissens in 20 Bänden,* vol. 13 (Leipzig, 1932), 687.

18. *Handbuch der neuzeitlichen Wehrwissenschaften,* vol. 1, *Wehrpolitik und Kriegführung,* Hrsg. im Auftrage der Deutschen Gesellschaft für Wehrpolitik und Wehrwissenschaften und unter umstehend aufgeführter Sachverständiger von Hermann Franke (Berlin, 1936).

19. *Der Grosse Brockhaus,* vol. 8 (Wiesbaden, 1955), 568.

20. Cf. *Brockhaus Enzyklopädie,* vol. 16 (Mannheim, 1991), and *Brockhaus Enzyklopädie,* vol. 16 (Mannheim, 1998).

21. Cf. *Duden Fremdwörterbuch (Der Duden in 12 Bänden),* vol. 5 (Mannheim, 1997).

22. Reinhard Stumpf, ed., *Kriegstheorie und Kriegsgeschichte: Carl von Clausewitz, Helmuth von Moltke,* Bibliothek der Geschichte und Politik 23 (Frankfurt a.M., 1993), 795f.

23. Georg Heinrich von Berenhorst, *Aphorismen* (Leipzig, 1805), 539.

24. Georg Wilhelm Freiherr von Valentini, *Die Lehren vom Krieg,* part 1, *Der kleine Krieg* (Berlin, 1820), 97.

25. Adam Dietrich Freiherr von Bülow, *Geist des neuern Kriegssystems hergeleitet aus dem Grundsatze einer Basis der Operationen auch für Laien in der Kriegskunst fasslich vorgetragen von einem ehemaligen preussischen Offizier* (Hamburg, 1805), 110.

26. Clausewitz, *Vom Kriege,* 169.

27. Werner Hahlweg, "Der klassische Begriff der Strategie und seine Entwicklung," in *Strategie-Handbuch,* Schriften des Instituts für Sicherheitspolitik an der Christian-Albrechts-Universität zu Kiel 8 (Bonn, 1990), 1:9–29.

28. Jehuda L. Wallach, *The Dogma of the Battle of Annihilation: The Theories of Clausewitz and Schlieffen and Their Impact on the German Conduct of Two World Wars* (Westport, Conn., 1986), 14f.

29. Henri Jomini, *Précis de l'art de la guerre, ou noveau tableau analytique des principales combinaisons de la stratégie, de la grande tactique et de la politique militaire.* 2 vols., new revision of the 1855 ed., with an introduction by H. R. Kurz (Osnabrück, 1974), 155f.

30. Helmuth von Moltke, "Über Strategie," in *Moltkes Taktisch-strategische Aufsätze aus den Jahren 1857 bis 1871,* by Helmuth von Moltke, edited by the Great General Staff, Department for War History, *Moltke's Militärische Werke, Die Thätigkeit als Chef des Generalstabes der Armee im Frieden,* Zweiter Teil (Berlin, 1900), 291–293.

31. Ulrich Marwedel, *Carl von Clausewitz. Persönlichkeit und Wirkungsgeschichte seines Werks bis 1918,* Militärgeschichtliche Studien 25 (Boppard a.Rh., 1978), 117.

32. For recent literature on Clausewitz's reception, cf. Beatrice Heuser, *Clausewitz*

lesen! Eine Einführung. Beiträge zur Militärgeschichte (Munich, 2005); and Hew Strachan, *Clausewitz's on War: A Biography* (Cambridge, U.K., 2007).

33. Peter Paret, "Clausewitz," in *Makers of Modern Strategy from Machiavelli to the Nuclear Age,* ed. Peter Paret (Princeton, N.J., 1986), 186–213.

34. *Meyers Grosses Konversations-Lexikon,* 15:105.

35. Burkhard Köster, *Militär und Eisenbahn in der Habsburgermonarchie 1825–1859* (Munich, 1999), 25.

36. Edward N. Luttwak, *Strategy: The Logic of War and Peace* (Cambridge, Mass., 2002), 15. Luttwak stresses that there is no good definition for strategy because in a military-political context it may be understood alternatively as a plan, a fixed doctrine, or an actual practice.

37. Hans Hitz, "Taktik und Strategie. Zur Entwicklung kriegswissenschaftlicher Begriffe," *Wehrwissenschaftliche Rundschau, Zeitschrift für Europäische Sicherheit* (1956), 611–628.

38. Georg von Sodenstern, "Operationen," *Wehrwissenschaftliche Rundschau. Zeitschrift für Europäische Sicherheit* 3 (1953): 1–10.

39. *Handbuch für Heer und Flotte,* 1:872.

40. Friedrich Meinert, *Über den Krieg, die Kriegswissenschaften und die Kriegskunst. Für das Militär und solche, welche vom Kriegswesen unterrichtet sein wollen* (Halle, 1798), 50, 58.

41. Georg Venturini, *Lehrbuch der angewandten Taktik oder eigentlichen Kriegswissenschaft,* vol. 1 (Schleswig, 1798–1800), 387–405.

42. Ernst Klink, *Die Begriffe Operation und operativ in ihrer militärischen Verwendung in Deutschland.* Studie MGFA, 12 December 1958, page 1.

43. Bülow, *Geist des neuern Kriegssystems,* 11.

44. Ernst August Nohn, *Der unzeitgemässe Clausewitz. Notwendige Bemerkungen über zeitgemässe Denkfehler,* Wehrwissenschaftliche Rundschau, Beiheft 5 (Frankfurt a.M., 1956), 10.

45. Carl von Clausewitz, *Strategie aus dem Jahr 1804 mit Zusätzen von 1808 und 1809,* ed. Eberhard Kessel (Hamburg, 1937), 49.

46. Only in 1939 did the Luftwaffe define the term "operation" in their manual of army tactics.

47. H.Dv. 100/900 *Führungsbegriffe,* 1977.

48. The term "operational" was also used by the *Staatssicherheitsdienst* (Stassi) of the German Democratic Republic (DDR).

49. Klink, *Die Begriffe Operation und operativ,* 18.

2. Factors and Constants: Space, Time, and Forces

The epigraph to this chapter is drawn from Hagen Schulze, *Weimar: Deutschland 1917–1933* (Berlin, 1982, 1998), 16.

1. Hermann Foertsch, *Kriegskunst heute und morgen* (Berlin, 1939), 50f.

2. Gerhard P. Gross, "Der 'Raum' als operationsgeschichtliche Kategorie im Zeitalter der Weltkriege," in *Perspektiven der Militärgeschichte. Raum, Gewalt und Repräsentation in historischer Forschung und Bildung,* ed. Jörg Echternkamp, Beiträge zur Militärgeschichte 67 (Munich, 2010), 115–140.

3. In 1913 the survey division was divided into a trigonometric section, a topographic section, a cartographic section, and a photogrammetric section, as well as into a colonial section. It was headed by the *Chef der Landesaufnahme*. Since 1 April 1894, his title had been Oberquartiermeister und Chef der Landesaufnahme. At the beginning of the war in 1914 the Prussian *Landesaufnahme* had a staff of 911, which included 31 officers; 367 civilian military administrators; 29 office workers; and 120 laborers—for a total permanent staff of 547. It also had an additional seconded 51 officers and 313 soldiers. The extraordinary importance which the German General Staff attached to geography was certainly noted abroad. See also Halford John Mackinder, *Democratic Ideals and Reality: A Study in the Politics of Reconstruction* (London, 1919), 26f.

4. The argument advanced by Patrick O'Sullivan shows that the factors continued to exist exclusively as natural phenomena. See "War Is a Geographical Phenomenon" in Patrick O'Sullivan, *Terrain and Tactics* (Westport, Conn., 1991), 16.

5. Otto von Bismarck, *Bismarck Gespräche,* vol. 2, *Von der Reichsgründung bis zur Entlassung,* ed. Willy Andreas (Basel, 1980), 525.

6. Wolfgang J. Mommsen, "Der Topos vom unvermeidlichen Krieg. Aussenpolitik und öffentliche Meinung im Deutschen Reich im letzten Jahrzehnt vor 1914," in *Bereit zum Krieg. Kriegsmentalität im Wilhelminischen Deutschland 1890–1914,* ed. Jost Dülffer and Karl Holl, Beiträge zur historischen Friedensforschung (Göttingen, 1986), 194–224; Friedrich von Bernhardi, *Deutschland und der nächste Krieg* (Berlin, 1912), 6.

7. Remarks by Beck on the minutes prepared by Colonel Rossbach from a meeting in the Reich Chancellery on 5 November 1937, dated 12 November 1937. Cf. Klaus-Jürgen Müller, *Generaloberst Ludwig Beck: Eine Biographie* (Potsdam, 2008), 499.

8. The Curzon Line was the line of demarcation suggested in 1920 by British foreign minister George Nathaniel Curzon between the Soviet Union and Poland to conclude the Polish-Soviet War.

9. Generaloberst Graf von Schlieffen, *Die grossen Generalstabsreisen—Ost—aus den Jahren 1891–1905,* Dienstschriften des Chefs des Generalstabes der Armee Generalfeldmarschall Graf von Schlieffen 2. General Staff of the Army, Seventh Department (War Science) (Berlin, 1938), 2:222.

10. Ludwig Beck, *Studien,* Introduction by Hans Speidel, ed. (Stuttgart, 1955), 56.

11. Hartmut Rosa, *Beschleunigung. Die Veränderung der Zeitstrukturen in der Moderne* (Frankfurt a.M., 2005), 318.

12. Ibid., 316.

13. Friedrich von Bernhardi, "Über angriffsweise Kriegführung," *Beiheft zum Militärischen Wochenblatt* 4 (1905): 138.

14. "Germany's fight against superiority is a biological necessity for our political development." Friedrich von Bernhardi, *Vom heutigen Kriege,* vol. 2 (Berlin, 1912), 189.

3. The Beginnings: Planning, Mobility, and a System of Expedients

1. Examples are: Brand, "Grundsätze operativer Führung," 31; John English, "The Operational Art: Developments in the Theories of War," in *The Operational Art: Developments in the Theories of War,* ed. Brian J. C. McKercher and Michael A. Hennessy (Westport, Conn., 1996), 7–28; Kutz, *Realitätsflucht und Aggression,* 27; Sandrart, "Vorwort zu

den Denkschriften," 13; Dennis E. Showalter, "German Grand Strategy: A Contradiction in Terms?" *Militärgeschichtliche Mitteilungen* 48 (1990): 65–102; Sodenstern, "Operationen," 1; Terence Zuber, *The Moltke Myth: Prussian War Planning, 1857–1871* (Lanham, Md., 2008). Zuber correctly criticizes the Moltke myth, but this criticism is overstated in essential passages.

2. This fact was largely regretted during the period of the Reich. On the occasion of Moltke's one hundredth birthday, Schlieffen gave a formal address in which he remarked on this subject with regret that "the immortalized field marshal did not treat the essence of war in a scientific way, that, unlike others before him, he did not write a theory of war" (Helmuth Graf von Moltke, *Ausgewählte Werke,* vol. 1, *Feldherr und Kriegslehrmeister,* ed. Ferdinand von Schmerfeld [Berlin, 1925], 241).

3. Heuser, *Clausewitz lesen!* 70–72.

4. Gerhard P. Gross, "There Was a Schlieffenplan," in *Der Schlieffenplan. Analysen und Dokumente,* ed. Hans Ehlert, Michael Epkenhans, and Gerhard P. Gross (Paderborn, 2007), 117–160.

5. Roland G. Foerster, "Das operative Denken Moltkes des Älteren und die Folgen," in *Ausgewählte Operationen und ihre militärhistorischen Grundlagen,* ed. Hans-Martin Ottmer and Heiger Ostertag, Operatives Denken und Handeln in deutschen Streitkräften 4 (Im Auftrag des Militärgeschichtlichen Forschungsamtes, Bonn, 1993), 255.

6. Moltke, "Über Strategie," in *Moltkes Taktisch-strategische Aufsätze aus den Jahren 1857 bis 1871,* 429–432.

7. Ibid., 429.

8. Ibid. He is, therefore, in contrast to Clausewitz, for whom the entire act of war is marked by politics. For more information on Moltke's attitude toward the primacy of politics and the conflict with Bismarck, see Heuser, *Clausewitz lesen!* 72–75; Dietmar Schoessler, "Die Weiterentwicklung in der Militärstrategie. Das 19. Jahrhundert," in *Strategie-Handbuch,* Schriften des Instituts für Sicherheitspolitik an der Christian-Albrechts-Universität zu Kiel 8 (Bonn, 1990), 1:31–62; Jehuda L. Wallach, *Kriegstheorien. Ihre Entwicklung im 19. und 20. Jahrhundert* (Frankfurt a.M., 1972), 84–86.

9. Cf. Wilhelm von Blume, *Strategie: Eine Studie* (Berlin, 1882).

10. Klink, *Die Begriffe Operation und operativ,* 3.

11. Moltke, "Über Strategie," in *Moltkes Taktisch-strategische Aufsätze aus den Jahren 1857 bis 1871,* 430.

12. Ibid., 431.

13. Hans Delbrück, "Moltke," *Erinnerungen, Aufsätze und Reden* (Berlin, 1902), 546–575.

14. Besides Alexander von Humboldt, Carl Ritter (1779–1859) is regarded as the founder of modern scientific geography in Germany.

15. Stumpf, ed., *Kriegstheorie und Kriegsgeschichte,* 876f.

16. Cf. Karl Ernst Freiherr von Canitz und Dallwitz, *Nachrichten und Betrachtungen über die Taten und Schicksale der Reiterei in den Feldzügen Friedrichs II. und in denen neuerer Zeit,* vol. 2 (Berlin, 1823–1824).

17. Eberhard Kessel, *Moltke* (Stuttgart, 1957), 109f.

18. On the mid-nineteenth-century Prussian army reform, see the convincing work by

Dierk Walter, *Preussische Heeresreform 1807–1870. Militärische Innovation und der Mythos der "Roonschen Reform,"* Krieg in der Geschichte 16 (Paderborn, 2003).

19. Ibid., 445. The claim, which can often be found in the older literature, that these reforms primarily served the purpose of making the army less bourgeois does not hold up under more recent studies. The military-technical aspect outweighed the existing anti-bourgeois reflexes by far.

20. Ibid., 612.

21. Helmuth von Moltke, *Moltkes Militärische Werke*, vol. 2, part 2, *Die Thätigkeit als Chef des Generalstabes der Armee im Frieden,* ed. Great General Staff, Department for War History I (Berlin, 1900), 173.

22. Ibid. The first time Moltke the Elder explained these thoughts was in the article *"Betrachtungen über Konzentrationen im Kriege,"* which was published anonymously in reaction to Austrian criticism, but which can be attributed to him.

23. Helmuth von Moltke, "Essay of 16 September 1865, 'Über Marschtiefen,'" *Moltkes Militärische Werke,* vol. 2, part 2, pages 235–246.

24. Ernst-Heinrich Schmidt, "Zur Genesis des konzentrischen Operierens mit getrennten Heeresteilen im Zeitalter des ausgehenden Ancien Régime, der Französischen Revolution und Napoleons," in *Ausgewählte Operationen und ihre militärhistorischen Grundlagen,* ed. Hans-Martin Ottmer and Heiger Ostertag, Operatives Denken und Handeln in deutschen Streitkräften 4 (Bonn, 1993), 51–105.

25. Gerhard von Scharnhorst, "Über die Schlacht von Marengo," in *Denkwürdigkeiten der militärischen Gesellschaft,* vol. 1, ed. Joachim Niemeyer (Osnabrück, 1985), 52–59.

26. Waldemar Erfurth, *Der Vernichtungssieg. Eine Studie über das Zusammenwirken getrennter Heeresteile* (Berlin, 1939), 14–17; Schmidt, "Zur Genesis," 83–97.

27. Deutscher Kaiser und König von Preussen Wilhelm I, *Militärische Schriften weiland Kaiser Wilhelms des Grossen,* vol. 1, *1821–1847* (Berlin, 1897), 117.

28. Stumpf, ed., *Kriegstheorie und Kriegsgeschichte,* 902.

29. On the Prussian railway system, see Klaus-Jürgen Bremm, *Von der Chaussee zur Schiene. Militärstrategie und Eisenbahnen in Preussen von 1833 bis zum Feldzug von 1866* (Munich, 2005); and Dennis E. Showalter, *Railroads and Rifles: Soldiers, Technology, and the Unification of Germany* (Hamden, Conn., 1975).

30. Bremm, *Von der Chaussee zur Schiene,* 72.

31. Ibid., 178f.

32. Martin L. Van Creveld, *Supplying War: Logistics from Wallenstein to Patton* (Cambridge, U.K., 1997), 87f.

33. Dennis E. Showalter, "Soldiers into Postmasters? The Electric Telegraph as an Instrument of Command in the Prussian Army," *Military Affairs* 37 (1973): 48–52.

34. The Prussian supply problems during the war of 1866 are examples for this. Cf. Bremm, *Von der Chaussee zur Schiene,* 213–215; Creveld, *Supplying War,* 83–85.

35. For a still classical explanation of this development, cf. Stephan Leistenschneider, *Auftragstaktik im preussisch-deutschen Heer 1871 bis 1914,* ed. Militärgeschichtliches Forschungsamt (Hamburg, 2002), 23–62; for a more pointed description, cf. Walter, *Preussische Heeresreformen,* 545–547.

36. Moltke explains that point as follows: "The higher the agency the shorter and more

general the orders will be; the bigger the main divisions, the more freedom they must get." Helmuth von Moltke, "Verbindungen," in Helmuth von Moltke, *Moltkes Militärische Werke,* vol. 4, part 2, *Moltkes Kriegslehren. Die taktischen Vorbereitungen zur Schlacht* (Berlin, 1911), 19–24.

37. Moltke to the supreme command of Second Army, Berlin, 22 June 1866, in Moltke, *Moltkes Militärische Werke,* vol. 2, part 2, pages 234 ff.

38. Kessel, *Moltke,* 429f., 449f.

39. Helmuth von Moltke, *Moltkes Militärische Werke,* vol. 2, part 2, *Aus den Verordnungen für die höheren Truppenführer vom 24. Juni 1869,* ed. Great General Staff, Department for War History I (Berlin, 1900), 174.

40. Helmuth von Moltke, "Aufsatz vom Jahre 1859 'Über Flankenstellungen,'" in Moltke, *Moltkes Militärische Werke,* vol. 2, part 2 (Berlin, 1900), 261–266.

41. Moltke, *Moltkes Militärische Werke,* vol. 2, part 2, *Aus den Verordnungen für die höheren Truppenführer vom 24. Juni 1869,* 173.

42. Ibid., vol. 2, part 1, 97.

43. Ibid., vol. 4, part 3, 163.

44. Ibid., 227f.

45. Ibid., vol. 2, part 2, *Aus den Verordnungen für die höheren Truppenführer vom 24. Juni 1869,* 207. For the issues of the battle of annihilation and the war of annihilation in German operational thinking, see chapter 4, "The Sword of Damocles: A Two-Front War."

46. Clausewitz, *Vom Kriege,* 113. See also Panajotis Kondylis, *Theorie des Krieges. Clausewitz—Marx—Engels—Lenin* (Stuttgart, 1988), 116–120.

47. "The nature of today's warfare is characterized by the pursuit of a major and quick decision. . . . Everything presses towards a swift end of the war." Moltke, *Moltkes Militärische Werke,* vol. 2, part 2, *Aus den Verordnungen für die höheren Truppenführer vom 24. Juni 1869,* 173.

48. Ibid., vol. 4, part 3, 214.

49. See Michael Howard, *War in European History* (Oxford, 1976), 134; Marwedel, *Carl von Clausewitz,* 147–150; Wallach, *Kriegstheorien,* 86; Hans-Ulrich Wehler, "Der Verfall der deutschen Kriegstheorie: Vom 'Absoluten' zum 'Totalen' Krieg oder von Clausewitz zu Ludendorff," in *Geschichte und Militärgeschichte. Wege der Forschung,* ed. Ursula von Gersdorff (Mit Unterstützung des Militärgeschichtlichen Forschungsamtes, Frankfurt a.M., 1974), 286.

50. Cf. Stig Förster, "Helmuth von Moltke und das Problem des industrialisierten Volkskriegs im 19. Jahrhundert," in *Generalfeldmarschall von Moltke. Bedeutung und Wirkung,* ed. Roland G. Foerster (Munich, 1991), 103–115. Kondylis also writes very convincingly about this in *Theorie des Krieges.*

51. Concerning the development of operational thinking in the Wehrmacht during the Third Reich—which will be discussed later—it is worth pointing out that today's universal fundamental equating of politics with something good, lawful, and, at the same time, moderating seems questionable against the backdrop of the primacy of politics of National Socialism. It would surely be useful either to define "good" politics or to replace politics with civilian authority. Also see Kondylis, *Theorie des Krieges,* 110–115.

52. See also Wehler, "Der Verfall der deutschen Kriegstheorie," 287.

53. Helmuth Graf von Moltke, *Die deutschen Aufmarschpläne 1871–1890*, ed. Ferdinand von Schmerfeld (Berlin, 1929), 83.

54. The Battle of Gravelotte-St. Privat is an example of this. Walter, *Preussische Heeresreformen*, 544.

55. Arden Bucholz, *Moltke, Schlieffen and the Prussian War Planning* (New York, 1991), 18–25.

56. Kondylis, *Theorie des Krieges*, 105–107.

57. Wehler, "Der Verfall der deutschen Kriegstheorie," 289.

58. Geoffrey Wawro, *The Austro-Prussian War: Austria's War with Prussia and Italy in 1866* (New York, 1996), 12–25.

59. Bucholz, *Moltke, Schlieffen and the Prussian War Planning*, 8–12.

60. Christian Millotat, *Das preussisch-deutsche Generalstabssystem. Wurzeln—Entwicklung—Fortwirken* (Zürich, 2000). Despite all the distance, historians such as Hans-Ulrich Wehler in *Deutsche Gesellschaftsgeschichte*, vol. 3, *Von der "Deutschen Doppelrevolution" bis zum Beginn des Ersten Weltkriegs: 1849–1914* (Munich, 1996), 322, or Wolfgang J. Mommsen in *Das Ringen um den nationalen Staat. Die Gründung und der innere Ausbau des Deutschen Reiches unter Otto von Bismarck 1850–1890*, Prophyläen Weltgeschichte Deutschlands 7/1 (Berlin, 1993), 235, have not been able to completely escape from the fascination with the General Staff.

61. Martin Raschke, *Der politisierende Generalstab. Die friderizianischen Kriege in der amtlichen deutschen Militärgeschichtsschreibung 1890 bis 1914* (Freiburg i.Br., 1993), 39.

62. Gerhard P. Gross, "Gerhard von Scharnhorst oder historische Bildung," *Truppenpraxis Wehrausbildung. Zeitschrift für Führung, Ausbildung und Erziehung* 3 (1995): 207–213.

63. Ibid.

64. On the Battle of Königgrätz, see Thorsten Loch and Lars Zacharias, "Königgrätz 1866. Die Operationen zwischen dem 22. Juni und 3. Juli 1866," *Österreichische Militärische Zeitschrift* 48, no. 6 (2010): 707–715.

65. Friedrich Engels, "Betrachtungen," in Karl Marx and Friedrich Engels, *Werke*, vol. 16 (Berlin, 1962), 182–184.

66. It is important to note, however, that Moltke's undeniably excellent operational leadership was preceded by a disastrous mistake by his French enemy.

67. Walter, *Preussische Heeresreformen*, 105. For the revitalization of the concept, see pages 167–186.

68. Förster, "Helmuth von Moltke und das Problem," 103–115.

69. Volkmar Regling, "Grundzüge der Landkriegführung zur Zeit des Absolutismus und im 19. Jahrhundert," in *Deutsche Militärgeschichte*, vol. 6, *Grundzüge der militärischen Kriegführung 1648–1939* (Stuttgart, 1983), 423.

70. Helmuth von Moltke, "Geschichte des Deutsch-Französischen Krieges von 1870–71," in Helmuth von Moltke, *Gesammelte Schriften und Denkwürdigkeiten des General-Feldmarschalls Grafen Helmuth von Moltke*, vol. 3, edited by Lescynski (Berlin, 1891), 1.

71. Otto von Bismarck, *Die politischen Reden des Fürsten Bismarck*, ed. Horst Kohl, 14 vols. (Berlin, 1892–1905), 5:156.

72. Ibid.

73. On the calls for a preventive war by Moltke the Elder and his successors, see Michael Epkenhans, "'Wir Deutsche fürchten Gott'—Zur Rolle des Krieges in Bismarcks Aussenpolitik," *Politische Studien. Zweimonatsschrift für Politik und Zeitgeschehen* 391 (2003): 54–63.
On the role of war in Bismarck's foreign policy, see Karl-Ernst Jeismann, *Das Problem des Präventivkrieges im europäischen Staatensystem mit besonderem Blick auf die Bismarck-zeit* (Munich, 1957), 83–152; see also Stig Förster, "Optionen der Kriegführung im Zeitalter des 'Volkskrieges.' Zu Helmuth von Moltkes militärisch-politischen Überlegungen nach den Erfahrungen der Einigungskriege," in *Militärische Verantwortung in Staat und Gesellschaft. 175 Jahre Generalstabsausbildung in Deutschland,* ed. Detlef Bald (Koblenz, 1986), 94–99.

74. On the discussion of preventive war plans, see Gross, "There Was a Schlieffenplan," 153f.; Ivo Nikolai Lambi, *The Navy and German Power Politics, 1862–1914* (Boston, Mass., 1984), 241–245; Annika Mombauer, "Der Moltkeplan. Modifikation des Schlieffenplans bei gleichen Zielen?" in *Der Schlieffenplan. Analysen und Dokumente,* ed. Hans Ehlert, Michael Epkenhans, and Gerhard P. Gross (Paderborn, 2007), 79f.; Heiner Raulff, *Zwischen Machtpolitik und Imperialismus. Die deutsche Frankreichpolitik 1904–06* (Düsseldorf, 1976), 126–144; Gerhard Ritter, *Der Schlieffenplan. Kritik eines Mythos. Mit erstmaliger Veröffentlichung der Texte und 6 Kartenskizzen* (Munich, 1956), 102–138.

75. For more on this topic, see Annika Mombauer, *Helmuth von Moltke and the Origins of the First World War* (Cambridge, U.K., 2001), 110–175.

76. On the assessment from the point of view of international law, see Martin Kunde, *Der Präventivkrieg. Geschichtliche Entwicklung und gegenwärtige Bedeutung* (Frankfurt a.M., 2007).

77. Moltke, "Geschichte des Deutsch-Französischen Krieges von 1870–71," 3:84f.

78. Ibid., 3:4, Memorandum of 27 April 1871, *Aufmarsch gegen Frankreich–Russland.*

79. For a two-front war against Austria and France, the General Staff developed various Aufmarschpläne in January 1877, December 1878, and January 1879.

80. For a two-front war against Russia and France, the General Staff developed several Aufmarschpläne in April 1871, February 1877, April 1879, January 1880, and February 1888.

81. Moltke, *Ausgewählte Werke,* 1:1.

82. In the following, the German Army is understood as the contingent army of the German Reich.

83. Memorandum of 27 April 1871, *Aufmarsch gegen Frankreich—Russland,* see Moltke, *Ausgewählte Werke,* 4–20.

84. *Reflections of December 1878 and January 1879: War against France and Austria,* see Moltke, *Ausgewählte Werke,* 67–74, here page 68.

85. Kessel, *Moltke,* 706–710.

4. The Sword of Damocles: A Two-Front War

1. Cf. Ritter, *Der Schlieffenplan.*

2. Cf. Terence Zuber, *Inventing the Schlieffen Plan: German War Planning, 1871–1914* (New York, 2002).

3. For the recent research on the Schlieffen Plan, see Ehlert, Epkenhans, and Gross, eds., *Der Schlieffenplan.* This volume is the first to include the newly discovered tran-

scripts of the Aufmarschanweisungen of the German General Staff from 1893–1894 to 1914–1915.

4. See Mombauer, *Helmuth von Moltke and the Origins of the First World War.*

5. Reichsarchiv, *Der Weltkrieg 1914–1918. Die militärischen Operationen zu Lande,* 14 vols. (Produced by the Reichsarchiv, Berlin, 1925–1944), 1:4.

6. Moltke the Younger wrote in his mobilization schedule of 1913–1914, "Considering the popular mood in France, a war waged by Germany against England or Russia alone is not expected" (Ehlert, Epkenhans, and Gross, eds., *Der Schlieffenplan,* 467).

7. See chapter 3; also see Bucholz, *Moltke, Schlieffen and the Prussian War Planning,* 58–108.

8. Albert von Boguslawski, *Betrachtungen über Heerwesen und Kriegführung* (Berlin, 1897).

9. Colmar Freiherr von der Goltz, *Kriegführung. Kurze Lehre ihrer wichtigsten Grundsätze und Formen* (Berlin, 1895).

10. Leistenschneider, *Auftragstaktik,* 57–123.

11. For an extensive view of the strategy debate, see Sven Lange, *Hans Delbrück und der "Strategiestreit." Kriegführung und Kriegsgeschichte in der Kontroverse 1879–1914* (Freiburg i.Br., 1995).

12. Markus Pöhlmann, *Kriegsgeschichte und Geschichtspolitik: Der Erste Weltkrieg. Die amtliche deutsche Militärgeschichtsschreibung 1914–1956* (Paderborn, 2002), 42–44.

13. Eberhard Kessel, "Napoleonische und Moltkesche Strategie," *Wissen und Wehr* 2 (1929): 171–181.

14. Werner Gembruch, "General von Schlichting," *Wehrwissenschaftliche Rundschau* (1960): 186–196.

15. Heinz-Ludger Borgert, "Grundzüge der Landkriegführung von Schlieffen bis Guderian," in *Deutsche Militärgeschichte in sechs Bänden 1648–1939* (Munich, 1983), 6:435.

16. Goltz, *Kriegführung,* 7–21.

17. Jay Luvaas, *The Military Legacy of the Civil War: The European Inheritance* (Chicago, 1959).

18. Roger Chickering, "The American Civil War and the German Wars of Unification: Some Parting Shots," in *On the Road to Total War,* ed. Stig Förster and Jörg Nagler (New York, 1997), 683.

19. Cf. Markus Pöhlmann, "Das unentdeckte Land. Kriegsbild und Zukunftskrieg in deutschen Militärzeitschriften," in *Der Grosse Krieg. Europäische Militärzeitschriften und die Debatte über den Krieg der Zukunft, 1880–1914,* ed. Stig Förster (in preparation).

20. Sigismund von Schlichting, "Über das Infanteriegefecht," *Militär-Wochenblatt* 2 (1879): 64.

21. Rudolf von Caemmerer, *Die Entwicklung der strategischen Wissenschaft im 19. Jahrhundert* (Berlin, 1904), 28 (English translation: *The Development of Strategical Science,* trans. Karl von Donat [London, 1905], 35–36).

22. Friedrich von Bernhardi, *Vom heutigen Kriege,* vol. 2 (Berlin, 1912), 93.

23. Friedrich von Bernhardi, *Deutschland und der nächste Krieg* (Berlin, 1912), 216.

24. Colmar Freiherr von der Goltz, *Das Volk in Waffen: ein Buch über Heerwesen und Kriegführung unserer Zeit* (Berlin, 1895), 239.

25. Bernhardi, *On War of Today,* 2:453.

26. Dieter Storz, *Kriegsbild und Rüstung vor 1914. Europäische Landstreitkräfte vor dem Ersten Weltkrieg* (Herford, 1992), 226–237.

27. Gross, "Das Dogma der Beweglichkeit," 144–148.

28. Bernhardi, *On War of Today,* 2:27.

29. William Balck, "Die Taktik der Infanterie und der verbundenen Waffen," in *Löbells Jahresberichte über die Veränderungen und Fortschritte im Militärwesen* 33 (1906): 283–316.

30. Marwedel, *Carl von Clausewitz,* 167–172.

31. Bernhardi, *Vom heutigen Kriege,* 1:94–98.

32. Today especially, it is necessary to explain to people that numerical superiority can be defeated. As Bernhardi noted, "For it is the spirit which decides in war today, it is the spirit of command and the spirit of the troops. Resolution and boldness have the same ascendency as of yore" (*Vom heutigen Kriege,* 2:190).

33. Oliver Stein, *Die deutsche Heeresrüstungspolitik 1890–1914. Das Militär und der Primat der Politik* (Paderborn, 2007), 170–331.

34. Ludwig Freiherr von Falkenhausen, "Die Bedeutung der Flanke," *Vierteljahreshefte für Truppenführung* (1908): 601.

35. Cf. Ludwig Freiherr von Falkenhausen, *Der grosse Krieg in der Jetztzeit. Eine Studie über Bewegung und Kampf der Massenheere des 20. Jahrhunderts* (Berlin, 1909).

36. "Conducting war under these conditions can scarcely be any longer called an art. It becomes a trade, and the commander is, as it were, a mechanic. . . . This essentially mechanical conception of war limits the will of the commander to the utmost by subjecting him to the force of outward conditions" (Bernhardi, *On War of Today,* 2:163). Bernhardi used these words to criticize Schlieffen's ideas of a modern war (which the field marshal had postulated in his essay "Krieg in der Gegenwart") without actually mentioning Schlieffen's name.

37. Bernhardi, *On War of Today,* 2:172.

38. For greater detail, see Gross, "There Was a Schlieffenplan," 134, 175.

39. The newly discovered final taskings and final discussions of the General Staff rides, the studies by Wilhelm Dieckmann and Helmuth Greiner, and the copies of the German deployment plans (*Aufmarschplanungen*) of 1893–1894 to 1914–1915 deserve particular mention. See Gross, "There Was a Schlieffen Plan," 117–152, and the deployment plans from 1893–1894 to 1914–1915 in Ehlert, Epkenhans, and Gross, eds., *Der Schlieffenplan,* 341–484.

40. Kessel had already pointed out that the records of the war games, exercise rides, and taskings, which unfortunately were destroyed, were much more important for the evaluation of Schlieffen's operational thinking than his plan of 1905. Alfred Graf von Schlieffen, *Briefe,* ed. Eberhard Kessel (Göttingen, 1958), 10.

41. Wallach, *Kriegstheorien,* 125f.

42. Ferdinand M. von Senger und Etterlin, "Cannae, Schlieffen und die Abwehr," *Wehrwissenschaftliche Rundschau* (1963): 27.

43. "Curiously enough, the current focus is on the frontal attack. Undecided battles, long protracted wars will be the consequence. But this will be impossible to bear with armies of millions. The nations' state of culture, the expense of the immense means

required to maintain such masses demand a rapid decision, a speedy conclusion" (Alfred Graf von Schlieffen, *Die taktisch-strategischen Aufgaben aus den Jahren 1891–1905* [Berlin, 1937], 86).

44. Stig Förster, "Der deutsche Generalstab und die Illusion des kurzen Krieges, 1871–1914. Metakritik eines Mythos," *Militärgeschichtliche Mitteilungen* 54 (1995): 61–95. Despite the lack of forces, Schlieffen had provided for troop contingents to suppress potential labor unrest in the deployment plan of 1906–1907, the last under his responsibility. See Ehlert, Epkenhans, and Gross, eds., *Der Schlieffenplan*, 412.

45. Förster, *Der deutsche Generalstab*, 61–95; Hew Strachan, "Die Ostfront. Geopolitik, Geographie und Operationen," in *Die vergessene Front. Der Osten 1914–15. Ereignis, Wirkung, Nachwirkung*, ed. Gerhard P. Gross (Paderborn, 2006), 20.

46. Schlieffen did not provide exact dates for the two front war he had planned. Therefore we can only speculate regarding his thoughts on the duration of his planned short war. The six-month duration of a war mentioned in the established literature, and also by Ritter, is certainly too short. The calculation of Burchardt (Lothar Burchardt, *Friedenswirtschaft und Kriegsvorsorge. Deutschlands wirtschaftliche Rüstungsbestrebungen vor 1914* [Boppard a.Rh., 1968], 15) is based on the wrong basic assumption that Schlieffen's memorandum of 1905 was a plan for a two-front war. This, however, is not correct. The Schlieffen Plan mentioned again and again is the deployment plan for a one-front war in the west. Therefore, it is not possible simply to apply the dates indicated in this plan to a two-front war. In contemporary military publications many authors shared the idea of a short war. In the last two decades before the outbreak of the war in 1914, a growing number of people expected a long war lasting more than eighteen months if the war was not decided in speedy, decisive battles. Schlieffen's successor, Moltke the Younger, also assumed that the war would last longer, up to two years. Several changes in Schlieffen's plans for an attack against France (for example, forgoing transit through the Netherlands) are based on this conviction. Cf. Burchardt, *Friedenswirtschaft und Kriegsvorsorge*, 21; Förster, *Der deutsche Generalstab*, 89f.

47. Schlieffen, *Die grossen Generalstabsreisen*, 222.

48. Gross, "Das Dogma der Beweglichkeit," 143–166.

49. Strachan, "Die Ostfront," 21f.

50. Schlieffen considered surprise an important parameter for the success of a battle. As he explained to his General Staff officers: "Nevertheless, these [other] factors alone do not bring victory. It is necessary that the enemy surprised by the suddenness of the attack is more or less caught up in confusion, ruining the execution of his decisions through the hastiness of their implementation" (Chef des Generalstabes der Armee, Kriegsspiel November/Dezember 1905, Berlin, 23 December 1905, BArch, PH 3/646, f. 1–36, here 34).

51. A note on the 2nd Grosse Reise in 1901 reads: "The transfer of a major contingent of the western army to the Vistula following decisive successes had been intended in the operations plan" (2. Grosse Reise, BArch, N 323/7, Boetticher Posthumous Papers, 6).

52. Martin Kutz, "Schlieffen contra Clausewitz. Zur Grundlegung einer Denkschule der Aggression und des Blitzkrieges," in *Realitätsflucht und Aggression*, ed. Martin Kutz (Baden-Baden, 1990), 31.

53. Heuser, *Clausewitz lesen!* 104–107.

54. Grossen Generalstab, *Der Schlachterfolg. Mit welchen Mitteln wurde er erstrebt?* (Berlin, 1903), 309.

55. Bernhardi, *Vom heutigen Kriege*, 2:419.

56. Jack Snyder, *The Ideology of the Offensive: Military Decision Making and the Disasters of 1914* (Ithaca, N.Y., 1984), 104–107.

57. Colmar Freiherr von der Goltz, *Krieg- und Heerführung* (Berlin, 1901), 14.

58. See the pointed criticism of this development in Kondylis, *Theorie des Krieges*, 136.

59. Cf. Wallach, *The Dogma of the Battle of Annihilation*.

60. Heuser, *Clausewitz lesen!* 134.

61. Isabel V. Hull, *Absolute Destruction: Military Culture and the Practices of War in Imperial Germany* (Ithaca, N.Y., 2005), 324–333.

62. In the following, Imperial Army refers to the army of the German Reich.

63. Stig Förster, "Der Vernichtungsgedanke in der militärischen Tradition des Deutschen Kaiserreiches. Überlegungen zum Problem historischer Kontinuität," in *Krieg, Frieden und Demokratie. Festschrift für Martin Vogt zum 65. Geburtstag*, ed. Christof Dipper (Frankfurt a.M., 2001), 262f.

64. Wilhelm von Blume, *Militärpolitische Aufsätze* (Berlin, 1906), 34.

65. Grosse Generalstabsreise 1898, BArch, N 323/30, Boetticher Posthumous Papers, 8.

66. Schlussaufgaben 1905, BArch, N 323/48, Boetticher Posthumous Papers 8.

67. Grosse Generalstabsreise September 1899, BArch, N 323/7, Boetticher Posthumous Papers, 13.

68. Letter to Hugo Freiherr von Freytag-Loringhoven, 14 August 1912, in Schlieffen, *Briefe*, 317.

69. Raschke, *Der politisierende Generalstab*, 126–129.

70. Erfurth, *Der Vernichtungssieg*, 69–72.

71. Kutz, *Realitätsflucht und Aggression*, 35f.; Wallach, *Kriegstheorien*, 101–110.

72. Alfred Graf von Schlieffen, *Cannae. Mit einer Auswahl von Aufsätzen und Reden des Feldmarschalls sowie einer Einführung und Lebensbeschreibung von General der Infanterie Freiherrn von Freytag-Loringhoven* (Berlin, 1925), 262.

73. Ibid.

74. Ibid., 9.

75. Raschke, *Der politisierende Generalstab*, 127f.

76. Cf. Stein, *Die deutsche Heeresrüstungspolitik*.

77. Gross, "There Was a Schlieffenplan," 141–144, 158f.

78. Millotat, *Das preussisch-deutsche Generalstabssystem*, 79–83.

79. This was the 2nd "German Department." This department mainly dealt with the deployment of the German Army.

80. Wilhelm Groener, *Lebenserinnerungen. Jugend—Generalstab—Weltkrieg*, ed. Friedrich Freiherr Hiller von Gaertringen (Göttingen, 1957), 72.

81. For the working routine in the General Staff, cf. Groener, *Lebenserinnerungen*, 70–74; Erich Ludendorff, *Mein militärischer Werdegang. Blätter der Erinnerung an unser stolzes Heer* (Munich, 1924), 73f., 93–95.

82. Mombauer, *Helmuth von Moltke*, 39f.; Ludendorff, *Mein militärischer Werdegang*, 74.

83. During Schlieffen's tenure 162 officers served in the General Staff.

84. Schlieffen, *Briefe,* 16.

85. Barry R. Posen, *The Sources of Military Doctrine: France, Britain, and Germany between the World Wars* (Ithaca, N.Y., 1984), 47–51.

86. Kriegsspiel 1905, BArch, N 323/10, Boetticher Posthumous Papers, 49.

87. Ibid., 48.

88. Jürgen Osterhammel, *Die Verwandlung der Welt. Eine Geschichte des 19. Jahrhunderts* (Munich, 2009), 694.

89. For the few consultations between general staff and admiralty staff, see Theobald von Schäfer, *Generalstab und Admiralstab. Das Zusammenwirken von Heer und Flotte im Weltkrieg* (Berlin, 1931); and Gerhard P. Gross, "German Plans to Occupy Denmark, 'Case J,' 1916–1918," in *The Danish Straits and German Naval Power, 1905 1918,* ed. Michael Epkenhans and Gerhard P. Gross (Potsdam, 2010), 155–166.

90. Friedrich von Boetticher, "Der Lehrmeister des neuzeitlichen Krieges," in *Von Scharnhorst zu Schlieffen 1806–1906. Hundert Jahre preussisch-deutscher Generalstab,* ed. Friedrich von Cochenhausen (Berlin, 1933), 257.

91. Gerhard Ritter melodramatically paraphrases Moltke's criticism as the last word in military matters. Ritter, *Der Schlieffenplan,* 20.

92. Gross, "There Was a Schlieffenplan," 144, 175.

93. Ritter, *Der Schlieffenplan,* 19–25.

94. Ibid., 36.

95. Dieckmann, *Der Schlieffenplan,* BArch, RH 61/347, f. 115; see also Ritter, *Der Schlieffenplan,* 39.

96. Gerhard P. Gross, "Im Schatten des Westens. Die deutsche Kriegführung an der Ostfront bis Ende 1915," in *Die vergessene Front. Der Osten 1914–15. Ereignis, Wirkung, Nachwirkung,* ed. Gerhard P. Gross (Paderborn, 2006), 50f.; Lothar Höbelt, "Schlieffen, Beck, Potiorek und das Ende der gemeinsamen deutsch-österreichisch-ungarischen Aufmarschpläne im Osten," *Militärgeschichtliche Mitteilungen* 2 (1984): 7–30; Martin Schmitz, "Verrat am Waffenbruder? Die Siedlice-Kontroverse im Spannungsfeld von Kriegsgeschichte und Geschichtspolitik," *Militärgeschichtliche Zeitschrift* 67, no. 2 (2008): 385–407.

97. Ritter, *Der Schlieffenplan,* 40.

98. Dieckmann, *Der Schlieffenplan,* BArch, RH 61/347, pages 156–159.

99. "Here as anywhere neither the frontal attack nor the envelopment, nor a bypass alone may result in a victory; it requires the combination of both" (Schlieffen remarks of 16 May 1902 cited in Dieckmann, *Der Schlieffenplan,* BArch, RH 61/347, f. 159).

100. Ritter, *Der Schlieffenplan,* 41.

101. Greiner, *Nachrichten,* BArch, RH 61/398, f. 95.

102. Übersicht über die Operationen der 1. Grossen Generalstabsreise 1904, Schlussbesprechung, BArch, N 323/8, Boetticher Posthumous Papers, 5–8.

103. See Aufmarsch 1906–07 in Ehlert, Epkenhans, and Gross, eds., *Der Schlieffenplan,* 413.

104. Holger H. Herwig, *The Marne, 1914: The Opening of World War I and the Battle that Changed the World* (New York, 2009), 37.

105. Dieckmann, *Der Schlieffenplan,* BArch, RH 61/347, f. 106

106. For more details on the history of this memorandum, see Gross, "There Was a Schlieffenplan," 120–130.

107. Wallach, *The Dogma of the Battle of Annihilation,* 92.

108. For more details on the differences between Schlieffen and Moltke the Younger, see Gross, "There Was a Schlieffenplan," 133f.

109. While the right wing consisted of 23 army corps, 12.5 reserve corps, and 8 cavalry divisions, a mere 3.5 army corps, 1.5 reserve corps, and 3 cavalry divisions were earmarked for the left wing.

110. "Schlieffen's Memorandum of 28 December 1912," Ritter, *Der Schlieffenplan,* 186.

111. Siegfried von Auwers, "Die Strategie des Schlieffenplanes. Eine Erwiderung," *Archiv für Politik und Geschichte* 10 (1928): 16–22, 508–516.

112. Ritter, *Der Schlieffenplan,* 157. An English translation is available at http://ghdi.ghi-dc.org/print_document.cfm?document_id=796.

113. Eric Dorn Brose, *The Kaiser's Army: The Politics of Military Technology in Germany During the Machine Age, 1870–1918* (Oxford, 2001), 69-III.

114. Gross, "Das Dogma der Beweglichkeit," 146f.

115. Hermann Giehrl, *Der Feldherr Napoleon als Organisator. Betrachtungen über seine Verkehrs- und Nachrichtenmittel, seine Arbeits- und Befehlsweise* (Berlin, 1911), 155.

116. Brose, *The Kaiser's Army,* 43-III.

117. At the end of the war in 1918, some two hundred thousand Allied trucks faced a mere forty thousand German trucks at the Western Front.

118. Ritter, *Der Schlieffenplan,* 158.

119. Creveld, *Supplying War,* 109–141.

120. Wilhelm von Blume, *Strategie, ihre Aufgaben und Mittel, zugl. 3., erw. u. umgearb. Aufl. Strategie. Eine Studie* (Berlin, 1912), 58.

121. Grossen Generalstab, *Heeresverpflegung* (Berlin, 1913), 290.

122. Strachan, "Die Ostfront," 19f.

123. The French "élan" found expression in War Plan XVII. The *Offensive à Outrance* was the focus of military thinking in France. "The moral forces are the most powerful pillars of success. Honor and patriotism instill the noblest devotion in the troops. Self-sacrifice and the will to win ensure victory" (cited in Hans Linnenkohl, *Vom Einzelschuss zur Feuerwalze. Der Wettlauf zwischen Technik und Taktik im Ersten Weltkrieg* [Koblenz, 1990], 40f.; and Storz, *Kriegsbild und Rüstung,* 79–84, 207–249).

124. Chef des Generalstabes der Armee, Kriegsspiel November/Dezember 1905, Schlussbesprechung, Berlin, 23 December 1905, BArch, PH 3/646, f. 34.

125. Schlieffen, *Briefe,* 10.

126. Kriegsspiel 1905, BArch, N 323/10, Boetticher Posthumous Papers, 21–23.

127. Chef des Generalstabes der Armee, Kriegsspiel November/Dezember 1905, Berlin, 23 December 1905, BArch, PH 3/646, f. 1–36. See also Gross, "There Was a Schlieffen Plan," 134f.

128. During the Great General Staff Ride West (Grosse Generalstabsreise West) of 1904, Schlieffen and his successor disagreed considerably on operational issues: "Graf Schlieffen occasionally asks for my opinion, and it almost never coincides with his. No greater

contrasts are imaginable than our mutual opinions" (Helmuth von Moltke, *Erinnerungen, Briefe, Dokumente 1877–1916. Ein Bild vom Kriegsausbruch, erster Kriegführung und Persönlichkeit des ersten militärischen Führers des Krieges*, ed. Eliza von Moltke [Stuttgart, 1922], 292). See also Ernst Buchfinck, "Der Meinungskampf um den Marnefeldzug," *Historische Zeitschrift* 152 (1935): 294. On the differences between Schlieffen and Moltke, see Gross, "There Was a Schlieffen Plan," 133f.

129. Schlieffen was deeply vexed about the disregard of his person (Gross, "There Was a Schlieffen Plan," 158f.).

130. For Moltke's operational and strategic plans in greater detail, see Mombauer, *Helmuth von Moltke and the Origins of the First World War*, and Mombauer, "Der Moltkeplan," 79–99.

131. Moltke, *Erinnerungen, Briefe, Dokumente*, 308; see also Förster, *Der deutsche Generalstab*, 61–95, and Mombauer, "Der Moltkeplan," 90.

132. For the French operations plans, see Robert A. Doughty, "France," in *War Planning 1914*, ed. Holger H. Herwig and Richard F. Hamilton (New York, 2010), 143–174. Stefan Schmidt, "Frankreichs Plan XVII. Zur Interdependenz von Aussenpolitik und militärischer Planung in den letzten Jahren vor dem Ausbruch des grossen Krieges," in *Der Schlieffenplan. Analysen und Dokumente*, ed. Hans Ehlert, Michael Epkenhans, and Gerhard P. Gross (Paderborn, 2007), 221–256.

133. Bucholz, *Moltke, Schlieffen and the Prussian War Planning*, 266.

134. Mombauer, "Der Moltkeplan," 89–91.

135. Ibid., 91f.

136. Groener, *Lebenserinnerungen*, 132f.

137. Dieter Storz, "'Dieser Stellungs- und Festungskrieg ist scheusslich!' Zu den Kämpfen in Lothringen und den Vogesen im Sommer 1914," in *Der Schlieffenplan. Analysen und Dokumente*, ed. Hans Ehlert, Michael Epkenhans, and Gerhard P. Gross (Paderborn, 2007), 161–204.

138. Wallach, *The Dogma of the Battle of Annihilation*, 133. It is astonishing to what extent Wallach's work shaped the historical debate on the Schlieffen Plan and operational thinking in the era of world wars even though his interpretations of key issues were incorrect.

139. Mombauer, "Der Moltkeplan," 79–99; Stig Förster, "Der Krieg der Willensmenschen. Die deutsche Offizierselite auf dem Weg in den Weltkrieg, 1871–1914," in *Willensmenschen. Über deutsche Offiziere*, ed. Ursula Breymayer, Bernd Ulrich, and Karin Wieland (Frankfurt a.M., 1999), 23–36.

140. Storz, "Dieser Stellungs- und Festungskrieg ist scheusslich!" 170.

141. Dieter Degreif, "Der Schlieffenplan und seine Nachwirkung" (Master's thesis, Johannes Gutenberg University, Mainz, 1973), 109.

142. The remarks of Moltke's aide-de-camp, Friedrich von Mantey, that there had been no differences between the operational thinking of Moltke the Younger and Schlieffen, primarily served to defend his former boss in view of the tribute paid to Schlieffen on the one hundredth anniversary of his birth in 1933. Friedrich von Mantey, "Graf Schlieffen und der jüngere Moltke," *Militär-Wochenblatt* 120 (1935–1936): 395–398. Mantey's efforts to gain access to the war plan files for a war-historical study were thwarted by Wolfgang Foerster. See Pöhlmann, *Kriegsgeschichte und Geschichtspolitik*, 319f.

143. Mombauer, *Helmuth von Moltke*, 287f.

144. Hermann Gackenholz, *Entscheidung in Lothringen 1914. Der Operationsplan des jüngeren Moltke und seine Durchführung auf dem linken deutschen Heeresflügel* (Berlin, 1933), 121.

145. Bernhardi even published an attack plan against France that was considerably consistent with the Schlieffen Plan, although he did not know of Schlieffen's memorandum. Even Clausewitz had proposed an operations plan against France in 1830–1831 that was based on an attack through Belgium.

146. One has to concur completely with Kutz, "Schlieffen contra Clausewitz," 12–48.

5. Bitter Awakening: World War I

The epigraph to this chapter is drawn from Clausewitz, *Vom Kriege*, 781.

1. Letter by Musketeer Gotthold Schneider from the Battle of Flanders, 31 October 1917, BArch, W 10/50684, page 9.

2. On the German advance, see Herwig, *The Marne, 1914*, 159–224.

3. After the war, this measure was criticized as a major deviation from the Schlieffen Plan. Yet the "Grosse Generalstabsreise West 1905: Case Freytag" shows that Schlieffen himself contemplated passing Paris to the east as a variation in his planning. The decision by Colonel General Alexander von Kluck, whose chief of staff, Major General Hermann von Kuhl, had played the "Case Kuhl" option against Schlieffen when he was a major in 1905, to lead the German First Army past Paris to the east in August 1914 was thus no sudden inspiration of the leadership on the spot, but was based on operational considerations developed by Schlieffen during the Generalstabsreise of 1905.

4. For French operation plans, see Doughty, "France," 143–174.

5. As noted by Colonel Gerhard Tappen, head of the Operations Department of OHL in a letter to his wife dated 7 September 1914. Cf. Herwig, *The Marne, 1914*, 245.

6. For details on the battle, see Herwig, *The Marne, 1914*, 225–306.

7. For a detailed distribution of the units of the Eighth Army, see Reichsarchiv, *Der Weltkrieg 1914–1918*, 2:358–365.

8. Thus it was only in 1909 that Moltke explained the German focus on the west to the chief of the Austro-Hungarian General Staff, General Franz Freiherr Conrad von Hötzendorff. The German plan merely held out the prospect of a relief attack on the Narew River in support of the planned Austrian offensive in Galicia, and only when the situation would allow. See Höbelt, "Schlieffen, Beck, Potiorek und das Ende," 7–30; Hans Meier-Welcker, "Strategische Planungen und Vereinbarungen der Mittelmächte für den Mehrfrontenkrieg," *Österreichische Militärische Zeitschrift*, Sonderheft 2 (1964): 15–22; Helmut Otto, "Zum strategisch-operativen Zusammenwirken des deutschen und österreichisch-ungarischen Generalstabes bei der Vorbereitung des ersten Weltkrieges," *Zeitschrift für Militärgeschichte* (1963): 423–440.

For the Austro-Hungarian operations plans, see Günther Kronenbitter, "Die militärischen Planungen der k.u.k. Armee und der Schlieffenplan," in *Der Schlieffenplan. Analysen und Dokumente*, ed. Hans Ehlert, Michael Epkenhans, and Gerhard P. Gross (Paderborn, 2007), 205–220.

9. As for their combat power, the German infantry divisions of thirteen thousand

men were considered to be slightly superior to the Russian divisions of seventeen thousand men, as the former were equipped with better weapons, particularly heavy artillery.

10. Secret memorandum of the German General Staff from the year 1913, "Mitteilungen über russische Taktik," in Walter Elze, *Tannenberg. Das deutsche Heer von 1914. Seine Grundzüge und deren Auswirkung im Sieg an der Ostfront* (Breslau, 1928), 168.

11. Cf. Schlieffen, *Die grossen Generalstabsreisen—Ost.*

12. "Aufmarschanweisung 1914/15 für Oberkommando der 8. Armee," in Elze, *Tannenberg,* 193.

13. Reichsarchiv, *Der Weltkrieg 1914–1918,* 2:45.

14. See "Aufmarschanweisung 1914/15 für Oberkommando der 8. Armee," in Elze, *Tannenberg,* 195.

15. Norman Stone, *The Eastern Front, 1914–1917* (London, 1975), 47–49.

16. On Russian planning, see Jan Kushber, "Die russischen Streitkräfte und der deutsche Aufmarsch beim Ausbruch des Ersten Weltkrieges," in *Der Schlieffenplan. Analysen und Dokumente,* ed. Hans Ehlert, Michael Epkenhans, and Gerhard P. Gross (Paderborn, 2007), 257–268; Bruce W. Menning, "War Planning and Initial Operations in the Russian Context," in *War Planning 1914,* ed. Holger H. Herwig and Richard F. Hamilton (New York, 2010), 80–142.

17. On the Russian plans, see Stone, *The Eastern Front,* 51–59.

18. For details on the course of the battle, see Dennis E. Showalter, *Tannenberg: Clash of Empires* (Hamden, Conn., 1991), 172–210; Reichsarchiv, *Der Weltkrieg 1914–1918,* 2:79–102.

19. In German postwar military publications, the replacement of Prittwitz was discussed at great length. An example of this discussion and the inherent criticism of Prittwitz can be found in Ernst Kabisch, *Streitfragen des Weltkrieges 1914–1918* (Stuttgart, 1924).

20. For details on the course of the battle, see Elze, *Tannenberg,* 116–148; Showalter, *Tannenberg,* 213–319; Hew Strachan, *The First World War,* vol. 1, *To Arms* (Oxford, U.K., 2001), 324–334; Wolfgang Venohr, *Ludendorff. Legende und Wirklichkeit* (Frankfurt a.M., 1993), 32–52.

21. Afflerbach points out that Ludendorff was generally held to be the intellectual successor of the Schlieffen tradition within the General Staff. Holger Afflerbach, *Falkenhayn. Politisches Denken und Handeln im Kaiserreich* (Munich, 1994), 212.

22. Lothar Höbelt, "'So wie wir haben nicht einmal die Japaner angegriffen.' Österreich-Ungarns Nordfront 1914–15," in *Die vergessene Front. Der Osten 1914–15. Ereignis, Wirkung, Nachwirkung,* ed. Gerhard P. Gross (Paderborn, 2006), 90–96.

23. Gross, "Im Schatten des Westens," 54–58.

24. Storz, "Dieser Stellungs- und Festungskrieg ist scheusslich!" 181.

25. Peter Graf von Kielmansegg, *Deutschland und der Erste Weltkrieg* (Stuttgart, 1980), 38.

26. On 23 August, the German forces still outnumbered the Allies, with 24.5 divisions against 17.5 Allied divisions on the right wing. Hew Strachan, *Der Erste Weltkrieg. Eine neue illustrierte Geschichte* (Munich, 2004), 82.

27. In the course of the German advance through Belgium, atrocities were committed by German forces against the Belgian civilian population. In order to suppress any resis-

tance to the German advance, Belgian citizens offering resistance were treated as irregulars, owing to the German Army's widespread fear of Franc-tireur forces. More than sixty-five hundred civilians fell victim to this action, which was in contravention of international law. See John Horne and Alan Kramer, *Deutsche Kriegsgreuel 1914. Die umstrittene Wahrheit* (Hamburg, 2004). These excesses, however, were no indication of an extermination campaign, but rather a result of the highly overwrought atmosphere during the first months of the war, and the excessive nervous tension of soldiers under terrible strain. At no further point in the war did similar events occur, on either the Western or the Eastern Front. See Sönke Neitzel, *Blut und Eisen. Deutschland im Ersten Weltkrieg* (Zürich, 2003), 55–56.

28. For more detailed information concerning these communication problems, see Herwig, *The Marne, 1914*, 245–247.

29. There was a profound personal conflict between the aristocrat Bülow and Kluck, a self-made man who had never been a member of the General Staff and had only been raised to the nobility at the age of fifty. This conflict emerged clearly during the campaign. See Barbara W. Tuchman, *The Guns of August* (New York, 1962), 274; Herwig, *The Marne, 1914*, 124.

30. Storz, "Dieser Stellungs- und Festungskrieg ist scheusslich!" 171.

31. Michael Salewski, "'Weserübung 1905?' Dänemark im strategischen Kalkül Deutschlands vor dem Ersten Weltkrieg," in *Politischer Wandel, organisierte Gewalt und nationale Sicherheit. Beiträge zur neueren Geschichte Deutschlands und Frankreichs. Festschrift für Klaus-Jürgen Müller*, ed. Ernst Willi Hansen, Gerhard Schreiber, and Bernd Wegner (Munich, 1995), 47–62.

32. The Imperial Navy entered the war without a clear definition of the rights and responsibilities of the various commands at the highest level. The single central command authority was the Kaiser, as the supreme commander. In the case of the navy—unlike the army—Wilhelm II insisted on directly exercising his command role. At the outbreak of the war, the peacetime organization of the navy established by Admiral Alfred von Tirpitz abruptly turned out to be ineffective in war. The Admiralty Staff, which he had relegated to near insignificance, was both personally and materially overtaxed by the conduct of naval warfare. Only in the summer of 1918 did the Kaiser relinquish his command authority with the establishment of a central naval warfare command. See Gerhard P. Gross, *Die Seekriegführung der Kaiserlichen Marine im Jahre 1918* (Frankfurt a.M., 1989), 347–428.

33. In addition to OHL, the Kaiser, the chancellor of the Reich, the state secretary of the foreign office, the Prussian war minister, the chief of the Admiralty Staff, the state secretary of the Imperial Naval Office, and the Kaiser's cabinet chiefs were all part of the *Grossen Hauptquartier* (Grand Headquarters). There were also the personal retinue of the Kaiser, the military representatives of the federal states, and the representatives of allied nations. However, the representatives of the political leadership elite of the Reich were only present in the Grand Headquarters during the first few months of the war.

34. Kaiser Wilhelm II as *Oberster Kriegsherr* (Supreme Commander).

35. *Kriegs-Rundschau. Zeitgenössische Zusammenstellung der für den Weltkrieg wichtigen Ereignisse, Urkunden, Kundgebungen, Schlachten- und Zeitberichte*, vol. 1 (Berlin, 1914–1915), 201.

36. During the first days of September, the Guards Reserve Corps, the XI Army Corps,

and the 8th Cavalry Division arrived in East Prussia. These units had been given their marching orders by Moltke on the night of 28/29 August 1914. See Reichsarchiv, *Der Weltkrieg 1914–1918*, 2:207.

37. Franz Uhle-Wettler, *Höhe- und Wendepunkte deutscher Militärgeschichte, überarb* (Hamburg, 2000), 201–253.

38. In contrast to the supposition which Tirpitz had elevated to the level of a dogma—that the Royal Navy would enforce a close blockade of the German coast in case of war and thus provide the High Seas Fleet with an opportunity for a decisive battle—the British fleet established an effective long-distance blockade without exposing itself to the risk of an engagement with the High Seas Fleet. This change in British strategy had been known in the navy since 1912–1913. Consequently, Tirpitz's strategic concept was the basis of faulty planning.

39. An exception was the capture of the Baltic islands in 1917. See Gerhard P. Gross, "Unternehmen 'Albion.' Eine Studie zur Zusammenarbeit von Armee und Marine während des Ersten Weltkrieges," in *Internationale Beziehungen im 19. und 20. Jahrhundert. Festschrift für Winfried Baumgart zum 65. Geburtstag,* ed. Wolfgang Elz and Sönke Neitzel (Paderborn, 2003), 171–186.

40. Falkenhayn was not alone in this belief. Colonel Max Hoffmann, chief of staff for the supreme commander in the east (Oberost), also doubted that Germany would be able to defeat Russia in a two-front war. "The Russian Army cannot be crushed completely; we would only be able to do so if we were at war only with Russia." See Max Hoffmann, *Die Aufzeichnungen des Generalmajors Max Hoffmann,* vol. 2, ed. Karl Friedrich Nowak (Berlin, 1929), 64.

41. For details of the battles, see Stone, *The Eastern Front,* 103–107; Reichsarchiv, *Der Weltkrieg 1914–1918*, 6:98–226; Venohr, *Ludendorff,* 86–107.

42. For details of the Winter Battle of the Masurian Lakes, see Reichsarchiv, *Der Weltkrieg 1914–1918*, 7:172–242.

43. Reichsarchiv, *Der Weltkrieg 1914–1918*, 6:254.

44. Concerning the military leadership crisis in the winter of 1914–1915, see Gross, "Im Schatten des Westens," 58f.; Afflerbach, *Falkenhayn,* 211–223.

45. Concerning the operations of the Austro-Hungarian Army in Galicia and the Carpathian mountains, see Höbelt, "So wie wir haben nicht einmal die Japaner angegriffen," 87–119.

46. See Stachelbeck, *Militärische Effektivität im Ersten Weltkrieg,* 63–96.

47. A brilliant analysis of the chances of success of both undertakings is to be found in Max von Gallwitz, *Meine Führertätigkeit im Weltkrieg 1914–1916. Belgien—Osten—Balkan* (Berlin, 1929), 373–378.

48. For details of the differences between the supreme commander in the east (Oberost) and Falkenhayn, see Afflerbach, *Falkenhayn,* 305–313; Volker Ullrich, "Entscheidung im Osten oder Sicherung der Dardanellen: das Ringen um den Serbienfeldzug 1915. Beitrag zum Verhältnis von Politik und Kriegführung im Ersten Weltkrieg," *Militärgeschichtliche Mitteilungen* 32, no. 2 (1982): 45–63.

49. Gallwitz evaluates the achievements of the Russian soldiers as follows: "Once again, the Russian soldier proved to be hardworking, undemanding, tough, and relatively unaf-

fected by pressure and casualties. Their tremendous casualties, losses to death and injury and through capture, never until the end managed to completely break the morale of the troops. In every new tract of terrain, we found them in defensive readiness. Their rates of march were impressive" (Gallwitz, *Meine Führertätigkeit,* 378).

50. Gallwitz explains that the motor pool of the 54th Infantry Division, which had been redeployed there from the west, was not up to the traffic and weather conditions in Russia; this led to delays in the advance. Ibid., 309.

51. Moltke, *Die deutschen Aufmarschpläne 1871–1890,* 80.

52. In a cabinet order dated 9 December 1916, Wilhelm II laid the foundations for this type of interpretation: "The Romanian campaign, which with the help of God has even now resulted in such a brilliant victory, will be regarded as a splendid example of inspired military strategy in the military history of future days" (Gundula Gahlen, "Deutung und Umdeutung des Rumänienfeldzuges in Deutschland zwischen 1916 und 1945," in *Der Erste Weltkrieg auf dem Balkan. Perspektiven der Forschung,* ed. Jürgen Angelow [Berlin, 2011], 293).

53. Gerhard P. Gross, "Ein Nebenkriegsschauplatz. Die deutschen Operationen gegen Rumänien 1916," in *Der Erste Weltkrieg auf dem Balkan. Perspektiven der Forschung,* ed. Jürgen Angelow (Berlin, 2011), 143–158.

54. Making use of the element of surprise, which was also central to German operational thinking, General Alexei Brusilov executed a frontal attack on a wide front instead of a narrow breakthrough. See Stone, *The Eastern Front,* 232–256.

55. Concerning the situation assessment by OHL in the weeks preceding the entry into the war, see Afflerbach, *Falkenhayn,* 446–448.

56. Ibid., 447.

57. Concerning the change in OHL, see ibid., 437–450.

58. Manfried Rauchensteiner, *Der Tod des Doppeladlers. Österreich-Ungarn und der Erste Weltkrieg* (Köln, 1993), 362–370.

59. It is one of the ironies of German military history that Falkenhayn, Hindenburg, and Ludendorff virtually changed roles during that summer. As was only to be expected, Falkenhayn—as Hindenburg and Ludendorff did earlier—rejected any interference from OHL.

60. Concerning the fighting in Romania, see Gross, "Ein Nebenkriegsschauplatz," 143–158; Reichsarchiv, *Der Weltkrieg 1914–1918,* 11:220–299. The latter also lists the organizational structure of the German units.

61. Friedrich Ratzel, *Politische Geographie oder die Geographie der Staaten, des Verkehrs und des Krieges* (Munich, 1903), 375; Strachan, "Die Ostfront," 18f.

62. In the case of the Ottoman Empire, this went to the point where Major General Hans von Seeckt became chief of the General Staff of the Ottoman Army and Falkenhayn became commander in chief in Palestine.

63. Günther Kronenbitter, "Von 'Schweinehunden' und 'Waffenbrüdern.' Der Koalitionskrieg der Mittelmächte 1914/15 zwischen Sachzwang und Ressentiment," in *Die vergessene Front. Der Osten 1914–15. Ereignis, Wirkung, Nachwirkung,* ed. Gerhard P. Gross (Paderborn, 2006), 121–143.

64. Strachan, "Die Ostfront," 23.

65. Peter Hoeres, "Die Slawen. Perzeptionen des Kriegsgegners bei den Mittelmächten. Selbst- und Feindbild," in *Die vergessene Front. Der Osten 1914–15. Ereignis, Wirkung, Nachwirkung,* ed. Gerhard P. Gross (Paderborn, 2006), 187.

66. Hans-Erich Volkmann, "Der Ostkrieg 1914/15 als Erlebnis- und Erfahrungswelt des deutschen Militärs," in *Die vergessene Front. Der Osten 1914–15. Ereignis, Wirkung, Nachwirkung,* ed. Gerhard P. Gross (Paderborn, 2006), 269.

67. The description which Lieutenant Tröbst, who was aide-de-camp in the 147th Infantry Regiment (Hindenburg) in July 1915, gave to Field Marshal von Hindenburg of the crossing of the Narew River by the regiment's 2nd Battalion on 23 July 1915 may serve as an example for the fierceness of the fighting: "Half an hour later, the companies began to leave their former positions and withdraw in small parties or singly, exhausted and worn-out, more like a flock with no will of its own than like human beings. . . . The first thing Kramme did was to order that our casualties should be listed. Altogether, the number of our dead, wounded, and missing amounted to three officers and 261 enlisted personnel. The plain truth was that more than half the battalion had gone down the drain" (Excerpts from the diary of Captain Hans Tröbst, courtesy of Mr. Cord Christian Tröbst).

68. Dieckmann, *Der Schlieffenplan,* BArch, RH 61/347, f. 106.

69. By then, the infantry no longer defended a line but a defense zone organized in depth. As required in mobile defense, the defenders yielded to the enemy thrust, particularly the preliminary artillery bombardment, and, echeloned in depth, contained the attack, only to break up the attacking forces with a hasty counterattack (*Gegenstoss*) or a deliberate counterattack (*Gegenangriff*), recapturing the lost terrain. Concerning the development of area defense, see Gross, "Das Dogma der Beweglichkeit," 148–150.

70. Konrad Krafft von Dellmensingen, *Der Durchbruch. Studie an Hand der Vorgänge des Weltkrieges 1914–1918* (Hamburg, 1937), 12.

71. "A massed thrust for the purpose of achieving a tactical breakthrough is impossible with the fire effect possible today" (Wenninger, "Über den Durchbruch als Entscheidungs-form," *Vierteljahreshefte für Truppenführung und Heereskunde* 10 [1913]: 639).

72. Alfred Graf von Schlieffen, *Über die Aussichten des taktischen und operativen Durchbruchs aufgrund kriegsgeschichtlicher Erfahrungen,* BArch, N 43/108, 30f.

73. Borgert, "Grundzüge der Landkriegführung," 490.

74. Ibid.

75. Krafft, *Der Durchbruch,* 405.

76. Burkhard Köster, "Ermattungs- oder Vernichtungsstrategie? Die Kriegführung der 2. und 3. Obersten Heeresleitung (OHL)," *Militärgeschichte. Zeitschrift für militärische Bildung* 2 (2008): 11.

77. Robert T. Foley, *German Strategy and the Path to Verdun: Erich von Falkenhayn and the Development of Attrition, 1870–1916* (Cambridge, Mass., 2005), 157f.

78. Ibid., 159f; Reichsarchiv, *Der Weltkrieg 1914–1918,* 7:318–322.

79. Afflerbach, *Falkenhayn,* 360; Erich von Falkenhayn, "Christmas Memorandum," *Die Oberste Heeresleitung 1914–1916 in ihren wichtigsten Entschliessungen* (Berlin, 1920), 180.

80. At the end of 1915, OHL had an operational reserve of 25.5 divisions at its disposal.

81. Afflerbach, *Falkenhayn,* 360–375; Foley, *German Strategy,* 181–236; Neitzel, *Blut*

und Eisen, 83–86. For details on the fighting, see German Werth, *Verdun: Die Schlacht und der Mythos* (Bergisch Gladbach, 1979). Stachelbeck, *Militärische Effektivität,* 97–126, describes the development of the attack procedure, using the 11th Bavarian Infantry Division as an example.

82. Stachelbeck, *Militärische Effektivität,* 61–195.

83. Erich Ludendorff, *Meine Kriegserinnerungen 1914–1918* (Berlin, 1919), 474.

84. Ibid., 472.

85. Kronprinz von Bayern Rupprecht, *Mein Kriegstagebuch,* 3 vols., ed. Eugen von Frauenholz (Berlin, 1929), 2:372.

86. Dieter Storz, "'Aber was hätte anderes geschehen sollen?' Die deutschen Offensiven an der Westfront 1918," in *Kriegsende 1918. Ereignis, Wirkung, Nachwirkung,* ed. Jörg Duppler and Gerhard P. Gross (Munich, 1999), 64.

87. Despite all training efforts, it was impossible to train all units to perfection in the new infiltration tactics. For that reason, many units still attacked in mass formation. Ibid., 66f., 76; Gross, "Das Dogma der Beweglichkeit," 151–153.

88. For details of the procedure developed by Major Pulkowski, see Linnenkohl, *Vom Einzelschuss zur Feuerwalze,* 277f.; see also Storz, "Aber was hätte anderes geschehen sollen?" 65f. Also see David T. Zabecki, *Steel Wind: Colonel Georg Bruchmüller and the Birth of Modern Artillery* (Westport, Conn., 1994), 49–50, 53, 70, 82, 99.

89. The preliminary artillery bombardment lasting for days, which had been used previously, always enabled the defender to prepare a defense and to bring up reserves.

90. Details on this can be found in the study presently being compiled by Dr. Markus Pöhlmann, *Geschichte der militärischen Mechanisierung von Landstreitkräften in Deutschland im Zeitalter der Weltkriege.* I am grateful to Dr. Pöhlmann for his information on the development of the German tank force.

91. The motorization rate of the German Army was considerably lower than that of its opponents. Its stock in horses, too, had decreased significantly in the war years. See Storz, "Aber was hätte anderes geschehen sollen?" 68f.

92. For details on the German 1918 offensives, see Martin Müller, *Vernichtungsgedanke und Koalitionskriegführung. Das deutsche Reich und Österreich-Ungarn in der Offensive 1917–1918* (Graz, 2003), 105–399. A more comprehensive treatment can be found in David T. Zabecki, *The German 1918 Offensives: A Case Study in the Operational Level of War* (London, 2006), 97–328.

93. Herman von Kuhl, *Der Weltkrieg 1914–1918. Dem deutschen Volke dargestellt,* 2 vols. (Berlin, 1929), 2:341; Venohr, *Ludendorff,* 295–299; Zabecki, *The German 1918 Offensives,* 160–164.

94. For details on the individual attacks, see Zabecki, *The German 1918 Offensives,* 97–328.

95. Cf. Gross, "Unternehmen 'Albion.'"

96. In the months of March and April, the German Army lost more than 310,000 men in casualties. In April, the troops had to cope with the highest loss rate per month since the beginning of the war. See Reichsarchiv, *Der Weltkrieg 1914–1918,* 14:300, 354, 516.

97. A similar picture can be seen in the Admiralty Staff of the Imperial Navy. However, in contrast to the General Staff, the Admiralty Staff intentionally had been reduced in peacetime by Tirpitz to the status of a poorly staffed planning organization.

98. Brose, *The Kaiser's Army,* 225, 240.

99. Groener, *Lebenserinnerungen,* 437.

100. Ibid., 449.

6. Old Wine in New Wineskins: Operational Thinking in the Reichswehr and the Wehrmacht between Reality and Utopia

1. Waldemar Erfurth, "Die Überraschung im Kriege," *Militärwissenschaftliche Rundschau* (1938): 342.

2. For the interpretation of the defeat, see Markus Pöhlmann, "Von Versailles nach Armageddon. Totalisierungserfahrung und Kriegserwartung in deutschen Militärzeitschriften," in *An der Schwelle zum Totalen Krieg. Die militärische Debatte über den Krieg der Zukunft 1919–1939,* ed. Stig Förster (Paderborn, 2002), 335.

3. Erwin Hermann, "Die Friedensarmeen der Sieger und der Besiegten des Weltkrieges," *Wissen und Wehr* 3 (1922): 269.

4. Hugo von Freytag-Loringhoven, "Irreführende Verallgemeinerungen," *Militär-Wochenblatt* 12 (1919): 219.

5. Lange, *Hans Delbrück und der "Strategiestreit,"* 125–130.

6. Apart from the Reichsarchiv, examples from the many writings and articles of the "Schlieffen disciples" include Wilhelm Groener's works *Das Testament des Grafen Schlieffen* and *Der Feldherr wider Willen,* as well as Friedrich von Boetticher's *Der Lehrmeister des neuzeitlichen Krieges.*

7. See Wallach (*The Dogma of the Battle of Annihilation,* 305–334) for more details on the work of the Schlieffen School in the 1920s and 1930s. Page 330 includes a selection of the most important writings of the Schlieffen School from the period between the two world wars. In his writings Wallach, however, only focused one-sidedly on the Schlieffen School and did not give any space to Schlieffen's critics during those years. Pöhlmann, in contrast to Wallach, convincingly sets new standards in *Kriegsgeschichte und Geschichtspolitik,* 284–321. Unlike Wallach, he also quotes Schlieffen's critics and discusses a partial revision of the Schlieffen School.

8. Within the Reichsarchiv, it was particularly the action officer for the German deployment planning until 1914, Lieutenant Colonel (Ret.) Wolfgang Foerster, a disciple of Schlieffen, who continued along the same path as his former superior. Thanks to his immediate access to the records in the 1920s and 1930s, Foerster became the greatest expert on Schlieffen's and Moltke's deployment and operations plans. His most important publications on this subject area are *Graf Schlieffen und der Weltkrieg* (Berlin, 1921) and *Aus der Gedankenwerkstatt des deutschen Generalstabes* (Berlin, 1931). At the same time, Foerster used his leading position as a director to restrict further research. See Pöhlmann, *Kriegsgeschichte und Geschichtspolitik,* 317.

9. Wetzell kept defending Moltke's decisions and openly criticized the Reichsarchiv's statement on the first weeks of the war at the Western Front. See Georg Wetzell, "Das Kriegswerk des Reichsarchivs: 'Der Weltkrieg 1914/1918.' Kritische Betrachtungen zum I. Band: Die Grenzschlachten im Westen," *Wissen und Wehr* 6 (1925): 1–43. Concerning this debate and the partial revision of the Schlieffen School, see Pöhlmann, *Kriegsgeschichte und Geschichtspolitik,* 284–321.

10. In order to support this position, the Research Institute even had Falkenhayn psychologically examined post mortem by means of a graphological and stylistic analysis and with the aid of photographs. As was to be expected, the psychologists attested that Falkenhayn had suffered from a "failure of volition," and had therefore been incapable as the chief of the Second OHL. See Pöhlmann, *Kriegsgeschichte und Geschichtspolitik,* 180, 256.

11. Wilhelm Marx, "Das 'Cannä-Oratorium,'" *Militär-Wochenblatt* 8 (1932): 246.

12. Lecture delivered on 5 May 1935 at the Wehrmacht Academy: "Unsere hauptsächlichen militärpolitischen, strategischen kriegswirtschaftlichen und psychologischen Fehler in der Vorbereitung des Weltkrieges selbst. Welche allgemeine Erkenntnisse ergeben sich daraus für die Kriegführung?" BArch RW 13/4, f. 51 f., 56.

13. It was not possible, however, to stifle the debate entirely. Delbrück, for example, repeatedly made the operational dogmatism of the General Staff a topic of discussion.

14. Wolfram Wette, *Militarismus in Deutschland. Geschichte einer kriegerischen Kultur* (Darmstadt, 2008), 150.

15. The Treaty of Versailles also laid down the force structure of the Reichsheer. Altogether, Germany was allowed to establish seven infantry and three cavalry divisions.

16. See James S. Corum, *The Roots of Blitzkrieg: Hans von Seeckt and German Military Reform* (Lawrence, Kans., 1992); Wilhelm Deist, "Die Reichswehr und der Krieg der Zukunft," *Militärgeschichtliche Mitteilungen* 45 (1989): 82–85.

17. Deist, "Die Reichswehr," 82–85.

18. See Stig Förster, ed., *An der Schwelle zum Totalen Krieg. Die militärische Debatte über den Krieg der Zukunft 1919–1939,* Krieg in der Geschichte 13 (Paderborn, 2002).

19. Cf. George Soldan, *Der Mensch und die Schlacht der Zukunft* (Oldenburg, 1925); Ernst Buchfinck, *Der Krieg von gestern und morgen* (Langensalza, 1930).

20. Cf. Max Schwarte, *Die militärischen Lehren des grossen Krieges* (Berlin, 1920).

21. See Friedrich von Rabenau, *Operative Entschlüsse gegen eine Zahl überlegener Gegner* (Berlin, 1935); Foertsch, *Kriegskunst.* For a summary of the journalistic debate, see Karl-Volker Neugebauer, "Operatives Denken zwischen dem Ersten und Zweiten Weltkrieg," in *Operatives Denken und Handeln in deutschen Streitkräften im 19. und 20. Jahrhundert,* ed. Horst Boog (Herford, 1988), 100; also Michael Geyer, *Aufrüstung oder Sicherheit. Die Reichswehr in der Krise der Machtpolitik 1924–1936* (Wiesbaden, 1980), 464–466.

22. William Mulligan, *The Creation of the Modern German Army: General Walther Reinhardt and the Weimar Republic, 1914–1930* (New York, 2005), 218f. In his writing, the author speaks of tactics, but what he refers to is operational warfare. See also Corum, *The Roots of Blitzkrieg,* 55–57.

23. Herbert Rosinski, *The German Army* (New York, 1966), 212.

24. Matthias Strohn, *The German Army and the Defence of the Reich: Military Doctrine and the Conduct of the Defensive Battle, 1918–1939* (Cambridge, U.K., 2011), 102.

25. Ibid., 106.

26. See Manfred Zeidler, *Reichswehr und Rote Armee 1920 bis 1933. Wege und Stationen einer ungewöhnlichen Zusammenarbeit* (Munich, 1993), 29–155.

27. "The larger mass had finally crushed the smaller; but it had taken time and for the winner it cost a pernicious consumption of forces. It was an attritional victory, not an annihilation one. The quality of the armies had not kept pace with their growth. The

mass restricted mobility. The difficulty of commanding them through a single will grew to monstrous proportions. Thus began the requirement for quick and decisive recovery from errors" (Hans von Seeckt, *Die Reichswehr* [Leipzig, 1933], 35).

28. Goltz, *Das Volk in Waffen,* 4; Falkenhausen, *Der grosse Krieg,* 7.

29. Hans von Seeckt, *Landesverteidigung* (Berlin, 1930), 65.

30. Ibid., 69.

31. Hans von Seeckt, "Generaloberst v. Seeckt über Heer und Krieg der Zukunft," *Militär-Wochenblatt* 113 (1928): 1459.

32. Strohn, *The German Army and the Defence of the Reich,* 102.

33. Hans Meier-Welcker, *Seeckt* (Frankfurt a.M., 1967), 533.

34. For details on the development, structure, and content of the regulation, see Wilhelm Velten, *Das deutsche Reichsheer und die Grundlagen seiner Truppenführung: Entwicklung, Hauptprobleme und Aspekte. Untersuchungen zur deutschen Militärgeschichte der Zwischenkriegszeit* (Bergkamen, 1994), 53–269.

35. "The spirit that animates the F.u.G. is the ruthless will to attack. Despite all materiel considerations, we owe all of our greatest and most significant victories to this will" (Ernst Jünger, "Die Ausbildungsvorschrift der Infanterie," *Militär-Wochenblatt* 108 [1923]: 53).

36. Seeckt explained: "As chief of the General Staff of II Army Corps I had the sense of the absolute superiority of all our military undertakings against the French during the August and September struggles. That principle is what I now see as the main task of our present education and training" (quoted in Meier-Welcker, *Seeckt,* 529).

37. Karl-Volker Neugebauer, introduction to H.Dv. 487 *Führung und Gefecht der verbundenen Waffen (F.u.G.).* (Berlin, 1921–1924; reprint, Osnabrück, 1994), ix.

38. Gross, "Das Dogma der Beweglichkeit," 154.

39. For more details on Seeckt's ideas, see Robert M. Citino, *The Path to Blitzkrieg: Doctrine and Training in the German Army, 1920–1939* (Boulder, Colo., 1999); Neugebauer, "Operatives Denken," 97–122; Wallach, *The Dogma of the Battle of Annihilation,* 335–351; Corum, *The Roots of Blitzkrieg.*

40. *Heeresdienstvorschrift 487 Command and Control of the Combined Arms in Combat (F.u.G.)* (1921), page 10, paragraph 12.

41. See Citino, *The Path to Blitzkrieg,* 8–72; Corum, *The Roots of Blitzkrieg,* 30–50.

42. Hans von Seeckt, *Gedanken eines Soldaten* (Berlin, 1929), 93–95.

43. Seeckt in a letter to Lieutenant General von Watter in 1926, cited in Meier-Welcker, *Seeckt,* 529.

44. Seeckt, *Gedanken eines Soldaten,* 122. Nevertheless, Seeckt did not ignore the progressive motorization and he repeatedly pointed out its significance for a rapid and mobile conduct of operations. See Hans von Seeckt, *Bemerkungen des Chefs der Heeresleitung, Generaloberst von Seeckt, bei Besichtigungen und Manövern aus den Jahren 1920 bis 1926* (Reichswehr Ministry, Berlin, 1927), 38–41.

45. Seeckt, *Gedanken eines Soldaten,* 150.

46. For more details on this debate, see Pöhlmann, "Von Versailles nach Armageddon," 361.

47. On the discussion in military publications, see Pöhlmann, "Von Versailles nach Armageddon," 358–366.

48. Hew Strachan, *European Armies and the Conduct of War* (London, 1983); Winfried Heinemann, "The Development of German Armoured Forces, 1918–1940," in *Armoured Warfare,* ed. J. P. Harris and F. H. Tiase (London, 1990), 51–69.

49. *Leitlinien für die obere Führung im Kriege,* Colonel Hierl, 1923, BArch, RH 2/2901, f. 2–117.

50. Ibid., 18.

51. Ibid., 96.

52. Ibid., f. 57.

53. Ibid., f. 66.

54. Pöhlmann, "Von Versailles nach Armageddon," 359.

55. Concerning this topic, the most important contributions are Jochim, "Hinhaltendes Gefecht," *Wissen und Wehr* 5 (1924): 106–114; Karl Linnebach, "Der Durchbruch. Eine kriegsgeschichtliche Untersuchung (1. Teil)," *Wissen und Wehr* 11 (1930): 448–471; Krafft, *Der Durchbruch.*

56. Chief of the Truppenamt to Section T-1 on 30 August 1924, BArch RH 2/2901, f. 127. For the time being, the project was put on ice, but it was revived later.

57. Meier-Welker, *Seeckt,* 636.

58. Deist, "Die Reichswehr," 85.

59. Wallach, *Kriegstheorien,* 176.

60. Anon., "Der Mensch und die Schlacht der Zukunft," *Militärwochenblatt* 30 (1926): 1067.

61. For details on Stülpnagel's theses, see Geyer, *Aufrüstung oder Sicherheit,* 84–97; Michael Geyer, "German Strategy in the Age of Machine Warfare, 1914–1945," in *Makers of Modern Strategy from Machiavelli to the Nuclear Age,* ed. Peter Paret (Princeton, N.J., 1986), 557–560; Gil-li Vardi, "Joachim von Stülpnagel's Military Thought and Planning," *War and History* 2 (2010): 193–216.

62. Lieutenant Colonel Joachim von Stülpnagel, "Gedanken über den Krieg der Zukunft," February 1924, BArch, N 5/10, Nachlass Stülpnagel, 38.

63. Chief of the Army Department to the Truppenamt, No. 270/24, T-1 Branch, secret, Berlin, 18 March 1924, BArch, N 5/20, Nachlass Stülpnagel, f. 27.

64. The Truppenamt expected a loss rate of approximately 75 percent of these troops deployed in the border regions. Geyer, *Aufrüstung oder Sicherheit,* 87.

65. Deist, "Die Reichswehr," 86.

66. Lieutenant Colonel Joachim von Stülpnagel, "Gedanken über den Krieg der Zukunft" (Thoughts on the War of the Future), February 1924, BArch, N 5/10, Nachlass Stülpnagel, f. 23.

67. Deist, "Die Reichswehr," 86.

68. Chief of the Army Department to the Truppenamt, No. 270/24, T-1 Branch, secret, Berlin, 18 March 1924, BArch, N 5/20, Nachlass Stülpnagel, f. 27.

69. Lieutenant Colonel Joachim von Stülpnagel, "Gedanken über den Krieg der Zukunft," February 1924, BArch, N 5/10, Nachlass Stülpnagel, f. 37.

70. Geyer, *Aufrüstung oder Sicherheit,* 87.

71. Vardi, "Joachim von Stülpnagel's Military Thought," 202.

72. Geyer, *Aufrüstung oder Sicherheit,* 86.

73. Stülpnagel to T-2, 10 March 1924, BArch RH 2/2901, f. 130.

74. The regulation project for the higher commands was temporarily stopped and put on hold because of Stülpnagel's criticism, but also because T-2, for reasons of confidentiality, did not want to lay down the German operational plans for a future war in a regulation. Also, the thinking was that operational training was assured by the Commander and General Staff rides. T-2 to the head of the Truppenamt, 2 July 1924, ibid., f. 125f.

75. Vardi, "Joachim von Stülpnagel's Military Thought," 193–216.

76. See Geyer, *Aufrüstung oder Sicherheit,* 92.

77. Schlussbesprechung Truppenamtsreise 1930, BArch, RH 2/363, f. 817.

78. Map exercises, sand table exercises, staff exercises, staff rides, battlefield tours, command post exercises, and special exercises.

79. For details on the evolution of the Kriegsspiel, see General (Ret.) Rudolf Hofmann's paper "Kriegsspiele," BArch, ZA 1/2014. A graphic definition of Kriegsspiel is included in the final discussion of the navy's Kriegsspiel A of 1938. "A Kriegsspiel is fictitious war history experienced on the intellectual level. It does not try to unveil the future by indicating a result—the next war is going to proceed exactly like this—but, based on a set task and by highlighting the problems we can perceive today, it will give future leaders the intellectual, volitional, and conceptual bases for decisions that are only made at the moment of the act" (Final Discussion of Kriegsspiel A of 1938, BArch, RM 20/1100, f. 6f).

80. Conclusions from the Truppenamt studies of the winters of 1927–1928 and 1928–1929, 26 March 1929, BArch, RH 2/384, f. 2.22.

81. For the discussions on the Territorial Reserve organization, see Jun Nakata, *Der Grenz- und Landesschutz in der Weimarer Republik 1918 bis 1933. Die geheime Aufrüstung und die deutsche Gesellschaft* (Freiburg i.Br., 2002), 128–142, 187–342.

82. Conclusions from the Truppenamt studies of the winters of 1927–1928 and 1928–1929, 26 March 1929, BArch, RH 2/384, f. 18.

83. See Geyer, *Aufrüstung oder Sicherheit,* 189f.

84. Conclusions from the Truppenamt studies of the winters of 1927–1928 and 1928–1929, 26 March 1929, BArch, RH 2/384, f. 5.

85. For the results of Locarno, see Zeidler, *Reichswehr und Rote Armee,* 129–134.

86. Johannes Hürter, *Wilhelm Groener. Reichswehrminister am Ende der Weimarer Republik (1928 bis 1932)* (Munich, 1993), 23.

87. Geyer, *Aufrüstung oder Sicherheit,* 207–213.

88. Hürter, *Wilhelm Groener,* 97f.

89. For the cooperation between the navy and the army, see Geyer, *Aufrüstung oder Sicherheit,* 194–198; Hürter, *Wilhelm Groener,* 108–110.

90. Draft letter by Groener to Brüning, 13 April 1932, BArch, RH 15/19, f. 39.

91. Blomberg was replaced by Colonel General Kurt Freiherr von Hammerstein-Equord. For details on changes of personnel, see Hürter, *Wilhelm Groener,* 89.

92. Geyer, *Aufrüstung oder Sicherheit,* 193.

93. Final discussion of the Truppenamt staff ride of 1930, BArch, RH 2/363, f. 817 (original emphasis).

94. Karl-Volker Neugebauer analyzed the Kriegsspiele of 1930 in detail in his essay "Operatives Denken zwischen dem Ersten und Zweiten Weltkrieg," in *Operatives Denken*

und Handeln in deutschen Streitkräften im 19. und 20. Jahrhundert, ed. Horst Boog (Herford, 1988), 97–122.

95. Final discussion of the leaders' ride of 1933, BArch, RH 2/360, f. 131.

96. For the history and significance of command and control up through the Bundeswehr, see Werner von Scheven, *Die Truppenführung. Zur Geschichte ihrer Vorschrift und zur Entwicklung ihrer Struktur von 1933 bis 1962. Eine Untersuchung der taktischen Führungsvorschriften des deutschen Heeres von der HDv 300 (1933/34) bis zur HDv 100/1(1962),* Ms Archiv der Lehrgangsarbeiten der Führungsakademie der Bundeswehr, Nr. JA 0388 (Hamburg, 1969).

97. Borgert, "Grundzüge der Landkriegführung," 558.

98. H.Dv. 300 *Truppenführung,* part 1, page 133, para. 340 (1933). See also David T. Zabecki and Bruce Condell, trans. and eds., *On the German Art of War: Truppenführung* (Boulder, Colo., 2001), 96.

99. Borgert, "Grundzüge der Landkriegführung," 562.

100. H.Dv. 300 *Truppenführung,* part 1, page 1 (1933). See also Zabecki and Condell, *Truppenführung,* 17.

101. Kutz, *Realitätsflucht und Aggression,* 42.

102. Statement on the principles of high-level military leadership by Mantey, 12 August 1930, BArch, RH 2/2901, f. 132–147.

103. Chief T-1 to Chief T-4, 21 January 1931. BArch, RH 2/2901, f. 306.

104. Martin L. Van Creveld, *Kampfkraft. Militärische Organisation und militärische Leistung 1939 bis 1945* (Freiburg i.Br., 1982), 34.

105. As stated from the Marxist point of view by Gerhard Förster, *Totaler Krieg und Blitzkrieg: Die Theorie des totalen Krieges und des Blitzkrieges in der Militärdoktrin des faschistischen Deutschlands am Vorabend des Zweiten Weltkrieges* (Berlin [Ost], 1967); Paul Heider, "Der totale Krieg—seine Vorbereitung durch Reichswehr und Wehrmacht," in *Der Weg der deutschen Eliten in den zweiten Weltkrieg,* ed. Ludwig Nestler (Berlin, 1990), 35–80; Uwe Bitzel, *Die Konzeption des Blitzkrieges bei der deutschen Wehrmacht* (Frankfurt a.M., 1991), 217–235; Wehler, "Der Verfall der deutschen Kriegstheorie."

106. Wallach, *The Dogma of the Battle of Annihilation,* 352. Modern research also questions the theory, which was accepted for a long time, that there was a historical development from Ludendorff's book to Goebbels's *Sportpalast* speech of 1943. Roger Chickering, "The Sore Loser: Ludendorff's Total War," in *The Shadows of Total War: Europe, East Asia, and the United States, 1919–1939,* ed. Roger Chickering and Stig Förster (Cambridge, Mass., 2003), 151–178.

107. Karl Linnebach, "Zum Meinungsstreit über den Vernichtungsgedanken in der Kriegführung," *Wissen und Wehr* 15 (1934): 743.

108. Pöhlmann, "Von Versailles nach Armageddon," 349.

109. On the etymology of total war, see ibid., 346.

110. Truppenamt, T-2, "Aufbau des künftigen Friedensheeres," 14 December 1933, reproduced in Klaus-Jürgen Müller, *General Ludwig Beck. Studien und Dokumente zur politisch-militärischen Vorstellungswelt und Tätigkeit des Generalstabschefs des deutschen Heeres 1933–1938* (Boppard, 1980), doc. 9.

111. Müller, *Generaloberst Ludwig Beck,* 187.

112. As a result of Germany's equality, which became apparent as a consequence of the Geneva disarmament negotiations, the minister of the Reichswehr, Kurt Schleicher, had planned, in 1932, to increase the Reichsheer to 147,000 troops and establish a wartime army of twenty-one divisions.

113. Truppenamt, T-2, "Aufbau des künftigen Friedensheeres," 14 December 1933, reproduced in Müller, *General Ludwig Beck. Studien und Dokumente,* doc. 9.

114. Beck's memorandum was also a clear challenge to the SA and their efforts to transform the army politically and militarily under their leadership. Cf. Müller, *Generaloberst Ludwig Beck,* 188; Geyer, *Aufrüstung oder Sicherheit,* 350–354.

115. The analogy with Tirpitz's fleet buildup and the "Risk Theory" linked to it is quite clear. Cf. Müller, *Generaloberst Ludwig Beck,* 615, anno. 18. A comparative study on this most complex of questions is still pending.

116. Geyer, *Aufrüstung oder Sicherheit,* 355–358.

117. Ibid., 403.

118. Beck in his memorandum on the improvement of the army's offensive power of 30 December 1935, printed in Müller, *General Ludwig Beck. Studien und Dokumente,* doc. 37.

119. The General Staff believed that their ideas were corroborated by the Wehrmachtskriegsspiel of 1934. Based on an analysis of the Wehrmacht's supply situation, the Army Weapons Office concluded that the German industrial areas along the Rhine should be protected at the very least. If such were not possible, then it would be necessary either to secure a favorable situation through foreign policy, with the possibility of importing raw materials, or a military decision would have to be brought about within four months. Cf. Wehrmachtskriegsspiel of 1934, presentation by the director of the Defense and Armaments Commission, BArch, RH 2/385, f. 102.

120. For a synopsis on the cooperation between the Luftwaffe and the army, see Bitzel, *Die Konzeption des Blitzkrieges bei der deutschen Wehrmacht,* 239–265.

121. Horst Boog, *Die deutsche Luftwaffenführung 1935–1945. Führungsprobleme, Spitzengliederung, Generalstabsausbildung* (Stuttgart, 1982), 152–156.

122. Bitzel, *Die Konzeption des Blitzkrieges bei der deutschen Wehrmacht,* 292–296.

123. Erfurth, *Der Vernichtungssieg.*

124. M. Ludwig, "Gedanken über den Angriff im Bewegungskrieg," *Militärwissenschaftliche Rundschau* (1936): 156f.

125. F. Lindemann, "Feuer und Bewegung im Landkrieg der Gegenwart," *Militärwissenschaftliche Rundschau* (1937): 363.

126. Herhudt von Rhoden, "Betrachtungen über den Luftkrieg," *Militärwissenschaftliche Rundschau* (1937): 200.

127. Lieutenant Colonel Matzky, "Critical Analysis of the Teachings of Douhet, Fuller, Hart, and Seeckt," Wehrmacht Academy, 29 November 1935. Matzky tears von Seeckt's operational ideas on a small, elite army into pieces, favoring the establishment of a mass military force, BArch, RW 13/20, f. 57.

128. Ibid., f. 25.

129. Colonel Karl-Heinrich von Stülpnagel, "The Future War in the View of Foreign Countries," 15 January 1934, BArch, RH 1/78, f. 3–35.

130. Ibid., 5f.

131. A short synopsis of this study can be found in Neugebauer, "Operatives Denken," 104f.

132. Stülpnagel, "The Future War in the View of Foreign Countries," BArch, RH 1/78, 59f.

133. Lieutenant Colonel Willi Schneckenburger, Lecture on "Control and the Operational and Tactical Use of Rapidly Mobile Formations and How Must We Organize Them," February 1936, BArch, RW 13/21, f. 1–47.

134. Ibid., 25.

135. Friedrich von Bernhardi, *Vom Kriege der Zukunft. Nach den Erfahrungen des Weltkrieges* (Berlin, 1920), 224.

136. For the discussion in German military journals, see Pöhlmann, "Von Versailles nach Armageddon," 358–366.

137. Heinz Guderian, "Bewegliche Truppenkörper (Eine kriegsgeschichtliche Studie, Part 5)," *Militär-Wochenblatt* 22 (1927): 822.

138. Bernhard R. Kroener, *"Der starke Mann im Heimatkriegsgebiet"—Generaloberst Friedrich Fromm. Eine Biographie* (Paderborn, 2005), 246–248.

139. Ibid., 836, n. 102.

140. George Soldan, "Irrwege um die Panzerabwehr, Part 3," *Deutsche Wehr* 40 (1936): 323.

141. For information on the development of this concept, see Heinz Guderian, *Achtung—Panzer! Die Entwicklung der Panzerwaffe, ihre Kampftaktik und ihre operativen Möglichkeiten* (Stuttgart, 1937); Heinz Guderian, "Schnelle Truppen einst und jetzt," *Militärwissenschaftliche Rundschau* (1939): 229–243; Bitzel, *Die Konzeption des Blitzkrieges bei der deutschen Wehrmacht*, 266–287; Citino, *Blitzkrieg to Desert Storm*, 105–249; Heinemann, "The Development of German Armoured Forces," 51–56; Richard L. DiNardo, *Germany's Panzer Arm* (Westport, Conn., 1997); Richard L. DiNardo, "German Armor Doctrine: Correcting the Myths," *War in History* 4 (1996): 384–397; and Hubertus Senff, *Die Entwicklung der Panzerwaffe im deutschen Heer zwischen den beiden Weltkriegen* (Frankfurt a.M., 1969).

142. On the tactics of Stormtroops and battle groups, see Gross, "Das Dogma der Beweglichkeit," 150–152.

143. Karl-Heinz Frieser, *The Blitzkrieg Legend: The 1940 Campaign in the West* (Annapolis, Md., 2005), 8–10.

144. For assault tactics, see Guderian, *Achtung—Panzer!* 174–181; Guderian, "Schnelle Truppen einst und jetzt," 229–243; Peter Graf von Kielmansegg, "Feuer und Bewegung. Der Durchbruch einer Panzerdivision," *Die Wehrmacht* 22 (1938): 11–14.

145. Quoted from Bitzel, *Die Konzeption des Blitzkrieges bei der deutschen Wehrmacht*, 277.

146. German officers—among them Guderian—were, without any doubt, inspired by works of Fuller and de Gaulle. The often cited argument that the German armored doctrine was based on Liddell Hart's ideas is no longer tenable. See Corum, *The Roots of Blitzkrieg*, 141–143; DiNardo, "German Armor Doctrine," 385f.; and Naveh, *In Pursuit of Military Excellence*, 108–115, which show in detail how Guderian and Liddell Hart created this legend after World War II.

147. See Corum, *The Roots of Blitzkrieg*, 136–143; and DiNardo, "German Armor Doctrine," 391.

148. Senff explained that Guderian had more or less been the first officer in history to demonstrate the use of armored formations operationally. Senff, *Die Entwicklung der Panzerwaffe,* 26.

149. Quoted in Wolfgang Sagmeister, "General der Artillerie Ing. Ludwig Ritter von Eimannsberger. Theoretiker und Visionär der Verwendung von gepanzerten Grossverbänden im Kampf der verbundnen Waffen" (Unpublished doctoral diss., Vienna, 2006), 277.

150. Rolf Barthel, "Theorie und Praxis der Heeresmotorisierung im faschistischen Deutschland bis 1939" (Doctoral diss., University of Leipzig, 1967), 300–311.

151. Corum, *The Roots of Blitzkrieg,* 138.

152. Ibid., 140.

153. Müller, *Generaloberst Ludwig Beck,* 217–219.

154. Ibid., 217.

155. "Reflections on the Use of the Armored Corps During the Truppenamt Staff Ride of 13 June 1925," Chief of the General Staff, Berlin, 25 July 1935, printed in Müller, *General Ludwig Beck. Studien und Dokumente,* doc. 35, page 465.

156. "Erhöhung der Angriffskraft des Heeres," Berlin, 30 January 1936, printed in ibid., doc. 39.

157. Heinemann, "The Development of German Armoured Forces," 53–56.

158. Müller, *Generaloberst Ludwig Beck,* 227.

159. Helmut Schnitter, *Militärwesen und Militärpublizistik. Die militärische Zeitschriftenpublizistik in der Geschichte des bürgerlichen Militärwesens in Deutschland.* (Berlin [Ost], 1967), 148; Bitzel, *Die Konzeption des Blitzkrieges bei der deutschen Wehrmacht,* 282.

160. Wilhelm Ritter von Leeb, *Die Abwehr* (Berlin, 1938).

161. "For as we cannot rely on superiority in terms of numbers and means of war in a potential future war, the defense must contribute to the support and preparation of the attack, which alone can bring about a decision" (Leeb, *Die Abwehr,* 109).

162. Ibid.

163. Schlieffen, *Cannae,* v.

164. Wehrmachtskriegsspiel 1934, BArch, RH 2/385 f., 1–142.

165. Chief T-3, Colonel Carl-Heinrich von Stülpnagel, commented on this subject in a memo about the present political-military situation: "In a future war, the factor of the surprising opening of the war will play a special role" (Müller, *Generaloberst Beck. Studien und Dokumente,* doc. 27).

166. Geyer, *Aufrüstung oder Sicherheit,* 417f.

167. Geyer, "German Strategy," 569.

168. Müller, *Generaloberst Ludwig Beck,* 236. See also Truppenamtsreise 1935, BArch, RH 2/374, f., 1–170.

169. Documents on this Kriegsspiel can be found in BArch, RW 19/1243, f. 1–105.

170. In January 1938 these included three armored divisions, three motorized divisions, two armored brigades, two light brigades, and several independent tank regiments.

171. For plans for the attack on Czechoslovakia, see Müller, *General Ludwig Beck. Studien und Dokumente,* 272–311.

172. Ibid., 300–302. Beck, who formally and unsuccessfully objected to these ideas, resigned on 18 August 1938.

173. Winter training of the General Staff officers, Army General Staff, Berlin, 9 November 1938, BArch, RH 2/2819, f. 2–5.

174. Korpsgeneralstabsreise 1938, Münster, 18 May 1938, BArch, ZA 1/2779, 39.

175. Ibid., 52.

176. Bitzel, *Die Konzeption des Blitzkrieges bei der deutschen Wehrmacht,* 310.

177. Wehrmachtskriegsspiel 1934, BArch, RH 2/385, f. 59.

178. For the organization of the General Staff, see Burkhart Müller-Hillebrand, *Das Heer 1933–1945. Entwicklung des organisatorischen Aufbaus,* vol. 1, *Das Heer bis zum Kriegsbeginn* (Frankfurt a.M., 1954–1969), 172; Waldemar Erfurth, *Die Geschichte des deutschen Generalstabes von 1918 bis 1945* (Göttingen, 1957), 166–168.

179. For the dispute over the Wehrmacht top-level organization, see Bitzel, *Die Konzeption des Blitzkrieges bei der deutschen Wehrmacht,* 310–326; Klaus-Jürgen Müller, *Das Heer und Hitler. Armee und nationalsozialistisches Regime 1933 bis 1940* (Stuttgart, 1969), 222–244; Müller, *General Ludwig Beck. Studien und Dokumente,* 103–137; Wilhelm Deist, "Die Aufrüstung der Wehrmacht," in *Das Deutsche Reich und der Zweite Weltkrieg,* vol. 1, *Ursachen und Voraussetzungen der deutschen Kriegspolitik,* ed. Wilhelm Deist, Manfred Messerschmidt, Hans-Erich Volkmann, and Wolfram Wette (Stuttgart, 1991), 500–512.

180. "Wehrmachtspitzengliederung und Führung der Wehrmacht im Kriege," reproduced in Wilhelm Keitel, *Generalfeldmarschall Keitel. Verbrecher oder Offizier? Erinnerungen, Briefe, Dokumente des Chefs des OKW,* ed. Walter Görlitz (Göttingen, 1961), 142. In 1935, Beck went even further and called for the participation of the army commander in chief in the war cabinet.

181. Keitel, *Generalfeldmarschall Keitel,* 143–166.

182. Udo Traut, *Die Spitzengliederung der deutschen Streitkräfte von 1921 bis 1964. Ein Beitrag zum Problem der Kollision von politisch-zivilem und militärischem Bereich* (Diss. jur., Karlsruhe, 1965), 148–176.

183. Eckart Busch, *Der Oberbefehl. Seine rechtliche Struktur in Preussen und in Deutschland seit 1848* (Boppard a.Rh., 1967), 104–106.

184. It was renamed *Wehrmachtführungsstab* (Wehrmacht Operations Staff) on 8 August 1940.

185. Müller, *Das Heer und Hitler,* 242.

186. Andreas Hillgruber, "Kontinuität und Diskontinuität," in *Grossmachtpolitik und Militarismus im 20. Jahrhundert. Drei Beiträge zum Kontinuitätsproblem,* by Andreas Hillgruber (Düsseldorf, 1974), 23. For the political objectives of the military elite, see Wolfram Wette, "Die deutsche militärische Führungsschicht in den Nachkriegszeiten," in *Lernen aus dem Krieg? Deutsche Nachkriegszeiten 1918–1945,* ed. Gottfried Niedhart and Dieter Riesenberger (Munich, 1992), 39–66.

187. Frieser, *Blitzkrieg Legend,* 7–14.

188. Deist, "Die Aufrüstung der Wehrmacht," 520.

7. Lost Victories, or the Limits of Operational Thinking

The epigraph to this chapter is drawn from Beck, *Studien,* 63.

1. For the history of the term Blitzkrieg and a summary of the literature, see Frieser, *Blitzkrieg Legend,* 5–14. See also William J. Fanning Jr., "The Origin of the Term 'Blitzkrieg':

Another View," *Journal of Military History* 61 (1997): 283–302. Naveh, *In Pursuit of Military Excellence,* 105–109, also addresses this term. Surprisingly, he consulted neither older German literature nor Frieser's *Blitzkrieg Legend* for his study.

2. George Raudzens, "Blitzkrieg Ambiguities: Doubtful Usage of a Famous Word," *War and Society* 7 (1989): 77–79.

3. The most important representatives of the Blitzkrieg strategy are Alan S. Milward and, among the German scholars, Andreas Hillgruber and Ludolf Herbst.

4. Michael Salewski, "Knotenpunkt der Weltgeschichte? Die Raison des deutsch-französischen Waffenstillstandes vom 22. Juni 1940," in *La France et l'Allemagne en guerre. Septembre 1939–November 1942,* ed. Claude Carlier and Stefan Martens (Paris, 1990), 119.

5. Strachan, *European Armies,* 163.

6. Cf. Wallach, *The Dogma of the Battle of Annihilation.*

7. Friedrich von Rabenau, "Revolution der Kriegführung," printed in Wallach, *The Dogma of the Battle of Annihilation,* 380–384.

8. Ibid., 383.

9. Ibid., 384.

10. Cited in ibid.

11. Georg Thomas, "Operatives und wirtschaftliches Denken," in *Kriegswirtschaftliche Jahresberichte,* ed. Kurt Hesse (Hamburg, 1937), 11–18.

12. The Truppenamt staff ride was conducted under the theme "Conduct of an Offensive War against Czechoslovakia, Including Deployment." Its objective was to determine the operational options for an attack on Czechoslovakia.

13. Cf. chapter 6, 183–184.

14. "Preparations in the west will not extend beyond a security manning of the Siegfried Line. There can and will not be a war with the Western Powers over Poland" (Bernhard von Lossberg, *Im Wehrmachtführungsstab. Bericht eines Generalstabsoffiziers* [Hamburg, 1950], 27). According to Manstein's personal war diary, on 3 September 1939, two hours prior to reception of the British declaration of war, Keitel would not tolerate a belief in a declaration of war by the Western Powers (war diary of General Field Marshal Erich von Manstein, entry of 24 October 1939, MGFA).

15. Günther Blumentritt, *Von Rundstedt: The Soldier and the Man* (London, 1952), 42f.

16. Report on the Army General Staff ride 1939, Luftgaukommando 3, Führ.Abt./Ia opl., Munich, 17 May 1939, BArch, RL 7/158, f., 1–28.

17. Ibid., 5 (italics in the original document).

18. Ibid., 8.

19. On a potential German-Soviet war subsequent to the war against Poland, see Rolf-Dieter Müller, *Der Feind steht im Osten. Hitlers geheime Pläne für einen Krieg gegen die Sowjetunion im Jahre 1939* (Berlin, 2011).

20. Winfried Baumgart, "Zur Ansprache Hitlers vor den Führern der Wehrmacht am 22. August 1939," *Vierteljahrshefte für Zeitgeschichte* 16 (1968): 120–149.

21. Christian Hartmann, *Halder. Generalstabschef Hitlers 1938–1942* (Paderborn, 1991), 134.

22. Torsten Diedrich, *Paulus. Das Trauma von Stalingrad. Eine Biographie* (Paderborn, 2008), 131.

23. Printed in Rolf Elble, *Die Schlacht an der Bzura im September 1939 aus deutscher und polnischer Sicht* (Freiburg i.Br., 1975), 236–239.

24. On the operations in Poland, see Elble, *Die Schlacht an der Bzura*; and Horst Rohde, "Hitlers erster 'Blitzkrieg' und seine Auswirkungen auf Nordosteuropa," in *Das Deutsche Reich und der Zweite Weltkrieg,* vol. 2, *Die Errichtung der Hegemonie auf dem europäischen Kontinent,* ed. Klaus A. Maier, Horst Rohde, Bernd Stegemann, and Hans Umbreit (Stuttgart, 1991), 79–156.

25. Der Einsatz der Luftwaffe im polnischen Feldzug, Chef des Generalstabes der Luftflotte 1, Prague, 16 November 1939, BArch, RL 7/4, 15.

26. Frieser, *Blitzkrieg Legend,* 21.

27. Manstein war diary, entry of 24 October 1939, MGFA. See also Mungo Melvin, *Manstein: Hitler's Greatest General* (London, 2010).

28. Frieser, *Blitzkrieg Legend,* 39. On German armament production, see Rolf-Dieter Müller, "Die Mobilisierung der deutschen Kriegswirtschaft für Hitlers Kriegführung," in *Das Deutsche Reich und der Zweite Weltkrieg,* vol. 5, *Organisation und Mobilisierung des deutschen Machtbereichs,* Part 1, *Kriegsverwaltung, Wirtschaft und personelle Ressourcen 1939 bis 1941,* ed. Bernhard R. Kroener, Rolf-Dieter Müller, and Hans Umbreit (Stuttgart, 1992), 406–556.

29. Richard L. DiNardo, *Mechanized Juggernaut or Military Anachronism? Horses and the German Army of World War II* (New York, 1991), 21–32.

30. Frieser, *Blitzkrieg Legend,* 39.

31. Ibid., 33–41.

32. Hans Reinhardt, "Die 4. Panzerdivision vor Warschau und an der Bzura vom 9.–20.9.1939," *Wehrkunde* 5 (1958): 246; Williamson Murray, "The German Response to Victory in Poland. A Case Study in Professionalism," *Armed Forces and Society* 7 (1981): 285–298.

33. This happened without Hitler's influence. On 14 September 1939, the chief of the General Staff, Colonel General Halder, wrote into his diary: "Kill delaying resistance." He elaborated: "This much-practiced form of combat in 100,000-soldier armies should be abolished because circumstances changed and the resoluteness of the defense suffered much by it in the Polish Campaign" (Franz Halder, *Kriegstagebuch. Tägliche Aufzeichnungen des Chefs des Generalstabes des Heeres 1939–1942,* 3 vols., ed. Hans-Adolf Jacobsen [Stuttgart, 1962–1964], 1:75).

34. For details on the development of infantry tactics, see Gerhard Elser, "Von der 'Einheitsgruppe' zum 'Sturmzug.' Zur Entwicklung der deutschen Infanterie 1922–1945," *Militärgeschichte* 1 (1995): 3–11.

35. Murray, "The German Response to Victory in Poland," 285–298; Jürgen Förster, "The Dynamics of Volksgemeinschaft: The Effectiveness of the German Military Establishment in the Second World War," in *Military Effectiveness,* vol. 3, *The Second World War,* ed. Williamson Murray and Allan R. Millette (Boston, Mass., 1988), 209.

36. See the 1939 instruction "Angriff gegen eine ständige Front" [Attack against a Fixed Front] and the 1940 H.Dv. 130/9 *Ausbildungsvorschrift für die Infanterie,* H. 9, *Führung und Kampf der Infanterie. Das Infanterie-Bataillon* [Army Manual 130/9 Regulations for the Infantry, Section H. 9, Command and Combat of the Infantry. The Infantry Battalion].

37. Elser, "Von der 'Einheitsgruppe,'" 5.

38. Frieser, *Blitzkrieg Legend,* 28–30.

39. Halder, *Kriegstagebuch,* 1:180, entry 4 February 1940.

40. Storz, "Dieser Stellungs- und Festungskrieg ist scheusslich!" 61–204.

41. Frieser, *Blitzkrieg Legend,* 106–110.

42. Walther Hubatsch, ed., *Hitlers Weisungen für die Kriegführung 1939–1945. Dokumente des Oberkommandos der Wehrmacht* (Frankfurt a.M., 1962), 32.

43. For general information on the various deployment directives, see Frieser, *Blitzkrieg Legend,* 71–77.

44. Gerhard Engel, *Heeresadjutant bei Hitler 1938–1943. Aufzeichnungen des Majors Engel.* Hildegard von Kotze, ed. (Stuttgart, 1975), 75.

45. Generalfeldmarschall Erich von Manstein, *Kriegstagebuch,* Entry 24 October 1939, MGFA (italics as in the original document).

46. Manstein never forgave Halder that he and not Manstein himself became Beck's successor as chief of Army General Staff.

47. On the various planning steps of the later "Sickle Cut," see Frieser, *Blitzkrieg Legend,* 78–116.

48. Ibid., 79–81, elaborates on which ways Manstein exploited the opportunity to present his operational plan to Hitler.

49. Ibid., 41–65, for a comparison of personnel, materiel, and quality strength of the warring parties.

50. For discussion on the halt order in front of Dunkirk, see ibid., 363–393.

51. Ibid., 393.

52. Wallach, *The Dogma of the Battle of Annihilation,* 379.

53. On the course of the German offensive, see Frieser, *Blitzkrieg Legend,* 117–400.

54. On the significance of combined arms warfare, see DiNardo, "German Armor Doctrine," 386–390.

55. On the collaboration of tanks and dive-bombers, see Rudolf Steiger, *Panzertaktik im Spiegel deutscher Kriegstagebücher 1939 bis 1941* (Freiburg i.Br., 1975), 87–95.

56. Naveh incorrectly draws this conclusion in *In Pursuit of Military Excellence,* 132. Guderian was a trained General Staff officer, and Rommel regularly participated in operational map exercises.

57. Ernst Klink, "Die militärische Konzeption des Krieges gegen die Sowjetunion," in *Das Deutsche Reich und der Zweite Weltkrieg,* vol. 4, *Der Angriff auf die Sowjetunion,* ed. Horst Boog, Jürgen Förster, Joachim Hoffmann, Ernst Klink, Rolf-Dieter Müller, and Gerd R. Ueberschär (Stuttgart, 1987), 205–213.

58. Georg Meyer's argument that the Eastern Campaign had been "Hitler's War" is hard to verify. See Georg Meyer, *Adolf Heusinger. Dienst eines deutschen Soldaten 1915 bis 1964* (Hamburg, 2001), 149.

59. Andreas Hillgruber, *Hitlers Strategie. Politik und Kriegführung 1940–1941* (Frankfurt a.M., 1965), 209.

60. For a discussion of the preventive war concept, see Gerd R. Ueberschär, "Das 'Unternehmen Barbarossa' gegen die Sowjetunion. Ein Präventivkrieg? Zur Wiederbelebung der alten Rechtfertigungsversuche des deutschen Überfalls auf die UdSSR 1941," in

Wahrheit und "Auschwitzlüge." Zur Bekämpfung "revisionistischer" Propaganda, ed. Brigitte Bailer-Galanda, Wolfgang Benz, and Wolfgang Neugebauer (Wien, 1995), 163–182.

61. Halder, *Kriegstagebuch,* 2:49, entry 31 July 1940.

62. Hartmann, *Halder,* 236.

63. Klink, "Die militärische Konzeption des Krieges," 319–327.

64. Horst Boog, "Die Luftwaffe," in *Das Deutsche Reich und der Zweite Weltkrieg,* vol. 4, *Der Angriff auf die Sowjetunion,* ed. Horst Boog, Jürgen Förster, Joachim Hoffmann, Ernst Klink, Rolf-Dieter Müller, and Gerd R. Ueberschär (Stuttgart, 1987), 277–319, 652–712.

65. On the war for food, see Müller, "Die Mobilisierung der deutschen Kriegs-wirtschaft," 394–400.

66. "Der Wirtschaftskrieg" [The Economic War], briefing by Colonel Becker during Wehrmacht High Command exercise staff ride on 20 June 1939, BArch, RW 19/1272, f. 3–16. See also Müller, "Die Mobilisierung der deutschen Kriegswirtschaft," 395.

67. Halder, *Kriegstagebuch,* 2:454, entry 3 June 1941.

68. Marcks initially had prepared an operations draft that coincided with Hitler's. Halder rejected this draft. A few days later Marcks presented a draft with Halder's concept. For details on the development of the various operational plans, see Albert Beer, *Der Fall Barbarossa. Untersuchungen zur Geschichte der Vorbereitungen des deutschen Feldzuges gegen die Union der Sozialistischen Sowjetrepubliken im Jahre 1941* (Diss., Westphalian Wilhelms University, Münster, 1978), 27–72; Hillgruber, *Hitlers Strategie,* 219–231; Friedhelm Klein and Ingo Lachnit, "Der "Operationsentwurf Ost" des Generalmajor Marcks vom 5. August 1940," *Wehrforschung* 2, no. 4 (1972): 114–123; Klink, "Die militärische Konzeption des Krieges," 219–245; David Stahel, *Operation Barbarossa and Germany's Defeat in the East* (Cambridge, U.K., 2009), 39–69.

69. Diedrich, *Paulus. Das Trauma von Stalingrad,* 161–170.

70. Halder, *Kriegstagebuch,* 2:214, entry 5 December 1940.

71. On Hitler's strategy in the Mediterranean, see Gerhard Schreiber, "Der Mittelmeer-raum in Hitlers Strategie 1940. 'Programm' und militärische Planungen," in *Militärge-schichtliche Mitteilungen* 28 (1980): 69–90; Ralf Georg Reuth, *Entscheidung im Mittelmeer. Die südliche Peripherie Europas in der deutschen Strategie des Zweiten Weltkrieges 1940–1942* (Koblenz, 1985); and Jürgen Förster, "Hitlers Entscheidung für den Krieg gegen die Sowjetunion," in *Das Deutsche Reich und der Zweite Weltkrieg,* vol. 4, *Der Angriff auf die Sowjetunion,* ed. Horst Boog, Jürgen Förster, Joachim Hoffmann, Ernst Klink, Rolf-Dieter Müller, and Gerd R. Ueberschär (Stuttgart, 1987), 3–37.

72. Hartmann, *Halder,* 218–224.

73. Hubatsch, ed., *Hitlers Weisungen,* Directive No. 21, 18 December 1940, 84–88.

74. Stahel, *Operation Barbarossa,* 89f.; Klink, "Die militärische Konzeption des Krieges," 246.

75. For details on the *Aufmarschanweisung* BARBAROSSA, see Klink, "Die militärische Konzeption des Krieges," 246f.

76. Heinz Guderian, *Panzer Leader* (Cambridge, Mass., 2001), 142.

77. Hartmann, *Halder,* 239.

78. Cf. Manfred Messerschmidt, "Introduction," in *Das Deutsche Reich und der Zweite Weltkrieg,* vol. 4, *Der Angriff auf die Sowjetunion,* ed. Horst Boog, Jürgen Förster, Joachim

Hoffmann, Ernst Klink, Rolf-Dieter Müller, and Gerd R. Ueberschär (Stuttgart, 1987), xiii–xix.

79. Klink, "Die militärische Konzeption des Krieges," 224f.

80. Andreas Hillgruber, "Der Zenit des Zweiten Weltkrieges: Juli 1941," in *Die Zerstörung Europas. Beiträge zur Weltkriegsepoche, 1914 bis 1945,* ed. Andreas Hillgruber (Frankfurt a.M., 1988), 283.

81. At the beginning of the campaign on 22 June 1941 the Wehrmacht mobilized three quarters of the army in the field and two thirds of the Luftwaffe, altogether more than 3 million soldiers, for the assault. The 150 German divisions with 3,650 tanks were opposed in the western military districts of the Soviet Union by 2.9 million Red Army soldiers in 179 infantry divisions, 10 tank divisions, 33.5 cavalry divisions, and 45 tank or motorized brigades with more than 10,000 tanks and 8,000 airplanes. In total, German reconnaissance calculated approximately 209 Soviet infantry divisions and 32 cavalry divisions. The number of regiments with armored fighting vehicles was not known. Klink, "Die militärische Konzeption des Krieges," 191–202, 275.

82. On the negative evaluation of military strength of the Red Army, see Johannes Hürter, *Hitlers Heerführer. Die deutschen Oberbefehlshaber im Krieg gegen die Sowjetunion 1941–1942* (Munich, 2006), 230–235.

83. Ibid., 282.

84. See chapter 8 of this volume for a discussion on the firm roots of this illusion among German General Staff officers, even after the lost war.

85. Rüdiger Bergien, "Vorspiel des 'Vernichtungskrieges'? Die Ostfront des Ersten Weltkriegs und das Kontinuitätsproblem," in *Die vergessene Front. Der Osten 1914–15. Ereignis, Wirkung, Nachwirkung,* ed. Gerhard P. Gross (Paderborn, 2006), 396–398.

86. The Great General Staff had acknowledged the Russian soldier's abilities for tenacious defense, even prior to World War I—a fact that was again and again confirmed during the fighting. Gross, "Im Schatten des Westens," 32, 61.

87. Volkmann, "Der Ostkrieg," 292f.

88. The commander in chief of the Soviet troops was General (later Marshal of the Soviet Union) Georgy Konstantinovich Zhukov.

89. As Falkenhayn did with the infantry divisions in 1915, the number of Panzer divisions was increased by detaching the third tank regiment from the existing divisions and forming new Panzer divisions around those detached regiments.

90. On the controversies about tank use, see Heinz Guderian, *Erinnerungen eines Soldaten* (Heidelberg, 1951), 132; Hans Höhn, "Zur Bewertung der Infanterie durch die Führung der deutschen Wehrmacht," *Zeitschrift für Militärgeschichte* 4 (1965): 427f.

91. General Fridolin von Senger und Etterlin saw Cannae as a prime example of a battle of defense. Senger und Etterlin, "Cannae, Schlieffen und die Abwehr," 27–29.

92. On the tactical-operational conduct of encirclement battles, see Edgar F. Röhricht, *Probleme der Kesselschlacht, dargestellt an Einkreisungs-Operationen im zweiten Weltkrieg* (Karlsruhe, 1958), 173–182.

93. See chapter 6 of this volume.

94. During World War I, the German troops lacked mobile means of transport, such as trucks. In contrast to the Entente, the level of motorization of the Kaiser's army was

very low. This significantly retarded the German 1918 offensives. See chapter 4 of this volume.

95. On the weaknesses of the German railroad system, see Klaus A. Friedrich Schüler, *Logistik im Russlandfeldzug. Die Rolle der Eisenbahn bei Planung, Vorbereitung und Durchführung des deutschen Angriffs auf die Sowjetunion bis zur Krise vor Moskau im Winter 1941/42* (Frankfurt a.M., 1987), 59–88.

96. Elisabeth Wagner, ed. *Der Generalquartiermeister. Briefe und Tagebuchaufzeichnungen des Generalquartiermeisters des Heeres, General der Artillerie Eduard Wagner* (Munich, 1963), 177.

97. Hermann Teske, *Die silbernen Spiegel. Generalstabsdienst unter der Lupe* (Heidelberg, 1952), 96; see also Schüler, *Logistik im Russlandfeldzug*, 37–39.

98. Wagner, *Der Generalquartiermeister*, 176.

99. Schüler, *Logistik im Russlandfeldzug*, 640.

100. In the fully motorized divisions bulk transport assets carried the unit's basic load and accompanied the attack force. The empty bulk transport convoys were then leapfrogged forward to the supply bases established directly behind the front to ensure the continuous supply of the fast divisions. Wagner, *Der Generalquartiermeister*, 285.

101. On the organization of the bulk transport, see Klink, "Die militärische Konzeption des Krieges," 248–259; Creveld, *Supplying War*, 143–180; Rolf-Dieter Müller, "Das Scheitern der wirtschaftlichen 'Blitzkriegsstrategie,'" in *Das Deutsche Reich und der Zweite Weltkrieg*, vol. 4, *Der Angriff auf die Sowjetunion*, ed. Horst Boog, Jürgen Förster, Joachim Hoffmann, Ernst Klink, Rolf-Dieter Müller, and Gerd R. Ueberschär (Stuttgart, 1987), 936–1029.

102. Only the U.S. Army in World War II was able to establish a fully motorized supply organization independent of the railways. Cf. Müller, "Das Scheitern der wirtschaftlichen 'Blitzkriegsstrategie.'"

103. When commanders in chief of the armies and army groups learned prior to the offensive on Moscow in October 1941 that the supply situation for the attack was not guaranteed, they commented to the senior quartermaster of Army Group Center, Colonel Otto Eckstein: "Your calculations are surely correct, but we do not wish to hold back [Field Marshal Fedor von] Bock if he has the confidence to proceed. . . . A bit of luck always belongs to the warrior" (Wagner, *Der Generalquartiermeister*, 213).

104. On the logistics for Operation BARBAROSSA, see Creveld, *Supplying War*, 142–180.

105. Joseph Goebbels, *Tagebücher 1924–1945*, vol. 4, *1940–1942*, ed. Ralf Georg Reuth (Munich, 1992), 1601, entry 16 June 1941.

106. Halder, *Kriegstagebuch*, 3:38, entry 3 July 1941.

107. The Soviet Third and Tenth Armies, totaling 43 divisions, 325,000 soldiers, and 3,300 tanks, were destroyed in the battle of encirclement. The number of destroyed tanks roughly equals to the number the German Army had started the attack with. For details on the double battle, see Klink, "Die militärische Konzeption des Krieges," 451–462.

108. More than three hundred thousand Red Army soldiers with three thousand tanks were encircled in the Battle of the Smolensk Pocket between 24 July and 5 August 1941. For details on the Battle of Smolensk, see Klink, "Die militärische Konzeption des Krieges," 451–462; Stahel, *Operation Barbarossa*, 260–360.

109. Hürter, *Hitlers Heerführer*, 284f.

110. Halder, *Kriegstagebuch,* 3:118, entry 25 July 1941.

111. Ibid., 3:170, entry 11 August 1941.

112. Adolf Heusinger, "In memoriam, Franz Halder 30.6.1884–2.4.1972," *Wehrforschung* (1972): 79.

113. Halder, *Kriegstagebuch,* 3:159, entry 7 August 1941; Stahel, *Operation Barbarossa,* 395.

114. Hartmann, *Halder,* 278–284; Klink, "Die militärische Konzeption des Krieges," 486–507; Stahel, *Operation Barbarossa,* 273–280.

115. Halder, *Kriegstagebuch,* 3:12, entry 26 July 1941.

116. On the Battle of Leningrad and the subsequent siege, see David M. Glantz, *The Battle for Leningrad, 1941–1944* (Lawrence, Kans., 2002); Jörg Ganzenmüller, *Das belagerte Leningrad 1941–1944. Die Stadt in den Strategien der Angreifer und Angegriffenen.* (Diss. phil., Paderborn, 2005); Johannes Hürter, "Die Wehrmacht vor Leningrad. Krieg und Besatzungspolitik der 18. Armee im Herbst und Winter 1941/42," *Vierteljahrshefte für Zeitgeschichte* 49 (2001): 377–440.

117. For details on the Battle of Kiev, see Klink, "Die militärische Konzeption des Krieges," 508–522.

118. On the German side, the importance of the rail for supply deliveries had been underestimated completely. For details, see Schüler, *Logistik im Russlandfeldzug,* 308–605.

119. For details on the double battle of Vyazma and Bryansk, see Klaus Reinhardt, *Die Wende vor Moskau. Das Scheitern der Strategie Hitlers im Winter 1941/42* (Stuttgart, 1972), 49–122; Klink, "Die militärische Konzeption des Krieges," 568–585.

120. For details on the fighting in front of Moscow, see Reinhardt, *Die Wende vor Moskau,* 123–171; Ernst Klink, "Der Krieg gegen die Sowjetunion bis zur Jahreswende 1941/42," in *Das Deutsche Reich und der Zweite Weltkrieg,* vol. 4, *Der Angriff auf die Sowjetunion,* ed. Horst Boog, Jürgen Förster, Joachim Hoffmann, Ernst Klink, Rolf-Dieter Müller, and Gerd R. Ueberschär (Stuttgart, 1987), 585–600.

121. On the plans, see Bernd Wegner, "Der Krieg gegen die Sowjetunion 1942/43," in *Das Deutsche Reich und der Zweite Weltkrieg,* vol. 6, *Der globale Krieg. Die Ausweitung zum Weltkrieg und der Wechsel der Initiative 1941 bis 1943,* ed. Horst Boog, Werner Rahn, Reinhard Stumpf, and Bernd Wegner (Stuttgart, 1993), 761–815.

122. Hartmann, *Halder,* 314f.

123. Müller, "Das Scheitern der wirtschaftlichen 'Blitzkriegsstrategie,'" 1023.

124. Wegner, "Der Krieg gegen die Sowjetunion," 791.

125. Hans Meier-Welcker, *Aufzeichnungen eines Generalstabsoffiziers 1939 bis 1942* (Freiburg i.Br., 1982), 142, entry 1 December 1941.

126. Müller, "Das Scheitern der wirtschaftlichen 'Blitzkriegsstrategie,'" 999.

127. Hartmann, *Halder,* 325.

128. Wegner, "Der Krieg gegen die Sowjetunion," 892.

129. On the Battle of Stalingrad, see Antony Beevor, *Stalingrad* (London, 1999); Manfred Kehrig, *Stalingrad. Analyse und Dokumentation einer Schlacht* (Stuttgart, 1974); Sabine Arnold, Wolfgang Ueberschär, and Wolfram Wette, eds., *Stalingrad. Mythos und Wirklichkeit einer Schlacht* (Frankfurt a.M., 1992); Bernd Ulrich, *Stalingrad* (Munich, 2005); Wegner, "Der Krieg gegen die Sowjetunion," 962–1063.

130. Gerd R. Ueberschär, "Die militärische Kriegführung," in *Hitlers Krieg im Osten 1941–1945. Ein Forschungsbericht,* by Rolf-Dieter Müller and Gerd R. Ueberschär (Darmstadt, 2000), 126.

131. On the fighting in Africa, see Reinhard Stumpf, "Probleme der Logistik im Afrikafeldzug 1941–1943," in *Die Bedeutung der Logistik für die militärische Führung von der Antike bis in die neueste Zeit,* ed. Militärgeschichtliches Forschungsam (Bonn, 1968), 569–739.

132. Hubatsch, ed., *Hitlers Weisungen,* Directive No. 32, "Vorbereitungen für die Zeit nach Barbarossa," 129–134.

133. Percy Ernst Schramm and Helmuth Greiner, eds., *Kriegstagebuch des Oberkommandos der Wehrmacht (Wehrmachtführungsstab) 1940–1945,* 4 vols. (Frankfurt a.M., 1961–1965), 1:328; see also Hartmann, *Halder,* 273f.; Hillgruber, *Hitlers Strategie,* 383f.

134. Halder, *Kriegstagebuch,* 3:39.

135. Army General Staff, Operations Division War Diary (KTB GenStdH/Op.Abt), 13 July 1941, BArch, RH 2/311.

136. Meier-Welcker, *Aufzeichnungen eines Generalstabsoffiziers,* 172, entry 26 August 1942.

137. On the military strength of the Red Army, see David M. Glantz, *Colossus Reborn: The Red Army at War, 1941–1943* (Lawrence, Kans., 2005).

138. Meyer, *Adolf Heusinger,* 150.

139. Reinhardt, *Die Wende vor Moskau,* 144.

140. On the coordination between infantry and tanks, see Steiger, *Panzertaktik,* 57–76.

141. Ibid., 47–56.

142. Röhricht, *Probleme der Kesselschlacht,* 33–38; Steiger, *Panzertaktik,* 145–162.

143. Bernd Wegner, "Die Aporie des Krieges," in *Das Deutsche Reich und der Zweite Weltkrieg,* vol. 8, *Die Ostfront 1943/44. Der Krieg im Osten und an den Nebenfronten,* ed. Karl-Heinz Frieser (Munich, 2007), 32–38.

144. Cited in ibid., 8:35.

145. Führer Order 26 December 1941, printed in *Wehrmacht High Command War Diary* (KTB OKW), vol. 1, part 1, doc. 113, page 1086f.

146. Führer Order 8 September 1942 on "General Tasks of the Defense," *Wehrmacht High Command War Diary* (KTB OKW), vol. 2, part 1, doc. 22, pages 1292–1297.

147. On trench warfare in many sections of the Eastern Front, see Christian Hartmann, *Wehrmacht im Ostkrieg. Front und militärisches Hinterland 1941/1942* (Munich, 2009), 403–423.

148. Führer Order 8 September 1942 on "General Tasks of the Defense," *Wehrmacht High Command War Diary* (KTB OKW), vol. 2, part 1, doc. 22, pages 1292–1297.

149. *Wehrmacht High Command War Diary* (KTB OKW), 6:324.

150. For details on the planning and sequence of the operation, see Eberhard Schwarz, *Die Stabilisierung der Ostfront nach Stalingrad. Mansteins Gegenschlag zwischen Donez und Dnjepr im Frühjahr 1943* (Göttingen, 1986), 122–231.

151. Friedhelm Klein and Karl-Heinz Frieser, "Mansteins Gegenschlag am Donec. Operative Analyse des Gegenangriffs der Heeresgruppe Süd im Februar/März 1943," *Militärgeschichte* 9 (1999): 12–18; David M. Glantz, *From the Don to the Dnepr. Soviet Offensive*

Operations, December 1942 to August 1943 (London, 1991); Ottmar Hackl, "Das 'Schlagen aus der Nachhand.' Die Operationen der Heeresgruppe Don bzw. Süd zwischen Donez und Dnepir 1943," *Truppendienst* (1983): 132–137; Ferdinand M. von Senger und Etterlin, "Die Gegenschlagsoperation der Heeresgruppe Süd, 17.–25. Februar 1943," in *Wehrgeschichtliches Symposium an der Führungsakademie der Bundeswehr. 9. September 1986. Ausbildung im operativen Denken unter Heranziehen von Kriegserfahrungen, dargestellt an Mansteins Gegenangriff Frühjahr 1943,* ed. Dieter Ose (Hamburg, 1987), 132–182; Dana V. Sadarananda, *Beyond Stalingrad: Manstein and the Operations of Army Group Don* (New York, 1990).

152. At the height of the renaissance of operational thinking in the Bundeswehr in 1987 a military history symposium was held at the Bundeswehr Command and Staff College in Hamburg. Under the theme "Training in Operational Thinking under Consideration of War Experiences Exemplified by Manstein's Counterattack in the Spring of 1943," the operation was analyzed in the presence of contemporary witnesses like retired generals Johann-Adolf Graf von Kielmansegg and Ferdinand Maria von Senger und Etterlin. Although the situation was not at all comparable to the situation of the late Cold War, the lessons learned for the Bundeswehr's mobile defense were deduced.

153. Bernd Wegner, "Von Stalingrad nach Kursk," in *Das Deutsche Reich und der Zweite Weltkrieg,* vol. 8, *Die Ostfront 1943/44. Der Krieg im Osten und an den Nebenfronten,* ed. Karl-Heinz Frieser (Munich, 2007), 62–64.

154. Karl-Heinz Frieser, "Die Schlacht im Kursker Bogen," in *Das Deutsche Reich und der Zweite Weltkrieg,* vol. 8, *Die Ostfront 1943/44. Der Krieg im Osten und an den Nebenfronten,* ed. Karl-Heinz Frieser (Munich, 2007), 83–172.

155. Jürgen Förster, *Die Wehrmacht im NS-Staat. Eine strukturgeschichtliche Analyse* (Munich, 2007), 185.

156. Karl-Heinz Frieser, "Die Rückzugskämpfe der Heeresgruppe Nord bis Kurland," in *Das Deutsche Reich und der Zweite Weltkrieg,* vol. 8, *Die Ostfront 1943/44. Der Krieg im Osten und an den Nebenfronten,* ed. Karl-Heinz Frieser (Munich, 2007), 672–677.

157. Erich von Manstein, *Verlorene Siegen* (Bonn, 1955), 615.

158. Quoted in Karl-Heinz Frieser, "Irrtümer und Illusionen: Die Fehleinschätzungen der deutschen Führung," in *Das Deutsche Reich und der Zweite Weltkrieg,* vol. 8, *Die Ostfront 1943/44. Der Krieg im Osten und an den Nebenfronten,* ed. Karl-Heinz Frieser (Munich, 2007), 523.

159. Ibid., 8:283f.

160. On Führer Order 8 March 1944, "Firm Positions," see ibid., 8:521–525.

161. Ibid., 8:518f.

162. The restructuring of the Panzer divisions into large battle divisions for defense purposes was completed under the "Basic Structure of the Panzer and Panzergrenadier Division 1945" issued by the chief of staff of Panzer troops on 25 March 1945. After this restructuring the number of tanks was reduced from the 1944 number of 165 to 54, and the number of armored fighting vehicles from 288 to 90. The infantry's strength was increased by one battalion. The Panzer division so organized was not capable of conducting operational attacks. Adalbert Koch and Fritz Wiener, "Die Panzer-Division 1945," *Feldgrau* (1960): 33–39.

163. On the role of the antitank defense, see Eike Middeldorf, *Taktik im Russlandfeldzug. Erfahrungen und Folgerungen* (Darmstadt, 1956), 132–135.

164. Cf. Ferdinand M. von Senger und Etterlin, *Der Gegenschlag. Kampfbeispiele und Führungsgrundsätze der beweglichen Abwehr* (Heidelberg, 1959).

165. The return to the tactical ideas of World War I is indicated by the 15 January 1945 reissue of *Merkblatt* (Instruction Sheet) 18b/43, "Der Sturmangriff. Kriegserfahrungen eines Frontoffiziers von 1917" (The Assault: War Experiences of a Front-Line Officer of 1917).

166. On the "Grosskampfverfahren" (Large Battle Procedure), see Heinz Magenheimer, "Letzte Kampferfahrungen des deutschen Heeres an der West- und Ostfront," *Österreichische Militärische Zeitschrift* 4 (1985): 317–320. On the criticisms of this procedure, see Eike Middeldorf, "Die Abwehrschlacht am Weichselbrückenkopf Baranow. Eine Studie über neuzeitliche Verteidigung," *Wehrwissenschaftliche Rundschau* 4 (1953): 201.

167. This procedure was used successfully for the last time at the Battle of the Seelow Heights. Richard Lakowski, *Seelow 1945. Die Entscheidungsschlacht an der Oder* (Berlin, 1995), 51–55.

168. H.Dv. 130/20 *Die Führung des Grenadier-Regimentes* (Command of the Infantry Regiment), of 21 March 1945, introduced new procedures for the conduct of defensive battles based on the latest experiences and ideological factors. Accordingly, the main front line had to be held under all circumstances and intruding enemy forces destroyed by immediate counterattack. The ideological tone of the regulation is reflected in the notion that the main front line had to be "holy to every soldier" and the enemy had to be "shot down together." H.Dv. 130/20, 74, No. 224.

169. "Since his first appearance in history, the German has always proved to be an excellent and hard fighter. This comes from his disposition, given him by providence, and is therefore imperishable. His most important characteristics are his vigorous offensive spirit, loyalty to success, and comradeship" (Ludwig, "Der Geist des deutschen Soldaten," *Militär-Wochenblatt* 42 [1941]: 1709).

170. Jürgen Förster, "Weltanschauung als Waffe. Vom 'Vaterländischen Unterricht' zur 'Nationalsozialistischen Führung,'" in *Erster Weltkrieg—Zweiter Weltkrieg. Ein Vergleich. Krieg, Kriegserlebnis, Kriegserfahrung in Deutschland,* ed. Bruno Thoss and Hans-Erich Volkmann (Paderborn, 2002), 287–300.

171. Commander in Chief of the Western Army, *Befehl für die Ausbildung des Westheeres* (Order for the Training of the Western Army), extract, 24 November 1941, BArch, RH 2/2836, f. 1.

172. See Der Chef des Oberkommandos der Wehrmacht, Aufgaben, Befugnisse, Einsatz der Feldjägerdienstkommandos, copy, 8 January 1944, BArch, RW 4/v. 493.

173. George Soldan, "Cauchemar allemand! Von der Unbesiegbarkeit des deutschen Soldaten," *Deutsche Wehr* 8 (1942): 113–116.

174. H.Dv. 130/20, page 12, No. 6 (italics as in the original document).

175. See the examples cited by Senger und Etterlin in *Der Gegenschlag.*

176. For details on this operation, see Karl-Heinz Frieser, "Der Zusammenbruch der Heeresgruppe Mitte im Sommer 1944," in *Das Deutsche Reich und der Zweite Weltkrieg,* vol. 8, *Die Ostfront 1943/44. Der Krieg im Osten und an den Nebenfronten,* ed. Karl-Heinz

Frieser (Munich, 2007), 570–587; Karl-Heinz Frieser, "Ein zweites 'Wunder an der Weichsel?' Die Panzerschlacht vor Warschau im August 1944 und ihre Folgen," in *Der Warschauer Aufstand 1944,* ed. Bernd Martin and Stanisława Lewandowska (Warszawa, 1999), 45–64.

177. Up to the present, dispute remains about why Stalin stopped his units. Cf. Jerzy Kochanowski and Bernhard Chiari, *Die polnische Heimatarmee. Geschichte und Mythos der Armia Krajowa seit dem Zweiten Weltkrieg* (Munich, 2003); Martin and Lewandowska, eds., *Der Warschauer Aufstand 1944*; Włodzimierz Borodziej, *Der Warschauer Aufstand 1944* (Frankfurt a.M., 2001); Norman Davies, *Aufstand der Verlorenen. Der Kampf um Warschau 1944* (Munich, 2004).

178. AOK 19, *Gedanken über den Einsatz der grossen mot. Verbände im Ob. West-Bereich,* 29 January 1944, reproduced in Dieter Ose, *Entscheidung im Westen 1944. Der Oberbefehlshaber West und die Abwehr der alliierten Invasion* (Stuttgart, 1982), 316f.

179. On the deployed units, see ibid., 228.

180. On the decoding of the German radio messages encrypted with the rotor cipher machine Enigma, see Michael Smith, *Enigma entschlüsselt. Die "Codebreakers" vom Bletchley Park,* ed. Helmut Dierlamm (Munich, 2000), 256f. On the German side, there were some thoughts about the possibility that the enemy seemed to be informed beforehand about many German operations. In a meeting at the Führer Headquarters, Hitler elaborated on 31 July 1944: "How does the enemy find out about our thoughts? Why does he impede us so much? Why does he counteract [us] so quickly on so many moves?" The dictator answered his own questions. He referred to traitors in the higher command echelons of the army, specifically in the General Staff. Even Hitler's reaction was the result of the assassination attempt of 20 July 1944 a few days earlier, and his distrust of the army leadership had grown over the years, and although Hitler's statements referred primarily to the eastern theater of war, they demonstrate that the German leadership regarded the German encryption system as secure. Helmut Heiber, ed., *Hitlers Lagebesprechungen. Die Protokollfragmente seiner militärischen Konferenzen 1942–1945* (Stuttgart, 1962), 587.

181. Ose, *Entscheidung im Westen,* 230.

182. On Operation LIEGE, see ibid., 221–232; Detlef Vogel, "Deutsche und alliierte Kriegführung im Westen," in *Das Deutsche Reich und der Zweite Weltkrieg,* vol. 7, *Das Deutsche Reich in der Defensive. Strategischer Luftkrieg in Europa, Krieg im Westen und in Ostasien 1943 bis 1944/45,* ed. Horst Boog, Gerhard Krebs, and Detlef Vogel (Stuttgart, 2001), 558f.

183. Heinz Magenheimer, "Die Abwehrschlacht an der Weichsel 1945. Planung und Ablauf aus der Sicht der deutschen operativen Führung," in *Ausgewählte Operationen und ihre militärhistorischen Grundlagen,* ed. Hans-Martin Ottmer and Heiger Ostertag (Bonn, 1993), 168.

184. Traut, *Die Spitzengliederung,* 134f.

185. Klink, "Die militärische Konzeption des Krieges," 244f.

186. A more up to date task description of the General Staff is contained in Megargee, *Inside Hitler's High Command,* 55–66.

187. Hartmann, *Halder,* 346.

188. Engel, *Heeresadjutant,* 36, war diary entry 8 September 1938.

189. Hartmann, *Halder,* 106.

190. Ian Kershaw, *Hitler 1936–1945* (Stuttgart, 2000), 461.

191. *Wehrmacht High Command War Diary* (KTB OKW), vol. 1, part 2, 1062.

192. Kershaw, *Hitler 1936–1945*, 558. Within only a few weeks he also dismissed Rundstedt, Guderian, and Hoeppner and retired Leeb and Bock.

193. Meyer, *Adolf Heusinger,* 149, 227.

194. John Strawson, *Hitler as Military Commander* (London, 1971), 230.

195. Engel, *Heeresadjutant,* 125, entry 4 September 1942. [Editor's note: During World Wars I and II the *Verwundetenabzeichen* was awarded in three classes; Black for one and two wounds; Silver for three and four wounds; and Gold for five or more wounds.]

196. John Keegan, *The Mask of Command* (London, 1987), 300, indicated this was the case for the commanders in chief of Army Groups South and Center, Rundstedt and Bock. But his reference to Leeb is not correct. As Ia (Operations Officer) of the 11th Bavarian Infantry Division, Leeb indeed had front experience, and in contrast to Hitler that experience was mostly on the Eastern Front.

197. Keegan, *The Mask of Command,* 300–309.

198. Adolf Heusinger, *Befehl im Widerstreit. Schicksalstunden der deutschen Armee 1923–1945* (Tübingen, 1957), 132–135.

199. Wagner, *Der Generalquartiermeister,* 204, letter 5 October 1941.

200. Franz Halder, *Hitler als Feldherr* (Munich, 1949), 45.

201. Ibid.

202. Megargee, *Inside Hitler's High Command,* 220. Goebbels also strongly criticized the generals. They did not believe in the Führer, were not able to handle stress, were infected by doubts, and failed morally. Joseph Goebbels, *Die Tagebücher von Joseph Goebbels, Diktate 1941–1945,* 15 vols., ed. Elke Fröhlich (Munich, 1993–1996), 11:227, entry 3 February 1944.

203. Hitler was not alone in his criticism within the National Socialist leadership. Goebbels commented on Manstein's dismissal with the words: "This finally solves the issue with Manstein, the most critical among the army leaders" (Goebbels, *Die Tagebücher,* 11:589, entry 31 March 1944).

204. Ibid., 11:403, entry 4 March 1944.

205. Hans Frank, *Im Angesicht des Galgens* (Munich, 1952), 243.

206. Heiber, *Hitlers Lagebesprechungen,* 587.

207. A summary of Hitler's military personnel politics is in Förster, *Die Wehrmacht im NS-Staat,* 93–130.

208. Wegner, "Die Aporie des Krieges," in *Das Deutsche Reich und der Zweite Weltkrieg,* 8:227.

209. Hartmann, *Halder,* 328.

210. Engel, *Heeresadjutant,* 129, war diary entry 30 September 1942.

211. Hartmann, *Halder,* 339. [Hitler Youth Quex, a mocking reference to a 1933 Nazi propaganda film of the same name.]

212. Chef GenStdH/GZ/OpAbt. (I), Nr. 10010/42, 6 January 1942, BArch, RH 20–16/80.

213. Halder, *Kriegstagebuch,* 3:489, entry 23 July 1942.

214. Keegan, *The Mask of Command,* 286–304. Citing the example of the lunchtime briefing on 12 December 1942 Keegan describes how acerbically Hitler was concerned about every tactical detail.

215. Quoted in Meyer, *Adolf Heusinger,* 149, 227.

216. Winfried Baumgart, "Das 'Kaspi-Unternehmen'—Grössenwahn Ludendorffs oder Routineplanung des deutschen Generalstabes," *Jahrbücher für die Geschichte Osteuropas* 18 (1970): 47–126, 231–278.

217. The Caucasus area was of importance for Hitler only in terms of economic resources for the prosecution of the war. Since the end of World War I, this area had achieved a nearly legendary importance in the strategic planning as a "bridge into the Orient." The following statement by Seeckt illustrates how the German side assessed the geographic situation of the Caucasus area: "When I was standing on the railroad tracks to Tiflis and Baku, my thoughts were flying further, across the Caspian Sea and the cotton fields of Turkestan. They were flying to the Olympic Mountains, and if—as I must hope—the war will continue for a long time, we will finally knock at the gateway to India" (quoted in Winfried Baumgart, *Deutsche Ostpolitik 1918. Von Brest-Litowsk bis zum Ende des Ersten Weltkrieges* [Munich, 1966], 181, n. 30).

218. Quoted in Wegner, "Der Krieg gegen die Sowjetunion," 897.

219. Frieser, *Der Zusammenbruch der Heeresgruppe Mitte,* 597.

220. Förster, *Die Wehrmacht im NS-Staat,* 192.

221. It should not be forgotten that Rommel on the one hand was a perfect media showman, and on the other hand his achievements were exaggerated as his opponents emphasized the importance of his conqueror, General Sir Bernard Montgomery.

222. Stumpf, "Probleme der Logistik"; Creveld, *Supplying War,* 181–201.

223. Wegner, *Von Stalingrad nach Kursk,* 37 n. 156.

224. On the modernist and antimodernist elements in Hitler's world view, see Rainer Zitelmann, *Hitler. Selbstverständnis eines Revolutionärs* (Stuttgart, 1991), 306–378.

225. The planned partition of the Soviet Union into backward sub-republics under German authority, with simultaneous detachment of the non-Russian western areas of the USSR, was far beyond the classical war objectives of the German dreams of becoming a great European power, and even beyond Germany's war objectives toward the end of World War I.

226. For details on Hitler's speech, see Hürter, *Hitlers Heerführer,* 1–13; and Hartmann, *Wehrmacht im Ostkrieg,* 469. The dictator did not elaborate directly on the annihilation of the Jews. However, Hitler's criticism of the Wehrmacht justice system for initiating proceedings against an SS officer for murdering Jewish hostages during the Poland Campaign signaled Hitler's intentions to all concerned.

227. Hürter, *Hitlers Heerführer,* 9.

228. Halder, *Kriegstagebuch,* 2:337, entry 30 April 1941.

229. The postwar criticisms by the senior generals of Hitler's alleged intentions for the conduct of a war of annihilation are improbable. See Hürter, *Hitlers Heerführer,* 10f.

230. Appendix, "Was ist der Krieg der Zukunft?" on the Wehrmacht High Command memorandum "Die Kriegführung als Problem der Organisation," 19 April 1938, in International Military Tribunal, *Trial of the Major War Criminals Before the International Military Tribunal Nuremberg, 14 November 1945–1 October 1946,* 42 vols. (Nuremberg, 1947–1949), 38:48–50.

231. During the Poland Campaign there had been systematic murders behind the front

lines by the police and the SS. Individual Wehrmacht elements also exhibited extensive willingness to use violence against the civilian population. As a consequence of those atrocities, SS members and soldiers were subjected to courts-martial.

232. See Dieter Pohl, *Die Herrschaft der Wehrmacht. Deutsche Militärbesatzung und einheimische Bevölkerung in der Sowjetunion 1941–1944* (Munich, 2008), 55.

233. Cf. Jochen Böhler, *Auftakt zum Vernichtungskrieg. Die Wehrmacht in Polen 1939* (Frankfurt a.M., 2006); Alexander B. Rossino, *Hitler Strikes Poland: Blitzkrieg, Ideology, and Atrocities* (Lawrence, Kans., 2003).

234. Förster, *Die Wehrmacht im NS-Staat*, 86–88.

235. Jürgen Förster, "Das Unternehmen 'Barbarossa' als Eroberungs- und Vernichtungskrieg," in *Das Deutsche Reich und der Zweite Weltkrieg*, vol. 4, *Der Angriff auf die Sowjetunion*, ed. Horst Boog, Jürgen Förster, Joachim Hoffmann, Ernst Klink, Rolf-Dieter Müller, and Gerd R. Ueberschär (Stuttgart, 1987), 413–447.

236. Christian Hartmann, "Verbrecherischer Krieg—verbrecherische Wehrmacht? Überlegungen zur Struktur des deutschen Ostheeres 1941–1944," *Vierteljahrshefte für Zeitgeschichte* 52 (2004): 29; Pohl, *Die Herrschaft der Wehrmacht*.

237. Pohl, *Die Herrschaft der Wehrmacht*, 64–66.

238. Ritter, *Der Schlieffenplan*, 158.

239. Halder, *Kriegstagebuch*, 3:53, entry 8 July 1941.

240. Quoted in Hartmann, *Halder*, 286.

241. Hürter, "Die Wehrmacht vor Leningrad," 393.

242. Hartmann, "Verbrecherischer Krieg," 55.

243. Army Group North War Diary, Ia, entry 27 October 41, cited in Ueberschär, "Das 'Unternehmen Barbarossa' gegen die Sowjetunion," 336.

244. Hürter, "Die Wehrmacht vor Leningrad," 401.

245. Cited in ibid., 415.

8. Operational Thinking in the Age of the Atom

The epigraph to this chapter is drawn from "Die Führungsvorschriften des deutschen Heeres in Vergangenheit, Gegenwart und Zukunft unter besonderer Betonung der Gegenwart," presentation by Colonel i.G. Ernst Golling, November 1960, page 4, Military History Research Institute.

1. See Gerhart Haas, "Zum Bild der Wehrmacht in der Geschichtsschreibung der DDR," in *Die Wehrmacht. Mythos und Realität*, ed. Rolf-Dieter Müller and Hans-Erich Volkmann (Munich, 1999), 1100–1112; Dorothee Wierling, "Krieg im Nachkrieg. Zur öffentlichen und privaten Präsenz des Krieges in der SBZ und frühen DDR," in *Der Zweite Weltkrieg in Europa. Erfahrung und Erinnerung*, ed. Jörg Echternkamp and Stefan Martens (Paderborn, 2007), 247f.

2. It would last until the 1990s, when the myth of the unblemished Wehrmacht was broken in public under great political controversy as a consequence of the so-called *Wehrmachtausstellung* (Exhibitions Focusing on War Crimes of the Wehrmacht). From that point on, crimes committed by individual units of the Wehrmacht could be addressed.

3. Not everybody could turn his "hobby into a business," as did Ulrich de Maizière, the former Bundeswehr chief of staff who worked as a sheet music salesman. See Mat-

thias Molt, *Von der Wehrmacht zur Bundeswehr. Personelle Kontinuität und Diskontinu-ität beim Aufbau der Deutschen Streitkräfte 1955 bis 1966* (Diss., University of Heidelberg, 2007); John Zimmermann, *Ulrich de Maizière. General der Bonner Republik 1912 bis 2006* (Munich, 2012), 123–134.

4. Jörg Echternkamp, "Wut auf die Wehrmacht? Vom Bild der deutschen Soldaten in der unmittelbaren Nachkriegszeit," in *Die Wehrmacht. Mythos und Realität,* ed. Rolf-Dieter Müller and Hans-Erich Volkmann (Munich 1999), 1068.

5. Bernd Wegner, "Defensive ohne Strategie. Die Wehrmacht und das Jahr 1943," in *Die Wehrmacht. Mythos und Realität,* ed. Rolf-Dieter Müller and Hans-Erich Volkmann (Munich 1999), 197–209; Bernd Wegner, "Erschriebene Siege. Franz Halder, die 'Historical Division' und die Rekonstruktion des Zweiten Weltkrieges im Geiste des deutschen Gen-eralstabes," in *Politischer Wandel, organisierte Gewalt und nationale Sicherheit. Beiträge zur neueren Geschichte Deutschlands und Frankreichs. Festschrift für Klaus-Jürgen Müller,* ed. Ernst Willi Hansen, Gerhard Schreiber, and Bernd Wegner (Munich, 1995), 292.

6. See Halder, *Hitler als Feldherr*; Heusinger, *Befehl im Widerstreit.*

7. The work of the section ended in 1961. See Wegner, "Erschriebene Siege," 291.

8. Ibid., 290f.

9. See the studies by Georg von Sodensterns, "Der Feldherr, Adolf Hitler" and "Das Ende einer Feldherrnrolle," BArch, N 594/9.

10. Quoted in Wegner, "Erschriebene Siege," 295.

11. The first issue of the *Wehrwissenschaftliche Rundschau,* as the central postwar mili-tary periodical, appeared in 1951.

12. "Zur Einführung," *Wehrwissenschaftliche Rundschau* 1 (1951): 1.

13. Wolfgang Foerster, "Zur geschichtlichen Rolle des preussisch-deutschen General-stabs," *Wehrwissenschaftliche Rundschau* 8 (1951): 7–20.

14. Kurt Zeitzler, "Das Ringen um die militärische Entscheidung im 2. Weltkriege," *Wehrwissenschaftliche Rundschau,* vol. 6 (1951): 44–48; vol. 7 (1951): 20–29.

15. Sodenstern, "Operationen," 1–10.

16. Ibid., 9.

17. See Torsten Diedrich and Rüdiger Wenzke, *Die getarnte Armee. Geschichte der Kas-ernierten Volkspolizei der DDR 1952 bis 1956* (Berlin, 2001).

18. Bruno Thoss, *NATO-Strategie und nationale Verteidigungsplanung. Planung und Aufbau der Bundeswehr unter den Bedingungen einer massiven atomaren Vergeltungsstrat-egie 1952 bis 1960* (Munich, 2006), 2.

19. Rudolf J. Schlaffer, "Preussisch-deutsch geprägtes Personal für eine in der NATO integrierte Armee: Der personelle Aufbau der Bundeswehr," in *Entangling Alliance. 60 Jahre NATO: Geschichte—Gegenwart—Zukunft,* ed. Werner Kremp, Berdhold Meyer, and Wolfgang Tönnesmann (Trier, 2010), 115.

20. On the evolution of leadership development and civic education (*innere Führung*), see Frank Nägler, *Der gewollte Soldat und sein Wandel. Personelle Rüstung und Innere Füh-rung in den Aufbaujahren der Bundeswehr 1956 bis 1964/65* (Munich, 2010); and Rudolf J. Schlaffer, *Der Wehrbeauftragte 1951 bis 1985. Aus Sorge um den Soldaten* (Munich, 2006).

21. Both the first chief of staff of the Bundesluftwaffe, Lieutenant General Josef Kammhuber, and the acting head of the Naval Directorate and later second chief of staff,

Navy, Vice Admiral Karl-Adolf Zenker, served primarily in the operations divisions of their respective Wehrmacht services during the war.

22. For Heusinger's curriculum vitae, see Adolf Heusinger, *Ein deutscher Soldat im 20. Jahrhundert,* Bundesministerium der Verteidigung (Bonn, 1987), and Meyer, *Adolf Heusinger.*

23. Pöhlmann, *Kriegsgeschichte und Geschichtspolitik,* 250.

24. Following Beck's resignation, a great deal of animosity arose between Halder and Manstein. Halder was appointed as chief of the General Staff, but Manstein had hoped to be Beck's successor.

25. For a discussion of the Blank Office, see Dieter Krüger, *Das Amt Blank. Die schwierige Gründung des Bundesministeriums für Verteidigung* (Freiburg i.Br., 1993).

26. Frank Buchholz, *Strategische und militärpolitische Diskussionen in der Gründungsphase der Bundeswehr 1949–1960* (Frankfurt a.M., 1991), 305.

27. Schlaffer, "Preussisch-deutsch geprägtes Personal," 115–120.

28. Krüger, *Das Amt Blank,* 52.

29. Meyer, *Adolf Heusinger,* 535–527. Neither the statement in *Strategische und militärpolitische Diskussionen* (114) that Heusinger was accepted because of his operational capabilities, which could not be allowed to be lost, nor Meyer's assertion that there had been no political reasons for the limitations placed on the selection board can be verified, because the files of the board were destroyed.

30. Axel F. Gablik, *Strategische Planungen in der Bundesrepublik Deutschland 1955–1967: Politische Kontrolle oder militärische Notwendigkeit?* (Baden-Baden, 1996), 40–50.

31. On the threat situation from the Western point of view and the expected Soviet potential, see Christian Greiner, "Die alliierten militärstrategischen Planungen zur Verteidigung Westeuropas 1947–1950," in Militärgeschichtlichen Forschungsamt, *Anfänge westdeutscher Sicherheitspolitik 1945–1956,* vol. 1 (Munich, 1982), 197–206; and Helmut R. Hammerich, Dieter H. Kollmer, Martin Rink, and Rudolf Schlaffer, *Das Heer 1950 bis 1970. Konzeption, Organisation und Aufstellung* (Munich, 2006), 38–45.

32. On the geographic situation of the Federal Republic, see Hammerich, Kollmer, Rink, and Schlaffer, *Das Heer,* 46–48, especially the map showing the structure of the natural environment.

33. For details on the operational considerations, see Hans-Jürgen Rautenberg and Norbert Wiggershaus, *Die "Himmeroder Denkschrift" vom Oktober 1950* (Karlsruhe, 1985), 39–41. Also summarized in Helmut R. Hammerich, "Kommiss kommt von Kompromiss. Das Heer der Bundeswehr zwischen Wehrmacht und U.S. Army (1950 bis 1970)," in *Das Heer 1950 bis 1970. Konzeption, Organisation und Aufstellung,* by Helmut R. Hammerich, Dieter H. Kollmer, Martin Rink, and Rudolf Schlaffer (Munich, 2006), 73–92.

34. Christian Greiner, "Die militärische Eingliederung der Bundesrepublik Deutschland in die WEU und die NATO 1954 bis 1957," in Militärgeschichtliches Forschungsamt, *Anfänge westdeutscher Sicherheitspolitik 1945–1956,* vol. 3 (Munich, 1993), 604.

35. Gregory W. Pedlow, ed., "NATO Strategy Documents, 1949–1969," in collaboration with the NATO International Staff Central Archives, http://www.nato.int/archives/strategy.htm (Brussels, 1997), xiv.

36. Comment by Graf von Schwerin on the memorandum of the committee of mili-

tary experts, 28 October 1950, printed in Rautenberg and Wiggershaus, *Die "Himmeroder Denkschrift,"* 58–60.

37. Quoted in Christian Greiner, "General Adolf Heusinger (1897–1982). Operatives Denken und Planen 1948 bis 1956," in *Operatives Denken und Handeln in deutschen Streitkräften im 19. und 20. Jahrhundert,* ed. Horst Boog (Herford, 1988), 231.

38. Hammerich, *Kommiss kommt von Kompromiss,* 88–90.

39. Greiner, "General Adolf Heusinger," 231f.

40. Gablik, *Strategische Planungen,* 63.

41. The "Bonin Plan" is printed in Heinz Brill, *Bogislaw von Bonin im Spannungsfeld zwischen Wiederbewaffnung—Westintegration—Wiedervereinigung. Ein Beitrag zur Entstehungsgeschichte der Bundeswehr 1952–1955,* 2 vols. (Baden-Baden, 1987), 1:117–161.

42. Bonin planned to deploy about eleven hundred guns in this defensive zone.

43. Thoss, *NATO-Strategie,* 96.

44. Buchholz, *Strategische und militärpolitische Diskussionen,* 182–185.

45. Gablik, *Strategische Planungen,* 48–51.

46. Daniel Niemetz, *Das feldgraue Erbe. Die Wehrmachteinflüsse im Militär der SBZ/DDR* (Published by Militärgeschichtliches Forschungsamt, Berlin, 2006), 53–55. On the broadening of access to the Wehrmacht officer corps, see Reinhard Stumpf, *Die Wehrmacht-Elite. Rang- und Herkunftsstruktur der deutschen Generale und Admirale 1933 bis 1945* (Boppard a.Rh., 1982), 241–248; and Bernhard R. Kroener, "Auf dem Weg zu einer 'nationalsozialistischen Volksarmee.' Die soziale Öffnung des Heeresoffizierkorps im Zweiten Weltkrieg," in *Von Stalingrad zur Währungsreform. Zur Sozialgeschichte des Umbruchs in Deutschland,* ed. Martin Broszat, Klaus-Dietmar Henke, and Hans Woller (Munich, 1988), 651–683.

47. Niemetz, *Das feldgraue Erbe,* 41–43.

48. Ibid., 53–55.

49. Ibid., 113.

50. The Russians increased the level of motorization of their infantry divisions by 3.5 times within the space of five years. See Diedrich and Wenzke, *Die getarnte Armee,* 102f.

51. Zeidler, *Reichswehr und Rote Armee,* 165f.

52. In addition to Zeidler, *Reichswehr und Rote Armee,* the topic is considered from the standpoint of German-Soviet cooperation in the 1920s and 1930s in Mary R. Habeck, *Storm of Steel: The Development of Armor Doctrine in Germany and the Soviet Union, 1919–1939* (London, 2003).

53. Erich F. Pruck, "Die Rehabilitierung von Kommandeuren der Roten Armee," *Osteuropa* 14, no. 3 (1964): 208.

54. Quoted in Zeidler, *Reichswehr und Rote Armee,* 262.

55. Ibid., 264f.

56. John Erickson, *The Soviet High Command: A Military Political History, 1918–1941* (London, 1962), 266–269.

57. For an overview, see Christian Greiner, "Die Entwicklung der Bündnisstrategie 1949 bis 1958," in *Die NATO als Militärallianz. Strategie, Organisation und nukleare Kontrolle im Bündnis 1949 bis 1959,* by Christian Greiner, Klaus A. Maier, and Heinz Rebhan, ed. Bruno Thoss (Munich, 2003), 17–174; and Klaus A. Maier, "Die politische Kontrolle

über die amerikanischen Nuklearwaffen. Ein Bündnisproblem der NATO unter der Doktrin der Massiven Vergeltung," in *Die NATO als Militärallianz. Strategie, Organisation und nukleare Kontrolle im Bündnis 1949 bis 1959,* by Christian Greiner, Klaus A. Maier, and Heinz Rebhan, ed. Bruno Thoss (Munich, 2003), 253–396.

58. Greiner, "Die militärische Eingliederung," 604f.; Greiner, "General Adolf Heusinger," 234f.

59. Hammerich, *Kommiss kommt von Kompromiss,* 93–121; Thoss, *NATO-Strategie,* 40–52.

60. Greiner, "Die militärische Eingliederung," 608.

61. On NATO's operational and strategic planning, see Hammerich, *Kommiss kommt von Kompromiss,* 93–121; Thoss, *NATO-Strategie*; and Dieter Krüger, "Schlachtfeld Bundesrepublik? Europa, die deutsche Luftwaffe und der Strategiewechsel der NATO 1958 bis 1968," *Vierteljahrshefte für Zeitgeschichte* 56 (2008): 171–225.

62. Greiner, "Die militärische Eingliederung," 615.

63. Gablik, *Strategische Planungen,* 101f.

64. On the course of the development and the public perception, see Buchholz, *Strategische und militärpolitische Diskussionen,* 241–244.

65. Ingo Trauschweizer, *The Cold War U.S. Army: Building Deterrence for Limited War* (Lawrence, Kans., 2008), 39.

66. Greiner, "General Adolf Heusinger," 246.

67. Trauschweize, *The Cold War U.S. Army,* 70.

68. On the nuclear strategy pursued by the NATO alliance between 1958 and 1968, see Krüger, "Schlachtfeld Bundesrepublik?"

69. For a detailed discussion of the public controversy on rearmament, see Hans Ehlert, "Innenpolitische Auseinandersetzungen um die Pariser Verträge und die Wehrverfassung 1954 bis 1956," in Militärgeschichtliches Forschungsamt, *Anfänge westdeutscher Sicherheitspolitik 1945–1956,* vol. 3 (Munich, 1982), 235–560; and Thoss, *NATO-Strategie,* 354–370.

70. Nägler, *Der gewollte Soldat und sein Wandel,* 269–289; Rudolf J. Schlaffer, "Anmerkungen zu 50 Jahren Bundeswehr. Soldat und Technik in der 'totalen Verteidigung,'" *Militärgeschichtliche Zeitschrift* 64 (2005): 487–502.

71. Buchholz, *Strategische und militärpolitische Diskussionen,* 137. The operations experts adopted American ideas.

72. In a passing comment on this topic Heusinger noted: "It all the more continues to be *art.*" He emphasized the term "art" by underlining it. Heusinger, *Ein deutscher Soldat,* 134.

73. Ibid.

74. The details of these plans are discussed in Hammerich, *Kommiss kommt von Kompromiss,* 139–141.

75. For a discussion of the importance of the Luftwaffe in the Bundeswehr's internal power struggles, see Krüger, "Schlachtfeld Bundesrepublik?" 185–188.

76. Martin Rink, "'Strukturen brausen um die Wette.' Zur Organisation des deutschen Heeres," in *Das Heer 1950 bis 1970. Konzeption, Organisation und Aufstellung,* by Helmut R. Hammerich, Dieter H. Kollmer, Martin Rink, and Rudolf Schlaffer (Munich, 2006), 419–423.

77. Ibid., 414–418.

78. Ibid., 355–483, on the structure and development of the German brigade and division organizations.

79. As in the 1920s and 1930s, there were at least three attempts to prepare a doctrinal regulation on operational command and control. However, the studies for the planned Joint Service Regulation Z.Dv. 1/4 *Richtlinien für die obere Führung* were not completed, as happened during the eras of the Reichswehr and the Wehrmacht.

80. Army Regulation H.Dv. 100/1 *Truppenführung* (*T.F.*), revised in 1952 by General of Infantry (Ret.) Theodor Busse.

81. Army Regulation H.Dv. 100/1 *Grundsätze der Truppenführung des Heeres,* 1956, para. 17.

82. Ibid., para. 1.

83. H.Dv. 100/2 *Führungsgrundsätze des Heeres im Atomkrieg,* 1956, para. 4. Emphasis in the original.

84. Scheven, *Die Truppenführung,* 27.

85. Ibid., 30f.

86. "Die Führungsvorschriften des deutschen Heeres in Vergangenheit, Gegenwart und Zukunft unter besonderer Betonung der Gegenwart," presentation by Colonel i.G. Ernst Golling, November 1960, page 3, Military History Research Institute.

87. Army Regulation H.Dv. 100/1 *Truppenführung,* October 1962.

88. Scheven, *Die Truppenführung,* 26f.

89. Hammerich, *Kommiss kommt von Kompromiss,* 179.

90. Krüger, "Schlachtfeld Bundesrepublik?" 187.

91. Thoss, *NATO-Strategie,* 726.

92. Ibid., 723.

93. Pedlow, ed., "NATO Strategy Documents," XXI f.

94. See *Atomkrieg in St. Louis. Ein Jahr danach. Ein Bericht aufgrund der Anhörung von Sachverständigen vor dem Kongressauschuss* (Military History Research Institute, December 1959). I thank Lieutenant Colonel Dr. Rudolf Schlaffer for pointing out this document to me.

95. Ingo Trauschweizer, "Learning with an Ally: The U.S. Army and the Bundeswehr in the Cold War," *Journal of Military History* 72 (2008): 477–508.

96. Heusinger to Müller-Hillebrand, Washington, 27 March 1962, Federal Archives, Bw 2/20030e. I thank Lieutenant Colonel Dr. Helmut R. Hammerich for indicating this document to me.

97. For basic remarks on the development of the nuclear strategy of NATO, see Beatrice Heuser, *NATO, Britain, France and the FRG: Nuclear Strategies and Forces for Europe, 1949–2000* (London, 1997).

98. Hans-Peter Sertl, "Generalfeldmarschall Erich von Manstein. Der Schlieffen des Zweiten Weltkrieges," *Der Landser* 28 (1961).

99. Report by the Chief of Staff, Führungsstab der Bundeswehr to Defense Minister Franz-Josef Strauss, 16 August 1960, quoted in Thoss, *NATO-Strategie,* 727.

Conclusion

1. Ludendorff on 22 February 1918 in his letter to Friedrich Naumann, printed in Herbert Michaelis and Ernst Schraepler, eds., *Ursachen und Folgen. Vom deutschen Zusammenbruch 1918 und 1945 bis zur staatlichen Neuordnung Deutschlands in der Gegenwart.*

Eine Urkunden- und Dokumentensammlung zur Zeitgeschichte, vol. 2, *Der militärische Zusammenbruch und das Ende des Kaiserreichs* (Berlin, 1958–1978), 250.

2. Gottfried Niedhart, "Lernfähigkeit und Lernbereitschaft nach Kriegen. Beobachtungen im Anschluss an die deutschen Nachkriegszeiten im 20. Jahrhundert," in *Historische Leitlinien für das Militär der neunziger Jahre,* ed. Detlef Bald and Paul Klein (Baden-Baden, 1989), 3–27; and Wette, "Die deutsche militärische Führungsschicht," 39–66.

3. Merkblatt 18b/43, "Der Sturmangriff. Kriegserfahrungen eines Frontoffiziers von 1917," 15 January 1945, page 2.

4. Letter from Commander in Chief of Army Group B to his commanders, 29 March 1945, BArch, RH 41/603, page 13f. (italics as in the original document).

5. Hans Wolf Rode, "Das Kriegserlebnis von 1939 und 1914," *Militär-Wochenblatt* 125, no. 46 (1941): 1827.

6. Oberbefehlshaber, Heeresgruppe A, An alle Generale (Divisionskommandeure) H.Qu., 20 January 1945, BArch, RH 19, f. 203f.

7. Commemorative ceremony on the fiftieth anniversary of Schlieffen's death, 21 December 1962, BArch, N 673/517b, unpublished works of Ulrich de Maizière. I thank Lieutenant Colonel Dr. John Zimmermann for pointing this file out.

Bibliography

Unpublished Sources

Bundesarchiv/Militärarchiv (BArch) Freiburg i.Br.

Bw 2/20030e	Heusinger an Müller-Hillebrand, Washington, 27 March 1962.
N 323/7	Nachlass Boetticher, Grosse Generalstabsreise, September 1899.
N 323/7	Nachlass Boetticher, 2. Grosse Reise.
N 323/8	Nachlass Boetticher, Übersicht über die Operationen der 1, Grossen Generalstabsreise 1904, Schlussbesprechung.
N 323/10	Nachlass Boetticher, Kriegsspiel 1905.
N 323/30	Nachlass Boetticher, Grosse Generalstabsreise 1898.
N 323/48	Nachlass Boetticher, Schlussaufgaben 1905.
N 43/108	Nachlass Alfred Graf von Schlieffen, *Über die Aussichten des taktischen und operativen Durchbruchs aufgrund kriegsgeschichtlicher Erfahrungen.*
N 5/10	Nachlass Stülpnagel, "Gedanken über den Krieg der Zukunft," February 1924, von Oberstleutnant Joachim von Stülpnagel.
N 5/20	Nachlass Stülpnagel, Chef Heeresabteilung an Truppenamt, Nr. 270/24, T. 1 I B, geh, Berlin, 18 March 1924.
N 594/9	Studien von Georg von Sodenstern, "Der Feldherr, Adolf Hitler" and "Das Ende einer Feldherrnrolle."
N 673/517b	Nachlass Ulrich de Maizière.
PH 3/646	Chef des Generalstabes der Armee, Kriegsspiel November/Dezember 1905, Berlin, 23 December 1905.
PH 3/646	Chef des Generalstabes der Armee, Kriegsspiel November/Dezember 1905, Schlussbesprechung, Berlin, 23 December 1905.
RH 1/78	Oberst Karl-Heinrich von Stülpnagel, "Der künftige Krieg nach den Ansichten des Auslandes," 15 January 1934.
RH 2/311	KTB GenStdH/Op.Abt., 13 July 1941.
RH 2/360	Schlussbesprechung Führerreise 1933.
RH 2/363	Schlussbesprechung Truppenamtsreise 1930.
RH 2/374	Truppenamtsreise 1935.
RH 2/384	Folgerungen aus den Studien des T.A. im Winter 27/28 und 28/29, 26 March 1929.
RH 2/385	Wehrmachtskriegsspiel 1934, Vortrag Chef We.Rü.A.
RH 2/2819	Winterausbildung des Generalstaboffiziere, Generalstab des Heeres, Berlin, 9 November 1938.
RH 2/2836	Oberbefehlshaber des Westheeres, Befehl für die Ausbildung des Westheeres, Auszugsweise Abschrift, 24 November 1941.
RH 2/2901	Stülpnagel an T-2, 10 March 1924.
RH 2/2901	Chef Truppenamt an T-1, 30 August 1924.

RH 2/2901	Chef T-1 an Chef T-4, 21 January 1931.
RH 2/2901	*Leitlinien für die obere Führung im Kriege*, Oberst Hierl, 1923.
RH 2/2901	Stellungnahme zu Grundzügen der höheren Truppenführung, von Mantey, 12 August 1930.
RH 2/2901T	2 an Chef des Truppenamtes, 2 July 1924.
RH 15/19	Schreiben Groener an Brüning (Entwurf), 13 April 1932.
RH 20-16/80	Der Chef GenStdH/GZ/Op.Abt. (I), Nr. 10010/42, 6 January 1942 (Abschrift).
RH 41/603	Schreiben Oberbefehlshaber der Heeresgruppe B an seine Kommandeure, 29 March 1945.
RH 61/347	Dieckmann, *Der Schlieffenplan.*
RH 61/398	Greiner, *Nachrichten.*
RL 7/4	Der Einsatz der Luftwaffe im polnischen Feldzug, Chef des Generalstabes der Luftflotte 1, Prague, 16 November 1939.
RL 7/158	Bericht über die Heeresgeneralstabsreise 1939, Luftgaukommando 3, Führ.Abt./Ia opl., Munich, 17 May 1939.
RM 20/1100	Schlussbesprechung des Kriegsspiels A von 1938.
RW 4/v. 493	Der Chef des Oberkommandos der Wehrmacht, Aufgaben, Befugnisse, Einsatz der Feldjägerdienstkommandos, Abschrift, 8 January 1944.
RW 13/4	Vortrag vom 5 May 1935 an der Wehrmachtakademie, "Unsere hauptsächlichen militärpolitischen, strategischen, kriegswirtschaftlichen und psychologischen Fehler in der Vorbereitung des Weltkrieges selbst. Welche allgemeine Erkenntnisse ergeben sich daraus für die Kriegführung?"
RW 13/20	Vortrag Oberstleutnant Matzky, Kritische Untersuchung der Lehre von Douhet, Fuller, Hart und Seeckt, 29 November 1935.
RW 13/20	Oberstleutnant Matzky (Wehrmachtsakademie gehaltenen Vortrages, 29 November 1935), "Kritische Untersuchung der Lehre von Douhet, Fuller, Hart, und Seeckt."
RW 13/21	Oberstleutnant Willi Schneckenburger, Vortrag "Führung, operative und taktische Verwendung schneller Verbände, wie müssen sie organisiert sein?" February 1936.
RW 19/203	Oberbefehlshaber, Heeresgruppe A, An alle Generale (Divisionskommandeure) H.Qu., 20 January 1945.
RW 19/1243	Unterlagen zum Kriegsspiel 1938.
RW 19/1272	Der Wirtschaftskrieg. Vortrag von Oberst Becker auf der Übungsreise des OKW, 20 June 1939.
W 10/50684	Brief Musketier Gotthold Schneider von der Flandernschlacht, 31 October 1917.
ZA 1/2014	Ausarbeitung von General a.D. Rudolf Hofmann über "Kriegsspiele."
ZA 1/2779	Korpsgeneralstabsreise 1938, Münster, 18 May 1938.

Zentrum für Militärgeschichte und Sozialwissenschaften der Bundeswehr(ZMSBw)

Atomkrieg in St. Louis. Ein Jahr danach. Ein Bericht aufgrund der Anhörung von Sachverständigen vor dem Kongressauschuss. December 1959.
"Die Führungsvorschriften des deutschen Heeres in Vergangenheit, Gegenwart und Zukunft unter besonderer Betonung der Gegenwart." Presentation by Oberst i.G. Ernst Golling, November 1960.
Klink, Ernst. *Die Begriffe Operation und operativ in ihrer militärischen Verwendung in Deutschland.* Studie MGFA, 12 December 1958.
Kriegstagebuch Generalfeldmarschall Erich von Manstein. (Unpublished).

Manuals

BMVg *Leitlinie für die operative Führung von Landstreitkräften in Mitteleuropa,* 1987.
H.Dv. 100/1 *Grundsätze der Truppenführung des Heeres,* 1956.
H.Dv. 100/1 *Truppenführung* (TF), Neubearbeitung 1952 durch General der Infanterie a.D. Theodor Busse.
H.Dv. 100/1 *Truppenführung,* 1959.
H.Dv. 100/1 *Truppenführung,* October 1962.
H.Dv. 100/2 *Führungsgrundsätze des Heeres im Atomkrieg,* 1956.
H.Dv. 100/2 *Führungsgrundsätze des Heeres für die atomare Kriegführung,* 1961.
H.Dv. 100/900 *Führungsbegriffe,* 1977.
H.Dv. 130/9 *Ausbildungsvorschrift für die Infanterie,* 1940.
H.Dv. 130/20 *Die Führung des Grenadier-Regimentes,* 1945.
H.Dv. 300 *Truppenführung* (*T.F.*), 1933.
H.Dv. 487 *Führung und Gefecht der verbundenen Waffen* (*F.u.G.*), 1921–1924; reprint, Osnabrück, 1994.
Merkblatt, *Angriff gegen eine ständige Front,* 1939.
Merkblatt 18b/43, "Der Sturmangriff. Kriegserfahrungen eines Frontoffiziers von 1917," 15 January 1945.

Published Literature

Afflerbach, Holger. *Falkenhayn. Politisches Denken und Handeln im Kaiserreich.* Beiträge zur Militärgeschichte 42. Munich, 1994.
———, ed. *Kaiser Wilhelm II. als Oberster Kriegsherr im Ersten Weltkrieg. Quellen aus der militärischen Umgebung des Kaisers 1914–1918.* Deutsche Geschichtsquellen des 19. und 20. Jahrhunderts 64. Munich, 2005.
Angelow, Jürgen, ed. *Der Erste Weltkrieg auf dem Balkan. Perspektiven der Forschung.* Berlin, 2011.
Anon. "Der Mensch und die Schlacht der Zukunft." *Militärwochenblatt* 30 (1926): 1066f.
Arbeitsgruppe Joint and Combined Operations und dem Service Historique de l'Armée de Terre. *Grundsätze der Truppenführung im Lichte der Operationsgeschichte von vier Jahr-*

hunderten. Eine Sammlung von Beispielen der Kriegs- und Operationsgeschichte vom Dreissigjährigen Krieg bis heute. Hamburg and Paris, 1999.

Arnold, Sabine, Wolfgang Ueberschär, and Wolfram Wette, eds. *Stalingrad. Mythos und Wirklichkeit einer Schlacht.* Frankfurt a.M., 1992.

Auwers, Siegfried von. "Die Strategie des Schlieffenplanes. Eine Erwiderung." *Archiv für Politik und Geschichte* 10 (1928): 16–22, 508–516.

Bailer-Galanda, Brigitte, Wolfgang Benz, and Wolfgang Neugebauer, eds. *Wahrheit und "Auschwitzlüge." Zur Bekämpfung "revisionistischer" Propaganda.* Wien, 1995.

Balck, William. "Die Taktik der Infanterie und der verbundenen Waffen." In *Löbells Jahresberichte über die Veränderungen und Fortschritte im Militärwesen* 33 (1906): 283–316.

———. *Entwicklung der Taktik im Weltkriege.* Berlin, 1922.

———. *Taktik,* vol. 1, *Einleitung und formale Taktik der Infanterie.* Berlin, 1908.

Bald, Detlef, ed. *Militärische Verantwortung in Staat und Gesellschaft. 175 Jahre Generalstabsausbildung in Deutschland.* Koblenz, 1986.

Bald, Detlef, and Paul Klein, eds. *Historische Leitlinien für das Militär der neunziger Jahre.* Militär und Sozialwissenschaften 2. Baden-Baden, 1989.

Barthel, Rolf. "Theorie und Praxis der Heeresmotorisierung im faschistischen Deutschland bis 1939." Doctoral diss., University of Leipzig, 1967.

Baumgart, Winfried. "Das 'Kaspi-Unternehmen'—Grössenwahn Ludendorffs oder Routineplanung des deutschen Generalstabes." *Jahrbücher für die Geschichte Osteuropas* 18 (1970): 47–126, 231–278.

———. *Deutsche Ostpolitik 1918. Von Brest-Litowsk bis zum Ende des Ersten Weltkrieges.* Munich, 1966.

———. "Zur Ansprache Hitlers vor den Führern der Wehrmacht am 22. August 1939." *Vierteljahrshefte für Zeitgeschichte* 16 (1968): 120–149.

Beck, Ludwig. *Studien.* Introduction by Hans Speidel, ed. Stuttgart, 1955.

Beer, Albert. *Der Fall Barbarossa. Untersuchungen zur Geschichte der Vorbereitungen des deutschen Feldzuges gegen die Union der Sozialistischen Sowjetrepubliken im Jahre 1941.* Dissertation, Westphalian Wilhelms University, Münster, 1978.

Beevor, Antony. *Stalingrad.* London, 1999.

Berenhorst, Georg Heinrich von. *Aphorismen.* Leipzig, 1805.

Bergien, Rüdiger. "Vorspiel des 'Vernichtungskrieges'? Die Ostfront des Ersten Weltkriegs und das Kontinuitätsproblem." In *Die vergessene Front. Der Osten 1914–15. Ereignis, Wirkung, Nachwirkung,* edited by Gerhard P. Gross, 393–408. Paderborn, 2006.

Bernhardi, Friedrich von. *Deutschland und der nächste Krieg.* Berlin, 1912.

———. "Über angriffsweise Kriegführung." *Beiheft zum Militärischen Wochenblatt* 4 (1905): 125–151.

———. *Vom heutigen Kriege.* 2 vols. Berlin, 1912.

———. *Vom Kriege der Zukunft. Nach den Erfahrungen des Weltkrieges.* Berlin, 1920.

Birken, Andreas, and Hans-Henning Gerlach. *Atlas und Lexikon zum Ersten Weltkrieg.* Königsbronn, 2002.

Bismarck, Otto von. *Bismarck Gespräche,* vol. 2, *Von der Reichsgründung bis zur Entlassung.* Edited by Willy Andreas. Basel, 1980.

———. *Die politischen Reden des Fürsten Bismarck.* 14 vols. Edited by Horst Kohl. Berlin, 1892–1905.

Bitzel, Uwe. *Die Konzeption des Blitzkrieges bei der deutschen Wehrmacht.* Europäische Hochschulschriften, Reihe III: Geschichte und Hilfswissenschaften 477. Frankfurt a.M., 1991.

Blume, Wilhelm von. *Militärpolitische Aufsätze.* Berlin, 1906.

———. *Strategie. Eine Studie.* Berlin, 1882.

———. *Strategie, ihre Aufgaben und Mittel, zugl. 3., erw. u. umgearb. Aufl. Strategie. Eine Studie.* Berlin, 1912.

Blumentritt, Günther. *Von Rundstedt: The Soldier and the Man.* London, 1952.

Boetticher, Friedrich von. "Der Lehrmeister des neuzeitlichen Krieges." In *Von Scharnhorst zu Schlieffen 1806–1906. Hundert Jahre preussisch-deutscher Generalstab,* edited by Friedrich von Cochenhausen, 249–319. Berlin, 1933. Auf Veranlassung des Reichswehrministeriums.

Boguslawski, Albert von. *Betrachtungen über Heerwesen und Kriegführung.* Berlin, 1897.

———. *Strategische Erörterungen betreffend die von General von Schlichting vertretenen Grundsätze.* Berlin, 1901.

Böhler, Jochen. *Auftakt zum Vernichtungskrieg. Die Wehrmacht in Polen 1939.* Frankfurt a.M., 2006.

———. *Der Überfall. Deutschlands Krieg gegen Polen.* Frankfurt a.M., 2009.

Bömelburg, Hans-Jürgen, Eugeniusz Cezary Król, and Michael Thomae, eds. *Warschauer Aufstand 1944. Ereignis und Wahrnehmung in Polen und Deutschland.* Im Auftrag des Militärgeschichtlichen Forschungsamtes und des Zentrums für Historische Forschung der Polnischen Akademie der Wissenschaften. Paderborn, 2010.

Boog, Horst. *Die deutsche Luftwaffenführung 1935–1945. Führungsprobleme, Spitzengliederung, Generalstabsausbildung.* Beiträge zur Militär- und Kriegsgeschichte 21. Stuttgart, 1982.

———. "Die Luftwaffe." In *Das Deutsche Reich und der Zweite Weltkrieg,* vol. 4, *Der Angriff auf die Sowjetunion,* edited by Horst Boog, Jürgen Förster, Joachim Hoffmann, Ernst Klink, Rolf-Dieter Müller, and Gerd R. Ueberschär, 277–319, 652–712. Stuttgart, 1987.

Boog, Horst, Jürgen Förster, Joachim Hoffmann, Ernst Klink, Rolf-Dieter Müller, and Gerd R. Ueberschär, eds. *Das Deutsche Reich und der Zweite Weltkrieg,* vol. 4, *Der Angriff auf die Sowjetunion.* Stuttgart, 1987.

Boog, Horst, Werner Rahn, Reinhard Stumpf, and Bernd Wegner, eds. *Das Deutsche Reich und der Zweite Weltkrieg,* vol. 6, *Der globale Krieg. Die Ausweitung zum Weltkrieg und der Wechsel der Initiative 1941 bis 1943.* Stuttgart, 1993.

Boog, Horst, Gerhard Krebs, and Detlef Vogel, eds. *Das Deutsche Reich und der Zweite Weltkrieg,* vol. 7, *Das Deutsche Reich in der Defensive. Strategischer Luftkrieg in Europa, Krieg im Westen und in Ostasien 1943 bis 1944/45.* Stuttgart, 2001.

Borgert, Heinz-Ludger. "Grundzüge der Landkriegführung von Schlieffen bis Guderian." In *Deutsche Militärgeschichte in sechs Bänden 1648–1939,* 6:427–584. Munich, 1983.

Borodziej, Włodzimierz. *Der Warschauer Aufstand 1944.* Frankfurt a.M., 2001.

Brand, Dieter. "Grundsätze operativer Führung." In *Denkschriften zu Fragen der operativen Führung,* 29–80. N.p: n.p., 1987.

Braun. "Der Strategische Überfall." *Militär-Wochenblatt* 18 (1939): 1134–1136.

Bremm, Klaus-Jürgen. *Von der Chaussee zur Schiene. Militärstrategie und Eisenbahnen in Preussen von 1833 bis zum Feldzug von 1866.* Militärgeschichtliche Studien 40. Munich, 2005.

Breymayer, Ursula, Bernd Ulrich, and Karin Wieland, eds. *Willensmenschen. Über deutsche Offiziere.* Frankfurt a.M., 1999.

Brill, Heinz. *Bogislaw von Bonin im Spannungsfeld zwischen Wiederbewaffnung—Westintegration—Wiedervereinigung. Ein Beitrag zur Entstehungsgeschichte der Bundeswehr 1952–1955.* 2 vols. Militär, Rüstung, Sicherheit 49. Baden-Baden, 1987.

Brockhaus Bilder-Conversations-Lexikon, vol. 3. Leipzig, 1839.

Brockhaus Enzyklopädie, vols. 16, 19. völlig neubearb. Aufl., Mannheim, 1991; 20., überarb. und aktual. Aufl. Mannheim, 1998.

Brockhaus' Kleines Konversations-Lexikon, vol. 2, 5th ed. Leipzig, 1911.

Brose, Eric Dorn. *The Kaiser's Army: The Politics of Military Technology in Germany during the Machine Age, 1870–1918.* Oxford, 2001.

Broszat, Martin, Klaus-Dietmar Henke, and Hans Woller, eds. *Von Stalingrad zur Währungsreform. Zur Sozialgeschichte des Umbruchs in Deutschland.* Munich, 1988. (Quellen und Darstellungen zur Zeitgeschichte, 26); 2. Aufl. 1989; 3. Aufl. 1990.

Bruckmüller, Ernst, ed. *Putzger—Atlas und Chronik zur Weltgeschichte.* Berlin, 2002.

Brühl, Reinhard, ed. *Wörterbuch zur deutschen Militärgeschichte,* vol. 1, A-Me. Schriften des Militärgeschichtlichen Instituts der DDR. Berlin (Ost), 1985.

Buchfinck, Ernst. *Der Krieg von gestern und morgen.* Schriften zur politischen Bildung, VI. Reihe, H. 11. Langensalza, 1930.

———. "Der Meinungskampf um den Marnefeldzug." *Historische Zeitschrift* 152 (1935): 286–300.

Buchholz, Frank. *Strategische und militärpolitische Diskussionen in der Gründungsphase der Bundeswehr 1949–1960.* Europäische Hochschulschriften, Reihe III: Geschichte und ihre Hilfswissenschaften 458. Frankfurt a.M., 1991.

Bucholz, Arden. *Moltke, Schlieffen and the Prussian War Planning.* New York, 1991.

Bülow, Adam Dietrich Freiherr von. *Geist des neuern Kriegssystems hergeleitet aus dem Grundsatze einer Basis der Operationen auch für Laien in der Kriegskunst fasslich vorgetragen von einem ehemaligen preussischen Offizier.* Hamburg, 1805.

Burchardt, Lothar. *Friedenswirtschaft und Kriegsvorsorge. Deutschlands wirtschaftliche Rüstungsbestrebungen vor 1914.* Militärgeschichtliche Studien 6. Boppard a.Rh., 1968.

———. "Operatives Denken und Planen von Schlieffen bis zum Beginn des Ersten Weltkrieges." In *Operatives Denken und Handeln in deutschen Streitkräften im 19. und 20. Jahrhundert,* edited by Horst Boog, 45–71. Herford, 1988.

Busch, Eckart. *Der Oberbefehl. Seine rechtliche Struktur in Preussen und in Deutschland seit 1848.* Militärgeschichtliche Studien 5. Boppard a.Rh., 1967.

Caemmerer, Rudolf von. *Die Entwicklung der strategischen Wissenschaft im 19. Jahrhundert.* Berlin, 1904.

Canitz und Dallwitz, Karl Ernst Freiherr von. *Nachrichten und Betrachtungen über die Taten und Schicksale der Reiterei in den Feldzügen Friedrichs II. und in denen neuerer Zeit,* vol. 2. Berlin, 1823–1824.

Carlier, Claude, and Stefan Martens, eds. *La France et l'Allemagne en guerre. Septembre 1939–November 1942.* Paris, 1990.

Chickering, Roger. "The American Civil War and the German Wars of Unification: Some Parting Shots." In *On the Road to Total War,* edited by Stig Förster and Jörg Nagler, 683–691. New York, 1997.

———. "The Sore Loser: Ludendorff's Total War." In *The Shadows of Total War: Europe, East Asia, and the United States, 1919–1939,* edited by Roger Chickering and Stig Förster, 151–178. Cambridge, Mass., 2003.

Chickering, Roger, and Stig Förster, eds. *The Shadows of Total War. Europe, East Asia, and the United States, 1919–1939.* Cambridge, Mass., 2003.

Citino, Robert M. *Blitzkrieg to Desert Storm. The Evolution of Operational Warfare.* Lawrence, Kans., 2004.

———. *The Path to Blitzkrieg: Doctrine and Training in the German Army, 1920–1939.* Boulder, Colo., 1999.

Clausewitz, Carl von. *Strategie aus dem Jahr 1804 mit Zusätzen von 1808 und 1809.* Edited by Eberhard Kessel. Hamburg, 1937.

———. *Vom Kriege. Hinterlassenes Werk des Generals Carl von Clausewitz,* 16th ed. Vollst. Ausg. im Urtext mit erneut erw. historisch-kritischer Würdigung. Edited by Werner Hahlweg. Bonn, 1952.

Cochenhausen, Friedrich von, ed. *Von Scharnhorst zu Schlieffen 1806–1906. Hundert Jahre preussisch-deutscher Generalstab.* Auf Veranlassung des Reichswehrministeriums. Berlin, 1933.

Conversations-Lexikon, oder kurzgefasstes Handwörterbuch für die in der gesellschaftlichen Unterhaltung aus den Wissenschaften und Künsten vorkommenden Gegenstände mit beständiger Rücksicht auf die Ereignisse der älteren und neueren Zeit. 6 vols., 2 subsequent vols. Leipzig, 1809–1811.

Corum, James S. *The Roots of Blitzkrieg: Hans von Seeckt and German Military Reform.* Lawrence, Kans., 1992.

Creveld, Martin L. Van. *Kampfkraft. Militärische Organisation und militärische Leistung 1939 bis 1945.* Inzelschriften zur Militärgeschichte 31. Freiburg i.Br., 1982.

———. *Supplying War: Logistics from Wallenstein to Patton.* Cambridge, U.K., 1997.

Davies, Norman. *Aufstand der Verlorenen. Der Kampf um Warschau 1944.* Munich, 2004.

Degreif, Dieter. "Der Schlieffenplan und seine Nachwirkung." Master's thesis, Johannes Gutenberg University, Mainz, 1973.

Deist, Wilhelm. "Die Aufrüstung der Wehrmacht." In *Das Deutsche Reich und der Zweite Weltkrieg,* vol. 1, *Ursachen und Voraussetzungen der deutschen Kriegspolitik,* edited by Wilhelm Deist, Manfred Messerschmidt, Hans-Erich Volkmann, and Wolfram Wette, 371–532. Stuttgart, 1991.

———. "Die Reichswehr und der Krieg der Zukunft." *Militärgeschichtliche Mitteilungen* 45 (1989): 81–92.

Deist, Wilhelm, Manfred Messerschmidt, Hans-Erich Volkmann, and Wolfram Wette, eds. *Das Deutsche Reich und der Zweite Weltkrieg,* vol. 1, *Ursachen und Voraussetzungen der deutschen Kriegspolitik.* Stuttgart, 1991.

Delbrück, Hans. *Erinnerungen, Aufsätze und Reden.* Berlin, 1902.

Denkschriften zu Fragen der operativen Führung. N.p.: n.p.: 1987.

Denkwürdigkeiten der militärischen Gesellschaft zu Berlin, 5 vols. Berlin, 1802–1805. New edition with introduction by Joachim Niemeyer. Bibliotheca Rerum Militarium 37. Osnabrück, 1985.

Diedrich, Torsten. *Paulus. Das Trauma von Stalingrad. Eine Biographie.* Paderborn, 2008.

Diedrich, Torsten, and Rüdiger Wenzke. *Die getarnte Armee. Geschichte der Kasernierten Volkspolizei der DDR 1952 bis 1956.* Militärgeschichte der DDR 1. Militärgeschichtliches Forschungsamt, Berlin, 2001.

DiNardo, Richard L. "German Armor Doctrine: Correcting the Myths." *War in History* 4 (1996): 384–397.

———. *Germany's Panzer Arm.* Westport, Conn., 1997. Pages 73–86.

———. *Mechanized Juggernaut or Military Anachronism? Horses and the German Army of World War II.* Contributions in Military Studies 113. New York, 1991.

Dipper, Christof, ed. *Krieg, Frieden und Demokratie. Festschrift für Martin Vogt zum 65. Geburtsgag.* Frankfurt a.M., 2001.

Domarus, Max. *Hitler. Reden und Proklamationen 1932–1945. Kommentiert von einem deutschen Zeitgenossen,* 2 vols., 3rd ed. Wiesbaden, 1973.

Doughty, Robert A. "France." In *War Planning 1914,* edited by Holger H. Herwig and Richard F. Hamilton, 143–174. New York, 2010.

Duden Fremdwörterbuch (Der Duden in 12 Bänden), vol. 5. Mannheim, 1997.

Dülffer, Jost, and Karl Holl, eds. *Bereit zum Krieg. Kriegsmentalität im Wilhelminischen Deutschland 1890–1914.* Beiträge zur historischen Friedensforschung, Göttingen, 1986.

Duppler, Jörg, and Gerhard P. Gross, eds. *Kriegsende 1918. Ereignis, Wirkung, Nachwirkung.* Beiträge zur Militärgeschichte 53. Im Auftrag des Militärgeschichtlichen Forschungsamtes. Munich, 1999.

Dupuy, Trevor N. *A Genius for War: The German Army and General Staff, 1807–1945.* New York, 1977.

Echternkamp, Jörg, ed. *Perspektiven der Militärgeschichte. Raum, Gewalt und Repräsentation in historischer Forschung und Bildung.* Beiträge zur Militärgeschichte 67. Munich, 2010.

———. "Wut auf die Wehrmacht? Vom Bild der deutschen Soldaten in der unmittelbaren Nachkriegszeit." In *Die Wehrmacht. Mythos und Realität,* edited by Rolf-Dieter Müller and Hans-Erich Volkmann, 1058–1080. Munich, 1999.

Echternkamp, Jörg, and Stefan Martens, eds. *Der Zweite Weltkrieg in Europa. Erfahrung und Erinnerung.* Im Auftrag des Deutschen Historischen Instituts Paris und des Militärgeschichtlichen Forschungsamtes Potsdam. Paderborn, 2007.

Ehlert, Hans. "Innenpolitische Auseinandersetzungen um die Pariser Verträge und die Wehrverfassung 1954 bis 1956." In Militärgeschichtliches Forschungsamt, *Anfänge westdeutscher Sicherheitspolitik 1945–1956,* vol. 3, 235–560. Munich, 1982.

Ehlert, Hans, Christian Greiner, Georg Meyer, and Bruno Thoss. *Die NATO-Option.* Munich, 1993.

Ehlert, Hans, Michael Epkenhans, and Gerhard P. Gross, eds. *The Schlieffen Plan: International Perspectives on the German Strategy for World War I.* English translation editor David T. Zabecki. Lexington, Ky., 2014.

Einmannsberger, Ludwig Ritter von. *Der Kampfwagenkrieg.* Berlin, 1933.

Elble, Rolf. *Die Schlacht an der Bzura im September 1939 aus deutscher und polnischer Sicht.* Einzelschriften zur militärischen Geschichte des Zweiten Weltkrieges 15. Freiburg i.Br., 1975.

Elser, Gerhard. "Von der 'Einheitsgruppe' zum 'Sturmzug.' Zur Entwicklung der deutschen Infanterie 1922–1945." *Militärgeschichte* 1 (1995): 3–11.

Elz, Wolfgang, and Sönke Neitzel, eds. *Internationale Beziehungen im 19. und 20. Jahrhundert. Festschrift für Winfried Baumgart zum 65. Geburtstag.* Paderborn, 2003.

Elze, Walter. *Tannenberg. Das deutsche Heer von 1914. Seine Grundzüge und deren Auswirkung im Sieg an der Ostfront.* Breslau, 1928.

Engel, Gerhard. *Heeresadjutant bei Hitler 1938–1943. Aufzeichnungen des Majors Engel.* Edited by Hildegard von Kotze. Schriftenreihe der Vierteljahrshefte für Zeitgeschichte 29. Stuttgart, 1975.

English, John. "The Operational Art: Developments in the Theories of War." In *The Operational Art: Developments in the Theories of War,* edited by Brian J. C. McKercher and Michael A. Hennessy, 7–28. Westport, Conn., 1996.

Epkenhans, Michael. "'Wir Deutsche fürchten Gott'—Zur Rolle des Krieges in Bismarcks Aussenpolitik." *Politische Studien. Zweimonatsschrift für Politik und Zeitgeschehen* 391 (2003): 54–63.

Epkenhans, Michael, and Gerhard P. Gross, eds. *The Danish Straits and German Naval Power, 1905–1918.* Potsdamer Schriften zur Militärgeschichte 13. Potsdam, 2010.

Erfurth, Waldemar. *Die Geschichte des deutschen Generalstabes von 1918 bis 1945.* Göttingen, 1957.

———. "Die Überraschung im Kriege." *Militärwissenschaftliche Rundschau* (1937): 597–622, 750–776; (1938): 171–202, 313–346.

———. *Der Vernichtungssieg. Eine Studie über das Zusammenwirken getrennter Heeresteile.* Berlin, 1939.

———. "Das Zusammenwirken getrennter Heeresteile." *Militärwissenschaftliche Rundschau* (1938): 156–178, 291–314, 472–499.

Erickson, John. *The Soviet High Command: A Military Political History, 1918–1941.* London, 1962.

Europäischen Publikation e.V. *Vollmacht des Gewissens.* 2 vols. Berlin, 1965.

Falkenhausen, Ludwig Freiherr von. "Die Bedeutung der Flanke." *Vierteljahreshefte für Truppenführung* (1908): 583–605.

———. *Der grosse Krieg in der Jetztzeit. Eine Studie über Bewegung und Kampf der Massenheere des 20. Jahrhunderts.* Berlin, 1909.

Falkenhayn, Erich von. *Die Oberste Heeresleitung 1914–1916 in ihren wichtigsten Entschliessungen.* Berlin, 1920.

Fanning, William J., Jr. "The Origin of the Term 'Blitzkrieg': Another View." *Journal of Military History* 61 (1997): 283–302.

Felleckner, Stefan. *Kampf. Ein vernachlässigter Bereich der Militärgeschichte.* Berlin, 2004.

Foerster, Roland G. "Das operative Denken Moltkes des Älteren und die Folgen." In *Ausgewählte Operationen und ihre militärhistorischen Grundlagen,* edited by Hans-Martin Ottmer and Heiger Ostertag, 251–274. Operatives Denken und Handeln in deutschen Streitkräften 4. Im Auftrag des Militärgeschichtlichen Forschungsamtes, Bonn, 1993.

———, ed. *Generalfeldmarschall von Moltke. Bedeutung und Wirkung.* Beiträge zur Militärgeschichte 33. Im Auftrag des Militärgeschichtlichen Forschungsamtes, Munich, 1991.

Foerster, Roland G., Christian Greiner, Georg Meyer, Hans-Jürgen Rautenberg, and Norbert Wiggershaus. *Von der Kapitulation bis zum Pleven-Plan.* Munich, 1982.

Foerster, Wolfgang. *Aus der Gedankenwerkstatt des Deutschen Generalstabes.* Berlin, 1931.

———. *Graf Schlieffen und der Weltkrieg.* 3 parts. Berlin, 1921.

———. "Zur geschichtlichen Rolle des preussisch-deutschen Generalstabs." *Wehrwissenschaftliche Rundschau* 8 (1951): 7–20.

Foertsch, Hermann. *Kriegskunst heute und morgen.* Berlin, 1939.

Foley, Robert T. *German Strategy and the Path to Verdun: Erich von Falkenhayn and the Development of Attrition, 1870–1916.* Cambridge, Mass., 2005.

Förster, Gerhard. *Totaler Krieg und Blitzkrieg: Die Theorie des totalen Krieges und des Blitzkrieges in der Militärdoktrin des faschistischen Deutschlands am Vorabend des Zweiten Weltkrieges.* Militärhistorische Studien 10. Berlin (Ost), 1967.

Förster, Jürgen. "The Dynamics of Volksgemeinschaft: The Effectiveness of the German Military Establishment in the Second World War." In *Military Effectiveness,* vol. 3, *The Second World War,* edited by Williamson Murray and Allan R. Millette, 180–230. Boston, Mass., 1988.

———. "Hitlers Entscheidung für den Krieg gegen die Sowjetunion." In *Das Deutsche Reich und der Zweite Weltkrieg,* vol. 4, *Der Angriff auf die Sowjetunion,* edited by Horst Boog, Jürgen Förster, Joachim Hoffmann, Ernst Klink, Rolf-Dieter Müller, and Gerd R. Ueberschär, 3–37. Stuttgart, 1987.

———. "Das Unternehmen 'Barbarossa' als Eroberungs- und Vernichtungskrieg." In *Das Deutsche Reich und der Zweite Weltkrieg,* vol. 4, *Der Angriff auf die Sowjetunion,* edited by Horst Boog, Jürgen Förster, Joachim Hoffmann, Ernst Klink, Rolf-Dieter Müller, and Gerd R. Ueberschär, 413–447. Stuttgart, 1987.

———. *Die Wehrmacht im NS-Staat. Eine strukturgeschichtliche Analyse.* Beiträge zur Militärgeschichte. Militärgeschichte kompakt 2. Munich, 2007.

———. "Weltanschauung als Waffe. Vom 'Vaterländischen Unterricht' zur 'Nationalsozialistischen Führung.'" In *Erster Weltkrieg—Zweiter Weltkrieg. Ein Vergleich. Krieg, Kriegserlebnis, Kriegserfahrung in Deutschland,* edited by Bruno Thoss and Hans-Erich Volkmann, 287–300. Paderborn, 2002.

Förster, Stig, ed. *An der Schwelle zum Totalen Krieg. Die militärische Debatte über den Krieg der Zukunft 1919–1939.* Krieg in der Geschichte 13. Paderborn, 2002.

———. *The Battlefield: Towards a Modern History of War.* Annual Lecture, German Historical Institute London, 2007. London, 2008.

———. "Der deutsche Generalstab und die Illusion des kurzen Krieges, 1871–1914. Metakritik eines Mythos." *Militärgeschichtliche Mitteilungen* 54 (1995): 61–95.

———. *Der doppelte Militarismus. Die deutsche Heeresrüstungspolitik zwischen Status-quo-Sicherung und Aggression 1890–1913.* Veröffentlichungen des Instituts für europäische Geschichte Mainz 118. Stuttgart, 1985.

———, ed. *Der Grosse Krieg. Europäische Militärzeitschriften und die Debatte über den Krieg der Zukunft, 1880–1914.* In preparation.

———. "Helmuth von Moltke und das Problem des industrialisierten Volkskriegs im 19. Jahrhundert." In *Generalfeldmarschall von Moltke. Bedeutung und Wirkung,* edited by Roland G. Foerster, 103–115. Beiträge zur Militärgeschichte 33. Im Auftrag des Militärgeschichtlichen Forschungsamtes, Munich, 1991.

———. "Der Krieg der Willensmenschen. Die deutsche Offizierselite auf dem Weg in den Weltkrieg, 1871–1914." In *Willensmenschen. Über deutsche Offiziere,* edited by Ursula Breymayer, Bernd Ulrich, and Karin Wieland, 23–36. Frankfurt a.M., 1999.

———. "Optionen der Kriegführung im Zeitalter des 'Volkskrieges.' Zu Helmuth von Moltkes militärisch-politischen Überlegungen nach den Erfahrungen der Einigungskriege." In *Militärische Verantwortung in Staat und Gesellschaft. 175 Jahre Generalstabsausbildung in Deutschland,* edited by Detlef Bald, 83–108. Koblenz, 1986.

———. "Der Vernichtungsgedanke in der militärischen Tradition des Deutschen Kaiserreiches. Überlegungen zum Problem historischer Kontinuität." In *Krieg, Frieden und Demokratie. Festschrift für Martin Vogt zum 65. Geburtsgag,* edited by Christof Dipper, 253–265. Frankfurt a.M., 2001.

———. "'Vom Kriege.' Überlegungen zu einer modernen Militärgeschichte." In *Was ist Militärgeschichte?,* edited by Benjamin Ziemann and Thomas Kühne, 265–282. Paderborn, 2000.

Förster, Stig, and Jörg Nagler, eds. *On the Road to Total War: The American Civil War and the German Wars of Unification, 1861–1871.* New York, 1997.

Forstmeier, Friedrich, and Hans-Erich Volkmann, eds. *Wirtschaft und Rüstung am Vorabend des Zweiten Weltkrieges.* Düsseldorf, 1975.

Frank, Hans. *Im Angesicht des Galgens.* Munich, 1952.

Freuding, Christian. "Organizing for War: Strategic Culture and the Organization of High Command in Britain and Germany, 1850–1945. A Comparative Perspective." *Defence Studies* 10, no. 3 (2010): 431–460.

Freytag-Loringhoven, Hugo von. "Irreführende Verallgemeinerungen." *Militär-Wochenblatt* 12 (1919): 213–220.

Frieser, Karl-Heinz. *The Blitzkrieg Legend: The 1940 Campaign in the West.* Annapolis, Md., 2005.

———, ed. *Das Deutsche Reich und der Zweite Weltkrieg,* vol. 8, *Die Ostfront 1943/44. Der Krieg im Osten und an den Nebenfronten.* Im Auftrag des Militärgeschichtlichen Forschungsamtes, Munich, 2007.

———. "Die deutschen Blitzkriege: Operativer Triumph—strategische Tragödie." In *Die Wehrmacht. Mythos und Realität,* edited by Rolf-Dieter Müller and Hans-Erich Volkmann, 182–196. Munich, 1999.

———. "Ein zweites 'Wunder an der Weichsel?' Die Panzerschlacht vor Warschau im August 1944 und ihre Folgen." In *Der Warschauer Aufstand 1944,* edited by Bernd Martin and Stanisława Lewandowska, 45–64. Warszawa, 1999.

———. "Irrtümer und Illusionen: Die Fehleinschätzungen der deutschen Führung." In *Das Deutsche Reich und der Zweite Weltkrieg,* vol. 8, *Die Ostfront 1943/44. Der Krieg im Osten und an den Nebenfronten,* edited by Karl-Heinz Frieser, 493–525. Munich, 2007.

———. "Die Rückzugskämpfe der Heeresgruppe Nord bis Kurland." In *Das Deutsche Reich und der Zweite Weltkrieg,* vol. 8, *Die Ostfront 1943/44. Der Krieg im Osten und an den Nebenfronten,* edited by Karl-Heinz Frieser, 623–678. Munich, 2007.

———. "Die Schlacht im Kursker Bogen." In *Das Deutsche Reich und der Zweite Weltkrieg,* vol. 8, *Die Ostfront 1943/44. Der Krieg im Osten und an den Nebenfronten,* edited by Karl-Heinz Frieser, 83–208. Munich, 2007.

———. "Der Zusammenbruch der Heeresgruppe Mitte im Sommer 1944." In *Das Deutsche Reich und der Zweite Weltkrieg,* vol. 8, *Die Ostfront 1943/44. Der Krieg im Osten und an den Nebenfronten,* edited by Karl-Heinz Frieser, 526–603. Munich, 2007.

Gablik, Axel F. *Strategische Planungen in der Bundesrepublik Deutschland 1955–1967: Poli-

tische Kontrolle oder militärische Notwendigkeit? Nuclear History Program, 5; Internationale Politik und Sicherheit, 30. Baden-Baden, 1996.

Gackenholz, Hermann. *Entscheidung in Lothringen 1914. Der Operationsplan des jüngeren Moltke und seine Durchführung auf dem linken deutschen Heeresflügel.* Schriften der kriegsgeschichtlichen Abteilung im historischen Seminar der Friedrich-Wilhelms-Universität Berlin 2. Berlin, 1933.

Gahlen, Gundula. "Deutung und Umdeutung des Rumänienfeldzuges in Deutschland zwischen 1916 und 1945." In *Der Erste Weltkrieg auf dem Balkan. Perspektiven der Forschung,* edited by Jürgen Angelow, 289–310. Berlin, 2011.

Gallwitz, Max von. *Meine Führertätigkeit im Weltkrieg 1914-1916. Belgien—Osten—Balkan.* Berlin, 1929.

Ganzenmüller, Jörg. *Das belagerte Leningrad 1941-1944. Die Stadt in den Strategien der Angreifer und Angegriffenen.* Krieg in der Geschichte 22. Diss. phil., Mit Unterstützung des Militärgeschichtlichen Forschungsamtes, Paderborn, 2005.

Gembruch, Werner. "General von Schlichting." *Wehrwissenschaftliche Rundschau* (1960): 186–196.

Gersdorff, Ursula von, ed. *Geschichte und Militärgeschichte. Wege der Forschung.* Mit Unterstützung des Militärgeschichtlichen Forschungsamtes, Frankfurt a.M., 1974.

Geyer, Michael. *Aufrüstung oder Sicherheit. Die Reichswehr in der Krise der Machtpolitik 1924-1936.* Veröffentlichungen des Instituts für Europäische Geschichte Mainz, Abteilung Universalgeschichte 91. Wiesbaden, 1980.

———. "Eine Kriegsgeschichte, die vom Tod spricht." In *Physische Gewalt. Studien zur Geschichte der Neuzeit,* edited by Thomas Lindenberger and Alf Lüdtke, 136–161. Frankfurt a.M., 1995.

———. "German Strategy in the Age of Machine Warfare, 1914–1945." In *Makers of Modern Strategy from Machiavelli to the Nuclear Age,* edited by Peter Paret, 527–597. Princeton, N.J., 1986.

———. "Das Zweite Rüstungsprogramm (1930–1934)." *Militärgeschichtliche Mitteilungen* 17 (1975): 125–172.

Giehrl, Hermann. *Der Feldherr Napoleon als Organisator. Betrachtungen über seine Verkehrs- und Nachrichtenmittel, seine Arbeits- und Befehlsweise.* Berlin, 1911.

Glantz, David M. *After Stalingrad: The Red Army's Winter Offensive, 1942-1943.* Solihull, U.K., 2008.

———. *The Battle for Leningrad, 1941-1944.* Lawrence, Kans., 2002.

———. *Colossus Reborn: The Red Army at War, 1941-1943.* Lawrence, Kans., 2005.

———. *From the Don to the Dnepr: Soviet Offensive Operations, December 1942 to August 1943.* Cass Series on Soviet Military Experience 1. London, 1991.

Glantz, David M., and Jonathan M. House. *The Battle of Kursk.* Lawrence, Kans., 1999.

Goebbels, Joseph. *Tagebücher 1924-1945,* vol. 4, *1940-1942.* Edited by Ralf Georg Reuth. Munich, 1992.

———. *Die Tagebücher von Joseph Goebbels, Diktate 1941-1945.* 15 vols. Edited by Elke Fröhlich. Im Auftrag des Instituts für Zeitgeschichte und mit Unterstützung des Staatlichen Archivdienstes Russlands, Munich, 1993–1996.

Goltz, Colmar Freiherr von der. *Krieg- und Heerführung.* Berlin, 1901.

———. *Kriegführung. Kurze Lehre ihrer wichtigsten Grundsätze und Formen.* Berlin, 1895.

———. *Das Volk in Waffen. ein Buch über Heerwesen und Kriegführung unserer Zeit.* Berlin, 1895.

Görlitz, Walter. *History of the German General Staff 1657–1945*. New York, 1953.

Greiner, Christian. "Die alliierten militärstrategischen Planungen zur Verteidigung West-europas 1947–1950." In Militärgeschichtliches Forschungsamt, *Anfänge westdeutscher Sicherheitspolitik 1945–1956*, vol. 1, 119–323. Munich, 1982.

———. "Die Entwicklung der Bündnisstrategie 1949 bis 1958." In *Die NATO als Mil-itärallianz. Strategie, Organisation und nukleare Kontrolle im Bündnis 1949 bis 1959*, by Christian Greiner, Klaus A. Maier, and Heinz Rebhan, ed. Bruno Thoss, 17–174. Munich, 2003.

———. "General Adolf Heusinger (1897–1982). Operatives Denken und Planen 1948 bis 1956." In *Operatives Denken und Handeln in deutschen Streitkräften im 19. und 20. Jahr-hundert*, edited by Horst Boog, 225–261. Herford, 1988.

———. "Die militärische Eingliederung der Bundesrepublik Deutschland in die WEU und die NATO 1954 bis 1957." In Militärgeschichtliches Forschungsamt, *Anfänge west-deutscher Sicherheitspolitik 1945–1956*, vol. 3, 561–850. Munich, 1993.

Greiner, Christian, Klaus A. Maier, and Heinz Rebhan. *Die NATO als Militärallianz. Strat-egie, Organisation und nukleare Kontrolle im Bündnis 1949 bis 1959*. Edited by Bruno Thoss. Entstehung und Probleme des Atlantischen Bündnisses bis 1956, 4. Im Auftrag des Militärgeschichtlichen Forschungsamtes, Munich, 2003.

Groener, Wilhelm. *Der Feldherr wider Willen. Operative Studien über den Weltkrieg*. Ber-lin, 1930.

———. *Lebenserinnerungen. Jugend—Generalstab—Weltkrieg*. Edited by Friedrich Freiherr Hiller von Gaertringen. Deutsche Geschichtsquellen des 19. und 20. Jahrhunderts 41. Göttingen, 1957.

———. *Das Testament des Grafen Schlieffen*. Berlin, 1927.

Gross, Gerhard P. "Das Dogma der Beweglichkeit. Überlegungen zur Genese der deutschen Heerestaktik im Zeitalter der Weltkriege." In *Erster Weltkrieg—Zweiter Weltkrieg. Ein Ver-gleich. Krieg, Kriegserlebnis, Kriegserfahrung in Deutschland*, edited by Bruno Thoss and Hans-Erich Volkmann, 143–166. Im Auftrag des Militärgeschichtlichen Forschungs-amtes, Paderborn, 2002.

———, ed. *Führungsdenken in europäischen und nordamerikanischen Streitkräften im 19. und 20. Jahrhundert*. Vorträge zur Militärgeschichte 19. Im Auftrag des Militärge-schichtlichen Forschungsamtes, Bonn, 2001.

———. "Gerhard von Scharnhorst oder historische Bildung." *Truppenpraxis Wehrausbil-dung. Zeitschrift für Führung, Ausbildung und Erziehung* 3 (1995): 207–213.

———. "German Plans to Occupy Denmark, 'Case J,' 1916–1918." In *The Danish Straits and German Naval Power, 1905–1918*, edited by Michael Epkenhans and Gerhard P. Gross, 155–166. Potsdamer Schriften zur Militärgeschichte 13. Potsdam, 2010.

———. "Ein Nebenkriegsschauplatz. Die deutschen Operationen gegen Rumänien 1916." In *Der Erste Weltkrieg auf dem Balkan. Perspektiven der Forschung*, edited by Jürgen Angelow, 143–158. Berlin, 2011.

———. "Der 'Raum' als operationsgeschichtliche Kategorie im Zeitalter der Weltkriege." In *Perspektiven der Militärgeschichte. Raum, Gewalt und Repräsentation in historischer Forschung und Bildung*, edited by Jörg Echternkamp, 115–140. Beiträge zur Militärge-schichte 67. Munich, 2010.

———. "Im Schatten des Westens. Die deutsche Kriegführung an der Ostfront bis Ende

1915." In *Die vergessene Front. Der Osten 1914–15. Ereignis, Wirkung, Nachwirkung,* edited by Gerhard P. Gross, 49–64. Im Auftrag des Militärgeschichtlichen Forschungsamtes, Paderborn, 2006.

———. *Die Seekriegführung der Kaiserlichen Marine im Jahre 1918.* Europäische Hochschulschriften, Reihe III 387. Frankfurt a.M., 1989.

———. "There Was a Schlieffenplan." In *Der Schlieffenplan. Analysen und Dokumente,* edited by Hans Ehlert, Michael Epkenhans and Gerhard P. Gross, 117–160. Im Auftrag des Militärgeschichtlichen Forschungsamtes und der Otto-von-Bismarck-Stiftung. Paderborn, 2007.

———. "Unternehmen 'Albion.' Eine Studie zur Zusammenarbeit von Armee und Marine während des Ersten Weltkrieges." In *Internationale Beziehungen im 19. und 20. Jahrhundert. Festschrift für Winfried Baumgart zum 65. Geburtstag,* edited by Wolfgang Elz and Sönke Neitzel, 171–186. Paderborn, 2003.

———, ed. *Die vergessene Front. Der Osten 1914–15. Ereignis, Wirkung, Nachwirkung.* Zeitalter der Weltkriege 1. Im Auftrag des Militärgeschichtlichen Forschungsamtes, Paderborn, 2006.

Der Grosse Brockhaus. Vols. 8 and 17. Wiesbaden, 1955.

Der Grosse Brockhaus: Handbuch des Wissens in 20 Bänden. Vols. 13 and 15., völlig neubearb. Aufl. Leipzig, 1932.

Grossen Generalstab. *Der Schlachterfolg. Mit welchen Mitteln wurde er erstrebt?* Studien zur Kriegsgeschichte und Taktik 3. Berlin, 1903.

———. *Heeresverpflegung.* Studien zur Kriegsgeschichte und Taktik 6. Berlin, 1913.

Guderian, Heinz. *Achtung—Panzer! Die Entwicklung der Panzerwaffe, ihre Kampftaktik und ihre operativen Möglichkeiten.* Stuttgart, 1937.

———. "Bewegliche Truppenkörper (Eine kriegsgeschichtliche Studie, 5 Teile)." *Militär-Wochenblatt* 18 (1927): 649–653; 19 (1927): 687–694; 20 (1927): 728–731; 21 (1927): 772–776; 22 (1927): 819–822.

———. *Erinnerungen eines Soldaten.* Heidelberg, 1951.

———. *Panzer Leader.* Cambridge, Mass., 2001.

———. "Schnelle Truppen einst und jetzt." *Militärwissenschaftliche Rundschau* (1939): 229–243.

Haas, Gerhart. "Zum Bild der Wehrmacht in der Geschichtsschreibung der DDR." In *Die Wehrmacht. Mythos und Realität,* edited by Rolf-Dieter Müller and Hans-Erich Volkmann, 1100–1112. Munich, 1999.

Habeck, Mary R. *Storm of Steel. The Development of Armor Doctrine in Germany and the Soviet Union, 1919–1939.* London, 2003.

Hackl, Ottmar. "Das 'Schlagen aus der Nachhand.' Die Operationen der Heeresgruppe Don bzw. Süd zwischen Donez und Dnepir 1943." *Truppendienst* (1983): 132–137.

Hahlweg, Werner. "Der klassische Begriff der Strategie und seine Entwicklung." In *Strategie-Handbuch,* vol. 1, edited by Gerhard Fels, 9–29. Schriften des Instituts für Sicherheitspolitik an der Christian-Albrechts-Universität zu Kiel 8. Bonn, 1990.

Halder, Franz. *Hitler als Feldherr.* Munich, 1949.

———. *Kriegstagebuch. Tägliche Aufzeichnungen des Chefs des Generalstabes des Heeres 1939–1942.* 3 vols. Edited by Hans-Adolf Jacobsen. Stuttgart, 1962–1964.

Hammerich, Helmut R. "Kommiss kommt von Kompromiss. Das Heer der Bundeswehr zwischen Wehrmacht und U.S. Army (1950 bis 1970)." In *Das Heer 1950 bis 1970. Konzeption, Organisation und Aufstellung,* by Helmut R. Hammerich, Dieter H. Kollmer, Martin Rink, and Rudolf Schlaffer, 17–351. Sicherheitspolitik und Streitkräfte der Bundesrepublik Deutschland 3. Unter Mitarb. von Michael Poppe, Munich, 2006.

Hammerich, Helmut R., Dieter H. Kollmer, Martin Rink, and Rudolf Schlaffer. *Das Heer 1950 bis 1970. Konzeption, Organisation und Aufstellung.* Sicherheitspolitik und Streitkräfte der Bundesrepublik Deutschland 3. Unter Mitarb. von Michael Poppe, Munich, 2006.

Handbuch der neuzeitlichen Wehrwissenschaften, vol. 1, *Wehrpolitik und Kriegführung.* Im Auftrage der Deutschen Gesellschaft für Wehrpolitik und Wehrwissenschaften und unter umstehend aufgeführter Sachverständiger von Hermann Franke, Berlin, 1936.

Handbuch für Heer und Flotte: Enzyklopädie der Kriegswissenschaften und verwandter Gebiete, vol. 1. Edited by Georg von Alten. Leipzig, 1909.

Handbuch für Heerestaktik, vol. 1, *Grundbegriffe.* Berlin, 1939.

Hansen, Ernst Willi, Gerhard Schreiber, and Bernd Wegner, eds. *Politischer Wandel, organisierte Gewalt und nationale Sicherheit. Beiträge zur neueren Geschichte Deutschlands und Frankreichs. Festschrift für Klaus-Jürgen Müller.* Beiträge zur Militärgeschichte 50. Im Auftrag des Militärgeschichtlichen Forschungsamtes, Munich, 1995.

Harris, J. P., and F. H. Tiase, eds. *Armoured Warfare.* London, 1990.

Hartmann, Christian. *Halder. Generalstabschef Hitlers 1938–1942.* Paderborn, 1991.

———. "Verbrecherischer Krieg—verbrecherische Wehrmacht? Überlegungen zur Struktur des deutschen Ostheeres 1941–1944." *Vierteljahrshefte für Zeitgeschichte* 52 (2004): 1–75.

———. *Wehrmacht im Ostkrieg. Front und militärisches Hinterland 1941/1942.* Quellen und Darstellungen zur Zeitgeschichte 75. Munich, 2009.

Hartmann, Christian, Johannes Hürter, and Ulrike Jureit, eds. *Verbrechen der Wehrmacht. Bilanz einer Debatte.* Munich, 2005.

Hartmann, Christian, Johannes Hürter, Peter Lieb, and Dieter Pohl. *Der deutsche Krieg im Osten 1941–1944. Facetten einer Grenzüberschreitung.* Quellen und Darstellungen zur Zeitgeschichte 76. Munich, 2009.

Heiber, Helmut, ed. *Hitlers Lagebesprechungen. Die Protokollfragmente seiner militärischen Konferenzen 1942–1945.* Quellen und Darstellungen zur Zeitgeschichte 10. Stuttgart, 1962.

Heider, Paul. "Der totale Krieg—seine Vorbereitung durch Reichswehr und Wehrmacht." In *Der Weg der deutschen Eliten in den zweiten Weltkrieg,* edited by Ludwig Nestler, 35–80. Berlin, 1990.

Heinemann, Winfried. "The Development of German Armoured Forces, 1918–1940." In *Armoured Warfare,* edited by J. P. Harris and F. H. Tiase, 51–69. London, 1990.

Herbst, Ludolf. *Der Totale Krieg und die Ordnung der Wirtschaft. Die Kriegswirtschaft im Spannungsfeld von Politik, Ideologie und Propaganda 1939–1945.* Studien zur Zeitgeschichte 21. Stuttgart, 1982.

Herders Conversations-Lexikon, vol. 4. Freiburg i.Br., 1856.

Hermann, Erwin. "Die Friedensarmeen der Sieger und der Besiegten des Weltkrieges." *Wissen und Wehr* 3 (1922): 268–282.

Herwig, Holger H. *The Marne, 1914: The Opening of World War I and the Battle that Changed the World.* New York, 2009.

Herwig, Holger H., and Richard F. Hamilton, eds. *War Planning 1914.* New York, 2010.

Heuser, Beatrice. *Clausewitz lesen! Eine Einführung. Beiträge zur Militärgeschichte.* Militärgeschichte kompakt 1. Munich, 2005.

———. *NATO, Britain, France and the FRG: Nuclear Strategies and Forces for Europe, 1949–2000.* London, 1997.

Heusinger, Adolf. *Befehl im Widerstreit. Schicksalstunden der deutschen Armee 1923–1945.* Tübingen, 1957.

———. *Ein deutscher Soldat im 20. Jahrhundert.* Schriftenreihe Innere Führung, Beih. 3/87 zur Information für die Truppe. Bundesministerium der Verteidigung, Bonn, 1987.

———. "In memoriam, Franz Halder 30.6.1884–2.4.1972." *Wehrforschung* (1972): 79.

Hillgruber, Andreas. *Grossmachtpolitik und Militarismus im 20. Jahrhundert. Drei Beiträge zum Kontinuitätsproblem.* Düsseldorf, 1974.

———. *Hitlers Strategie. Politik und Kriegführung 1940–1941.* Frankfurt a.M., 1965.

———, ed. *Probleme des Zweiten Weltkrieges.* Neue wissenschaftliche Bibliothek, 20: Geschichte. Köln, 1967.

———. "Der Zenit des Zweiten Weltkrieges: Juli 1941." In *Die Zerstörung Europas. Beiträge zur Weltkriegsepoche, 1914 bis 1945,* edited by Andreas Hillgruber, 273–295. Frankfurt a.M., 1988.

Hitz, Hans. "Taktik und Strategie. Zur Entwicklung kriegswissenschaftlicher Begriffe." *Wehrwissenschaftliche Rundschau. Zeitschrift für Europäische Sicherheit* (1956): 611–628.

Höbelt, Lothar. "Schlieffen, Beck, Potiorek und das Ende der gemeinsamen deutsch-österreichisch-ungarischen Aufmarschpläne im Osten." *Militärgeschichtliche Mitteilungen* 2 (1984): 7–30.

———. "'So wie wir haben nicht einmal die Japaner angegriffen.' Österreich-Ungarns Nordfront 1914–15." In *Die vergessene Front. Der Osten 1914–15. Ereignis, Wirkung, Nachwirkung,* edited by Gerhard P. Gross, 87–119. Zeitalter der Weltkriege 1. Im Auftrag des Militärgeschichtlichen Forschungsamtes, Paderborn, 2006.

Hoeres, Peter. "Die Slawen. Perzeptionen des Kriegsgegners bei den Mittelmächten. Selbst- und Feindbild." In *Die vergessene Front. Der Osten 1914–15. Ereignis, Wirkung, Nachwirkung,* edited by Gerhard P. Gross, 179–200. Zeitalter der Weltkriege 1. Im Auftrag des Militärgeschichtlichen Forschungsamtes, Paderborn, 2006.

Hoffmann, Max. *Die Aufzeichnungen des Generalmajors Max Hoffmann,* vol. 2. Edited by Karl Friedrich Nowak. Berlin, 1929.

Höhn, Hans. "Zur Bewertung der Infanterie durch die Führung der deutschen Wehrmacht." *Zeitschrift für Militärgeschichte* 4 (1965): 417–432.

Horne, John, and Alan Kramer. *Deutsche Kriegsgreuel 1914. Die umstrittene Wahrheit.* Hamburg, 2004.

Howard, Michael. *War in European History.* Oxford, 1976.

Hubatsch, Walther, ed. *Hitlers Weisungen für die Kriegführung 1939–1945. Dokumente des Oberkommandos der Wehrmacht.* Frankfurt a.M., 1962.

Hübner, Johann. *Johann Hübners Zeitungs- und Conversations-Lexikon: Ein vaterländisches Handwörterbuch,* Part 3, M–R, 31st ed. Leipzig, 1826.

Hull, Isabel V. *Absolute Destruction: Military Culture and the Practices of War in Imperial Germany.* Ithaca, N.Y., 2005.

Hürter, Johannes. *Hitlers Heerführer. Die deutschen Oberbefehlshaber im Krieg gegen die Sowjetunion 1941–1942.* Quellen und Darstellungen zur Zeitgeschichte 66. Munich, 2006.

———. "Die Wehrmacht vor Leningrad. Krieg und Besatzungspolitik der 18. Armee im Herbst und Winter 1941/42." *Vierteljahrshefte für Zeitgeschichte* 49 (2001): 377–440.

———. *Wilhelm Groener. Reichswehrminister am Ende der Weimarer Republik (1928 bis 1932).* Beiträge zur Militärgeschichte 39. Munich, 1993.

Ideen und Strategien 1940. Ausgewählte Operationen und deren militärgeschichtliche Aufarbeitung. Operatives Denken und Handeln in deutschen Streitkräften 3. Bonn, 1990.

International Military Tribunal. *Trial of the Major War Criminals before the International Military Tribunal Nuremberg, 14 November 1945–1 October 1946.* 42 vols. Nuremberg, 1947–1949.

Jeismann, Karl-Ernst. *Das Problem des Präventivkrieges im europäischen Staatensystem mit besonderem Blick auf die Bismarckzeit.* Munich, 1957.

Jochim. "Hinhaltendes Gefecht." *Wissen und Wehr* 5 (1924): 106–114.

Jomini, Henri. *Précis de l'art de la guerre, ou noveau tableau analytique des principales combinaisons de la stratégie, de la grande tactique et de la politique militaire.* 2 vols. New revision of the 1855 ed., with an introduction by H. R. Kurz. Osnabrück, 1974.

Jünger, Ernst. "Die Ausbildungsvorschrift der Infanterie." *Militär-Wochenblatt* 108 (1923): 51–53.

Justrow, Karl. *Feldherr und Kriegstechnik. Studien über den Operationsplan des Grafen Schlieffen und Lehren für unseren Wehraufbau und unsere Landesverteidigung.* Oldenburg, 1933.

Kabisch, Ernst. *Streitfragen des Weltkrieges 1914–1918.* Stuttgart, 1924.

Keegan, John. *The Mask of Command.* London, 1987.

Kehrig, Manfred. *Stalingrad. Analyse und Dokumentation einer Schlacht.* Beiträge zur Militär- und Kriegsgeschichte 15. Stuttgart, 1974.

Keitel, Wilhelm. *Generalfeldmarschall Keitel. Verbrecher oder Offizier? Erinnerungen, Briefe, Dokumente des Chefs des OKW.* Edited by Walter Görlitz. Göttingen, 1961.

Kershaw, Ian. *Hitler 1889–1936. Hubris.* London, 2001.

———. *Hitler 1936–1945.* Stuttgart, 2000.

Kessel, Eberhard. *Moltke.* Stuttgart, 1957.

———. "Napoleonische und Moltkesche Strategie." *Wissen und Wehr* (1929): 171–181.

Kielmansegg, Peter Graf von. *Deutschland und der Erste Weltkrieg.* Stuttgart, 1980.

———. "Feuer und Bewegung. Der Durchbruch einer Panzerdivision." *Die Wehrmacht,* 22 (1938): 11–14.

Klein, Friedhelm, and Karl-Heinz Frieser. "Mansteins Gegenschlag am Donec. Operative Analyse des Gegenangriffs der Heeresgruppe Süd im Februar/März 1943." *Militärgeschichte* 9 (1999): 12–18.

Klein, Friedhelm, and Ingo Lachnit. "Der 'Operationsentwurf Ost' des Generalmajor Marcks vom 5. August 1940." *Wehrforschung* 2, no. 4 (1972): 114–123.

Klink, Ernst. "Der Krieg gegen die Sowjetunion bis zur Jahreswende 1941/42." In *Das Deutsche Reich und der Zweite Weltkrieg,* vol. 4, *Der Angriff auf die Sowjetunion,* edited by Horst Boog, Jürgen Förster, Joachim Hoffmann, Ernst Klink, Rolf-Dieter Müller, and Gerd R. Ueberschär, 451–1088. Stuttgart, 1987.

. "Die militärische Konzeption des Krieges gegen die Sowjetunion." In *Das Deutsche Reich und der Zweite Weltkrieg*, vol. 4, *Der Angriff auf die Sowjetunion*, edited by Horst Boog, Jürgen Förster, Joachim Hoffmann, Ernst Klink, Rolf-Dieter Müller, and Gerd R. Ueberschär, 190–326. Stuttgart, 1987.

Koch, Adalbert, and Fritz Wiener. "Die Panzer-Division 1945." *Feldgrau* (1960): 33–39.

Kochanowski, Jerzy, and Bernhard Chiari. *Die polnische Heimatarmee. Geschichte und Mythos der Armia Krajowa seit dem Zweiten Weltkrieg*. Beiträge zur Militärgeschichte 57. Im Auftrag des Militärgeschichtlichen Forschungsamtes, Munich, 2003.

Kondylis, Panajotis. *Theorie des Krieges. Clausewitz—Marx—Engels—Lenin*. Stuttgart, 1988.

Köster, Burkhard. "Ermattungs-oder Vernichtungsstrategie? Die Kriegführung der 2. und 3. Obersten Heeresleitung (OHL)." *Militärgeschichte. Zeitschrift für historische Bildung* 2 (2008): 10–13.

. *Militär und Eisenbahn in der Habsburgermonarchie 1825–1859*. Militärgeschichtliche Studien 37. Munich, 1999.

Krafft von Dellmensingen, Konrad. *Der Durchbruch. Studie an Hand der Vorgänge des Weltkrieges 1914–1918*. Hamburg, 1937.

Kraus, Hans-Christof, and Thomas Nicklas, eds. *Geschichte der Politik. Alte und neue Wege*. Historische Zeitschrift, Beih. 44. Munich, 2007.

Kremp, Werner, Berdhold Meyer, and Wolfgang Tönnesmann, eds. *Entangling Alliance. 60 Jahre NATO: Geschichte—Gegenwart—Zukunft*. Trier, 2010.

Kriegs-Rundschau. Zeitgenössische Zusammenstellung der für den Weltkrieg wichtigen Ereignisse, Urkunden, Kundgebungen, Schlachten- und Zeitberichte, vol. 1. Berlin, 1914–1915.

Kroener, Bernhard R. "Auf dem Weg zu einer 'nationalsozialistischen Volksarmee.' Die soziale Öffnung des Heeresoffizierkorps im Zweiten Weltkrieg." In *Von Stalingrad zur Währungsreform. Zur Sozialgeschichte des Umbruchs in Deutschland*, edited by Martin Broszat, Klaus-Dietmar Henke, and Hans Woller, 651–683. Munich, 1988.

. "Der 'erfrorene' Blitzkrieg. Strategische Planungen der deutschen Führung gegen die Sowjetunion und die Ursachen ihres Scheiterns." In *Zwei Wege nach Moskau. Vom Hitler-Stalin-Pakt bis zum "Unternehmen Barbarossa,"* edited by Bernd Wegner, 133–148. Munich, 1991.

. *"Der starke Mann im Heimatkriegsgebiet"—Generaloberst Friedrich Fromm. Eine Biographie*. Paderborn, 2005.

Kroener, Bernhard R., Rolf-Dieter Müller, and Hans Umbreit, eds. *Das Deutsche Reich und der Zweite Weltkrieg*, vol. 5, *Organisation und Mobilisierung des deutschen Machtbereichs*. Part I, *Kriegsverwaltung, Wirtschaft und personelle Ressourcen 1939 bis 1941*. Stuttgart, 1992.

Kronenbitter, Günther. "Austria-Hungary." In *War Planning 1914*, edited by Holger H. Herwig and Richard F. Hamilton, 24–47. New York, 2010.

. "Die militärischen Planungen der k.u.k. Armee und der Schlieffenplan." In *Der Schlieffenplan. Analysen und Dokumente*, edited by Hans Ehlert, Michael Epkenhans, and Gerhard P. Gross, 205–220. Paderborn, 2007.

. "Von 'Schweinehunden' und 'Waffenbrüdern.' Der Koalitionskrieg der Mittelmächte 1914/15 zwischen Sachzwang und Ressentiment." In *Die vergessene Front. Der*

Osten 1914–15. Ereignis, Wirkung, Nachwirkung, edited by Gerhard P. Gross, 121–143. Zeitalter der Weltkriege 1. Im Auftrag des Militärgeschichtlichen Forschungsamtes, Paderborn, 2006.

Krüger, Dieter. *Das Amt Blank. Die schwierige Gründung des Bundesministeriums für Verteidigung.* Einzelschriften zur Militärgeschichte 38. Freiburg i.Br., 1993.

———. "Schlachtfeld Bundesrepublik? Europa, die deutsche Luftwaffe und der Strategiewechsel der NATO 1958 bis 1968." *Vierteljahrshefte für Zeitgeschichte* 56 (2008): 171–225.

Kuhl, Herman von. *Der Weltkrieg 1914–1918. Dem deutschen Volke dargestellt.* 2 vols. Berlin, 1929.

Kühne, Thomas, and Benjamin Ziemann, eds. *"Was ist Militärgeschichte?" In Verbindung mit dem Arbeitskreis Militärgeschichte e.V.* Krieg in der Geschichte 6. Paderborn, 2000.

Kunde, Martin. *Der Präventivkrieg. Geschichtliche Entwicklung und gegenwärtige Bedeutung.* Frankfurt a.M., 2007.

Kushber, Jan. "Die russischen Streitkräfte und der deutsche Aufmarsch beim Ausbruch des Ersten Weltkrieges." In *Der Schlieffenplan. Analysen und Dokumente,* edited by Hans Ehlert, Michael Epkenhans, and Gerhard P. Gross, 257–268. Paderborn, 2007.

Kutz, Martin, ed. *Realitätsflucht und Aggression im deutschen Militär.* Baden-Baden, 1990.

———. "Schlieffen contra Clausewitz. Zur Grundlegung einer Denkschule der Aggression und des Blitzkrieges." In *Realitätsflucht und Aggression,* edited by Martin Kutz, 12–48. Baden-Baden, 1990.

Lakowski, Richard. *Seelow 1945. Die Entscheidungsschlacht an der Oder.* Berlin, 1995.

Lambi, Ivo Nikolai. *The Navy and German Power Politics, 1862–1914.* Boston, Mass., 1984.

Lange, Sven. *Hans Delbrück und der "Strategiestreit." Kriegführung und Kriegsgeschichte in der Kontroverse 1879–1914.* Einzelschriften zur Militärgeschichte 40. Freiburg i.Br., 1995.

Leeb, Wilhelm Ritter von. *Die Abwehr.* Berlin, 1938.

Leistenschneider, Stephan. *Auftragstaktik im preussisch-deutschen Heer 1871 bis 1914.* Edited by the Militärgeschichtliches Forschungsamt. Hamburg, 2002.

Lešin, Michail G. "Führungsdenken im russisch-sowjetischen Militärwesen—Genesis, Ansprüche, Grenzen." In *Führungsdenken in europäischen und nordamerikanischen Streitkräften im 19. und 20. Jahrhundert,* edited by Gerhard P. Gross, 209–218. Bonn, 2001.

Lindemann, F. "Feuer und Bewegung im Landkrieg der Gegenwart." *Militärwissenschaftliche Rundschau* (1937): 362–377.

Lindenberger, Thomas, and Alf Lüdtke, eds. *Physische Gewalt. Studien zur Geschichte der Neuzeit.* Frankfurt a.M., 1995.

Linnebach, Karl. "Der Durchbruch. Eine kriegsgeschichtliche Untersuchung (1. Teil)." *Wissen und Wehr* 11 (1930): 448–471.

———. "Zum Meinungsstreit über den Vernichtungsgedanken in der Kriegführung." *Wissen und Wehr* 15 (1934): 726–751.

Linnenkohl, Hans. *Vom Einzelschuss zur Feuerwalze. Der Wettlauf zwischen Technik und Taktik im Ersten Weltkrieg.* Koblenz, 1990.

Loch, Thorsten, and Lars Zacharias. "Betrachtungen zur Operationsgeschichte einer Schlacht." *Österreichische Militärische Zeitschrift* 49, no. 4 (2011): 436–444.

———. "Königgrätz 1866. Die Operationen zwischen dem 22. Juni und 3. Juli 1866." *Öster-reichische Militärische Zeitschrift* 48, no. 6 (2010): 707–715.

———, eds. *Wie die Siegessäule nach Berlin kam. Eine kleine Geschichte der Reichseinigungs-kriege (1864 bis 1871). In Zusammenarb. des Militärgeschichtlichen Forschungsamtes, Potsdam, und des Napoleonmuseums Thurgau.* Freiburg i.Br., 2011.

Lossberg, Bernhard von. *Im Wehrmachtführungsstab. Bericht eines Generalstabsoffiziers.* Hamburg, 1950.

Ludendorff, Erich. *Meine Kriegserinnerungen 1914–1918.* Berlin, 1919.

———. *Mein militärischer Werdegang. Blätter der Erinnerung an unser stolzes Heer.* Munich, 1924.

———. *Der totale Krieg.* Munich, 1935.

Ludwig, M. "Der Geist des deutschen Soldaten." *Militär-Wochenblatt* 42 (1941): 1709.

———. "Gedanken über den Angriff im Bewegungskrieg." *Militärwissenschaftliche Rund-schau* (1936): 153–164.

Luttwak, Edward N. *The Pentagon and the Art of War. The Question of Military Reform.* New York, 1984.

———. *Strategy: The Logic of War and Peace.* Cambridge, Mass., 2002.

Luvaas, Jay. *The Military Legacy of the Civil War: The European Inheritance.* Chicago, 1959.

Mackinder, Halford John. *Democratic Ideals and Reality: A Study in the Politics of Recon-struction.* London, 1919.

Magenheimer, Heinz. "Die Abwehrschlacht an der Weichsel 1945. Planung und Ablauf aus der Sicht der deutschen operativen Führung." In *Ausgewählte Operationen und ihre militärhistorischen Grundlagen,* edited by Hans-Martin Ottmer and Heiger Ostertag, 161–182. Operatives Denken und Handeln in deutschen Streitkräften 4. Bonn, 1993.

———. "Letzte Kampferfahrungen des deutschen Heeres an der West- und Ostfront." *Österreichische Militärische Zeitschrift* 4 (1985): 317–320.

Maier, Klaus A. "Die politische Kontrolle über die amerikanischen Nuklearwaffen. Ein Bündnisproblem der NATO unter der Doktrin der Massiven Vergeltung." In *Die NATO als Militärallianz. Strategie, Organisation und nukleare Kontrolle im Bündnis 1949 bis 1959,* by Christian Greiner, Klaus A. Maier, and Heinz Rebhan, edited by Bruno Thoss, 251–420. Munich, 2003.

Maier, Klaus A., Horst Rohde, Bernd Stegemann, and Hans Umbreit, eds. *Das Deutsche Reich und der Zweite Weltkrieg,* vol. 2, *Die Errichtung der Hegemonie auf dem europäischen Kontinent.* Stuttgart, 1991.

Manstein, Erich von. *Verlorene Siegen.* Bonn, 1955.

Mantey, Friedrich von. "Graf Schlieffen und der jüngere Moltke." *Militär-Wochenblatt* 120 (1935–1936): 395–398.

Marholz, Josef. "Die Entwicklung der operativen Führung." *Österreichische Militärische Zeitschrift* (1973): 107–113, 195–204, 369–376, and 458–461.

Martin, Bernd, and Stanisława Lewandowska, eds. *Der Warschauer Aufstand 1944.* Warszawa, 1999.

Marwedel, Ulrich. *Carl von Clausewitz. Persönlichkeit und Wirkungsgeschichte seines Werks bis 1918.* Militärgeschichtliche Studien 25. Boppard a.Rh., 1978.

Marx, Karl, and Friedrich Engels. *Werke,* vol. 16. Berlin, 1962.

Marx, Wilhelm. "Das 'Cannä-Oratorium.'" *Militär-Wochenblatt* 8 (1932): 246f.

Mason, Timothy W. "Innere Krise und Angriffskrieg 1938/1939." In *Wirtschaft und Rüstung am Vorabend des Zweiten Weltkrieges,* edited by Friedrich Forstmeier and Hans-Erich Volkmann, 158–188. Düsseldorf, 1975.

McKercher, Brian J. C., and Michael A. Hennessy, eds. *The Operational Art: Developments in the Theories of War.* Westport, Conn., 1996.

Megargee, Geoffrey P. *Inside Hitler's High Command.* Lawrence, Kans., 2000.

Meier-Welcker, Hans. *Aufzeichnungen eines Generalstabsoffiziers 1939 bis 1942.* Einzelschriften zur militärischen Geschichte des Zweiten Weltkrieges 26. Freiburg i.Br., 1982.

———. *Seeckt.* Frankfurt a.M., 1967.

———. "Strategische Planungen und Vereinbarungen der Mittelmächte für den Mehrfrontenkrieg." *Österreichische Militärische Zeitschrift,* Sonderheft 2 (1964): 15–22.

Meinert, Friedrich. *Über den Krieg, die Kriegswissenschaften und die Kriegskunst. Für das Militär und solche, welche vom Kriegswesen unterrichtet sein wollen.* Halle, 1798.

Melvin, Mungo. *Manstein: Hitler's Greatest General.* London, 2010.

Menning, Bruce W. "War Planning and Initial Operations in the Russian Context." In *War Planning 1914,* edited by Holger H. Herwig and Richard F. Hamilton, 80–142. New York, 2010.

Messerschmidt, Manfred. "Introduction." In *Das Deutsche Reich und der Zweite Weltkrieg,* vol. 4, *Der Angriff auf die Sowjetunion,* edited by Horst Boog, Jürgen Förster, Joachim Hoffmann, Ernst Klink, Rolf-Dieter Müller, and Gerd R. Ueberschär, xiii–xix. Stuttgart, 1987.

Meyer, Georg. *Adolf Heusinger. Dienst eines deutschen Soldaten 1915 bis 1964.* Published with the cooperation of the Clausewitz-Gesellschaft and the Militärgeschichtliches Forschungsamtes, Hamburg, 2001.

Meyers Grosses Konversations-Lexikon, vol. 15. Leipzig, 1908.

Meyers Neues Konversations-Lexikon: Ein Wörterbuch des allgemeinen Wissens. vol. 15. Hildburghausen, 1867.

Michaelis, Herbert, and Ernst Schraepler, eds. *Ursachen und Folgen. Vom deutschen Zusammenbruch 1918 und 1945 bis zur staatlichen Neuordnung Deutschlands in der Gegenwart. Eine Urkunden- und Dokumentensammlung zur Zeitgeschichte,* vol. 2, *Der militärische Zusammenbruch und das Ende des Kaiserreichs.* Berlin, 1958–1978.

Middeldorf, Eike. "Die Abwehrschlacht am Weichselbrückenkopf Baranow. Eine Studie über neuzeitliche Verteidigung." *Wehrwissenschaftliche Rundschau* 4 (1953): 187–203.

———. *Taktik im Russlandfeldzug. Erfahrungen und Folgerungen.* Darmstadt, 1956.

Miksche, Ferdinand Otto. *Blitzkrieg.* London, 1942.

Militärgeschichtliches Forschungsamt. *Anfänge westdeutscher Sicherheitspolitik 1945–1956.* 4 vols. Munich, 1982–1997.

———. *Deutsche Militärgeschichte 1648–1939,* vol. 6, *Grundzüge der militärischen Kriegführung 1648–1939.* Munich, 1983.

———, ed. *Die Bedeutung der Logistik für die militärische Führung von der Antike bis in die neueste Zeit.* Vorträge zur Militärgeschichte 7. Bonn, 1968.

———, ed. *Operatives Denken und Handeln in deutschen Streitkräften im 19. und 20. Jahrhundert.* Vorträge zur Militärgeschichte 9. Herford, 1988.

Militär-Lexikon: Handwörterbuch der Militärwissenschaften. Berlin, 1901.

Millotat, Christian. *Das preussisch-deutsche Generalstabssystem. Wurzeln—Entwicklung—Fortwirken.* Zürich, 2000.

Milward, Alan S. "Hitlers Konzept des Blitzkrieges." In *Probleme des Zweiten Weltkrieges,* edited by Andreas Hillgruber, 19–40. Köln, 1967.

Molt, Matthias. *Von der Wehrmacht zur Bundeswehr. Personelle Kontinuität und Diskontinuität beim Aufbau der Deutschen Streitkräfte 1955 bis 1966.* Diss., University of Heidelberg, 2007.

Moltke, Helmuth von. "Aufsatz vom Jahre 1859 'Über Flankenstellungen.'" In *Moltkes Militärische Werke,* vol. 2, part 2, pages 261–266. Berlin, 1900.

Moltke, Helmuth von. "Aufsatz vom 16. September 1865 'Über Marschtiefen.'" In *Moltkes Militärische Werke,* vol. 2, part 2, pages 235–246. Berlin, 1900.

Moltke, Helmuth von. *Ausgewählte Werke,* vol. 1, *Feldherr und Kriegslehrmeister.* Edited by Ferdinand von Schmerfeld. Berlin, 1925.

Moltke, Helmuth von. *Die deutschen Aufmarschpläne 1871–1890.* Edited by Ferdinand von Schmerfeld. Forschungen und Darstellungen aus dem Reichsarchiv 7. Berlin, 1929.

Moltke, Helmuth von. "Betrachtungen über Konzentrationen im Kriege von 1866." *Militär-Wochenblatt* 18 (1867): 187–189.

Moltke, Helmuth von. *Erinnerungen, Briefe, Dokumente 1877–1916. Ein Bild vom Kriegsausbruch, erster Kriegführung und Persönlichkeit des ersten militärischen Führers des Krieges.* Edited by Eliza von Moltke. Stuttgart, 1922.

Moltke, Helmuth von. *Gesammelte Schriften und Denkwürdigkeiten des General-Feldmarschalls Grafen Helmuth von Moltke.* 8 vols. Edited by Lescynski. Berlin, 1891–1893; vol. 3, Berlin, 1891.

Moltke, Helmuth von. "Geschichte des Deutsch-Französischen Krieges von 1870–71." In *Gesammelte Schriften und Denkwürdigkeiten des General-Feldmarschalls Grafen Helmuth von Moltke,* vol. 3, by Helmuth von Moltke, edited by Lescynski. Berlin, 1891.

Moltke, Helmuth von. "Über Strategie." In *Kriegstheorie und Kriegsgeschichte: Carl von Clausewitz, Helmuth von Moltke,* edited by Reinhard Stumpf, 429–432. Frankfurt a.M., 1993.

Moltke, Helmuth von. "Über Strategie." In *Moltkes Taktisch-strategische Aufsätze aus den Jahren 1857 bis 1871,* by Helmuth von Moltke, edited by the Great General Staff, Department for War History, 291–293. Berlin, 1900. (*Moltke's Militärische Werke, Die Thätigkeit als Chef des Generalstabes der Armee im Frieden,* Zweiter Teil.)

Moltke, Helmuth von. *Vom Kabinettskrieg zum Volkskrieg. Eine Werkauswahl.* Edited by Stig Förster. Bonn, 1992.

Moltke, Helmuth von. *Moltkes Militärische Werke.* 15 vols. Grossen Generalstab, Berlin, 1892–1912.

Moltke, Helmuth von. *Moltkes Militärische Werke,* vol. 2, part 2, *Die Thätigkeit als Chef des Generalstabes der Armee im Frieden.* Edited by the Great General Staff, Department for War History I. Berlin, 1900.

Moltke, Helmuth von. *Moltkes Militärische Werke,* vol. 2, part 2, *Aus den Verordnungen für die höheren Truppenführer vom 24. Juni 1869.* Edited by the Great General Staff, Department for War History I, 165–215. Berlin, 1900.

Moltke, Helmuth von. *Moltkes Militärische Werke,* vol. 4, part 2, *Moltkes Kriegslehren. Die taktischen Vorbereitungen zur Schlacht.* Edited by the Great General Staff, Department for War History I. Berlin, 1911.

Moltke, Helmuth von. *Moltkes Taktisch-strategische Aufsätze aus den Jahren 1857 bis 1871.* Edited by the Great General Staff, Department for War History. *Moltke's Militärische*

Werke, Die Thätigkeit als Chef des Generalstabes der Armee im Frieden, Zweiter Teil. Berlin, 1900.

Mombauer, Annika. "German War Plans." In *War Planning 1914,* edited by Holger H. Herwig and Richard F. Hamilton, 48–79. New York, 2010.

———. *Helmuth von Moltke and the Origins of the First World War.* Cambridge, U.K., 2001.

———. "Der Moltkeplan. Modifikation des Schlieffenplans bei gleichen Zielen?" In *Der Schlieffenplan. Analysen und Dokumente,* edited by Hans Ehlert, Michael Epkenhans, und Gerhard P. Gross, 79–99. Im Auftrag des Militärgeschichtlichen Forschungsamtes und der Otto-von-Bismarck-Stiftung. Paderborn, 2007.

Mommsen, Wolfgang J. *Das Ringen um den nationalen Staat. Die Gründung und der innere Ausbau des Deutschen Reiches unter Otto von Bismarck 1850–1890.* Prophyläen Weltgeschichte Deutschlands 7/1. Berlin, 1993.

———. "Der Topos vom unvermeidlichen Krieg. Aussenpolitik und öffentliche Meinung im Deutschen Reich im letzten Jahrzehnt vor 1914." In *Bereit zum Krieg. Kriegsmentalität im Wilhelminischen Deutschland 1890–1914,* edited by Jost Düllfer and Karl Holl, 194–224. Beiträge zur historischen Friedensforschung, Göttingen, 1986.

Müller, Klaus-Jürgen. *General Ludwig Beck. Studien und Dokumente zur politisch-militärischen Vorstellungswelt und Tätigkeit des Generalstabschefs des deutschen Heeres 1933–1938.* Schriften des Bundesarchivs 30. Boppard, 1980.

———. *Generaloberst Ludwig Beck: Eine Biographie.* Militärgeschichtliches Forschungsamtes, Potsdam, 2008.

———. *Das Heer und Hitler. Armee und nationalsozialistisches Regime 1933 bis 1940.* Beiträge zur Militär- und Kriegsgeschichte 10. Stuttgart, 1969.

Müller, Martin. *Vernichtungsgedanke und Koalitionskriegführung. Das deutsche Reich und Österreich-Ungarn in der Offensive 1917–1918.* Graz, 2003.

Müller, Rolf-Dieter. "Die Mobilisierung der deutschen Kriegswirtschaft für Hitlers Kriegführung." In *Das Deutsche Reich und der Zweite Weltkrieg,* vol. 5, *Organisation und Mobilisierung des deutschen Machtbereichs,* Part 1, *Kriegsverwaltung, Wirtschaft und personelle Ressourcen 1939 bis 1941,* edited by Bernhard R. Kroener, Rolf-Dieter Müller, and Hans Umbreit, 406–556. Stuttgart, 1992.

———. "Das Scheitern der wirtschaftlichen 'Blitzkriegsstrategie.'" In *Das Deutsche Reich und der Zweite Weltkrieg,* vol. 4, *Der Angriff auf die Sowjetunion,* edited by Horst Boog, Jürgen Förster, Joachim Hoffmann, Ernst Klink, Rolf-Dieter Müller, and Gerd R. Ueberschär, 936–1029. Stuttgart, 1987.

———. *Der Feind steht im Osten. Hitlers geheime Pläne für einen Krieg gegen die Sowjetunion im Jahre 1939.* Berlin, 2011.

Müller, Rolf-Dieter, and Gerd R. Ueberschär. *Hitlers Krieg im Osten 1941–1945. Ein Forschungsbericht.* Darmstadt, 2000.

Müller, Rolf-Dieter, and Hans-Erich Volkmann, eds. *Die Wehrmacht. Mythos und Realität.* Im Auftrag des Militärgeschichtlichen Forschungsamtes, Munich, 1999.

Müller-Hillebrand, Burkhart. *Das Heer 1933–1945. Entwicklung des organisatorischen Aufbaus,* vol. 1, *Das Heer bis zum Kriegsbeginn;* vol. 2, *Die Blitzfeldzüge 1939–1941. Das Heer im Kriege bis zum Beginn des Feldzuges gegen die Sowjetunion im Juni 1941;* vol. 3, *Der Zweifrontenkrieg. Das Heer vom Beginn des Feldzuges gegen die Sowjetunion bis zum Kriegsende.* Frankfurt a.M., 1954–1969.

Mulligan, William. *The Creation of the Modern German Army: General Walther Reinhardt and the Weimar Republic, 1914–1930.* Monographs in German History 12. New York, 2005.

Murray, Williamson. "The German Response to Victory in Poland: A Case Study in Professionalism." *Armed Forces and Society* 7 (1981): 285–298.

Murray, Williamson, and Allan R. Millette, eds. *Military Effectiveness,* vol. 3: *The Second World War.* Boston, Mass., 1988.

Nägler, Frank. *Der gewollte Soldat und sein Wandel. Personelle Rüstung und Innere Führung in den Aufbaujahren der Bundeswehr 1956 bis 1964/65.* Sicherheitspolitik und Streitkräfte der Bundesrepublik Deutschland 9. Munich, 2010.

Nakata, Jun. *Der Grenz- und Landesschutz in der Weimarer Republik 1918 bis 1933. Die geheime Aufrüstung und die deutsche Gesellschaft.* Einzelschriften zur Militärgeschichte 41. Militärgeschichtliches Forschungsamt, Freiburg i.Br., 2002.

Naveh, Shimon. *In Pursuit of Military Excellence: The Evolution of Operational Theory.* London, 1997.

Neitzel, Sönke. *Blut und Eisen. Deutschland im Ersten Weltkrieg.* Deutsche Geschichte im 20. Jahrhundert. Zürich, 2003.

———. "Des Forschens noch wert? Anmerkungen zur Operationsgeschichte der Waffen-SS." *Militärgeschichtliche Zeitschrift* 61, no. 2 (2002): 403–429.

———. "Militärgeschichte ohne Krieg? Eine Standortbestimmung der deutschen Militärgeschichtsschreibung über das Zeitalter der Weltkriege." In *Geschichte der Politik. Alte und neue Wege,* edited by Hans-Christof Kraus and Thomas Nicklas, 287–308. Historische Zeitschrift, Beih. 44. Munich, 2007.

Nerter, Ludwig, and Paul Heider. *Der Weg der deutschen Eliten in den zweiten Weltkrieg.* Berlin, 1990.

Neugebauer, Karl-Volker, ed. *Grundkurs deutsche Militärgeschichte,* vol. 1, *Die Zeit bis 1914. Vom Kriegshaufen zum Massenheer.* Im Auftrag des Militärgeschichtlichen Forschungsamtes, Munich, 2006.

———, ed. *Grundkurs deutsche Militärgeschichte,* vol. 2, *Das Zeitalter der Weltkriege 1914 bis 1945. Völker in Waffen.* Im Auftrag des Militärgeschichtlichen Forschungsamtes, Munich, 2007.

———, ed. *Grundzüge der deutschen Militärgeschichte,* vol. 2, *Arbeits- und Quellenbuch.* Im Auftrag des Militärgeschichtlichen Forschungsamtes, Freiburg i.Br., 1993.

———. Introduction to H.Dv. 487, *Führung und Gefecht der verbundenen Waffen (F.u.G.).* Berlin, 1921–1924. Reprint, Osnabrück, 1994. Pages vii–xxvi.

———. "Operatives Denken zwischen dem Ersten und Zweiten Weltkrieg." In *Operatives Denken und Handeln in deutschen Streitkräften im 19. und 20. Jahrhundert,* edited by Horst Boog, 97–122. Herford, 1988.

Niedhart, Gottfried. "Lernfähigkeit und Lernbereitschaft nach Kriegen. Beobachtungen im Anschluss an die deutschen Nachkriegszeiten im 20. Jahrhundert." In *Historische Leitlinien für das Militär der neunziger Jahre,* edited by Detlef Bald and Paul Klein, 3–27. Baden-Baden, 1989.

Niedhart, Gottfried, and Dieter Riesenberger, eds. *Lernen aus dem Krieg? Deutsche Nachkriegszeiten 1918–1945.* Munich, 1992.

Niemetz, Daniel. *Das feldgraue Erbe. Die Wehrmachteinflüsse im Militär der SBZ/DDR.*

Militärgeschichte der DDR 13. Published by Militärgeschichtliches Forschungsamt, Berlin, 2006.

Nohn, Ernst August. *Der unzeitgemässe Clausewitz. Notwendige Bemerkungen über zeitgemässe Denkfehler.* Wehrwissenschaftliche Rundschau, Beiheft 5. Frankfurt a.M., 1956.

Ose, Dieter. *Entscheidung im Westen 1944. Der Oberbefehlshaber West und die Abwehr der alliierten Invasion.* Beiträge zur Militär- und Kriegsgeschichte 22. Stuttgart, 1982.

———, ed. *Wehrgeschichtliches Symposium an der Führungsakademie der Bundeswehr. 9. September 1986. Ausbildung im operativen Denken unter Heranziehen von Kriegserfahrungen, dargestellt an Mansteins Gegenangriff Frühjahr 1943.* Hamburg, 1987.

Osterhammel, Jürgen. *Die Verwandlung der Welt. Eine Geschichte des 19. Jahrhunderts.* Munich, 2009.

O'Sullivan, Patrick. *Terrain and Tactics.* Westport, Conn., 1991.

Ottmer, Hans-Martin, and Heiger Ostertag, eds. *Ausgewählte Operationen und ihre militärhistorischen Grundlagen.* Operatives Denken und Handeln in deutschen Streitkräften 4. Im Auftrag des Militärgeschichtlichen Forschungsamtes, Bonn, 1993.

Otto, Helmut. "Zum strategisch-operativen Zusammenwirken des deutschen und österreichisch-ungarischen Generalstabes bei der Vorbereitung des ersten Weltkrieges." *Zeitschrift für Militärgeschichte* (1963): 423–440.

Paret, Peter. "Clausewitz." In *Makers of Modern Strategy from Machiavelli to the Nuclear Age,* edited by Peter Paret, 186–213. Princeton, N.J., 1986.

———, ed. *Makers of Modern Strategy from Machiavelli to the Nuclear Age.* Princeton, N.J., 1986.

Pedlow, Gregory W., ed. "NATO Strategy Documents, 1949–1969." In collaboration with the NATO International Staff Central Archives. Brussels, 1997. http://www.nato.int/archives/strategy.htm.

Pierer's Universal-Lexikon, vol. 12. Altenburg, 1861.

Pohl, Dieter. *Die Herrschaft der Wehrmacht. Deutsche Militärbesatzung und einheimische Bevölkerung in der Sowjetunion 1941–1944.* Quellen und Darstellungen zur Zeitgeschichte 71. Munich, 2008.

———. "Die Kooperation zwischen Heer, SS und Polizei in den besetzten sowjetischen Gebieten." In *Verbrechen der Wehrmacht. Bilanz einer Debatte,* edited by Christian Hartmann, Johannes Hürter, and Ulrike Jureit, 106–116. Munich, 2005.

Pöhlmann, Markus. *Geschichte der militärischen Mechanisierung von Landstreitkräften in Deutschland im Zeitalter der Weltkriege.* In preparation.

———. *Kriegsgeschichte und Geschichtspolitik: Der Erste Weltkrieg. Die amtliche deutsche Militärgeschichtsschreibung 1914–1956.* Paderborn, 2002.

———. "Das unentdeckte Land. Kriegsbild und Zukunftskrieg in deutschen Militärzeitschriften." In *Der Grosse Krieg. Europäische Militärzeitschriften und die Debatte über den Krieg der Zukunft, 1880–1914,* edited by Stig Förster. In preparation.

———. "Von Versailles nach Armageddon. Totalisierungserfahrung und Kriegserwartung in deutschen Militärzeitschriften." In *An der Schwelle zum Totalen Krieg. Die militärische Debatte über den Krieg der Zukunft 1919–1939,* edited by Stig Förster, 323–391. Paderborn, 2002.

Posen, Barry R. *The Sources of Military Doctrine: France, Britain, and Germany between the World Wars.* Cornell Studies in Security Affairs. Ithaca, N.Y., 1984.

Poten, Bernhard von. *Handwörterbuch der gesamten Militärwissenschaften,* vol. 7. Leipzig, 1878.

Pruck, Erich F. "Die Rehabilitierung von Kommandeuren der Roten Armee." *Osteuropa* 14, no. 3 (1964): 202–209.

Rabenau, Friedrich von. *Operative Entschlüsse gegen eine Zahl überlegener Gegner.* Berlin, 1935.

Raschke, Martin. *Der politisierende Generalstab. Die friderizianischen Kriege in der amtlichen deutschen Militärgeschichtsschreibung 1890 bis 1914.* Einzelschriften zur Militärgeschichte 36. Freiburg i.br., 1993.

Raths, Ralf. *Vom Massensturm zur Stosstrupptaktik. Die deutsche Landkriegtaktik im Spiegel von Dienstvorschriften und Publizistik 1906 bis 1918.* Einzelschriften zur Militärgeschichte 44. Berlin, 2009.

Ratzel, Friedrich. *Politische Geographie oder die Geographie der Staaten, des Verkehrs und des Krieges.* Munich, 1903.

Rauchensteiner, Manfried. *Der Tod des Doppeladlers. Österreich-Ungarn und der Erste Weltkrieg.* Köln, 1993.

———. "Zum 'operativen Denken' in Österreich 1814–1914." *Österreichische Militärische Zeitschrift* (1974): 121–127, 207–210, 285–291, 379–389, 473–478; *Österreichische Militärische Zeitschrift* (1975): 46–53.

Raudzens, George. "Blitzkrieg Ambiguities: Doubtful Usage of a Famous Word." *War and Society* 7 (1989): 77–94.

Raulff, Heiner. *Zwischen Machtpolitik und Imperialismus. Die deutsche Frankreichpolitik 1904–06.* Düsseldorf, 1976.

Rautenberg, Hans-Jürgen, and Norbert Wiggershaus. *Die "Himmeroder Denkschrift" vom Oktober 1950.* Karlsruhe, 1985.

Regling, Volkmar. "Grundzüge der Landkriegführung zur Zeit des Absolutismus und im 19. Jahrhundert." In *Deutsche Militärgeschichte 1648–1939,* vol. 6, *Grundzüge der militärischen Kriegführung 1648–1939,* by Militärgeschichtliches Forschungsamt, 11–425. Munich, 1983.

Reichsarchiv. *Der Weltkrieg 1914–1918. Die militärischen Operationen zu Lande.* 14 vols. Berlin, 1925–1944.

Reinhardt, Hans. "Die 4. Panzerdivision vor Warschau und an der Bzura vom 9.–20.9.1939." *Wehrkunde* 5 (1958): 237–247.

Reinhardt, Klaus. *Die Wende vor Moskau. Das Scheitern der Strategie Hitlers im Winter 1941/42.* Beiträge zur Militär- und Kriegsgeschichte 13. Stuttgart, 1972.

Reuth, Ralf Georg. *Entscheidung im Mittelmeer. Die südliche Peripherie Europas in der deutschen Strategie des Zweiten Weltkrieges 1940–1942.* Koblenz, 1985.

Rhoden, Herhudt von. "Betrachtungen über den Luftkrieg." *Militärwissenschaftliche Rundschau* (1937): 198–214, 347–361, 504–517, 623–632.

Rink, Martin. "'Strukturen brausen um die Wette.' Zur Organisation des deutschen Heeres." In *Das Heer 1950 bis 1970. Konzeption, Organisation und Aufstellung,* by Helmut R. Hammerich, Dieter H. Kollmer, Martin Rink, and Rudolf Schlaffer, 353–483. Munich, 2006.

Ritter, Gerhard. *Der Schlieffenplan. Kritik eines Mythos. Mit erstmaliger Veröffentlichung der Texte und 6 Kartenskizzen.* Munich, 1956.

———. *Staatskunst und Kriegshandwerk. Das Problem des Militarismus.* 4 vols. Munich, 1965–1968.

Rode, Hans Wolf. "Das Kriegserlebnis von 1939 und 1914." *Militär-Wochenblatt* 125, no. 46 (1941): 1825–1827.

Rohde, Horst. "Hitlers erster 'Blitzkrieg' und seine Auswirkungen auf Nordosteuropa." In *Das Deutsche Reich und der Zweite Weltkrieg,* vol. 2, *Die Errichtung der Hegemonie auf dem europäischen Kontinent,* edited by Klaus A. Maier, Horst Rohde, Bernd Stegemann, and Hans Umbreit, 79–156. Stuttgart, 1991.

Röhricht, Edgar F. *Probleme der Kesselschlacht, dargestellt an Einkreisungs-Operationen im zweiten Weltkrieg.* With a Foreword by Colonel General (Ret.) Franz Halder. Deutsche Truppenführung im 2. Weltkrieg. Studien. Karlsruhe, 1958.

Rosa, Hartmut. *Beschleunigung. Die Veränderung der Zeitstrukturen in der Moderne.* Frankfurt a.M., 2005.

Rosinski, Herbert. *The German Army.* New York, 1966.

Rossino, Alexander B. *Hitler Strikes Poland: Blitzkrieg, Ideology, and Atrocities.* Lawrence, Kans., 2003.

Rupprecht, Kronprinz von Bayern. *Mein Kriegstagebuch.* 3 vols. Edited by Eugen von Frauenholz. Berlin, 1929.

Sadarananda, Dana V. *Beyond Stalingrad: Manstein and the Operations of Army Group Don.* New York, 1990.

Sagmeister, Wolfgang. "General der Artillerie Ing. Ludwig Ritter von Eimannsberger. Theoretiker und Visionär der Verwendung von gepanzerten Grossverbänden im Kampf der verbundnen Waffen." Unpublished doctoral diss., Vienna, 2006.

Salewski, Michael. "Knotenpunkt der Weltgeschichte? Die Raison des deutsch-französischen Waffenstillstandes vom 22. Juni 1940." In *La France et l'Allemagne en guerre. Septembre 1939–November 1942,* edited by Claude Carlier and Stefan Martens, 115–129. Paris, 1990.

———. "'Weserübung 1905?' Dänemark im strategischen Kalkül Deutschlands vor dem Ersten Weltkrieg." In *Politischer Wandel, organisierte Gewalt und nationale Sicherheit. Beiträge zur neueren Geschichte Deutschlands und Frankreichs. Festschrift für Klaus-Jürgen Müller,* edited by Ernst Willi Hansen, Gerhard Schreiber, and Bernd Wegner, 47–62. Munich, 1995.

Sandrart, Hans-Henning von. "Vorwort zu den Denkschriften." In *Denkschriften zu Fragen der operativen Führung,* 11–17. N.p.: n.p., 1987.

Schäfer, Theobald von. *Generalstab und Admiralstab. Das Zusammenwirken von Heer und Flotte im Weltkrieg.* Berlin, 1931.

Scharnhorst, Gerhard von. "Über die Schlacht von Marengo." In *Denkwürdigkeiten der militärischen Gesellschaft zu Berlin,* vol. 1, pages 52–59. Berlin, 1805. New edition with introduction by Joachim Niemeyer. Bibliotheca Rerum Militarium 37. Osnabrück, 1985.

Scheven, Werner von. *Die Truppenführung. Zur Geschichte ihrer Vorschrift und zur Entwicklung ihrer Struktur von 1933 bis 1962. Eine Untersuchung der taktischen Führungsvorschriften des deutschen Heeres von der HDv 300 (1933/34) bis zur HDv 100/1(1962).* Ms Archiv der Lehrgangsarbeiten der Führungsakademie der Bundeswehr, Nr. JA 0388. Hamburg, 1969.

Schlaffer, Rudolf J. "Anmerkungen zu 50 Jahren Bundeswehr. Soldat und Technik in der 'totalen Verteidigung.'" *Militärgeschichtliche Zeitschrift* 64 (2005): 487–502.

———. "Preussisch-deutsch geprägtes Personal für eine in der NATO integrierte Armee: Der personelle Aufbau der Bundeswehr." In *Entangling Alliance. 60 Jahre NATO: Geschichte—Gegenwart—Zukunft*, edited by Werner Kremp, Berdhold Meyer, and Wolfgang Tönnesmann, 111–126. Trier, 2010.

———. *Der Wehrbeauftragte 1951 bis 1985. Aus Sorge um den Soldaten.* Sicherheitspolitik und Streitkräfte der Bundesrepublik Deutschland 5. Munich, 2006.

Schlichting, Sigismund von. "Über das Infanteriegefecht." *Militär-Wochenblatt* 2 (1879): 37–67.

Schlieffen, Alfred Graf von. *Briefe.* Edited by Eberhard Kessel. Göttingen, 1958.

———. *Cannae. Mit einer Auswahl von Aufsätzen und Reden des Feldmarschalls sowie einer Einführung und Lebensbeschreibung von General der Infanterie Freiherrn von Freytag-Loringhoven.* Berlin, 1925.

———. *Die grossen Generalstabsreisen—Ost—aus den Jahren 1891–1905.* Dienstschriften des Chefs des Generalstabes der Armee Generalfeldmarschall Graf von Schlieffen. General Staff of the Army, Seventh Department (War Science), Berlin, 1938.

———. *Die taktisch-strategischen Aufgaben aus den Jahren 1891–1905.* Dienstschriften des Chefs des Generalstabes der Armee Generalfeldmarschalls Graf von Schlieffen. General Staff of the Army, Seventh Department (War Science), Berlin, 1937.

Schmidt, Ernst-Heinrich. "Zur Genesis des konzentrischen Operierens mit getrennten Heeresteilen im Zeitalter des ausgehenden Ancien Régime, der Französischen Revolution und Napoleons." In *Ausgewählte Operationen und ihre militärhistorischen Grundlagen*, edited by Hans-Martin Ottmer and Heiger Ostertag, 51–105. Operatives Denken und Handeln in deutschen Streitkräften 4. Bonn, 1993.

Schmidt, Stefan. "Frankreichs Plan XVII. Zur Interdependenz von Aussenpolitik und militärischer Planung in den letzten Jahren vor dem Ausbruch des grossen Krieges." In *Der Schlieffenplan. Analysen und Dokumente*, edited by Hans Ehlert, Michael Epkenhans, and Gerhard P. Gross, 221–256. Im Auftrag des Militärgeschichtlichen Forschungsamtes und der Otto-von-Bismarck-Stiftung. Paderborn, 2007.

Schmitz, Martin. "Verrat am Waffenbruder? Die Siedlice-Kontroverse im Spannungsfeld von Kriegsgeschichte und Geschichtspolitik." *Militärgeschichtliche Zeitschrift* 67, no. 2 (2008): 385–407.

Schnitter, Helmut. *Militärwesen und Militärpublizistik. Die militärische Zeitschriftenpublizistik in der Geschichte des bürgerlichen Militärwesens in Deutschland.* Militärhistorische Studien 9. Berlin (Ost), 1967.

Schoessler, Dietmar. "Die Weiterentwicklung in der Militärstrategie. Das 19. Jahrhundert." In *Strategie-Handbuch*, 1:31–62. Schriften des Instituts für Sicherheitspolitik an der Christian-Albrechts-Universität zu Kiel 8. Bonn, 1990.

Schönrade, Rüdiger. *General Joachim von Stülpnagel und die Politik. Eine biographische Skizze zum Verhältnis von politischer und militärischer Führung in der Weimarer Republik.* Potsdam, 2007.

Schramm, Percy Ernst, and Helmuth Greiner, eds. *Kriegstagebuch des Oberkommandos der Wehrmacht (Wehrmachtführungsstab) 1940–1945.* 4 vols. Im Auftrag des Arbeitskreises für Wehrforschung, Frankfurt a.M., 1961–1965.

Schreiber, Gerhard. "Der Mittelmeerraum in Hitlers Strategie 1940. 'Programm' und militärische Planungen." *Militärgeschichtliche Mitteilungen* 28 (1980): 69–90.

Schüler, Klaus A. Friedrich. *Logistik im Russlandfeldzug. Die Rolle der Eisenbahn bei Planung, Vorbereitung und Durchführung des deutschen Angriffs auf die Sowjetunion bis zur Krise vor Moskau im Winter 1941/42.* Europäische Hochschulschriften, Reihe III: Geschichte und ihre Hilfswissenschaften 331. Frankfurt a.M., 1987.

Schulze, Hagen. *Weimar: Deutschland 1917–1933.* Deutsche Geschichte 10. Berlin, 1982; Berlin, 1998.

Schwarte, Max. *Die militärischen Lehren des grossen Krieges.* Berlin, 1920.

———. *Die Technik im Weltkriege.* Berlin, 1920.

Schwarz, Eberhard. *Die Stabilisierung der Ostfront nach Stalingrad. Mansteins Gegenschlag zwischen Donez und Dnjepr im Frühjahr 1943.* Studien und Dokumente zur Geschichte des Zweiten Weltkrieges 17. Göttingen, 1986.

Seeckt, Hans von. *Bemerkungen des Chefs der Heeresleitung, Generaloberst von Seeckt, bei Besichtigungen und Manövern aus den Jahren 1920 bis 1926.* Reichswehr Ministry, Berlin, 1927.

———. *Gedanken eines Soldaten.* Berlin, 1929.

———. "Generaloberst v. Seeckt über Heer und Krieg der Zukunft." *Militär-Wochenblatt* 113 (1928): 1457–1460.

———. *Landesverteidigung.* Berlin, 1930.

———. *Die Reichswehr.* Leipzig, 1933.

Senff, Hubertus. *Die Entwicklung der Panzerwaffe im deutschen Heer zwischen den beiden Weltkriegen.* Frankfurt a.M., 1969.

Senger und Etterlin, Ferdinand M. von. "Cannae, Schlieffen und die Abwehr." *Wehrwissenschaftliche Rundschau* (1963): 26–43.

———. *Der Gegenschlag. Kampfbeispiele und Führungsgrundsätze der beweglichen Abwehr.* Die Wehrmacht im Kampf 22. Heidelberg, 1959.

———. "Die Gegenschlagoperation der Heeresgruppe Süd, 17.–25. Februar 1943." In *Wehrgeschichtliches Symposium an der Führungsakademie der Bundeswehr. 9. September 1986. Ausbildung im operativen Denken unter Heranziehen von Kriegserfahrungen, dargestellt an Mansteins Gegenangriff Frühjahr 1943,* edited by Dieter Ose, 132–182. Hamburg, 1987.

Sertl, Hans-Peter. "Generalfeldmarschall Erich von Manstein. Der Schlieffen des Zweiten Weltkrieges." *Der Landser* 28 (1961).

Showalter, Dennis E. "German Grand Strategy: A Contradiction in Terms?" *Militärgeschichtliche Mitteilungen* 48 (1990): 65–102.

———. *Railroads and Rifles: Soldiers, Technology, and the Unification of Germany.* Hamden, Conn., 1975.

———. "Soldiers into Postmasters? The Electric Telegraph as an Instrument of Command in the Prussian Army." *Military Affairs* 37 (1973): 48–52.

———. *Tannenberg: Clash of Empires.* Hamden, Conn., 1991.

Smith, Michael. *Enigma entschlüsselt. Die "Codebreakers" vom Bletchley Park.* Edited by Helmut Dierlamm. Munich, 2000.

Snyder, Jack. *The Ideology of the Offensive: Military Decision Making and the Disasters of 1914.* Ithaca, N.Y., 1984.

Sodenstern, Georg von. "Operationen." *Wehrwissenschaftliche Rundschau. Zeitschrift für Europäische Sicherheit* 3 (1953): 1–10.

Soldan, George. "Cauchemar allemand! Von der Unbesiegbarkeit des deutschen Soldaten." *Deutsche Wehr* 8 (1942): 113–116.

———. "Irrwege um die Panzerabwehr, Part 3." *Deutsche Wehr* 40 (1936): 323–325.

———. *Der Mensch und die Schlacht der Zukunft.* Oldenburg, 1925.

Stachelbeck, Christian. *Militärische Effektivität im Ersten Weltkrieg. Die 11. Bayerische Infanteriedivision 1915 bis 1918.* Zeitalter der Weltkriege 6. Paderborn, 2010.

Stahel, David. *Operation Barbarossa and Germany's Defeat in the East.* Cambridge, U.K., 2009.

Steiger, Rudolf. *Panzertaktik im Spiegel deutscher Kriegstagebücher 1939 bis 1941.* Einzelschriften zur militärischen Geschichte des Zweiten Weltkrieges 12. Freiburg i.Br., 1975.

Stein, Oliver. *Die deutsche Heeresrüstungspolitik 1890–1914. Das Militär und der Primat der Politik.* Paderborn, 2007.

Stenger, Alfred. *Schicksalswende. Von der Marne bis zur Vesle 1918, Oldenburg.* Schlachten des Weltkrieges 35. Berlin, 1930.

Stone, Norman. *The Eastern Front, 1914–1917.* London, 1975.

Storz, Dieter. "'Aber was hätte anderes geschehen sollen?' Die deutschen Offensiven an der Westfront 1918." In *Kriegsende 1918. Ereignis, Wirkung, Nachwirkung,* edited by Jörg Duppler and Gerhard P. Gross, 51–95. Munich, 1999.

———. "'Dieser Stellungs- und Festungskrieg ist scheusslich!' Zu den Kämpfen in Lothringen und den Vogesen im Sommer 1914." In *Der Schlieffenplan. Analysen und Dokumente,* edited by Hans Ehlert, Michael Epkenhans, and Gerhard P. Gross, 161–204. Im Auftrag des Militärgeschichtlichen Forschungsamtes und der Otto-von-Bismarck-Stiftung. Paderborn, 2007.

———. *Kriegsbild und Rüstung vor 1914. Europäische Landstreitkräfte vor dem Ersten Weltkrieg.* Herford, 1992.

Strachan, Hew. *Clausewitz's on War: A Biography.* Cambridge, U.K., 2007.

———. *Der Erste Weltkrieg. Eine neue illustrierte Geschichte.* Munich, 2004.

———. *European Armies and the Conduct of War.* London, 1983.

———. *The First World War,* vol. 1, *To Arms.* Oxford, U.K., 2001.

———. "Die Ostfront. Geopolitik, Geographie und Operationen." In *Die vergessene Front. Der Osten 1914–15. Ereignis, Wirkung, Nachwirkung,* edited by Gerhard P. Gross, 11–26. Zeitalter der Weltkriege 1. Im Auftrag des Militärgeschichtlichen Forschungsamtes, Paderborn, 2006.

Strategie-Handbuch, vol. 1. Schriften des Instituts für Sicherheitspolitik an der Christian-Albrechts-Universität zu Kiel 8. Bonn, 1990.

Strawson, John. *Hitler as Military Commander.* London, 1971.

Strohn, Matthias. *The German Army and the Defence of the Reich: Military Doctrine and the Conduct of the Defensive Battle, 1918–1939.* Cambridge, U.K., 2011.

Stumpf, Reinhard. "Der Krieg im Mittelmeerraum 1942/43: Die Operationen in Nordafrika und im mittleren Mittelmeer." In *Das Deutsche Reich und der Zweite Weltkrieg,* vol. 6, *Der globale Krieg. Die Ausweitung zum Weltkrieg und der Wechsel der Initiative 1941 bis 1943,* edited by Horst Boog, Werner Rahn, Reinhard Stumpf, and Bernd Wegner, 569–757. Stuttgart, 1993.

———, ed. *Kriegstheorie und Kriegsgeschichte: Carl von Clausewitz, Helmuth von Moltke.* Bibliothek der Geschichte und Politik 23. Frankfurt a.M., 1993.

———. "Probleme der Logistik im Afrikafeldzug 1941–1943." In *Die Bedeutung der Logistik für die militärische Führung von der Antike bis in die neueste Zeit,* edited by Horst Boog, 211–239. Vorträge zur Militärgeschichte 7. Bonn, 1968.

———. *Die Wehrmacht-Elite. Rang- und Herkunftsstruktur der deutschen Generale und Admirale 1933 bis 1945.* Militärgeschichtliche Studien 29. Boppard a.Rh., 1982.

Supplemente zum Conversations-Lexikon für Besitzer der ersten, zweiten, dritten und vierten Auflage, 3. Abteilung. Leipzig, 1820.

Teske, Hermann. "Die Eisenbahn als operatives Führungsmittel im Krieg gegen Russland." *Wehrwissenschaftlichen Rundschau* 1, nos. 9–10 (1951). 51–55.

———. *Die silbernen Spiegel. Generalstabsdienst unter der Lupe.* Heidelberg, 1952.

Thomas, Georg. "Operatives und wirtschaftliches Denken." In *Kriegswirtschaftliche Jahresberichte,* edited by Kurt Hesse, 11–18. Hamburg, 1937.

Thoss, Bruno. *NATO-Strategie und nationale Verteidigungsplanung. Planung und Aufbau der Bundeswehr unter den Bedingungen einer massiven atomaren Vergeltungsstrategie 1952 bis 1960.* Sicherheitspolitik und Streitkräfte der Bundesrepublik Deutschland 1. Munich, 2006.

Thoss, Bruno, and Hans-Erich Volkmann, eds. *Erster Weltkrieg—Zweiter Weltkrieg. Ein Vergleich. Krieg, Kriegserlebnis, Kriegserfahrung in Deutschland.* Im Auftrag des Militärgeschichtlichen Forschungsamtes, Paderborn, 2002.

Trauschweizer, Ingo. *The Cold War U.S. Army: Building Deterrence for Limited War.* Lawrence, Kans., 2008.

———. "Learning with an Ally: The U.S. Army and the Bundeswehr in the Cold War." *Journal of Military History* 72 (2008): 477–508.

Traut, Udo. *Die Spitzengliederung der deutschen Streitkräfte von 1921 bis 1964. Ein Beitrag zum Problem der Kollision von politisch-zivilem und militärischem Bereich.* Diss. jur. Karlsruhe, 1965.

Tuchman, Barbara W. *The Guns of August.* New York, 1962.

Ueberschär, Gerd R. "Die militärische Kriegführung." In *Hitlers Krieg im Osten 1941–1945. Ein Forschungsbericht,* by Rolf-Dieter Müller and Gerd R. Ueberschär, 73–143. Darmstadt, 2000.

———. "Das 'Unternehmen Barbarossa' gegen die Sowjetunion. Ein Präventivkrieg? Zur Wiederbelebung der alten Rechtfertigungsversuche des deutschen Überfalls auf die UdSSR 1941." In *Wahrheit und "Auschwitzlüge." Zur Bekämpfung "revisionistischer" Propaganda,* edited by Brigitte Bailer-Galanda, Wolfgang Benz, and Wolfgang Neugebauer, 163–182. Wien, 1995.

Ueberschär, Gerd R., and Wolfram Wette, eds. *"Unternehmen Barbarossa." Der deutsche Überfall auf die Sowjetunion 1941.* Paderborn, 1984.

Uhle-Wettler, Franz. *Höhe- und Wendepunkte deutscher Militärgeschichte, überarb.* Hamburg, 2000.

Uhlig, Heinrich. *Das Einwirken Hitlers auf Planung und Führung des Ostfeldzuges.* In Europäischen Publikation e.V., *Vollmacht des Gewissens,* 2:147–286. Berlin, 1965.

Ullrich, Volker. "Entscheidung im Osten oder Sicherung der Dardanellen. das Ringen um den Serbienfeldzug 1915. Beitrag zum Verhältnis von Politik und Kriegführung im Ersten Weltkrieg." *Militärgeschichtliche Mitteilungen* 32, no. 2 (1982): 45–63.

Ulrich, Bernd. *Stalingrad*. Munich, 2005.

Valentini, Georg Wilhelm Freiherr von. *Die Lehren vom Krieg*, part 1, *Der kleine Krieg*. Berlin, 1820.

Vardi, Gil-li. "Joachim von Stülpnagel's Military Thought and Planning." *War and History* 2 (2010): 193–216.

Velten, Wilhelm. *Das deutsche Reichsheer und die Grundlagen seiner Truppenführung: Entwicklung, Hauptprobleme und Aspekte. Untersuchungen zur deutschen Militärgeschichte der Zwischenkriegszeit*. Bergkamen, 1994.

Venohr, Wolfgang. *Ludendorff. Legende und Wirklichkeit*. Frankfurt a.M., 1993.

Venturini, Georg. *Lehrbuch der angewandten Taktik oder eigentlichen Kriegswissenschaft*, vol. 1. Schleswig, 1798–1800.

Vogel, Detlef. "Deutsche und alliierte Kriegführung im Westen." In *Das Deutsche Reich und der Zweite Weltkrieg*, vol. 7, *Das Deutsche Reich in der Defensive. Strategischer Luftkrieg in Europa, Krieg im Westen und in Ostasien 1943 bis 1944/45*, edited by Horst Boog, Gerhard Krebs, and Detlef Vogel, 419–639. Stuttgart, 2001.

Volkmann, Hans-Erich. "Der Ostkrieg 1914/15 als Erlebnis- und Erfahrungswelt des deutschen Militärs." In *Die vergessene Front. Der Osten 1914–15. Ereignis, Wirkung, Nachwirkung*, edited by Gerhard P. Gross, 263–293. Zeitalter der Weltkriege 1. Im Auftrag des Militärgeschichtlichen Forschungsamtes, Paderborn, 2006.

Vornholt, Holger. *Der grosse Ploetz-Atlas zur Weltgeschichte*. Göttingen, 2009.

Wagner, Elisabeth, ed. *Der Generalquartiermeister. Briefe und Tagebuchaufzeichnungen des Generalquartiermeisters des Heeres, General der Artillerie Eduard Wagner*. Munich, 1963.

Wallach, Jehuda L. *The Dogma of the Battle of Annihilation: The Theories of Clausewitz and Schlieffen and Their Impact on the German Conduct of Two World Wars*. Westport, Conn., 1986.

———. *Kriegstheorien. Ihre Entwicklung im 19. und 20. Jahrhundert*. Frankfurt a.M., 1972.

Walter, Dierk. *Preussische Heeresreform 1807–1870. Militärische Innovation und der Mythos der "Roonschen Reform."* Krieg in der Geschichte 16. Paderborn, 2003.

Warlimont, Walter. *Im Hauptquartier der deutschen Wehrmacht 1939–1945. Grundlagen, Formen, Gestalten*. Munich, 1978.

Wawro, Geoffrey. *The Austro-Prussian War: Austria's War with Prussia and Italy in 1866*. New York, 1996.

Wegner, Bernd. "Die Aporie des Krieges." In *Das Deutsche Reich und der Zweite Weltkrieg*, vol. 8, *Die Ostfront 1943/44. Der Krieg im Osten und an den Nebenfronten*, edited by Karl-Heinz Frieser, 21–274. Munich, 2007.

———. "Defensive ohne Strategie. Die Wehrmacht und das Jahr 1943." In *Die Wehrmacht. Mythos und Realität*, edited by Rolf-Dieter Müller and Hans-Erich Volkmann, 197–209. Im Auftrag des Militärgeschichtlichen Forschungsamtes, Munich, 1999.

———. "Erschriebene Siege. Franz Halder, die 'Historical Division' und die Rekonstruktion des Zweiten Weltkrieges im Geiste des deutschen Generalstabes." In *Politischer Wandel, organisierte Gewalt und nationale Sicherheit. Beiträge zur neueren Geschichte Deutschlands und Frankreichs. Festschrift für Klaus-Jürgen Müller*, edited by Ernst Willi Hansen, Gerhard Schreiber, and Bernd Wegner, 287–302. Munich, 1995.

———. "Der Krieg gegen die Sowjetunion 1942/43." In *Das Deutsche Reich und der Zweite*

Weltkrieg, vol. 6, *Der globale Krieg. Die Ausweitung zum Weltkrieg und der Wechsel der Initiative 1941 bis 1943,* edited by Horst Boog, Werner Rahn, Reinhard Stumpf, and Bernd Wegner, 761–1102. Stuttgart, 1993.

———. "Von Stalingrad nach Kursk." In *Das Deutsche Reich und der Zweite Weltkrieg,* vol. 8, *Die Ostfront 1943/44. Der Krieg im Osten und an den Nebenfronten,* edited by Karl-Heinz Frieser, 3–79. Munich, 2007.

———. "Wozu Operationsgeschichte?" In *Was ist Militärgeschichte?,* edited by Benjamin Ziemann and Thomas Kühne, 105–113. Paderborn, 2000.

———, ed. *Zwei Wege nach Moskau. Vom Hitler-Stalin-Pakt bis zum "Unternehmen Barbarossa."* Serie Piper, 1346. Im Auftrag des Militärgeschichtlichen Forschungsamtes, Munich, 1991.

Wehler, Hans-Ulrich. *Deutsche Gesellschaftsgeschichte,* vol. 3, *Von der "Deutschen Doppelrevolution" bis zum Beginn des Ersten Weltkriegs: 1849–1914.* Munich, 1996.

———. "Der Verfall der deutschen Kriegstheorie: Vom 'Absoluten' zum 'Totalen' Krieg oder von Clausewitz zu Ludendorff." In *Geschichte und Militärgeschichte. Wege der Forschung,* edited by Ursula von Gersdorff, 273–311. Mit Unterstützung des Militärgeschichtlichen Forschungsamtes, Frankfurt a.M., 1974.

Wenninger. "Über den Durchbruch als Entscheidungsform." *Vierteljahreshefte für Truppenführung und Heereskunde* 10 (1913): 593–640.

Werth, German. *Verdun: Die Schlacht und der Mythos.* Bergisch Gladbach, 1979.

Wette, Wolfram. "Die deutsche militärische Führungsschicht in den Nachkriegszeiten." In *Lernen aus dem Krieg? Deutsche Nachkriegszeiten 1918–1945,* edited by Gottfried Niedhart and Dieter Riesenberger, 39–66. Munich, 1992.

———. *Militarismus in Deutschland. Geschichte einer kriegerischen Kultur.* Darmstadt, 2008.

Wetzell, Georg. "Das Kriegswerk des Reichsarchivs: 'Der Weltkrieg 1914/1918.' Kritische Betrachtungen zum I. Band: Die Grenzschlachten im Westen." *Wissen und Wehr* 6 (1925): 1–43.

Wierling, Dorothee. "Krieg im Nachkrieg. Zur öffentlichen und privaten Präsenz des Krieges in der SBZ und frühen DDR." In *Der Zweite Weltkrieg in Europa. Erfahrung und Erinnerung,* edited by Jörg Echternkamp and Stefan Martens, 239–276. Paderborn, 2007.

Wilhelm I, Deutscher Kaiser und König von Preussen. *Militärische Schriften weiland Kaiser Wilhelms des Grossen,* vol. 1, *1821–1847.* Auf Befehl seiner Majestät des Kaisers und Königs, vom Königlich Preussischen Kriegsministerium, Berlin, 1897.

Wrochem, Oliver von. *Erich von Manstein: Vernichtungskrieg und Geschichtspolitik.* Krieg in der Geschichte 27. Paderborn, 2006.

Young, Peter, and Richard Natkiel, eds. *The Cassell Atlas of the Second World War.* London, 1999.

Zabecki, David T. *The German 1918 Offensives: A Case Study in the Operational Level of War.* London, 2006.

———. *Steel Wind: Colonel Georg Bruchmüller and the Birth of Modern Artillery.* Westport, Conn., 1994.

Zabecki, David T., and Bruce Condell, translators and eds. *On the German Art of War: Truppenführung.* Boulder, Colo., 2001.

Zeidler, Manfred. *Reichswehr und Rote Armee 1920 bis 1933. Wege und Stationen einer ungewöhnlichen Zusammenarbeit.* Beiträge zur Militärgeschichte 36. Munich, 1993.

Zeitzler, Kurt. "Das Ringen um die militärische Entscheidung im 2. Weltkriege." *Wehrwis-senschaftliche Rundschau,* vol. 6 (1951): 44–48; vol. 7 (1951): 20–29.

Zentner, Christian. *Illustrierte Geschichte des Ersten Weltkriegs.* Eltville a.Rh., 1990.

Zimmermann, John. *Ulrich de Maizière. General der Bonner Republik 1912 bis 2006.* Munich, 2012.

Zitelmann, Rainer. *Hitler. Selbstverständnis eines Revolutionärs.* Stuttgart, 1991.

Zuber, Terence. *Inventing the Schlieffen Plan: German War Planning, 1871–1914.* New York, 2002.

———. *The Moltke Myth: Prussian War Planning, 1857–1871.* Lanham, Md., 2008.

"Zur Einführung." *Wehrwissenschaftliche Rundschau* 1 (1951): 1.

Index

Military units are listed at the beginning of the index in numerical and then alphabetical order. Page numbers in *italics* refer to illustrations and information in their captions. The abbreviation "pl." in **bold** refers to maps that appear on color plates at the center of the book.